A MANUAL

OF THE

ANCIENT HISTORY OF THE EAST,

TO THE COMMENCEMENT OF THE MEDIAN WARS.

THE

Student's Manual of Oriental History.

A MANUAL

OF THE

ANCIENT HISTORY OF THE EAST

TO THE COMMENCEMENT OF THE MEDIAN WARS:

BY

FRANCOIS LENORMANT,

Librarian of the Institut de France,

AND

E. CHEVALLIER,

Member of the Royal Asiatic Society, London.

VOL. I

COMPRISING THE HISTORY OF THE ISRAELITES, EGYPTIANS, ASSYRIANS, AND BABYLONIANS.

NEW EDITION.

PHILADELPHIA: J. B. LIPPINCOTT & CO.

MDCCCLXXI.

TABLE OF CONTENTS.

PREFACE.

THE one great fact of the last fifty years in the scientific world has certainly been the revival of historical studies, and especially that conquest which has been achieved of the ancient past of the East by modern criticism, which has been able to throw light into the darkest recesses of annals long buried in obscurity.

But a short half century ago, little was known of the ancient world beyond the Greeks and Romans. Accustomed to look on these two great nations as the representatives of ancient civilisation, it was easy to ignore all that had taken place beyond the regions of Greece and Italy. It was almost agreed that one entered the domain of positive history, only in setting foot on the soil of Europe. It was known, however, that in this immense tract of country, lying between the Nile and the Indus, there had once been great centres of civilisation—monarchies embracing vast territories and innumerable tribes; capitals more extensive than our modern western capitals; palaces as sumptuous as those of our own kings, on which, as some vague traditions said, their proud builders had inscribed the pompous history of their deeds. It was also known that these ancient nations of Asia had left behind them mighty traces of their passage o'er the earth. Heaps of ruins in the desert, and on the river banks, temples, pyramids, monuments of every kind, covered with inscriptions in strange and unknown characters, and the tales of travellers in these countries—all bore witness to a really great development of social culture. But this greatness was to be found only in ruins, in fragmentary stories of Grecian historians, and in some passages in the Bible. And as everything belonging to the primitive eastern world assumes colossal proportions, it was but natural to infer that fiction occupied a large place in Biblical story, and in the pages of Herodotus. To-day everything is quite changed. In all its branches the science of antiquities has soared to a height previously unknown, and its discoveries have changed the page of history. From the great works of the learned men of the Renaissance, the civilisation of Greece and Rome was supposed to be known to its very base; and yet on that very civilisation Archæology has been found to throw an unexpected light. The study and correct understanding of the ornamented remains, the history of art, dates, so to speak, but from yesterday. Winckelman closes the eighteenth, and Visconti inaugurates the present, century. The innumerable painted vases, and monuments of every description which have been and still are furnished by the burial places of Etruria, of Greece, of Cyrene, and of the Crimea, constitute an immense field of research unknown fifty years ago, and which has prodigiously extended the horizon of science.

But these advances in the domain of the classical world are nothing when compared with the new worlds suddenly revealed to our eyes; with Egypt, opened up to us first by the French, and which has supplied remains to fill the museums of Europe, and initiate us into the minutest details of the oldest civilisation of the world; with Assyria, whose monuments, discovered also by a Frenchman, have been disinterred from the grave where they have lain for more than 2,000 years, and open to our view an art and culture of which but the faintest indication is to be found in historical literature.

Nor is this all. Phœnician art, intermediate between that of Egypt and Assyria, has been revealed to us, and invaluable treasures have been recovered from the catacombs. Aramæan Syria has given us its ancient inscriptions and memorials. Bold explorers, too, have made us acquainted with the traces of all the various nations so closely packed in the narrow territory of Asia Minor. Cyprus with its strange writing and the sculptures of its temples; Lycia with its peculiar language, its inscriptions, coins, sepulchral grottoes; Phrygia with its great rock, sculptured bas-reliefs, and the tombs of the kings of the family of Midas; Arabia contributes to science ancient monuments of times anterior to Islamism, texts engraven by pilgrims on the rocks of Sinai, and the numerous inscriptions which abound in Yemen. Nor let Persia be forgotten with the remains of its kings, Achæmenian and Sassanian. Nor India, where our knowledge has been entirely renewed by the study of the Vedas. But it is not only the length of the course that has been increased, the progress of science has been so great that its domain is now also widely extended. Everywhere, by new routes, enterprising and successful pioneers have pushed their researches, and thrown light into the darkest recesses. Europe in our age takes definite possession of the world. What is true of the events of the day, is also true in the region of learning; science regains possession of the ancient world, and of ages long forgotten.

This resuscitation of the earliest epochs of civilisation commenced with Egypt. The hand of Champollion has torn down the veil which concealed mysterious Egypt from our eyes, and has added lustre to the name of France by the greatest discovery of our age. Thanks to him, we have at last the key to the enigma of the Hieroglyphs. And henceforth we may tread boldly on solid and well-known ground, where those who preceded us wandered among swamps and pitfalls. Champollion's discovery has been the starting point for those learned and ingenious researches to which we owe the restoration of Egyptian History. Through the whole extent of the Nile Valley the monuments have been examined, and in reply they have told us all the deeds of the kings who governed Egypt from the most ancient times.

Science has penetrated the dark catacombs where sleep the Pharaohs, and has restored to us many dynasties whose only traces were to be found in some mutilated remains of the old historian Manetho. At the commencement of the present century, we knew little beyond the names of a few sovereigns, whose reigns were far apart and connected with but a small number of events, distorted by the statements of credulous Greek travellers, or magnified by national vanity. We now know nearly the whole series of monarchs who reigned over Egypt during more than 4,000 years. The art of the Pharaohs has been appreciated in all its diverse forms, architecture, sculpture, painting; and the law which governed the inspiration of Egyptian genius has been discovered. Their religion, under its double character, sacerdotal and popular, has been studied, and it has been proved that under the strange and confused symbolism which ordained the worship of animals, was hidden a profound theology, which in its conceptions embraced the entire universe, and was based on the grand idea of the unity of God, the vague and faint echo of a primitive revelation. We can also form an estimate of the state of science in this famous nation. The most important fragments of its literature have been translated into modern languages, and in style closely resemble the Bible. In a word, Egypt has completely resumed its place in positive history, and we can now relate its annals on the authority of original and contemporary documents exactly as we relate the history of any modern nation.

The resurrection of Assyria has been, if possible, yet more extraordinary. Nineveh and Babylon have not, like Thebes, left gigantic ruins above the surface of the ground. Shapeless masses of rubbish, now crumbled into mounds, are all that remain for travellers to see. One might then readily have believed that the last vestiges of the great Mesopotamian civilisation had for ever perished, when the spades of Mr. Botta's excavators, and subsequently those of Mr. Layard and Mr. Loftus, opened to the light those majestic sculptures which we admire at the Louvre and the British Museum; guarantees of discoveries still more brilliant and extensive, when explorations can be pushed on into all parts of Assyria and Chaldæa. So now those pious kings, who led entire nations into captivity, live again, as it were, before our very eyes, on the bas-reliefs of their palaces. These are the figures which seem so terrible in the burning words of the Hebrew seers. We have found again the gates where, to quote the prophet's expression, people passed like the waters of the river. These are the beautifully wrought idols which corrupted the people of Israel, and caused them so soon to forget Jehovah. There, reproduced in a thousand different phases, is the daily life of the Assyrians; their religious ceremonies, domestic habits; their splendid furniture, and rich vases. There are their battles, the beleaguered cities, the war machines that shook the ramparts.

Innumerable inscriptions cover the walls of the Assyrian edifices that have been laid bare by excavations. They are written in those strange cuneiform characters so complicated as to seem likely to baffle the sagacity of interpreters. But there is no philological mystery that can defy the methods of modern science. The sacred writing of Nineveh and Babylon has been, like that of Egypt, compelled to give up its secrets. The learned labours of Sir Henry Rawlinson, Dr. Hincks, and, above all, of M. Oppert, have given us the key to the graphic system in use on the banks of the Euphrates and Tigris. We read now—following an established principle—the annals of the kings of Assyria and Babylon, engraved on alabaster or impressed on clay, for the instruction of posterity. We read the accounts they themselves have given of their wars, their conquests, their cruelties. We there decipher the official Assyrian version of events of which the Bible, in the Books of Kings, gives us the Jewish version; and the comparison of the two, places in the clearest light the incomparable veracity of the Sacred Volume.

These discoveries in Assyrian antiquity have thrown invaluable and most unexpected light on the origin and progress of civilisation. It was impossible that such brilliant culture should remain imprisoned in the narrow limits of Assyria. And so we find, in fact, that the influence of Assyrian art and civilisation followed everywhere the conquering Ninevite arms. To the east and north she made her influence felt in Media and Persia, where, combining with the subtle and delicate genius of the Persians under the Achæmenians, she gave birth to the marvellous creations of Persepolis. The origin of Grecian art, vainly sought in Egypt, is found at Nineveh. Assyrian influence penetrated into Syria, Asia Minor and the Islands of the Mediterranean; through the Greek cities of the coast it found its way into the heart of the Hellenic tribes. The early Greek sculptors thus received the inspirations and precepts of sculptors of the Assyrian school, who approached them step by step, and selected Asiatic works for their models. From Asia Minor this influence passed with the Lydian colonists into Italy, where it formed the base of the development of the Etruscan civilisation, while this, in its turn, furnished to that of Rome the elements of its primitive grandeur. Thus are explained the monuments, the luxury, and the riches of the cities of Etruria, which for so long a time excited the fierce desires of the rude sons of Romulus. Thus the history of the oldest empires in the world, of those birth-places of civilisation, is rendered henceforward accessible to Europe, under conditions now admitted to be the only guarantees for real historical study—that is, with the assistance and guidance of original documents.

We can now appreciate at their true value the ideas—crude and con-used in even the best of them—which the writers of classical antiquity have left us of nations whose languages they did not know, and of an historical tradition probably already falsified when they gathered the few fragments which they have preserved. Nevertheless, we both may and ought still to speak with respect of the accuracy with which Herodotus has related what was told him by the Egyptians and Persians, and with sympathy for the zeal which Diodorus Siculus has shown for learned researches. We are also bound to accept those traces of manners and customs which they have collected. But to reproduce as a whole the facts which they relate, and to give them as an account of the chain of principal events in Egyptian or in Assyrian History, is not to give a summary of that history suitable for young people, for it would convey an absolutely untrue idea.

The stories of Herodotus and Diodorus about Egypt and Assyria are no more a real history than one of our own country would be which suppressed the invasion of the barbarians, the feudal period, the renaissance; which made Philip Augustus the predecessor of Charlemagne, and Napoleon, the son of Louis XIV., and which explained the financial difficulties of Philippe le Bel by the disaster of the battle of Pavia. Nevertheless, such, with some corrections borrowed from Josephus, is the character of the majority of the standard works. Doubtless there are some who, to a certain extent, have advanced with the progress of science, and have eliminated gross errors. But at the point to which knowledge has advanced—when the history of Oriental nations can be related in a connected and precise manner, and furnishes lights which can be no longer passed by, on the origin of our arts and civilisation, it is not sufficient to suppress a few incongruities. There is no longer any reason to leave great gaps, to ignore facts of the highest interest, and to preserve, by the side of important rectifications, errors which falsify the general result. It is therefore indispensable to introduce amongst us, and into standard works, a complete reform in all that relates to the first period of ancient history, to the annals of the ancient empires of the East, to the first dawn of civilisation.

The immense conquests of science must be made common property, their principal results must be made part of that sum of knowledge which no one can be permitted to ignore, and which is the foundation of all real education. At the present day, one cannot, without unpardonable ignorance, adhere to such a history as has been written by good old Rollin, and all the tribe of his followers. What would be said of any professor, or man of the world, who would now speak of four elements, or of the three quarters of the habitable globe—who would with Ptolemy, make the sun move round the world? And yet it is much in this style that the great majority of our historical works speak even now on the subject of Egypt and Assyria. The absolute necessity of the reform of which we speak must, therefore, be obvious to every one. There is no one master of science but has loudly proclaimed it, and the opinion is becoming general. But the historical archæological sciences now require popular works, manuals such as have been produced in great quantities for the physical sciences, and have carried ideas into every grade of society.

The results of the wonderful progress in antiquities and Oriental philology during the last fifty years have not been sufficiently communicated to the general public. They have to be sought out in special, voluminous, and costly works, written in a style so learned as to make them available for only a small number. How often have we not heard in the world, and from the cleverest men of education, "Yes, we know that primitive Oriental History, that history which is the starting-point for every other, has been completely reconstructed, has assumed an entirely new aspect in the last half-century; but where shall we find, brought together and clearly expressed, all the facts which science is now able to establish?" This is the gap we have attempted to fill in the Manual now put forth. Doubtless, we are not the first to make the attempt; besides M. Henry de Riancy, who, in his "Histoire du Monde," has embodied some of the results of modern researches, two distinguished members of the University, M. Guillemin, rector of the Academy of Nancy, and M. Robiou, professor of history, have attempted to introduce into public instruction the true history of the ancient empires of the East.

These books have paved the way for us, and on more than one point we have followed their lead. But in spite of all their merit, they do not seem to us to fulfil all requirements. They still present serious deficiencies, and useful and ample as they are for students of public schools, they are not so for men of the world and professors, to whom they do not supply sufficient means for rectifying previous impressions. It is but too easily perceived that the authors have but partly studied the sciences, —the results of which they profess to give—that their knowledge on some points is second-hand, and not always from the best sources. Moreover, these books have been published several years; science has advanced in the meanwhile, and they are now out of date.

We hope we may state confidently that the reader will find in the present Manual a complete *résumé* of the state of knowledge at the present time—saving only those imperfections which no man—and ourselves less than any other, can hope to avoid. The science whose results I have set forth is one in which an illustrious father, whose labours I attempt to continue, has educated me, and which forms the aim and occupation of my life. There is no one branch comprised in the present publication to which I have not devoted direct and profound study.

In the history of every nation, we have taken as guides those authorities who command the greatest respect, those whose opinions give law to the learned world. For that of the Israelites during the periods of the Judges and of the Kings, in all cases where the interpretation of Egyptian and Assyrian inscriptions has not given new and unexpected light, our guides have been M. Munk, removed far too early from those Biblical studies in which he was an acknowledged master in our country, and M. Ewald, in whose writings so many brilliant flashes of genius and profound poetic sentiment shine out among ideas often rash and capricious. For Egypt, we have followed the traces of the disciples of Champollion, of De Rongé and Mariette, in France; Lepsius and Brugsch, in Germany; and Birch, in England. But chiefly we have used the great Histoire d'Egypt of M. Brugsch, and still more the excellent abridgment composed by M. Mariette, for the schools of Egypt, a real masterpiece of historic sense, clear explanation, prudent method, and substantial conciseness. We have borrowed entire pages from this last book, particularly in relation to the dynasties of the ancient and middle empires, for we have nothing to add to what the learned director of excavations to the Egyptian government has said, and we could not possibly say it better. The writings of Sir H. Rawlinson, Dr. Hincks, and, above all, of M. Oppert, have furnished us with the elements necessary for the re-construction of the annals of Assyria and Babylonia, of which M. Oppert has commenced a comparative statement, unfortunately still incomplete. The translations of the historical inscriptions of the kings of Nineveh, which we have inserted in the text, are borrowed from the works of that eminent Orientalist whom France has brought from Germany, to make him our fellow countryman; but we have ourselves compared the whole with the original monuments, and in offering them to our readers, we do not hesitate "jurare in verba magistri."

Our own immortal Eugene Burnouf, M. Spiegel, the German commentator of the Zend Avesta, Westergaard, and, finally, M. Oppert, are the authorities to whom we have had recourse on the subject of the antiquities, doctrines, and institutions of Persia. Lastly, as to Phœnicia, the admirable studies of Morris have been, naturally, our starting-point; but we have amplified or modified his results with the assistance of the writings of the Duke de Luynes, M. Munk, M. de Saulcy, Dr. A. Levy of Breslau, and the Count de Vogüé. The summary, then, of the works of the masters of science, of the conquests of European learning during the last fifty years in the field of Oriental literature, forms the foundation of our book, and constitutes its chief value; but, in these studies, which are peculiarly our own, it has been impossible to confine ourselves to the mere part of a copyist. In this Manual will be found a large mass of personal researches, and also some assertions for which we must be held personally responsible. But we have at least always taken care to indicate our own hypotheses and individual opinions. One last word on the principles and ideas which are reflected on every page of this book.

I am a Christian, and proclaim it loudly; but my faith fears none of the discoveries of criticism when they are true. A son of the Church, submissive in all things necessary, I for that very reason claim from her with even greater ardour the rights of scientific liberty. And it is just because I am a Christian that I regard myself as being more in accord with the true meaning and spirit of science than are those who have the misfortune to be without faith. In history, I am of the school of Bossuet. I see in the annals of humanity the development of a providential plan running through all ages and all vicissitudes of society. In it I recognise the designs of God, permitting the liberty of man, and infallibly doing His work by their free hands, almost always without their knowledge, very often against their will. For me, as for every Christian, all ancient history is the preparation for,—modern history the consequence of,—the Divine sacrifice of Calvary.

Thus it is that, faithful to the traditions of my father, I have a passion for liberty and for the dignity of man. Thus it is that I have a horror of despotism and oppression, that I have no admiration for those great scourges of humanity, called conquerors—those men whom the materialist historian elevates to the honours of an apotheosis—be they called Sesostris, Sennacherib, Nebuchadnezzar, Cæsar, Louis XIV., or Napoleon. Thus, above all, it is that I am almost invincibly attached to the doctrine of the constant and unlimited progress of humanity—a doctrine unknown to paganism, a doctrine born of Christianity, and whose whole law is found in the words of the evangelist, "BE YE PERFECT."

AUTHOR'S PREFACE

TO THE ENGLISH EDITION.

THIS Manual, as originally published last year in Paris, found greater favour with the public than I had ventured to anticipate. Two editions sold in a few months; and a version, published in Germany, proved to me that the Work supplied what had been long and generally required. I am also especially proud and thankful to acknowledge the kind reception the Manual met with from men of the highest authority on the subject of historical study—the encouragement which such men as Guizot, Mignet, Vitet, and Guigniaut have given to my attempt to introduce to the general public, and for educational purposes, the results of those discoveries in Oriental Archæology which have in the last fifty years entirely remodelled Ancient History.

The Work, too, has been honoured by the award of the prize of the Academie Française, and is thus stamped with the approval of the highest possible authority.

In England the Work was most favourably received, and in some reviews the publication of an English translation was recommended.

Such encouragement imposed on me the duty of leaving nothing undone that may render my Book as deserving as possible of the approval it had met with; to revise it carefully, and to correct and complete it as far as possible.

This I have endeavoured to do in the present Edition, which has been entirely revised, in many parts re-written, and so extended as to be much larger than the original work, from which it differs considerably in some respects, to which it is desirable I should refer.

In the first place, I have deferred to the opinion expressed by many persons, that the absence of references to authorities was a serious defect; as the reader was unable to refer to original works, and to verify the statements made in the Book. It was, however, found impossible in every case to refer to authorities in notes, as the size of the book would have been enormously increased; I have therefore confined myself, except for very important facts, to prefixing to each chapter a list of every book from which information has been drawn.

The chief fault, however, found with the "Manuel d'Histoire Ancienne de l'Orient" in its original form was, that it had no distinctly defined character; that it was neither a book entirely suited to pupils, nor perfectly fitted for teachers. Some parts, the first chapter for instance, were too elementary, and others too much in detail and too scientific, to be comprehended by children. This fault I have endeavoured to repair. As now published, the Manual is intended for teachers, for senior pupils, and for men of education who desire to keep pace with the advance of Oriental historical studies.

The First Book is entirely new; in this, as a preface to the others, I have endeavoured to collect the small number of facts at present ascertained as to the condition of the primitive races of men. As required both by the principles of sound criticism, and by my own conviction, I have given the first place to the Biblical narration, and have appended to this the parallel traditions preserved among other ancient nations. I have next given a rapid sketch of the discoveries of prehistoric archæology, bearing on facts totally apart from those contained in the Bible, and giving us an insight into the daily conditions of the life of the first men. And this book closes with an enumeration of the facts relating generally to the races of mankind, and to the principal families of languages—a necessary introduction to the historical narrative.

In the Second Book, on the history of the Israelites, little change has been made; it has been slightly expanded, and advantage has been taken of the admirable work in which M. Oppert has definitely fixed the chronology of the kings of Israel and Judah, by means of solar and lunar eclipses, mentioned in the Assyrian inscriptions.

In the history of the Israelites two things run side by side: one, the constant, direct, and supernatural interference of the Almighty with the destiny of that nation to whom He had entrusted the sublime mission of preserving religious truth, and from which the Redeemer was to come; the other, events arising from ordinary and natural causes apart from this supernatural interference. In writing Sacred History, it would be natural to give prominence to this Divine government of Israel; but in introducing the Israelites into a picture of the whole civilisation of Ancient Asia, it was necessary to look more at the merely human aspect of their history, without, however, for a moment losing sight of the entirely exceptional character of that history.

The Third Book, on Egypt, has been only slightly modified. Some few additions have been made, amongst others, a short analysis of the Funereal Ritual, or Book of the Dead; and a few errors have been corrected.

The Fourth Book, however, on the History of the Assyrians and Babylonians, has been doubled in size, and has been entirely re-written. In the past year science has continued to advance, and I have been compelled to keep pace with its progress. I have, moreover, especially devoted myself to the study of Assyrian texts, and have therefore been able to bring a larger amount of knowledge to bear on Assyrian history, and to add translations of some hitherto unpublished documents. As the greater part of these translations are from tablets in the British Museum, I have been careful to insert their distinctive marks, in order that Assyriologists may compare my versions with the originals.

The two following Books treat, the one of the Annals of the Medes and Persians to the time of the first disagreement between the Greeks and Darius, son of Hystaspes; the other, of the History of the Phœnicians to the period of the first rise of the Carthaginian power. No essential change has been made in this portion of the work, but it has been carefully revised, and has received numerous additions and corrections.

The Seventh and Eighth Books are entirely new, the nations of whom they treat were not mentioned in the original editions. The Seventh Book contains the History of Ancient Arabia, considered chiefly with reference to its intermediate position between the civilisations of India and of Western Asia; it is founded on the admirable work of M. Caussin de Percival, on the History of the Arabs previous to the rise of Islamism, and on the newly ascertained facts from the monumental texts of Egypt and Assyria, as well as from the ancient inscriptions of Yemen.

The absence of any history of India in my original work was universally regarded as an omission, as leaving a vacant space requiring to be filled. India no doubt had no political relations with Western Asia, but was, nevertheless, not entirely isolated from the nations bordering on the Mediterranean. From the time of Darius that country was brought into relations with Persia, and from the time of Alexander with Greece; moreover, Arian India exercised too great an influence on the progress of the human mind in periods of remote antiquity to permit us to omit her entirely in a general view of the great ancient civilisations of Asia.

I could not but acknowledge the justice of this criticism; and the History of India forms the Eighth Book of this Manual—a book a little longer than the others on account of the importance of the subject, and founded on the successive labours of Sir W. Jones, Colebrooke, Schlegel, Eugene Burnouf, Lassen, Max Müller, and Weber.

With India I have ended. I was urged to add a chapter on the early

Annals of China; but in the first place I have not considered myself competent to deal with the subject; and in the second, it appeared to me that China has always been so completely isolated from the rest of the world that it could claim no place in a book on the subject of civilisations that have influenced, even indirectly, our own.

This English edition has had the advantage of my latest revisions, and in one or two instances includes discoveries made too late for insertion in the French work.

THE

Student's Manual of Oriental History.

BOOK I.

PRIMITIVE TIMES.

CHAPTER I.

THE BIBLE NARRATIVE.

Authority.—Genesis Chapters I.—XI.

SECTION I.—THE HUMAN RACE BEFORE THE DELUGE.

1. WE have no precise and consecutive history of the first men, or of the origin of our species, but that of Holy Scripture. This sacred story, even without the assured and solemn authority which it derives from the inspired character of the book in which it is found, would always form in sound criticism the base of all history; for, merely considered from a human point of view, it contains the most ancient tradition as to the first days of the human race, the only one which has not been disfigured by the introduction of fantastic myths of disordered imagination run wild. The chief features of that tradition, which was originally common to all mankind, and which the special care of Providence has preserved in greater purity among the chosen people than among other races, are preserved, though changed, in countries far distant from each other, and whose inhabitants have had no communication for thousands of years. And the only clue which can guide us through the labyrinth of these scattered fragments of tradition, is the Bible Story. This it is to which the historian must first turn, recognising its distinctive character; whilst for the Christian it has a dogmatic value, permitting him, indeed, to interpret it in conformity with the light furnished by the progress of science, but at the same time giving him a fixed point round which to group the results of human investigation.

The historical interpretation of this narrative presents, however, serious difficulties. The most able and orthodox theologians have repeatedly discussed the degree of latitude which may be allowed for exegesis. In very many places it is impossible to know absolutely how far that allegorical style of language, which is so largely employed in the Bible, has been used in these passages. We may remark also, that gaps which appear in the Bible story, leave open a very large field for scientific speculation. Our high respect for the authority of the sacred books must prevent us from seeking in them what they were not intended to contain, what never entered the minds of those who wrote under the divine inspiration. Moses has never pretended to write a complete history of primitive man, and certainly not of the origin and progress of material civilisation. He has confined himself to recording a few of the essential and principal features of that history, in a form suitable to the people whom he addressed. His object has been to elucidate the descent of the Patriarchs who were chosen by God to preserve, from age to age, the primitive revelations, and above all, to show, in opposition to the monstrous cosmogonies of the nations who surrounded the Hebrews, those great truths which idolatry had obscured, the creation of the world from nothing by the mere will of an Almighty being, the unity of the human race sprung from one couple, the fall of that race, the origin of evil in the world, the promise of a Redeemer, and, finally, the constant interference of Providence in the affairs of the world.

2. The story of creation itself, and its agreement with the discoveries of the natural sciences, are things beyond the scope of our work. It is only from the moment when God, having created the world and all the beings which inhabit it, put the seal to his work by creating man, that we shall take up the story of the first book of the Bible, "Genesis," so called in Europe, from a Greek word, which signifies "beginning," because this book commences with the history of the creation of the Universe. "God said, Let us make man in our image, after our likeness: and let them have dominion over the fish of the sea, and over the fowl of the air, and over the cattle, and over all the earth, and over every creeping thing that creepeth upon the earth. So God created man in his own image, in the image of God created he him; male and female created he them." "And the Lord God formed man of the dust of the ground, and breathed into his nostrils the breath of life; and man became a living soul."

The story of the fall of the first human pair immediately succeeds that of their creation. The father of all mankind, Adam (whose name in the Semitic languages means "Man" *par excellence*), created by God in a state of absolute innocence and happiness, disobeyed the Lord by his presumption in the delicious gardens of Eden where he had at first been placed, and this disobedience condemned him and his race to pain, grief, and death. God had created him for work, as the inspired book expressly says, but it was in expiation of his fall that his work became painful and difficult. "In the sweat of thy face shalt thou eat bread," said the Lord to him, and this condemnation still rests upon all men.

This is how the book of Genesis recounts the temptation and fall, the consequences of which have fallen on all the descendants of our first parents: — "Now the serpent was more subtile than any beast of the field which the Lord God had made. And he said unto the woman, Yea, hath God said, Ye shall not eat of every tree of the garden. And the woman said unto the serpent, We may eat of the fruit of the trees of the garden: but of the fruit of the tree which is in the midst of the garden (the tree of the knowledge of good and evil) God hath said, Ye shall not eat of it, neither shall ye touch it, lest ye die. And the serpent said unto the woman, Ye shall not surely die: for God doth know that in the day ye eat thereof, then your eyes shall be opened, and ye shall be as gods, knowing good and evil. And when the woman saw that the tree was good for food, and that it was pleasant to the eyes, and a tree to be desired to make one wise, she took of the fruit thereof, and did eat, and gave also unto her husband with her; and he did eat. And the eyes of them both were opened, and they knew that they were naked; and they sewed fig leaves together and made themselves aprons."

"Prodigious, overwhelming truth," says Chateaubriand, "man dying, poisoned with the fruit of the tree of life. Man lost, for having tasted of the tree of knowledge; for having dared too well to know both good and evil. Should we suppose a prohibition from God, relative to any other desire of the soul, how could the wisdom, the depth of the providence of the Most High be vindicated. It would then be only a caprice unworthy of the Deity, and no moral lesson would result from Adam's disobedience. As it is, all the history of the world is the consequence of the law imposed on our first parents. The secret of the moral and political existence of nations, the profoundest mysteries of the human heart, are contained in the tradition of that wonderful, that fatal tree."

3. The Bible assigns no precise date to the origin of the human species, it gives no positive time for that event. It has in reality no chronology for the early epochs of man's existence, neither for that which extends from the creation to the deluge, nor for that which reaches from the deluge to the call of Abraham The dates which commentators have attempted to fix are purely arbitrary, and have no dogmatic authority. They belong to the domain of historical hypothesis, and one might mention a hundred attempts to make the calculation, each with a different result. What alone the sacred books state, in which science is in complete agreement with them, is that the appearance of man on the earth (however remote the date may be) is

recent, when contrasted with the immense duration of the geological periods of creation; and that the antiquity of many thousands of years, which some people, as for instance the Egyptians, Chaldæans, Indians and Chinese, have self-complacently claimed in their mythological traditions, is entirely fabulous.

Equally useless, equally devoid of solid foundation, as are these calculations regarding the date of man's creation, would be the attempt to determine from the Bible the exact place of the cradle of our species, or of the garden of Eden. The sacred story furnishes no precise indications on that point. The most learned and orthodox commentators of the holy books have left the question undecided. Everything bids us imitate their reserve and hold the common opinion which places in Asia the origin of the first human family, and the source of all civilisation.

4. Adam and Eve (Chavah) the first human couple who came from the hands of God, had two sons, Cain and Abel (Habel).*

They led, the one an agricultural, the other a pastoral life, the origin of which modes of life the Bible thus places at the very first footstep of humanity. Cain killed his brother Abel, being jealous of the blessings with which the Lord had recompensed his piety, but became an exile in the despair of his remorse, and retired with his family to the east of Eden, where he built the first city, which after the name of his first-born he called "Enoch." God had created man with gifts of mind and body fitted to enable him to accomplish the object of his existence, and consequently to form regular and civilised societies. The book of Genesis attributes to the family of Cain the first invention of the industrial arts. To Enoch, son of Cain, was born, it is said, in the fourth generation, Lamech, who in his turn had many sons. Jabal, "the father, of such as dwell in tents and of such as have cattle;" Jubal the inventor of music, Tubalcain the discoverer of the art of casting and working in metals, and lastly a daughter Naamah, inventor of that of spinning the wool of the flocks, and weaving the thread into cloth. (This last tradition is not found in the Bible, but is mentioned in the Jerusalem Talmud as a very ancient Jewish legend.)

---

* These names have meanings in the Semitic languages, as have all those names applied in the Bible narrative to the first ancestors of our race; they are in reality descriptive epithets which express the part played, and the position assumed, by each person in the original family. Adam, as we have already said, means "Man," Eve "Life," "because she was the mother of all living," says the sacred text. Cain signifies "Creature," "Shoot." Habel is the word which in the most ancient Semitic idioms expressed the idea of "Son," and is preserved in the Assyrian; and lastly, Seth, as the Bible expressly says, is "Substitute," whom God had given to his parents in place of the much loved son they had lost.

The Bible ascribes to Lamech the origin of those sanguinary customs of revenge which played so great a part in the life of ancient nations; "Lamech said to his wives, Adah and Zillah, 'Hear my voice; ye wives of Lamech, hearken unto my speech: I would slay a man in my wound, and a young man in my hurt: if Cain shall be avenged sevenfold, truly Lamech seventy and sevenfold.'"*

5. Adam had a third son named Seth, and God afterwards gave him a great many more children. Seth lived 912 years and had a numerous family, who, whilst all other men gave themselves up to idolatry and vice of every kind, preserved faithfully, down to the time of the deluge, those religious traditions of the primitive revelation, which after that event passed into the race of Shem.

The descendants of Seth were Enos, Cainan, Mahalaleel, Jared, Enoch, who walked with God 365 years, and "was not, for God took him," Methuselah who of all men lived the longest life, 969 years, Lamech, and lastly Noah, who was the father of Shem, Ham and Japhet. Each of these three was the head of a numerous family.

Section II.—The Deluge.

1. In the meanwhile the corruption of mankind went on increasing and passed all bounds. Their iniquities were such that the Lord was angered and determined to exterminate their race. The just Noah, descendant of Seth, alone "found grace in the eyes of the Lord" (Gen. vi. 8). God caused him to build an ark into which He shut him, and his family and seven couples of every kind of animal clean and unclean, and then the deluge commenced. "The fountains of the great deep were broken up, and the windows of heaven opened, and rain was upon the earth forty days and forty nights . . . And the waters increased and bare up the ark, and it was lift up above the earth; . . and the waters prevailed exceedingly upon the earth, and all the high hills that were under the whole heaven were covered; fifteen cubits upward did the waters prevail, and the mountains were covered. And all flesh died that moved upon the earth, both of fowl, and of cattle, and of beast, and of every creeping thing that creepeth upon the earth, and every man. All in whose nostrils was the breath of life, of all that was in the dry land died . . . Noah only remained alive, and they that were

---

* Genesis iv. 23, 24, marginal reading. The author's rendering of this passage in which the learned De Sacy concurs is, "Ecoutez ma voix, femmes de Lamech, soyez attentives à mes paroles; J'ai tué un homme parce qu'il m'avait blessé, un jeune homme parce qu'il m'avait fait une plaie. Cain sera vengé soixante et dix fois et Lamech septante fois sept fois."—Tr.

with him in the ark. And the waters prevailed upon the earth an hundred and fifty days" (Gen. vii. 11, 12, 17, 19—24).

There are some observations which it is in the highest degree important to make on this narrative. The distinction between *clean* and *unclean* animals proves that the species taken into the ark were only those useful to man, and capable of domestication, for to these only, does the division into two such classes, apply among the Hebrews. The manner in which the deluge was brought about, an idea quite distinct from the fact itself, is related in accordance with the crude notions on physical science which were current with the contemporaries of Moses; and here the wise words of one of the most eminent catholic theologians of Germany, Dr. Reusch, are particularly applicable, "God gave to the writers of the Bible a supernatural inspiration, but the object for which this supernatural inspiration was given was, as in all revelation, the teaching of religious truth, not of secular science; and we may, without trenching on the respect due to these sacred writers, without weakening the truth of divine inspiration, freely admit that in secular, and consequently in physical science, these writers were not above the level of their contemporaries; that they were liable to the errors of their time and of their nation . . . Moses was not raised by revelation above the intellectual level of his time; and further, nothing proves to us that it was possible for him to raise himself above that level by study or thought."*

Finally, the expressions used by the author of the book of Genesis, if interpreted by comparison with other similar expressions, will not necessarily lead us to suppose that he intended to mean that the deluge was really, and in the literal sense of the word, universal. The words, "all the high hills that were under the whole heaven were covered," and "all flesh died that moved upon the earth," are not stronger than the words of the same author, "And the famine was over all the face of the earth;" "and all countries came to Egypt for to buy corn" (Gen. xli. 56, 57). "This day will I begin to put the dread of thee and the fear of thee upon the nations that are under the whole heaven" (Deut. ii. 25).

It is quite clear that the expressions in these last three passages are not to be understood literally, that Moses did not intend to convey the idea that Joseph's famine extended to China, or that the red men of America were to be in fear of the Jews. And we may without violence to the sacred text extend the same limited interpretation to the account of the deluge. We shall see as we proceed whether the limitation should be carried even farther.

2. "And God remembered Noah, and every living thing, and all the

---

* *La Bible et la Nature*, French Translation, p. 27.

cattle that was with him in the ark, and God made a wind to pass over the earth, and the waters assuaged. The fountains also of the deep and the windows of heaven were stopped, and the rain from heaven was restrained; and the waters returned from off the earth continually: and after the end of the hundred and fifty days the waters were abated. And the ark rested . . . upon the mountains of Ararat . . . And it came to pass at the end of forty days that Noah opened the window of the ark which he had made: and he sent forth a raven, which went forth to and fro, until the waters were dried up from off the earth. Also he sent forth a dove from him, to see if the waters were abated from off the face of the ground; but the dove found no rest for the sole of her foot, and she returned unto him into the ark, for the waters were on the face of the whole earth: then he put forth his hand, and took her, and pulled her in unto him into the ark. And he stayed yet other seven days; and again he sent forth the dove out of the ark; and the dove came in to him in the evening; and, lo, in her mouth was an olive leaf pluckt off. So Noah knew that the waters were abated from off the earth" (Gen. viii. 1—4, 10).*

On quitting the ark with his three sons, Shem, Ham and Japhet, and their wives, Noah sacrificed to the Lord, who made a covenant with him and his race, and commenced to cultivate the earth. His posterity was very numerous, for he lived three hundred and fifty years after the deluge, and died at the age of nine hundred and fifty years.

SECTION III.—THE CONFUSION OF TONGUES.

1. THE family of Noah multiplied rapidly; but from this time the life of man was much shortened, and as a rule did not exceed our present average. Shem, nevertheless, (and probably also his brothers) lived on during many centuries; and according to the testimony of Holy Scripture, the family whence Abraham sprung (thanks no doubt to the temperate habits of patriarchal life) enjoyed up to his time far more than the ordinary length of human life.

2. All men being of one family still used the same language. Some generations after the deluge the mass of the descendants of Noah, who had become very numerous, had fixed their dwellings on the immense plains watered by the Tigris and Euphrates, in the country originally called Shinar, that is in the Semitic idiom, "the land of the two rivers." Proud of their numbers and strength, they believed themselves all powerful, and their insolent audacity led them to defy God himself.

---

* On the Bible narrative of the Deluge and its relations with the facts of science, see the recent essay of the Abbé Lambert, *Le Déluge Mosaïque, l'histoire, et la géologie.* Paris, 1868.

"They said one to another, 'Go to, let us build us a city and a tower whose top may reach unto heaven,'" (Gen. xi. 4). But God punished their pride by confusing their language. No longer able to understand one another, they were compelled to disperse, each family or group of families, carrying with it the new language, from that time to become its own, and whence the idioms, science now attempts to classify according to their analogies, are descended. Thus were formed the three great races who have peopled the world—the children of Ham in parts of Asia and in Africa, of Shem in Asia, and of Japhet in Europe. The Tower remained unfinished, and was called Babel, that is, "confusion," on account of the confusion of languages which took place there.*

3. The confusion of tongues and general dispersion of mankind are to be placed, according to the natural sense of a passage in Scripture which has afforded much exercise to the sagacity of commentators, in the time of Peleg the fifth from Shem, and about the time of his birth, because that name, which means *division*, was given him in commemoration of that event. Nothing, however, in the Bible forbids us to suppose that some families had already separated themselves from the mass of the descendants of Noah, and had gone to a distance and formed colonies apart from the common centre, while the greater number of the families destined to repeople the earth still remained united.

CHAPTER II.

TRADITIONS PARALLEL TO THE BIBLE STORY.

Chief authorities.—Ph. Buttmann, *Mythologie oder gesammelte Abhandlungen über die Sagen des Alterthums*, vol. i.—De Beauvoir Priaulx. *Quæstiones Mosaicæ; or, the Book of Genesis compared with the remains of ancient religions.* London, 1842.—Cantu, *Histoire Universelle*, vol. i.—L'Abbé Darras, *Histoire de l'Eglise*, vol. i.—Luken, *Traditions de l'humanité traduit par Vander Hœgen*, Bruxelles, 1862.—De Rougemont, *Le Peuple primitif*, vol. i.

SECTION I.—THE CREATION—THE FALL—AND THE ANTEDILUVIAN PATRIARCHS.

1. THE Bible narrative, which we now resume, is not one isolated tale unconnected with the traditions of other nations, and proceeding only from the pen of Moses. It is on the contrary, as we have already said, the most complete and authentic form of a grand primitive tradi-

* See page 23.

tion, which can be traced back to the earliest ages of humanity, and has originally been common to all races and all people, and been carried all over the world, by the dispersion of these races on the surface of the earth. In his narrative of this history the Hebrew legislator has faithfully reproduced the ancient memories preserved from age to age among the Patriarchs, and, by a special dispensation of Providence, favoured by the isolated and nomadic life led by the family of Abraham, less corrupted among them than among the surrounding nations. He has, assisted by the light of inspiration, restored their true character to facts elsewhere frequently obscured by polytheism and idolatry; but, as St. Augustine has said, without attempting to make the Hebrews a nation of scholars, either in ancient history, or in physics and geology. Let us now seek in various parts of the world, among people spread over the most distant latitudes, the scattered fragments of this primitive tradition, which the Mosaic narrative has taught us how to piece together.

We shall find in one place or another all its essential features, even those parts of the tradition that are difficult to understand literally, and where we may be allowed to suppose allegorical and figurative expressions. But the search presents difficulties, and must necessarily be restricted by the severest rules of criticism. Otherwise we may be in danger of receiving, like some indiscreetly zealous defenders of Holy Scripture, legends arising from more or less direct communication, from a sort of infiltration of the Mosaic narrative, in place of those ancient and genuine traditions which coincide in a most striking manner with the sacred story. It is necessary then before all, and for our greater security, to leave out everything that comes to us from nations on whose traditions, Jewish, Christian, or even Moslem writings, may be suspected of having exercised an influence. It is necessary to select traditions of proved antiquity founded on ancient written monuments; and when savage nations are in question, who have no books, to admit only such as have been collected by witnesses worthy of entire belief, and prior to the arrival of any missionary.

2. And first, among many people, we find the idea that man was formed of the dust of the earth. The Greeks in their legends represented Prometheus as playing the part of a demiurgus or secondary Creator, who moulded from clay the first individuals of our species, and gave them life by means of the fire which he stole from heaven. In the cosmogony of Peru the first man created by the Divine power was called Alpa Camasca "animated earth." Among the tribes of North America, the Mandans believed that the Great Spirit formed two figures of clay, which he dried and animated by the breath of his mouth, the one received the name of the "first man," the other that of "companion." The great God of Otaheite "Tœroa" made man of

red earth; and the Dyacks of Borneo, stubbornly opposed to all Moslem influences, repeated from generation to generation, that man had been formed of earth.

The religion of Zoroaster is the only one among the elaborate religious systems of the ancient world which admits the creation of man by the exercise of the almighty power of a personal God, distinct from primordial matter. The fundamental ideas of the pantheistic and emanative theories which were the basis of all religion in Chaldæa and in Egypt, as well as in India, left everything uncertain as to the creation of mankind.

Men, as well as all other created beings, were supposed to have issued from the very substance of the Deity—a substance hardly distinguished from the matter of the world—and they came into being spontaneously, as successive emanations were developed, not by a free and predetermined action of creative will; and those who held this faith gave themselves little trouble to define, except under a symbolical and mythological form, the why and wherefore of the emanation.

3. Zoroastrian Mazdeism alone, among the nations of the ancient world, preserved the idea of the original sin and of the fall of the human race. The sacred book called Bundehesh contains a story of the temptation of the first human pair, almost exactly like that of the Bible, in which all the essential features are found, even to that of the tempter having assumed the form of a serpent; and nevertheless it is no more possible that the Bundehesh has borrowed from the Bible, than the Bible from Zoroastrian religion. We shall give this story further on in that chapter of our manual in which we explain the system of the religious legislator of the Persians.

We should seek in vain for the same belief among the Egyptian, Chaldæan, or Indian priests. Doubtless as Pascal has so eloquently said, "The problem of our existence is complicated in this dark abyss, and it is as impossible to imagine man without this mystery, as for man himself to understand it;" but the doctrine of the fall and of original sin is one of those against which human pride has constantly revolted, and from which it has first tried to escape. And so, everywhere, the primitive tradition as to the first step of humanity has been the first to be obliterated. As soon as men have felt the sentiment of pride arise, which their progress in civilisation, their conquests in the material world, inspired, they cast off that tradition. All religious philosophy which has arisen beyond the limits of the revelation preserved among the chosen people, has rejected the doctrine of the fall. And, indeed, how was it possible for such a doctrine to agree with the dreams of pantheism and of emanation. And thus the tradition of the fall of our first parents has not been preserved beyond the Zoroastrians and the Mosaic narrative, except among some savage nations whose miserable condition had made them still feel all the consequences of the fall. Thus the inhabitants of the Caroline Islands, in the legends which the first European navigators collected from them, said, "In the beginning there was no death, but a certain Erigiregers, who was one of the evil spirits, one of the Elus Melabut, and who was aggrieved by the happiness of mankind, contrived to get for them a sort of death from which they should wake no more."*

The Hottentots also said that "their first parents had committed so great a fault, and so grievously offended the supreme God, that he had cursed both them and their posterity."†

3. But if the doctrine of original sin and of the fall is, of all the facts in the Mosaic narrative, the one least found among the traditions of other nations—if this is the point where the Christian should recognise most clearly the marks of divine inspiration as bearing most directly on the instruction which Holy Scripture is designed to give us, as to our origin, our destiny, and our duties—the circumstances with which Moses relates the fault which brought about that fall, are nevertheless found divested indeed of all meaning, without moral signification, and intermixed with entirely material ideas, in the most ancient legends of many people. It is in fact impossible not to recognise a close connection in their origin, between the forms though not between the ideas, of the biblical tradition of the tree of the knowledge of good and evil, and a series of ancient myths common to all the branches of the Arian race, to which a learned German, Adalbert Kuhn, has devoted a book of the highest interest.‡

We speak of those containing the idea of the discovery of the use of fire, and of the water of life; they are found in their most ancient state in the Vedas; they have passed, more or less modified by the lapse of time, to the Greeks, Romans, Slavonians, Iranians, and Indians. The fundamental fact of these myths, which are complete only in their most ancient forms, represents the Universe as an immense tree, whose roots embrace the earth, and whose branches form the vault of heaven. The fruit of the tree is fire, indispensable to the life of man, and also the material symbol of intelligence; from its leaves distils the water of life. The gods have reserved for themselves the possession of fire; it falls sometimes to the earth as lightning, but man cannot produce it for himself. He, who like the Greek Prometheus, discovers the means of producing fire artificially and gives

---

* *Histoire Générale des Voyages*, vol. xvii.

† KOLBE, *Description du Cap de Bonne Esperance*, vol. i.

‡ *Die Herabkunft des Feuers und des Göttertranks.* Berlin, 1859. See also some important articles by M. F. Baudry in the *Revue Germanique*, 1861.

it to other men, is an impious being who has robbed the sacred tree of its forbidden fruit; he is accursed, and the wrath of the gods pursues him and his race.

The analogy between the form of these myths, and that of the Bible story, is very close. It is in fact the same tradition, but perverted to another meaning to symbolise the introduction of material progress, instead of applying to a fundamental principle of moral government, and further disfigured by that monstrous conception, too common in Paganism, which represents the Deity as a formidable power, and a jealous enemy of human happiness and progress. The spirit of error had altered among the Gentiles the mysterious remembrance of the event which decided the lot of humanity; Moses reproduced it in the form evidently preserved among the Hebrews, the same form as among the Arian nations,—in spite of the alteration in sense—but he restored to it its true meaning, and caused it to reassume its solemnly instructive character.

4. So far we have been advancing on uncertain ground and in constant danger of falling into error. The lights of the primitive traditions which we have been able to catch from right and left, have been so few and far between, that it would have been wiser not to tread that road, had we not been sure of soon entering on a plainer path. But we have now reached solid ground. In place of a few isolated tales, scattered links of a chain whose unity is likely to be contested, we now come suddenly on a multitude of concordant proofs, which, coming from the four winds of heaven, arrange themselves so as to put beyond doubt that these stories were identical in the early ages of the world.

In the number given by the Bible for the antediluvian patriarchs, we have the first instance of a striking agreement with the traditions of various nations. Ten are mentioned in the Book of Genesis, and a remarkable concidence gives the same number, ten, in the legends of a great number of people, for those primitive ancestors whose history is lost in a mist of fable. To whatever epoch they carry back these ancestors, whether before or after the deluge, whether the mythical or historical character prevails in the picture, they are constant to this sacred number ten, which some have vainly attempted to connect with the speculations of later religious philosophers, on the mystical value of numbers. In Chaldæa, Berosus enumerates ten antediluvian kings, of whom we shall speak in the chapter on the history of Babylon, and whose fabulous reign extended to thousands of ordinary years, forming ten cosmic days. The legends of the Iranian race commence with the reign of ten Peisdadien kings, "men of the ancient law," who lived on "pure Homa (water of life), and who preserved their sanctity." In India we meet with the nine Brahmadikas, who with Brahmah, their founder, make ten, and who are called the Ten Petris or Fathers. The Chinese count ten emperors, partakers of the divine nature, before the dawn of historical times. And finally, not to multiply instances, the Germans and Scandinavians believed in the ten ancestors of Odin, and the Arabs in the ten mythical kings of the Adites, the primordial people of their peninsula. Such an agreement cannot be accidental, and must lead us back to a common origin for all these traditions.

SECTION II.—THE DELUGE.

1. THE one tradition which is really universal, among those bearing on the history of primitive man, is that of the Deluge. It would, perhaps, be too much to say that it is found among all people; but it occurs among all the great races of the human species, with one important exception, the black race, among whom no trace of the tradition has been found, either among the African tribes or the populations of Polynesia. This absolute silence of a whole race as to the memory of an event so important, in the face of the unanimous voice of all others, is a fact which science should carefully note, for it may involve most important consequences.

Faithful to the plan which we have laid down, we shall pass in review the chief traditions of the deluge, collected from the various branches of humanity. Their agreement with the Bible narrative, will clearly prove their original unity, and we shall see that the tradition is one of those which date from before the confusion of tongues; that it goes back to the earliest ages of the world, and can be nothing but an account of a real and well-authenticated fact.

But we must first eliminate some legends which have been erroneously connected with the Biblical Deluge, whose essential features however compel sound criticism to reject them. They refer to merely local phenomena, of an historical date, relatively very near our own. Doubtless the tradition of a great primitive cataclysm may have been confused with these stories, and have led to the exaggeration of their importance; but the characteristic features of the recital given by Moses are not found in them, and this fact clearly shows, even under the legendary form of the traditions, their restricted and local character. To class traditions of this nature with those which really refer to the deluge, would be to weaken rather than strengthen the argument to be drawn from the concurrence of the latter.

Such is the character of the great inundation placed by the historical records of China, under the reign of Yao. It has no real connection with, and not even any resemblance to, the Biblical deluge; it was an event purely local, and its date even can be determined as long subsequent to the commencement of historical times in Egypt and

Babylon. The Chinese scribes mention *Yu*, a minister and engineer engaged in re-establishing the water courses, elevating the banks, digging canals, and regulating the taxes of all the provinces in China. A learned Sinologue, Edouard Biot, has proved, in a memoir on the changes in the lower course of the Hoang Ho, that this catastrophe arose from frequent inundations of this river. The primitive Chinese settlements on its banks had suffered much from these overflows. The works which *Yu* carried out were only the commencement of the embankments necessary for restraining the water, and which were continued in after ages.

Not less clear is the local character of the legend of Bochica related by the Muyscas, ancient inhabitants of the province of Cundinamarca, in South America, though the fabulous element is here in greater proportion to the historical foundation. Huythaca, wife of the divine man Bochica, gave herself up to abominable sorceries, to cause the river Funzha to leave its bed. All the plain of Bogota was inundated, men and animals perished in this catastrophe, a few only escaped by reaching the high mountains. The tradition adds that Bochica broke open the rocks which form the valley of Canoas and Tequendama, to allow of the escape of the waters; afterwards he re-assembled the dispersed people of the Muyscas tribe, taught them the worship of the sun, and died.

2. Of all the true traditions relative to the great deluge, by far the most curious is that of the Chaldæans, made known to the Greeks by the historian Berosus, and which will be found at length in the chapter on the Babylonians. It is a story more exactly parallel to that of the Bible than any other, omitting no characteristic particular in the detail, even to the birds sent out of the ark. It must be evident to anyone who compares the two narratives, that they were one up to the time when Abraham went out from among the Chaldæans, to journey to Palestine. But in the Chaldæan cosmogony, the tradition embodies no moral lesson, as does the Bible narrative. The deluge is but an accidental event, a sort of fatal accident in the history of the world, in place of being a punishment sent for the sins of mankind. The man chosen by heaven to escape the deluge is called by Berosus, Xisuthrus, a name the original form of which we do not know, and therefore cannot guess its meaning. The Chaldæan legend adds one incident, not to be found in the Bible:—Xisuthrus, warned by the gods of the approaching deluge, buried at Sippara, the city of the Sun, tables, on which were engraven the revelation of the mysteries of the origin of the world, and of religious ordinances. His children dug them up after the deluge, and they became the basis of the sacerdotal institutions of Chaldæa.

On the other hand, the original monuments and texts of Egypt, amidst all their speculations on the cosmogony, do not contain one single, even distant, allusion, to the recollection of a deluge. It is true that the religious theories of the Egyptians said much more on the origin of the Universe, and of celestial bodies, than of the creation, and the early days of the human race. According to a passage in Manetho, open however to much suspicion as interpolated, Thoth or Hermes Trismegistus, had himself inscribed on tablets, before the deluge, in hieroglyphics and in the sacred tongue, the elements of all knowledge. After the deluge, the second Thoth translated the contents of these tablets into the vulgar tongue. This is the only allusion to the deluge which can be produced from an Egyptian source. Manetho has no mention of it in his Dynasties, the only authentic part of his work we now possess. The absence of this tradition from among the myths of the Pharaonic religion, renders it probable that this was only a recent foreign introduction, and, without doubt, of Asiatic and Chaldæan origin. So the Siriadic land where, according to the passage in question, the columns of hieroglyphics were placed, may well have been no other than Chaldæa. This tradition, though not found in the Bible, was current as a popular tale among the Jews at the commencement of the Christian era—a circumstance which confirms our supposition, as the Hebrew people may have received it during the Babylonian captivity. Josephus tells us that the patriarch Seth, unwilling that the wisdom and astronomical discoveries of the ancients should perish in the double destruction of the world, by fire and by water, which Adam had predicted, set up two pillars, one of brick the other of stone, on which were engraven records of this wisdom, and which still remained in the land of "Siriad."*

The tradition of the deluge, in less exact conformity indeed with the Mosaic record than that of Chaldæa, but still preserving all essential points, and clearly characteristic, exists in the most ancient recollections of all the branches of the Arian or Japhetic race, without exception. We shall give the versions peculiar to the Indians, Iranians, to the Celts and Slavonians in the chapter on the primitive Arians, on their organisation and religious ideas. The importance of the tradition of the deluge among all the Arian people, is the greater when we remember that the name of "Noah," unlike those of the other primitive patriarchs, bears no appropriate meaning in any of the Semitic idioms, and appears to derive its origin from some one of the languages of the Arian stock. Its fundamental root is Na, to which, in all the languages of the latter race, is attached the meaning of water—*νάειν*, to flow, *νᾶμα* water, *νήχειν*, to swim; Nympha, Neptunus, water deities, Nix, Nick, the Undine of the northern races. It seems then to have been applied by tradition, precisely on account of the deluge, to that righteous man who was spared by the Divine will, and may consequently be

---

* Jos. *Ant.*, 1, 2, 3.

compared to the name Ogyges, embodying a similar idea, which one of the forms of the Greek legend connects with the deluge.

This observation on the probability of an Arian origin for the name Noah, makes it easy to see why we find it, with the slight modification of a reduplication of the first syllable, in that of the King Nannachus, under whom the Phrygian tradition placed the deluge.*

The memory of this event had a great place in the legends of Phrygia; the city of Apamea, drew from it its surname of "Kibotos" or "Ark," professing to be the place where the ark rested. Also the history of Noah, with his name, was inscribed on certain medals which issued from the mint of Apamea in the third century of our era, when Christian ideas had spread over all the Roman world, and began to infuse themselves into the minds of those even who remained attached to Paganism.

3. "It is a fact well worthy of remark," says M. Maury, "to meet in America with traditions relative to the deluge, infinitely closer to those of the Bible and the Chaldæan religion than those of any people of the ancient world. We can hardly admit that the emigrations which certainly took place from Asia into Northern America, by the Kurile and Aleutian Islands, and which have taken place again in our own days, could have carried such remembrances, for no trace of them has been found among the Mongolian and Siberian populations,† who mixed with the aborigines of the New World. . . No doubt some American nations, the Mexicans and Peruvians, had attained, at the time of the Spanish conquest, to a very advanced social state. But that civilisation had its own peculiar and distinctive character, and seems to have developed itself on the soil where it flourished. Many very simple inventions, such as scales, for example, were unknown to these nations, and this fact proves that they derived their knowledge neither from India nor Japan. The attempts which have been made to discover in Asia, among the Buddhists, the origin of Mexican civilisation, have not as yet led to any satisfactory conclusion. Moreover, had Buddhism penetrated into America, which seems at least doubtful, it could not have carried with it a story not to be found in its books. The cause of the likeness of the diluvian traditions of the people of the New World to those of the Bible, remains still an unexplained fact." This avowal, from the pen of a man of immense learning, and who, in the very book whence we borrow our quotation, attempts to destroy the authority of the Mosaic narrative of the deluge, is doubly valuable.‡

But to us this fact, inexplicable to M. Maury, is capable of a very

---

* SUID. v.—Ναννακός.

† The tradition of the Deluge is nevertheless found very distinctly among the Calmucs; MALTE BRUN, *Précis de Géographie*, vol. lx.

‡ Art. 'Deluge,' *Encyclopédie Moderne.*

simple, and the only possible explanation. It clearly proves that the tradition of the deluge is one of the oldest of humanity, a tradition so old as to be anterior to the dispersion of the human families, and to the first developments of material civilisation; and that the red races, the people of America, brought it with them from the common cradle of our species, to their new abodes, at the same time that the Semites, the Chaldæans, and the Arians carried it, each one, to its own new settlement.

Among the American legends on the deluge, the most important are those of Mexico, as they existed in a written and definite form, previous to any contact with Europeans. Don Fernando d'Alva Extlilxochitl, in his history of the Chichimeques entirely founded on native documents, says, that according to the traditions of that people, the first age called Atonatiuh, that is, "The sun of the waters," was terminated by a universal deluge. The Noah of the Mexican cataclysm is Coxcox, called by some people Teo Cipactli, or Tezpi. He saved himself with his wife Xochiquetzal in a bark, or according to other traditions a raft of cypress wood. Pictures representing the deluge of Coxcox have been found among the Aztecs, the Miztecs, the Zapotecs, the Tlascalans and the Mechoacaneses. The tradition of the last-named people in particular bears a yet more striking resemblance to the Biblical narrative. It is said that Tezpi embarked in a spacious vessel with his wife, his children, and many animals, and such seeds as were necessary for the subsistence of mankind. When the Great Spirit Tezcatlicopa ordered the waters to subside, Tezpi sent out of the ark a vulture. That bird, which lived on dead bodies, did not come back, on account of the great number of corpses scattered on the recently dried earth. Tezpi sent other birds, among whom the humming bird alone returned, holding in its mouth a branch with leaves. Then Tezpi seeing that the soil was beginning to be covered with new verdure came out of his ship on the mountain Colhuacan.* According to another tradition, current among the Indians of Cholula (and related in a manuscript now in the Vatican, by Pedro de los Rios, a Dominican monk, who in 1566 copied in the country all the hieroglyphic pictures which he could procure),† before the great inundation which took place 4,800 years after the creation of the world, the country of Anahuac was inhabited by giants; all those who did not perish were transformed into fish with the exception of seven persons who took refuge in some caverns.

The Peruvians, whose civilisation was not below that of the Mexicans

* HUMBOLDT, *Monuments des Peuples indigènes de l'Amérique*, vol. ii., p. 77.

† HUMBOLDT, vol. i., p. 144.

also had a tradition of the deluge, and placed that event under King Viracocho, first of the Incas of Cuzco.*

The traditions of those American tribes who remained in a savage state must, from their very nature, be to a certain extent open to doubt. As they did not exist in a written form they were not secure from foreign influence; they were collected only in later times, when the tribes had long been in contact with Europeans, and when many an adventurer who had lived among them might have introduced new elements into their traditions. These tales, nevertheless, are worthy of mention, but must be received with some reserve. In the songs of the inhabitants of New California there is mentioned a far distant time when the sea left its bed and covered the earth. All men and all animals perished in this deluge, sent by the supreme God Chinigchinig, with the exception of a few persons who took refuge upon a high mountain which the water could not reach.†

According to Father Charlevoix, the tribes of North America related in their rude legends that all mankind had been destroyed by a deluge, and that then God, to repeople the earth, had changed animals into men. The traveller Henry repeats a tradition which he had heard from the Indians of the lakes. Formerly the Father of the Indian tribes lived towards the rising sun. Having been warned by a dream that a deluge was coming to destroy the earth, he constructed a raft on which he saved himself with his family, and all the animals. He floated thus many months on the water. The animals, which then had the power of speech, complained aloud and murmured against him. At last a new earth appeared, and he stepped down on it with all the creatures, who thenceforward lost the power of speech as a punishment for their murmurs against their preserver.‡

Mr. Catlin thinks he has found, in the great American tribe the Mandans, traditions entirely analogous to those of the Bible, especially a remembrance of sending out the dove, and of the exit from the ark. Resemblances of the same kind have been pointed out by other travellers, but they are too vague to enable us to rely on the details with which the narrators have surrounded them. In the Polynesian islands the diluvian tradition is not found among the black or Australian race, but among the Polynesians, originally an Asiatic people, it is met with, mixed up with incidents borrowed from the ravages of high tides, which are among the most constant plagues of those islands. The most

* ULLOA, *Memoires sur la découverte de l'Amerique.* Villebrane, vol. ii. p. 346 *sq.*

† DUFLOT DE MOFRAS, *Exploration du territoire de l'Oregon*, vol. ii., p. 366 *sq.*

‡ THATCHER, *Indian Traits*, vol. ii. p. 108, *et sq.*

striking of these Polynesian tales is from Otaheite, which some features connect positively with the great traditions of primitive times. But the diluvian stories from this part of the world are all of that childish character pervading all the legends of canoe-using races.

This long review, which we now conclude, enables us to state positively, as we have already said, that the narrative of the deluge is a universal tradition, pervading all branches of the human family, always excepting the black race. A remembrance so precise, and everywhere in such perfect agreement, cannot possibly be a myth, invented for a purpose. It must of necessity be the recollection of a real, of a terrible event, so strongly impressed on the imagination of our first ancestors, as never to be forgotten by their descendants.

SECTION 3.—THE CRADLE OF POST-DILUVIAN HUMANITY.

As to traditions on this subject, see chiefly Eckstein, "*De quelque Légendes Brahminiques qui se rapportent au berceau de l'Espèce humaine,*" Paris, 1856. Renan, "*De l'origine du langage,*" 2nd edit., pp. 218—233. Obry, "*Le Berceau de l'espèce humaine selon les Indiens, les Perses et les Hébreux,*" Amiens, 1838.

1. THE place where the Bible narrative states that the ark rested after the deluge, the starting point for the sons of Noah, is mount Ararat. From a remote time this name has been applied to the highest mountain in the Armenian range, which in the course of the various migrations of which that country has been the scene has received the name of Ararat, after having been called Mount Masis by the indigenous inhabitants. The greater number of the interpreters of Scripture have taken this view, but others in the early days of the Christian era preferred to follow the Chaldæan tradition, after Berosus, who placed the descent of Xisuthrus in another part of the same range, at the Gordiæan (Kurdish) Mountains.

Nevertheless, if we attentively examine the sacred text, it is impossible to admit that Moses thought that the Ararat of the deluge was situated in Armenia—in fact a few verses further on it is distinctly said that it was "as they journed from the east" that the descendants of Noah arrived at the plains of Shinar. This compels us, in searching for the high land on which the ark rested, to seek it in the chain of the Hindoo Koosh, or perhaps rather in the mountains where we find the sources of the Indus. This, too, is exactly the point to which the traditions of the Indians and Persians converge—the traditions of those two great ancient nations who have preserved the clearest and most circumstantial recollections of the primitive ages.

2. In all the legends of India, the origin of mankind is placed at Mount Merou—the abode of the Gods—the pillar that unites heaven with earth. Merou is situated north, even with reference to the primitive location of the Indian Arian tribes in the Punjaub and on the Upper Indus. This is not a fabulous mountain, unknown to terrestrial geography. Baron Eckstein has proved that it actually exists, and is situated near the "Serica" of the ancients—or the south-west of Thibet.

But the indications of the Iranians are still more precise, still more in agreement with those of the Bible, because as these people have not migrated so far as others, the tradition of the primitive cradle has not assumed for them so misty a form. The invaluable enumeration of the successive halting places of this race, which is contained in the most ancient chapters of the books attributed to Zoroaster, characterises "Aryanem Vaedjo,"* the original "starting point" of mankind, and particularly of the Iranians as a northern region cold and mountainous whence the Persian race descended southward towards Sogdiana. There is the centre of the world, the Holy Mountain Berezat of the Zend Avesta, the Alboraj of the modern Persians, from whose side flows the not less sacred river, Arvand, whose waters gave drink to the first men. The illustrious Eugene Burnouf has shown in a perfectly convincing manner that the Berezat is the Bolor or Belourtagh, and that the Arvand is the Jaxartes.†

It is true that the names Berezat and Arvand have been attached in later times to mountains and rivers far from Bactria, we find them applied successively to mountains and rivers in Persia, Media, Mesopotamia, Syria, and Asia Minor, and with no little surprise we recognise them in the classical names of the "Orontes" of Syria, and the "Berecynthus" of Phrygia. But this is the effect of the displacement all the localities of legendary geography underwent in the early ages. Races carried with them in their migrations those ancient names to which their ancient traditions were attached, and bestowed them anew on the mountains and rivers they found in the countries where they settled. This happened to the name of Ararat. M. Obry has shown that the mountain which the Japhetic tribes regarded as the sacred cradle of humanity originally bore in their traditions the name of Aryaratha, the origin of that of Ararat, and that it was only in later times that the Armenians in their migration transported the name to

---

* RITTER *Erdkunde*, vol. viii., 1st part, pp. 29—31, 50—69. "*Haug der erste Kapitel des Vendidad* in the last vol. of Bunsen's "Egypt." KIEPERT in the *Bulletin de l'Academie de Berlin*, December, 1855. SPIEGEL *Avesta*, vol. i., p. 4, *sq*.

† *Commentaire sur le Yaçna*, vol. i., p. 239 *sq*.

Mount Masius. Thus the Biblical statement of an Ararat situated east of the land of Shinar, coincides exactly with the traditions of the Arian race.

We find, then, the sacred tradition and the most reliable of the popular traditions are agreed that the mountain mass of Little Bokhara and Western Thibet was the place whence the human race issued. There the largest rivers of Asia, the Indus, the Oxus, and the Jaxartes, take their rise ; the culminating points are the Belourtagh, and the vast plateau of Pamir, so fitted for sustaining the primitive populations while still in a pastoral condition, and whose name in its primitive form was Upa Merou, the land of the summit of Merou. To this locality, too, point some Greek traditions, particularly the expression μέροπες ἄνθρωποι, which can only mean the "men sprung from Merou." The legends of other people also, as to the original country of their ancestors, tend in the same direction, though without reaching the central point, being partly obscured by the distance they have travelled. The Mongolian tribes attach their most ancient legends to the Thian Chan and to the Altai, the Finnish tribes to the Oural, because these two chains hide more distant mountains from their view. But if we prolong the two lines of migration indicated by this tradition, we shall find that they meet in Little Bokhara.

3. These localities, having been the cradle of post-diluvian humanity, nations who had preserved the remembrance were naturally led to place there also the cradle of antediluvian man. Among the Indians, men before the deluge like those after it, descended from Mount Merou. There is found the Outtara Kourou, the true terrestrial paradise. There also we are led by the Greek paradisiacal myth of the Meropes, the people of Merou. The Persians described the "Aryanem Vaedjo," situated on Mount Berezat, as a paradise exactly resembling that of the book of Genesis, until the day when the fall of our first parents and the wickedness of Ahriman the spirit of evil, transformed it into an abode of insupportable cold. The name also of Eden has been applied at one time to this region, for it is clearly found in the name of the kingdom of Oudyana, or "the garden," near Cashmere, watered by four rivers precisely as was the Mosaic Eden.

It is certain that two of the rivers of Paradise, in the Bible narrative, are two of the largest rivers which take their rise in the mountain mass of Belourtagh and Pamir, the one to the north, the other to the south. Gihon is the Oxus, still called Djihoun by the people on its banks. In Pison we must recognise the Upper Indus, and the land of Havilah, rich in gold and precious stones, which it "compassed," seems to be the country of Darada, near Cashmere, so celebrated for its riches. But must we conclude with some scholars the absolute identity of the Biblical Eden with the Outtara Kourou and the Aryanem

Vaedjo? Need we suppose, with these critics, that the occurrence of the names of the Tigris and Euphrates, as the other rivers of Paradise, are the result of subsequent confusion? We think not; it seems to us, as to M. Bunsen, that in the mind of Moses Eden had a far greater extent than the Paradise of the Indians and Iranians. If we take literally the indications of the Bible as to the four rivers which went out of Eden, they clearly mark out a vast region stretching from the mountains, where to the east rise the Oxus and the Indus, to those mountains whence on the west flow the Tigris and Euphrates—a fertile and temperate land—a really delicious abode, situated between regions burned up by heat, or wasted by cold. It is there that the inspired Hebrew legislator most probably thought that our species first saw the light.

SECTION 4.—THE TOWER OF BABEL.

1. The traditions in agreement with the Bible which we have hitherto examined have a really universal character, and are found among people of various races, and in far distant countries. This is not the case with the tradition of the confusion of tongues at the Tower of Babel. The Bible narrative places the scene of this event in the plains of Shinar or Chaldæa, and the legend is peculiar to the inhabitants of that country, and to nations who are known to have emigrated from thence. The story of the "Tower of the Tongues" was among the most ancient recollections of the Chaldæans, and was one of the national traditions of the Armenians, who had received it from the civilised nations inhabiting the Tigro-Euphrates basin. Berosus gives the story in a form almost identical with that of the Bible, which will be found further on in the chapter on the Babylonians.

2. As far as the Chaldæans are concerned, though the tradition itself remained immutable, its locality was not always the same. A very valuable gloss, introduced by the LXX. into the text of the Prophet Isaiah,* leads us to suppose that one version of the story placed the

---

* Isaiah x. 9. In the LXX. version the expression is used "Calneh, where the tower was built." The names mentioned are Babylon, Calneh, Arabia, Damascus, and Samaria.

In the Hebrew the names are Calno, Carchemish, Hamath, Arpad, Samaria, and Damascus.

The name Carchemish is not found in the LXX., and as that word, according to Fuerst's Lexicon, means "The Tower of Chemosh," is it not possible that the reference in the Greek to the "Tower" may have arisen from a translation, instead of a transcription of the word?—TR.

"Tower of Tongues" in the city of Calneh, now Nipur, one of the most ancient cities of southern Chaldæa. This was handed down from the most remote ages, when the civilisation of the Tigro-Euphrates basin had its chief seat in the provinces bordering on the Persian Gulf. But the tradition most generally current among the Chaldæans, in agreement with the Bible, placed that famous Tower in the immediate vicinity of Babylon. It is found in the great pyramid of the seven stages at Borsippa. Some years since an inscription of King Nebuchadnezzar was recovered and translated, in which he boasts of having repaired and completed the tower in honour of one of his gods.* He calls it "The Tower of the Seven Stages, the Eternal House, the Temple of the Seven Luminaries of the Earth (the seven planets) to which is attached the most ancient legend of Borsippa, which the first king built, but without being able to finish the work."

Nebuchadnezzar adds, "Men had abandoned it since the days of the deluge, speaking their words in disorder. The earthquake and lightning had shaken the crude brickwork and split the burnt brickwork of the revetment, the crude brick of the upper stories had crumbled down into mere piles." The discovery of this inscription points out to us, among the ruins still lifting their heads around the site of ancient Babylon, the still gigantic remains of a monument which, in the days of Nebuchadnezzar, was believed to be the Tower of Babel. It is this that the inhabitants of the country still call "Birs Nimrod," "the

---

* In the translation of this inscription, the author, whose version is supported by the high authority of M. Oppert, differs from Sir H. C. Rawlinson, who renders it as follows:—"Behold now the building named 'The Stages of the Seven Spheres,' which was the wonder of Borsippa, had been built by a former king. He had completed 42 ammas (of the height) but he did not finish its head. From the lapse of time it had become ruined, they had not taken care of the exits of the waters, so the rain and wet had penetrated into the brickwork, the casing of burnt brick had bulged out, and the terraces of crude brick lay scattered in heaps; (then) Merodach, my great lord, inclined my heart to repair the building. I did not change its site, nor did I destroy the foundation platform, but in a fortunate month, and on an auspicious day, I undertook the rebuilding of the crude brick terraces and the burnt brick casing (of the temple). I strengthened its foundation, and I placed a titular record in the part that I had rebuilt. I set my hand to build it up, and to finish its summit. As it had been in former times, so I built up its structure. As it had been in former days, thus I exalted its head," etc. RAW. *Her.* ii. 485. It will be seen that, in Sir H. C. Rawlinson's version, the damaged state of the temple is ascribed to defective drainage, instead of, as in the author's and M. Oppert's translation, to the effects of the deluge. It is necessary to add that the author is about to devote a special work to the defence of his opinion.—TR.

tower of Nimrod," and, in the midst of the plains, it still looks like a mountain. The description given by Nebuchadnezzar of the state in which he found it, when he undertook the repairs, suits exactly the state in which it now is. It is no more than a prodigious, shapeless mass of sun-dried bricks which have crumbled away into ruinous heaps.

2. The decipherment of the cuneiform inscriptions has given us an etymology for the name of Babel different from that which seems to follow from the Bible text—that is Bab-ilu, "The gate of the god Ilu." The derivation Babylon, "confusion," is the result of an alliteration inspired by the legend told of the place. But, on the other hand, our knowledge of the Assyrian tongue has revealed that the name "Borsippa" meant, in that idiom, "the tower of tongues." Babylon is often designated in the cuneiform texts by a symbolical name, ideographically written, meaning "the town of the root of languages." Borsippa by another meaning "the town of the dispersion of tribes." These names seem almost like medals struck to commemorate the ancient tradition of the plains of Shinar.

CHAPTER III.

MATERIAL VESTIGES OF PRIMITIVE HUMANITY.

SECTION I.—REMAINS OF THE ARCHÆOLITHIC EPOCH.

THUS far we have been listening to the great voice of humanity, relating, in both sacred and profane tradition, the memories it has retained of its early ages. We must now address ourselves to an enquiry of an entirely different nature, in order to gather all possible information as to the actual conditions of man's primitive existence.

The stones are now about to speak. We shall ask the successive layers which compose our soil to give up the secrets which lie hid in them. We shall carefully examine the material traces left by the passage of races long anterior to history, and thus place by the side of general facts transmitted by tradition, numerous details of the life of the first men, as well as of the successive phases of their material progress. We avail ourselves of an entirely new science which as yet has not existed twenty years, called "prehistoric archæology." It is, like all sciences which are still in their infancy, presumptuous, and claims, at any rate in the case of some of its adepts, to overturn tradition, to abolish all authority, and to be the only exponent of the problem of our origin. These are bold pretensions which will never be realised.

Without aiming so high, the new science, within the limits of the possible, has a part to play sufficiently great and brilliant to satisfy its ambition. To fill up with certainty, the enormous gaps in tradition, to give to doubtful statements the authority of facts proved by science—this is what it will one day accomplish, and has already partly achieved. Prehistoric archæology, moreover, is as yet but in its infancy, it still leaves great gaps, and many problems without solution. There is too often a desire to establish a system, and many scholars hasten to build theories on an insufficient amount of observations. Finally, all the facts of this science are not yet established with perfect certainty.

But in spite of these imperfections, inevitable in a study so recently commenced, the science of the archæological vestiges of primitive humanity has taken rank among the positive sciences. It has already brought together a great number of absolutely certain facts, and has commenced to synthetise them. Its researches have already brought to light the scenes of the rude and savage life of the first men, and from its successes up to the present time, we may infer its future achievements. Henceforth it will be impossible to write a book such as we have undertaken, and to embody in it the actual state of knowledge, without giving a place to the results of this study. It is necessary that none but facts satisfactorily proved should be admitted to such a manual as this, and therefore we have taken the greatest care to distinguish between facts proved, and things which still remain doubtful. Unfortunately the researches of prehistoric archæology have not yet been prosecuted in all parts of the globe. In fact at present only in Western Europe, and more particularly in France and England. This is far from the place where the human race first appeared, or where our first parents lived. Here the science presents a most lamentable gap, which no doubt will be one day filled up. But, as we shall see, the facts proved in Europe, although they cannot be regarded as absolutely primordial, possess so high an amount of interest as to prevent our passing them over in silence.

2. To find the most ancient vestiges of the existence and industry of man in Western Europe, we must go back to that period which geologists call quaternary, the period immediately preceding the commencement of the present geological epoch. The form of our continents was then very nearly the same as at present. America has not changed. In Africa the ocean entirely covered the vast plains which now form the desert of Sahara, and which everything proves to be the bed of a recently dried sea—recently being of course understood in the sense of the geologists, for whom, in comparison with the periods employed in the formation of the earth, facts long anterior to history, are quite modern. The mountain range of Morocco, Algeria, and Tunis, formed a long peninsula stretching from east to west, connected

with Spain, and the Straits of Gibraltar did not then exist. A continent submerged at the same time that the Sahara tract was raised, and of which the legend of Atlantis preserves a vague recollection, has left as its last relics, and as indications of its extent, the Canary and Azores islands. Sicily was attached to the extremity of Italy, the British isles to the north of France. In the north of Asia a vast Mediterranean Sea, which subsequent elevations of the soil have removed, occupied the whole basin of the Caspian and Sea of Aral, covered great part of the Steppes situated between the Oural mountains and the Volga, as well as the country of the Kalmuks, and reached southward to the base of the Caucasus. Its eastern limits are uncertain, but according to the observations of travellers, and indications drawn from the annals of China, it seems to have occupied all the desert of Gobi to the north of Thibet.

The conditions of climate, and consequently of the Fauna and Flora, were then entirely different from what they have been during any part of historical times. After having experienced a degree of heat much greater than we at present have, our continents about this time suffered a considerable abatement of temperature, which led to the "glacial period" of the geologists. The change must have been sudden, and we need not here seek for its causes, which are very imperfectly explained. Southern Europe, as far as the latitude of Sicily, had then much the same appearance as Siberia has now. Immense glaciers covered the whole of Ireland, Scotland, and Scandinavia. Those of the Alps advanced into the plains of Piedmont and Lombardy, part of which was still under water. The glaciers of the Rhone touched the Jura. All the valleys of the Carpathian, the Balkan, Pyrenees, Apennines, were filled with ice. These conditions of climate were the same for the whole northern hemisphere, a great part of which was emerging from the waters, in consequence of an alteration of level which submerged great tracts of land in the southern hemisphere. Indications have been found in America of the passage of glaciers not smaller than those of Europe. Asia shows traces of them, almost as far south as tropical latitudes, for we see clearly that a great glacier occupied the place of the upper waters of the Tigris and Euphrates, and moved towards Assyria.

It was not until a little later, when the effect of the return to a less rigorous climate had been felt, that vegetation became sufficiently abundant to nourish the numerous animals characterising the close of this period of excessive cold. Then the earth, partly cleared of snow and ice, was occupied by mammoths or maned elephants, and the rhinoceros (Tichorinus), whose thick fur enabled them to live in a very rigorous climate, and who wandered south as far as Spain and Greece; aurochs, wild bulls, stags, all larger than those of our days, associated with gigantic cave bears, hyenas, and enormous carnivora of the feline race, larger and stronger than any tiger or lion. At this time the hippopotamus and beaver inhabited our rivers. Marmots, wild goats, and chamois, now confined to the summit of the Alps or Pyrenees, inhabited the lower plains of the Mediterranean. The musk ox, not now found south of the 60th parallel in North America, wandered in the plains of Perigord. The reindeer, more arctic still, abounded in the same latitude. What especially marked this particular epoch, immediately after the glacial period, was the extraordinary moisture of the climate, due, no doubt, to the melting of the great glaciers and the almost unimaginable abundance of water, spread over the northern hemisphere. Nearly all the elevated valleys were occupied by lakes, which gradually burst their natural barriers and emptied themselves into the valleys. The rivers were enormous, and occupied the entire breadth of the valleys through which their successors now run, these valleys being for the most part only the ancient river beds deeply eroded by the passage of such masses of water. To imagine the Somme, the Rhine, and the Rhone of that age, it is necessary to raise the level of the water of the first, 100 metres, of the second 60, and at least 50 for the last.

3. Such was the aspect of our countries, such were the rigorous conditions which the climate and the monstrous animals still remaining imposed on the existence of man on his first appearance. The bones of the animals we have mentioned are found associated with chipped flints, and other stone implements, evidencing the rudest workmanship, and the most rudimentary social state, in the sand and fluviatile gravels of the counties of Suffolk and Bedford, and in the transported beds of the valleys of the Somme and Oise, and in the sand of the Champ de Mars at Paris. Of this age also seem to be the bone caverns of the Pyrenees, which are from 150 to 250 metres above the present level of the valleys, and some grottoes in Perigord, that of Moustier for example, where the worked flints resemble those found at Saint Acheul and Abbeville.

The arms and utensils of this primitive age are for the most part pointed axes of flint, formed by breaking off large splinters. We can easily see that these flints, whose white coating proves their great antiquity, were intended to cut, to cleave, and to pierce. When the points are sharpened it has been by striking off smaller chips. Some of these stones are scrapers, which were used, no doubt, to clean the inside of the skins which the savages of the first stone age used as a defence against the cold.

We may even form a pretty correct idea of their mode of life. The cultivation of the soil and domestication of animals were unknown; they wandered in the forest, and inhabited natural caverns in the mountains. Those who dwelt by the sea shore lived on fish, which they harpooned among the rocks, and on shell fish; the inland people subsisted on the flesh of animals killed by stone weapons. This is proved by the accumulation of animal bones in the caves, some of which still bear marks of the instrument used to cut off the flesh. But the men of this epoch did not confine themselves to eating the flesh of ruminant, hoofed, pachydermatous, or even carnivorous animals; they were very fond of the marrow, as the long bones are almost constantly found to be cracked. This is a taste which has been noticed among most savages. The men, therefore, whose traces are found in the quaternary deposits, were savages little above the level of those now inhabiting the Andaman Islands, or New Caledonia. Their life was profoundly miserable, but still they were men; even in their abject state the divine spark was still in them. Already man was in possession of fire, that primordial and wonderful discovery which places a gulf between him and even the most sagacious animal. Let us not forget also that even the most rudimentary inventions require the exercise of the greatest intelligence, as being the first, without precedent or pattern. In the earliest days of mankind it required a greater exercise of genius to contrive the cutting out of a rude stone hatchet, such as we find in the sand of the fluviatile alluvium, than it does in our days to construct the most complicated and ingenious machine. Moreover, if we look at the same time in our museums at the only arms of primitive man, and at the skeletons of the formidable animals among whom he had to live, we must see that, so feeble and so ill-armed, he needed all the resources of the intelligence with which his Creator had gifted him, to escape rapid annihilation under such conditions. Imagination may almost exactly depict the terrible combats of the first men against the monsters who then lived, but have since disappeared. Every moment it was necessary to defend their caverns against carnivora, larger and stronger than those of our age, bears, tigers, and hyenas. Often surprised by these terrible beasts, they became their prey. By force of cunning and tact they contrived, however, to conquer carnivora before whom they were so weak and feeble, and by slow degrees drove them back before mankind. The savages of the quaternary period dug pits as traps for the elephant and rhinoceros, and the flesh of these giants of the animal kingdom formed an important part of their food.

4. A second stage in the development of humanity is marked by an improvement in the workmanship of the stone implements, but its zoological character has not varied. The remains of this epoch are found more particularly in caverns, in those at the foot of the Pyrenees, and in those of Perigord, where excavations have supplied many thousand vestiges of men, still savage, but more advanced than those who lived at the date of the formation of the deposits of the valleys of the Somme and Oise. During this age the great carnivora seem to have disappeared, thus accounting for the enormous increase of herbi-

vora. The mammoth and rhinoceros still existed, but were gradually becoming extinct. The reindeer abounded in the South of France in vast herds, which roamed in the pastures of the forests. The men of this second epoch used bones and the horns of animals, as well as stone, and their utensils were better formed. All the objects dug up in the grottoes of Perigord and Angoumoise proved that our species had made great progress in the manufacture of tools and utensils. Their arrows are barbed. Some flints are notched, so as to form a sort of saw. Ornaments merely for show are found made of teeth and flints. In many grottoes have been found phalangal bones of ruminant animals hollowed and pierced with a hole evidently intended to serve as whistles, for which purpose they can even now be used. But the men who in these caves led the life of Troglodytes, not only managed to cut with facility, they succeeded also with stone tools in carving and engraving ivory and reindeer's horn, as is proved by numerous specimens. Finally, it is most remarkable that they had already the instinct of design, and drew with the point of flint on slate, ivory, or horn, the pictures of the animals which surrounded them.

The species most frequently delineated in these essays of prehistoric, one might almost say antediluvian, art are the wild goat and the reindeer, either singly or in groups. One tablet of slate gives us an excellent picture of the cave bear. But unquestionably the most remarkable of all these designs is one on a slab of fossil ivory which has been discovered in the grotto of the Madelein (commune of Turzac in the arrondissement of Sarlat). On it is drawn, by a very inexperienced hand, and evidently after many failures, a figure, clearly that of a mammoth, with the long mane which distinguished it from every living species of elephant. The greater part of the representations thus drawn by men who were contemporary with the enormous spread of reindeer in our countries are extremely rude. But there are some which are really works of art. We could never have expected to find in these works of mere savages such firm designs, so bold an outline, such truth to living nature, such fidelity in giving to each animal its own appropriate attributes. Thus art preceded the earliest development of material civilisation. In that primitive age, though man had not yet risen above a savage state, he already showed artistic spirit and a love of the beautiful. This sublime faculty, which God had given him when He "made man after His image," was aroused, even before he felt the desire to ameliorate the hard conditions of his life. Man had then also a religious belief, for the sitting position of the skeletons in the sepulchral grottoes of these primitive times, such as that of Aurignac, incontestably denotes some funeral rites, the origin of which is necessarily connected with some idea of a future life. From the first days of his appearance on earth man has borne his head erect and looked up to heaven. "Os homini sublime dedit cœlumque tueri."

5. We have as yet spoken only of facts relating to France, for there only has the study of the remains of mankind previous to the present geological period, been completely carried out, there alone have the observations been sufficiently numerous, and properly tested. In more than thirty departments of France settlements of the "reindeer age" have been found. They have been discovered also in Belgium, Germany, England, Spain, Italy, and Greece, in smaller number indeed, but sufficient to prove that in these countries, man appeared about the same time as in France, and that he lived at first under the same conditions. Europe, too, is not the only part of the world where discoveries have been made to prove the extreme antiquity of the presence of man, his co-existence with the extinct mammalia, and his original ignorance of the use of metals. M. Louis Lartet has found in the Lebanon, near Beyrout, caves, where chipped flints are mixed with the remains of bones of ruminant animals. In India quaternary deposits at the foot of the Himalayas furnish axes of the same type as those of the valley of the Somme. They have also been found in America. A French naturalist, M. Marcou, has discovered in the States of Mississippi, Missouri, and Kentucky, human bones, stone arrowheads and axes, in beds below those which contain the remains of the mastodon, megatherium, megalonyx, hipparion, and other animals, which have disappeared from the present fauna. Thus we see that the human species was already spread over the greater part of the surface of the globe, during the quarternary geological period. We therefore bring together under our general head and into one group the two successive ages of the great carnivora, and of the reindeer, which both belong to that geological period, and are both characterised by the co-existence of man with species of animals now extinct under conditions of climate quite different from the present, and give to these two united ages the name of the "Archæolithic epoch," an expression taken from the Greek, and distinguishing the epoch thus named as the most ancient of those in which man, still ignorant of the art of working metals, exclusively employed chipped flints for his arms and utensils.

SECTION 2.—REMAINS OF THE NEOLITHIC EPOCH.

1. THE third age in the gradual progress of man is marked by the appearance of polished stone, for it must be noted that, however great are the evidences of skill in working stone and bone in the preceding epoch, no one specimen of any weapon or utensil has been found bear-

ing traces of polish. The quaternary alluvium and the caverns of that age do not supply polished stone axes of flint, serpentine, nephrite, and obsidian: these are found in the peat pits, and in mounds, doubtless of great antiquity, but which are raised above the level of the soil; in sepulchres very ancient, but later than the commencement of our geological period, and in some entrenched camps, at a later time occupied by the Romans. They have been found by thousands nearly all over France, in Belgium, Switzerland, England, in Italy, Greece, Spain, Germany and Scandinavia.

We must not suppose, however, that an abrupt and sudden change separated the "reindeer age" from the "polished stone age." They passed from one to the other by successive gradations, which proves that the new period of the development of human industry was the result of slow and continued progress. Modern geology has noticed an exactly parallel fact, that the transition from the quaternary to the present geological period was not sudden and violent, but gradual. It was the result of successive and local phenomena, which gave our continents their present form, and changed though by slow degrees the climate so as to lead to the extinction or drive to northern latitudes some species of animals.

2. The axes of the polished stone period differ in form from those of the Archæolithic epoch, which are sharpened almost to a point, whereas those of the later age have a broad cutting edge. Some of the axes of this period had handles of stag's horn, or of wood, whilst others seem to have been held in the hand itself, and to have been used as knives or saws, for bone, horn, or wood. With that exception the nature of the weapons and utensils is the same in both ages, the only difference being in the skill and perfection of the workmanship, for there are axes, knives, barbed arrowheads, scrapers, awls, sling stones, disks, rude pottery, necklace beads of shells or earth, which belong to the preceding epoch. Although the name "polished stone age" is given to the third phase of the prehistoric period, it must not be imagined that everything belonging to it, is polished, the finish, the perfection of execution of unpolished weapons and utensils, often show that they belong to the new period. It will therefore be better to use the expression "Neolithic" epoch, as sufficient to denote the relatively recent character of this new age of the stone period.

In different parts of Europe unmistakable remains have been observed of workshops where the stone implements of this epoch were made, their site being shown by numerous unfinished pieces found side by side with weapons of the same material completely finished. The flints seem generally to have been chipped to shape in the quarry, and then carried elsewhere to be polished. There were, therefore, in that age centres of industry, special manufactories, and as a consequence there must have been commerce. The people who manufactured arms and utensils on so large a scale could not have lived in a complete state of isolation, or they could not have disposed of the fruits of their labour. They must have carried them to people who were not in possession of materials so suitable for the purpose, and exchanged them for some produce of the soil. Thus it is that man's requirements established step by step the various relations of social life. Axes have been found in Brittany, of fibrolite, a material which in France is only found in Auvergne and the neighbourhood of Lyons. In the Isle of Elba a great number of implements of stone have been found, the use of which was certainly anterior to the opening of the iron mines by the Etruscans, the greater part of these weapons are made of flint, which is not found on the island, and must therefore have been brought by sea.

The remains of the animals found with works of human art belonging to the Neolithic age, agree with other indications in showing that they do not belong to the quaternary, but to our own geological epoch, and we are thus on the threshold of historical times. The great carnivora, and pachydermata, such as the elephant and rhinoceros no longer existed. The Urus (*bos primigenius*), which was still living at the commencement of history, is the only animal of that age belonging no longer to our contemporary fauna. The bones found with the polished stone utensils are those of the horse, stag, sheep, goat, chamois, wild boar, wolf, dog, fox, badger and hare. The reindeer no longer inhabits our countries. On the other hand, we begin to find domestic animals, which were absolutely wanting in the caves of Perigord. It is evident that the climate of our countries had become what it now is.

3. Every one must have seen in France or in England one of those strange monuments of enormous rough stones known as Dolmens and Cromlechs, and which have been long regarded as Druidical altars or sanctuaries. A careful examination of these monuments has shown them to be tombs, originally almost always covered by a tumulus, under which the construction of rough stones was buried. The greater part of them have been plundered ages ago; but in the small number laid bare by the excavations of our days, there has been an entire absence of any kind of metal. Nothing has been found with the bones and ashes of the dead, except weapons of flint, quartz, jade, serpentine, and some earthenware. There are however some few in which articles of bronze have been found, and this shows that the use of these monuments was continued down to the period when the use of metals was known. All indications concur in proving that the Dolmens and Cromlechs of France were the sepulchres of a race distinct from the Celts who at a later time inhabited Gaul, and that the Celts annihilated, or rather subjugated and amalgamated with themselves, this earlier race. Many conjectures have been made as to the branch of the

human family to which these people belonged, but they are at present premature, and without solid foundation.

It is not only in France and in England that monuments of this kind have been found. They have been observed in Syria, in Algeria, and even in Hindustan. Axes and knives of flint, obsidian, and compact quartz, which have been taken from the tombs of Attica, Bœotia, Achaia, and of the Cyclades, are identical with similar weapons found on the soil of France; those which have been found in the various provinces of Russia are exactly of the same type. Scandinavia has its Dolmens, its funeral mounds, which present a complete analogy to those of France. The bodies have been buried in the tomb without being burned; bronze is found even less frequently in them than in the French Dolmens. The objects in stone and in bone in these tombs have great variety of form, and are of peculiar delicacy of execution. But a notable portion of the Danish collections come not from Dolmens, but from peat pits, where the objects are found in the lowest beds, with trunks of partly decomposed pine trees, a fact of the highest importance for establishing the antiquity of the Neolithic age, for this tree has for ages disappeared from the forests of Denmark, and has been replaced by the oak and beech. Two circumstances will explain the peculiar degree of perfection attained in the Scandinavian stone work,—first, the period of the exclusive use of stone tools was more prolonged there than in any other part of Europe, so that human industry had more time to perfect the work; secondly, the flint found there is of superior quality, and fractures more readily than that of other countries.

4. Again, Scandinavia has opened to the study of science other most curious deposits of the same phase in the history of man. On the coasts of Denmark, Sweden and Norway, in various places, considerable quantities of shells of oysters and of other eatable mollusca are found. These deposits have not been brought together by the waves; they are manifestly remains of feasts, whence the name *Kjækken mœddinger*, kitchen middens, under which they are known in the country, they are often hundreds of yards in extent, and nearly ten feet thick. No metallic object has ever been met with, but quantities of chipped flints, fragments of worked bone and horn, and rude hand-made pottery; the rudeness of the workmanship of these objects resembles the cavern period, the second age of the Archæolithic epoch. But the style of the weapons and utensils should not be the only criterion by which to arrive at the date of deposits of this nature. Above all, the fauna which they disclose must be taken into serious consideration. Now in the kitchen middens we meet with no remains of species of a former geological age excepting the lynx and urus, both of which have disappeared only since historical times. No bones of animals which have ceased to inhabit those countries have been discovered, but indications have even been

found of the pig and dog in a domesticated state. The kitchen middens then must be placed with the most ancient of the Dolmens. If art was so rudimentary, it is only because the tribes, who have left on the borders of the North Sea the relics of their rude feasts, were behind their neighbours, who, more favourably situated, had already begun to advance on the road to civilisation.

Deposits analogous to the kitchen middens have lately been discovered in other countries. They have been found in Cornwall, on the north coast of Scotland, in the Orkney islands, and very far from these, on the coasts of Provence. The "terramarre" of the banks of the Po, a mass composed of cinders, burnt wood, worked flints and bone,—bones of animals whose flesh seems to have been eaten,—fragments of pottery, and other vestiges of the life of the early ages, show great analogy with the deposits of Denmark, Norway and Sweden, and seem evidently to have belonged to the same period in the development of humanity.

5. But the most interesting remains of the Neolithic age, those which evidence the most advanced state of society and mark the last phase of the progress of the people of Western Europe before the introduction of the use of metal, are the lake villages.

In 1853 the unusually low level of the Lake of Zurich brought to light the remains of dwellings on piles which seemed of very high antiquity. Dr. F. Keller having called attention to this discovery, the exploration of other lakes was commenced to see if they contained any similar remains. The investigations, conducted by M. Troyon, were crowned with complete success. Not only were these lake villages found in a great number of Swiss lakes, but in those of Savoy, Dauphiny, of Northern Italy, and even of Greece. The dwellings of these lake villages were near the banks, constructed on a vast platform formed by layers of trunks of trees and poles, bound together by interlaced branches, and made solid with clay, the whole supported by piles driven down in the water. Herodotus exactly describes habitations of this kind which existed in his time in the lakes of Macedonia.* Modern travellers have found entire villages constructed in the same way in New Guinea.

The custom of building dwellings on piles in the midst of the water was continued in Helvetia and the neighbouring countries for many centuries, for the objects which have been recovered from these lake villages belong to very different ages. Whilst from the most recent, utensils have been recovered of bronze and iron—metals the use of which determines a new period in the progress of human inventions—in the others, and by far the greater number, weapons and utensils of

* HERODOTUS, Book V., chap. 16.

polished stone and bone only have been found. In form and workmanship, these much resemble the objects furnished by the Dolmens and peat pits of France, Great Britain, Belgium and Scandinavia, only they are in greater variety. The animals whose bones have been dredged up from under the lake villages are the same as still inhabit Switzerland—brown bears, badgers, aurochs, pole-cats, otters, wolves, dogs, foxes, wild cats, beavers, wild boars, pigs, goats, sheep. The elk, the urus, the auroch only are wanting among the present fauna of the country, but we know from written testimony that they were found there at the commencement of the Christian era. Thus the lake villages clearly characterise in Western Europe the close of the Neolithic age, and the people who had built them continued still to live there up to the time when they first learned the use of metals from more advanced nations. The collection of objects which the Swiss savants have obtained from their sites prove also in many ways that even in most ancient times there was a real civilisation. Pottery was still hand-made, but attained to a great variety of forms, and exhibited some taste in ornament. The largest vases served for storing grain for winter—and wheat, barley, oats, peas, and lentiles, have been recovered in them. The inhabitants of the lake villages were therefore given to agriculture, an art absolutely unknown to the men whose remains are preserved in the caves of Perigord. They domesticated animals, and they knew the use of the mill. Finally, in the lake villages of the earliest age shreds of stuffs have been met with, which prove that, no longer content with skins as clothing, men even then knew how to spin and weave the threads of flax.

SECTION III.—CHRONOLOGY OF THESE TWO EPOCHS.

1. THE chronological succession of the different periods of the exclusively stone-using age is thus now positively and precisely established. We find there the three first steps of the human race in the march of civilisation, after which the use of metal marked a new advance, and one of the highest importance. Not but what it is quite possible to exaggerate the state of advancement to which the first use of metals corresponds. The ancients tell us that the Massagetæ,* who were barbarous in the highest degree, were in possession of metallic implements, and among the tribes of Ugrian race, the working of mines certainly commenced in a social state but very little advanced. In the Oural and Altai mountains traces have been found of ancient excavations sometimes more than thirty metres deep. Some negro people, also,

* HERODOTUS, Book I., chap. 201, 215, 216.

know how to work metals, and even to manufacture steel, and that without being really civilised. Nevertheless it is incontestable that the art of working metals has been one of the most powerful agents of progress, and it is precisely among people whose civilisation is oldest that we find this invention known at the earliest date.

Except in the Bible where the individual is specified who first practised this art, the history of the discovery of metals is among all ancient nations surrounded by fables. The invention appeared so marvellous and beneficial, that the popular imagination saw in it a gift from the gods. Thus almost always the pretended inventor who is named is only the mythological personification of fire, which is the natural agent of the work. Such is the Twachtri of the Vedas, the Hephæstus of the Greeks, and the Vulcan of the Romans. The first metal employed for weapons and utensils was copper, the ore of which is most easily reduced to a metallic state, and which men soon learned how to harden by an alloy of tin, so as to form bronze. The employment of iron, which is more difficult to work, marked a new progress in this invention.

2. Every branch of the human race, without exception, has passed through the three stages of the age of stone, and its traces have everywhere been found. But, though each people and each country present to the observer the same succession of three ages, corresponding to three periods of social development, we should greatly err were we to suppose that these different people passed through these stages at the same time. There is no necessary synchronism between these three stages in different parts of the world ; the stone age is not an epoch which can be chronologically determined, but a state of human progress which, in different countries, varied enormously in date. Entire populations have been discovered who, at the close of the last century, and even in our own days, had not passed out of the stone age. Such was the case with the greater number of the Polynesian tribes, when discovered by Captain Cook in the Pacific. A French traveller in 1854 found on the banks of the river Colorado, in California, an Indian tribe who used weapons and utensils of stone and wood only. The races of the north of Europe had no civilisation till long after those of Greece and Italy. The lake villages of Switzerland certainly continued to exist, after Marseilles and other Greek cities had been founded on the shores of Provence. All appearances seem to indicate that when in Europe the Dolmens of the age of stone were first constructed, the people of Asia had for centuries been in possession of bronze, iron, and all the secrets of a very advanced material civilisation. In fact, the use of metals in Egypt, Chaldæa, and China can be traced back to a very remote antiquity.

As we have already seen, the Biblical tradition mentions a son of the patriarch Lamech, Tubalcain, as the first who worked in copper and iron, a statement which carries back the use of metals among some races for more than one thousand years before the deluge. The knowledge of the art no doubt spread at first slowly, and for a long time remained an exclusive monopoly in the hands of some nations, whose progress was from various causes in advance of that of others. The Chalybes were already renowned for weapons of iron and bronze, which they fabricated in their mountains, whilst at the same time there were nomadic tribes in Central Asia who still remained contented with stone. Moreover positive proofs have been discovered that the invention of working in metals did not at once cause the disappearance of stone weapons. Metal articles were very valuable, and before their use became completely general, many people continued for economy's sake to use for some time the old utensils to which they were accustomed. Among most half-savage tribes who know the art of working metals, as do the negroes, the process even in the tribe itself is a sort of secret, preserved in certain families, transmitted traditionally from father to son, and never communicated to those who surround them and buy their manufactures. Everything leads us to suppose that this was the case during a long succession of generations in the primitive world, and consequently it might, and must, have happened that some of the swarms of emigrants, who threw themselves first into the forests of the still desert world, although they started from centres where some families had already learned to work in metals, knew themselves only how to make stone implements, and carried with them no remembrance of the arts of their original and far distant establishments. There is therefore no necessary contradiction to the Bible narrative, which dates the first discovery of metallurgic art before the deluge; in the fact that the red race of America, which certainly did not separate from the birthplace of humanity on the plateau of Pamir till after the deluge—the recollection of which event they preserved—arrived at its last settlement, still using utensils of stone, and that it invented for itself the art of working in metals, as is proved by the originality of the character of the work, so totally distinct from that of the Old World. And this could not only have been the case among the people of the New World, for whoever studies the ancient method of working metals must find indications of three distinct centres of invention, whence the art spread into different countries;—one, most ancient of all, that of which the Bible speaks, situated in Asia,—the second in Africa, among the black race, where the use of bronze seems never to have prevailed, and where the nature of the minerals of the country permitted them to arrive at once at the production of iron,—the third in America, among the red races.

There has even occurred in certain cases, and under exceptional circumstances, a return to the use of stone by people who, at the time of their emigration, were aware of the use of metals, but had not entirely abandoned the usages of a previous state of civilisation. This seems to have been the case with the Polynesian race. These people, as has been proved by the valuable researches of M. de Quatrefages, were originally Malays, and so far as we can approximately determine the date of their first emigration, it occurred in comparatively modern times, when we know from positive proof that the fabrication and use of metals were generally known among the Malay Islands, but without having entirely superseded the employment of stone utensils. But the islands where the ancestors of the Polynesians first established themselves, in the neighbourhood of Otaheite, and where they multiplied for many ages before spreading over the rest of the Australasian Archipelago, contained no metallic veins in their soil. The secret of metallurgy, even supposing that some of the emigrants possessed it, was in a few generations lost for want of use, and no recollection was preserved but of the stone which they had occasion to use every day. So the swarms of the Polynesian race remained in the "stone age," even when they came to establish themselves, as in New Caledonia, in countries abounding in metals.

3. These remarks on the impossibility of considering the "stone age" as an historical epoch, at a fixed time, the same for all countries, are applicable to the present geological period, particularly to the Neolithic or "polished stone" age, certainly very short, and which perhaps did not occur at all among people who learned early to work metals; whilst, on the contrary, among other races it has lasted thousands of years. But they do not apply to the Archæolithic age, corresponding to the quaternary period. The changes in the climate of the globe, and in the elevation of the continents, mark positive and synchronous epochs in time with determinable limits, although it is not possible to estimate their duration either in years or in ages.

The glacial period was simultaneous in Western Europe, in Asia, and in America. Those conditions of climate and of the superabundance of water which immediately succeeded it, and in the midst of which we find the most ancient vestiges of mankind, were common to the whole northern hemisphere, and had ceased to exist—had been replaced by the present conditions—in the most ancient times to which we can follow back the civilisation of Egypt or Chaldæa. Geological remains do not permit us to suppose—and this simple argument is a sufficient one—that our countries can have been still in that condition of climate peculiar to the age of the great pachyderms and of the reindeer, when Asia had arrived at the state in which it now is. The quaternary period was simultaneous on the whole surface of the globe. But we repeat, the change of climate and of the fauna is anterior to all remains of the most ancient oriental civilisation, to all real history. It follows that the remains of human industry which are found in the quaternary beds and in caverns of the same epoch, whether in France or in the Himalayas, certainly belong to primitive humanity, to the most ancient ages of the existence of man on the earth. They throw direct light on the mode of life of primitive man, whilst it is only by analogy that we can draw from the remains of the Neolithic epoch information as to ages really primordial, just as we may do from the study of the life of nations who are still leading a savage life.

SECTION IV.—PREHISTORIC ARCHÆOLOGY OF THE BIBLE.

1. Do the statements of the Biblical tradition, corroborated by the universal recollections of mankind, agree with, or contradict, the positive facts relative only to the material life of the first men, inscribed on the quaternary beds of the crust of the earth? If we take the facts themselves in their simplicity, apart from the rash conclusions which some scholars have drawn from them to suit a preconceived theory, that by no means follows necessarily from them—if we examine at the same time the Bible story with that breadth of historical exegesis which is admitted by the most severe orthodoxy, and is refused only by those who would at any price destroy the authority of the Sacred Books—no contradiction can be found. But as the attempt to prove such a contradiction has been made with marked persistency in a great number of books recently devoted to the discoveries of the new science of prehistoric archæology, it becomes the duty of the historian to pause and carefully examine the three questions on which it is possible that grave difficulties may exist, and where a certain school has pretended to find that the Bible is contradicted by the discoveries of the remains of fossil man. These three questions are; the antiquity of man,—the savage and miserable state of the first men of whom traces have been found,—and finally, the absence of geological traces of the Deluge.

2. *The Antiquity of Man.*—Undoubtedly positive facts prove that the antiquity of man on the earth is much greater than has been inferred from an inexact and too narrow interpretation of the Biblical narrative. But even if the historical interpretation, always susceptible of modification, and on which the Church pronounces no doctrinal opinion, must not be such as is now generally admitted, will the authority of the narrative itself be in the least shaken? Will it be contradicted on any one point? Assuredly not, for the Bible gives no fixed date for the creation of man.

One of the most learned men of our age in oriental literature, and who was at the same time an eminent Christian, Silvester de Sacy, was in the habit of saying, "There is no Biblical chronology." The wise and venerable ecclesiastic, who was the oracle of sacred exegesis in France, M. l'Abbé Le Hir, says also, "Biblical chronology is uncertain; it is left to human science to fix the date of the creation of our species." The calculations which have been attempted on Biblical chronology rest in fact solely on the genealogy of the Patriarchs from Adam to Abraham, and on the statements as to the duration of their lives. But first the primary element in a real and scientific chronology is absolutely wanting. We have no means of determining the measure of time by which the length of each Patriarch's life is computed, and nothing in the world is more vague than the word "year," when it has no precise explanation. Moreover, between the different versions of the Bible, between the text of the Hebrew and Septuagint (whose authority in chronology is equal), there are, in the generations from Noah to Abraham, and in the years of life, differences so great that interpreters may arrive at calculations which differ by more than 2,000 years, according to the version which they select as their guide. In the text, as it has come down to us, the numbers are anything but certain ; they have been subjected to alterations which have rendered them discordant; alterations the extent of which we cannot estimate ; alterations which, however, need not trouble the mind of any Christian, for the more or less exact transcription of a number must not be confounded with the question of the Divine inspiration, which has given Holy Scripture to teach man his origin, his way, his duty, and his end. Moreover, besides the want of certainty as to the original reading of the numbers given in the Bible for the existence of each of the Patriarchs from Noah to Abraham, the genealogy of these Patriarchs can be considered by a good critic only as having the same character as the genealogies habitually preserved among Semitic people—among the Arabs for instance—which establish direct affiliation by the enumeration of the most remarkable personages, omitting many intermediate steps.

These decisive arguments prove that there is no real Biblical chronology, and therefore no contradiction between that chronology and the discoveries of science. However distant may be the date to which researches on fossil man may one day carry back the existence of the human race (as well as the Egyptian monuments, even now incompatible with the number of 4,000 years hitherto generally accepted), the narrative of the sacred books will be neither shaken nor contradicted, for it assigns no positive date, either for the creation of man or for the deluge. All that the Bible expressly says is, that man was the last creature whom God placed on the earth, and this the discoveries of science, far from denying, confirm in the clearest manner.

But while we admit that religion need not limit the freedom of scientific speculations as to the antiquity of man, we are bound to state that science can as yet assign no date to, however far it may carry back, this antiquity. We have no standard by which to determine, even approximately, the number of ages which have elapsed since the time of the first men whose remains have been found in the quaternary deposits. We are in fact treating of geological formations, whose rate of deposit may be accelerated or retarded by widely different causes which we have no means of estimating. Nothing, even in the present day, is so variable as the rate of deposit of fluviatile alluvium, like that of the quaternary epoch. And moreover, the occurrences of that period cannot be compared with those of the present time, as causes were then in operation on a scale which no longer exists. So that the hundreds of thousands of years, which some authors with too lively imaginations have reckoned, from the first traces of fossil man to our own times, are really baseless hypotheses, and mere guesses. The date of the appearance of the human species, according to the geological record, is still unknown, and will probably remain so for ever.

3. *The miserable Condition of Primitive Man.*—Here again no contradiction is found between the Mosaic record and prehistoric Archæology. The writers who have attempted to prove a contradiction have but little studied Christian doctrines, and have lost sight of one important fact; the doctrine of the fall. They have believed that the miserable state of the life of the savages of the quaternary epoch was a contradiction of the happy and cloudless life of Eden, of the state of absolute perfection in which the first man issued from the hands of his Creator. Thus they ignored the great gulf between the Eden life of our first ancestors, and that of these human races, however ancient they may be, fixed by disobedience, that original fault which changed the condition of man and condemned him to painful toil, to sorrow, and death.

Nothing, however, can be more instructive for the Christian who sees them by the light of sacred tradition, than the facts brought to light by geological discoveries among the quaternary deposits. The condemnation pronounced by the Divine anger is imprinted in a striking manner on the hard and toilsome life which it is evident that the tribes scattered on the surface of the earth then led, under the conditions of climate of that epoch, and in the midst of formidable animals against whom it was necessary every moment to defend their lives. It seems that the weight of that sentence fell then, immediately after the fall, more heavily upon our race than it has since done. And when science shows us the first men who came to our countries, living in the midst of ice, under conditions of climate analogous to those under which the Esquimaux now live,—conditions which up till then had not been produced in the temperate zone, and which have not since appeared there,

—we are naturally led to recall the ancient Persian tradition, in complete agreement with the statements of the Bible, on the subject of the fall of mankind through the fault of their first ancestor, which places in the first rank among the punishments which followed that fault, as well as death and sickness, the appearance of intense and permanent cold which man could hardly bear, and which rendered the earth almost uninhabitable.*

We must not, however, exaggerate this picture. If geological discoveries reveal the hard and miserable conditions of the life of aboriginal man, they do not show him at all in an abject state. Far from this, man in the quaternary age was in full possession of those faculties which are the sublime heritage of our species. He had high aspirations, noble instincts, in entire contrast with merely savage life. He believed in a future state. He was already a thinking, an inventive being; and that impassable gulf which the possession of a soul has fixed between him and those animals who most nearly approach him in organisation, was then as wide as it ever was to be. Finally, we must not forget that we have as yet found traces only of thinly scattered tribes who had launched out into the midst of forests and deserts, who lived by hunting and fishing, at an enormous distance from the cradle of humanity, round which were still concentrated the chief settlements of the children of Adam. Thus though these first adventurous explorers of the "wide, wide world" were ignorant of agriculture, and had no domesticated animals, we must not absolutely conclude that the agricultural and pastoral modes of life did not exist in the more compactly grouped settlements, naturally more advanced, which had not left their original habitations. There exists, then, nothing to contradict the Bible statement, which mentions Cain and Abel, the one a cultivator of the soil, the other a shepherd, in the neighbourhood of Eden, in the second generation of mankind. To assert that such a contradiction follows from the discoveries in France or in America, would be to fall into a mistake, similar to that of confounding the trappers of the backwoods of Canada, with the agricultural population round Quebec and Montreal.

But besides this, was not the life of those men whose remains have been preserved in the quaternary deposits exactly in all its details what the Bible narrative tells us of the first generation of men after leaving Paradise? For protection against the cold they had but the skins of the animals they contrived to kill; and this is what the book of Genesis expressly says of Adam and Eve. For arms and utensils they had only rudely cut stones; and the Bible names the first worker in metal six generations after Adam, and we know how many centuries these antediluvian generations represent in the Bible narrative. The facts collected by prehistoric Archæology prove that the progress of material

* *Vendidad Sadé*, chap. i.

civilisation is the special work of man, and the result of successive inventions. Our sacred tradition does not, like the Pagan cosmogonies, assert that the arts of civilisation were supernaturally taught to mankind by special revelation from heaven ; it represents them as purely human inventions, and names their authors ; shows the gradual progress of our species to be the work of the free hand of man, fulfilling, most often unconsciously, the plans of Divine Providence.

4. *The Deluge.*—This point is the only one on which there is, we must acknowledge, a serious difficulty. There is however no radical and irreconcilable contradiction between the Bible narrative and geological facts ; but there is a problem, the key to which has not yet been found, and on this we can but speculate,—the place of the Mosaic Deluge, among the phenomena which our earth witnessed during the quaternary period.

It has now been proved, in a manner rendering discussion impossible, that no one of the three chief deposits constituting the quaternary strata have, as a merely superficial observation had led geologists to suppose, been produced by a great universal cataclysm, such as the deluge must have been, if we understand the expressions of the Bible literally. These different deposits are the results of partial and local deluges, produced by similar conditions of climate successively in all parts of the earth, but which have not affected the whole surface, their effects never being visible more than 300 metres above the actual level of the sea. It is true that if the interpretation now generally received, which makes the flood universal, as to man and the regions which he inhabited, not as to the whole surface of the globe, be admitted, these statements of science will not raise any insurmountable difficulties for exegesis, because any one of the partial deluges, so frequent during the quaternary period, would fulfil the conditions of the deluge which chastised the iniquities of the human race.

But this is how the difficult problem arises. On one hand we have the Bible narrative, supported by the universal tradition of all races of mankind, with one exception, proclaiming the great fact of the deluge. On the other, geological discoveries show man already spread over nearly the whole surface of the earth in the time of the great carnivora and pachydermata of extinct species ; since which no trace can be found of a cataclysm so universal as to destroy all mankind. Moreover, no violent interruption is found since this epoch in the course of the progress of humanity, which advances step by step towards perfection ; and the species of animals, then living but now extinct, disappeared gradually and by slow degrees. Neither of these propositions can be disproved, and it is therefore necessary to attempt to reconcile them. But we must repeat that the definite solution has not yet been found, we can but suggest hypotheses. Three seem possible. We shall explain them carefully, without pronouncing in favour of either, and without attributing to them a certainty which they cannot claim.

The first consists in throwing back the probable date of the deluge, and regarding it as anterior to the quaternary epoch. The absence of precise chronology in the Bible between the deluge and the time of Abraham renders this possible. This hypothesis rests on the vestiges of the existence of man, which scholars of great merit, M. Desnoyers and the Abbé Bourgeois, think they have found in the upper beds of the tertiary strata, but which, though probable, nevertheless require further confirmation. If man had already appeared in our countries at the close of the tertiary geological period, a sudden, entire, and prolonged interruption separates these primeval men from those of the quaternary epoch. The Mosaic deluge may then be identified with that immense irruption of waters over great part of Europe and Asia which closed the tertiary period, and produced what geologists know as the northern erratic block phenomena, when floating icebergs carried over all parts of England, the plains of Germany, and Russia, enormous boulders brought from the neighbourhood of the Pole.

The second hypothesis is that which has been recently supported by the Abbé Lambert.* It consists in regarding the universality of the deluge as to the men spread on the face of the earth, as comprising successive events, and in including all the partial diluvian phenomena of the quaternary period.

And finally, the third limits the universality of the deluge, both with regard to man and the extent of terrestrial surface, and would consider this great fact, which has left such lively remembrances in the mind ot mankind, as having extended only to the principal centre of humanity, to those who had remained near its primitive cradle, without reaching the scattered tribes who had already spread themselves far away in almost desert regions. It thus explains the absence of all tradition of the deluge among the black race, whilst all other people are agreed as to the event itself. It is certain that the Bible narrative commences by relating facts common to the whole human species, confining itself subsequently to the annals of the race peculiarly chosen by the designs of Providence. The theory of which we speak, only makes this narrowing of the story commence at an earlier period than has been usual. The hypothesis is a very bold one, and discards some universally received ideas. But we find it sustained by scholars of the greatest merit, and who are well known as sincere Christians, M. Schœbel† and M. d'Omalius d'Halloy.‡

* *Le Déluge Mosaïque, l'histoire, et la géologie*, Paris, 1868.

† *De l'universalité du Déluge*, Paris, 1858.

‡ *Discours prononcé à la classe des Sciences de l'Académie de Belgique*, Bruxelles, 1866.

This theory is supported by one of the most eminent authorities on anthropology, M. de Quatrefages, as well as by Cuvier, who has expressly taught it in his famous discourse on the "Revolutions du Globe," an attempt to prove the agreement between sacred tradition and geology. An eminent naturalist of the order of Jesuits, the R. P. Bellynck, without going so far as to adopt it, finally admits that it has nothing expressly opposed to orthodoxy. This hypothesis is best received by anthropologists, that is, students of the natural history of man, because it leaves them greater latitude to explain the immense changes which have taken place in certain races of mankind, by dating back the separation of these races from the main stem of the descendants of Adam, and placing it in a period when climatic and atmospheric influences were much more powerful in their action than at present, because phenomena both terrestrial and atmospheric had then much greater intensity. It is not opposed to the sense which the poetical expressions in many parts of the Bible permit us to place on the story of the deluge, many passages in the sacred books can be brought together, in which the words "all men," "all the earth," are used, and where it is impossible to understand them literally. An attentive examination of the first chapters of Genesis, a careful weighing of the words, furnishes indications from which it may be presumed that Moses did not intend to describe the deluge as absolutely universal, but on the contrary admitted that some portions of the human race had been preserved. "The author of the book of Genesis," says M. Schœbel, "in speaking of the men who were swallowed up by the deluge, always describes them as 'Haadam,' 'Adamite humanity.' Does not this show that he speaks of one single family, not yet divided into different nations, 'Goim'? But this division was already known to the human race."

"The author, in the 4th chapter of Genesis, has shown the race of Cain, living and multiplying, separated from the race of Seth both by distance and by religion and manners. This family was not then in the Adamite unity, it was really a people distinct from the race of Seth. Why, if this distinct people were comprised in the punishment of the deluge, did not the author say so? Why did he not in any way imply it? The crime which brought the deluge on mankind, as the author tells us, was an excess of corruption, of depravity, in the sons of "Jehovah,"* his worshippers. Thus those who knew Jehovah, who invoked his name, were the cause of the deluge. The descendants of Cain did not know Jehovah, they never called on His name, for "Cain went out

* It will be well to bear in mind, with regard to this quotation from M. Schœbel, that the expression is Sons of God (Elohim) the name Jehovah does not occur in the passage Gen. vi. 4.—Tr.

from the presence of Jehovah." What is still more significant is that when Moses, speaking of Jabal, son of Lamech, says that he was "the father of such as dwell in tents," the construction of the Hebrew phrase implies the *present*, "those who dwell," at the time when the author was writing.

Moreover the question whether, according to the Bible itself, some who were not in the ark with Noah may not have escaped the deluge, has in ancient times been discussed among Jews as well as Christians, and the Church has not pronounced formally on the subject. According to the text of the LXX., Methuselah must have lived six years after the deluge, whereas the Hebrew text places his death in the same year as that event.* The statements of the Greek text have been followed by many Hebrew teachers. Some Christian writers of the early ages have also adopted it, amongst others chronologers such as Eusebius. St. Jerome, in his "Questions upon Genesis," tells us that in his time this famous difficulty was the subject of many controversies.

5. To resume—Biblical tradition, and the discoveries made by the researches of modern science on the most ancient remains of man, have thrown light on the history of the primitive ages of our species, from two opposite points of view. The Bible has chiefly enunciated the facts which have some moral bearing, whence religious teaching may be extracted. Prehistoric archæology, from the nature of its only sources of information, is exclusively confined to material facts. The two domains of religion and of science here, as everywhere else, adjoin without

* The date of the death of Methuselah, as compared with that of the deluge, according to the received chronology of the three principal versions of Scripture, is as shown in the following calculation :—

	Hebrew.	Septuagint.	Samaritan.
	Years.	Years.	Years.
Adam (age at the birth of his son)	130	230	130
Seth ,, ,,	105	205	105
Enos ,, ,,	90	190	90
Cainan ,, ,,	70	170	70
Mahalaleel ,, ,,	65	165	65
Jared ,, ,,	162	162	162
Enoch ,, ,,	65	165	65
Methuselah (whole life) . .	969	969	720
	1656	2256	1407
Date of flood (B.C.) .	1656	2262	1427
Methuselah survived flood . .		6	20

—Tr.

encroaching on each other's ground; but in their points of contact, as we have shown, sacred tradition and science nowhere contradict each other. The deluge is a problem not yet indeed definitely solved, but there is nothing in the narrative irreconcilable with science. We cannot better conclude this difficult chapter than in the words of the Abbé Lambert:—"Science has no right to ask from the inspired writer reasons for all it may discover, for all it may suppose it has discovered, in the material universe which it studies. All that can reasonably be asked is that facts proved by science should not be contradicted by Scripture. It is not therefore necessary to prove the *agreement* of scientific facts with the sacred text; it is enough to prove that there is no incompatibility, no contradiction; that nothing in the sacred narrative is contrary to scientific truth or reason, and that the discoveries of science may without danger be employed to fill the vacant spaces in the Mosaic narrative."

CHAPTER IV.

HUMAN RACES AND THEIR LANGUAGES.

Chief authorities for General Ethnography:—Memoirs of the Ethnological Societies of Paris and New York.—Publications of the Société Ethnologique de Paris.—Pritchard, *Researches into the Natural History of Mankind.*— Pickering, *The Races of Man and their Geographical Distribution*, London, 1851.—Latham, *The Natural History of the Varieties of Man*, London, 1850.—Edwards, *Des charactères physiologiques des Races humaines*, Paris, 1829.—Nott and Gliddon, *Types of Mankind*, Boston, 1854.—D'Omalius d'Halloy, *Des Races humaines*, Paris, 1845.—Hollard, *De l'homme et des Races humaines*, Paris, 1853.—A. De Gobineau, *Essai sur l'inégalité des Races humaines*, Paris, 1855.—Knox, *The Races of Men*, London, 1850.—Bonstetten, *L'homme du Midi et l'homme du Nord*, chap. 5, Geneva, 1824.—Foissac, *De l'influence des climats sur l'homme*, Paris, 1837.—Hotz, *The moral and intellectual diversity of Races*, Philadelphia, 1856.—Camper, *Dissertation sur les variétés naturelles qui charactérisent la physionomie des hommes*, 1791.—A. Maury, *La Terre et l'homme*, Paris, 1857.—De Quatrefages, *Rapport sur les progrès de l'anthropologie*, Paris, 1868.

For Linguistic Science:—Michaelis, *De l'influence des opinions sur le langage*, Bremen, 1762.—Adelung, *Mithridates*, Berlin, 1806–1817.—Bopp, *Grammaire comparée des langues Indo-Européennes*, (Breal's translation), Paris, 1865–67.—Balbi, *Atlas ethnographique du Globe*, Paris, 1826.—Rapp, *Versuch einer Physiologie der Sprache*, Stuttgard, 1836.—Pott, *Etymologische Forschungen*, Lemgo, 1833-6.—Nève,

Introduction à l'histoire générale des littératures Orientales, Louvain, 1845.—Marcel, *Language as a means of Mental Culture*, London, 1853.—Obry, *Etude historique et philologique sur le participe passé et les verbes auxiliaires*, Paris, 1852.—Egger, *Notions élémentaires de grammaire comparée*, Paris, 1854.—Renan, *Histoire générale des langues sémitiques*, Paris, 1855.—*De l'origine du langage*, Paris, 1858.—Pott, *Die Ungleichheit Menschlicher Rassen*, Lemgo, 1856.—A. Maury, *La Terre et l'homme*, Paris, 1857.—Max Müller, *Lessons on the Science of Language*.—F. Baudry, *Grammaire comparée des langues classiques*, Paris, 1868.—*Le Journal de philologie comparée*, Berlin, edited by M. Adalbert Kuhn.

Section I.—The Unity of the Human Race and its Varieties.

1. Sacred tradition teaches us that the whole human race and all its varieties descend from one single original pair. Divine inspiration alone could pronounce in a definite and precise manner on a point of such primary importance in a religious, as well as in a philosophical, point of view; for in this is involved the fundamental doctrine of Christianity,—redemption. Human knowledge cannot venture on positive assertions in a matter such as this, which is too deep for research. It is only by induction that reason can trace the human race back to an original couple; the only result its investigations have attained is to demonstrate the fact, that all the varieties of mankind belong to one single species, which almost necessarily supposes one single couple for its original authors.

There are now two schools of naturalists devoted to the study of the physical organisation of man; the one admits, in conformity with sacred tradition, the unity of the human race; the other supposes that many species of men appeared, and in different places, but the authorities of the latter persuasion are not agreed as to the number of these species, which are variously stated from two to sixteen. The two theories are called Monogenistic and Polygenistic. The professors of the latter opinion follow as a rule preconceived philosophical ideas, and are really less naturalists, than enemies to Bible doctrines. All scholars who have approached the subject without opinions formed beforehand, and investigated it apart from other considerations, according to the laws of scientific method and with the assistance of observation, have decidedly pronounced, as the result of their studies, for the Monogenistic theory. The proofs which permit science to affirm and demonstrate the unity of the human species have been recently admirably collected by M. de Quatrefages, the most eminent anthropologist of France, and having profited by recent discoveries, he has presented these proofs in a more satisfactory form than they have ever before assumed. From him we borrow the materials for a rapid *résumé* of these proofs, which though they belong rather to physiology, must not be neglected by history; for the question whether all men are brothers, or whether differences of species create between them impassable barriers, must exercise a most serious influence on the facts and interpretation of history. Moreover, our origin is necessarily the first chapter in our history.

2. Mankind, considered from the naturalist's point of view, is subject to the same laws as all other organic beings. When man therefore exhibits phenomena which cannot be solved by considering him alone, we must question animals and even vegetables, and argue up from them to him. By this method we may establish in a scientific manner the unity of our species. But first, it is necessary to define what is meant by "species." "A species is an assemblage of individuals more or less like each other, who are descended, or may be considered as descended, from one single primitive pair by an uninterrupted succession of families." Individuals who differ in a marked manner from the general type are "varieties." A "race" is a variety which has been propagated by parentage. The characters peculiar to each of the human races must not be considered as characters of "species;" for the variations which we observe in one species among animals, especially among domestic animals, and which even affect the most essential parts of the skeleton, are much more considerable than those separating the white man from the negro, the two most widely differing types of humanity. Moreover, it is not possible to establish a well defined separation between the different races of men, which graduate insensibly one into the other. Now when we look at *species* of animals, however near they may be to each other, we may fix on one or more characteristics absent in one, present in the other, and clearly distinguishing them; and this is never the case with *races*. These characteristics so assimilate, that even when they are numerous we can hardly say which one is really the distinguishing trait. If we study "crosses," they reveal in their turn the fundamental difference between a *species* and a *race*. A cross between two *species* is very rare in nature. When it is brought about by the interference of man, it is, in an immense majority of cases, unfertile. A cross between *races* is always fertile. Now unions between the most widely differing types of humanity constantly present the latter character; it even sometimes happens that the fertility of races thus united, is increased.

A *race*, as we have said, is a variety which is propagated. The action of the conditions of existence in the midst of which an animal is developed, is chief among the causes tending to produce in a species, varieties, and originate a race. These influences of climate, soil, and mode of life, are very evidently those which have given rise to the different races of mankind. It is true that we no longer see the same causes bring about the same effects on the Europeans who emigrate in our times. But this is because civilised man knows so well how to defend himself against the effects of the climate in which he resides. This is his constant care, even in the native country of his race; as an emigrant his precautions are redoubled. The inhabitant of the temperate zone who goes to Siberia takes every care to keep himself warm. In India or Senegal he uses every means to escape the heat, and succeeds to a very great extent. Everywhere he carries with him manners, customs, and practices, that become part of the atmosphere in which he lives, and tend to diminish the effect of the change. Nevertheless these precautions are in some degree useless. Man in spite of all is, to some extent, affected by the new climate and new country where he fixes his abode. A European, when he ceases to resist these influences, will soon become so changed as not to be recognisable by his former countrymen. The English race, which more than any other carries with it the means of protection against exterior influences, is affected after the first generation in Australia, where nevertheless it prospers wonderfully. In the United States it has been so transformed as to be considered almost a new race.

If it is thus in our days, when man is provided with all the means of defence the most refined civilisation furnishes, what effect must these influences, which he can never completely resist, have had on the primitive families who spread themselves in a savage state over the world? In the conditions of that age of humanity, climatic influences must have had the same effect on man as on animals; and changes as great as any differences separating the races of humanity, have taken place in many species of animals when transported to new climates. Moreover, a complete change in the mode of life of a people, even under the same climate, has been found to produce facts analogous to those thus brought about in the early days of the human species, and which have given rise to its races. We have a striking example in Ireland, at the end of the war of the seventeenth century. Entire populations, driven into the wild lands of the island and exposed for generations to misery, hunger, and ignorance, have, we may almost say, returned to a savage state, and their physical characteristics, completely altered or modified, have made of them a race perfectly distinct from the people from whom they sprung, and who are to be found in their original condition in the neighbouring counties.

3. Besides, nothing more manifestly proves the unity of the human species, its descent from one stock, and that its varieties have been caused by climatic influences, than the consideration of the geographical distribution of different branches of mankind over the surface of the

globe, and the comparison of their types, with the physical and social conditions by which each is surrounded. "All traditions concur in placing the formation of the white race, that is of the race most elevated in the intellectual scale, that which possesses in the highest degree beauty, proportion, perfect balance of forces, and of physical organisàtion, in the northern part of the ancient world, situated, so to speak, at equal distances from its two extremities. The study of the migrations of races, the comparison of languages, and historical testimony, concur in making the white race radiate from the country situated at the foot of the Caucasus, comprised between the Mediterranean, the Red Sea, the Indian Ocean, the steppes of Central Asia, and the Himalaya mountains. The farther we remove from that cradle of our race, the more the characteristics of that noble race are altered or effaced. In Europe it best maintains itself. Nevertheless we no longer find, even among European people, that perfect regularity of feature, that noble symmetry, which strikes us so much in thè faces of Eastern people, among the Armenians, Persians, or the women of Georgia, or Circassia. Among Europeans there is more animation, more mobility, more expression; their beauty, in a word, is less physical than moral.

"In Africa we meet with alterations of another kind. Already the Arab inhabiting the neighbourhood of the Isthmus of Suez, peopling both shores of the Red Sea, and advancing towards the banks of the Mediterranean, has less intelligent and regular features. His brow is more receding and his head more elongated; his face has neither the beauty of complexion, the rounded contour of the Persian or Armenian, nor the freshness of the European; his skin is yellowish and sometimes brown. Advancing to the south towards the Tropic of Cancer, colour takes a still darker tint, the hair becomes crisp, the lips thick. Such is the physiognomy of the Gallas and Abyssinians.

"Further south, on the Eastern coast of Africa, the type becomes uglier still. There we find the Caffre with woolley hair, thick lips, and prominent jaws. And, finally, at the very extremity, at the farthest point in that part of the world which the human race can reach, moral and physical characteristics have arrived at their extremest point of degradation. The Hottentot presents the ugliest and least intelligent type of humanity.

"On the opposite coast of Africa, at distances still greater from the cradle of the white race, degeneration proceeds even more rapidly. The Berber races of the Sahara, are certainly descended from a white stock, but amongst them we find the first commencement of the change that has taken place in Soudan. The head is elongated, the mouth forms a salient projection, the limbs are thin and ill-proportioned, and the colour of the skin is darkened. The Fellatah of the Soudan is already a negro, but a negro whose face denotes intelligence. This remnant of nobility in the features disappears among the blacks of Senegambia, and is replaced by an increase of ugliness. The negro of Congo gives us the pure type of his race—forehead low and receding, lower jaw prominent, lips thick, nose flat, hair woolly, occiput large, intelligence limited, and almost entirely confined to manual dexterity. Lastly, at the extremity of this Western coast of Africa, the Bushman or Bosjesman, presents features more offensive, if possible, than the Hottentot.

"This gradual degeneration of the human type which may, so to speak, be stated in degrees of latitude, from the borders of the Caspian Sea to the Cape of Good Hope, is not less decided if we travel east or south-east from the same original centre. If we penetrate the steppes of Central Asia, we meet with the Mongolians, with prominent cheek bones, small sunken eyes obliquely cut, triangular faces, square and thickset figures. All harmony in the outline has disappeared. The Dravidian race were driven by the white man, from the greater part of Hindustan, and took refuge in the mountains of their ancient country. The Malays, their advance guard, who have spread from the Peninsula beyond the Ganges into the islands, from the Moluccas to Madagascar, present features even more savage than the Mongolians, and are a darker coloured race. Among the most barbarous of them the skin is almost black, and the limbs already show that meagreness, that shrivelled type, which in Africa announces nearness to the negro. The Alfourou varies from light to dark brown, and his hair grows in enormous tufts, as among the most brutalised of the Malay people. Finally, beyond the Alfourou race, expelled by them, and spread here and there in the interior of the islands from the Andamans to the Philippines,—the Australians and the Negritos, whose country extends as far as Van Dieman's Land, exhibit the last degree of rudeness, deformity, stupidity, and degradation.

"If, instead of travelling south-east, we advance beyond the Mongolians to the north and north-east, we find an alteration of another kind indeed, but not less marked. As less extent of ground was open for the migration of nations, so that our species could not pass so far from the place where it attained its highest degree of development, there has not been so large a field open for the process of degeneration. The Ugro-finnish, who are spread over the whole north of the globe, from Lapland to the country of the Esquimaux, still resemble the Mongolian race; but their eyes are generally less oblique, their skin is not so decided a yellow, their hair is more abundant, their forehead lower, their face denoting less intelligence.

"America, if we exclude the northern part inhabited by the Arctic race, comprises another people, whose mode of distribution is not always in complete correspondence with the law we are attempting to prove. In North America, man has a peculiarly energetic character in his features. The outline of his face is angular, the forehead extraordinarily receding, without however being depressed like that of the negro; the skin is red, he has little or no beard, the eyes are slightly projecting, the cheek bones prominent. This type reaches its culminating point of beauty and intelligence in the tropical regions of Mexico and Peru. Beyond these countries, as we descend southward, the skin darkens, or rather embrowns, the features become ugly, the outline loses its curve and regularity, the limbs their handsome shape. Such is the character of the Guaranas, of the Botocondos, of the Aymaras. When we arrive at the southern extremity of America, we find only most deformed, most miserable creatures, the brutalised and stupid people of Terra del Fuego.

"This new and apparently anomalous distribution of the races of the New World, far from being an exception to the law which shows us the human race most perfect where the climatic conditions are most favourable, does in fact only confirm it. America has its temperate regions situated farther south than Europe, because the continent is colder; the mountain chain, traversing it like a backbone, forms a succession of elevated plateaus. It is in fact in Mexico and Peru, that is, in the countries which, on account of their elevation, possess those conditions most favourable for life, that the indigenous civilisation of America attained to its highest degree of development."—A. MAURY.

4. The distribution of mankind in all parts of the world, and in all climates, that we have just sketched, is another of the facts in which the science of anthropology, guided by the analogies shown by most recent observations on the geographical distribution of animals, finds a decisive proof of the unity of our species, in the fact that, however widely it has spread, it must have come from that one single spot where man first appeared. Animals, like plants, are not distributed haphazard over the globe. Observation teaches us that each region has its species, its genera, its peculiar types. Experience proves that some species may be transported from one region to another, where they will live and prosper. But there is no one species which is naturally cosmopolitan. So that, as far as animals and plants are concerned, we must give up the idea of one single centre, and accept that of very many centres of creation.

The partisans of the Polygenistic theory are obliged, from the moment that they divide man into more than one species, to admit for him these many centres of creation. But there again they are in opposition to the laws which science demonstrates to have presided over the distribution of organised beings. In fact, though they have a more extended area than the *species*, the *genera* do not the less present analogous facts of localisation; for, as M. de Candolle has so well said, "The same causes have affected both species and genera." The more perfect the organisation of a vegetable, or of an animal becomes, the more restricted is its area. With regard to mammalia particularly, we can trace step by step the contraction of the area coincident with the improvement in organisation. When we arrive at the great anthropomorphic apes, which are nearest to man in a physical point of view, we find that nearly every genus is represented by one single species, that no one of these genera is common to both Asia and Africa, no one has spread over the whole of that part of the world which it inhabits, and finally, that the habitat of each one is remarkably limited. If then we suppose that the human race can be divided into many species, each of distinct origin,—if we admit that this type, the most perfect of all, even in a merely organic point of view, can have arisen in more than one centre of creation, and that it is not characteristic of any one in particular, we should make man the sole exception to the laws of nature. Thus direct observation and the science of physiology, whilst they enable us to state, in accordance with the ingenious expression of M. de Quatrefages, that "everything is as if the whole of mankind had commenced with one original and single pair," teach us nothing with regard to the existence of this original and single pair. Divine revelation alone can instruct us on that subject.

SECTION II.—THE FOUR GREAT RACES OF MANKIND.

1. THE numerous varieties of the human species whose geographical distribution we have described, divide into four principal races, four great types, which comprise secondary and mixed races, each of them including a certain number, first of families, and then of nations. These four races are :—

The White, also but erroneously called Caucasian, by some authors. We have already pointed out its original centre, whence it has spread into India, Arabia, Syria, Asia Minor, and Egypt.

The Red, exclusively inhabiting America.

The Yellow, which has existed in China, from very remote antiquity, and has spread into all the countries inhabited by Mongolian populations, as well as into the Malacca Peninsula, and the Malay Islands.

Lastly, the Black, which belongs to Central and Western Africa, and is distributed over the tropics from the east coast of Africa to Australia.

2. The negroes of the most characteristic type have the skull elongated and narrow, especially at the temples. The upper jaw bone projects forward, after the fashion called by naturalists prognathism, and gives rise to the most striking traits of the black face, the slightly projecting nose, broad at the base of the nostrils, and the exaggerated

development of lip. The hair is black, short, and woolly, and is in general very scanty, as is the case also with the various mammalia of the Negro country. With some peculiarities in the form of the body, and a perceptible curve of the legs, these are the essential and distinctive characteristics of the black race, much more so than colour, as there are some people of white race, such as the Abyssinians, to whom long residence in equatorial Africa has given an equally dark coloured skin.

The skull of the yellow race is rounded in form, the oval of the head is larger than with Europeans. The cheek bones are very projecting, the cheeks rise towards the temples, so that the outer corners of the eyes are elevated, the eyelids seem half closed. The forehead is flat above the eyes. The bridge of the nose flat, the chin short, the ears disproportionately large, and projecting from the head. The colour of the skin is generally yellow, and in some branches turns to brown. There is little hair on the body, beard is rare, the hair of the head is coarse and, like the eyes, almost always black.

We have already mentioned the principal features which distinguish the red man's face ; in skeleton he is very like the white. He is distinguished by his colour, always reddish brown, or approaching to copper, more or less deep in tone, and by the scarcity of hair, for all American races have scanty and short hair, and are beardless.

As for our white race, it is, above all, characterised by the beauty of the oval which forms the head. The eyes are horizontal, with more or less widely opened lids ; the nose rather projects than is large, the mouth small or moderately pierced, the lips thin : the beard is ample, the hair long, smooth, or curled, and its colour variable. The skin is of a rosy white, with more or less transparency, according to the climate, habits, or temperament. Morally and intellectually the white race has a marked superiority over all others. In the nations of this race, we find, from remote antiquity, the greatest development of civilisation and the most progressive tendencies.

3. It would be most interesting if we could determine, among these four types of humanity,—and, in the most ancient times to which history and the monuments of civilisation go back, they are found as distinct as they are to-day ;—which is the most ancient, and whether either of them can claim to represent, with any certainty, the primitive man. Unfortunately this is a question science is unable positively to answer. There are no certain elements for determining the primitive type of our species. It appears very probable that this type no longer exists in the world, and that no actual race entirely resembles it. The conditions of climate under which man first appeared on the earth, have now entirely changed, for they belonged to another geological period. How is it possible that these great changes can have left unchanged the

primitive type of humanity? Some anthropologists have wished to seek the type of primitive man in the lowest ranks of the human species, among the Hottentots or the Aborigines of Australia; but such an opinion is not scientifically admissible; these tribes show, in their physical characteristics, such a state of degradation as to prove that they were once in a more elevated condition, from which they have gradually declined. On the other hand, it is almost impossible not to admit that the advance of the white race towards perfection is in a great measure due to the exceptionally favourable conditions of climate in which it has lived, as well as to the long continued influence of civilisation, when we see, as occasionally we do see, how much this race degenerates, how near it approaches to a savage state, when these favouring circumstances are removed.

We see among all species of animals, presenting numerous varieties, phenomena which naturalists have designated by the name "Atavism." This is the sporadic appearance in all varieties of individuals who reproduce the type, not of their direct ancestors, but of the original species, before the formation of varieties. Certain facts occurring from time to time among the different races of humanity, seem entitled to be considered as instances of Atavism. The most able Anthropologists, such as M. de Quatrefages, and Dr. Pruner Bey, consider that they throw light on the primitive ancestry of our species. Two points at any rate seem to be proved; that the faces of the first men were to some extent prognathic, and their colour was not black. The anatomical trait of prognathism, especially of the upper jaw, exists in all the families of the black race, and is not less apparent among part of the yellow race. A decided tendency in that direction is seen in the Ugro-finnish races. It frequently appears in isolated individuals of the purest branches of the white race. Those remains of human heads which have, at present, been recovered from caverns of the close of the quaternary period, are decidedly prognathic. "Every thing seems to indicate," says M. de Quatrefages, "that this characteristic must have existed in the first ancestors of mankind." We are enabled to be more positive on the next point, that the first ancestors of our species were not black; the darkened colour of the skin, the excessive development of the black matter or *pigment* which forms under the epidermis, is unquestionably an effect of a burning climate and of the sun's power, produced only in tropical regions which were certainly not the primitive cradle of humanity. Moreover, we often see individuals, white or yellow, appear from the result of "Atavism" among negro nations; while no negro was ever born from white or yellow people. M. de Quatrefages is also of opinion that we might go still farther, and conjecture, from some other facts of the same nature, that the original type of humanity approached that of the yellow races, whose languages also are still preserved in the most primitive state. But we do not venture to follow him on ground still so insecure; and prefer to confine ourselves to the two points—one probable, the other certain—which we have just explained.

SECTION III.—THE DESCENDANTS OF NOAH, ACCORDING TO THE BOOK OF GENESIS.

Authorities:—Bochart, *Phaleg*, vol. i. of his complete works, Leyden, 1712.—Ch. Lenormant, *Introduction à l'Histoire de l'Asie Occidentale*, Paris, 1838.—Knobel, *Die Völkertafel der Genesis*, Giessen, 1851.

1. NOAH, as we have already said, had three sons, Shem, Ham, and Japhet. In the 10th chapter of the book of Genesis, Moses gives us a table of the nations known in his time, as affiliated to these three great chiefs of the new race of postdiluvian humanity. This is the most ancient, the most precious, the most complete document which we possess on the distribution of the ancient nations of the world. We may even consider it as anterior to Moses, for it represents nations in positions which the Egyptian monuments show us to have been much changed in several important points, before the time of the Exodus. Moreover, the enumeration is made there in regular geographical order, from Babylon and Chaldæa as a centre, not from Egypt or Palestine. It seems therefore probable that this table of nations and their origin was part of the tradition brought by the family of Abraham from Chaldæa, and that it represents the distribution of nations known to the civilised world at the time when the Patriarch left the banks of the Euphrates, that is about 2,000 years before the Christian Era.

This document furnishes an inestimably valuable basis for the researches of ethnography, that is the science which investigates the relationships of nations with each other, and their origin. The attentive study of historical tradition, the comparison of languages, and the examination of the physiological characteristics of different nations, lead to results in complete accordance with the inspired volume. We are about to explain, as briefly as possible, the facts resulting from the ethnographic teachings of the book of Genesis, and those which modern science has supplied, to complete or supplement them.

2. *Family of Ham.*—Ham, whose name signifies the "Sun-burned," was the father of the great family from whom the people of Phœnicia, of Egypt, and Ethiopia, were primarily descended. These nations are now represented by the Fellahs of Egypt, the Nubians, the Abyssinians, and the Tuaricks, and possess all the characteristics of the white race, but are distinguished by their dark colour, passing from light brown to bronze, and almost into black; by their short stature, receding chin,

thick, though not prominent lips, scanty beard, and very curly though never quite woolly hair. The classifications of anthropology, founded entirely on physical characteristics, place them exactly as does the sacred text.

According to the book of Genesis, Ham had four sons, Cush, Mizraim, Phut, and Canaan. The identity of the race of Cush with the Ethiopians is certain. The hieroglyphic inscriptions of Egypt always designate the people of the Upper Nile, south of Nubia, by the name of Cush. In Scripture, Mizraim is the name constantly applied to Egypt, and in our own times the Arabs still use the name Mizr, both for the capital of Egypt and for the country itself. The identity of the descendants of Phut with the people who inhabited the northern coasts of Africa, has not been established in quite so certain a manner. The most competent critics are however of opinion that this name, in its most extended signification, applies to the primitive Libyans, amongst whom some Japhetic tribes subsequently settled. Under the name of Canaan are comprised the Phœnicians and all the tribes in their vicinity, who, before the establishment of the Hebrews, inhabited the country called Canaan, from Sidon and Gaza to Sodom and Gomorrah, that is, the territory lying between the Mediterranean and the Dead Sea, which in later times was called the "Holy Land."

It seems certain that the Hamitic race inhabited at first a great part of Western and Southern Asia, before the arrival of the children of Shem, who drove them out from thence. Nimrod, a descendant of Cush, reigned in Babylon, built Erech and Calneh, in the land of Shinar, and established there the first of all empires. The Hamites were the first inhabitants of the country bordered by the Oxus, extending towards the upper course of the Indus, whence is derived the name Hindoo Koosh, always given to the mountain chain of this region. All scholars are now agreed that the banks of the Tigris, Southern Persia, and part of India itself (where the tribes of this race were called Kausikas) were peopled by the Cushite family, before being occupied by the descendants of Shem, and by the Arians of the race of Japhet. There are also good reasons for believing that the Carians, the original inhabitants of great part of Asia Minor, were of the race of Ham. And lastly, the same race exercised in early times an uncontested sovereignty on the coasts of Carmania and Gedrosia, along the Indian Ocean, and over all the south of the Arabian Peninsula.

We see that, of the three great races who separated after the confusion of tongues, the Hamites were the first to leave the common centre of the human race, and that they spread themselves over a vast extent of territory, and founded the earliest monarchies. Amongst them material civilisation made at first the most rapid progress. But Noah had laid a curse on his son Ham for having been wanting in filial respect, and for having exposed him to derision during a fit of drunkenness. "A servant of servants shall he be to his brethren" had been the sentence, and the curse has been fulfilled in all its completeness. The Empires founded by the Hamites soon came in contact with the two other races, who, in the contest which ensued, were victorious, and dispossessed the original inhabitants of the countries they had occupied. The Semites replaced them in Chaldæa, Assyria, Palestine, and Arabia; the Arian race in India and Persia. The descendants of the cursed son maintained their power only in Africa, particularly in Egypt, where the most flourishing of their colonies sprung up. The descendants of Ham were the first after the deluge to make progress in material civilisation, which they carried to a high degree of development. But beneath it all their nature was unchanged; their race always retained the trace of the grossness and depravity which had drawn down on Ham his father's curse. The Hamitic people were always deeply corrupt. Their religion never advanced beyond the most absolute materialism, shamelessly expressed by most revolting myths, and by symbols of inconceivable obscenity. Thus it was that the triumph of the races of Shem and Japhet always resulted in the substitution of a higher and purer civilisation for that of the Hamites, the introduction of greater moral purity, and of a religion more spiritual, even when tainted with the errors of idolatry.

3. *Race of Shem.*—The descendants of Shem were the next to disperse themselves over the world, leaving the country where man had originally dwelt after the deluge. They occupied the countries extending from Upper Mesopotamia to the southern extremities of Arabia, and from the borders of the Mediterranean Sea to the country beyond the Tigris. The first-born of Shem, according to the book of Genesis, was Elam, representing the Elamites of Susiana. The first settlement of a mixed Hamitic and Turanian population in that country was in fact replaced by inhabitants of Semitic race; but these last were not able to maintain themselves there, and at a later period were conquered by the Arians, descendants of Japhet. Susiana, between Persia properly so called and the Tigris, always had these elements in its population, which seems to have been an essentially mixed race. Asshur, the second son of Shem, was the founder of that powerful nation who, under the name of Assyrians, played so great a part in the history of Western Asia. "Asshur," says the Bible, "builded Nineveh and Calah and Resen." At Babylon and throughout Chaldæa the language, as we know now by the monuments, was the same as at Nineveh; the preponderating influence also was that of the race of Asshur, but the mass of the population seems to have remained Hamitic, of the Cushite branch, which had formed the primitive empire of Nimrod, itself also containing a mixture of other elements.

The book of Genesis next mentions Arphaxad, whose name means "border of the Chaldæans," or rather "neighbourhood of the Chaldæans." This name, like the greater number of those given to the grandsons of Noah, is rather the geographical designation of the country where he founded a settlement, than the proper name of the individual. It determines the localities which were inhabited in the first age after the deluge, by those nearly related families, who, in later times, became the parent stock of the Hebrews and Arabs. In fact, among the descendants of Arphaxad we find Eber, the direct ancestor of Abraham and the Hebrew nation, and also Joktan, who was the progenitor of the most ancient Arab tribes, of those with whom in later times the children of Ishmael amalgamated, and over whom they obtained supremacy. Moreover, we shall see presently that at the moment of his call Abraham was still living in the midst of the Chaldæans. Lud was the fourth son of Shem. He personifies the ancient inhabitants of Lydia. According to all appearances this people originally dwelt in the neighbourhood of Assyria and Mesopotamia, whence in later times they migrated to the western extremity of Asia Minor. The most recent investigations of the little we know of the Lydian language, and of their traditions, goes far to prove their Semitic blood. The last of the children of this Patriarch, according to the Bible enumeration, was Aram. He was the parent of the Syrian race, which occupied all the country between the Mediterranean and the Euphrates. There were also Aramæans in the western part of Mesopotamia. The Hebrews therefore divided the country of Aram into several regions; 1st. Aram Naharaim, or "Aram of the two rivers," that is, the "Mesopotamia" of the Greeks, between the Euphrates and the Tigris; 2nd. Aram properly so called, that is, Syria, whose most ancient and important city was Damascus; and 3rd. Aram Zobah, or the region in which in later times was formed the kingdom of Palmyra.

The group of Semitic nations, whose chief representatives in our days are the Arabs and the Jews, present a purer and handsomer type of the white race than any of the Hamitic nations; the beard is fuller, the complexion clearer though still dark, the stature loftier, with a spare habit of body. The face is generally long and thin, the forehead rather low, the nose aquiline, the mouth and chin receding, so as to give a rounded rather than a straight profile, the eyes sunken, black and bright.

4. *Race of Japhet.*—The name of this youngest born of the sons of Noah, signifies "extension," because that his posterity was to occupy an immense extent of country. His family remained longest united, and was the last to leave the neighbourhood of the place where Noah had fixed his residence after the deluge. The book of Genesis gives the

names of his seven sons as Gomer, Magog, Madai, Tubal, Meshech, Tiras, and Javan. Gomer personifies the families originally established on the northern coast of the Euxine, and north of Greece. From these were in due course of time to spring a people well known to the Greek and Roman historians, as Cimmerians, Cimbri, or Kymry, who were for ages the terror of Asia and Europe, and who even made Rome tremble at the summit of her power. Three sons of Gomer are mentioned: Ashkenaz, whose name seems composed of the Gothic roots *As chunis*, "the race of Ases," and which represents the Germanic and Scandinavian nations not yet separated, and inhabiting a limited district to the north-east of the Black Sea; Riphath, that is, the group of Celts or Gauls, then established in their first European settlement on the Riphæan mountains—the present Carpathians, before entering on their last migration towards the France of our days; and lastly, Togarmah, in whom tradition has always recognised the Armenians.

That Madai is synonymous with the Medes is certain. He represents the great Iranian family which holds so important a place among the Japhetic and Arian populations. The identity of Tubal and the Tibareni is equally well established; these people as late as the classical ages inhabited the mountains bordering on Colchis; from them are descended the isolated races who still live in the valleys of the Caucasus. Meshech seems to correspond with the Moschi of Herodotus, who occupied the territory between the country of the Tibareni and Phrygia. To the same race would seem to belong the neighbouring nations of the north of Asia Minor, Paphlagonians, and Meriandynians, inhabitants of Pontus. Tiras can only be the ancestor of the Thracians. The Greek historians also have informed us that the Thracians came originally from Asia Minor, and that having left Bithynia at some unknown epoch, they came across the Hellespont to seek a settlement in the countries to the north of Macedonia.

Javan, or Ioun, was the father of the Ionians and Greeks; leaving the southern parts of Asia Minor, the sons of Javan spread themselves over the coasts and islands of the Ægæan Sea. From these primitive Ionians came Elishah, Tarshish, Kittim, and Dodanim. Elishah is Hellas, that is, Greece. Dodanim personifies the Pelasgic race of the Epirotes, whose most important religious centre was at Dodona. Kittim represents the inhabitants of the islands of the Archipelago, and Cyprus, where this people had founded the town of Citium. Finally, Tarshish ought probably to be the Tyrrhenian Pelasgians, a branch of whom were established in Greece, and who formed the primitive population of a great part of Italy.

Moses in enumerating the sons of Japhet, naturally only mentioned those whose descendants were likely to be known to the Hebrews of his time. But the science of our days, guided by physiological and linguistic affinities, is enabled to complete the testimony of the book of Genesis on this point, and to assign a still larger number of nations to the Japhetic stock. It is universally agreed to recognise as descendants of Japhet in Europe, the Greeks and Romans, the Germans, the Celts, Scandinavians, and Slavonians ; in Asia, the Persians, the Medes, the Bactrians, and the higher castes of India. These last nations, known by the collective name of "Arians," remained for a long time concentrated in the countries watered by the Oxus and Jaxartes, that is in Bactria and Sogdiana, the region which was the original dwelling of the whole race. Thence one branch directed its course to the south, crossed the Hindoo Koosh, and penetrated into India, destroying or subjugating the earlier Hamitic population. The other established itself in the country which lies between the Caspian Sea and the Tigris, and in the mountains of Media and Persia. We see that in very ancient times they mixed with the Assyrians, and that they even ruled over them for several centuries.

The race of Japhet is then that which is also designated, to indicate the extent of its domain, the *Indo-European race.* To this race we ourselves belong. It is a race noble beyond all others, the race to which Providence has assigned the mission of carrying to a degree of perfection, unknown to other races, arts, sciences, philosophy. "God," said Noah, according to the Bible, "shall enlarge Japhet, and he shall dwell in the tents of Shem, and Canaan shall be his servant." That blessing and prophecy are accomplished, for the race of Japhet has not only become the most numerous and the most widely spread, but it is also the dominant race of the world which day by day advances toward universal sovereignty.

5. There is one of the sons of Japhet of whom we have not yet spoken, for the subject requires rather more detailed explanation. He represents a group of nations more extensive than the others, and of very peculiar physiognomy—we speak of Magog. This name in sacred Scripture is almost always associated with Gog. The very frequent allusions in the Hebrew prophets to the incursions and ravages of the sons of Gog and Magog, induce us to recognise them as the nomadic tribes of the north-east, near the Caspian Sea. Their name has been compared to that of the Massagetæ. The historian Josephus, the recorder of the traditions of the Jewish nation, calls them Scythians. Everything seems then to prove that the inspired writer of the book of Genesis, under the name of Magog, intended to represent the numerous tribes composing the secondary race now designated by science, "Turanian." This race, one of the largest, both numerically, and with regard to the extent of territory which it occupies, is divided into two great branches, the Ugro-finnish and the Dravidian. The first must be again subdivided into the Turkish, including the populations of

Turkestan, and of the Steppes of Central Asia, as well as the Hungarians, who have been for a long time settled in Europe; and the Uralo-finnish group, comprising the Finns, the Esthonians, the Tchoudes, and in general, nearly all the tribes of the north of Europe and Asia. The country of the Dravidian branch is, on the contrary, to the south. This branch is in fact composed of the indigenous people of the Peninsula of Hindustan, Tamuls, Telingas, Carnates, who were subjugated by the Arian race, and who appear to have originally driven before them the negroes of the Australian group, the original inhabitants of the soil, who are now represented by the almost savage tribe of the Khonds.

The Turanian race is one of the oldest in the world, and appears to have migrated at the same time as the Hamitic; it might even be possible to restore the chief features of an epoch, when the sons of Turan and of Cush alone occupied the greater part of Europe and Asia, whilst the Semites and the Arians had not yet left the regions which were the cradle of our species. The skulls discovered in France, England and Belgium, in caves of the close of the quaternary epoch, appear, from their characteristics, to belong to a Turanian race, to the Uralo-finnish group, and particularly resemble those of the Esthonians. Wherever the Japhetic or pure Indo-European race extended, it seems to have encountered a Turanian population which it conquered and finally amalgamated with itself. This was the course of events in Western Europe, where the Basques, the descendants of the ancient Iberians, are possibly the last remains of this original population; in Hindustan; in the interior of Persia, and in Carmania, where the southern coast was occupied by Cushites. In Media and Susiana the Turanian element struggled more successfully and managed to maintain itself almost on a footing of equality with the Arian. We shall see as we proceed that it composed a considerable portion of the original population of Chaldæa and Babylonia, and that it appears to have furnished the dominant and especially the sacerdotal class.

Both ethnography and linguistic science attest the fundamental unity of the Turanian race, which, in spite of its extent, presents itself to us as a mixed race, intermediate between the white and yellow, passing gradually from one to the other. At each extremity of the scale, we find types which coincide almost completely with those of the other races. The Uzbecs, the Osmanli Turks, and the Hungarians, are not to be distinguished in appearance from the most perfect branches of the white race. On the other hand the Tchoudes almost exactly resemble the Tongouses, who belong to the yellow race. The intermediary physiognomy of the Turanians may arise from two causes. Either they spring from a mixture of white and yellow elements, or, if the conjecture of M. de Quatrefages, as to the original characteristics of some of the features peculiar to the yellow race be correct, the Turanian race results from a stoppage of development during the progress from the primitive human type to the complete perfection of the civilised white man. In any case, the presence of this race among the descendants of Japhet, in the 10th chapter of Genesis, is justified by its close approach, at any rate on one side, to the white race, particularly to the Japhetic family, as has been proved by scholars who have so successfully employed themselves in fixing the place of the Turanian languages in comparative philology, —M. Pott in Germany, M. Max Müller in England, and M. Oppert in France. All appearances would lead us to regard the Turanian race as the first branch of the family of Japhet, which went forth into the world, and by that premature separation, by an isolated and antagonistic existence, took, or rather preserved, a completely distinct physiognomy. We are especially led to consider the Turanian as a type of the white race, imperfectly developed, rather than the result of a cross between the two races, by the marked disposition to prognathism existing in all its branches and which, as we have already said, appears to be a very primitive peculiarity, gradually effaced by favourable conditions of life, and by civilisation.

6. The descendants of Shem, Ham and Japhet, so admirably catalogued by Moses, include then, as we have seen, one only of the races of humanity, the white race, whose three chief divisions he gives us as now recognised by anthropologists. The other three races, yellow, black and red, have no place in the Bible list of the nations sprung from Noah. We need not be surprised at this, in the case of the first and third. The inspired author of the book of Genesis could only speak to the men of his time of nations whom they knew. Now, in the days of Moses, no one in Egypt, or among the Israelites, had any idea of the existence of the Chinese, or of the red American race. The negroes, however, were perfectly well known. Moses especially, educated in Egypt, must have seen very many of them, for the Pharaohs of his day made wars on them, and led thousands away captive into the Egyptian cities. It was not then from ignorance or omission that he did not mention them in his enumeration of the descendants of the three sons of Noah; it was voluntarily, and doubtless with some express intention, though we may not be able to explain it. Those who suppose that the inspired author believed that the deluge was not universal as to all the then formed branches of the human species, that there were tribes, besides the family of Noah, who escaped the flood, find in this fact one of their most specious arguments. The text of the Bible, however, has nothing expressly opposed to the supposition that Noah might have had, after the deluge, other sons besides Shem, Ham and Japhet, from whom might have sprung the races which do not appear in the genealogy of these three personages. It does not, as we have already

said, in any way oppose the hypothesis that some families sprung from the three Noachian patriarchs may have left the common centre of humanity before the building of the Tower of Babel, and the confusion of tongues, and may have given birth to those great races who, becoming developed in absolute isolation, have assumed a perfectly distinct physiognomy and have remained shut out from the history of the rest of mankind. In the table of affiliation in the 10th chapter of Genesis, Moses has professed only to include those nations who after having lived together, speaking the same language, in the land of Shinar, were dispersed in consequence of the disaster of Babel. And these were the nations who composed the white race, the superior and dominant race, to whom, over all others, pre-eminence must be conceded and the glory of representing humanity in its noblest aspect.

SECTION IV.—THE PRINCIPAL FAMILIES OF LANGUAGES.

1. WE cannot, in a book of this kind, discuss that most difficult philosophical problem—the origin of language. It forms no part of our plan, and is not practically useful for historical purposes. Whatever opinion we may hold on this subject, it is certain that the gradual development of language, rendering it for every age the perfect expression of thought, and its adaptability to the manners and state of civilisation of each people, are purely human results produced by those especial and sublime faculties with which the Creator has endowed our species. To study and compare the infinitely varied languages which are spoken by mankind, to discover their general laws, to group them in families, to seek out their relationships and affinities, are the objects of comparative philology, as yet quite a new science, but one holding a foremost place among the acquirements of our age in the domain of learning. It takes for the object of its investigations, languages as they now exist, and does not attempt to trace back their origin beyond the region of positive fact.

The questions of primary origin, by revelation, by voluntary agreement among mankind, or by the necessary and spontaneous effect of their organisation, so much debated among philosophers, do not belong to this science ; if at any time it does approach this problem, it is merely as a corollary to its observations. We have not, unfortunately, space to give to this subject all the development it deserves. We cannot even attempt a complete sketch, however rapid, but can only indicate the chief points of interest. We must confine ourselves to enumerating in few words the principal families of the idioms spoken on the earth, and afterwards adding some details as to the most perfect languages, those most advanced in their development, those also which have had most effect on civilisation—for in no others is there any literature worthy of the name—that is the inflected languages of the Semitic, and of the Japhetic, or Indo-European nations.

2. Ever since man began to speak, that is, ever since he began to exist, the languages of various races have passed through innumerable modifications, caused by the progress of knowledge among those by whom they were spoken, by intercommunication, and by the reciprocal influence of one idiom on another. It is therefore as impossible to trace back to a primitive language, as we have found it impossible to trace back to a primitive race. Too many changes have been in operation since man left the birth-place of his race. The utmost we can do is to recover from some ancient languages a few traces of the original idiom, in other words, to find a certain number of the processes by which the earliest men made known their thoughts. "The earliest feature in these primitive languages," says M. Maury, in agreement with all philologers, "was doubtless the predominance of outward impression in the formation of signs, and the pre-eminently concrete form in which thought was embodied. Just as the human mind clothes its first perceptions, not in the abstract and general form that can only be obtained by elimination and analysis, but in the particular form, in one sense more synthetic, including and confounding mere accessories with absolute truth; so primitive language almost entirely ignored metaphysical abstraction. No doubt, pure reason is reflected in this, as in all other results of human faculties. The most humble exercise of intelligence implies most elevated notions. Speech, even its most simple state, pre-supposes absolute and eminently pure models, but all was expressed in a concrete and tangible form."

In designating objects, imitation, or "onomatopœia," seems to have been the ordinary method employed. The human voice, being at once both sign and sound, it was natural to take the sounds of the voice to designate the sounds of nature. Moreover, as the choice of appellations was not arbitrary, and as man has never chosen sounds at haphazard as signs of his thoughts, we may be sure that of all words actually in use there is not one for which there is not a sufficient reason, either as a primitive fact, or as a remnant of a more ancient language. Now, the primitive fact that must have determined the choice of words is, without doubt, the attempt to imitate the object wished to be expressed, especially if we consider the perceptive instincts that must have governed the first steps of the human mind. The comparative study of various languages and the traces of their elementary forms, may also give a certain idea of the language of the first men. This study has enabled a celebrated philologist, Jacob Grimm,* to trace the following sketch of what primi-

* *Mémoire sur l'origine du langage* in the *Mémoires de l'académie de Berlin*, 1852.

tive language must have been. "Language on its first appearance was simple, without artificial processes, full of life and the energy of youth. All the words were short, monosyllabic, generally formed of short vowels and simple consonants. Words were joined and agglomerated in speech, like blades of grass in turf. All its conceptions resulted from perception, from clear intuition, forming one thought, and becoming in its turn the starting point for a host of other equally simple ideas. The connections between the words and the ideas were simple, but were frequently disfigured by the addition of unnecessary words. At each progressive step, spoken language assumed more fulness and flexibility, but was still wanting in rhythm and harmony. Thought had not as yet become fixed, and therefore primitive speech could leave no monument of its existence." The languages that emerged from this primitive idiom underwent modifications in accordance with fixed laws, in the same way as all other natural phenomena. Comparative philology has been enabled to discover the most essential of these laws, and the varying effects in the different languages, the development of which they have governed.

"Three distinct epochs mark the history of language: the monosyllabic, the agglutinative, and the inflected. Not that all languages have necessarily passed through these three phases, but because the idioms belonging to the last epoch, that of inflexion, bear the marks of a more developed organisation than those of the intermediate epoch corresponding to that of agglutination; these latter languages being themselves better organised than the monosyllabic tongues. Among all languages, ancient and modern, some have passed through the three phases, others have been arrested in their development. Thus agglutination includes the monosyllabic state, and inflection includes both the agglutinative and the monosyllabic states. Exactly as among species of animals, some remain as elementary organisms, whilst others progress during the period of gestation from that organism, to a higher and more developed organisation."—A. MAURY.

3. Monosyllabic languages consist only of simple words, expressed by one single emission of the voice. These words are both substantives and verbs; they express the notion, the idea, independently of the employment, namely, the way in which the word is put into relation with other words, indicating its categorical sense in the phrase.

The majority of the languages of the yellow race have stopped at this stage of development. The ancient Chinese is perhaps the best and purest example. The modern Chinese is also in the monosyllabic state, but tendencies to agglutination begin to appear. This is also the case in Annamese, Siamese, Burmese, and in general in all the Indo-Chinese idioms; in the Thibetan, as well as in the languages of some primitive tribes of the north of India, who have been driven by Arian conquest into the valleys of the Himalayas.

From the dialects we have just named we pass, by an almost insensible transition, to the agglutinated languages. These, in the Old World—for we leave out the indigenous languages of America, and their peculiar process of agglutination—constitute a vast group, embracing the idioms spoken by all the Turanian nations, which have received from Professor Max Müller and Mr. Logan the name of "Turanian group of languages." The fundamental character of this group, and of the state of language it represents, is the use of monosyllabic particles, indicating all the modifications of language, all the ideas of relation possible between the different words in a phrase. These particles or "post positions" are "glued" to the root, which remains invariable, defining its meaning, lengthening it out almost indefinitely, without any fusion or contraction, either with each other, or with the root or primitive word. The Turanian or agglutinated languages of the Old World are generally very harmonious in their vocalisation, and exhibit a marked tendency to avoid the junction of many consonants, always terminating the fundamental word or root with a vowel. The grammatical laws, the characteristic method of formation, are the same for all, and clearly prove the essential unity of this group. But the vocabularies vary almost infinitely between one and the other, a circumstance, moreover, to be observed in all the languages of uncivilised people who, from their mode of life, are completely isolated from one another, even when near neighbours.

The Turanian languages may be divided into families, corresponding exactly to the divisions of the Turanian nations. The two principal are the Tartaro-finnish and Dravidian. The first is composed of three branches, each subdivided into a great number of small groups and idioms; first, the Turkish, which, as its name indicates, is formed of the languages of all the tribes of Turkestan, and of those who, like the Osmanlis, have descended from them. Next the Uralo-finnish branch, represented in Europe by the Finlandish, the Magyar, the Esthonian, and the Lapponese; in Asia, by the dialects spoken in the regions of the Oural and Altai, such as the Ostiak and the Samoiede. Finally, the Tartar branch, properly so called, spoken by the northern people of the yellow race, Mongols and Tongouses. We might add a fourth branch, formed by the Japanese and Corean, which have also sprung from the same source. The Dravidian family is composed of the languages of the southern part of Hindustan, the principal being the Tamil, the Telinga, and the Canarese.

The Tartaro-finnish presents a state of language slightly more advanced than that of the Dravidian family. The roots are generally of two syllables, accented on the first; but in this dissyllable we find the unmistakable trace of the primitive monosyllable that still exists in the roots of the Dravidian family. These last languages are more harmonious, and, compared with them, the Tartaro-finnish tongues are hard and roughened, so to speak, by the cold of the countries where they are spoken, above all the Magyar. The Finnish only is an exception; it equals in softness and harmony the most musical of the languages of Hindustan.

4. Inflected languages are peculiar to the white race, and are those which have attained to the highest degree of development. They result from the most complete progress of thought and civilisation :—

"In these languages the root undergoes a phonetic alteration, destined to express the modifications resulting from the differences of the relations binding the root to the other words. The elements, which still possess a character so rigid and immutable in the agglutinated languages, become in the inflected more simple, more organic. An inflected language represents the highest degree of grammatical structure, and is best adapted to the expression and development of ideas. Nothing can better show the difference that separates the agglutinated from the inflected languages than the contrast between the respective declensions and conjugations of these two classes of idioms. In declension the agglutinated languages have but the slightest separation between the case and its post position; number is simply expressed by a termination; and there is as yet no blending of these words with the principal word or root. The genders are hardly distinguished. But in the inflected languages, all the circumstances of the word, gender, number, and case, are expressed by modifications affecting the substantive itself, and constantly changing its sound, form, and accent. In the verb the transformation of the root is still more complete. We no longer find, as in the agglutinated languages, a central syllable to which others are 'glued;' but the whole body of the word is modified in accordance with the several moods and tenses, preserving, however, some of the sound of the root, serving to recall the original sense modified by its relations with other words."—A. MAURY.

"The mode of indicating persons and numbers,"* writes M. Schleicher, "differs entirely in the inflected languages from the method of the agglutinated idioms. Among these last languages, the persons are indicated by a pronominal suffix, slightly altered, and the plural is often marked by the plural sign of the substantive. It cannot be otherwise, since the difference between the substantive and the pronoun had only just commenced. In the inflected languages, the personal terminations of the verb have no doubt a visible connection with the pronoun, but the forms of the inflected verbs are fundamentally distinguished from all others. In this case an energetic force has formed that indissoluble thing which we call '*a word*,' and in this we cannot mistake the respec-

* *Les langues de l'Europe moderne*, French translation, p. 153.

tive character of the substantive and verb. Just because the unity of the word is so rigorously maintained during inflection we cannot express many relations by one single word. Whilst the changes, the almost immeasurable elongations, which verbs and substantives undergo in the agglutinated tongues, can only take place at the expense of the unity of the word. The inflected verb then marks fewer relations than the agglutinated verb. Thence also arises the great difficulty of decomposing the inflected forms into their simple elements. The elements expressing relation undergo very considerable changes in inflected idioms, simply to preserve the unity of the word."

The inflected languages are divided into two great families, the Semitic, and the Indo-European or Arian. To these two families belong the languages of the great ancient civilisations whose history we have undertaken to relate. They are so important, that we must devote to each a special paragraph.

SECTION V.—THE SEMITIC LANGUAGES.

1. THE principal languages of the Semitic family are eight in number:—

1st. The Hebrew, spoken by the Israelites, by the Phœnicians, and probably also by other tribes of Canaan.

2nd. The Aramæan, formerly used in Syria; of this there were many dialects. The Biblical Aramæan, in which, in the sixth century before our era, some of the books of the Bible were composed, as for instance, part of the book of Daniel. The Aramæan of the Targum, found in the "Targums" or paraphrases of the Bible, dating from the commencement of our era. The Syro-Chaldee, the vulgar tongue formed among the Jews by alterations in the Hebrew, spoken in Palestine in the time of Christ, and used in the great Rabbinical work called the Talmud. The Nabathean, the dialect of the ancient inhabitants of Arabia Petræa; and finally, the Samaritan, a dialect formed in the old territory of the tribe of Ephraim, after the Assyrian conquest, which is preserved literally among the descendants of these dissenters from the Jewish worship.

3rd. The Sabæan, still used in the southern part of the basin of the Euphrates, among the Mendaites, a peculiar sect, a remnant of the ancient Assyro-persic paganism.

4th. The Syriac, the language used in writing in the countries of Edessa and Nisibis, the development and literary existence of which extended from the second to the sixth century of the Christian era.

5th. The Assyrian, a language common to Babylon and Nineveh, in which the cuneiform inscriptions of those two famous cities are composed.

6th. The Himyarite, or ancient idiom of Southern Arabia ; of this we possess nothing but a few inscriptions.

7th. The Ghez, the ancient language of Abyssinia. Its development and literary existence are subsequent to the establishment of Christianity in that country, that is, to the third century of our era.

8th. Finally, the Arabic, the only one of the Semitic tongues still a living language. It has but a small number of dialects, slightly differing from each other. Through the influence of the Koran, this idiom, originally peculiar to the Ishmaelite tribe, has spread from Babylonia to the extremity of Morocco, from Syria to Yemen.

2. These languages form a perfectly homogeneous group, and are not divided into so many branches as other linguistic families. The roots are all of two syllables, and the original monosyllable is found only, with great difficulty, in the inflexible form which the elements of the vocabulary have now assumed. The idioms termed Semitic are essentially analytical; instead of rendering the complex element of speech in its unity, they prefer to dissect it and give it term by term. There is a marked disposition to accumulate the expression of the relations round the root. This is particularly to be observed in Hebrew. These languages, then, are still partly in the agglutinated state, although they are very clearly also inflected. The subject, the case of the pronoun, the conjunctions, the article, form only one word with the idea itself. The principal idea is, as it were, encircled with particles which modify its relations and then form accessories. The vocabulary shows the closest resemblance between the different languages of the Semitic family. What has much contributed to maintain the close homogeneity in this family is, that its idioms never had that power of growth that the Indo-European or Arian languages have, so as to be unceasingly modified by continual development. They have always remained the same; and, to quote the expression of M. Renan, they have less lived than lasted. This impress of immutability distinguishes the Semitic languages in the highest degree, they have had a great conservative power, that has preserved the fixed form of the pronunciation of the consonants, and prevented alterations resulting from the softening of articulation and other changes which easily take place. It really seems as if a special dispensation of Providence had endowed them with that faculty of immutable preservation, to facilitate the discharge of the duty imposed on one of them—of preserving without alteration, from age to age, the inspired Book in which the principles of religious truth were embodied.

3. The name "Semitic," however, conferred by Eichhorn on this family of languages, and since universally adopted, is very improper, and even likely to lead to serious error. They were not really restricted to nations descended from Shem, a large part, if not the majority, of

the Hamitic nations spoke the so-called Semitic languages. Hebrew was originally only the language of the Canaanites, a people exclusively Hamitic, both in its disposition and physiognomy ; the family of Abraham, living for many generations in the midst of these people, adopted their language in place of that previously spoken by them,—a language probably more like Arabic, because of the original parentage of the races of Heber and Joktan. The Ghez is spoken by a population in which the Hamitic character largely predominates. The Semitic element that came from Yemen, and has been so infused as to become dominant, would, if the language came from there, have brought the Himyaritic, as they did bring the writing of Southern Arabia.

The monuments of Babylon and Chaldæa enable us to state that the language called Assyrian was originally that of the Cushites of the lower Euphrates, and that the Assyrians carried it with them when they formed their settlement in the north. The Himyaritic itself is the idiom of a country where the Cushite race preceded the descendants of Joktan, and at all times formed a considerable element in the population. If the Joktanites of Southern Arabia had at the time of their civilisation a language different from tribes of the same stock who were established in the remainder of the Peninsula, may it not have been owing to the influence of the race who preceded and mixed with them? We may, moreover, from a purely linguistic point of view, form, among the Semitic family, a group of languages composed of the Assyrian, Himyaritic, and Ghez, which we may call the Cushite group, marked by certain features peculiar to these three idioms, and unknown to the remainder of the family.

4. The other nations descended from Ham spoke languages closely related to each other and forming a special family, called Nilotic, the greater part of the languages, and especially the most important, having had the valley of the Nile as their birth-place. There is first the Egyptian, the most ancient language in which we possess written monuments. Although somewhat altered in the course of time, it remained in use, under the name of Coptic, up to the seventeenth century of our era, the period when it finally gave way to the Arabic, and was no longer used except in the liturgy of the native Egyptian Christians. Next come the idioms of the Gallas and of Abyssinia, and the whole series of dialects that must be grouped with them, spoken in the district between the White Nile and the Red Sea. The Malagasy, or language of Madagascar, seems to attach itself to them on one side, but is very much mixed with elements of Malay origin. The languages of Nubia and Kordofan form, in their turn, a peculiar group in the family ; they are numerous ; each colony has its own dialect ; and it would be impossible to enumerate them here. We shall only mention that one of them, the Bischari, seems to be the last remains of the idiom in which

hieroglyphic inscriptions of the Ethiopians of Meroe are composed. A last division of the same family is represented by the Berber, sprung from the ancient Libyan, and spoken by a great part of the people who are spread over the north and north-west of Africa. To this group belong the Kabyle-Algerian, and the Tuarick. A language nearly related to the Berber was spoken by the Guanches, ancient inhabitants of the Canary Isles.

All the idioms, the chief of which we have enumerated, composing the Nilotic family, present a very close original relationship with the family called Semitic. The grammatical structure is essentially the same; some of the most important parts of speech, such as the pronouns, are in both of them exactly similar. The organisation only is less complete and less perfect. In the vocabulary a large part at least of the roots are common to the two families. But the Nilotic languages have them in a more ancient form, the form which belonged to them before they underwent the modification that in the Semitic languages invariably put them into dissyllables. The remainder of the roots are derived from languages in reality African, spoken by various negro races.

It is difficult then not to admit with Charles Lenormant, M. Bunsen, and Mr. Stuart Poole, that the Nilotic languages spring from the same stock as the Semitic, and form with them one single class divided into two families. One language was originally common to the sons of Shem and of Ham. But the Egyptian and its allied idioms were first separated from the main stem, and in a less perfect state of development. In this separate state of existence they became, as it were, stereotyped by the fixed standard of the monuments of Egypt, whilst the Cushite languages of Asia, of the Canaanites, and Semitic people, continued to progress, arrived at a state of greater perfection, and assumed the character of a distinct family.

SECTION VI.—THE INDO-EUROPEAN LANGUAGES.

1. THE great family of Indo-European, Arian, or Japhetic languages, belongs exclusively to nations sprung from Japhet, who all speak, or have spoken its idioms. These languages are very numerous, for they have an inherent vitality that forces them into development, progress, and incessant change, in space and in time.

In them the mechanism of inflection is most perfect, most developed, and they retain no apparent trace of the original stage of agglutination. The organisation common to these languages is revealed by a systematic comparison of the idioms representing the most ancient and complete branches of the family. All the Indo-European idioms have more or less resemblance to the Sanscrit, the richest of all, and most like the primitive form. The further we travel east, the greater resemblance we find between the languages of this numerous and noble family, the nearer we get to that which may be considered its typical form. Thus the Celtic tongues, the most western of all the family, are least like the Sanscrit. The birth-place of these idioms is the country between the Caspian Sea and the Hindoo Koosh. There, before the dispersion of the various tribes of the sons of Japhet, was spoken the primitive language, the origin of all the others. Modern science calls this the Ariac, and can even partly reconstruct its most essential characteristics.

From the earliest times known to history the Arian languages have been essentially synthetic; the words are placed in a sentence according to the system of construction, for which the Latin is our type. Our Neo-Latin and English idioms have in modern times sprung from this family of languages, in consequence of the necessity for finding new forms of speech to express new forms of thought. In the most primitive state, in the little even that we know of the Ariac, the genius of the family has a complex character essentially distinguishing it from the Semitic, with which language its vocabulary has but a small number of words in common—and moreover this small common base may result from the identity of the method employed by both languages in their origin, that is, the onomatopoetic. It would nevertheless be exaggeration to assume it as impossible that these two linguistic families were originally sisters. Philologers of high authority have pronounced that the Arian tongues were produced by the modifying influence of the Semitic on the Turanian languages.

Without prejudging anything as to the reciprocal affiliation, more or less direct, of the Indo-European idioms, an affiliation which presents serious difficulties, we may divide them into six groups:—1st. the Indian; 2nd. Iranian; 3rd. Pelasgic or Greco-Latin; 4th. Slavonian; 5th. Germanic; and 6th. Celtic.

2. The Sanscrit forms the base of the Indian group; it is the sacred and scientific language of the Brahmins. Spoken for more than twenty centuries, it still lives as a literary language, and it must, from so long an existence, have become the most perfect type of an inflected language, as the meaning of the name which the Indians have given it signifies, *Sanscrita*, that is, "that which is complete in itself." This sonorous language, so rich in articulations, rendered so flexible by improvised poetry, is called by those who write it, "the language of the gods," and its alphabet "writing of the gods" *deva nâgari.* The language that we may consider the eldest daughter of the Sanscrit, is the Pali, once spoken on the east of Hindustan, and now become the learned and religious language of the Buddhists of Ceylon, of Madura

in the Burman empire, and of the Indo-Chinese provinces. The Pracrit dialects are of the second generation; this name Pracrita signifies "inferior," "imperfect," and has been given to idioms which were the vulgar tongues of India in the ages immediately anterior to the Christian era. These dialects are especially preserved in the Indian dramas, where they are put into the mouths of inferior personages.

Next come languages of later birth, and restricted to certain provinces, whence they take their names. These are still in use. The Hindui with its seven dialects—the Hindustani, the language of the upper classes of all Central India, from Calcutta to Bombay; the Cashmerian, the Bengali, the Guzerati, the Mahratta, the Nepalese. To these we must add the Zingari, the idiom of that strange race, originally Indian, who wander all over Europe, and are called according to the country, Zigeuner, Zingari, Gitanos, Bohemians, or Gipsies.

3. The most ancient type of the idioms of the Iranian group is found in the Zend, and the Persian of the cuneiform inscriptions of the Achæmenian kings. The Zend is originally from Bactria; it is the language of the books of Zoroaster. Like the Sanscrit, it had ceased to be a spoken language before the Christian era, and its use was confined entirely to literature. The scale of articulations is less varied in these languages than in the Sanscrit, as they have only three vowels, *a*, *i*, *u*.

About the time of the Sassanians the Persian language had already undergone great alterations, and still further modifications followed the Moslem invasion. The Parsee was then formed, the connecting link between the idiom of the Achæmenians and the modern Persian. This last, coming from the province of Fars, has been handed down by many generations of eminent poets, under the independent dynasties of Persia in the middle ages, but mixed in its phraseology with Turkish and Arabic words and forms of speech. Alterations of another kind in the Zend have given birth to the Gheber, spoken by the descendants of those obstinate dissenters from Zoroastrianism who took refuge in India.

To the Iranian group also are attached, among other still living idioms, the Affghan or Pushtoo, the Belochee, the Kurdish, the Armenian with its rich literature, which has flourished for fourteen centuries, and its many existing vulgar dialects, and finally the Ossitinian, spoken by a small nation dwelling in the centre of the chain of the Caucasus.

The Pehlvi has been produced by a mixture of Semitic and Iranian elements; the grammar is Aramæan, the vocabulary Persic. It was used at the court of the first Sassanian kings; and one of the books attributed to Zoroaster, the Bundehesh, exists only in that language.

4. "The Greco-Latin group comprehends the greater part of the languages of Southern Europe. The epithet 'Pelasgic' sufficiently characterises it, for Greece and Italy were first peopled by one common

race, the Pelasgi, whose idiom seems to have been the source of both Greek and Latin. The first of these languages is not in reality the mother of the other, as has been believed; they are two sisters, and if we must assign a different age to them, the Latin has a right to be considered the elder. This language, in fact, presents a more archaic character than classical Greek. The most ancient dialect of the Hellenic idiom, the Æolian, resembles Latin much more than more recent Greek dialects. The Latin has in no respect the character of a language formed from the decomposition of one more ancient, or by its mixture with others. It bears in a high degree the synthetic character of ancient idioms. The elements of grammar have not yet resolved themselves into so many different words, and the phraseology as well as the conjugation of the verb, and the most ancient of its declensions, present a striking likeness to the Sanscrit. Its vocabulary contains a host of words, the archaic form of which is entirely Ariac. The Latin belongs to a group of languages now lost, and which it seems to have gradually absorbed—the Sabine, which originally furnished many Latin words, the Umbrian, the Oscan spoken in Campania, the Messapian, and Iapygian.

The Etruscan, we know only from a small number of words, and it seems to have been a separate branch of the Pelasgic stem. The present language of the Albanians, although now very much mixed with Greek and Slavonic words, seems to be one of the least altered of those derived from the Pelasgic. In many of its forms it seems to point to a grammatical system nearer the Sanscrit than even the Greek."—A. MAURY.

The decomposition of the Latin during the middle ages, gave birth to the present languages of Southern Europe, grouped together under the common name of "Neo-Latin." The Italian, French, Provençal, Spanish, Portuguese, the language of the Grisons, and the Rouman of the Danubian Principalities.

5. The group of Lettic and Slavonic languages resembles very closely the Indian and Iranian languages. The genius of the primitive Ariac is remarkably conspicious in them; this group is divided into two branches, the Lettic and Slavonian properly so called. The first belongs to a period less advanced than the second. The Lithuanian substantive has, for example, only two genders, whilst the Slavonic has three. The Slavonic conjugation is also superior to the Lithuanian, in which the third person of the singular, dual and plural are not distinguished. The Lettic branch comprises first the Lithuanian, of all the spoken languages of Europe approaching nearest to the Sanscrit; next the Borussian or ancient Prussian, which has been displaced by the German; and finally the Lettic or Livonian. The Slavonic branch is by far the most extended; we may even say that of all the groups of languages in Europe, this is the one spoken by the greatest

number of persons. Its name Slave is derived from a word implying the idea of "glory," a term which all nations speaking its idioms apply to themselves. With the exception of the Bulgarian, which has undergone great alterations, the Slavonic idioms preserve a greater likeness to each other than, for example, the Germanic languages. A traveller who knows one of its dialects perfectly can make himself understood in the whole extent of territory where they are spoken—from Montenegro to Kamchatka.

The Slavonic languages must be divided into two great branches—the Eastern and Western. The most ancient known form of the first is the Slavonic, the liturgical language of the Russian church, which has ceased to be spoken since the end of the middle ages. By its side we must place the Bulgarian, also representing a very ancient state of language, and which has been carried from the neighbourhood of the Oural to the banks of the Danube, where it is gradually disappearing. The Russian, whose domain has been so prodigiously extended by conquest, and which is supplanting by degrees the Uralo-finnish and Tartar idioms; and finally the Servian, spoken between the Adriatic Sea and the Danube.

The Western Slavonic idioms are the Polish, the Tschekh or Bohemian, the Sorabian or Wendish, of Lower Lusatia, to which we must add some languages rooted out many ages ago by the German, such as the Cachoub of Lauenburg, the Polab and the Obotrite of the banks of the Elbe. Generally speaking, these idioms are harsher, less harmonious, and more full of consonants than those of the eastern branch, particularly the Tschekh.

6. "The vast family of Germanic languages, which has by degrees supplanted the Slavonic, embraces at present a great number of idioms, successors of others of the same family, now entirely lost. All these languages are distinguished by common characteristics springing from the Ariac grammar by regular and graduated alterations. One of the most celebrated of German Philologists—whose labours have made him almost a legislator in the comparative grammar of the German languages—Jacob Grimm—has distinguished four fundamental characteristics in this family. First, the tendency of the vowel to soften in pronunciation, to indicate a modification in the meaning or employment of a word. Secondly, the transformation of one consonant into another of the same class, softer, stronger, or aspirated. Thirdly, the existence of strong and weak conjugations, that is, conjugations in which the radical vowel changes according to certain rules, and of conjugations where it remains invariable."—A. MAURY.

The Germanic languages form two branches, Gothic and German. We know the ancient Gothic only by a small number of written remains, among which we must place in the first rank the fragments of the version of the Bible, by Bishop Ulphilas in the fourth century. To the same branch belong,—1st, the Norse idiom of the old Scandinavians, preserved almost unaltered in Iceland, and which by gradual alterations has formed the Danish and Swedish. 2nd. The Anglo-Saxon, which by its mixture with the old French, and in consequence of special modifications due particularly to Celtic influences, has produced the English. 3rd. The Low German, itself comprising many dialects; the Frison, the Dutch and the Flemish. These last languages are the remains of the Saxon, which was spoken, with slight differences, from state to state in the whole north-west of Germany, from the Elbe and Weser to the Rhine and the Scheldt. As for the German branch, properly so called, it comprises four dialects,—the High German, since Luther's time the language of letters and society in all Germany, the Swabian, the Austrian, and the Franconian.

7. The Celtic tongues, now restricted to a small number of provinces in France and the British Isles, are, of all the Indo-European languages, the furthest westward from the primitive settlements of man, and are also the most altered. These idioms doubtless do recall the Sanscrit grammar, but have no general resemblance to that language. Following the laws of the permutation of consonants, that we mentioned when speaking of the German languages, we may carry back the Celtic vocabularies to the Sanscrit and Ariac; but the grammatical forms have been so altered that it is often difficult to attach them, at any rate directly, to the ordinary types of the Indo-European family. The Gaulish has disappeared, supplanted by the Latin; there only remain a few inscriptions still imperfectly explained. The Celtic idioms which are still living, are classed in two groups, Cymric or Breton, and Gallic or Gælic. The first embraces the Cymric properly so called, or the Welsh, the language still used in a great part of Wales, and the Cornish, which up to the last century remained in use in the county of Cornwall; finally, the Armorican or Breton, in general use in France in the Departments of the Côtes du Nord, Finistère, Morbihan and part of Loire Inférieure. To the second belong the Irish, the Gælic properly so called, or Erse, spoken in the Highlands of Scotland, and lastly, the Manx or dialect of the Isle of Man.

The hasty view we have taken of the races of mankind and the various families of languages, has led us insensibly far from the primitive days of humanity to our own times. And thus we find ourselves led away from the history of ancient Oriental civilisation, to which these enquiries were nevertheless a necessary introduction. We now return to our proper subject, not again to deviate from it.

END OF BOOK I.

BOOK II.

THE ISRAELITES.

CHAPTER I.

THE PATRIARCHS—THE ISRAELITES IN EGYPT—MOSES.

Chief Authorities:—The Bible, Books of Genesis, Exodus, Leviticus, Numbers, and Deuteronomy.—Josephus, *Antiquities of the Jews.* Books I., II.—The dissertations attached to the Pentateuch in Dr. Calm's and M. Cahen's Bible.—Munk, *La Palestine*, Paris, 1845.—Ewald, *Geschichte des Volkes Israel*, Göttingen, 1851–64.—Wallon, *La Sainte Bible*, Paris, 1854.—J. Salvador, *Histoire des institutions de Moïse*, Third Edition, Paris, 1862.

SECTION I.—ABRAHAM.

1. BY degrees the various nations of the human race forgot the great traditions of their primitive history, or rather, they preserved the recollection only of some detached facts which, as time went on, became mixed up with purely imaginative stories. The idea of the existence of God was gradually obscured in their minds, and idolatry established itself all over the world.

"Man drowned in lust and passion," says Bossuet, "had nevertheless preserved a vague idea of the Divine power, which maintained itself by its own inherent force, but which, eclipsed by objects apparent to the senses, led him to worship all objects displaying activity and power. Thus the sun and the stars, that made their influence felt from such a distance, fire, and the elements whose effects were so universal, were the earliest objects of public worship."

To arrest the progress of so great an evil and to prevent its final triumph, which would have eliminated from the world the true conception of the Divinity, God in His great power and infinite mercy chose one family out of that race of Shem on whom the second father of the human race, Noah, had invoked special blessings; and, calling it to a sublime vocation, imposed on it the duty of preserving the ancient faith—no less as to the creation of the world, than as to that special Providence which governs all human affairs,—and made it the depository of the precepts delivered and promises made to the human race.

2. Terah, of the race of Arphaxad, lived in the district bearing the name of his ancestor, that is, in the south of Chaldæa; his residence was in the city of Ur, called also Calneh, the Mugheir of our time, the ruins of which have been explored by the English traveller Loftus.* He had three sons, Abram, Nahor, and Haran. The last died in his father's lifetime, whilst the family still dwelt in their original habitation, and left a son named Lot. The sterility of the country where they lived rendering it unsuited to a race entirely given to pastoral life, induced Terah to change his residence and to migrate with all his family to the northern countries. He came to the town of Haran in the north of Mesopotamia, settled there, and died at the age of 205 years.

Then God revealed His mission to Abram, the destiny by which he was to become the "father of the faithful." He was then 65 years old, and his father did not die till 60 years later. "Get thee out of thy country, and from thy kindred, and from thy father's house," said the Lord to him, "unto a land that I will show thee; and I will make of thee a great nation, and I will bless thee, and thou shalt be a blessing. And I will bless them that bless thee, and curse him that curseth thee; and in thee shall all families of the earth be blessed" (Gen. xii. 1—3). The popular traditions of the Jews and Arabs, which appear here to rest on an ancient foundation, add that this emigration was rendered necessary in consequence of the dangers which threatened the pious Abram in the midst of idolatrous populations, and even in the house of his father, a zealous worshipper of false gods.† The historian Josephus, the echo of the legends of the Synagogue, says that the inhabitants of the region of Haran took up arms against him, and wished to punish him for the contempt with which he had treated their divinities. We may also connect this event with the Elamite conquest that occurred about this time, and as we shall show in the fourth book, affected the whole basin of the Euphrates and Tigris.

3. Abram obeyed the commands of the Lord. Leaving in Haran

---

* In identifying the ruins now called "Mugheir," with both Ur and Calneh, the author differs from Sir H. Rawlinson and other English authorities, who believe Mugheir to represent Ur, and Calneh to be found at Nipur. (See Professor Rawlinson's *Five Great Monarchies*, vol. i. 20.) The reasons which have led the author to this conclusion are, that Ur must have been one of the cities of the primitive Chaldæan tetrapolis (Gen. x. 10), and that no other name in the list but Calneh can stand for Ur. Also, that the ideographic name of Ur in the cuneiform inscriptions means "dwelling of Oannes;" and that the name Calneh is a corruption of "Hekal Anu," with the same meaning.—Tr.

† Jos. *Ant.* I., vii. 2; *Koran*, ch. xxi. "The Prophets;" xxix. "The Spider;" vi. "Cattle."

his father, and Nahor his brother, he departed, directing his course to the south with Sarai his wife, Lot, his brother's son, and all that were his; he thus passed over the Euphrates, traversed Syria, and arrived at last in the country of Canaan (in after times Judæa), which name signified "the low country," in opposition to Aram, or the elevated district. It was then entirely occupied by Canaanitish tribes of the race of Ham, who had built cities, and lived in settled habitations, allowing the nomadic tribes of the Shemites to wander about, feeding their flocks in the pastures adjacent to the cities, just as in the present day the Bedouin tribes wander even up to the gates of the cities of Syria and Palestine. Arrived in the land of Canaan, Abram (Gen. xii. 6, 7), in the district of Sichem, had a vision in which God announced to him that the whole of that land should one day belong to his seed. He then built an altar to the Lord who had appeared to him, and also another between Bethel and Hai, in the place where he had pitched his tents, in the rich pastures of the lower Jordan, and after having called there upon the name of the Lord, he pursued his course towards the south.

A famine obliged him to go to Egypt and sojourn there some time (Gen. xii. 10, *seq.*) Fearing lest his wife Sarai, who was very beautiful, should be taken from him, and that he himself should be subjected to violence, he asked her to pass herself off for a sister, whose natural protector he would be. The king, whom the Bible designates (as it does all Egyptian kings mentioned in the books of Genesis and Exodus), only by his title Pharaoh (in Egyptian Pir aa), having heard of the beauty of Sarai, sent for her to the palace; he treated Abram with great distinction, and made him handsome presents of slaves and cattle. But, stopped in his project by a Divine chastisement, and having learned that Sarai was the wife of Abram, he restored her to her husband, and sent them out of the country with all that they had.

4. Abram returned, still accompanied by Lot, his brother's son, to the place of his former encampment between Bethel and Hai. Abram and Lot led a life similar in every respect to that of the Arab Sheikh of our days. A crowd of hereditary servants wandered as they now do, going from one pasture ground to another as soon as the first was exhausted, with the flocks and herds of their masters, or rather of their lords, for each patriarchal family formed a small nomadic state in which, in all probability, the shepherds were bound to the chief of the tribe by ties of relationship more or less distant (Gen. xiii. 1, *seq.*). The great number of the flocks and herds of the uncle and nephew rendered it difficult to feed them together, their servants began to quarrel on the subject, and a separation became necessary. Abram allowed Lot to choose the region in which he would dwell. He decided on the fertile banks of the Lower Jordan and the basin of the Dead Sea, which, at its southern extremity, offered a country of magnificent pasture

land in the plain now called Ghor Sâfieh, which the Bedouin tribes of that part of Syria still regard as a real terrestrial paradise (Gen. xiii. 10, *seq.*) This plain was in the immediate vicinity of Sodom, the chief of the five confederate cities, built round the inland sea; the four others were Gomorrah, Admah, Zeboim, and Segor, or Zoar. Their inhabitants seem to have been of Canaanitish blood; but they were horribly corrupt, given over to impiety, to iniquity of every kind, and to the most infamous vices, which drew down on them the Divine vengeance. In spite of that, Lot fixed his dwelling within the city of Sodom itself, leaving his flocks and herds in the Ghor (Gen. xiii. 14). After the departure of his nephew, Abram had another vision, in which God renewed to him the promise of an innumerable posterity, to whom the whole surrounding country should belong. He then came and dwelt in the grove of Mamre, near Hebron, a city then occupied by the Hittites, a Canaanitish race. He there built another altar to Jehovah.

5. In the meanwhile, Chedorlaomer, king of Elam, that is of Susiana, had conquered the valley of the Jordan, and brought into subjection to his sceptre the five towns of the borders of the Dead Sea, that is, the country where Lot had settled (Gen. xiv. 1, *seq.*). Twelve years he remained their master; but in the thirteenth year, the petty kings of that region, seeing that Chedorlaomer was occupied by wars in the north of Arabia, thought they could throw off the yoke. But the Elamite king came against them with his vassals, Amraphel, king of Shinar, Arioch, king of Ellasar, and Thargal, king of nations, or of the nomadic tribes.*

The battle took place in the vale of Siddim, on the borders of the Dead Sea, where were many wells of bitumen. The people of the country were routed. Sodom, Gomorrah, and the three other cities were pillaged, and Lot was led away captive. Of this Abram was informed by a fugitive. He was at the time living at Mamre, and was in alliance with the Canaanitish prince of the country. With his ally and the two brothers of that prince, and all his own servants, he commenced the pursuit of the enemy, who had begun to retreat. He overtook them at the northern extremity of Palestine, at the place where, in later times, was built the city of Dan. Attacking them by night, he gained the victory. The four kings were pursued to the neighbourhood of Damascus. Lot was rescued, and all the booty retaken. It was on this occasion that Abram received the blessing of Melchizedek, king of Salem, priest of the most high God, whose tribe, no doubt of Semitic origin, was one of the very few who in their pastoral life had been able

---

* We shall explain further on, in Book IV., the reason why we have preferred, for the name of this prince, the reading Thargal, from the Septuagint, to the Tidal of the Hebrew text.

to preserve intact the primitive belief in the unity of God.* Abram generously refused to receive for himself the smallest portion of the booty which the king of Sodom offered him, and accepted only a share for his allies. Abram, overpowered with gratitude for the success which by God's help he had obtained, had again at this time one of those visions which signalised every important event of his life, confirmed him in his faith, and inspired him with all confidence for the future. "I am thy shield" (Gen. xv. 1, *seq.*), said the Lord to him, "and thy exceeding great reward." "Lord God what wilt thou give me," said Abram, "seeing I go childless . . . and one born in my house is mine heir." "Look now towards heaven," was the reply, "and tell the stars, if thou be able to number them: and he said unto him, So shall thy seed be . . . . I am Jehovah, that brought thee out of Ur of the Chaldees to give thee this land to inherit it." Abram, then, by the command of God, performed the symbolical ceremony which sealed his covenant with the Eternal; he sacrificed a number of animals, and cut them in pieces; and, in a vision, he saw God himself, under the form of a flame of fire, pass between these pieces. This was the form by which, among the Orientals, solemn treaties were concluded; and St. Ephræm, the Syrian, in his commentary on Genesis, speaks of this practice as in use among the Chaldæans in his time. He who swore to the alliance by passing thus between the severed limbs of the victims, intimated that he consented to be thus treated if he violated his promise. From similar practices the Greek phrase ὅρκια τέμνειν, and the Latin *fœdus ferire*, are derived.

6. After a ten years' sojourn in the land of Canaan, Sarai, despairing of ever giving a son to Abram, wished him to take to wife her servant, the Egyptian woman Hagar. She, lifted up by pride, began to despise her mistress, who complained to Abram. The servant, given over to the bad treatment of a jealous mistress, took to flight. She was seated by a fountain in the desert when she was visited by an angel, who announced that the son she bore in her bosom should one day become powerful, and should have a numerous posterity, and ordered her to return and submit herself to her mistress. Returning to the dwelling of Abram, she bore him a son, who was called Ishmael (God shall hear). Abram was then eighty-six years old. Thirteen years after this event, God renewed His covenant with Abram. This name, which signifies "Exalted Father," was changed by God himself to Abraham, "Father of a great Multitude," signifying the immense posterity

* The commonly received opinion among the Jews, according to Jerome, and also among the Samaritans, according to Epiphanius, was that Melchizedek was the Patriarch Shem, who according to the commonly received chronology must have been alive at this time.—Tr.

which should spring from the patriarch; and circumcision was instituted as the symbol of this renewed covenant, and as the distinctive sign of the sons of Abraham. Sarai received the name of Sarah (mistress, princess), and God promised to Abraham another son by her in whom the Divine covenant should be perpetuated. As for Ishmael, the Lord announced that twelve princes should spring from him, and that his posterity should be very numerous.

7. By this time Abraham had arrived at the age of ninety-nine years, and Sarah ninety years. Without doubt, as we have already said, the life of men who led the active and frugal life of the patriarchs was still much longer than that of their contemporaries; but it was much more brief than life had been before the Deluge; and at the age to which Abraham and his wife had arrived, all natural appearances were against their having children. One day three strangers presented themselves before the tent of Abraham, who entreated them to enter, and hastened to fulfil towards them the duties of hospitality. They revealed themselves then to him as angels of God, and repeated the promise that next year Sarah should have a son. The aged woman, who from inside the tent heard this prediction, could not help laughing, but was blamed by the angels for doubting the Divine power which could perform in her a miracle (Gen. xx. 1, *seq.*).

8. At that time occurred the catastrophe of Sodom and the other border cities of the Dead Sea. Their iniquities and corruption had increased to such a degree, that God determined to make their punishment an example to the world. Abraham in vain interceded for the doomed cities; the ten righteous men, whose presence would have sufficed, according to God's word, to turn away the anger of the Lord, were not found in Sodom. Warned by the angels, Lot and his two daughters, whose betrothed husbands made light of the matter, and refused to follow, fled in all haste to Zoar. Then Sodom, Gomorrah, Admah, and Zeboim were reduced to ashes, without the escape of one inhabitant, by a fearful convulsion of nature, poetically termed in the Bible a rain of fire and brimstone, but which appears to have been in reality a prodigious volcanic eruption from a great number of craters at once, and of which the surrounding country shows traces to this day. Lot, fearing to remain at Zoar, where he did not consider himself free from danger, retired with his two daughters to a cave in the desert to the east of the Dead Sea. There the book of Genesis records the incestuous birth of Moab and Ammon, ancestors of the nations whom Moses and Joshua found established on the eastern banks of the Jordan and of the Dead Sea.

9. Continuing to lead the wandering life of a nomad shepherd, Abraham settled for a time in the country of Gerar, near Gaza, on the frontier between Egypt and Palestine. He made a treaty with the

king of that country, named Abimelech, beside a well which was called, in memory of the circumstance, Beersheba (the Well of the Oath). It was in that country that, in accordance with the promise of the messengers, Sarah brought into the world a son, who received the name of Isaac, from the Hebrew word "Yitschak" (laughing), for, said Sarah, "God hath made me to laugh, so that all that hear me will laugh with me." At a feast which Abraham made on the occasion of the weaning of Isaac, Sarah saw a mocking smile on the face of Ishmael, son of Hagar, and again she demanded the banishment of the servant and of her son. Hagar and Ishmael wandered in the wilderness of Beersheba, and they were on the point of dying with thirst, when a voice from heaven consoled and encouraged them. A fountain appeared before their eyes, and they slaked their thirst.

Ishmael grew up in exile and became a practised archer, and his mother took him a wife out of the land of Egypt. He became the head of the second race of Nomadic Arabs, who mixed with the first tribes sprung from Joktan, over whom in course of time they gained the supremacy. The most illustrious of all the Arab tribes directly descended from Ishmael was that of the Koreish, who inhabited Mecca, and possessed there the famous sanctuary of the Caabah, traditionally said to have been built by Ishmael and Abraham. From this tribe sprung Mahomet.

10. Abraham returned towards the north, and remained many years settled at Mamre. There it was that his faith was put to its most severe test; God commanded him to offer up his son Isaac in sacrifice. Though his heart was torn with grief, he, nevertheless, did not hesitate to obey; and when he was already on the point of consummating this cruel sacrifice, he was stayed by a voice from on high, telling him that God was satisfied with this proof of his obedience. At the same moment he saw behind him a ram, which he took and offered up in the stead of his son (Gen. xxii. 1, *seq.*). A short time afterwards Sarah died, at the age of one hundred and twenty-seven years. Abraham bought from the Hittites of Hebron, then called Kirjath Arba, a sepulchral cave near that city, to make it his family tomb, and there buried the body of Sarah.

SECTION II.—ISAAC AND JACOB.

1. WHEN Abraham found himself old, and perceived that his end approached, he wished to get a wife for his son Isaac, that he might become the progenitor of the chosen people. Unwilling to form an alliance with the daughters of the Canaanites, he sent his steward Eliezer to Mesopotamia, to choose for Isaac a wife from his own

people. Arrived at the gates of the city of Haran, where one branch of the family of Terah had remained after the departure of Abraham, Eliezer stayed by a well, and saw a very beautiful young woman who came there to draw water. When she was about to return, having filled her vessel, Eliezer asked her to give him to drink. She inclined the vessel towards him, and offering to draw also for his camels, she went for more water, which she gave them. In this mark of courteous and ingenuous manners, Eliezer recognised the sign which he had asked of the Lord, to point out to him the woman destined to inherit the Divine promises; he learned also that the damsel, whose name was Rebecca (Ribkah, fat heifer), was the daughter of Bethuel, son of Nahor, Abraham's brother, and consequently his master's niece. He accepted the hospitality which was offered him by Bethuel, imparted to him his mission, and Rebecca went off with him with the blessings of her family. Although Abraham was one hundred and forty years old, he took after his son's marriage another wife, named Keturah, by whom he had six sons. One was Midian, the father of the Midianites, who lived between the Dead Sea and the Elanitic gulf of the Red Sea, to the east of the Nabatheans. Abraham gave rich gifts to these sons, but sent them out of Palestine that his inheritance there might pass entire to Isaac. He, who was forty years old at the time of his marriage, remained twenty years without children. At last God heard his prayers, and Rebecca bore him twins. The first-born was called Esau, and also Edom (the red), on account of his colour; the second received the name of Jacob (the supplanter). Abraham lived long enough to see the Divine promise accomplished in the posterity of Isaac. He died fifteen years after the birth of the two brothers, at the age of one hundred and seventy-five years, and was buried by Isaac and Ishmael in the tomb of his family, by the side of Sarah. This tomb, it is said, pointed out by constant and unbroken tradition, still exists under the great Mosque at Hebron: but Christians are rigorously excluded by the Mahometans from the building.*

2. The life of Isaac presents no very noticeable event. Adopting his father's nomadic mode of life, the second patriarch passed all his existence partly in the pastures of Mamre and partly in those of Gerar; sometimes in strict friendship with the king of that country, who, like his predecessor in the time of Abraham, was called Abimelech; at others, exposed to the ill-will and jealousy of the inhabitants, who, like all people of settled and agricultural occupations, were ill enough

---

* The first European who entered this Mosque, which had been for centuries closed against all Christians, was H. R. H. the Prince of Wales. A most interesting account of the visit is given by Dean Stanley in his *Lectures on the Jewish Church.*—TR.

disposed toward nomadic shepherds. The book of Genesis ascribes to Isaac, during one of his visits to Gerar, the like adventure as befell Abraham in Egypt. This seems to be merely a double tradition, founded on one occurrence. Esau was the eldest son of Isaac, but Jacob was the particular favourite of his mother Rebecca. He one day bought the birthright from his elder brother, and afterwards, with his mother's assistance, contrived by stratagem to receive, in place of Esau, the blessing which should render him the heir of the promises of God to the race of Abraham. From that time he found himself exposed to the furious hatred of his brother ; and to escape the consequences, was compelled to fly to Mesopotamia, to Laban, Rebecca's brother ; and this, by the advice of his mother, and by order of his father, who, after the example of Abraham, was not willing that the heir of his race should marry a Canaanitish woman. During his flight, Jacob had at Luz that famous vision in which he saw a ladder, above it stood Jehovah, and the angels of God were ascending and descending on it (Genesis xxviii. 10). In memory of this event, he named the place Bethel (House of God,) which name was continued by his descendants.

3. Having crossed the Euphrates, Jacob met the shepherds of Haran, who showed him Rachel (the sheep), one of the daughters of Laban, who herself fed her father's flocks. Jacob made himself known, and was received in a most friendly manner by Laban ; but he would not give him his daughter Rachel until he had served him fourteen years, and had married Leah, Rachel's elder sister. Jacob had twelve sons, Reuben, Simeon, Levi, Judah, Dan, Naphtali, Gad, Asher, Issachar, Zebulon, Joseph, and Benjamin, who were the ancestors of the twelve tribes of Israel, and one daughter named Dinah. Reuben, Simeon, Levi, Judah, Issachar, Zebulon and Dinah were born of Leah ; Dan and Naphtali, of Bilhah, the handmaid of Rachel; Gad and Asher, of Zilpah, the handmaid of Leah ; and at the last, the youngest, Joseph and Benjamin, of Rachel herself, who had been barren for many years. After a long sojourn with Laban, Jacob determined at last to return to his father, who was still alive ; he became reconciled with Esau, who abandoned to him the possession and exclusive enjoyment of the pastures of the land of Canaan, and retired with his own people to Mount Seir, now Esh Sherah* to the north of the Elanitic gulf, where he became the founder of the Idumean or Edomite nation. One circumstance in the Bible narrative, as to this return of Jacob, shows us that idolatry existed in the house of Laban, as we have before seen was the case in that of his ancestor Terah. It is also during this journey that the Book of Genesis places

* The northern part is now called Jebâl; the southern, Esh Sherah; the latter name means merely "district," and has no connection with the Hebrew word Seir, "the hairy."—Tr.

the mysterious wrestling of Jacob with the angel, whence he obtained the name of Israel (one who has fought with God), a name borne only by his heirs, who called themselves children of Israel, or Israelites.

4. Very severe trials awaited Jacob after his return to the land of Canaan. Shechem, son of Hamor, prince of the Shechemites, carried off and outraged his daughter Dinah. He afterwards asked her in marriage, but the sons of Jacob conspired to take a terrible vengeance on all the Shechemites. They appeared to consent to the marriage, under conditions which facilitated a treacherous attack which Simeon and Levi made on the city, when they killed all the men; the other sons of Jacob then pillaged the city, and carried off the women and children, and flocks and herds. Jacob was much grieved at this event, and reproached them severely for their atrocious conduct and perfidy. The whole family left the district of Shechem, where they no longer believed themselves safe. At Ephrath, in later times called Bethlehem, Jacob had the misfortune to lose Rachel, who died in giving birth to a second son, Benjamin. Her tomb is still shown in the neighbourhood of Bethlehem. Jacob then repaired to Mamre, where his father Isaac still lived, and continued to live, to the age of one hundred and eighty years. He therefore must have been a witness of the incident which we have now to relate, and of the grief of his son Jacob.

5. Joseph, Rachel's eldest son, was regarded with peculiar affection by his father, who showed him frequent marks of tenderness, and seemed disposed to transfer to him the privileges which, by right of birth, belonged to the sons of Leah. Moreover, the three elder sons of Jacob had, by serious misconduct, incurred their father's anger. Joseph, beloved by his father, but regarded almost as an enemy by his brothers, brought accounts to Jacob of all the evil doings of his elder brothers. Attaching in his childhood great importance to dreams, in which he seemed to read the future, Joseph did not hesitate to relate to his brothers some of his nightly visions which seemed to presage for him a brilliant career. His brothers conceived mortal hatred for him, and conspired to bring about his ruin. One day Jacob sent Joseph to see his brethren, who were feeding their flocks in the neighbourhood of Shechem. Seeing him alone, they formed the plan of killing him; nevertheless, Reuben, the eldest, upon whom the chief weight of responsibility would have fallen, tried to save Joseph, and managed to persuade his brothers to put the lad into a dry well, whence he himself intended afterwards to release him. But, in his temporary absence, a caravan of Midianitish merchants passed on their way to Egypt. Judah persuaded his brothers to sell Joseph to these men, who in their turn sold him to Potiphar, or Petephra (belonging to the sun), an officer of the army of a king of Egypt, whom Holy Scripture designates only by his title of Pharaoh. The elder sons of Jacob made their father believe that some wild beast had devoured Joseph.

SECTION III.—JOSEPH IN EGYPT.

1. JOSEPH in slavery quickly acquired the good graces of his master, who entrusted to him the superintendence of his house. But, on a false accusation by the wife of Potiphar, he was put in prison, where God revealed to him the hidden meaning of the mysterious dreams of his two companions in captivity. One of the two, chief butler of the king, was soon restored to the favour of his master, as Joseph had foretold; but he did not, as he had promised, remember Joseph. Two years later, however, the king, in his turn, having seen in a dream seven lean kine, and seven withered ears of corn, which eat up seven fat kine, and seven full ears of corn, was much disturbed, and desired that the vision should be interpreted to him. The chief butler then remembered the Hebrew slave who had so truly predicted his own and his companion's fate. Joseph was brought out of prison and presented to the king, and informed him that seven years of famine should succeed seven years of plenty. Let us here remark, in passing, that the number of years—seven—must not be taken literally. The number seven was used by the Egyptians as an indeterminate number; the vision of seven fat and seven lean kine would the more naturally present itself to the mind of the king, because the "seven cows belonging to the divine bull" were among the most important symbols of Egyptian Paganism.* And also in an Egyptian inscription, dating from the twelfth dynasty (we shall explain this expression in our Third Book), and, consequently, many centuries older than Joseph, the governor of a province boasts of having provided granaries to meet the wants of seven years; that is, granaries capable of supplying many successive years of scarcity.

2. Egypt, at the time when Joseph was taken there, was divided into two kingdoms, in consequence of events which we shall relate in our Third Book, in the history of that country. It had its own native-born princes only in the Thebaid. Lower Egypt had been occupied for many centuries by invaders of Canaanitish race, known by the name of Shepherds, who had at last adopted Egyptian manners, and had established a dynasty of princes of their own blood. It was before one of these kings, named Apophis, or Apepi, that Joseph was brought. He had not, and was not likely to have, the same repugnance as an Egyptian for the services of a stranger, for he himself was likewise of foreign origin. Struck with the counsel of Joseph, and with his wisdom, the king judged that no one could be found better able to meet the predicted scourge than a man so favoured by heaven. He put a ring on his finger, a golden collar on his neck (a mark of honour frequently mentioned in

* Egyptian "Funeral Ritual," chap. cxlix.

the monuments of Egypt), clothed him with a robe of fine linen, and made him ride in a chariot, accompanied by a herald, who proclaimed to all the people to bow the knee before him, for that he was chosen governor of all the land of Egypt. The king conferred on Joseph an Egyptian name, which signifies "sustainer of the world" (*Zaph-n-to*); that is, nourisher of the country, for, in the Egyptian language, the country (*the* country Egypt), and the world were expressed by the same word (*to*). The new minister married the daughter of a priest of Heliopolis, named Petephra, the same as his old master; her name was, as the Bible tells us, Asenath, that is, "the precious Neith." Neith was an Egyptian goddess. By this marriage Joseph had two sons, Manasseh and Ephraim.

3. Joseph collected, in public granaries constructed for the purpose, a part of the superabundant harvest of the years of plenty, and distributed it on the king's part among the Egyptians in the years of famine. In return for this provision, and the assistance which had saved them, the son of Jacob required that the inhabitants of Egypt should surrender to the king what lawyers would call the "fee simple" of their lands, paying a quit rent of one-fifth of the produce for the right of tenancy. The priests were exempt, because they were entitled to maintenance from the public granaries.

The provision created by the foresight of Joseph was so considerable, that he could not only feed the entire people of Lower Egypt during the whole time of the famine, but was able to sell corn to the inhabitants of the neighbouring countries where the famine made itself felt. It was then that his brothers came, sent by Jacob into Egypt to buy food. At their second visit, he made himself known to them, forgave them, and invited all his family to reside in Egypt. In this he only put in practice the common policy of the Pharaohs, which had always been to attract the tribes of Palestine and Syria as colonists, into the land of Delta, in order that a scientific system of agriculture might gradually and laboriously reclaim the marsh land. And this policy, which had been that of the indigenous sovereigns, was to a still greater degree that of the Shepherd Kings, whose greatest interest was to establish in their states a non-Egyptian element, to assure themselves of support against a national reaction.

4. Jacob, with all that were his, accepted the invitation of Joseph. He was then 130 years old. Pharaoh received them with favour, and established them in the land of Goshen, which we believe to have been the territory around the present city of Belbeis, on the frontier line of the Delta and the desert, N.N.E. of Memphis, and of the modern city of Cairo. There Jacob died, seventeen years after his settlement. On his death-bed he blessed his sons, and declared that the inheritance of the Divine promises to the race of Abraham, and the position of head of the

family should fall to Judah, to the exclusion of his three elder brothers, Reuben, Simeon, and Levi, who had proved themselves unworthy of it by their crimes. His body, embalmed in the Egyptian manner, was conveyed to the tomb of Abraham, at Hebron. Joseph lived on for half a century, and always remained the active protector of the Israelite colony. He, at last, in his turn, died at the age of 110 years, and before his death, took an oath of such of his brethren as survived him, that his embalmed body should be carried up into the land of Canaan when the children of Israel left Egypt.

Section IV.—The Israelites in Egypt, and the Exodus.

1. The Hebrews remained 430 years in the fertile land of Goshen, and there multiplied exceedingly. They formed a small nation, separated from the Egyptians by their manners, their religious worship, their language, and their patriarchal government. The Bible is silent on the period, following immediately on the death of Joseph and his brethren, but it is certain that the Hebrews remained isolated from the Egyptians. Their business as shepherds, their nomadic habits, held in scorn by the native-born Egyptian population, had fixed between the two peoples an insurmountable barrier. The patriarchal worship was not, in truth, preserved in its primitive purity, but the idolatrous worship of the Egyptians was too much opposed to the traditions of the Israelites to permit its spread among the latter people. The children of Israel preserved a remembrance of the God of Abraham, of Isaac, and of Jacob, though they had but a very confused idea of that God. Subject to the kings of Egypt, they were nevertheless governed by their own proper chiefs. The tribes were divided into families, each of which had its "Zaken" (Exodus iii. 18), or Sheikh; and these heads of families were under the orders of the superior chiefs of their respective tribes, called in Egyptian "Hak." With these were also other officers bearing the title of "Shoterim" (Exodus v. 14), or Scribes, who, although chosen from the race of Israel, represented among them the authority of the Egyptian government, and were personally responsible for the collection of the imposts laid on the Hebrew colony.

2. Nevertheless, the life of the Israelites in Egypt was far from being at all times as happy as it had been at first. Great revolutions had taken place in the country, which we shall relate in detail when we come to treat of Egypt. The stranger kings had been driven out of Lower Egypt; the unity of the country and its full independence had been re-established; a native dynasty, a glorious dynasty, warlike and victorious, had mounted the throne. These kings appear to have left the Hebrews in peace, and even to have favoured them. It even seems that the

children of Israel were concerned on several occasions in the early Asiatic campaigns of that dynasty, and had taken advantage of that circumstance to attempt to make settlements in the land promised to their race—attempts which failed. Thus mention is made of an expedition of the sons of Ephraim against the people of Gath, whose cattle they tried to drive off, but who slew them (1 Chron. vii. 21). A daughter of Ephraim built several cities in the land of Canaan (1 Chron. vii. 24). Lastly, it is mentioned, that the family of Shelah, son of Judah, had made conquests on the territory of Moab (1 Chron. iv. 21, 22).

But some time afterwards, in consequence of disturbances, which, as we shall see further on, it is possible were not quite free from Israelitish influence,* another new dynasty, that which counts in Egyptian history as the Nineteenth, came into power. "Another king," says Scripture, "arose, who knew not Joseph." The services he had rendered were forgotten; the sons of Jacob, regarded as dangerous because of their number and their origin, were exposed to the most unjust and cruel persecutions. The Pharaoh, who commenced to persecute them with the view of reducing their power, was called Ramses, as we know from documents of Egyptian origin. He was a warlike prince, and at the same time an implacable despot and tyrant. He overburdened the Israelites with work, and employed them under taskmasters in all the rough operations of the building of cities. It was the custom of the kings of Egypt to employ prisoners of war in forced labour of this kind; paintings in many Egyptian tombs represent scenes where prisoners of Semitic race are seen making bricks and building walls, under the eye of the Egyptian superintendents, armed with long whips—scenes which may serve to illustrate the story of the Bible as to the servitude of the Israelites. A hieroglyphic inscription, dated in the reign of Ramses, enumerates the populations thus employed on public works, and mentions amongst them the Aberiou, or Hebrews. They built in their servitude two cities to the east of the Delta, Pithom and Raamses, the last so-called after the name of the king, cities which are both frequently mentioned in the Egyptian monuments. Pharaoh had hoped to crush the Israelites by force of bad treatment. Seeing, on the contrary, that their number went on always increasing, he ordered all the male infants that were born to be thrown into the Nile.

3. It was at this time that Moses came into the world; he was the son of Amram and Jochebed, both of the tribe of Levi, who had already had two children, a son named Aaron and a daughter named Miriam. His mother hid him three months. At last, no longer able to conceal his existence, she exposed him on the bank of the river in an ark, covered

---

* See Book III., ch. iii., sec. 2–5.

with bitumen and pitch. The daughter of Pharaoh, whom the historian Josephus calls Thermouthis (in Egyptian T-ouer-maut, "the great mother"), going down to bathe, saw the ark and rescued the child, for whom Jochebed offered herself as nurse. She gave him the name of Moses, which means "drawn out of the water." Afterwards, when the child was grown, the mother brought him back to the princess, who caused him to be educated at court. Holy Scripture says nothing about the youth of Moses and his education; but we may, with a certain amount of confidence, receive the Jewish tradition related by Josephus (Jos. *Ant.* II., ix. 5). According to that tradition, the princess caused the child, whom she had saved from the Nile, to be educated by the priests in all the science of the Egyptians, and she was also compelled to protect him from the plots of the sacerdotal caste, and from the diviners who predicted to the king that Egypt would have reason to dread that child. He was, also, according to the same authority, taught warlike arts, and held an important command in an expedition to Ethiopia.

4. The favour he enjoyed at court did not prevent Moses, on reaching manhood, from feeling sensibly the oppression of his countrymen; he often went among them to console them. One day, in his indignation, he killed an Egyptian who was beating a Hebrew. Threatened with the consequence of this deed, he fled into Arabia Petræa. Whilst he was there, wandering as a fugitive, he once, finding himself in the vicinity of a Midianitish tribe, had occasion to defend the seven daughters of Jethro, chief and priest of the tribe, who had come to water their father's flocks, from the violence of the shepherds who wished to drive them away from the well. Jethro having learned from his daughters the generous conduct of Moses, invited him to his home, and offered him hospitality. Moses consented to live with Jethro, who gave him as a wife his daughter Zipporah. Moses passed many years among the Midianites, leading the life of a shepherd. During that time no change had occurred in the situation of his brethren in Egypt. Another king, who the monuments tell us was named Merenphtah, had mounted the throne, but he continued, with regard to the Hebrews, the iniquitous system of his predecessor. In solitude by his flocks and herds Moses could meditate on the lot of the Israelites; patriarchal traditions filled his mind, and the thought of Jehovah, the God of his fathers, was ever present with him.

5. One day, when he had wandered near Mount Horeb, he saw a bush which was on fire, and was not consumed. Not being able to account for this wonder, he turned aside to examine it more closely, but he heard a voice from the midst of the bush which told him that he stood on ground sanctified by the presence of God himself. We consider the facts of Sacred History here only in a purely and exclusively historical aspect; and, therefore, do not insert the sublime dialogue

which the Bible gives between Moses and the Lord. All the sentiments of the future liberator, his faith in God, his distrust of his own abilities, his hesitation, are depicted in this dialogue in which God, to use the expression of Bossuet, "made himself more fully known to this great man than he ever had before to any human being." God commanded Moses to return to Egypt, and revealed to him that he had been chosen to deliver his people from slavery, and to make them know the God of their fathers anew as the Absolute Being—"I AM THAT I AM," such is the name under which God was pleased to cause Himself to be announced to His people, in making Himself known as the God of Abraham, of Isaac, and of Jacob.

6. Moses then rejoined his brother Aaron, whose assistance he had been promised by the Divine voiçe in the burning bush, and who, more eloquent than himself, was to be the interpreter of inspirations from on high, to the Hebrews and to the king of Egypt. They returned at once to Egypt, and after having assembled the chiefs of the tribes of Israel, to encourage them and ensure their obedience, they presented themselves before Pharaoh. Although they had only demanded for their countrymen leave to go and sacrifice in the desert, their request was contemptuously refused, and far from permitting the least relaxation to the people of Israel, the labours imposed on them were increased. Then God, by the ministry of Moses and Aaron, inflicted on the country the various scourges so well known by the name of the plagues of Egypt. The evils which then were sent to afflict the valley of the Nile and terrify the Egyptians are thus enumerated in the Bible :—1st. The waters of the Nile became red like blood, and the river stank, so that the Egyptians digged round about the river for water to drink. 2nd. Frogs multiplied so as to cover all the land, and to become an insupportable nuisance to the people. 3rd. Clouds of lice tormented both men and beasts. 4th. Swarms of noxious insects infested the houses and fields, and damaged the harvests. 5th. An epizootic disease carried off the greater part of the cattle. 6th. Boils broke out on the bodies both of man and beast. 7th. A terrible hailstorm, accompanied by lightning and thunder, ravaged the country. 8th. Clouds of locusts came up and devoured all that the hail had left. 9th. Thick darkness, produced possibly by clouds of sand which the wind brought from the desert, covered the whole of Egypt. 10th. A sudden epidemic carried off the first-born of each family. These plagues, it must be remarked, are such as from time to time occur in the climate of Egypt. What made them miraculous was their extraordinary violence, and that they followed each other with such rapidity at the call of Moses. More than once the king, touched with repentance or fear, entreated the two brothers to obtain from God the cessation of these disasters; but no sooner had the plague ceased, than the hardness of his heart returned.

At last, the death of the first-born throughout his kingdom, and of his own son, broke his resolution, and he allowed Israel to go. On the night of their departure, Moses instituted, in memory of that event, the feast of the Passover ; the Hebrews amounted then to 600,000 adult men, without counting women and children. They all set out under the leadership of Moses.

7. Their march was necessarily very slow, they were three days in gaining the banks of the Red Sea, by a route and by stations which are difficult now to determine precisely. Pharaoh, changing his mind, and regretting the permission which he had given them to depart, pursued after them with 600 war chariots, and a great mass of infantry. He overtook them on the sea shore. The Hebrews had before them on the east the sea, to the right and left inaccessible mountains, and behind them they saw the Egyptian army. Without miraculous assistance they were lost. Already they had abandoned themselves to despair, when Moses promised them, on behalf of the Almighty, a wonderful deliverance. When night came on, Moses stretched out his hand over the sea, a violent tempest from the east began to blow, separated the waters of the gulf at the place where the Israelites were encamped, and opened a passage in the midst of the waters, which were rolled back on each side. The Hebrews at once entered the road thus miraculously opened, and the whole night was occupied in the passage, which took place probably in the neighbourhood of Mount Attaka. The exact spot it is now impossible to identify, but as the Red Sea at this period probably extended many miles north of the present head of the Gulf of Suez (the tongue of the Egyptian Sea (Is. xi. 15), which has been dried up), and was much narrower to the north than to the south of Suez, the balance of probability seems in favour of Israel having crossed the sea at this narrower part.

The Egyptians ventured to follow the fugitives into the bed of the gulf, with their chariots and horses, but the chariot wheels could not roll, and the advance was very difficult. When morning appeared, Moses again extended his hand over the sea. At once the east wind ceased to blow, and the "sea returned to his strength," and cut off the retreat of the Egyptian army, which was swallowed up by the waves. It is generally added that Pharaoh perished in the waters with his army, but this is one of those interpretations, one of those developments, which are too often added to the Bible story. The Sacred Volume says nothing of the kind ; nor do any of its expressions justify, or give any ground for, such an assertion. The army, not the king, was engulfed ; and, in fact, we shall see in the chapter on the History of Egypt that the Pharaoh Merenphtah survived this disaster, and died in his bed.

SECTION V.—THE ISRAELITES AT SINAI.

1. IT was not without deep consideration and mature reflection that Moses had conducted the Israelites towards the Red Sea and the Peninsula of Sinai. The shortest and easiest route from Egypt to the land of Canaan was northward along the coast of the Mediterranean, and past Rhinocorura (El Arish) to Gaza. But this road was throughout its whole extent guarded by strong fortresses, garrisoned by Egyptian troops, who could have opposed the passage of the Hebrews (Ex. xiii. 17). The army of Pharaoh, accustomed to use that road on its expeditions into Asia, would easily have overtaken them, and as undoubtedly have cut them to pieces. Moreover, it would have been imprudent in the highest degree to bring the people of Israel, debased by long continued slavery, and with no practice in the use of arms, directly into collision with the warlike Canaanitish nations, who, if the war had been prolonged, could have called for the powerful assistance of the King of Egypt, at that time their sovereign. Moreover, before entering into possession of the Promised Land, and forming an independent state, it was absolutely necessary for the Hebrews to serve an apprenticeship, and to be regenerated in solitude. To become worthy of its high destinies, it was necessary for the nation to be kept separate for some time in the desert, far away from the Pagan populations, in the midst of whom it had so long lived; and, above all, from the vices of cities. In this way only could faith in the God of their fathers, so long forgotten in this slavery, be re-awakened among them. It was only in this way that it was possible for Moses to form a new people, obedient to the Divine will, to give them laws, to subject them to discipline, and to put them in a condition, not only to conquer the land which the Lord had promised them, but to establish themselves there, so as to be able to fulfil the sublime destiny to which Providence had called them. Such were the reasons which decided Moses, guided by Divine inspiration, to lead the children of Israel into the desert of Sinai; to avoid, as much as possible, any rencontre with hostile nations; to keep them there as long as was necessary for the establishment of the law and the complete organisation of the nation; and, finally, to lead them to the south-eastern frontier of Palestine, which was not covered by Egyptian fortresses.

2. The enterprise offered, moreover, enormous difficulties; and the constant and direct aid of Providence could alone ensure its success. We have already stated what was the number of the Hebrews at the time of the Exodus. But they were not alone; the Bible tells us that a mixed multitude of people had followed them. These were, to all appearance, people of tribes foreign to the Egyptian race, who also

being oppressed, had seized this opportunity to free themselves from servitude. We cannot therefore estimate below three millions the number of individuals who followed Moses. This immense multitude found itself, with numerous flocks and herds, in a desert which barely afforded a scanty pasturage and little water to the few Arab tribes who wandered there. From the very first, God began to provide for the subsistence of His people, by causing Moses to sweeten the bitter water of Marah, a station which seems to correspond to the situation of Howara, a short distance south of the place where the Israelites passed the sea—a place where the water to this very day is unfit to drink on account of its bitterness. Afterwards, when they had left the fountains of Elim to cross the desert of Sin, in the neighbourhood of Rephidim, near Mount Horeb, God sent a flight of quails, of which the people ate too greedily; and he made water to come out of a rock in the valley, now called Wady Mokatteb, a miracle which, at a later time, was repeated to save the people from certain death.

It was then also that God began to shower down manna, which furnished the Hebrews with food during the forty years they were detained in the desert as a punishment for their want of faith. Manna fell every morning in the camp. Every one collected quickly (for it melted with the first rays of the sun) the quantity required for the day's consumption, but not more, for by the next day it became putrid. Nevertheless, on the eve of the Sabbath, enough for two days might be gathered without fear of its spoiling, in order that they might scrupulously observe the day consecrated to the Lord. The country in which we must seek for the desert of Sin has even now many tamarisk shrubs, from the branches of which a resinous substance exudes when punctured by an insect. This the Arabs of the country eat, instead of honey, with bread; and modern writers have named this "manna." Several travellers have also found a species of manna which seems to fall from the sky, and attaches itself to stones, bushes, and shrubs; this is the vegetable manna carried about by the wind. May we suppose this to be the substance which fed the Hebrews? In any case, the natural facts observed by travellers are insufficient to explain the Bible narrative; for this manna is only found in the Sinaitic peninsula, and only during the months of June and July; whilst, according to the Bible, the Hebrews gathered what was their principal article of food every day for forty years, and over the whole of their route, as far as Edrei and Gilgal. Moreover, the quantity is very far short of what would suffice to feed so great a multitude of men.

The Hebrews were still at Rephidim when they were attacked by the Amalekites, one of the most ancient and powerful tribes of Arabia Proper, who were descended from Aram, and who have been mentioned in the story of the conquests of Chedorlaomer. God gave the victory to the Israelites, who were led to battle by Joshua, the future conqueror of the Promised Land.

Having left Rephidim, the children of Israel arrived, the third month after their departure from Egypt, at Mount Sinai, where God gave them the Law, announced by the roar of thunder, by lightning, and clouds and smoke which covered the mountain. He promulgated first the fundamental duties of man towards God, his neighbour, and himself; that which we call the Decalogue, or Ten Commandments. To these were added very many precepts more in detail, and the people promised to obey the Law of the Lord.

But when Moses had returned to Sinai, where he was lost to sight enveloped in a cloud, and where he remained forty days and forty nights, receiving the commands which God gave him for the celebration of His worship, the ignorant and fickle people of Israel had not patience to submit to this first and easy proof of their fidelity to the supreme law which was about to be their national institution, the fundamental principle of their constitution. During the short absence of the prophet they forgot both the majesty of God, who had delivered them from slavery, and their own covenant. They said to Aaron, "Make us gods, which shall go before us." Aaron made them a golden calf, in imitation of the Egyptian worship of Apis; and the Israelites, when they saw it, said, "These be thy gods, O Israel, which brought thee up out of the land of Egypt." Aaron built an altar, and offered victims to this abominable idol. Moses interceded with the Lord, that this impious and faithless people should not be annihilated; but, in the transport of his indignation, he threw down and broke on the ground the tables of stone on which God himself had written the Law. He cast the idol into the fire, and sent the tribe of Levi to fall on those rebels against the Divine Law—the law of the nation itself, that God had miraculously freed, and almost, as it were, created. A great number fell by the sword. Other tables of stone were made by Moses, by the Lord's command, and the Ten Commandments were written on them afresh.

SECTION VI.—THE LAW OF MOSES.*

1. WE cannot here explain in all its details the legislation dictated to Moses at various times by the Divine Word, and destined to teach the Hebrew people the essential principles of faith, laws and morality, the forms of worship, political and civil institutions, which were to make them a separate people among the nations of the ancient world. But it is at least necessary to explain here, as briefly as possible, its fundamental principles and most essential provisions.

* See MICHAELIS "Mosaisches Recht," Frankfort, 1775.

The Mosaic Law presents the spectacle, unique in the history of the world, of a legislation which was complete from the origin of a nation, and subsisted for long ages. In spite of frequent infractions, it was always restored, even although in its very sublimity it was in direct opposition to the coarse inclinations of the people whom it governed. He alone could impose it on the Israelites who could say, "I am the Lord thy God," and confirm the words by forty years of miracles. Doubtless, there are in this code some things which do not bear the direct imprint of the Divine perfection; we find sanction given there to customs imperfect, or even to be regretted, which had formerly existed among a people who had come out from the midst of idolaters. These the law partly tolerated (compare Matt. xix. 8; Mark x. 4), confining itself to prescribing rules for restraining abuses.

But however far it may be from that evangelical perfection, reserved for an epoch when the example of the Saviour and the institution of sacraments might give to the human race a moral power previously unknown, the Law of Moses yet surpasses, by the distance of heaven from earth, the institutions of all ancient nations, without excepting those who surpassed the Hebrews in quickness of intellect or elevation of character.

2. The fundamental principle of this legislation is the supreme authority of God over the people of Israel (1 Sam. viii. 7, xii. 12). He was in the literal sense of the word their Sovereign; and all other authority, both in political and civil affairs, was subordinate to the continual acknowledgment of His own. The other powers were instituted by God to administer affairs in accordance with His laws, but were not ordinarily chosen among the priests, descendants of Aaron, nor from the tribe of Levi, consecrated to the various functions of public worship. Each tribe (Ex. xviii. 21—27) had its civil authorities, although certain causes were reserved for the supreme central tribunal; but the unity of the nation was, above all, founded on unity in faith and worship—on the mighty recollections recalled each year by the solemn feasts: the Passover, or Feast of Unleavened Bread (commemorating the Exodus from Egypt), Pentecost (the Promulgation of the Law), and the Feast of Tabernacles, or Tents (the Sojourn in the Desert). The one tabernacle, where the solemn sacrifices were offered, and where was deposited the Ark, the symbol of the covenant made between God and His people, was equally the political and religious centre of the nation.

3. The penal laws promulgated by Moses allowed neither extraordinary punishments nor torture, by which (miserable heritage of Roman law) modern nations, even as late as a century ago, endeavoured to force confession from an accused person by the infliction of pain. The punishment of death could not be inflicted on the testimony of a single

witness (Numb. xxxv. 30; Deut. xvii. 6); and (contrary to the political custom of Asia), the punishment of a father did not entail that of the children (Deut. xxiv. 16). But idolatry, which in these countries, as in every or nearly every other, was indissolubly connected with frightful debauchery — idolatry, which was both an affront to the Divinity itself and also a formal attack on the constitution of the nation and on the essential condition of its unity, was punished with death (Deut. xiii. 9; xvii. 2—5). The same punishment was also decreed for divination (Lev. xx. 7), another form of idolatry, for incest and unnatural crimes, for rebellion of a son against his father (Deut. xxi. 18, *seq.*), for stealing and selling as a slave a free man (Ex. xxi. 16; Deut. xxiv. 7), and for infidelity in a betrothed or married woman. Moreover, the influence of the almost barbarous manners and customs of the Israelites are very apparent in some of the penal laws.

By the side of most equitable regulations as to theft and loss, there are others of most implacable severity—such as the law of retaliation applied to malicious or accidental wounding—"eye for eye, tooth for tooth, hand for hand, foot for foot" (Ex. xxi. 24; Lev. xxiv. 20). A terrible law, but one which possibly in its administration may have been commuted for a pecuniary fine. The murderer, on the same principle, was punished with death; but here the ancient rule admitted of no composition; even in the case of involuntary manslaughter; however accidental was the cause of death, it must be revenged by a death. The relations of the victim were obliged, as a point of honour, to require this sanguinary expiation (Numb. xxxv. 10—24). Moses, unable to abolish this custom entirely, strove to find means of rendering it practically inoperative. He established cities of refuge.

Six cities were named after the conquest of the Promised Land, three on either bank of the Jordan, to receive those who fled to escape these terrible reprisals; and the situations of the towns, the facilities of approach to them, directions placed at the cross roads, all contributed to facilitate the escape of the fugitive. On his arrival within the gate of the protecting city, he was required to submit to the judgment of its elders as to the death he had caused. If declared guilty of murder, he was given up to the members of the family of the deceased, who, in satisfying their vengeance, were only ministers of justice. If pronounced innocent he was admitted to the city, a dwelling was assigned him, and land to cultivate for his subsistence. If he left the precinct, he was exposed to the revenge of the relations of the dead man, but within the precinct they could not strike him without being themselves guilty of murder. And not only did the legislator impose these limits of place on family feuds, he also limited them as to time. At the death of the high priest, the refugees could return home without fear of future molestation.

4. Property in land was subject to conditions, restrictions which, in their beneficent wisdom, must have often recalled to the Israelite the direct and special gift which God had given him, in employing his nation to chastise the corruption of the Canaanites, and giving him possession of their territories. Not only was the tenth part of the produce (Lev. xxvii. 26—34; Numb. xviii. 21), a sort of tax levied in the name of God himself as Sovereign of the Hebrew people, set apart for the support of the Levites, who were excluded by law from all share in the possession of the land, and had only certain cities set apart for them with a small extent of town lands, but every seventh or Sabbatical year the land rested, and the natural produce without cultivation was shared with servants and strangers (Lev. xxv. 1—7). The year of Jubilee too, that is the fiftieth year, or more correctly, the seventh Sabbatical year (representing the fiftieth, including the year from which the calculation started, according to the usage of most ancient people), was to put each family again in possession of the inheritance that had been assigned to it at the time of the conquest (Lev. xxv. 8—17). Thus the sale of landed property could only be an assignment for the number of years which had to run to the next year of Jubilee; so that improvidence, prodigality, or the bad conduct of a father, could only temporarily injure the prospects of his family. At the end of a fixed term they recovered their former competence, and this without injury to the rights of anyone. Neither could the father exercise the power of life and death over his children, as among the Romans (Deut. xxi. 18—21).

5. But the Sabbatical years and years of Jubilee had yet another intent and still higher aim—they restored liberty to all Hebrew slaves (Lev. xxv. 40). The lot of a slave among the Israelites was not in the least like what it was among the most polished of ancient European nations. The Law of Moses punished with death the master who murdered his slave (Ex. xxi. 20), and freed, without any indemnity, the slave wounded by his master (Ex. xxi. 26). The rest of the Sabbath, and of the feasts, belonged to him as much as to the free man. "That thy man-servant and thy maid-servant," said the law, "may rest as well as thou;" and it added this touching reason, "Remember that thou wast a servant in the land of Egypt" (Deut. v. 14, 15; xv. 15; xvi. 12; xxiv. 18, 22). But this servitude, thus lightened, and which could only arise from punishment for a crime, or for payment of a debt by the labour of a family otherwise insolvent—this servitude could not in any case exist longer than six years, because on the seventh year, by which, it seems, we must understand the Sabbatical year (Deut. xv. 12—18), the Israelite slave recovered his liberty, unless he refused it himself, in which case the servitude was prolonged to the next Jubilee.

It is true that foreign slaves were excluded from this beneficent arrangement, the Hebrews applying to them the laws which were in force among their own nations (Ex. xii. 44; Lev. xxv. 44, 46). But by declaring himself a proselyte—by opening his eyes to the light and embracing the Divine Law of Sinai, every stranger was admitted to an equality with the children of Israel. The slave of foreign birth, therefore, found himself, by the mere fact of his conversion, entitled to the benefit of all provisions made in favour of those Hebrews who had fallen to the condition of slaves.

6. A loan by an Israelite to a foreigner might bear interest (Deut. xxiii. 20), the rate of which was not limited by law; the matter was, in fact, considered as a commercial transaction. But loans between Israelites were to be made without interest (Ex. xxii. 25; Lev. xxv. 35—37), as people leading an agricultural life, each with his own little property would not borrow for speculation, but from necessity. Now to wish capital to produce interest when, far from being productive in the hands of the borrower, it was itself consumed for the wants of his family, would be to desire to make a living out of the property of the unfortunate, to traffic in his misfortune. In such a case, interest, however small its amount, is detestable usury. The pledge was the object of delicate and affecting regulations (Deut. xxiv. 10—13, 17)—"When thou dost lend thy brother anything, thou shalt not go into his house to fetch his pledge. Thou shalt stand abroad, and the man to whom thou dost lend shall bring out the pledge abroad to thee. And if the man be poor, thou shalt not sleep with his pledge. In any case, thou shalt deliver him the pledge again when the sun goeth down, that he may sleep in his own raiment and bless thee; and it shall be righteousness unto thee before the Lord thy God. . . . . Thou shalt not take a widow's raiment to pledge."

7. "The most perfect charity was also prescribed to the Israelites towards strangers, contrary to the customs of all other ancient people. 'The stranger that dwelleth with you shall be unto you as one born among you,' said the law, 'and thou shalt love him as thyself; for ye were strangers in the land of Egypt.' They had a share of the tithes, and, equally with the widow and orphan, had the right of gleaning; a right formally established by law. Jewish legislation was essentially partial to the poor; it forbade usury, commanded almsgiving, prescribed kindness even towards animals, and admitted the stranger to the Temple and sacrifices. Whatever was abased and trodden down by the ancient world, was elevated by the Mosaic Law. In the society it founded, the foreigner was no longer an enemy; the slave was still a man; and woman, seated honourably by the side of the head of the family, was there treated with equal consideration."—ROBIOU.

SECTION VII.—THE TABERNACLE.

1. THE law once promulgated, Moses occupied himself in organising the external and visible worship of Jehovah, which it was necessary to institute as quickly as possible, in order to retain in the faith a people fond of outward pomps, and the more inclined, from that very love of ceremonies, to relapse into idolatry. He communicated his Divine inspirations on this subject, first to Aaron and the chiefs of the tribes, then to the whole nation; he explained to them the plan of a portable Temple, in which worship might for the future be performed for the whole nation.

Aaron and his four sons were designated as the priests of this worship; and the duty of assisting them in their functions was assigned to the entire tribe of Levi, as a recompense for the devotion they had manifested for the cause of Divine unity. On an appeal which Moses made to the generosity of the nation, materials—metals, and other valuables—necessary for the construction of the Tabernacle (for so it is customary to call this portable Temple), the altars, sacred vessels, etc., were contributed in abundance. Numerous artificers undertook the task, under the direction of two artists, Bezaleel, of the tribe of Judah, and Aholiab, of that of Dan. The work advanced rapidly, and on the first day of the second year the Tabernacle was erected and consecrated.

2. It resembled the very handsome tent of a nomadic chief, but the hangings were backed by a frame-work of planks to make them firmer. The edifice was oblong, its longer sides running east and west, and was composed of the Sanctuary proper, called Mishcan (habitation), and of a large court surrounding it on all sides. In this court, in the open air, was the altar of sacrifices, of wood covered with bronze, on which the slain victims were burned, and the great basin of bronze, mounted on a pedestal of the same metal, in which the priests washed their hands and feet before approaching the altar or entering the sanctuary.

The Sanctuary proper was divided by an embroidered veil of magnificent stuffs into two parts—the Holy Place, and the Holy of Holies. The Holy Place contained the sacred utensils; the table of shew-bread, made of wood and covered with gold, on which were placed, every sabbath day, twelve loaves of unleavened bread offered by the twelve tribes; the famous golden candlestick with seven branches; and, finally, the small portable altar of wood covered with golden plates, on which incense was burned. The table of shew-bread and the seven-branched candlestick are represented on the arch of Titus at Rome, among the trophies brought from Jerusalem after the capture of that city by the

Romans. There is also, in several Egyptian monuments, a representation of a table of offerings, from which it appears that the table of shew-bread was copied.

The Holy of Holies, into which the High Priest and Moses had alone the right to enter, and that only on certain fixed days, contained nothing but the "Ark of the Covenant"— the symbol of the covenant made between God and His chosen people. It was of very durable wood covered with plates of gold. The description given in the Book of Exodus is very obscure and incomplete, but everything seems to show that the Ark was made on the model of the Naos, or portable wooden chapels, which the sanctuary of every Egyptian Temple contained, and which their bas-reliefs often represent.

In the Naos, or Egyptian Arks, whose doors were always shut, was enclosed the image, hidden from profane eyes, of the Deity, to whom each was consecrated, and who was supposed to reside there. In the Ark of the Mosaic Tabernacle there was no image of that kind, for the Law, to avoid the danger of idolatry, forbade the representation of God under any visible and material figure whatever. Moses had placed there the two stone tables of the Decalogue, as if they were the deed of the compact between God and the Israelites. The two emblematical figures which covered the Ark with their extended wings, and which the Bible calls Cherubim, must have been, from their name, which means bulls, and from some passages which attribute to them a human face and wings, related to those winged human-headed bulls whose gigantic images have been found at the doors of all the palaces of Assyria. An additional proof of this fact is found in the employment of the word Kirub, in very many Assyrian texts, to designate these winged bulls, and, in an extended sense, the gateways which they ornamented.

One is often astonished at the magnificence of the Tabernacle, as it is described in the Book of Exodus; and, above all, at the amount of work in metal which had been executed for it. Such works cannot be produced by a nation of nomadic shepherds, wandering about in tents. They require perfect apparatus and fixed and extensive establishments. Anti-religious criticism has been quick to draw occasion from this difficulty to tax the Sacred Volume with exaggeration and even with falsehood, and to say that the works of the Tabernacle should be consigned to the domain of fable. But now these specious objections fall before the progress of knowledge, and the truthfulness of the Divine Book is as clearly apparent in this as in all its other statements.

The most recent explorers of Arabia Petræa, the Count de Labord, M. Lepsius, and M. Lottin de Laval, have found in the mountain range of Sinai, near the place where the Hebrews sojourned under the leading of Moses during the two years which were employed in the work on the Tabernacle, in a place now called Wady Mogharah, important copper mines worked by the Egyptians from the time of their oldest dynasties; and the ruins are still perfectly recognisable of vast metallurgic factories which they had established there. Inscriptions abound in these ruins.

It seems, then, quite clear, that the Israelites when at Sinai, and wishing to manufacture the vessels required in their worship, took possession of the workshops of Wady Mogharah, and very probably made the Egyptian workmen assist, under the direction of the two overseers named in the Bible. It was there, no doubt, that Aaron made the golden calf, and that with the furnaces established by order of the Pharaohs, and the utensils belonging to them, Bezaleel and Aholiab cast the numerous golden and bronze articles for the furnishing of the Tabernacle.

SECTION VIII.—SOJOURN IN THE DESERT.

1. WHEN the Tabernacle was dedicated, a few days after the second Paschal anniversary of the Exodus from Egypt, Moses broke up the camp and recommenced the journey. He had chosen for his guide, in the part of the desert which remained to be traversed, and which he did not know personally, his brother-in-law Hobab the Midianite, who had rejoined him at Sinai, and had brought to him his wife and children.

The route taken was to the North, towards the Desert of Paran and the southern frontier of Palestine. But at the commencement of the journey murmurs re-commenced. The heat (for it was about the end of May) made a number of victims in that crowded mass of people; soon the lowest of the people complained of want of nourishment, and began to regret the abundance they had enjoyed in Egypt. Numerous flocks of quails again arrived in the camp; the Hebrews fell on them with such avidity that they soon paid the penalty of their greediness with their lives. They arrived at last at Kadesh Barnea, near the southern extremity of the Dead Sea, in the Deserts of Paran.*

2. Thence Moses sent twelve men, one from each tribe, to explore the land of Canaan, and to make a report on its inhabitants, on the cities they occupied and on the general aspect of the country. Returning after forty days, they praised the fertility of the land of Canaan, but represented the conquest of it as an impossibility, on

---

* The true situation of Kadesh Barnea has not yet been definitely settled. The most interesting supposition is that of Dean Stanley, who conjecturally identifies it with Petra. Kadesh Barnea was probably the En Mishpat, smitten by Chedorlaomer (Gen. xiv. 7).—TR.

account of the strength of its inhabitants, men of gigantic stature, and established in well fortified towns. At this report discouragement seized on the people. In vain Joshua and Caleb, who had been among the explorers, attempted to calm the exasperation of the mob, and to overcome their fears by more favourable accounts.

A general revolt threatened to overturn completely the plans of Moses, and the people even spoke of electing another leader, to return to Egypt. Moses then perceived the impossibility of carrying out his work with that generation so inured to slavery and incapable of heroic self-devotion. He severely reproached the people for their mistrust of God, who had manifested Himself to them by so many miracles, and announced to them the Divine decree, which condemned all the men above twenty years old, except Caleb and Joshua, to die in the wilderness, and reserved the conquest of Canaan for the new generation. At the words of Moses, the Hebrews perceived the criminality of their conduct, and wished at once to march against the Canaanites, but the decree had been irrevocably pronounced. In spite of being forbidden by Moses, who refused to leave the camp, they attempted an attack; the Israelites were repulsed with loss by the Canaanites and Amalekites who combined against them, and were compelled to resign themselves to a continuance of their nomadic life in the desert.

The postponement for forty years of the entry into the Land of Promise was a Divine punishment for the want of faith of the Hebrews, and was so ordered by the wise disposal of Providence, as greatly to facilitate, from a merely human point of view, the conquest of the land of Canaan. Not only did it bring to the fight with the warlike people of Canaan a generation hardy, trained to war, and born in the enjoyment of liberty, in place of that which had been born and grown up in slavery, but it ensured the invasion taking place at the exact historical time most favourable to success. If the Hebrews had entered the land of Canaan two years after the Exodus, they would have had to deal, not with the Canaanites alone, but with the whole force of the Egyptian empire, at that time very strong, and master of all Palestine.

Forty years later, however, circumstances had changed. Egypt was subject to kings who did not trouble themselves about warlike matters, and who allowed the Israelites and the Canaanites to fight as they would in Palestine, confining themselves to claiming a purely nominal suzerainty over the country, which neither the one nor the other cared to contest.

3. During thirty-eight years, the Hebrews—sadly resigned to their nomadic life—traversed the Desert to which the Arabs have given the name of El Tyh, or Tyh Beni Israel (wanderings of the children of Israel), going from north to south as far as Eziongeber, on the Elanitic Gulf, and returning thence northward to Kadesh Barnea. They do not

appear to have been troubled there by attacks of any kind. This long space of time passed away without any incidents sufficiently remarkable to deserve being handed down to posterity. At least the historical documents of the Pentateuch only relate one event of this period of any importance—the revolt excited by the Levite Korah, the cause of which is attributed to the privileges of the priesthood given to Aaron and his family. We know what was the Divine punishment that fell on Korah and his principal accomplices. The people having thought this chastisement too severe, God punished their murmurs by a pestilence which carried off very many victims.

4. At the commencement of the fortieth year after the Exodus, Aaron, the brother of Moses, died at Masera, in Mount Hor. He was then 123 years old, and the high priesthood was transmitted to his son Eleazar. The entry to the Promised Land was refused to him, as well as to Moses, by a Divine decree, because they had wavered in their faith when God had commanded them to speak to the rock in Kadesh to give water to His people. Mount Hor is on the frontier of the country then occupied by the Edomites, descendants of Esau, from whom Moses requested a free passage, appealing to the memory of their common origin, and to the visible marks of the Divine protection with which God had favoured the Israelites. The legislator, in fact, feeling his end approaching, wished to secure the completion of the work of his life, by himself conducting the people to the left bank of the Jordan, where the borders of Canaan were defended only by that river, which was fordable in many places.

In asking a passage across Idumæa, Moses had promised that the Hebrews should not stray from the highway, and that the people should pay even for the water that they drank. The Edomites refused; and thus the Hebrews, who were forbidden by God to fight against their brethren, were obliged to turn away to the south-east, as far as the head of the Elanitic Gulf, and then again to turn to the north. Attacked on their march by the Canaanites of Arad, they were at first vanquished, but afterwards gained a brilliant victory. The Edomites permitted them to defile past their territories without disturbing them. God also forbade the Hebrews to attack the Moabites and Ammonites, descendants of Lot. They followed the skirt of the desert as far as the torrent of Zared (now Wady Karak), and then came to that of Arnon, which formed the frontier of the Moabites, and of the Amorites, a Canaanitish nation. The brook Arnon runs into the Dead Sea, towards the middle of the eastern bank of that sea; and the brook Zared also on the same side, more to the south.

SECTION IX.—CONQUEST OF THE COUNTRY EAST OF THE JORDAN.

1. A PEACEFUL embassy was then addressed by Moses to Sihon, king of the Amorites, to request a passage through the country, again promising not to stray from the road, and to do no damage. Sihon was a victorious adventurer who, a short time before, putting himself at the head of the Canaanitish tribes which up to that time had been living about Engadi on the west bank of the Dead Sea, had passed the Jordan, and formed, at the expense of the Ammonites and Moabites between Arnon and Jabbok, a kingdom, with Heshbon for its capital. He had ravaged the whole country of Moab, and had even taken its capital by assault. A great bas-relief on lava—in imitation of Egyptian work, but ruder in execution, which was discovered by M. De Saulcy in the ruins of a triumphal monument of this prince near Arnon, in a place to which the Arabs still give the very significant name of Tell Schihan, Hill of Sihon—has recently been brought to France by the Duke de Luynes, who has generously presented it to the Museum of the Louvre ; it represents the conqueror piercing a prostrate enemy with his lance. Puffed up beyond measure by his former successes, Sihon refused the request of the Israelites, assembled his troops, and advanced to the desert to fight with the people led by Moses. Completely conquered, the Amorites had all their cities taken, and their territory became the prize of the Hebrews.

After this first victory, Moses, without losing a moment, directed the forces of Israel against the kingdom of Bashan, which took up arms to avenge Sihon. This kingdom, whose capitals were Ashteroth—Karnaim, and Edrei, had also been founded at the expense of the Ammonites, who had been thrown back further east, towards Rabbath Ammon (in later times Philadelphia), and of the southern provinces of the Aramæan state of Damascus, by Amorite tribes under the leadership of an adventurer of enormous size and prodigious strength, named Og. He was descended from the people of the Rephaim, who had occupied part of Palestine before the arrival of the Canaanites, and whom tradition represents as giants. Og having set himself up as the adversary of Israel, shared the fate of Sihon ; he was conquered and killed. By his defeat the Hebrews found themselves masters of the left bank of the Jordan, from the Dead Sea to Mount Hermon, where that river has its source—that is, of all the country called by the Greeks in later times Peræa (the country beyond the river).

2. After these two victories, the people of Israel encamped on the tract that had been taken by Sihon from the Moabites, opposite Jericho. Balak, king of Moab, was terrified at their presence, and allied himself

for defence against them with the chiefs of the Midianites. Believing themselves, however, too weak to attack the Hebrews, the allies called in from the country of the Ammonites a famous diviner, named Balaam, to lay a curse on these redoubtable enemies, and devote them to an evil end. This scheme having failed of success, they invited the Hebrews to the sacrifices of Baal Peor their god.

The immoral and voluptuous worship of that idol seduced a great number of Israelites. Zimri, the chief of a family of the tribe of Simeon, dared to pass before Moses with the daughter of a Midianitish prince. They were both slain on the spot by Phinehas, son of Eleazar the high priest. Moses was obliged to show the most terrible severity; he ordered the judges to punish all the guilty with death. A war of extermination was at once commenced against the Midianites. Moses entrusted the command to Phinehas, who with 12,000 men attacked the enemy, and made great slaughter.* Phinehas did not take possession of the Midianite territory, he contented himself with devastating the country, and returned to the camp with an immense booty.

They then took a census of the families of Israel; the result showed 601,730 men fit to bear arms. New precepts were added to the law of the Hebrews, and Joshua was designated by God as the successor of Moses; but with the command to consult the high priest Eleazar as to the designs he might wish to adopt.

3. The moment for crossing the river approached. The tribes of Reuben and Gad, rich in flocks and herds, and charmed with the abundance of pasture which the country they had just conquered afforded, begged Moses to allow them to settle there. Moses reproached them, for thus sowing discouragement among the people; but these two tribes having promised to take part in the battles for the conquest of Canaan, without claiming any other part of the territory, the legislator gave his consent. The two tribes then established them-

---

* There may be a doubt whether Phinehas was in command. He was sent "with the holy instruments, and [even] the trumpets to blow in his hand" (Numb. xxxi. 6).

"Critics are not agreed what these holy vessels or instruments were which Phinehas carried with him to the war. Spencer contends that the Urim and Thummin are meant, while Geddes conjectures that the Ark and its appurtenances may be thus called. Le Clerk thinks the trumpets only are meant, and that we should render the '*and*' '*even.*' I deem this the most probable opinion."—BOOTHROYD, *Bib. Heb.*

It would seem, also, that if Phinehas had been in command, Moses would have been wroth with him (Numb. xxxi. 14), and not with the officers of the host.

Phinehas possibly went, as Hophni and Phinehas did (1 Sam. iv. 4), only in charge of the sacred utensils, which none but a priest might touch.—TR.

selves between Arnon and Jabbok, Reuben to the south and Gad to the north. One-half of the tribe of Manasseh, sprung from Joseph, obtained the same privilege, and received for its share the territory of Bashan.

4. Finally, Moses fixed the limits of the territory which was to be conquered; he charged Joshua, Eleazar, and the chiefs of the ten tribes, to watch over the partition of the lands which were to be assigned by lot. He directed that forty-eight cities in various districts should be assigned to the Levites, of which six should, at the same time, serve as an asylum for those who had accidently slain a man.

After having thus regulated in advance the work of the conquest, he felt the necessity of recalling to the new generation the miraculous preservation of the Hebrews in the desert, and all that he himself had done to lay the foundation for the well-being of his people in ages to come. He addressed to the Israelites a series of discourses, in which he recalled the principal points of his legislation, with some modifications and alterations which time had rendered necessary. He exhorted the Hebrews to piety and virtue, foretelling to them the misfortunes which neglect of the Divine Law would entail on them. The document containing the law was consigned to the Priests, with directions to read it to the people every seventh year at the feast of Tabernacles (Deut. xxxi. 10).

After having given his warnings afresh in a sublime song, which the Hebrews were to learn by heart, Moses installed Joshua in power. He then gave his benediction to the tribes of Israel, and retired to Mount Nebo, whence he cast his eyes over the country which his people were to conquer. He died on that mountain, at the age of 120 years; and "no man," says Scripture, "knoweth of his sepulchre unto this day."

CHAPTER II.

ESTABLISHMENT OF THE ISRAELITES IN THE PROMISED LAND.—THE JUDGES.

Chief Authorities:—The Bible, Books of Joshua and Judges, I. Book of Samuel (called in the Septuagint and Vulgate *I. Book of Kings*).—Josephus, *Antiquities*, Books V. and VI.

The modern writers mentioned at the beginning of Chapter I.

SECTION I.—CONQUEST OF THE LAND OF CANAAN—JOSHUA.

1. WHEN the thirty days of mourning, by which the Israelites showed their sorrow for the death of Moses, had expired—precisely forty years after their going out of Egypt—Joshua at the head of the twelve

tribes crossed the Jordan, whose waters opened of their own accord for their passage, and attacked Jericho, the walls of which, to follow the expressions of the Bible, fell down at the sound of the trumpets of Israel. The inhabitants of Ai (a city situated to the eastward, and near Bethel), drawn into an ambuscade, soon succumbed in their turn. Immediately after this double success, which gave them the keys of Canaan and proved their moral superiority, the Hebrews advanced to the heart of the country, to Shechem, which they seem to have carried without a blow. Joshua built on Mount Ebal, as a monument of the conquest, a great altar, on which was engraven a summary of the law of Moses.*

In the meanwhile, the kings of the different Canaanite tribes began to recover from the stupor into which they had at first been thrown by the invasion. A general coalition was formed against the Hebrews. The Hittites of the south (for there were others much more powerful in the valley of the Orontes and at the foot of Mount Amanus, who remained indifferent to the events in Palestine), the Jebusites, the Amorites of this side Jordan, who inhabited the mountains, the Canaanites properly so called, who lived on the plains bordering the sea and the river, combined together to give them battle.

2. The Hivites of Gibeon having made a separate peace on very advantageous terms with the Israelites, Adonizedek, king of Jebus (which was afterwards Jerusalem), called to him the people of Hebron, Jarmuth, Lachish, and Eglon; and these five nations, the

---

* The strategy displayed in the invasion of Canaan by the Israelites under Joshua—considering it only as an ordinary historical event—is worth notice. Had Israel advanced on Palestine from the south, however victorious they might have been, they would only have driven before them an ever-increasing mass of enemies, who after each repulse would gain reinforcements, and could fall back on new fortifications and an untouched country, more and more difficult at each step. The Canaanites, if defeated on the heights of Hebron, would have held in succession those of Jerusalem and of Mount Ephraim; and it is unlikely that the invaders would ever have reached the district of Gilboa and Tabor, or the Sea of Tiberias. In all probability Israel would have been compelled to turn off to the low country—the land of the Philistines—and with the Canaanites on the vantage ground of the mountains of Judah and Ephraim, the nation would in its infancy have been trodden down by the march of the Egyptian and Assyrian armies, whose military road this was.

By crossing Jordan, destroying Jericho, occupying the heights by a night march, and delivering the crushing blow of the battle of Beth-horon, Joshua executed the favourite manœuvre of the greatest captains by sea and land, down to the days of Nelson and Napoleon; he broke through and defeated the centre of the enemy's line, and then stood in a position to strike with his whole force successively right and left.—Tr.

strongest in the southern part of the country, attacked the Gibeonites, who appealed for help to Joshua. He pushed on and gained a brilliant victory, in which he annihilated the enemy's army. It is on the occasion of this victory that the Bible, quoting as it distinctly says a song from a collection of ancient poetry, the Book of Jasher, uses the poetical expression of the sun standing still to give Israel time to destroy the Canaanites.* The five kings made prisoners at the battle of Beth-horon were hanged. Immediately after the battle, the Hebrews took by storm the cities of Makkedah, Libnah, Lachish, Eglon, Hebron, and Debir, whose inhabitants they exterminated; and thus the south of Palestine was subjected to their power.

3. But a second and still more formidable coalition was formed, comprising the Canaanites of the east and west, and all the tribes of the North, Hittites, Perizzites, and Hivites, from the foot of Mount Hermon. It was under the direction of the most powerful prince of that part of the country, Jabin, King of Hazor. But God had resolved to punish the crimes of the Canaanite nation. Joshua was once again victorious in a battle delivered on the banks of the Lake Samochonitis (Merom), and pursued the enemy to the neighbourhood of Sidon, then the chief of the Phœnician cities of the coast. The King of Hazor fell into the hands of the Israelites, and was put to death, and a great number of the cities of the north were taken. An attack directed against the Anakim of the southern extremity of the Promised Land was attended with equal success. At last, after six or seven years of fierce battles, in which thirty-one of the principal Canaanite cities were destroyed, Palestine was almost completely in the power of the Hebrews, from Baal Gad, at the foot of Hermon, to the mountains which join those of Seir, that is, to the Land of Edom.

---

* The miracles which accompanied the entry of the Israelites into Palestine seem such as might have been produced by volcanic agency.

The bed of the Jordan was left dry for more than thirty miles. "The waters . . . stood and rose up upon an heap very far from the city Adam, that is beside Zaretan" (Josh. iii. 16). "The expression '*that is beside Zaretan*,'" says Dr. Lightfoot, "is to be understood of the waters, not of Adam." That city is said to have been twelve miles from Zaretan.

The fall of the walls of Jericho may most obviously have been caused by an earthquake.

The stones which fell on the defeated Amorites, were volcanic not ordinary hailstones; and the Talmudists believed that they were still to be seen. The passages are quoted at length in Dr. Lightfoot's *Horæ Hebraicæ*, etc. London, 1584.

If it be admitted that these events were brought about by agencies in the ordinary course of nature, they are not in any way less miraculous, as they occurred at the exact time when required, to help the chosen people, and even, in two instances, were promised to them beforehand.—Tr.

4. Nevertheless the Canaanites were able to maintain themselves in very many places, and particularly in a great number of fortified towns. Joshua, already very aged, was convinced that the work of the conquest could not be at once accomplished, and that he might consider his mission as terminated. Instead of making fresh attempts which would have required great efforts, he preferred to consolidate his conquests and organise the internal affairs of the Hebrews, leaving to each tribe the task of reducing the remaining cities which were to belong to them.

It was then that the two tribes who had obtained lands in Peræa, returned to occupy them, and that the soil conquered on this side Jordan was parted among the others by twenty-one commissioners. In the south-east there remained independent, Gaza, Gath, Ashdod, Ascalon, and Ekron; that is, the five cities which soon after came into the possession of the Philistines,* but which were at first, even at the time of the conquest, a refuge for the Anakim, driven from their mountains. The Jebusites retained Jerusalem in the territory which the tribe of Judah received, from the desert of Paran and the frontiers of Edom, the Dead Sea and the mouth of the Jordan, to the Mediterranean near Ekron. Of the Canaanites a large number still remained in the domains of Ephraim, and in lands which the half-tribes of Manasseh obtained on this side Jordan.

The country which was thus given to the descendants of Joseph was from the Jordan near Jericho, to the sea near Gaza. The land of Ephraim extended northwards, but was south of the portion of Manasseh. Higher up was Asher; to the east, Issachar, in whose territory were some plots given to Manasseh, amongst others, Megiddo. Zebulon was established to the north of Issachar, between the part occupied by the tribe of Asher and the territory of Naphtali, but a little more to the eastward. Naphtali followed the Jordan from its source to the Lake of Gennesaret, and occupied the eastern bank of the lake itself. Simeon obtained some cities at first destined for Judah, and occupied the extreme south-east of the Israelite territory on the frontier of the Philis-

---

* The Philistines are mentioned in Gen. xxi. 32, in Abraham's time; in Gen. xxvi., in Isaac's time; at the time of the Exodus, Ex. xiii. 17, and in Joshua xiii. 5.

The Author regards the mention in these texts rather as geographical expressions, defining the territory by what afterwards became its best known name, and considers that the statement in the text is proved by the fact, that when Moses (Deut. vii. 1) and Joshua (Josh. iii. 10) spoke to the Hebrews of the nations whom they were to fight against, the Philistines were not mentioned; and that the first arrival of the Philistines on the coast of Palestine is conclusively proved to have occurred in the reign of the Egyptian king, Ramses III.—Tr.

tines, and had on the north the tribe of Dan. As we have already said, the tribe of Levi had no share of the territory, but only certain isolated cities in the midst of various other tribes. The Tabernacle and the Ark of the Covenant, the central point of religious worship and of the nation itself, were established at Shiloh, a town of the territory assigned to Ephraim, to which tribe Joshua belonged.

5. Believing himself near death, Joshua assembled the people at Shechem, and, in a discourse which the Bible has preserved, recalled to them all the benefits which Jehovah had conferred on the Hebrews. He exhorted the Israelites to the faithful observance of the laws of Moses, and to the continuance of war with the Canaanites, predicting great misfortunes for them, if they abandoned the worship of the true God, and if they mixed themselves with the heathen, who were still very numerous in the country. The Hebrews promised to obey, and again renewed their covenant with Jehovah. Joshua prepared a record of it, which was written in the book of Moses ; moreover, he set up in the place of the assembly a monumental stone, to serve as a witness against the people, if they renounced their God.

Soon after Joshua died at the age of 110 years, 65 years after leaving Egypt. He was buried in the inheritance at Timnath Serah, which the people had assigned to him in recognition of his services, where a French traveller, M. Victor Guérin, has recently discovered his tomb, a vast excavation in the rock. He had been for twenty-five years the supreme chief of the people of Israel. The High Priest, Eleazar, followed him quickly to the tomb, and was buried on a hill which belonged to his son Phinehas, in the mountains of Ephraim. This was in the latter part of the fourteenth century before the Christian era, which is all that can be said in the absence of precise chronological statements. All the very positive dates which up to this time have been attempted to be established for the Exodus, the passage of the Jordan, and the death of Joshua, are purely hypothetical and destitute of any real value, to which no wise historian will commit himself without some fixed and solid basis for chronological calculation.

Section II.—Period of Repose—First Servitude—Commencement of the Judges.

1. While the elders lived, who had been contemporaries of Joshua, and who had assisted in the conquest, the Hebrews maintained their respect for the law and for the worship of Jehovah. In conformity with the last injunctions of Joshua, some of the tribes recommenced hostilities, either to make new conquests, or to re-conquer cities captured at the first invasion, but which the Canaanites had been able

again to occupy. Thus the tribes of Judah and Simeon attacked some Canaanite colonies near Bezek, a city whose precise position is unknown, but which must be between Jerusalem and the Jordan. Ten thousand Canaanites were defeated near that city, whose king, Adonibezek, had his thumbs and great toes cut off, a punishment which by his own account he had inflicted on seventy kings.

Jerusalem, it is true, they could not take from the Jebusites, but all the rest of the mountains of Judah were cleared of enemies, and they even possessed themselves for a time of the cities of Gaza, Ascalon, and Ekron. Bethel fell by treason into the hands of the Ephraimites. Nevertheless, the tribes wanted either the strength or the energy to expel completely or to exterminate the Canaanites, as Moses had commanded. Joshua had committed a great fault in not naming his successor; the want of a head, the absence of union and concert in their operations, paralysed the forces of the Hebrews. It was especially the northern tribes, those of Dan, Manasseh, Ephraim, Asher, Zebulon, and Naphtali, that could not take all the cities which had been assigned to them, or were obliged to content themselves with imposing tribute on the Canaanites, permitting them still to live in the midst of Israel. In general the coast cities successfully repulsed the efforts of the Israelites, and remained in the hands of their ancient possessors. This is the reason why the campaigns of the last great warrior king of Egypt, Ramses III., campaigns which took place at this time and touched only the sea coast of Palestine, have no place in the history of the Hebrews. In the Egyptian inscriptions which give accounts of these wars, there is no reference to the children of Israel, and at the same time the Book of Judges makes no mention of the passage of the Egyptian armies.

2. A messenger of the Divine will came to announce to the Hebrews the fatal consequences of their weakness (Judg. ii. 1). The people admitted the truth of all that was said by the man of God, but they could only answer the appeal by their tears. The Canaanites became more and more dangerous by their material force, which was not yet broken, still more by their religious worship so seductive to the senses, and also by their corrupt manners. The old men who had surrounded Joshua died off one by one; from the good old days of warlike spirit and religious enthusiasm there only survived the High Priest, Phinehas, whose aged arm could no longer avenge, as once it did, insults to the laws and name of Jehovah, and who was not capable of maintaining the political and religious unity of the tribes, and of preserving them from anarchy.

Idolatry and the corruption of manners increased from day to day; with no head, and no common centre, the tribes became estranged from one another, and their mutual indifference threatened to grow into hostility. Two events recounted in the Book of Judges, and which we must refer to the epoch following the death of Joshua and his companions, show how far, after so short a time, the sanguine anticipations of Moses and his successor had failed of realisation. The one is that of the Levite, whom the people of the tribe of Dan took with them when they captured from the Canaanites the city of Laish, and called it Dan, and who, representing Jehovah by an idol, in defiance of the first and most essential of the precepts of the decalogue, instituted in that city a religious worship to rival that of the Tabernacle at Shiloh. The other is the massacre of the tribe of Benjamin by the other confederate tribes, to avenge the outrage committed on the wife of a Levite of Mount Ephraim; the details of this last event present a miserable picture of the barbarous manners of the period. The infamous conduct of the inhabitants of Gibeah; the corpse of the Levite's wife cut in pieces, and sent to all the tribes to provoke them to the war; the slaughter of the Benjamites, wherein the innocent were confounded with the guilty; and, finally, the expedition against Jabesh Gilead, and the massacre of its inhabitants, who had remained quiet during these events, in order to give their daughters to the survivors of the tribe of Benjamin, and thus enable the tribe to recover itself—these all are actions unworthy of an organised community living under a regular government and civilised laws.

"In those days," says the Book of Judges (xxi. 25), after having related these two horrible incidents, "there was no king in Israel; every man did that which was right in his own eyes;" all united political life had in fact ceased with the life of Joshua; no central authority any longer existed. The Israelites had no other government than the separate tribal authorities. The tribe was divided into houses, the house into families, each comprising many individuals; each one of these divisions had its own chiefs, princes of tribes, of houses, of families. But it would have been vain to seek for any national institution besides the sacerdotal body, and this had no real and political power. Under such a system the bonds of nationality must soon have relaxed, and the tribes become estranged from each other. Two things only could and would have preserved the unity of the people; first, the unity of belief and worship, which brought all the tribes round the Tabernacle of Shiloh; secondly, the danger of division when surrounded on all sides by hostile nations. But these purely moral bonds were not sufficiently strong for a people like the Hebrews, and we shall soon see how slight was the power they preserved.

3. Enjoying the sweets of peace, the Hebrews allied themselves with the Canaanites, and neglected more and more the national sanctuary at Shiloh, and soon they did not fear even to give themselves over to the worship of Baal, Ashtaroth, and all the Phœnician divinities. That patriotic feeling, which should always have been strengthened by

religious unity and the solemn assemblies of the Mosaic feasts, became weaker every day, and soon the tribes, isolated and without a head, were attacked either by neighbouring nations, or by the enemies whom they had the imprudence to tolerate in the interior of the country, and who began to recover themselves and to gain strength. From time to time, it is true, an energetic man put himself at the head of certain tribes, or even of the entire nation, to revive the national spirit and throw off the foreign yoke; but he had not always the power nor even the will to revive religious feeling and the love of the Mosaic institutions, and after his death the people fell back again into anarchy.

During many centuries there were continual vicissitudes of reverses and prosperity, of anarchy and absolute government; but the institutions given to Israel at Sinai were no longer thought of. This period is usually termed that of the "Judges," a word intended as a translation of the Hebrew title given to those temporary liberators who became by their exploits the first magistrates of the nation, or more frequently of a part only of the nation. But the word is very ill chosen, for it in no way gives an exact idea of the functions and powers of the men to whom it is applied. It would be much better to employ here the Hebrew word itself, and to name the so-called judges (whose authority was in no way judicial), the Suffetes of Israel; for this name, Suffete, is set apart in Roman history as the designation of the first magistrates of the Carthaginian Republic, whose title was the same and their powers similar to those of these magistrates of Israel. For our part this is the designation to which we shall give the preference.

4. It was in the lifetime of the very generation which followed the conquest that we must place the first servitude of Israel, a punishment inflicted on them on account of the adoption by the majority of the people of the worship of the Canaanitish divinities. A king of Western Mesopotamia, named Chushan Rishathaim,* at that time extended his dominions from the west of the Euphrates to the frontiers of the land of Canaan. In the state in which the Hebrews then were they could not defend their independence, and became tributary to Chushan, who oppressed them for eight years. Moved by their prayers, the Lord raised up as a deliverer, Othniel, nephew of Caleb, who, by the defeat of the strangers, gave his countrymen liberty, which they enjoyed forty years.

This was the commencement of the alternations of servitude and

---

* Sir H. Rawlinson is disposed to conjecture that Cushan-rish-athaim—a name which has been a complete puzzle to etymologists—is a corrupt reading of the name of an Assyrian king, which Sir H. Rawlinson reads Asshur-ris-ilim (Asshur is the head of the gods), and M. Lenormant, Asshur-rish-ishi (Asshur lifts up his head).—Tr.

deliverance which answered, during the whole period of the Judges, or Suffetes, to the alternations of infidelity and return towards God. But we should fall into a great historical error, and into inextricable difficulties, if we were to believe that the years of servitude and independence extended always to all the people of Israel. That is a point long since cleared up; and if there are still difficulties left for science, it is only when she attempts to determine exactly the geographical limits of each of these invasions and their relative dates. As for that of Chushan, I see no motive to limit it, as some critics do, to the countries east of Jordan, to which this king would first have come. Besides that, it will not in any way embarrass the chronology to enter these eight years of servitude and forty of repose in the general history of the Jews; it is not likely that a people, whose mission was to punish the adhesion of the tribes of Israel to Phœnician rites, would have failed to invade Western Palestine, whence no doubt this worship spread to the eastern tribes.

5. It is, however, impossible to give a complete historical and, above all, chronological description of the epoch of the Judges, or Suffetes. The Book of Judges, which is our only authority for this period, is not properly an historical book. Everything in it is told in a discursive style, and the events are not placed in their proper order of succession; the author was far from being tied to an invariable order of time. It is, in fact, a collection of detached traditions of the republican period, collected, probably, from ancient poems and popular legends, which celebrated the glory of the heroes of the age. This collection, which dates from the first days of the kingdom, appears to have been intended above all to encourage the new government to finish the work commenced by Joshua, and to exhibit to the people the advantages of an hereditary monarchy. For this purpose it was sufficient to show by a series of examples how great had been the disorders from which the Hebrews suffered before the foundation of the kingdom; what a series of misfortunes had been occasioned by the forbearance of the Israelites towards the Canaanites, and how even the temporary power of one person had invariably rescued them from total ruin.

There was, therefore, no intention to state in exact chronological order the events and the period of the supremacy of each Suffete. Scholars who have attempted this, have given themselves infinite trouble without adequate result. Not only do the First Book of Samuel, and the First Book of Kings give two absolutely different computations for the duration of the period of the Judges, but the historian Josephus, the faithful reporter of the traditions of the Synagogue, has as many as three different ways of reckoning the same interval of time.

And now that the progress of knowledge in the domain of history allows us to cherish the hope of being able soon to determine with certainty, by synchronism with the annals of Egypt, the precise date of the Exodus, we are compelled to recognise the necessity of reducing the time which elapsed from the going out of Egypt to the establishment of the monarchy in Israel very much more than do any of the calculations hitherto proposed.

SECTION III.—EHUD, SHAMGAR, DEBORAH, GIDEON, JEPHTHAH.

1. Forty years after the first servitude, the invasion of Eglon, king of the Moabites, took place, who, united with the Ammonites and Amalekites, imposed his yoke on the unfaithful Israelites. It is evident that this great coalition did not confine itself to invading the territory of the eastern tribes, neighbours of the Ammonites. The country of Moab was to the south-east of the Dead Sea, and it was from the south that the Amalekites could most easily reach the Promised Land. These nations must, consequently, have attacked the tribe of Judah; and, moreover, the circumstances of the insurrection show that the enemy was established even in the heart of the country. In fact, Ehud, son of Gera, of the tribe of Benjamin, having, while presenting the tribute of his district, killed Eglon, called the people to arms, occupied the fords of Jordan, which formed the most direct road of communication between Central Palestine and the territory of Moab, and killed 10,000 Moabite soldiers who attempted to regain their country. But we must not apply to the whole of Palestine the twenty-four years of repose which were obtained by this exploit.

2. In fact, it is after this success of the Israelites that Scripture mentions the resistance opposed to the Philistines in the south by Shamgar, son of Anath, at the head of a body of labourers, armed only with agricultural implements. About the same time, too, it tells us of a new servitude, which also must apply to a portion only of the country. The Canaanites of the north, formerly conquered by Joshua, had again become very strong, and had retaken the greater part of the country conquered by the Hebrews. As in the time of Joshua, they had at their head a king, named Jabin, who resided at Hazor, their principal city, the gigantic ramparts of which were some years since discovered by M. de Saulcy.* With 900 war-chariots and a numerous army, he oppressed the northern tribes, on whom he imposed his yoke for twenty years. His troops were commanded by Sisera, who had his head-quarters in a city, called Harosheth of the Gentiles.

Barak, son of Abinoam, was called to arms by the Prophetess Deborah, who then administered justice and taught the precepts of the law to the people of her neighbourhood under a palm-grove, between Ramah

---

* *Voyage autour de la Mer Morte et dans les Terres Bibliques*, vol. ii.

and Bethel, in Mount Ephraim. He marched against the enemy, accompanied by the Prophetess, and completely defeated Sisera, who was assassinated during his flight by Jael, wife of a descendant of the brother-in-law of Moses. The famous song of Deborah and Barak, which the Bible has preserved, was composed in celebration of this victory. The Hebrews then took the city of Harosheth, and next that of Hazor, and killed Jabin, the king. The Bible says distinctly that it was only with the forces of Naphtali and Zebulon, with but 10,000 combatants, that Barak took the initiative in the war, and gained the battle of the River Kishon.

It follows, from the famous song of Deborah, that the Hebrew general received afterwards the help of Benjamin, of the tribe of Issachar, and of Ephraim. Reuben was divided ; one part of its chiefs refusing to take part in the war. The tribes of Judah and Simeon, far away to the south, were quite beyond these events. The land of Gilead, beyond Jordan, remained unmoved, and the maritime tribes of Dan and Asher, quite close to the theatre of war, did not leave their peaceful occupations. This is one of the most striking examples of the divisions and of the timidity and apathy among the tribes, which, resulting from the relaxation of the common faith, were more than once fatal to the Hebrews. God often makes use of our vices themselves as instruments of punishment.

3. Forty years of peace followed this struggle, but only for the tribes who had been in the fight ; for the sins of the rest of Israel brought on them another scourge, and they were given over for seven years to the tyranny of the Midianites. The Amalekites and Bedouin tribes of the East joined these people to make continual incursions into Palestine, overrunning the country from east to west, even to the neighbourhood of Gaza ; they encamped there with their cattle and their numerous camels ; they carried off the beasts of the Hebrews ; and, like clouds of locusts, they ravaged the country, destroyed the crops, and caused famine. The Israelites were obliged to put their cattle and the produce of their lands, for safety, into caves of the earth and into fortified cities. The people then were humbled, and implored the assistance of God ; and God, by the voice of an angel, appealed to the faith and courage of Gideon, son of Joash, of the tribe of Manasseh. He gave the signal of insurrection against the invaders, by overturning the altar which had been erected to Baal in his village. At the first news of this movement, the Midianites and their allies took the field. Gideon, calling to him the tribes of Manasseh, Asher, Zebulon, and Naphtali, who had felt the devastation less than the others, and who, consequently, were more in a state to make war, prepared for the fight.

But God did not will that His people should attribute the victory to the number of combatants. By His command, Gideon put aside 300 men only; the rest were kept in the rear as an army of reserve. The 300 chosen men, divided into three bodies, surprised by night the camp of the Midianites; they were armed with trumpets, and with torches enclosed in pitchers which they broke, crying out, "The sword of the Lord and of Gideon." The enemy, seized with panic, and seeing an Israelite in everyone they met, turned their swords against each other. The men of Naphtali, Asher, and Manasseh pursued them; the Ephraimites occupied the bank of Jordan; Gideon pursued to the river those who had escaped, and the hostile army was exterminated. This was undoubtedly one of the most complete and decisive victories which the Hebrews ever gained; for, from this day forward, history makes no more mention of the Midianites. Excesses, showing how barbarous the manners of the Israelites still were, sullied this success. Gideon, with his own hand, killed the two captive chiefs of the enemy. He also put to death by torture the elders of the two towns of Succoth and Penuel, who, fearing the vengeance of the Midianites, had refused provisions to his troops.

4. Gideon refused the royalty which a part of the Israelites offered him, but he ruled for a long time over the tribes who had followed him to war. The Book of Judges says forty years; but this expression, which is found on every page, must not be taken literally, and has been proved merely to indicate an indeterminate space of time, corresponding approximately to the duration of a generation. Fidelity to the Divine law, already much shaken under the government of Gideon, who thought to honour Jehovah by setting up an idol* to Him in his native place, disappeared altogether after his death, and Baal was worshipped by the people of God. One of the sons of the conqueror of the Midianites, Abimelech, supported by the inhabitants of Shechem, recruited a band of outlaws, with whom he killed nearly all his brothers, and formed for himself a small kingdom in the country of Shechem, which he retained three years, and then perished in civil war while besieging the city of Thebez. A piece of a millstone, thrown by a woman's hand, struck him on the head and killed him. Tola, his cousin, was recognised Suffete of Israel during twenty-three years, and after him, Jair, the Gileadite, during twenty-two years. We know no particulars of their government; but Scripture tells us that Israel, having given themselves over to the worship of the idols of Sidon, of Moab, of Ammon, and of the Philistines, God again gave them into the hand of their enemies.

5. The Ammonites invaded the territory of the tribes of Peræa, and kept them under their authority for eighteen years. Thence, crossing the Jordan, they made occasional incursions into the land of Judah, Benjamin, and Ephraim. The supplications of the sufferers were at

* See *Gesenius Thesaurus*, p. 135.

last heard by the Lord, who was willing to help His people, and the war commenced. The inhabitants of Gilead, which was the capital of Peræa, having no man among them capable of conducting warlike operations, addressed themselves to the chief of a band in the neighbourhood, named Jephthah. The position of a highway robber was not then more degrading in the eyes of the Hebrews than it is now-a-days in the opinion of the Arabs. He was recognised as general, and the negotiations which he attempted to open having failed, he gained great advantages over the Ammonites, and delivered the country. It was then that Jephthah, in fulfilment of his culpable and rash vow, sacrificed his own daughter. He had sworn to offer as a burnt offering, if he returned as conqueror, the first living being which he should meet at the door of his house. It was his only daughter who came to meet him with "timbrels and dances." Jephthah felt himself bound by his vow, and his daughter made no resistance. This was an impious sacrifice, and distinctly opposed to the law of Moses, which permitted the sacrifice only of certain animals, and utterly interdicted human sacrifices.* But such horrible immolations were common among the pagan populations who surrounded the Israelites, and the precepts of the law had fallen into complete oblivion.

The Ephraimites, who had not taken part in the war, ashamed of their conduct, laid the blame on Jephthah; they reproached him with not having called them to the battle. The quarrel became serious; they came to blows about it with the inhabitants of Gilead, who made great slaughter among them. The Gileadites, having occupied the Fords of Jordan during several days, slew all the Ephraimites who attempted to cross in order to regain their own country, and whom they recognised by certain peculiarities in pronunciation. After six years of a stormy administration, Jephthah died, and was succeeded by Ibzan of Bethlehem, Elon of the tribe of Zebulon; and lastly, Abdon of Pirathon, in Ephraim, whose governments embraced a space of about twenty-five years. But not one of these Suffetes extended his authority beyond the tribes of the north and of Peræa. Whilst they were governing those, other events, much more serious and more important, were passing among the tribes of the south and west.

---

* That Jephthah really offered up his daughter as a burnt offering has been doubted, and from the tenor of the narrative itself, Jephthah's vow may be read as in the margin of our Bible, "Whatsoever cometh forth . . . to meet me . . . shall surely be the Lord's, *or* I will offer it up for a burnt offering" (Judg. xi. 31).

The opinion of the Author that the sacrifice was consummated, is that of Josephus, of the Chaldee Paraphrast, who adds that if Jephthah had consulted the High Priest, his daughter might have been redeemed for a sum of money, and also of most of the fathers, some of whom even praise him for fulfilling his vow.—Tr.

SECTION IV.—ELI AND SAMUEL.

1. We must now look at a long and fierce contest which commenced in the south of Palestine,—a contest which was to bring on the Hebrews more extensive disasters than had been known in any previous epoch, but which in the end had the effect of reuniting all the tribes of Israel, and of reviving, together with the worship of Jehovah, the spirit of nationality and the love of their ancient institutions. At this epoch of their history, the Israelites found themselves suddenly brought into the presence of a new enemy, whom neither Moses nor Joshua appears to have foreseen, and whom they do not mention in the enumeration of the dangers against which the people were to guard, but who entered on the scene with almost irresistible power, and threatened to annihilate the whole independence and the whole national life of the Hebrews. The Canaanites from this moment disappear almost entirely from the history of Palestine; they no more menace Israel with oppression; they have ceased to be a danger; everything shows that their power was completely and finally broken, not so much by the last victory of Deborah and Barak, but by an external cause.

The Philistines, this new enemy, first appeared in the south. In the whole Pentateuch, Moses never once named them among the population, whom the Hebrews should expel from the Promised Land; they were not spoken of under Joshua, nor when, just after his death, the tribe of Judah possessed itself temporarily of the cities of Gaza, Askelon and Ekron, then held by the Anakim. The first mention of the Philistines which the Bible contains is on the occasion of the exploit of Shamgar; but they do not seem at that time to have been very formidable; nothing then indicated the great ascendancy which they were to attain in that period of the Hebrew annals, at the threshold of which we now are. It is chiefly in recent times, and by the aid of the Egyptian hieroglyphical documents, that the origin, the race, and early history of the Philistines have been definitely cleared up. But the achievements of science have been so considerable as to enable us now to speak positively on these different subjects. The Philistines had no connection in their origin with the other nations of Syria. They were neither of the race of Ham, like the Canaanites, nor of that of Shem, like the Israelites, but in reality of Japhetic origin. Closely related to the primitive colonies of Greece and the Archipelago, they also belonged to that great Pelasgic race which ruled for a time the whole basin of the Mediterranean, and their name, Philistin or Pilistin, contains the same essential elements as that of the Pelasgi.*

* The Pelasgic character of the Philistines was first established by HITZIG, *Urgeschichte und Mythologie der Philister*, Leipzig, 1845. STARK, *Forschungen zur Geschichte und Alterthumskunde der Hellenistischen Orients*. Jena, 1852.

A great number of evidences, both in sacred literature and in profane authors, concur in pointing out the island of Crete as having been their original habitation, or at least their earliest known settlement.*

It was thence that they came by sea to attack and occupy the country which from them received the name of Palestine. We shall see, in the Book of this Manual which treats of the history of Egypt, that the grand historical bas-reliefs of the palace of Medinet Habou at Thebes relate with precision all the vicissitudes of the furious and terrible war in which the Pharaoh Ramses III., some years after the conquest of Canaan by Joshua, strove to repel their invasion. The Philistines were then vanquished, but not completely; and, in exchange for their submission to his sceptre, the King of Egypt was obliged to agree to give them a territory on the coast where they had landed. This was the nucleus of their settlements and of their power. They began humbly, still weak, and subject to the government of Egypt; and such must have been their situation at the time of their attempt on the southernmost tribes of Israel, which Shamgar does not seem to have had much difficulty in repulsing with some bands of peasants, assembled in haste, and imperfectly armed.

But the rapid decay of the Egyptian power soon permitted the Philistines to free themselves from all subjection. New immigrations from Crete strengthened them. They became masters of the five strong cities of Gaza, Ashdod, Askelon, Gath, and Ekron, which formed the capitals of five principalities, united in a confederation. Whilst the Israelites and Canaanites were exhausting themselves in continual wars, this new power silently grew. A day came when they felt themselves sufficiently strong to aspire to dominion over the whole of the ancient land of Canaan. They had a considerable fleet, and employed it in the shameful practice of piracy. By sea they assailed the cities of the Phœnician coast, where all the life and national power of the Canaanites had concentrated itself, when their strength in the interior had been broken by Joshua. Such small Canaanitish principalities in the interior of the country as still remained were sustained only by the support of those maritime cities, which commerce had raised to unequalled opulence. In the year 1209 B.C., the Philistines took and reduced to ashes Sidon, the principal of the Phœnician cities, which was then supreme over all the others.† The disaster was so complete, that Phœnicia disappeared

* Tacitus expressly says that they came from Crete (*Hist.* v. 2). The Philistines are called Cherethites, that is, Cretans, in 1 Sam. xxx. 14, Ezekiel xxv. 16, and Zephaniah ii. 5. The geographer Stephen, of Byzantium, attributes the foundation of Gaza to the mythical Minos, the personification of the Cretan power; and, lastly, the great god of that city, Marnas, has always been identified with the Cretan Jupiter.

† JUSTIN, xviii. 3.

from history for half a century, till the time when Tyre had become sufficiently strong to reclaim the heritage of Sidon. It was about the same time, after having annihilated in this way the Phœnician power, that the Philistines attempted to subjugate the people of Israel.

2. When the Ammonites invaded Peræa, and there established that dominion which was destroyed by Jephthah, they were allied with the Philistines, who simultaneously entered the territory of the southern tribes, and imposed on them their yoke, the heavier because the tyranny of this people was exercised with order and method, in conformity with wise and regular administrative laws. When the northern and eastern tribes delivered themselves from the Ammonites, and enjoyed a momentary repose under the government of the three Suffetes, successors of Jephthah, the Philistines continued to oppress the southern provinces, and every day their power there became consolidated and extended, in spite of the resistance of the Israelitish population.

It is this popular resistance which the Book of Judges personifies in the exploits of Samson, who, as the learned historian of the Philistines, M. Stark,* has well said, always played in the south of Palestine the part of the people's defender, offering to the Israelites of these districts a centre for national resistance, and of unity in a particular locality, but without succeeding in forming any real political establishment. The particulars which are told in the Book of Judges as to his marriage with the Philistine woman at Timnath, the irregularities of his life, and, lastly, the manner in which he perished, a victim to the treachery of a woman, are too precisely detailed to be open to suspicion. But the story of his exploits, as it is given in that book, is, in its character, entirely unlike the merely human histories of the other Judges. In it are combined all the legendary mythological tales which had long been current among the people of Palestine and Syria. The narrative is entirely allegorical and emblematic, with no real and positive character. It represents the form which such exploits had taken in the popular memory, in which Samson was made the impersonation of all the heroes of whom so many tales were told. He, therefore, can find no place in a purely historical work such as ours.

3. Whilst these things were passing in the south, great efforts had been made in the north of the land of Israel to re-establish purity of religion, and that national unity of which it was the safeguard. A priest of the line of Ithamar, youngest son of Aaron, named Eli, had usurped the high priesthood from the line of Eleazar, to whom that function legitimately belonged by the choice of Moses.† His usurpation

* *Forschungen*, p. 156—160.

† There were only three high priests of the line of Eleazar between Phinehas and Eli. This furnishes abundant proof of the necessity of

might be pardoned, as he had restored the Tabernacle of Shiloh, abandoned for many generations, and which had fallen into the most deplorable state of dilapidation. By force of zeal and care he brought back the concourse of faithful worshippers to that only legal sanctuary for the worship of the true God, instituted by Moses as the real centre of the national life of the chosen people.

Abdon now dead, Eli was elected Judge, or Suffete, by the tribes of the north and east, who alone remained independent. Those of the south and west, crushed under the weight of Philistine domination, looked up to him, and considered him their legitimate chief, though deprived of his authority by foreign tyranny. This combination of civil and sacerdotal power in the person of Eli—this return of the Israelite people to the faith of their fathers, and to the ideas of unity—should have had most fortunate results. But Eli was not a man capable of at once saving religion and the state—of re-uniting all Israel, and conducting them to victory. He had none of the genius necessary for so magnificent a mission. Above all, towards the close of his life, the deplorable weakness of the high priest for his two sons, Hophni and Phinehas, undid all the good which he had been able to accomplish, and much aggravated the evils of the situation of the country. The sons of Eli profaned the sacred place, perverted the offerings made to the Lord, and caused all the people to murmur. The high priest contented himself with addressing to them mild remonstrances. In vain a prophet announced to Eli that he should be punished for his weakness, that his family should lose the power which he had not known how to exercise, and that his two sons should perish. A child, inspired by God, repeated many times, but without effect, to the unfortunate father the evils hanging over him. This was the young Samuel, of the tribe of Levi, son of a woman of Ramah, who had been given in answer to the prayers of his mother, after long-continued barrenness, and had been brought up in the Tabernacle, where he assisted the high priest at the sacrificial altar. He it was whom Providence had chosen to fulfil, at a later date, the mission of liberator.

4. The accomplishment of the oft-repeated prediction of Samuel was not long delayed. The Philistines, always ambitious, and resolved to get possession of the whole country, threatened the northern tribes.

---

reducing the usual calculation as to the length of the period of the Judges, or Suffetes. The most moderate of these calculations places three centuries between the death of Joshua and the accession of Eli to the high priesthood. It is impossible that such an interval could be filled by only three pontiffs, and the succession of high priests is the only element of positive and regular chronology which we have for this period of the history of Israel.

They assembled an army to attack them at Aphek, in the plain of Esdraelon, where the Hebrews were defeated, with the loss of 4,000 men. Then, as had not been done since the capture of Jericho, the Ark of the Covenant was brought into the camp of Israel, borne by Hophni and Phinehas, to give courage to the warriors in the battle which was to decide the national independence. But a fresh and yet more severe trial awaited the Hebrews. They were routed, with the loss of 30,000 men, on the field of battle; the two sons of Eli perished in defending the sacred Ark, which fell into the hands of the Philistines. Eli, at this last news, seized with despair and stupor, fell from his seat, broke his neck, and died.

In the meanwhile the hand of God fell heavily on the Philistines, who had deposited the Ark as a trophy at Ashdod, in the temple of their god Dagon. An epidemic ravaged their towns, which they knew to be the punishment of this profanation: and, after some hesitation, they decided on restoring to the Israelites the Ark, which was deposited first at Bethshemesh, one of the Levitical towns, and afterwards at Kirjath-jearim. But they did not, for all that, give up the power which their victory had given them over the conquered people. The battle fought near Aphek had thrown into their hands the entire territory of the northern tribes, which till then had been secure from them. The whole of Israel was subdued, deprived of independence, and grievously oppressed. But this very oppression prepared the way for their first deliverance, by making all Israel at last comprehend to what a condition the abandonment of the worship of the true God and of the precepts of the law had brought them, and by showing them that no safety was possible but in ranging themselves resolutely on the side of Jehovah.

5. The servitude lasted twenty years, which Samuel passed in solitude, preparing himself for the mission to which God called him, and meditating on the means of accomplishing it. When at last he thought that the time had come, he left his retreat to put himself at the head of his countrymen, and encourage them to re-conquer their independence. He first exhorted them to abandon idolatry of every kind, to adore only the God of Abraham and of Moses, who alone was able to deliver them from the yoke of the Philistines. Seeing the Hebrews sincerely disposed to submit to his guidance, and to form themselves into a compact body round the symbols of the only God, he convoked a general assembly at Mizpeh, on the territory of Gad, where they were not directly under the eyes of the Philistines.

Then the representatives of the different tribes confessed aloud that Israel had sinned in straying away from the worship of their God, and as a mark of penitence a fast-day was appointed. Then the assembly solemnly proclaimed Samuel as Suffete of Israel. The Philistines were enraged at this act of independence on the part of a nation whom they believed to be finally subjugated, and took the field to chastise the rebels. But God terrified them by a storm, and the Israelites, attacking them at Mizpeh, overthrew them and put them to flight, killing a very great number. Profiting immediately by this success, the Hebrews, by Samuel's advice, themselves took the offensive against the Philistines, beat them in every encounter, and forced them to restore the towns which they had taken, and to make a peace very advantageous for Israel, whose independence they were compelled to acknowledge, after having oppressed them during forty years. The treaty, nevertheless, left to the Philistines the right of maintaining an armed post at Gibeah, and another clause provided that the Hebrews of the districts bordering on the Philistine frontier should be disarmed, so as not to be in a position to make an attack.

6. While Samuel governed, to use the Bible expression, "the Philistines came no more into the coasts of Israel, and the hand of the Lord was against the Philistines." The Canaanitish colonies who lived among the tribes of the north, and whom the defeat of the Philistines had delivered from servitude equally with the Hebrews, lived in peace among them, and maintained with them friendly and neighbourly relations. Everything tended then to favour the projects of Samuel, who could, from that time, work in tranquillity at the restoration of the essentially spiritual Mosaic law, and the re-establishment of unity, both in government and religion. He fixed his residence at Ramah, his native town; but made year by year a round of visits to Bethel, to Gilgal near Jericho, and to Mizpeh, where he held assemblies of the people, and presided over councils on public affairs.

The most important and the most fruitful of the institutions of Samuel, whose position was very similar to that of Moses, as he was both the spiritual and temporal chief of the people, though not invested with the High Priesthood,* was the institution of the "Schools of the Prophets." This requires some explanation. The word prophet (in Hebrew, *Nabi*) has in the Bible two entirely distinct meanings. It is applied sometimes, and in its most general sense (adopted in our ecclesiastical language), to those men inspired by God, before whose eyes Divine grace unfolded the future, that they might exhort the people to penitence, and announce to the world the coming of the Redeemer, who was to take away the sins of the world. In this sense, prophet is synonymous with seer (in Hebrew, *Roeh*). But more commonly in the Bible, especially in ancient times, this word is the title of the members of religious corporations, who, among the Israelites, played the same part as the preaching orders in the Roman Catholic Church—corpora-

* Samuel, like Moses, was not a Priest.—Tr.

tions from among whom almost always the Seers came. Such were the institutions established by Samuel.

"The experience of what had passed since the death of Joshua did not permit him to deceive himself as to the force and stability of a written law with no other guarantee than the consent of the people, obtained by the force of circumstances, and without having at the head of the people men who could make the laws respected. He perceived, also, that the law of Moses needed to be developed and modified with the progress of the nation, notwithstanding that on the other hand it would be very dangerous to touch the letter of the law, protected by its sacred character. Men, therefore, were needed to interpret this law, to breathe life and soul into the dead letter; men who could enter into its true sense, and who could participate, so to speak, in the inspiration of the legislator; men, finally, who should devote themselves to constant preaching, who should reproach the people fearlessly for their shortcomings, and constantly set before them their duty towards God. This was the aim of Samuel in the organisation of the Schools of the Prophets.

"Far from the din of arms and the warrior's trumpet, the young prophets sang the praises of Jehovah to the sweet sounds of the lute, the flute, and harp, or 'kinnor,' in a peaceful retreat; they prepared their eloquent discourses in meditation on God, and on the true sense of the law. They occupied quarters set apart for them in several cities, generally those where the public assemblies were held, and which Samuel habitually visited. We find them at Ramah, where they occupied a quarter called Naioth (habitations) (1 Sam. xix. 18); there their assembly was presided over by Samuel himself, and also at Bethel, Jericho, and Gilgal. These Schools of the Prophets were destined to exercise, as long as the Hebrew people remained independent, a great influence, and to rank among the powers of the State, representing the law in its true and peculiarly spiritual aspect, as opposed to the Priests, who were frequently either too much attached to the rites of material worship, or permitted themselves to fall into remissness, and, above all, as opposed to the royal authority, whose encroachments it was their duty to withstand."—MUNK.

CHAPTER III.

KINGDOM OF ISRAEL—SAUL, DAVID, SOLOMON.

Chief Authorities:—The Bible, *I. and II. Books of Samuel*, *I. Book of Kings*, *I. and II. Books of Chronicles*.—Josephus, *Antiquities*, Books VII. and VIII.

The modern writers quoted at the commencement of Chapter I.

SECTION I.—ESTABLISHMENT OF ROYALTY—SAUL.
(1097—1058, B.C.)

1. SAMUEL having become old, and feeling himself too feeble to support alone the entire weight of the administration, wished to share his functions as supreme magistrate with his two sons, Joel and Abiah, whom he installed as Suffetes at Beersheba, at the southern extremity ot Palestine. But his sons did not walk in the ways of their father, and serious complaints were made against their administration, for they allowed themselves to be guided by their personal interest and their cupidity, instead of exhibiting the integrity of Samuel, and nothing was found with them but corruption and injustice. The Elders of Israel, fearful for the future, met, and came to Samuel at Ramah, to ask him to give them a king.

In vain the Lord expressed, by the mouth of His prophet, the anger which He felt at His people rejecting a constitution of which God himself was the author, a constitution which recognised God alone as the Sovereign of Israel. In vain He represented to the Hebrews, by Samuel, the abasement to which oriental nations are reduced under the dominion of an absolute master, who recognises neither personal liberty nor the rights of property. "He will take," said He, "your sons, and appoint them for himself, for his chariots, and to be his horsemen; and some shall run before his chariots. And he will appoint him captains over thousands, and captains over fifties; and will set them to ear his ground, and to reap his harvest, and to make his instruments of war and instruments of his chariots. And he will take your daughters to be confectionaries, and to be cooks, and to be bakers. And he will take your fields, and your vineyards, and your oliveyards, even the best of them, and give them to his servants. And he will take the tenth of your seed, and of your vineyards, and give to his officers, and to his servants. And he will take your menservants, and your maidservants, and your goodliest young men, and your asses, and put them to his work. He will take the tenth of your sheep: and ye shall be his servants" (1 Sam. viii. 11—17). The people would hear nothing. They required a king, like other nations, to rule them and lead them to war. God then chastised them, as He often does in His providence, by granting their imprudent wish. Saul, son of Kish, of the tribe of Benjamin, still quite a young man, and celebrated for his beauty, courage, and strength, was pointed out by Him, anointed by Samuel, and acknowledged by part of the Hebrews.

2. There had been, however, a numerous opposition to the establishment of royalty, so that it was considered prudent to defer for some time the solemn installation of Saul. But soon after this, Nahash, king of the Ammonites, threatened the city of Jabesh Gilead. When the news came to Saul, who still lived in his house at Gibeah, and was at that time driving a pair of oxen at their work, he killed those animals, cut them in pieces, and sent messengers to all Israel to say to the people, "Whosoever cometh not forth after Saul and after Samuel, so shall it be done unto his oxen." The whole people followed him. 300,000 Israelites passed in review; 30,000 men were furnished by the tribe of Judah, for, in very short campaigns, a *levée en masse* was quite practicable. The enemy, attacked at break of day, was cut to pieces and entirely destroyed.

Israel, carried away by enthusiasm, would have put to death those who at first refused to recognise Saul. But he, with a moderation which did not always distinguish him, would not consent to stain his victory with such excesses. "There shall not a man," said he, "be put to death this day: for to-day the Lord hath wrought salvation in Israel." His reign was then solemnly inaugurated at Gilgal by Samuel and the people.

3. In resigning the power with which he had been hitherto invested, Samuel by no means renounced all political influence; he intended, on the contrary, to watch over the new sovereign, and to withdraw his protection the moment the king ceased to be a faithful vassal to Jehovah and to his law. According to the ideas of Samuel, royalty was but a permanent and hereditary chieftainship, an especially military authority; and all institutions were, in spite of this change, to remain as they had been before. For a time the new chief of the government continued submissive to the influence of the sanctuary, and Samuel continued to direct him in his administration. The prophet himself had dictated the new constitution, the conditions of which were reduced to writing, and deposited in the Tabernacle. In conformity with the spirit of the law, it was only permitted to take up arms in the name of the Lord, whose Ark of the Covenant was in the midst of the camp. The king himself would be no more than a captain always under arms, without court or

fixed residence—always at the orders of Jehovah, whose mouthpiece Samuel remained.

But Saul did not very long remain submissive to Samuel's orders; he wished to be free from a tutelage which he began to feel irksome, and, above all, desired to usurp the functions of the priesthood which were united to the royal power in all the monarchies surrounding him in the neighbouring Pagan nations. After his solemn installation, Saul had sent the Israelites to their homes, keeping under arms only 3,000 men of the permanent militia, of whom he had 2,000 with himself, the other 1,000 being in the southern provinces, with his son Jonathan. The latter being very brave, and animated with the most ardent and patriotic zeal, found the presence of the military post of the Philistines at Gibeah, in the land of Benjamin, almost insupportable. One day he surprised and took it.

The Philistines, to revenge this insult, put an immense army into the field. Saul called the people to Gilgal for a levy which would enable him to repulse this invasion. Samuel was to join him there to sacrifice to the Lord before commencing the campaign. After waiting seven days, as he had not yet come, Saul, who saw that the people began to get impatient, thought the moment favourable for consummating his contemplated usurpation of the sacerdotal power. He himself offered sacrifice, instead of waiting with confidence for the help of the Lord, who had so often saved Israel. Soon after Samuel arrived. Indignant at the act of the king, all the significance of which he saw, for it aimed at establishing the monarchy of Israel on the same basis as heathen kingdoms, and placing the spiritual at the mercy of the caprice of the political chief, by giving the latter power in the affairs of the sanctuary, the prophet reproached Saul severely for his contempt of the precepts of the law.* Speaking in the name of the Lord, he announced to him that Divine help was withdrawn from him, that his dynasty should not last, and another royal house should be substituted for his. Saul nevertheless marched against his enemies, encamped at Michmash; but he had not taken time to bring with him the northern tribes, and on his arrival among those of the south he found himself in a position of great embarrassment.

By an arrangement subsisting together with Samuel's treaty, the Philistines had for a long time forbidden among these tribes the trades of armourer and smith, so that the people were disarmed, or at least had only agricultural implements to fight with, and even for the repair of these they had to resort to the Philistines. So completely dispirited were

---

* See Numb. xvi. 40, bearing in mind that Samuel himself was only a Levite, not of the seed of Aaron.—Tr.

they, that they furnished only 600 men to the king for his bold march. Nevertheless, Jonathan, accompanied only by his armour-bearer, scaled a post of the Philistines between Michmash and Gibeah. Panic-struck at this exploit, they, as once did the Midianites, turned their arms against each other. The Hebrews, great numbers of whom had been compelled by force to serve with the enemy, abandoned them to rejoin their countrymen, and those who were concealed in the mountains of Ephraim sallied out from their retreats. Saul soon found himself at the head of 10,000 men, and the enemy was pursued as far as Beth-aven.

4. The Philistines having re-entered their own country, Saul, during the following years, continued his part as a military chieftain, repulsing with equal success the aggressions of other neighbouring nations, such as the Ammonites, Moabites, Idumeans, and the Syrians of Zobah. The tribes of the east of Jordan, also, in his reign conquered the Hagareens, a tribe of nomadic Arabs, and spread themselves through the desert towards the Euphrates. Saul still expected long and hard contests with the Philistines, and tried to surround himself with all the men among Israel who were brave and skilled in war; he took measures to have experienced troops and armies easily assembled in case of necessity, and he gave the general command of his military forces to Abner, son of Ner, his own cousin-german. He is the only great dignitary whom we find about Saul. In general he had hitherto preserved his simplicity of manners, he had no court, and his household comprised only members of his own family.

One day, Samuel, now very near his end, came to Saul, and, reminding the king that he owed his crown to him, ordered him in the name of Jehovah to take up arms against the Amalekites, the earliest and most inveterate of the enemies of the Hebrews, and to wage against them a war of extermination. Saul obeyed, and his expedition was crowned with success; but in place of destroying all, as the prophet had ordered him, he carried off as booty the best of the cattle and other valuables. Agag, king of Amalek, was made prisoner; but the Amalekites were not entirely destroyed, as Moses himself had commanded, and there still might be some fear of fresh attacks from them; and the more so that Saul, tempted by the prospect of getting money, had entered into negotiations as to the ransom of Agag. Indignant at this disobedience to the commands of God, and at the cupidity which for a bribe could seriously endanger the future of the people and their security, Samuel went to meet Saul at Gilgal, and laid a curse on him in the name of the Lord, telling him that God rejected him from that time, and announcing prophetically an evil end for him and for his race. At the same time, to render impossible the scheme for setting free the king of the Amalekites on ransom, Samuel with his own hand killed Agag.

5. From this moment the rupture was final and complete between Saul on one side, and Samuel, backed by all the party who were sincerely attached to the law, on the other. The Divine protection abandoned the king of Israel. By God's command Samuel went to Bethlehem, and secretly anointed as heir to the throne, to the exclusion of the son of Saul, the youngest of the sons of Jesse, David, who had already proved his courage by defending his flock against lions and bears. This newly chosen one of God belonged to the tribe of Judah, and was directly descended from Nahshon, who had been the chief of the tribe in the desert. His grandmother was that Ruth whose touching story is related in the Bible, in the Book that bears her name.

From the moment of the prophet's curse, Saul became subject to fits of dark melancholy, from which he recovered only to give himself up to the committal of acts of cruelty. David alone, whom the secret influence of Samuel had introduced into the palace, could, by the melody which he drew from his harp, drive away his dark hallucinations. Thus the young shepherd, whose secret election was not yet known, soon became necessary to the king, who loaded him with favours and made him his armour-bearer.

6. A circumstance now occurred to bring out his valour. The war with the Philistines had been re-kindled. While the two armies were face to face, a warrior of gigantic stature, named Goliath, a native of the town of Gath, and sprung from the old race of the Anakim, came out each day from the camp of the Philistines to defy Israel. No one was found who dared to confront this redoubtable warrior. David, armed only with his sling, had the courage to measure himself with him ; the first stone slung killed the giant, and David, throwing himself on him, cut off his head. The Philistines, terrified at the death of their champion, fled away precipitately, and the Israelites pursued them as far as the gates of Ekron and Gath, making a great slaughter among their troops.

After this triumph, and some other exploits not less glorious against the same enemies, Saul gave David the hand of his daughter, and Jonathan conceived for him an affection to which he was always true. But jealousy entered the soul of the king when he heard the Israelites celebrate the victories of David by singing, "Saul has slain his thousands, and David his ten thousands." From that day he hated him deeply, and sought out every means to destroy him. Saved on many occasions by Michal his wife, by Jonathan, and by the high priest Ahimelech, David, warned by Jonathan, was obliged to flee to the king of Gath, when he feigned madness to escape the vengeance of the Philistines. But he did not long remain there ; having assembled a band of some hundreds of desperadoes, and lived some time in the land of Moab, he returned to the land of Judah, without, however, stirring up civil war. The forest of Hareth was his place of refuge. Samuel died at Ramah, mourned by all Israel, and at a very great age.

From that time Saul put no restraint on the sanguinary passions which took possession of him. He began to persecute without intermission and without pity, as friends and partisans of David, the priests, the Levites, the schools of the prophets—in a word, all that represented the authority of religion, and the power of the law.

He may almost be said in his folly to have declared war against Jehovah. Having arrested the high priest Ahimelech and the eighty-five priests who lived with him in the city of Nob, he caused them to be slain before his own eyes; and afterwards, as if maddened with slaughter, he put to the sword the whole population of Nob, men, women and children. One only of the sons of Ahimelech, named Abiathar, the heir to the high priesthood, escaped from the massacre, and took refuge with David.

Wandering from place to place to save his life, more than once betrayed in his misfortunes, betrayed too by the men of Keilah, whom he had saved by help of his men when attacked by the enemy, the son of Jesse nevertheless spared the life of the king which twice was in his power—once in the desert of Ziph, and once again near Engadi. In the course, however, of this wandering life he found time to marry two new wives, the widow of the rich Nabal, Abigail, who had afforded him most generous assistance, and Ahinoam of Jezreel;* whilst Saul, in contempt of both law and morality, gave his first wife, Michal, to another husband. At last he was obliged again to retire to Gath, whose king, Achish, received him favourably, and gave him the city of Ziklag. There David passed many years, making many incursions against the Amalekites, and thus, even in his exile, serving the cause of Israel.

7. After some time, the war recommenced between Saul and the Philistines. Achish, king of Gath, opened the campaign, and compelled David, whom he had in his power, to march with him. But happily the mistrust of the Philistine chiefs, by compelling Achish to dismiss from his camp the Israelitish hero, relieved him from the cruel alternative of either betraying his benefactor, or fighting against his country. The Philistines had advanced to Shunem, in Northern Palestine. Saul, at the head of his army, had taken up a position on the heights of Gilboa, within view of his enemies; there was fought a battle in which the Israelites were cut to pieces, and the forebodings of Samuel were fulfilled. Saul having lost Jonathan and two other of his sons, fell on his sword, so that he might not die by the hand of the

---

* This, of course, was the Jezreel in the south of Judah (mentioned Josh. xv. 56), not the more famous city of the same name in the plain of Esdraelon.—TR.

Philistines. The enemy cut off his head and deposited his arms as trophies at Ascalon, in the temple of the goddess Ashtaroth, the Asiatic Venus. He had reigned forty years.

SECTION II.—DAVID (1058—1019).

1. DAVID, at the news of the death of Saul, broke out into the most lively and sincere expressions of grief, the persecutions which he had suffered from that king had not caused him to forget the benefits he had at first received from him. Above all he lamented his friend Jonathan, and poured out his grief in the beautiful elegy preserved in the Second Book of Samuel :—

The beauty of Israel is slain upon thy high places :
How are the mighty fallen !
Tell it not in Gath,
Publish it not in the streets of Askelon ;
Lest the daughters of the Philistines rejoice,
Lest the daughters of the uncircumcised triumph.
Ye mountains of Gilboa let there be no dew,
Neither let there be rain upon you, nor fields of offerings :
For there the shield of the mighty is vilely cast away,
The shield of Saul, as though he had not been anointed with oil.
From the blood of the slain, from the fat of the mighty,
The bow of Jonathan turned not back,
The sword of Saul returneth not empty.
Saul and Jonathan
Were lovely and pleasant in their lives,
And in their death they were not divided ;
They were swifter than eagles, they were stronger than lions.
Ye daughters of Israel, weep over Saul,
Who clothed you in scarlet, with other delights,
Who put ornaments of gold on your apparel.
How are the mighty fallen in the midst of battle !
O Jonathan, thou art slain on thine high places.
I am distressed for thee, my brother
Jonathan ! Very pleasant hast thou been to me :
Thy love to me was wonderful, passing the love of women.
How are the mighty fallen,
And the weapons of war perished !

But, in spite of his regrets, he hastened to profit by an event which put him in a position to claim the rights resulting from the anointing with holy oil which he had received from Samuel. He returned to his country, and was proclaimed king at Hebron by his own tribe of Judah ; but the other tribes recognised Ishbosheth, son of Saul, whom Abner had hastened to proclaim at Mahanaim. A very sanguinary civil war followed, lasting seven years, and in which David and his captains found Abner a formidable antagonist. Irritated, however, by the conduct of Ishbosheth towards him, Saul's old general resolved to make advances to David, and to gain favour, brought with him to Hebron David's wife, Michal. Joab, the first of the lieutenants of David, fearing to find in Abner a rival in the king's favour, assassinated him at the gate of the city, and David, though exasperated by this crime, nevertheless did not dare to punish this man who was one of the firmest supporters of his crown.

A short time after, Ishbosheth was assassinated by two traitors, who came with his head to David, hoping for a reward. David indignantly refused all complicity with the crime, and had them executed on the spot. Ishbosheth, however, left only one son, lame and incapable of reigning, named Mephibosheth; his death re-established the unity of the Hebrew nation, for all the tribes who had supported him now hastened to recognise David.

The Philistines seem to have shown themselves at first inclined to be favourable to David during the time of the civil war. Themselves embarrassed by wars against the Syrians, Phœnicians, and other peoples, they had seen with pleasure divisions break out among the Hebrews, and perhaps believed that David, in remembrance of his exile, and the hospitality of Achish, intended to make his own people subordinate to them. But it was no longer the same when they saw him unanimously received by the Hebrews. They at once attacked him, and twice showed themselves in the valley of Rephaim near Jerusalem, but on both occasions they were routed.

2. The reign of David was the most glorious epoch in the history of the Israelites. The interior administration of the monarchy was organised, and the supremacy of the tribe of Judah over the other tribes was established. Beyond the limits of Palestine its preponderance was felt from the shores of the Mediterranean to the banks of the Euphrates. To establish definitively the national unity, and to be able to extend its limits, it was above all things necessary to obviate all risk of danger in the heart of the country, and to crush the few Canaanitish colonies which still lived isolated among the tribes. Thus, when David, at the age of thirty-seven, was left without a competitor for the throne, he commenced his actual reign. From the Jebusites, who were the most warlike of those colonies, he took their citadel Jebus, in the territory of the tribe of Benjamin, and changed its name to Jerusalem. On the hill of Sion was built "the City of David," and this he made the seat of his power, which had hitherto been at Hebron.

The great number of heroes who surrounded David at the beginning of his reign, and who for the most part had accompanied him in his wanderings, augured well for the success of his warlike enterprises. History has preserved us the names of thirty of these famous men, some of whom had performed prodigies of valour. The most celebrated was Joab, a man of ferocious character but of proved courage, and endowed with those qualities which make a leader. The court of David was also remarkable from its commencement for a certain amount of luxury in strong contrast with the simplicity of Saul's. David, when he became master of Jerusalem, built there a magnificent palace, for which Hiram, king of Tyre, with whom he had contracted an intimate alliance, sent him cedar-wood from Lebanon, as well as the necessary workmen and artificers. With regard to his domestic relations, he imitated the customs of other Oriental sovereigns. At Hebron, the number of his legitimate wives, without counting Michal, long separated from him, amounted to six, one of whom was the daughter of Talmai, king of Geshur, in Syria. Each of them had borne him a son. Michal alone had never any children.

Established at Jerusalem, David increased the number of his wives, and established a harem. This was the first infraction of the law of Moses (Deut. xvii. 17), but we shall see that in later times his love for women led the king to commit crimes much more serious. Apart from this weakness, against which the Mosaic law had not raised barriers sufficiently strong, David showed himself disposed to be a faithful vassal of Jehovah, in the sense in which Samuel, an interpreter of the true spirit of the law, had understood the position of royalty. Two prophets, disciples of Samuel, were his friends and intimate councillors; one was Gad, the other Nathan. These two men, inspired by God, were distinguished by their noble character, and by the frankness with which they reproached the king on every occasion with the faults of his private or public life, and the king always heard them with deference.

3. The reign of David was essentially a warlike one. New successes against the Philistines put an end to the tribute which some districts of the southern tribes were still paying. Gath even, and the towns of its territory were conquered and re-united to the Israelitish kingdom. It was then that David removed the Ark of the Covenant from the house of Abinadab at Kirjath-jearim, where it had been deposited ever since the disasters of the time of Eli, and brought it to Jerusalem (after a short stay in the house of Obed-Edom the Gittite), in solemn procession, depositing it in the Tabernacle which was set up in the Acropolis of Sion. He intended there to build a magnificent Temple, worthy of Jehovah, but Nathan dissuaded him, revealing to him that the duty of constructing the Temple was reserved by Providence for his successor, and that he, David, should devote himself entirely to warlike affairs, so as to establish firmly the power of Israel. He then turned his arms successively against the neighbouring nations. The Moabites were crushed, and became tributaries. The Syrians of

Zobah, under their king Hadadezer, were in their turn conquered ; those of Damascus who wished to assist them, were reduced to pay tribute, and the king of Hamath, named Toi, the enemy of the prince of Zobah, sent his own son to congratulate David on his victory. At the other extremity of the kingdom the power of the Amalekites and Idumæans was totally broken.

An insult offered to David's ambassadors by Hanun, king of the Ammonites, led to a serious war. Hanun obtained mercenaries from Syria to reinforce his army. Joab and Abishai his brother, David's generals, gave them battle. Joab, opposed to the Syrians, gained the first success, and the Ammonites, seeing their allies routed, took to flight into their town. But this defeat provoked a great coalition, embracing all the people between the Jordan and the Euphrates. David, however, fearlessly marched against them at the head of his army ; he vanquished all his enemies, and made himself master of the small Aramæan kingdoms of Damascus, Zobah, and Hamath, and subjugated the Eastern Idumæans, who met their final defeat in the Valley of Salt. By these victories, he extended his dominions as far as the Euphrates. At the same time, towards the south, he took from the Eastern Idumæans the ports of Eziongeber and Elath (the Ælana of the classical geographies,) at the extremity of the Elanitic Gulf, establishing a communication, by the Red Sea, with the remotest countries of Asia and Africa. Having obtained these results, David again attacked the Ammonites ; Rabbath, their capital, was besieged, and fell after a long defence. This success was chiefly due to Joab ; but it seems from his character and antecedents, that we ought also to attribute to him the atrocious executions which followed. Not only in the capital which was taken by assault, but in all the Ammonite cities, the conqueror, to exterminate the upper and warlike classes of the people, is said to have "put them under saws and under harrows of iron, and under axes of iron, and made them to pass through the brick-kiln."

4. In the midst of so many labours and conquests, David, led astray by his passions, fell suddenly into a double crime. He was in his palace during the siege of Rabbath-Ammon, when one day he saw Bathsheba, wife of Uriah the Hittite, one of his most valiant and devoted captains, who was then at the siege. He seduced and carried her off, and then Joab, by his orders, treacherously caused the death of Uriah in an encounter with the Ammonites. David then publicly married Bathsheba. For this odious conduct, for this first crime aggravated by a second, he was severely reproached by the prophet Nathan. David expressed a sincere and deep repentance, to which many of his Psalms bear testimony. But God did not permit so cruel an abuse of power to pass unpunished. David, who had so basely violated sacred family rights, saw himself punished by his own children,—

Bathsheba's first son died. After the birth of another son, named Solomon, the whole royal family was troubled by the disorders and crimes of its members. Amnon, eldest son of David, did violence to his sister Tamar, and was soon afterwards assassinated by her brother Absalom. Absalom himself revolted against his father, induced by the advice of Ahitophel, one of David's chief councillors, and led ten of the tribes after him into rebellion. David was compelled to leave Jerusalem on foot in the middle of the night; and in this precipitate flight had to submit also to the insults of Shimei, a relative of Saul, who cast stones at him, and overwhelmed him with curses. Nevertheless, all who remained faithful to David gathered around him, and the king was able with 20,000 men to offer battle to the rebels in the Forest Ephraim.* Absalom was defeated and killed by Joab, though David had expressly directed that the life of his guilty son should be spared.

5. But internal peace was not yet completely secured by this event. The jealousy of the tribes of Israel against the men of Judah, whom they accused of wishing to usurp the good graces of the king, and the animosity of the latter, brought about a new revolt. Sheba, of the tribe of Benjamin, raised an insurrection among the Israelites; but Joab marched against him and besieged him in Abel, whose inhabitants threw him the head of the rebel. The civil war was then stifled, and, except some campaigns against the Philistines, the remainder of the reign of David was peaceable. The population increased very considerably; but it appears that peace had enervated and corrupted it, for the Lord judged his people deserving of chastisement, and so permitted David to draw down on himself and his subjects a terrible scourge.† Pride, or perhaps the wish to increase his treasure by imposing new taxes and to ensure the means of recruiting a numerous permanent army, induced the king to order a general census. 1,100,000 adult men, without counting women and children, were found in Israel, 470,000 in Judah, and still Levi and Benjamin were not numbered. A terrible pestilence then came on the land of Israel; but it had scarcely lasted three days when God, pitying the misery of his people and the grief of their king, who humbled himself before Him, stayed the avenging angel.

6. Another attempt at revolt was made about this time by Adonijah, one of the king's sons. But David, who intended his crown to pass to

---

* Evidently no part of Mount Ephraim, properly so called, but in the land of Gilead beyond Jordan. The name "Wood of Ephraim" is conjectured by Dean Stanley to have been derived from the slaughter of the Ephraimites by Jephthah, in that neighbourhood (Judges xii. 6). —Tr.

† Compare Ex. xxx. 12, *seq.* It does not seem that David paid, or intended to pay, this ransom for his people.—Tr.

Solomon, caused the latter to be anointed and recognised by the people. Adonijah, abandoned by his partisans, submitted, and obtained pardon. But the aged king did not long survive this new trial. He died at the age of seventy years, thirty-three years after having established the seat of his power at Jerusalem. On his death-bed he gave wise counsels to his son Solomon, and left him the plans by which to build the Temple of the true God.

7. David had not only founded the political and material power of the Hebrew state, he had also firmly established its institutions. "Saul," says the learned Heeren, "had only been the general of an army, carrying out the orders of Jehovah as transmitted by Samuel, without a court, without a fixed residence. The nation was as yet only an agricultural and pastoral race, without riches, without luxury, but which became by insensible degrees a warlike people. Under David, were effected a total reform of the nation and change of the mode of government; the establishment of a fixed residence at Jerusalem, where was also the seat of the sanctuary; a rigorous observance of the worship of Jehovah as the exclusively national religion; a considerable increase to the state by conquest; a gradual development of despotism and of a palace government, whose political results manifested themselves towards the end of his reign, by the revolt of his sons." And in fact from the time when the government of David was completely constituted, an organised army; chiefs, who took their turn of service one month in each year, with 24,000 native soldiers; a foreign body-guard for the sovereign composed of Cretan and Philistine archers; governors of the tribes; a financial system, organised in all the towns and villages; ministers charged with the supervision of each branch of agriculture, both for the collection of taxes and the care of the royal domains; councillors of state; a general commanding the troops;—all these carry us far away from the time when Saul, already proclaimed king by one part of Israel, himself drove his own oxen to the field.

But David was not only the author of a political organisation and a successful general, he was also—and it is his greatest glory—a prophet-king. He saw far off into the future, and described, with incomparable magnificence of style, the splendours of that New Jerusalem one day to rise on the ruins of that which he was building. He was the author of the greater part of those Psalms in which repentance finds its most touching, and most sorrowful accents, prayer its most perfect and sublime form—beautiful sacred poems which furnish consolation for all ages, and support for every pious mind.

SECTION III.—SOLOMON (1019—978).

1. ALTHOUGH nominated by and anointed before the death of his father, Solomon did not enter on full possession of the throne without some difficulty. Adonijah put forth new pretensions, and Solomon, to free himself from this dangerous competitor, was compelled to put him to death. Joab was put to death as his accomplice, even though he had taken refuge at the altar, and Solomon also for the same reason deposed the high priest Abiathar. The reign of Solomon was, on the whole, peaceful. He preserved the regular habits of administration and the governmental system of his father, as we may see by a passage in the First Book of Kings (iv. 1—8), which mentions the king's scribes, the secretary of state, the commander-in-chief of the army or minister of war, the president of the council of state, the chief of the chamberlains, the king's "friend" (a name which we shall see further on was used in Asia and Egypt as a title or an office at court), the steward of the royal household, the minister of the public revenue, and finally twelve officers, who served in regular turn each for one month, to supply provisions for the king and his household.

Hardly was he in possession of royalty, when Solomon strengthened himself by foreign alliances with Tyre and with Egypt. Moreover, desirous of inaugurating his reign rather by religious acts than by war, he went to Gibeon, and there offered 1,000 burnt offerings to the Lord. Peaceably installed master of the countries conquered by his father, he saw his government recognised from the Euphrates to the Mediterranean, and to the river of Egypt. An unwarlike king, he lived in peace with the neighbouring nations; and Scripture has expressed the profound peace which Israel enjoyed in his reign, by the words "Judah and Israel dwelt safely, every man under his own vine and under his own fig-tree, from Dan to Beersheba (that is from the north to the south of the kingdom) all the days of Solomon."

2. Favoured by this peace, Solomon resolved to put into execution the great project of his father, and to build the temple of Jehovah at Jerusalem. Hiram, king of Tyre, the firm ally of Solomon, as he had been of David, furnished him, in exchange for oil and grain, abundant in the land of Israel, with the requisite timber cut in the cedar forests of Lebanon, of which there remain now only a few trees many centuries old. Solomon brought also from Tyre and from Gebal or Byblos workmen skilled in the art of stone cutting and working in wood, work in which the Israelites were then but little practised, but for which the Phœnicians were famous. There was also a Tyrian, born of a Jewish mother, and named like his king, Hiram, whom Solomon

brought to Jerusalem to execute the works of bronze, iron, gold, silver, and marble, for the service of the Temple, as well as to direct the dyeing of the precious stuffs, purple, and blue and crimson (2 Chron. ii. 14). Seven years and a half were occupied in the building of this famous edifice, which was commenced in the fourth year of the reign of Solomon, and on which the king lavished every sort of oriental gorgeousness. In the eighth year the dedication was held in the midst of an immense concourse of people; the Ark of the Covenant was then placed in the Holy of Holies, the inaccessible place,—symbol of the impenetrable majesty of God. 22,000 oxen and 120,000 sheep served for a feast to the entire nation convoked to this grand solemnity. In conformity with the strict spirit of the Mosaic law, it was forbidden to sacrifice elsewhere ; "the unity of God," says Bossuet, "was symbolised in the unity of His temple."

The description of the Temple, of its furniture and of its splendours, fills many chapters of the Book of Kings. From this description M. de Saulcy and the Count de Vogüé have lately attempted, in very interesting works, a complete and full description of it. Its foundations, constructed of gigantic stones, still exist over nearly the whole area of its site on Mount Moriah. The building of the Temple has contributed to the celebrity of the name of Solomon not less than the marvellous wisdom God gave him, and which was proved by all his actions, and all his words, especially in his administration of justice, a wisdom which the Queen of Sheba, in Southern Arabia, came from a far country to test and admire, and which the Arabs, in their fertile imagination, have transformed into a magic power that gave to Solomon the command of all the Genies.

3. Solomon married an Egyptian princess whom he permitted to exercise her own religious worship in a small chapel expressly built in the style of the religious edifices on the banks of the Nile, a chapel which a happy accident has preserved intact down to our own days in the village of Siloam, near the gates of Jerusalem. He built for himself and for her, in the Acropolis of Sion, a very magnificent palace, which the Bible describes in much detail. He enclosed Jerusalem with strong walls. He built or enlarged Megiddo, Gezer, and Baalath ; and lastly, he founded in the desert which extends from Anti-Lebanon to the Euphrates, the great city of Tadmor, afterwards Palmyra, intended as a halting-place for the caravans on the road between Damascus and Babylon.

More powerful than his father, Solomon was able, by the mere renown of his name, to keep in submission those who still remained in the interior of the country of the Canaanitish colonies once conquered by Joshua—the Amorites, Hittites, Perrizites and Hivites. He employed them, after the manner of the Egyptians, in the great works with which he enriched his kingdom, whilst he reserved the Israelites for the army and the administration.

4. But the principal enterprise of the reign of Solomon was that which opened to the Hebrews the navigation and commerce of the Southern Sea. Commerce with India dates back to the most remote antiquity. From the very earliest ages the refined civilisation of Egypt and Syria sought with avidity the spices, the aromatics, the metals, the precious and scented woods, the gems, the ivory—in a word, all the valuable merchandise which the rich soil of India supplies in abundance. But if commerce with India thus dates back to almost the earliest epochs of Egyptian civilisation, never before the time of Solomon had this commerce taken a direct route. The awkward and ill-constructed Indian ships availed themselves of the monsoon to cross the ocean, and bring the riches of their country to the ports of Yemen or Arabia Felix. Thence the merchandise of India was conveyed by caravans across Arabia to Babylon, or carried by sea to Egypt. The Egyptian vessels, which for a very long time alone ploughed the Red Sea, and had there uncontested dominion, shipped at the ports of Yemen and carried home these commodities.

Solomon was the first to conceive the happy idea of relieving this rich and important commerce from the shackles of a forced depôt in Southern Arabia, by making his ships double the southern point of the Arabian Peninsula, and steer straight to the Indian ports. He took advantage of the excellent harbours which his father's conquest of Idumæa had given him on the Red Sea, and of that weakening of the Egyptian power, hitherto irresistibly preponderant, which had been going on for many generations, and now permitted the creation of a new naval power on that sea. But Solomon was not able alone to carry out the plan which he had conceived ; the Hebrews had no experience in maritime affairs, nor had they those instincts which make seamen.* He engaged then with his ally Hiram, king of Tyre, to undertake at their common expense voyages to India. A fleet was built with timber from Judæa at Elath and Eziongeber ; it was manned by Phœnician sailors, the most skilful, hardy and famous of all ancient navigators. A first

---

* Dean Stanley (*Sinai and Palestine*, p. 261) observes, "To have planted the centres of national and religious life on the sea-shore was a thought which never seems to have entered even into the imperial mind of Solomon.

Far away at Eziongeber, on the Gulf of Akaba, was the chief emporium of his trade. Even Jaffa only received the rafts which floated down the coast from Tyre. To describe the capital as a place "where shall go no galley with oars, neither shall gallant ship pass by" (Is. xxxiii. 21) is not, as according to Western notions it would be, an expression of weakness and danger, but of prosperity and security."

expedition was conducted to Ophir, a country which the historian of ancient India, M. Lassen,* has conclusively demonstrated to be the country of Abhira, near the present province of Guzerat.† It was a great success, and many treasures were brought back, which the two kings divided.

From this time, as long as Solomon lived, the fleet sailed every three years for the same country, and returned thence, laden with spices, aromatics, gold, silver and ivory. In return for the share he had received of these Indian expeditions, Hiram made Solomon his partner in the long voyages which the Tyrian fleets regularly made every year as far as the southern coast of Spain, then called Tarshish (a name applied in earlier times to Italy), in search of tin, lead, cinnabar, and many other sorts of valuable merchandise. So the Bible says, "The king made silver to be in Jerusalem as stones, and cedars made he to be as sycamore trees that are in the vale for abundance" (1 Kings x. 27).

5. But that brilliant prosperity, that power, and those incalculable riches, depraved the heart of the king, who allowed himself to be seduced by the love of pleasure, and forgot the God of his fathers. Led away by the love of women, he opened his harem, already scandalously full, to a crowd of strange women of the Moabites, Ammonites, Edomites, Zidonians, and Hittites. "Of the nations," says the Bible, "concerning which the Lord said unto the children of Israel, Ye shall not go in unto them, nor they to you, for surely they will turn away your heart after their gods" (1 Kings xi. 2; Ex. xxxiv. 16; Deut. vii. 3, 4). In fact, we see that Solomon, giving way to the solicitations of his strange wives and concubines, so far forgot the majesty of the Creator as to serve Ashtoreth, the goddess of the Zidonians, Moloch, "the abomination of the Ammonites," and to build a temple to Chemosh "the abomination of the Moabites." Alliance with neighbouring nations, and toleration of the worship of strange gods, were things utterly at variance with the calling of Israel and the law of Moses.

The conduct of Solomon began very soon to cause great irritation to a large part of the people. Advice and threatenings were not wanting, but he turned a deaf ear to them all. When his fall was complete, when he had publicly shown himself unfaithful to the Divine precepts, the punishment of God began to fall on the head of this king, till then so fortunate; and before the tomb closed on him he saw that the threats he had despised were already on their way to accomplishment.

* *Indische Alterthumskunde*, vol. ii., p. 584—592.

† Sir E. Tennent, in his work on Ceylon, argues in favour of Ophir having been in that island. Sir H. Rawlinson seems to accept the fact as proved (see RAW. *Her.* i. 243, note).—TR.

His empire did not stand untouched, and he lived to see the first signs of its dismemberment. The Idumæan Hadad, assisted by the king of Egypt, took from him some of the provinces round the Red Sea. The Syrian Resin made himself independent at Damascus, and then assumed the crown. Jeroboam, in exciting the tribes of Israel to revolt, prepared the way for the division of the Hebrew people, and commenced its ruin. This last was the son of Nebat, of the tribe of Ephraim. His intelligence had attracted the attention of Solomon, who had given him an important administrative appointment. But the king, having learned by the voice of the prophet Ahijah that his protegée should come to reign over ten of the tribes, and receiving from another quarter the news that he was preparing an insurrection in the North, would have put him to death. Jeroboam fled to Sheshonk, king of Egypt (called Shishak in the Bible), and there lived till the death of Solomon, which took place after a reign of forty years, that is about the year 978 B.C.

The reign of Solomon is of the highest importance in the history of the Hebrews, and serves as the pivot of its whole chronology. The first precise and positive date which is met with in all that history is, in fact, that of the solemn dedication of the Temple. It is only after that event that we can possibly fix with certainty, by means of the facts furnished by the Books of Samuel and of Kings, the other dates of the reigns of Solomon, of David, and of Saul.

6. Solomon's wisdom, Scripture tells us, excelled the wisdom of all the children of the East country, and all the wisdom of Egypt. "For he was wiser (before his fall, be it clearly understood,) than all men; . . . And his fame was in all nations round about. And he spake 3,000 proverbs; and his songs were a thousand and five. And he spake of trees, from the cedar-tree that is in Lebanon, even unto the hyssop that springeth out of the wall: he spake also of beasts, and of fowl, and of creeping things, and of fishes" (1 Kings iv. 30, *seq.*). All these works are lost; there remain only the "Proverbs," or a collection of maxims which bear internal evidence of his authorship, and the Book called Ecclesiastes, in which all the circumstances, all the pleasures of human life are appreciated at their true value, and stamped with the motto, "All is vanity." This last work is assigned to the king of Israel with less certainty. The Song of Songs is also attributed to Solomon, a mystical poem, in which, under the forms of impassioned love, is figured the longing of the soul after God, an example copied in later times among the Arabs by some mystic sects of Islam.

CHAPTER IV.

SEPARATION OF THE TEN TRIBES.—KINGDOMS OF ISRAEL AND JUDAH.—FALL OF SAMARIA AND JERUSALEM.

Chief Authorities:—The Bible, *Books of Kings and Chronicles; The Prophets, particularly Isaiah, Jeremiah and Ezekiel.*—Josephus, *Antiquities*, Books VIII. and X.

The modern writers mentioned at the beginning of Chapter I.

SECTION I.—REHOBOAM AND JEROBOAM.—SEPARATION OF THE TEN TRIBES (978–957).

1. THE reigns of David and Solomon represent the highest degree of glory and political power to which the Hebrews have ever attained. But this very prosperity, and the corruption that it introduced at the court, the development of commercial relations with foreign powers, could not but react on the interior state of the kingdom of Israel, and exercise an evil influence on the manners and faith of the people. Religion, the only tie which bound the Hebrews together, was weakened by the prevalence of idolatry under Solomon. Royalty, powerful and respected as it was under David and his successor, was yet not firm enough to form the foundation of the unity of the nation, and to establish permanently the preponderance of Judah over the other tribes. Even at the close of the reign of David we have seen that an insurrection was attempted, from jealousy of the importance and prerogatives of the tribe from which the king had sprung.

The symptoms of revolt became again apparent, and in a much more menacing form, in the last years of Solomon. The prophet Ahijah had clearly announced to that monarch the division of his kingdom. The enormous expenses which the great works of his reign had entailed tended to alienate the Northern tribes from those of the South, and to excite a rupture. Solomon's successor was his son Rehoboam, who was forty-one years of age. The deputies of the tribes of Israel who came to do homage to the new king, wishing at the same time to dictate some conditions to him, and to require a diminution of the burdens of the people, thought it better not to present themselves at Jerusalem, and they assembled at Shechem, the capital of the powerful tribe of Ephraim. They recalled Jeroboam from Egypt, and put him at their head. Rehoboam was invited to Shechem, to be proclaimed king, and not in the least suspecting the trap which was laid for him, he presented himself before the assembly. Jeroboam spoke in the name of the deputies: "Thy father," said he to the king, "made our yoke grievous; now, therefore, make thou the grievous service of thy father, and his heavy yoke which he put upon us, lighter, and we will serve thee." Rehoboam surprised, asked a delay of three days. The old state councillors of Solomon were unanimous in advising him to give way, but the king preferred to their counsels the pernicious advice of his young courtiers, who, playing on his self-love, urged him to resistance.

When, on the third day, Jeroboam and the deputies presented themselves before him, he haughtily replied, "My father made your yoke heavy, and I will add to your yoke. My father chastised you with whips, but I will chastise you with scorpions." Then the people broke out into rebellion, crying out, "What portion have we in David . . . to your tents, O Israel: see now to thine own house, David" (1 Kings xii., 2 Chron. x.). Adoram, "who was over the tribute," sent by Rehoboam to calm the popular tumult, was stoned to death. Rehoboam had barely time to get into his chariot and fly in all haste to Jerusalem. The tribes of Judah and Benjamin alone remained faithful to the dynasty of David, whilst the others proclaimed Jeroboam king. The tribe of Benjamin, which had peculiar grievances against the house of David, would probably have joined with the tribes of Israel if its territorial position had not compelled it to hold to Judah. The city of Jerusalem was in fact partly in the land of Benjamin. Rehoboam attempted to resist; he assembled an army of 180,000 men to subdue the seceded tribes, but God caused him to be told by the prophet Shemaiah that this event was brought about in the order of His providence, and that the soldiers were not to fight against their brethren. The army was disbanded, and the separation was thus consummated.

2. The Bible gives us no detail as to the respective limits of the two kingdoms formed by this separation. It merely says that the ten tribes declared for Jeroboam—that is, Ephraim, which was at the head of the movement, Simeon, Dan, Manasseh, Issachar, Asshur, Zebulon, Naphtali, Reuben, and Gad. The new state, embracing the greater part of the nation, took by preference the name of Kingdom of Israel, which had already served in former times to designate the kingdom of Ish-bosheth. The land of Israel included, then, all Peræa with the tributary countries as far as the Euphrates and the greater part of Palestine on this side the Jordan. The kingdom of Rehoboam, called the kingdom of Judah, embraced only Southern Palestine, between Bethel and Beer-

sheba. The king of Judah had, besides, the suzerainty of Idumea and the land of the Philistines, but the whole of the provinces subject to his sceptre were in extent hardly a fourth part of the kingdom of Solomon.

The boundaries were not very exactly defined; and some frontier towns belonging to the tribes of one of the two kingdoms were in fact, either from the wish of the inhabitants, or the force of circumstances, found in the power of the other kingdom. Thus, for example, the towns of Bethel and Rama, although situated in the territory of Benjamin, belonged to the kingdom of Israel; but, in return, the southern cities of Dan, such as Ajalon, formed part of the kingdom of Judah. As for the towns which in the time of Joshua had been given to the tribe of Simeon, they all, from their geographical position, fell to the state of Judah. So then, in reality, as Simeon was one of the ten tribes who declared for Jeroboam, we must suppose that at any rate a part of the tribe had emigrated to the north. A passage in the Book of Chronicles appears in fact to indicate that the Simeonites, after the reign of David, no longer possessed the towns which had been given them by Joshua (1 Chron. iv. 31). Some remnants of that tribe, who had remained in the land of Judah, emigrated in later times, under Hezekiah, to the number of 500 families,* towards Mount Seir. A learned Dutch Orientalist, M. Dozy, has recently devoted a very learned and ingenious work to proving that they must have gone very far into Arabia, and have been the founders of the city of Mecca.†

3. The two kingdoms of Israel and Judah remained separate until the capture of Samaria by the Assyrians and the annihilation of the Israelitish state. It does not seem that, during the whole of this long space of time, any one conceived the idea of the re-establishment of national unity under one sceptre. The chronology of the two parallel kingdoms presents serious difficulties which St. Jerome has pronounced insuperable. They have been minutely considered by students, who have proposed numerous systems for their solution. We do not intend here to enter into a critical examination of the problem and the discussion of its elements; these are questions of detail which cannot be brought within the compass of the present work. Let us, then, confine ourselves to saying that the system most generally adopted by critics, and which seems preferable, arranges in the following manner the royal lists of the two monarchies formed from the ruins of that of David and Solomon:—

---

* 1 Chron. iv. 42. The reading is "men"; but there is no doubt that the emigration of 500 men would entail the removal of their families. —Tr.

† *Die Israeliten zu Mekkah*, Leyden, 1865.

KINGDOM OF JUDAH. *Commencement of the reign of—*		KINGDOM OF ISRAEL. *Commencement of the reign of—*	
	B.C.		B.C.
Rehoboam	978.	Jeroboam	978.
Abijam	961.		
Asa	958.		
		Nadab	957.
		Baasha	953.
		Elah	932.
		Zimri	931.
		Omri	930.
		Ahab	919.
Jehoshaphat	916.		
		Ahaziah, or Azariah	899.
		Jehoram, or Joram	898.
Jehoram	891.		
Ahaziah	887.		
Athaliah	886.	Jehu	886.
Joash or Jehoash	879.		
		Jehoahaz	858.
		Jehoash	842.
Amaziah	839.		
		Jeroboam II.	827.
Azariah	810.		
		Interregnum	784 to 773.
		Zachariah	773.
		Shallum	772.
		Manahem	772.
		Pekahiah	761.
		Pekah	759.
Jotham	758.		
Ahaz	742.	Manahem II.	742.
		Pekah (restored)	733.
		Hoshea	730.
Hezekiah	727.		
		Fall of the Kingdom of Israel	721.

It is necessary to place this comparative table of the succession of the princes of the two kingdoms before the eye of the reader, in order to avoid the confusion which might easily result from relating simultaneously, as we are obliged to do, the annals of Judah and of Israel, which appear at times to be extremely entangled. We now again take up the thread of events.

4. Jeroboam was hardly proclaimed king when he hastened to guard against any possible attack from the kingdom of Judah, by fortifying Shechem, his new capital, and some frontier cities. But he did not know how to make a proper use of the position in which he found himself. Instead of conducting himself as a prince chosen by God, instead of strengthening the state which he founded under Divine per-

mission, he permitted himself to be led astray by a narrow-minded and base feeling of distrustful policy, and became an apostate. Fearing lest the Israelites, if in conformity with the precepts of the law, they went to sacrifice in the Temple at Jerusalem, might again return to the authority of Rehoboam, and thus shake his throne, he resolved to interrupt all the relations of his subjects with the religious centre of the nation; and that he might better succeed in this project by calling to his aid the bad passions and gross tendencies of the people, he gave full sanction to a revolting system of idolatry. At the two extremities of his kingdom, at Dan and at Bethel, he built two Temples in which Jehovah was worshipped under the ignoble image of a golden calf, and thus renewed the crime of which the Hebrews had been guilty in the desert.

The people allowed themselves to be led into the seducing and entirely materialistic worship of these dumb gods; their altars were erected on all the high places, and new priests, strangers to the tribe of Levi, were consecrated for this new religion. The legitimate priests and Levites, driven out by Jeroboam, abandoned their possessions and sought refuge in the kingdom of Judah, followed by the few men, who, of the tribes of Israel, wished to remain faithful to the law, and preferred expatriation to apostasy. Divine warnings were not, however, wanting to induce Jeroboam to leave the criminal path he had entered; but he heeded them not. Thus, one day, a zealous prophet from the kingdom of Judah ventured to present himself in the Temple at Bethel, and to curse the altar at the moment when the king was offering incense on it. Abijah, son of the king, having become seriously ill, Jeroboam conceived the idea of sending his wife, disguised, to ask advice of the prophet Ahijah, who had predicted his accession to the throne, and in whom the king of Israel hoped to find a protector favoured by heaven. But Ahijah, far from showing a favourable disposition, reproached the queen in the most severe terms with the idolatry of Jeroboam, and predicted to her the coming end of his dynasty as well as the ruin of the kingdom of Israel, whose people were to be carried captive beyond the Euphrates, "and," added he, "when thy feet enter into the city the child shall die" (1 Kings xiv. 12).

5. The most ordinary political intelligence would have taught Rehoboam, with such conduct on part of his rival, to show great zeal for the orthodox Mosaic worship, which alone, even from a human point of view, could be to him the means of safety. He acted thus for three years. His zeal abated, however, but too soon, and gave place to a culpable indifference, quickly followed by the gradual introduction of Phœnician idolatry, together with all the abominable debaucheries which always accompanied it. At the same time, the schismatical worship of the high places spread in all parts of the kingdom, even

among those who remained faithful to the doctrine of the unity of God. Doubtless this worship was addressed to Jehovah; but the multiplication of sanctuaries itself was a violation of the precepts of the Law, and turned away worshippers from the one Temple, where alone sacrifice was permitted to be offered.

The indifference to the national sanctuary and to the Holy City became so great that, in spite of the fortresses guarding his southern frontier, Rehoboam could make no resistance to the Egyptian troops, who, in the fifth year of his reign (970 B.C.), invaded the kingdom of Judah, probably through the intrigues of Jeroboam, and penetrated to Jerusalem. Rehoboam trembled in his palace, and the prophet Shemaiah took advantage of the occasion to reproach the king, before all his court, for his infidelity towards Jehovah, the cause of this misfortune. The king and all his nobles who surrounded him showed sincere repentance, and said, "The Lord is righteous." Shemaiah then reassured them, by telling them that this was but a passing storm, and that they must accept with resignation the chastisement of Heaven (1 Chron. xii. 6). Shishak, king of Egypt, at the head of a numerous army, entered the capital without striking a blow, and plundered the treasures of the Temple. But as Shemaiah had announced, he had no other intent than to humble, and to extort money from the king of Judah; and his army retired when satisfied with their plunder. Rehoboam reigned twelve years after the Egyptian invasion. No memorable event marked that space of time. Constant hostilities went on between Rehoboam and Jeroboam; but they confined themselves to mutual small incursions; and it does not appear that there ever was any engagement of importance between the two kings.

6. After the death of Rehoboam, and the accession of his son Abijam, Jeroboam thought a time when the kingdom was passing from one hand to another favourable for attempting the conquest of the land of Judah. From two quarters he prepared to deliver decisive blows, and he had recourse to a *levée en masse* of the people. By this means Jeroboam put under arms 800,000 men, and Abijam 400,000. The two armies met on the mountains of Ephraim, near the heights of Samaria. In spite of an ambuscade which Jeroboam set behind the troops of Judah, they succeeded in possessing themselves of Bethel and some other Israelitish cities. Abijam, as little zealous as his father for religion, was guilty of the fault of not profiting by this event to abolish at Bethel the worship of the golden calf, and the town soon again fell into the power of Israel. Abijam died after a reign of three years. His son and successor, Asa, showed from his earliest years great zeal for the worship of Jehovah. Though still very young, he displayed great hatred for idolatry; he did not even spare his grandmother, Maacha, widow of Rehoboam, who favoured the Phœnician worship,

and attempted to domineer over him. Asa deprived her of all influence in the affairs of the government. The statue of Ashtaroth, which she had dared to set up at Jerusalem, was burned in the valley of Kidron. Everywhere the altars of the Canaanitish deities were destroyed, and the persons consecrated to that shameful worship were expelled from the land. The only reproach that Scripture addresses to Asa is, that he allowed the schismatical altars on the high places to remain, in order to give occupation and means of subsistence to the numerous priests whom the apostasy of the ten tribes had induced to return to Judah.

SECTION II.—DISORDERS AND REVERSES IN THE KINGDOM OF ISRAEL (957—919 B.C.).

1. JEROBOAM had reigned twenty-two years. After his death the prediction of the prophet Ahijah against his family was almost immediately accomplished. At the close of only two years of power his son, Nadab, was assassinated by one of his principal officers, named Baasha, of the tribe of Issachar, whilst besieging Gibbethon, a city of the tribe of Dan, which had fallen into the power of the Philistines. Baasha seized upon the crown, and to remove all danger of any possible competition, put to death all the near relatives of Jeroboam.

2. Whilst these events were occurring in the kingdom of Israel, Asa re-established in the land of Judah the worship of the true God; and reigning with wisdom and glory, promoted in every shape the national prosperity. One of his principal cares was the army, which he laboured to place on an improved footing. Events were soon to show how prudent and full of foresight his conduct had been. In the fifteenth year of the reign of Asa (943 B.C.), a formidable invasion menaced the southern frontiers of Palestine. Zerah, king of Ethiopia,* at the head of a numerous army, recruited amongst the barbarous people of the Upper Nile, had overrun Egypt. After having subjugated it for the moment, and carried devastation from south to north throughout its whole extent, he crossed the river Rhinocorura, and assailed the kingdom of Judah, hoping to pillage it also, as well as all Syria. Asa led his army to meet the Ethiopians, and gave them battle in the valley of Zephathah, near Mareshah. Zerah was vanquished and obliged to fly, leaving an immense booty to the Jewish soldiers.

---

* Some historians have erroneously confounded this prince with Tirhakah, king both of Ethiopia and Egypt, who lived nearly two centuries later. Others have supposed him to be Uaserken, king of Egypt, and not of Ethiopia, whose name could never be so transcribed into Hebrew. The Zerah of the Bible was the king Azerch-Amen, whose name is read on several Ethiopian monuments. This important correction in history is due to Dr. Brugsch.

The defeat of the king of Ethiopia was so complete that he could not even maintain himself in Egypt, but was obliged to retire in all haste into his own kingdom, above the Cataracts of the Nile. On the return of the victorious Asa to his capital, the prophet Azariah presented himself before the king, and in an address to him and to his army showed how their recent success was the recompense of their return to religious truth, just as the disasters of Rehoboam had been the just punishment of his infidelity. Asa continued to show great severity to idolatry ; he executed also important repairs in the Temple, and offered there splendid sacrifices in recognition of his victory over Zerah. Very many of the inhabitants of the land of Israel who still remained, in spite of the official schism, faithful to the God of their fathers, seeing the success of the pious Asa, came up to be present at that feast, and established themselves in the land of Judah.

3. Baasha, the usurper of the crown of Israel, could not without disquiet see the constantly increasing power of Asa and his kingdom. He commenced hostilities against him by fortifying the town of Ramah, and placing a garrison there, to prevent the people of Israel from communicating with the kingdom of Judah and going up to the Temple. Asa could not permit the establishment of this threatening fortress at a distance of only two leagues from Jerusalem. He emptied the royal treasury, and that of the Temple, to purchase the alliance of Ben-hidri,* king of Syria, who resided at Damascus, and had formed a considerable state of the Aramæan provinces, formerly subject to David and Solomon. His offers having been accepted, Ben-hidri invaded the north of Palestine, penetrating to the neighbourhood of the lake of Gennesaret, and possessed himself of many important towns. Asa at the same time marched on Ramah, took it, and having demolished the fortifications, already far advanced, employed the materials in constructing at Geba and Mizpeh two fortresses, to serve as the bulwarks of his state against the kingdom of Israel.

But the prophets were by no means pleased to see an alliance concluded with a pagan against the king of Israel, and at the expense of the sacred treasure. A prophet, named Hanani, bitterly reproached Asa with leaning on Syria, instead of trusting entirely to the help of Jehovah, who could have subdued both the Syrians and the Israelites.

* This name, borne successively by many kings of Syria, is written Ben-hadad in the Hebrew text of the Bible, and Ben-ader in the Septuagint (υἱὸς Ἄδερ). The reading we have adopted, Ben-hidri, that given by the Assyrian cuneiform inscriptions contemporary with these princes, is sufficiently near that which the LXX. followed. [Many Hebrew manuscripts give this name with a final R, as does also the Samaritan. The two letters R and D in Hebrew are not easily distinguishable.]

The words of the inspired speaker were not without influence on the people, and led to some troubles. Asa thought fit to use severity, and ventured even to cause Hanani to be arrested as a disturber of the public peace. From this moment to the end of his reign he found himself exposed to the ill-will of the whole order of prophets, who looked on him as a tyrant. Nevertheless, in spite of his rupture with this body, who represented the living and zealous element in the Mosaic religion, he did not swerve from religious truth, and was always a faithful servant of Jehovah. His orthodoxy, and vigilance in repressing every attempt to introduce the worship of strange gods, procured him a long succession of years of peaceable reign, and he did not die till 916 B.C., after forty-one years of prosperity, leaving in his son Jehoshaphat a worthy successor.

4. During this time disorder and crime, the just punishment of schism and apostasy, were raging in the kingdom of Israel. Baasha reigned for ten years after the invasion of the Syrians, but without ever recovering from that humiliation. The Bible mentions no more collisions between him and Asa, but the two kings remained in a permanent state of hostility. Baasha, it may be seen by what we have related of his life, was animated by a spirit of the greatest impiety; he had taken up the position of a declared enemy of Mosaic orthodoxy, in which he saw a danger to his own crown, and a source of strength to the king of Judah.

The prophet Jehu, son of the prophet Hanani who had braved the anger of Asa when condemning his alliance with the Syrians, ventured to present himself before Baasha, to reproach him with having imitated the sins of Jeroboam, after being exalted from the dust, to overturn his dynasty; he announced to him the divine decree by which, as a punishment for this impiety, he and his race should be cut off—"I will make thy house," said he, speaking in the name of the Lord, "like the house of Jeroboam, the son of Nebat" (1 Kings xvi. 2). Asa lived to witness the accomplishment of this prophecy, and to see a third dynasty mount the throne established by Jeroboam; for events followed each other quickly in the land of Israel. Baasha, nevertheless, transmitted the crown to his son Elah, dying, after having reigned nearly twenty-three years. But Elah succumbed in the second year of his reign, struck down, like the son of Jeroboam, by the hand of a conspirator.

Whilst the troops, commanded by the general-in-chief Omri, were occupied by a second siege of the town of Gibbethon, then held by the Philistines, Zimri, one of the two captains of the war chariots, assassinated King Elah, "as he was drinking himself drunk in the house of Arza, steward of his house" (1 Kings xvi. 9), at Tirzah, then the capital of Israel. The murderer having seized on the throne, massacred all the members of the royal family; and the prediction of the prophet Jehu was thus accomplished to the letter.

When the news of Zimri's crime arrived in the camp at Gibbethon, the troops, indignant, proclaimed their general Omri king of Israel. Omri at once abandoned the siege to march on Tirzah, and the usurper, seeing himself forced to surrender the city, set fire to the palace and burned himself alive there, after having reigned but seven days. Nevertheless, Omri, the elect of the army, found a rival in a certain Tibni, son of Ginath, on whom the people of the capital bestowed the crown. War broke out between the two pretenders, and as the party of Omri was the strongest, the death of Tibni left his competitor to be recognised by all Israel. The text of Scripture leaves us to infer that the civil war between Omri and Tibni lasted four years, for it makes the reign of Omri commence only in the thirty-first year of the reign of Asa (927 B C.), although it gives for the conspiracy of Zimri and his death the twenty-seventh year of that prince (931 B.C.), in which year Omri was proclaimed king by the army.

In the seventh year of his reign, two years after the death of Tibni, Omri, desirous of creating a new capital, doubtless because he distrusted the disorderly spirit and revolutionary tendencies of the inhabitants of Tirzah, bought, from an individual named Shemer, a hill, situated in a very strong position in the midst of the territory of Ephraim, and not far from Shechem; he paid for the site two talents of silver, and built there a city called Samaria. There, ever after, down to the time of the destruction of the kingdom of Israel by the Assyrians, the residence of its sovereigns was fixed. The foundation of Samaria is the only fact worthy of remark which is recorded of the reign of Omri, with the exception of an unfortunate war against the Syrians, in which he lost many towns. He governed in the same spirit as his predecessors, maintaining the schismatical worship established by Jeroboam. He died at last in the twelfth year of his reign, leaving the throne to his son Ahab.

Section III.—Ahab, Jehoshaphat, and their Sons (919—886 B.C.).

1. Jehoshaphat, son of Asa, ascended the throne of Jerusalem at the age of thirty-five years. Inheriting the virtues of his father, he manifested even a greater zeal for the national worship, and removed the last traces of idolatry. To inspire the people with stronger religious sentiments, he sent, in the third year of his reign, five of the principal persons of his court, accompanied by two priests and nine Levites, with the Book of the Law, to make the tour of the whole country, and instruct the inhabitants. At the same time Jehoshaphat built new forti-

fications, and filled the arsenals with munitions of all kinds; he also carefully re-organised the administration and the army. This last was to be henceforth composed of two very strong divisions—one of Judah, the other of Benjamin. The peace then reigning in the land of Judah, to which many neighbouring people paid tribute, much favoured the reforms of Jehoshaphat, which, as we shall see, were to be still further developed.

2. The court of Samaria exhibited then a complete contrast to that of Jerusalem. Whilst Jehoshaphat made unceasing efforts to re-establish the worship of Jehovah in all its purity, Ahab, who surpassed in impiety all the kings of Israel, not content with the worship of the golden calves, and influenced by his Phœnician wife Jezebel, daughter of Eth-baal, king of Tyre, had introduced the worship of Baal and of Ashtaroth, to whom she erected temples and altars, even in the town of Samaria. This irruption of Phœnician paganism brought trouble and disorder on the whole kingdom of Israel, and gave rise to sanguinary collisions between the worshippers of Baal and the small number of zealous partisans who still adhered to the true faith. The former party had become the strongest; Baal had no less than 450 priests or prophets in his service, and Ashtaroth 400, all maintained at the expense of Jezebel. Sustained by the energy of a fanatical and cruel queen, they persecuted with the utmost fury the prophets of Jehovah, whom they attempted to exterminate. These latter were still tolerably numerous; and in the persecution of which they were the objects, some of them exhibited such zeal and courage as had never previously been seen among them, and when occasion offered, they made sanguinary reprisals on their adversaries. Their chief was the celebrated prophet Elijah, and at court they had a secret protector in Obadiah, the governor of the king's house. But the mass of the people, undecided or indifferent, did not give a hearty support to either of the two parties, for which reason Elijah reproached them with "halting between two opinions," and declaring neither for Jehovah nor for Baal. The king Ahab himself, a man with no energy and no convictions, may be placed in the front rank of these waverers. At one time he bowed before Baal, and gave himself up to all the abominations of Canaanitish worship; at another, terrified by the words of the prophet, he rent his clothes and humbled himself before Jehovah. One day he permitted Jezebel to order the massacre of the prophets of Jehovah, and on another he gave up the prophets of Baal to the vengeance of Elijah.

The kingdom of Israel could not rise from this miserable position but by a violent revolution; it required an energetic man, inspired from on high, full of courage and devotion, to bring over the waverers, to ensure the triumph of the holy cause of Jehovah and of Hebrew nationality, against the tyrannical fury of the Phœnician princess. In this calamitous time Israel saw a saviour arise, who undertook alone, if not to accomplish, at any rate to prepare the way for, a revolution, and to overturn the impious dynasty, which sought to sweep away the very last traces of the worship of the true God. This man was the prophet Elijah, the hero of the epoch. Full of fierce enthusiasm, excited by almost continual Divine inspiration, he braved, by his constancy and courage, the fury of Jezebel, and frequently made King Ahab tremble, who, though he detested, could not help respecting him. Like Samuel, he was inflexible in his purpose, and feared not to show himself stern, and even cruel, to accomplish what he found to be necessary. Unfortunately, Israel had fallen too low for a complete regeneration to be possible. Even Elijah never raised his voice against the image worship of Bethel and Dan, but directed all his efforts to ensure the triumph of the name of Jehovah over the odious Phœnician worship; and when at the end of his days he was compelled to leave his work still unfinished, he chose a successor to continue and complete it.

3. Nevertheless, the throne of Ahab seemed to be strengthened by some brilliant victories. Ben-hidri, king of Syria, son of the one who had made war on Baasha and Omri, came, followed by thirty-nine princes, his vassals or allies, to besiege Samaria, which had become, as we have said, the capital of the kingdom. The king of Israel humbled himself before him, and offered to declare himself his vassal; but Ben-hidri replied with such insolence, that, by the counsel of the elders, Ahab resolved on resistance. God told him by a prophet—"Thus saith the Lord, Hast thou seen all this great multitude? behold, I will deliver it into thine hand this day, that thou mayest know that I am the Lord." Feeling his faith re-animated in this danger, he ordered a sally of 7,000 men, who surprising the enemy's camp when they were in the midst of an orgy, routed them completely.

But the courtiers of the king of Syria, as a salve to their own pride and that of their master, said to Ben-hidri, "Their gods are gods of the hills, therefore they are stronger than we; but let us fight against them in the plain, and surely we shall be stronger than they."* The king permitted himself to be persuaded to replace exactly the men,

* It may be noticed that the Hebrews were essentially Highlanders in all their instincts of fight; their first impulse in making war was to occupy the heights of some mountain. Joshua made his night-march for this purpose before the battle of Beth-horon. When resistance to Jabin, king of Hazor, was contemplated, the first command of the prophetess to Barak was, "Draw toward Mount Tabor." Gideon "went down" from the hill to his great victory over Midian. It added to David's grief for the loss of his friend Jonathan, that the defeat had been sustained "in *thine* high places." The same feeling seems to have influenced the Hebrews also in later times; the first Maccabæan victory and the last success against Rome were both in "the going down" to

horses, and war chariots which he had lost, and commenced the campaign the next year with troops incomparably superior in number to those of Ahab. But God showed that He could confound the blasphemies of the enemies of Israel. 100,000 Syrians were cut to pieces under the walls of Aphek, in the plain of Esdraelon, and Ben-hidri was forced to implore the clemency of the enemy whom he had so insolently defied.

Ahab, who could have made the king of Syria a prisoner, did not even confine himself to setting him at liberty. Under the guarantee of an article, which gave him the right of keeping a garrison in Damascus, he concluded a treaty of intimate alliance, which insured Ben-hidri the assistance of Israelitish troops in his wars. A most valuable inscription of Shalmanezer IV.,* king of Assyria, discovered near the source of the Tigris and now preserved in the British Museum, in relating a defeat which that prince inflicted the next year on Ben-hidri, near the city of Karkar, mentions among the troops who fought on the side of the latter 10,000 men of *Ahab of Israel.* A prophet severely reproached Ahab for this alliance with an infidel whom God had delivered into his hands, and threatened him with the Divine wrath; but he was not heeded.

4. A horrible crime, into which he was led by the queen Jezebel, brought on Ahab a still more dreadful prophecy from Elijah. A man named Naboth at Jezreel possessed a vineyard near to the palace of the king in that city. Ahab, desirous of joining that vineyard to his garden, asked Naboth to sell it to him in perpetuity. This was to introduce into the civil law a principle formally opposed to the Mosaic law, which did not permit the property of the soil to go for ever out of the hands of the family to whom it had been assigned at the conquest, but directed its return at the year of Jubilee.

Naboth, faithful to the spirit of the law, refused to sell the inheritance of his fathers: at this the king showed himself much aggrieved. Jezebel having learned the cause of his grief, consoled him by promising to give him the vineyard of Naboth. She sent orders in the king's name to the

---

Beth-horon, and even to the very last day of Jewish independence, when their "hold," Masada, fell before the Romans.

We find, too, that though the Hebrews frequently assembled large bodies of infantry, they were never strong in cavalry or war chariots; a fact well known, and alluded to by the Rabshakeh, whom Sennacherib sent to Hezekiah—"I will deliver thee," said he, "2,000 horses, if thou be able on thy part to set riders upon them."

This whole subject is treated at length by Dean Stanley, *Sinai and Palestine*, ch. ix.—Tr.

* This is the king who appears in Sir H. Rawlinson's list as Shalmanezer II. The cause of the difference between that high authority and the author will appear in the Book on the Assyrians.—Tr.

authorities of his city to accuse Naboth of high treason. They brought false witnesses, who swore that Naboth had blasphemed God and the king; he was condemned and stoned to death. Jezebel told her husband of the death of Naboth and persuaded him to confiscate the property of the condemned, in defiance of the precepts of the law. Ahab having gone to the vineyard of Naboth to take possession of it, the prophet Elijah met him. "Hast thou killed and also taken possession," said he to the king. "Thus saith the Lord, In the place where dogs licked the blood of Naboth, they shall lick thy blood, even thine." "Hast thou found me, O mine enemy," said the king. "I have found thee," replied the prophet, "because thou hast sold thyself to do evil in the sight of the Lord. Behold, I will bring evil upon thee, and will make thy house like the house of Jeroboam the son of Nebat, and like the house of Baasha son of Ahijah, and the dogs shall eat Jezebel by the wall of Jezreel" (1 Kings xxi. 19),

5. The accomplishment of the first part of this prophecy was not long delayed. Ben-hidri during the three years that had elapsed, since the treaty of peace had been concluded, after the battle at Aphek, had not executed its conventions. Ramoth, one of the most important cities of the land of Gilead or Peræa, still remained in the hands of the Syrians. Ahab showed his intention of recommencing war against the king of Syria, and taking from him by force the city, he was not willing to surrender. At this time Jehoshaphat, king of Judah, who since his accession to the throne had profited by the blessings of peace to continue his reforms in religious worship, and in the administration, had visited the king of Israel, with whom he had allied himself by marriage, his son Jehoram having married Athaliah, the daughter of Ahab and Jezebel. This was the first time since the separation of the two kingdoms that a king of Judah showed himself as a friend and ally on the territory of Israel; and we may well be surprised to find peace between the kingdoms, and family ties between the courts, of the pious Jehoshaphat and the impious Ahab.

It is possible that Jehoshaphat hoped to work on the facile character of Ahab, and lead him to better sentiments. At the moment of marching against the Syrians, Ahab expressed a wish that the king of Judah should take part in the expedition. Jehoshaphat consented, and promised the assistance of his troops, on the condition that the king of Israel should at once consult the prophets. Ahab brought together 400 of them at the gate of Samaria; they all with one voice declared that he ought to go to the war, and that the king of Israel should return a conqueror. But Jehoshaphat distrusted these 400 unanimous voices; it did not seem possible that, after so many persecutions, the call of Ahab could assemble so many true prophets of Jehovah, to speak with sincerity and independence. At his request Micaiah was sent for, who had not previously been called, and who announced a terrible disaster, and the death of Ahab. He nevertheless persisted in marching on Ramoth, and Jehoshaphat accompanied him there. The king of Israel, having learned that the Syrian officers had received orders to single him out personally for attack, disguised himself and mixed with the soldiers, whilst Jehoshaphat wore his royal robes. The Syrians, taking the latter for the king of Israel, directed their attack on him, and surrounded him. Jehoshaphat called for help, but the officers of Ben-hidri discovering their mistake at once retired. At the same time Ahab was mortally wounded by an arrow which a soldier had "shot at a venture"; he died at sunset, and the Israelite army at once retreated. The body of the king was carried to Samaria, where it was buried. His blood-stained chariot was washed in the pool at Samaria, and the words of Elijah were accomplished, that the dogs should lick the blood of Ahab. His son Ahaziah succeeded him.

6. Jehoshaphat returned to Jerusalem, when the prophet Jehu, son ot Hanani, blamed him mildly for having lent his help to the impious Ahab, which he said would have drawn on the king the wrath of Jehovah if he had not deserved the mercy of God, by exterminating idolatry in his kingdom. Jehoshaphat continued to rule over his people in the same spirit of piety, and to introduce notable improvements in the administration; he reformed the tribunals in the principal cities of the kingdom, directing them to observe the greatest impartiality, and he established at Jerusalem a supreme court of appeal, composed of Priests, Levites, and heads of families, as the last resort for difficult cases. After the example of Solomon, Jehoshaphat constructed vessels at Eziongeber, to recommence commercial expeditions to India, and especially to the land of Ophir, but he no longer had Phœnicians to man them, and the vessels being shipwrecked in the very gulf, quite close to Eziongeber, Jehoshaphat gave up the enterprise, in spite of the persuasions of Ahaziah, king of Israel, who wished to become his partner.

7. During the short reign of Ahaziah, which lasted hardly a year, Mesha, king of Moab, who, like his predecessors, had recognised the suzerainty of the king of Israel, refused to pay his tribute. He had formerly paid 100,000 lambs and 100,000 rams, with their wool; for the land of Moab had been at all times rich in flocks and herds, and is so to this day. A severe fall which Ahaziah had through the railing of the platform of the palace of Samaria, prevented him from taking measures for subjecting the Moabites. Brought up in the worship of Baal and in the superstitions of idolatry, Ahaziah sent messengers to Ekron, in the land of the Philistines, to enquire of the celebrated oracle of Baal-zebub what would be the result of his illness. The prophet Elijah, indignant at this insult to the God of Israel, stopped the messengers of

Ahaziah on their way. "Is it not because there is not a God in Israel," said the prophet to them, "that ye go to enquire of Baal-zebub the God of Ekron? Now, therefore, thus saith the Lord, Thou shalt not come down from the bed on which thou art gone up, but shalt surely die" (2 Kings i. 3). This in fact soon happened, and as Ahaziah had no son, his brother Jehoram succeeded him, 898 B.C.

8. The new king of Israel confirmed the alliance his father had concluded with Jehoshaphat, and overthrew the worship of Baal, which his two predecessors had observed, but without, nevertheless, becoming really faithful to the law of God. Jehoram having requested help from Jehoshaphat against the Moabitish rebels, the king of Judah replied, "I am as thou art, my people as thy people, my horses as thy horses." Assisted also by the king of the Idumæans, a vassal of Jehoshaphat, the two allies gained a brilliant victory over the Moabites, whose king was obliged to throw himself into a fortress. The king of Moab, in conformity with the frightful superstition of many oriental people, to propitiate the gods, sacrificed his own son on the wall, in the sight of the besiegers, who, struck with horror, raised the siege. Elisha, the successor of Elijah, showed himself for the first time in the camp on the occasion of this war, and there promised success to the combined arms of Israel and Judah.

Some months after this, the Moabites, having found allies in the Ammonites, and having succeeded in enlisting the Idumæan tribes of Mount Seir, desirous of revenging themselves on Jehoshaphat who had assisted their enemy, suddenly invaded the land of Judah and penetrated as far as Engedi. But a dispute having arisen as to the division of the booty among the undisciplined hordes of invaders, it was easy for the Jewish troops to put them to flight, and to drive them all, in four days, across the frontier. After this event Jehoshaphat still reigned five or six years in peace, blessed by his subjects and respected by the neighbouring people; in the last years of his reign his eldest son Jehoram, brother-in-law to Jehoram king of Israel (for the two Hebrew kingdoms had then at their head princes of the same name), took part in the affairs of state as co-regent. Jehoshaphat died at the age of sixty years (891 B.C.), his people whom he had led back to the true principles of religion, and whom he had endowed with useful institutions, placed on his seven sons their fairest hopes for the future, which but too soon proved false.

9. Jehoram, king of Judah, forgetful of the lessons of his father, and led by his wife, Athaliah, into the wicked ways of Ahab and Jezebel, commenced by the murder of his six brothers and of very many great personages, who probably did not share in his leaning towards Phœnician idolatry. As weak as he was cruel, he soon became an object of contempt to his subjects, and did not know how to make his authority

respected abroad. The Idumæans revolted, and set up an independent king, after having assassinated the Jewish vassal king. Jehoram then marched against the rebels, and obtained a success on the frontiers, but had not sufficient strength to reconquer Idumæa, which remained independent. At the same time, the sacerdotal city Libnah, in the low country of Judæa, refused to obey the impious king.

Hordes of Arabs from the south invaded the unfortunate land of Judah; assisted by the Philistines, they ravaged the country and pillaged the domains of the king, whose sons, with the exception of one named Jehoahaz, or Ahaziah, perished in the conflict. During this time serious dangers threatened the capital of the kingdom of Israel. War had been re-kindled between that kingdom and Damascus. Ben-hidri laid siege to Samaria; and the city, closely blockaded by the enemy, was reduced to such a fearful state of famine, that a mother killed and ate her own child.* Nevertheless, God was willing still to save the people of Israel and give them a great occasion to call to mind His wondrous works to themselves as well as to their fathers. In conformity with a prediction of Elisha, the besieging army, having heard a miraculous noise, was seized with panic; it fled away in the darkness of night, and the pillage of the camp by the Israelites at once restored plenty to Samaria.

10. Elijah, before his disappearance, had announced that the crown of Israel was to be transferred to Jehu, one of the generals of Ahab and Jehoram; and that of Damascus to Hazael, the chief councillor of Ben-hidri. The moment for the accomplishment of this double prophecy had come. Elisha went to Damascus, at a time when Ben-hidri was seriously ill. Informed of the arrival of the prophet, whose reputation was immense, he sent Hazael to him, to ask the issue of his illness (2 Kings viii. 10). "Go and say to him," replied Elisha, "Thou mayest certainly recover; howbeit the Lord hath showed me that he shall surely die." And after having pronounced these words, the prophet fixed for a long time his eyes on Hazael, with a look full of sorrow, and his eyes filled with tears. And Hazael said, "Why weepeth my lord?" And he answered, "Because I know the evil that thou wilt do unto the children of Israel; their strongholds wilt thou set on fire, and their young men thou wilt slay with the sword, and wilt dash their children." And Hazael said, "But what, is thy servant a dog, that he should do this thing?" And Elisha answered, "The Lord hath showed me that thou shalt be king over Syria."

The next day Hazael, impatient to realise the prophecy, suffocated Ben-hidri in his bed, by covering his face with a wet cloth. Having then mounted the throne of Damascus, he continued hostilities against

* See Deut. xxviii. 50—53, and JOSEPHUS, *Wars*, vi., 3, 4.

the kingdom of Samaria. At the same time Jehoram, king of Judah, died at the age of forty years, after horrible suffering from a disease which had lasted two years. His death excited no regret; his body was buried out of the sepulchre of the royal family, and refused the honours due to kings. His son Ahaziah, aged twenty-two years, succeeded him. Completely controlled by his mother, Athaliah, and by the advice of his relations of the family of Ahab, he persisted in the impious course of Jehoram, his father. His maternal uncle, Jehoram, king of Israel, persuaded him to take part in the new expedition he was about to make against the king of Syria, again to attempt the re-conquest of Ramoth-Gilead. Jehoram and Ahaziah went personally to the siege of that city. They managed to get possession of Ramoth; but king Jehoram was seriously wounded, and obliged to retire to Jezreel.

11. The prophet Elisha judged that the time had arrived for the revolution predicted by Elijah, since become even more necessary from the intimate alliance between the two kings of the Hebrew people, and their common tendency to Phœnician idolatry, which threatened to root out the worship of Jehovah. Elisha sent one of his disciples secretly to anoint Jehu as king of Israel. The disciple repaired to Ramoth, where Jehu was, with other captains of the army of Jehoram. No sooner had these officers, companions and friends of Jehu, learned the mission of the prophet, than they solemnly proclaimed him who had been anointed king with sound of the trumpets, and caused him to be recognised by the whole army. Jehu marched at once on Jezreel, where Jehoram was lying sick of his wounds, and where Ahaziah had gone to visit him. Jehoram got into his chariot, and went out of the city to meet the approaching squadron, accompanied by Ahaziah.

The two kings met Jehu near the field which had belonged to Naboth. "Is it peace?" asked Jehoram of his former general. "What peace?" replied Jehu, "so long as the whoredoms of thy mother Jezebel and her witchcrafts are so many." Then Jehoram turned his horses and fled, exclaiming, "There is treachery, O Ahaziah." But at the same instant an arrow, shot by Jehu, pierced him between the shoulders, and stretched him dead in his chariot. Jehu ordered one of his followers to cast the body of Jehoram into the field of Naboth, to avenge the innocent blood shed by Ahab and Jezebel. Ahaziah had taken to flight. Jehu ordered him to be pursued. He was overtaken near Ibleam, mortally wounded, and was carried to Megiddo, where he died. His body was taken to Jerusalem, and buried in the city of David. Jehu, pursuing his work of extermination, entered Jezreel. Lifting his eyes to the windows of the palace, he saw Jezebel, painted and adorned with her best ornaments, looking out. He caused her to be thrown from the window, and she was trodden under the feet of his horses. When a little afterwards he ordered her to be buried, they found only the head, hands, and feet; the rest of her body had been devoured by dogs, according to the prophecy of Elijah.

Seventy sons of Ahab remained at Samaria; they were massacred by the people, and their heads sent to Jezreel. All that remained of the house of Ahab, all the nobles of his court, his friends, and the priests of Baal, perished. The statue of that deity was burnt, and his temple demolished and "made a draft house." But in spite of his zeal for Jehovah, Jehu did not even attempt to re-establish His worship in all its purity; he allowed Jeroboam's golden calves to remain. The prophets, satisfied with their victory, and with the chastisement of the impiety of the royal race, promised continuance to his dynasty; but they were unable to preserve the kingdom of Israel from the attacks which menaced it from without, or to preserve for it that power which it had latterly been on many occasions able to employ, thanks to the close alliance existing between the two courts of Samaria and Jerusalem.

Events, not less sanguinary, had taken place at the same time in the kingdom of Judah. Ahaziah died at the age of twenty-three years. As all the sons he left behind him were under age, Athaliah, his mother, found herself legally invested with the government, as their guardian, with the title of regent. But she conceived the project of assuring the perpetuity of her power, and the final triumph of the worship of Baal at Jerusalem, by the extinction of the house of David. She did not shrink even from a frightful crime to attain that object, and caused all her grandsons, children of Ahaziah, to be slain before her own eyes. She reigned for six years after that odious act, and Baal replaced Jehovah in the worship of the city of David.

SECTION IV.—THE KINGDOMS OF JUDAH AND ISRAEL, FROM THE REIGN OF ATHALIAH TO THE DEATH OF AZARIAH (886—758).

1. NEVERTHELESS, a sister of Ahaziah, Jehosheba, wife of the high priest Jehoiada, had saved one of these victims devoted to death by the ambition of Athaliah, Jehoash, only one year old. The child remained for six years concealed in the Temple, unknown to all except Jehoiada. But in the seventh year, the high priest assembled in the Temple the Levites and the chiefs of the army, he told them that there still remained a son of Ahaziah, showed him to them, and made them swear to recognise and defend him. At this news, and at the sound of the acclamations of the people, who saluted Jehoash, Athaliah ran in, but was at once seized by the orders of the high priest, and put to death; her body, like that of Jezebel, was trodden under the feet of the horses. At the same time the people entered the temple of Baal, overturned his

altars, broke in pieces his images, and put Mattan, the high priest of Baal, to death before the altar.

Jehoash governed during his minority under the advice of the high priest Jehoiada, who found him a docile pupil, giving good hopes of the firm establishment of the national worship. When the king was of proper age, Jehoiada married him to two wives, by whom he had many children of both sexes. One of the first cares of the young prince was the restoration of the Temple of Jerusalem, which had been exposed to every sort of desecration under the preceding reigns. Jehoash directed the priests to employ for that purpose the money arising from redemptions and voluntary gifts, and that they should also make special collections for the repairs of the Temple.

2. During this time the kingdom of Israel grew weaker under the dominion of Jehu. The bravery of that king, and the support he received from the order of prophets, could not protect the country from the invasion of the Syrians, who, led by their king Hazael, occupied all the provinces situated east of the Jordan, and there exercised cruelties which were long remembered. It evidently was to obtain support against these redoubtable enemies that Jehu humbly solicited the favour of Shalmanezer IV., king of Assyria. In the cuneiform inscriptions on the "black obelisk," now preserved in the British Museum, this last prince says, "I received tribute from Jehu, son of Omri—silver, gold, plates of gold, cups of gold, vases of various kinds in gold, sceptres for the hand of the king;" and one of the bas-reliefs of the same monument shows Jehu prostrating himself, with his face to the earth, before the Assyrian monarch, as if acknowledging himself a vassal. Jehu died in the twenty-eighth year of his reign (858), leaving the throne to his son Jehoahaz.*

Hazael continued his attacks on the kingdom of Israel, under its new prince, who was far from showing his father Jehu's zeal for the worship of Jehovah; images of Ashtoreth were again seen even in Samaria. The army of Jehoahaz, decimated by continual battles, was reduced to 10,000 infantry, fifty horsemen, and ten war chariots. Nevertheless, with this feeble remnant, encouraged probably by the prophets, whose favour Jehoahaz managed to gain by his repentance, he contrived to hold the Syrian troops in check, and to re-establish tranquillity for a time. Jehoahaz died in the seventeenth year of his reign. His son Jehoash succeeded to the throne; and so, for the second time, the two Hebrew kingdoms were under the government of princes of the same name.

---

* The celebrity of Omri, the founder of Samaria, was such that the Assyrians believed that all the kings of Israel, as well as Jehu, were descended from him.

3. Jehoash, king of Judah, persevered in religious orthodoxy, in fidelity to the precepts of the law, and docility to the councils of the sanctuary, so long as the high priest Jehoiada survived, who lived, it is said, to the age of 130 years. The respect which Jehoiada had inspired was so great, that he was buried in the royal sepulchre. But after the death of the venerable high priest, the favourers of the Phœnician worship ventured again to hold up their heads, and Jehoash had the weakness to show them culpable toleration. It was in vain that the prophets lifted up their voices; the high priest Zachariah, son of Jehoiada, having dared one day, in the court of the Temple, to reproach the people with this defection, and to menace them with Divine chastisement, was stoned by order of the ungrateful king, and expired, crying out, "The Lord look upon it and require it" (2 Chron. xxiv. 22). The chastisement of Jehovah was not, in fact, long delayed. In the year following, Hazael having penetrated with his army as far as Gath, which he conquered, threatened to besiege Jerusalem; and the weak Jehoash could only escape from his enemies by paying to the king of Syria a disgraceful tribute, for which he employed the treasures of the Temple. This event caused a conspiracy to break out, contrived, it may be, by the priests, who wished to avenge the death of Zachariah. Jehoash was assassinated by two of his servants, after an inglorious reign, which had lasted forty years (839). He was refused burial in the royal sepulchre.

Amaziah, son of Jehoash, reigned next, for twenty-nine years; he made himself, no doubt, agreeable to the priests and prophets, by dealing severely with the partisans of the Phœnician worship, for the only accusation brought against him is, that he allowed the irregular sanctuaries of the high places still to exist. As soon as he was firm on his throne, he punished with death the murderers of his father; but he is praised for the pardon which, in conformity with the Mosaic law, he extended to the children of the guilty (2 Chron. xxv. 4). An expedition, he undertook against the Idumæans, was crowned with brilliant success; after having vanquished them in battle, he possessed himself of their capital, *Sela*, which, in later times, was called by the Greeks *Petra*.

4. About the same epoch Jehoash, king of Israel, gained equally signal advantages over the Syrians. Hazael had died at a very advanced age, and his son Ben-hidri, the third of the name who is mentioned in the Bible, had succeeded him. Jehoash, encouraged by the last dying words of the prophet Elisha, attacked and defeated Ben-hidri, and took from him all the cities which Hazael had taken from Jehoahaz. But he was arrested in the midst of these successes by the incursions of some Moabitish bands, which caused him much disquiet; afterwards war broke out between him and Amaziah, king of Judah. The troops of

the latter were totally defeated and put to flight, and Amaziah fell alive into the hands of his enemies. Jehoash marched at once on Jerusalem, and entered it through a breach in the wall; he carried off the treasures that remained in the Temple and in the king's palace, and returned to Samaria, taking with him numerous hostages, probably in exchange for Amaziah, whom he released. Scripture represents this misfortune of Amaziah as the just punishment of his infidelity to Jehovah, for it accuses him of having worshipped the deities of the Idumæans, after the victory which he had gained over that people, and of threatening the prophet who ventured to reprimand him.

Jehoash, king of Israel, died in the sixteenth year of his reign (827), leaving as successor his son Jeroboam II. Some years after this (810), Amaziah, like his father, was assassinated at Lachish, where he had taken refuge from conspirators; his body was brought to Jerusalem, and buried in the sepulchre of the kings.

5. Uzziah, otherwise called Azariah, his son and successor, whose accession was hailed with joy by all the people, calmed the disorders of parties, and promised Judah a time of good fortune and power. The young king displayed much attachment to the worship of Jehovah, and it appears that a prophet, named Zechariah, exercised a most happy influence over him. In the early years of his reign he secured the submission of the Idumæans, by retaking and fortifying the city of Elath, on the Elanitic Gulf. He also made conquests over the Philistines, retook Gath, and even possessed himself of Ashdod, which he fortified. He subdued lastly the Ammonites, whom he made to pay tribute, as well as the Arabs of Gurbaal.

In spite of his warlike character, Uzziah did not the less favour the arts of peace; whilst he renewed and augmented the defences of all the cities of his kingdom, he actively encouraged the progress of agriculture, and had in his service a number of agricultural labourers and vine dressers. His flocks covered the plains; in those parts of the deserts suitable for pasture he had many cisterns dug, and built towers to protect the shepherds. His reign, which lasted nearly fifty-two years, was one of the most glorious in the history of the Hebrews. But towards the close of his reign, Uzziah, puffed up by his military successes and his prosperity, attempted the same usurpation as Saul. He wished, in contempt of the law, and in spite of the protests of the priests, to assume sacerdotal functions. He was suddenly struck with leprosy, at the moment when he was himself offering incense at the altar of incense. He was obliged, king though he was, to shut himself up, in conformity with the Mosaic ordinances; and this prince was condemned to end his days in the most complete isolation. His son Jotham became regent.

6. The kingdom of Israel had again become very powerful under

Jeroboam II., who, following up the success obtained by his father over the Syrians, attacked them on their own territory, and made conquests in the neighbourhood of Damascus and Hamath. It appears even from a passage in the Book of Kings (2 Kings xiv. 28) that the Israelites occupied these two cities for some time. All the country east of the Jordan, from Hamath to the Dead Sea, was again brought under the dominion of the king of Samaria. The prophet Jonah, son of Amittai, of the tribe of Zebulon, had encouraged king Jeroboam to this war, and predicted its complete success. This sudden good fortune of the kingdom of Israel introduced into it riches and luxury, and all the evils of corrupt society were soon to be seen there. The prophet Amos, a simple shepherd of Tekoa, in the land of Judah, presented himself at Bethel, and in language full of energy, boldness, and ardent zeal for truth and justice, reproached Israel for the worship of the images at Bethel and Dan, their effeminacy and licentious luxury, and the injustice and oppression to which they subjected the poor; he threatened Jeroboam and the nobles of Samaria with the anger of heaven, and in the midst of their careless security he unfolded to them the distant prospect of exile and death. Already the Assyrian power was menacing, and all Western Asia trembled at the news of its rapid progress. Amaziah, high priest of Bethel, desired Jeroboam to put Amos to death; but the king confined himself to expelling the prophet from his territories.

7. From this time, especially, the noblest development of prophecy commences. Protesting against idolatry, and even against too strong an attachment to the purely exterior forms of the worship of Jehovah, against the corruption of morals, the faults or tyranny of kings; the prophets were at once preachers and political orators. Inspired by the Spirit of God, who unveiled to them the future, they began to predict the splendors of the new Jerusalem, and to announce in the most precise terms the advent of the Saviour promised to Israel and to all nations.

Together with Amos there was the prophet Joel, the son of Pethuel, whose predictions have come down to us. And at the same time, Isaiah began to prophesy, whose writings were deposited in the Temple at Jerusalem, and preserved with religious care. The words of this great prophet point above all to the promised and expected Messiah: "Behold my servant, whom I uphold; mine elect, in whom my soul delighteth; I have put my spirit upon him: he shall bring forth judgment to the Gentiles" (xlii. 1). "He shall see of the travail of his soul and be satisfied: by his knowledge shall my righteous servant justify many; for he shall bear their iniquities" (liii. 11). "Arise, shine; for thy light is come, and the glory of the Lord is risen upon thee. For behold, the darkness shall cover the earth, and gross darkness the people: but the Lord shall arise upon thee, and his glory shall be seen upon thee. And the Gentiles shall come to thy light, and kings to the brightness of thy rising" (lx. 1—3).

8. Jeroboam II. died in the forty-first year of his reign (784), and the dates of the Book of Kings leave us to infer that his son Zachariah did not ascend the throne till eleven or twelve years after (773). It is probable that at the death of Jeroboam the kingdom of Israel was divided by factions; either Zachariah was too young to reign, or he was too weak to put down the seditious, who disputed the throne with him, or wished to annihilate royalty. The words of the prophet Hosea, who partly belongs to this epoch, confirm these suppositions. The prophet says, "Their heart is divided; now shall they be found faulty; he shall break down their altars, he shall spoil their images. For now they shall say, We have no king, because we feared not the Lord; what then should a king do to us? They have spoken words, swearing falsely in making a covenant: thus judgment springeth up as hemlock in the furrows of the field" (Hos. x. 2).

Zachariah at last established himself on the throne of his father, in the thirty-eighth year of the reign of Uzziah, king of Judah, but he reigned only six months. A rebel, named Shallum, son of Jabesh, assassinated him in the presence of the people, probably during a riot, and possessed himself of the throne. Thus ended in its turn the dynasty of Jehu; for none of those families, who successively raised themselves to the throne of Israel, could ever keep it for more than a few generations. Shallum only maintained himself for a month. Menahem, son of Gadi, who commanded the army, and was then at Tirzah, marched against him, and, having taken Samaria, slew the assassin of the king, ascended the throne, and sat there for ten years. A town named Tiphsah, situated, according to all appearances, near Tirzah, which had not recognised Menahem as king, was taken by storm, and punished by the new king with the most implacable cruelty.

9. Pul, king of Chaldæa and Assyria, then invaded Syria and threatened the kingdom of Israel. Menahem, unable to fight against so powerful an enemy, extorted from the country 1,000 talents, or three millions of shekels of silver, to give to Pul, and thus ransomed his army at the price of fifty shekels of silver a head, which shows that it numbered 60,000 men.* In return for this humiliation, which recalls to us that of Jehu before Shalmaneser, Pul consented to withdraw his troops, and to give his powerful assistance to Menahem, against those internal enemies who contested his possession of the usurped throne.

But such conduct could only augment the hatred of the nation to

* It seems, however, doubtful whether the sum of fifty shekels was not the amount extorted from each individual rather than the ransom given for each soldier.—Tr.

Menahem and his family. His son Pekahiah succeeded him in the fiftieth year of the reign of Uzziah, king of Judah (761). After two years one of his officers, Pekah, son of Remaliah, with fifty men of Gilead, formed a conspiracy against and assassinated him in the palace of Samaria (759). After this crime, Pekah ascended the throne. The prophet Hosea unfolds to our eyes a dark picture of this period of anarchy and crime. "The Lord," says he, "hath a controversy with the inhabitants of the land, because there is no truth, nor mercy, nor knowledge of God in the land. By swearing, and lying, and killing, and stealing, and committing adultery, they break out, and blood toucheth blood. Therefore shall the land mourn, and every one that dwelleth therein shall languish, with the beasts of the field, and with the fowls of heaven; yea, the fishes of the sea also shall be taken away" (Hos. iv. 1—4). "They all are hot as an oven, and have devoured their judges; all their kings are fallen: there is none among them that calleth upon me" (vii. 7). "They have set up kings, but not by me: they have made princes, and I knew it not: of their silver and their gold have they made them idols, that they may be cut off" (viii. 4). Towards the end of the second year of Pekah (758), Uzziah, king of Judah, died in the hospital at Jerusalem, to which he had been compelled to retire, at the age of sixty-eight, and after a reign of fifty-two years. His son Jotham, the regent, succeeded him.

Section V.—Intervention of the Assyrians in Palestine. Decline of the Kingdom of Israel and Fall of Samaria. (758—721).

1. Jotham, who at the age of twenty-five years succeeded his father on the throne of Judah, distinguished himself by his energy and piety, and his reign was one of the happiest in the annals of Judah. The Bible nevertheless blames him for having allowed the high places still to exist, and permitting the people to offer sacrifices there. To the fortifications erected by his father, he added others as a preparation for the dangers threatening the land. He restored the Temple, and erected some important works at Jerusalem. He fought with success against the Ammonites, and compelled them during three years to pay a considerable tribute. During this time internal disorders, occasioned by the conflicting claims of many competitors for the throne, continued as violent as ever in the kingdom of Israel. The Book of Kings assigns eight years less for the reign of Pekah than the period which elapsed between his first accession to the throne and his death. But this strange circumstance

is explained by the Assyrian inscriptions,* the historical bearing of which was first pointed out by M. Oppert. It is found that the reign of Pekah was interrupted for more than seven years; that about 742 he was deposed by a second Menahem, probably a son of Pekahiah, who was placed on the throne by Tiglath-pileser II., king of Assyria, to whom he paid tribute as a vassal. In 733 a new revolution dethroned him and restored Pekah. The latter, openly hostile to the Assyrians, whose vassal he had dethroned, made an alliance with Resin, king of Damascus. These two princes, even in the time of Pekah's first reign, had formed the project of overturning the throne of the house of David and installing as king in Jerusalem a certain Ben Tabeal, a creature of their own,† in order, probably, to oppose a more compact force to the Assyrians; but the wise measures of Jotham did not permit them to carry their project into execution. Unfortunately, however, Jotham died, after a reign of sixteen years, when he was hardly forty-two years old (742).

2. His son and successor, Ahaz, a young man about twenty years of age, possessed none of his father's good qualities. He, by his own example, encouraged Phœnician idolatry; he erected statues of Baal, and went so far as even to take part in the abominable worship of Moloch, by making his son pass through the fire in the valley of Hinnom. Weak and timid, he could not compel the respect of his powerful neighbours; in the very beginning of his reign, Pekah and Resin invaded the land of Judah, and Jerusalem was threatened with a siege. Ahaz resolved to throw himself into the arms of the king of Assyria, and to purchase his help by a disgraceful tribute. The prophet Isaiah in vain attempted to deter him by advice and threats.

The danger passed away from Jerusalem itself, but Pekah inflicted serious losses on the troops of Ahaz. Carrying out, then, his unpatriotic project, the king of Judah called in to his assistance Tiglath-pileser, whose protection he purchased with the treasures of the Temple and of the palace. The Assyrian monarch, always anxious for new conquests, and desirous of adopting that policy of his predecessors of which Palestine had been the object, did not make him wait long. He invaded the kingdom of Damascus, took the capital, killed Resin, and united the states that prince had governed to his own vast empire. A great part of the inhabitants of the kingdom of Damascus were trans-

---

* LAYARD, *Cuneiform Inscriptions*, plate 50. *Cuneiform Inscriptions of Western Asia*, vol. ii., plate 67.

† This project seems to have been conceived and even attempted in the time of Jotham, but more fully carried out after the accession of Ahaz. Compare 2 Kings xv. 37, and Isaiah vii. 1—6.—TR.

ported into Armenia, to the banks of the river Cyrus.* From Syria Tiglath-pileser penetrated into the land of Israel, and occupied the whole of Galilee and Peræa, whence he transported the principal inhabitants to Assyria (732). This was the commencement of the captivity of the ten tribes, and the kingdom of Israel was henceforth confined to the limits of the small tract around Samaria. Pekah, the king, was shortly after assassinated, the victim of a conspiracy, at the head of which was Hoshea, son of Elah, who wished to place himself on the throne.

Ahaz visited the king of Assyria at Damascus, to pay homage as a vassal. On this occasion, having seen the great altar at Damascus, he sent the pattern of it to the high priest Urijah at Jerusalem, ordering him to set up a similar one in the court of the Temple.† The new altar, charged with idolatrous symbols, replaced that which Solomon had constructed. Not content with this profanation, Ahaz, on his return to Jerusalem, set up altars everywhere to Syrian deities, and ended by entirely closing the sanctuary of the true God. He had, however, no cause to congratulate himself on the Assyrian alliance, which he had so dearly purchased, and he soon found how galling were the bonds of vassalage he had voluntarily assumed. The Idumæans made incursions into the territory of Judah, for the purpose of pillage. At the same time the Philistines, profiting by the weakness of Ahaz, took some important cities. Ahaz died in the sixteenth year of his reign (727); though still young, he was not regretted, and was refused even the honours of royal sepulture. He left, in his son Hezekiah, a successor who afforded the brightest hopes to the kingdom. In his earliest years, the prophet Isaiah had announced him as a saviour to Judah, who should re-establish the renown of the house of David.

3. Hezekiah exhibited in every respect the most complete contrast to his father; he manifested the most ardent zeal for religion, from the moment of his accession to the throne; he re-opened the Temple, which had been closed by Ahaz. Everywhere the statues of Phœnician divinities were broken in pieces, and he even suppressed the high places, where worship, although addressed to Jehovah, was in illegal rivalry with the central sanctuary, and contrary to the prescriptions of the Mosaic law. Wishing to destroy all that could give occasion for

* Now the Kur, between the Caspian and Black Seas. A full description of this river and district is given in Sir R. Ker Porter's Travels, vol. i., 107—113.—Tr.

† The majority of Assyrian altars, however, seem to have been free from emblems of any kind. Some of them were square, ornamented with gradines; others triangular, with circular tops. One of the latter description, discovered by Mr. Layard, is in the British Museum.—Tr.

idolatry, Hezekiah broke in pieces the brazen serpent which Moses had made to set up in the desert, and which had become the object of superstitious worship to the people. The first Passover after the accession of Hezekiah was celebrated with extraordinary solemnity; the king sent messengers to Samaria, and to all that remained of the kingdom of Judah, to invite the attendance of all who were still faithful to the law of the Lord. A small number did come to Jerusalem, but the majority of the population insulted and maltreated Hezekiah's messengers. Completing his reforms, the pious king reorganised the body of priests and Levites, under the auspices of the high priest Azariah.

4. During this time the last hour of the kingdom of Samaria was fast approaching. "For so it was," says Scripture (2 Kings xvii. 7), "that the children of Israel had sinned against the Lord their God, which had brought them out of the land of Egypt." Ver. 16, 17—"And they left all the commandments of the Lord their God, and made them molten images, even two calves, and made a grove, and worshipped all the host of heaven, and served Baal. And they caused their sons and their daughters to pass through the fire, and used divination and enchantments, and sold themselves to do evil in the sight of the Lord, to provoke him to anger." In vain had the prophets multiplied their warnings, Israel had remained deaf to all threats; and even the invasion of the king of Assyria, carrying into captivity a part of the people, had not led the rest of them to repentance.

The day of Divine chastisement, therefore, had at last arrived. Hoshea, the assassin of Pekah, had succeeded in mounting the throne, three years before the accession of Hezekiah (730); he was a vassal of the king of Assyria, and paid tribute to Shalmaneser VII.,* successor of Tiglath-pileser. We know from the writings of the prophets of this epoch, that in the kingdom of Israel, as well as in that of Judah, there were always advocates of an alliance with Egypt, then governed by the warlike Shebek, the So of the Bible, who alone seemed able to oppose the invasions of Assyria, and who himself was interested in keeping at a distance from his frontiers a power whose thirst for foreign conquest seemed unable to confine itself to Asia. The prophets distrusted such an alliance, and expressed their disapprobation with energy. King Hoshea, nevertheless, expected to find in it a means of safety. He signed a treaty with So, and immediately refused his tribute to the king of Assyria. Shalmaneser, at this news, burst like a thunderbolt on the land of Israel, seized Hoshea and threw him into prison, occupied the whole country, and laid siege to Samaria, the capital, where

* Shalmaneser IV., according to Sir H. Rawlinson. See Tabular List of Assyrian Kings at the end of Book IV.

the turbulent and warlike Ephraimite aristocracy had fortified themselves (723). Samaria made an obstinate resistance to the enemy's attacks, and the siege operations were at length relaxed on the part of the Assyrians, and turned into a blockade. Important events had in fact occurred at Nineveh; Shalmaneser was dead, and Sargon had usurped power. At last, in the third year of the siege, the new king came himself to Samaria; he renewed the operations with vigor, and the last bulwark of Israelitish independence was swept away (721). According to the practice constantly adopted by the Assyrian conquerors of that epoch, all the principal inhabitants who could give any cause for apprehension, especially the rich and warlike, were compelled to emigrate, and the conquered country was re-peopled successively under Sargon and his successors, by different races of the vast Assyrian empire, chiefly from Chaldæa.

At the moment when the kingdom of Israel thus fell a victim to internal strife, to military revolutions, and to false policy, the kingdom of Judah was reanimated with new life under king Hezekiah. There, in spite of the failings of very many kings, and of a portion of the people, the central sanctuary and the dynasty of David had always withstood the irruption of the irreligion, and of the political passions which had proved so disastrous to Israel. The prophets were more listened to, the priests exercised a greater influence, and both the State and David's dynasty had owed to them their safety in the perilous days of Athaliah. Israel had but a few days of greatness and happiness under king Jeroboam II., whilst Judah enjoyed long years of glory and prosperity under the happy reigns of Asa, Jehoshaphat and Uzziah. Besides, the geographical position of Judah was much more advantageous, and Jerusalem above all occupied a very defensible position.*

Sargon did not attempt to subdue the kingdom of Judah; Samaria taken, he marched with all speed to the land of the Philistines, there to meet Shebek, king of Egypt, who, not having been able to come soon enough to save Israel, entered Palestine at that moment. After having vanquished him at Raphia, and compelled the Philistine cities to obedience, the Assyrian conqueror, retracing his steps, penetrated into Phœnicia, where he took all the cities with the exception of Tyre. But, occupied by these conquests, he left Hezekiah and the kingdom of Judah in tranquillity.

---

* See BERNHARDI. *Commentatio de causis quibus effectum sit ut Regnum Judæ diutius permaneret quam Regnum Israel.* Louvain, 1825.

SECTION VI.—THE KINGDOM OF JUDAH, FROM THE CAPTURE OF SAMARIA TO THE BATTLE OF MEGIDDO (721—610).

1. THE historical books of the Bible tell us nothing of what passed in the kingdom of Judah during the twenty years of profound peace which Hezekiah enjoyed after the terror the conquest of Samaria by Sargon and the establishment of Assyrian garrisons on the very frontiers of his state must have caused him. But the writings of the prophet Isaiah give us a lively picture of the moral and political condition of the people of Judah at this period of their history. Happy in its king, and trusting surely in the valour of its soldiers, Judæa was nevertheless troubled by the intrigues of a party who, instead of seeking safety in piety and faith in Jehovah, breathed only war, and counted on the chariots and horses of Egypt, which the prophet pronounced useless, and even dangerous, to Judah. This party, numbering in its ranks important personages, and even priests and prophets, misconceived the true spiritual sense of the religious precepts of the law, and attached itself almost entirely to outward observances. It abandoned itself to the indulgence of its passions, violated right, and oppressed the people. The land, said Isaiah, can never enjoy real happiness till God has punished these impious people with exemplary chastisement.

2. In spite of the influence which Isaiah exercised over king Hezekiah, the party for war at any price, and for an Egyptian alliance, prevailed at the court of Jerusalem, when in 704 Sargon died, leaving Babylon separated from his kingdom by a most serious revolt. All the nations of Palestine thought to find in this change of masters a favourable opportunity for throwing off the Assyrian yoke. A general coalition of their princes was organised under the auspices and with the concurrence of the Ethiopian Shabatok, the Sethos of Herodotus, who then reigned over Egypt. The petty sovereigns of the cities of Phœnicia, and of the Philistine towns, the kings of Ammon, Moab, and Edom, all at the same time refused tribute, and allied themselves with Hezekiah who opened hostilities by taking Migron,* a town of the tribe of Benjamin, on the frontier of the former kingdom of Israel, which Sargon had detached from the kingdom of Judah, and where he had installed one of his own creatures with the title of king.

But the new king who was about to mount the throne of Assyria was the terrible Sennacherib. He allowed more than three years to elapse before he came to chastise the audacity of the princes of Palestine, being occupied in putting down the insurrections of the Chaldæan

---

* It must be mentioned that Sir H. Rawlinson reads this name Ekron. See note to Book iv., chap. iii., sec. 3, 2.—TR.

Merodach Baladan, and in reducing Babylon to obedience, and afterwards in repressing the desire for revolt that had been manifested in the turbulent provinces situated to the north and east of Assyria. But as soon as he was thus well secured against all chance of insurrections, which, breaking out in his rear, might compel him to retrace his steps after reaching the territory of Palestine, he marched on that country at the head of all the forces of his empire. He threw himself first on Phœnicia, defeated Luliya (Eululæus) king of Tyre, who had then the suzerainty over the other Phœnician cities. All submitted to him, and the terrified kings of Ammon, Moab and Edom hastened—to use a modern Oriental expression—to beg *Amaun* without having attempted to fight. Sennacherib, advancing by the sea coast, entered the country of the Philistines, whom he crushed; defeated in their territory an Egyptian army advancing to help them, and finally arrived at Migron, where he re-established the prince, his creature, whom Hezekiah had dethroned.

3. Hezekiah was left alone after the defeat of his allies. From this time it is that the Bible narrative commences, for it is silent as to the events which led to the invasion of the kingdom of Judah by Sennacherib, and it is only from the inscriptions of the Assyrian king that we have been able to relate them.* Sennacherib, according to the Book of Kings, which here completely agrees with the inscribed monuments of Assyria, invaded the territory of Judah, possessed himself successively of all its fortresses, led away a considerable part of its people into captivity, and at last came in person to Jerusalem. Hezekiah, to save his capital and the Temple from the profanation with which they were menaced by Sennacherib's army, humbled himself before the king of Assyria, who imposed on him a tribute of 30 talents of gold and 300 talents of silver. To pay this, Hezekiah cut oft even the gold which covered the doors of the Temple, probably with the wish of making the Assyrians believe that his treasury was not sufficient to pay so considerable a sum, and that nothing more was possible, for, less than a year after, he was found making a parade of his treasures before the Babylonian ambassadors. Sennacherib left, after having received this tribute, to press the siege of the very strong fortress of Lachish, in the plain country of Judah, which was soon forced to surrender. At the same time his outposts were advanced as far as Pelusium, on the frontiers of Egypt, for he intended to invade that country after having completed the subjugation of Judæa.

But while encamped before Lachish, Sennacherib conceived the idea that it would be imprudent, just when he was about to march into Egypt, to leave behind him a city so important as Jerusalem without securing it

* See OPPERT, *Les Inscriptions des Sargonides*, p. 44, *seq.*

by a garrison. He therefore sent a strong body of troops to reduce the capital of Judah. Hezekiah decided on resistance by the advice of Isaiah, who had regained his legitimate ascendancy over him, and neglected nothing to put Jerusalem into a defensible state. He covered up the springs that might furnish the assailants with water, repaired the walls wherever there were breaches, demolished the houses likely to interfere with the defence, and diverted the water of the fountain of Siloam into the city.

Very soon the general-in-chief of the Assyrian army (Tartan), the grand cupbearer of the king (Rab-shakeh), and the chief of the eunuchs (Rab Saris),* presented themselves before the walls, bearing the summons of Sennacherib. Hezekiah sent three officers to confer with them. The grand cupbearer spoke, and in haughty language ridiculed the plans for defence, and the bravery which the king of Judah boasted of, and called Egypt, whence Hezekiah expected aid, a bruised reed, which could only wound the hand that should lean on it. "But if ye say unto me," he added, "We trust in the Lord our God, is it not he whose high places and whose altars Hezekiah hath taken away, and hath said to Judah and to Jerusalem, Ye shall worship before this altar in Jerusalem. Now therefore give pledges to my lord, the king of Assyria, and I will deliver to thee 2,000 horses if thou be able on thy part to set riders on them. * * Am I now come up without the Lord against this place to destroy it? The Lord said to me, Go up against this land and destroy it." The servants of Hezekiah asked him to speak in Syriac, so as not to be understood by the people who were on the wall, but the Assyrian replied that it was precisely to those men who were in danger of dying of hunger and thirst that his words were addressed; then raising his voice he spoke to the soldiers of Hezekiah in the Hebrew tongue, saying that their king was deceiving them, and that he had no power to save them; that the king of Assyria, on the other hand, offered them good fortune and tranquillity, and would lead them away to a land more fertile than their own, and moreover that Jehovah would no more save them than other gods had saved their own countries. This speech was listened to in profound silence, Hezekiah having forbidden any reply.

Hezekiah and the people went into the Temple, with their clothes rent, to prostrate themselves before Jehovah, and implore His compassion. Isaiah encouraged them, promising them in the name of God a speedy deliverance. Nevertheless Sennacherib, having taken Lachish, had encamped at Libnah on his way to Jerusalem. He there learned

---

* Most histories consider these as three personages, whom they call Tartan, Rab-shakeh and Rabsaris, taking their titles for proper names.

the approach of Tirhakah, prince royal of Ethiopia and Egypt, entrusted with the command of the army by Sabatok, the king, who, at the head of a numerous body of troops, recruited chiefly on the borders of the Upper Nile, advanced along the Delta, and was preparing to enter Palestine, there to engage the Assyrians. The position of Sennacherib might have become very perilous if Tirhakah had attacked him before he had completely subdued the kingdom of Judah. In this position of affairs he resolved to hasten the attack on Jerusalem, and sent to Hezekiah a new summons still more imperative than the former, and which left him hardly a few days for consideration. The king read the letter, and went to the Temple and addressed a fervent prayer to the Lord, asking Him to avenge the outrage done to His name. Then Isaiah, filled with Divine inspiration, announced to the king and people that Jehovah had heard his prayer, and that very soon Sion and Jerusalem would regard with scorn the humbled pride of Sennacherib, and that he should not even attempt to besiege Jerusalem. In fact, in the following night "the angel of the Lord went out, and smote in the camp of the Assyrians an hundred and four score and five thousand" (2 Kings xix. 35), killed by the plague, which suddenly broke out in the midst of the army.* With troops thus thinned by disease, Sennacherib could no longer think of taking Jerusalem, nor of making head against the numerous and fresh army Tirhakah was bringing up; he hastily gave orders to retreat, and during the remainder of his reign did not again appear in Palestine. Hezekiah again took possession of his devastated territory, and even of a number of the cities of Ephraim formerly belonging to the kingdom of Israel; and which, throwing off the Assyrian yoke, gave themselves up to him. As for the Egyptians, content with being no longer threatened, they do not appear to have pursued Sennacherib in his retreat, and they allowed him to retain possession of the land of the Philistines as far as Gaza.

When Herodotus visited Egypt the priests related to him this miraculous event, which had saved that country as well as the kingdom of Judah from an Assyrian invasion, only, as was natural, they attributed the prodigy to the power of their own gods (HER. ii. 141).

4. Judah was delivered from the Assyrians; but the army of Sennacherib in its retreat had left the plague, as a last scourge, behind it. Hezekiah was attacked, and his life was despaired of. The pious king implored the Lord with tears, begging to live long enough to have an heir who might ensure to the house of David the succession to the crown. God heard his prayer, and Isaiah was commissioned to announce

* It has been suggested that the number recorded as slain in the Assyrian camp may be read as 100 + 80 + 5,000 = 5,180, instead of 185,000 as usually understood.—TR.

to the king his speedy recovery, in spite of the prognostications of his physicians.

The check which Sennacherib had sustained had spread throughout all Asia the renown of the kingdom of Judah, the only one to escape the redoubtable conqueror before whom all trembled. So that before long ambassadors arrived at Jerusalem from Merodach-Baladan, who had revolted at Babylon against the Assyrian yoke, and expected an immediate attack from Sennacherib. They came under the pretext of congratulating Hezekiah on his recovery, but in reality to propose an alliance against the common enemy. Hezekiah, flattered by this proceeding, with most imprudent vanity exhibited to the envoys of the Babylonian prince his treasures, magazines and arsenals. Isaiah, the constant counsellor of the king, knew the fresh dangers to which an alliance with the Babylonian insurgents might expose the kingdom, and enlightened by prophetic foresight said to the king, "Behold the days come that all that is in thy house, and that which thy fathers have laid up in store unto this day, shall be carried into Babylon: nothing shall be left, saith the Lord. And of thy sons that shall issue from thee, which thou shalt beget, they shall take away; and they shall be eunuchs in the palace of the king of Babylon." The decisive defeat of Merodach-Baladan, only a few months later, did not, moreover, permit Hezekiah to carry out the desire which he seems to have had to listen to these proposals.

5. Hezekiah passed the rest of his life in profound peace and in endeavouring to repair the numberless evils which the army of Sennacherib had left behind it. He amassed, as provision for the future, great treasures, levied numerous troops, established magazines and arsenals, and rebuilt the fortifications of his cities. Three years after the Assyrian invasion his wife gave him a son, whom he named Manasseh, and who appears to have been associated with him on the throne from the time of his birth, for the Book of Kings counts the years of his reign from that time (697).

Under the reign of Hezekiah, Hebrew literature, which had declined since the epoch of Solomon, received a fresh impulse, and this became the golden age of prophetic poetry. By the side of Isaiah we find, at the court of the king, the prophet Micah, of Moresheth, near Gath. It most probably was towards the end of the reign of Hezekiah that Nahum pronounced the sublime prophecy, in which, at the very moment of the most brilliant prosperity of Nineveh, he announced its approaching ruin. A passage in the Book of Proverbs (Prov. xxv. 1), gives us to understand that Hezekiah established a sort of academy, charged with collecting and arranging ancient literary remains, and especially the proverbs attributed to Solomon. The beautiful poem composed by Hezekiah after his sickness, entitles the king to be reckoned among the best poets of the period. Hezekiah died at the age of fifty-four years, in the forty-first year of his reign (685).* His funeral was celebrated with great pomp, and amidst the universal regrets of his people.

6. Manasseh was but twelve years old when he ascended the throne of his father Hezekiah, 685. The prophet Isaiah was now too old to exercise a serious influence over the affairs of the country and the destinies of the young prince. The anti-religious party, who found a strong support in the evil passions of the masses, and whom Hezekiah had been able to put down for a time, but not to subdue permanently, again lifted its head, succeeded in influencing the young king, and gave itself up to disorders all the more assiduously that it had to revenge on the priests and prophets the severe restrictions from which it had suffered, and wished now to end for ever. It was under the influence of this party that Manasseh was educated, for in no other way can be explained the terrible reaction which took place under the son of the pious Hezekiah. Manasseh combined in himself the impiety of Ahab and the cruelty of Jezebel. He re-established the worship of Baal and of Ashtaroth, and even in the courts of the Temple he erected altars dedicated to the worship of the stars. At the entry of the Temple were horses and chariots, emblems of the god Baal, considered as the sun; and the sanctuary was profaned by the abominable mysteries of Ashtaroth, celebrated by debauchery. Manasseh made his son pass through the fire in honour of Moloch, and gave himself up to all sorts of evil and superstitious practices, such as divination and necromancy. Many prophets ventured to raise their voices against these abominations, and to predict for Jerusalem and for Manasseh the fate of Samaria and of the house of Ahab; but they were not heeded, and death was the reward of their devotion; for Manasseh, says Scripture, "shed innocent blood very much, till he had filled Jerusalem from one end to another."

A tradition of the synagogue, adopted by the early fathers, says that Isaiah was among the number of the martyrs of this epoch. Manasseh,

---

* This date is entirely different from that which we find in all histories up to this time (697). But the whole chronology of this epoch needs now to be re-cast, taking as a starting point the date of the expedition of Sennacherib, definitely fixed by the monuments for the year 700 B.C. Evidently, when the Book of Kings gives but twenty-nine years for the reign of Hezekiah, it stops its calculation at the birth of Manasseh, and his association on his father's throne in 697. It reckons, also, the years of Manasseh's reign from the same date, although he did not reign alone, and in reality till 685, when he was twelve years old, that is fifteen years after the invasion of the Assyrians, as the Bible expressly says.

wearied by his reproaches, caused him to be sawn asunder between two planks.

Conduct so wicked, of necessity drew down on the king of Judah the punishments which Divine Providence keeps always in reserve for great criminals. Esarhaddon, king of Assyria, one of the last of the great Assyrian conquerors, set on foot an expedition to reduce to obedience the revolted Phœnician cities. After having taken and burnt Sidon, and received the submission of the other cities, he marched on the kingdom of Judah, defeated the army, took Jerusalem, made Manasseh prisoner, and confined him at Babylon; there the latter repented of his conduct, and prayed to God, who heard him. Restored to Jerusalem after a captivity of some length, by order of Esarhaddon, and re-established on the throne, on the condition of recognising the suzerainty of the Assyrian monarch and paying him tribute, he overthrew the idols, and re-established the altar of Jehovah. But his repentance was not of long duration; after a time he recommenced the wicked ways which had led to his misfortunes, and Jeremiah attests that the end of the reign of Manasseh was as full of the same impiety and the same crimes as the commencement. Manasseh died in 642, at the age of fifty-five years. His corpse was refused royal sepulture.

7. His son Amon, who succeeded him at the age of twenty-two years, followed his example in favouring idolatry. Some officers of his court conspired against Amon, and killed him in his palace; he had hardly reigned two years (640). Burial in the royal sepulchre was refused to him as well as to his father. The people killed the assassins of Amon, and placed on the throne his son Josiah, who was but eight years old.

8. The reign of Josiah was the last brilliant epoch of the kingdom of Judah, so soon to be swallowed up in the great revolutions of which Asia became the theatre. The young king was no doubt educated by the priests and prophets, for we see that, while still very young, he manifested great zeal for the re-establishment of the orthodox worship, and that he made his ancestor David his model. He married early, and was hardly fourteen years old when his first wife Zebuda gave him a son, who received the name of Eliakim. Two years after, another wife, Hamutal, gave him a second son, called Jehoahaz, and about thirteen years later he had by the same wife a last son, named Mattaniah.

According to the Book of Chronicles, Josiah commenced in the twelfth year of his reign his religious reforms by severe measures against idolaters; and although the Book of Kings reports no act of Josiah previous to the eighteenth year of his reign, the repair of the Temple, which was ordered in that same year, presupposes the suppression of idolatry. Jeremiah, son of Hilkiah, a priest of the town of Anathoth, who commenced preaching as a prophet in the thirteenth year of the reign of Josiah, probably exercised by his discourses some influence on the mind of the king, for being persecuted in his native city, and even threatened with death, he repaired to Jerusalem. The prophet Zephaniah also lived under Josiah, and very probably during the early part of his reign.

9. The eighteenth year of Josiah was signalised by an important event, which contributed to render the zeal of the king for the re-establishment of the Mosaic worship still more ardent. The high priest Hilkiah, in superintending the repairs of the Temple, found hidden the Book of the Law, probably an ancient and valuable copy of the writings of Moses, hidden away from the fury of the king during the reign of Manasseh, and which was believed to have been lost. The book was carried to the king, who, but little acquainted with the Law, caused it to be read to him. Hearing all its precepts, so ill observed up to that time, and the menaces of the Divine chastisement awaiting transgressors, Josiah was struck with terror, and rent his clothes. He then convoked the elders of his council, and repaired with them to the courts of the Temple; the priests, the Levites, the prophets, and people of all ranks, came together in a crowd. Josiah read with a loud voice the Book of the Law, and made the people renew the oath of the covenant with Jehovah. He then ordered the total destruction of all the monuments of pagan worship, and of all that might recall the idolatry of former times. A great number of idols were burned, and their ashes cast into the brook Kedron. The high places on the south of the Mount of Olives, originally dedicated by Solomon to the various divinities of Asiatic paganism, were desecrated by human bones which were placed there. The high places and separate altars destined to the worship of the true God were treated in the same way, for the king, in conformity with the strict precepts of the Mosaic laws, would no longer tolerate any altar but that of the central sanctuary of the nation. The reforms of Josiah extended even to part of the ancient kingdom of Israel, reunited to Judah after the retreat of Sennacherib. Josiah went in person to Bethel, destroyed the temple of the golden calf established by Jeroboam, killed the priests, and defiled the altar. On his return to Jerusalem, he celebrated the Passover with a solemnity which had not been seen in that ceremony even under Hezekiah. The city of David again became the centre of religious worship, both for the inhabitants of the land of Judah and for the remains of the ten tribes, who were still left on the ancient territory of Israel. Jeremiah preached in the public places on the subject of this new covenant, and pronounced a curse on those who should attempt to violate it.

10. The piety and energy of Josiah, united to the courageous devotion of Jeremiah, would perhaps have been sufficient to re-establish

religious unity in a durable manner, and to establish the state firmly on the basis of the Mosaic law; but political movements in Asia, into which the land of Judah was drawn in spite of itself, hastened the ruin of the little kingdom, already weakened by so many struggles. Judah had escaped from the invasion of the Scythians, who, in 625 and 624, had traversed Palestine and threatened Egypt, and who, stopped in their progress by the entreaties and presents of Pharaoh, had in their retreat pillaged the Temple of Atergatis at Ascalon. No doubt the mountains of Judæa were found inaccessible by the Scythian horsemen, who could only act on the plains. The weakening of the Assyrian empire, fallen into decay in the weak and effeminate hands of Saracus, and whose capital had been once on the eve of falling into the hands of the Medes, had given the Hebrews some respite during the thirty years of Josiah's reign. But in the Chaldæan king of Babylon—Nabopolassar—who was beginning to form an empire for himself out of the ruins of that of Nineveh, and who already threatened the country on this side the Euphrates, Egypt saw the rise of a new and formidable enemy. Necho, son and successor of Psammeticus I., wishing to arrest the progress of the Chaldæans, and also to seize his share of the spoils of the Assyrian monarchy, marched on the Euphrates after the example of the Pharaohs of the eighteenth and nineteenth dynasties, to possess himself of the fortress of Carchemish, or Circesium, and thus make himself master of the point where for ages armies had most easily and most frequently crossed the Euphrates. Necho had no hostile intentions towards the kingdom of Judah, which he did not even cross in his march. He traversed the land of the Philistines, in great part subject to him, for Psammeticus had, after a siege of twenty-nine years, possessed himself of the town of Ashdod, and he himself had taken Gaza. The Egyptian army passed to the north of the kingdom of Judah over the ancient territory of Israel, intending to cross the plain of Esdraelon, but was stopped in its march by Josiah, who advanced to attack it near Megiddo, urged on by the foolish suggestions of the military party, who desired at any price an opportunity for a victory, which might again raise the fortunes of Judah. Necho told Josiah that he did not wish to meddle with his states; that he was marching in hot haste against his enemies, and that Josiah could not fight him unless he were determined to provoke a struggle which could but prove fatal to him. In spite of these warnings Josiah persisted in fighting the Egyptians, but his troops were beaten and himself mortally wounded by the arrow of an Egyptian archer. His body was conveyed to Jerusalem (610). The death of the pious king spread everywhere grief and consternation; in him the last support of religion went down to the sepulchres of Sion, and from that moment the kingdom of Judah, which might have had hopes of religious and political regeneration, advanced with rapid steps to total ruin.

Jeremiah and all the poets of the epoch composed lamentations on the death of king Josiah, which for a long time afterwards were recited on each anniversary of the fatal day of Megiddo.

SECTION VII.—LAST DAYS OF THE KINGDOM OF JUDAH—NEBUCHADNEZZAR—CAPTURE OF JERUSALEM—(610—588).

1. JEHOAHAZ, or Shallum, the second son of Josiah, succeeded his father at the age of twenty-three years, chosen by the people instead of his elder brother, Eliakim, the latter having possibly shown himself disposed to negotiate with the king of Egypt, whom they yet hoped to resist. During this time Necho had continued his march to the north, and had taken Kadesh on the Orontes, the Cadytis of Herodotus.* He had for the moment given up the capture of Carchemish, wishing first to conquer Syria and Palestine. He stopped at Riblah, a Syrian city on the territory of Hamath, and thence sent troops to occupy Jerusalem. The king Jehoahaz was carried to Riblah, and Necho sent him prisoner to Egypt, where he remained till his death. He had reigned but three months. Necho raised to the throne in his place Eliakim, the eldest son of Josiah, whose name he changed to Jehoiakim; at the same time he imposed on the land of Judah a tribute of one hundred talents of silver and one talent of gold.

2. Jehoiakim was not more fitted than his brother to raise the hopes of the priests and prophets; on the contrary, his tyranny and the protection which he extended to idolatry drew down on him the execration of all well-minded men. Not content with the tax which he was compelled to lay on the people to pay the tribute to Egypt, he further oppressed his people and made them submit to forced labour for the

---

* HER. ii. 159; iii. 5. Cadytis has been identified both with Jerusalem (named *Kadesh* or *Kadusha*, "the holy," the modern *El Kuds*), and also with Gaza. The identification with Jerusalem is accepted by the learned Lightfoot (*Horæ Hebraicæ*, London, 1584) as a "thing beyond controversy;" but Herodotus seems to have reached it travelling along the sea coast, and there are many indications which render it impossible to consider Cadytis as Jerusalem.

A more generally received opinion has made Cadytis Gaza (see Jer. xlvii. 1), to which there is only one (but that seems a fatal) objection—that Necho took Cadytis after defeating Josiah at Megiddo, and, as it would appear, on his way to Carchemish.

All the arguments in favour of Gaza will tell also in favour of the identification in the text; *and* Kadesh also was directly in Pharaoh's way from Megiddo to Carchemish, and a city of such importance that he would be unlikely to leave it in his rear untaken.—TR.

purpose of erecting sumptuous edifices, in spite of the miserable state of the people. Those who dared to resist the abominable tyranny of the king were in danger of death, and much innocent blood was shed in Jerusalem. Jehoiakim pursued the prophet Urijah even to Egypt, with the intention of putting him to death (Jer. xxvi. 21). Jeremiah would have shared the same fate if he had not been protected by some important personages, but the danger he was in did not daunt him; he ceased not to stigmatise in the most energetic terms the tyranny of Jehoiakim, the depravity of his courtiers, among whom were to be seen even men of priestly class, and some who even preached as prophets.

3. In the fourth year of the reign of Jehoiakim, Necho, after having subjected by degrees the people on this side the Euphrates, thought himself in a position to undertake the siege of Carchemish. But at this moment Nebuchadnezzar (Nabukudurussur), Prince Royal of Babylon, advanced against him at the head of a strong army, whilst his father, Nabopolassar, was engaged in the capture and destruction of Nineveh, in alliance with Cyaxares, king of the Medes. A great battle was fought before Carchemish, and Necho, being defeated, was obliged to retire hastily into Egypt, abandoning all his recent conquests. At this time Habakkuk pronounced his prophecy on the redoubtable power of the Chaldæans, which threatened to swallow up Judah, and which was to fall in its turn, after having served as the instrument of the wrath of heaven.

In the year following the battle of Carchemish, the Chaldæans advanced as far as the frontiers of Egypt, and brought all Syria into subjection, without however touching the kingdom of Judah; for they appeared before Pelusium in two columns, one of which had marched through the land of the Philistines and the other through Peræa, the land of the Ammonites and Moabites. The Egyptians no longer dared to advance beyond their own frontier. In the month of December of that year, 605, a public fast was proclaimed at Jerusalem to implore the help of God against the Chaldæans. Jeremiah took advantage of this occasion to make his secretary, Baruch, read publicly in the court of the Temple the book of his prophecies. Jehoiakim having heard of it sent for, and after having read the roll, burnt it; at the same time he ordered Jeremiah and Baruch to be arrested and put to death. But they succeeded in concealing themselves in a safe retreat, which they did not leave until after the death of Jehoiakim, and where Jeremiah dictated afresh the words of the book that had been burned, and added to it a prophecy full of menace to the king.

Jehoiakim nevertheless escaped the danger for the time; Nebuchadnezzar having received the news of the death of his father (604), took the road across the desert to return with all possible haste to Babylon, to be there proclaimed king, postponing to another time the subjection of

Jehoiakim, and of other allies of Egypt. He did not return to Syria till two years later, but he then penetrated into the heart of the kingdom of Judah, and made it tributary, took Jerusalem, and forced Jehoiakim to recognise him as suzerain (602). At that time Nebuchadnezzar took, for the first time, some of the sacred vessels of the Temple to Babylon, and carried off many young men of noble families—such as Daniel, Hananiah, Mishael and Azariah—as hostages for the fidelity of Jehoiakim, whom he at first intended to imprison, but finally decided on allowing to occupy the throne at Jerusalem. Three years later (599) Jehoiakim, seduced by the false policy of certain orators or false prophets, and reckoning on the assistance of Psammeticus II., king of Egypt, ventured to rebel against the king of Babylon. Nebuchadnezzar prepared a new expedition into Judæa, and whilst his preparations were going on, ravaged the country by bands of Chaldæan, Arab, Syrian and Ammonite cavalry. Jehoiakim died whilst these preliminary incursions were going on, at the age of thirty-six years, leaving his son Jehoiachin to bear all the weight of the consequences of his rebellion.

4. Jehoiachin, called also Jeconiah, then, at the age of eighteen years, mounted a throne surrounded by the most formidable dangers. The Chaldæan army did not long delay its appearance before Jerusalem, to which it laid siege; king Nebuchadnezzar soon followed. Jehoiachin was not in a state to sustain a long siege, and as the help he expected did not arrive from Egypt, he surrendered, and descended from the throne which he had occupied but three months and ten days (599). The Babylonians then entered the city, and seized upon all the treasures of the Temple and of the royal palace, and carried off all the utensils of gold which had been in the sanctuary ever since the time of Solomon. Ten thousand of the principal inhabitants, nobles and artisans, particularly smiths and armourers, were removed to Babylon. This was the commencement of the seventy years captivity of Judah. Amongst those carried off was Ezekiel, then twenty-five years old, who five years later began to preach and prophesy among his brother exiles at Babylon, and in Chaldæa. The king Jehoiachin, who had surrendered at discretion, was shut up in close prison at Babylon, where he remained more than thirty-six years, until Evil Merodach, son and successor of Nebuchadnezzar, released him, and permitted him to pass his last years at liberty. Mattanaiah, youngest son of Josiah, and uncle of the unfortunate Jehoiachin, was then made king of Judah by Nebuchadnezzar, who changed his name to Zedekiah, thus proving his own suzerainty, as Necho had done by Eliakim.

5. Zedekiah, last of the successors of David, was in reality nothing more than a Babylonian satrap. A young man without experience, devoid of judgment and of energy, he became the sport of the intriguers of the court, who by their evil counsels hastened his fall and the final

ruin of Judah. By keeping the faith he had sworn to the Babylonian monarch, Zedekiah might, to a certain extent, have enjoyed a time of tranquillity, during which the forces of his little kingdom might have recruited themselves. Jeremiah and some clear-sighted men showed that this was the only course to take in order to avoid the greatest misfortunes; but the aristocratic party was far from approving that prudent policy, and used all its influence with Zedekiah to induce him to throw off the Chaldæan yoke, by contracting alliances with the neighbouring nations and with Egypt. This advice was supported by the rash counsels which the exiles in Babylon gave in all their letters to Jerusalem, the effect of which on the minds of the priests and people Jeremiah took all possible pains to counteract.

In the fourth year of the reign of Zedekiah (595), ambassadors from the kings of Edom, Moab, Ammon, Tyre and Sidon, came to Jerusalem, to attempt to organise a general revolt against the common oppressor. Jeremiah, fearful of the consequences of these conspiracies, and preaching by act as well as by word, sent to each of the ambassadors a yoke of wood, emblematical of the Babylonian servitude, to signify to them that all the neighbouring peoples ought patiently to bear that yoke until the destined hour, not long to be delayed, should arrive to break the Babylonian power. He showed himself in the courts of the Temple, bearing the yoke on his shoulders. These speeches of Jeremiah diverted Zedekiah for a time from those imprudent projects; and the king himself repaired in person to Babylon, to do homage to his suzerain, and to dispel any suspicion which might have arisen as to his fidelity.

6. But Zedekiah did not long retain the peaceful dispositions with which the prophet had succeeded in inspiring him. Led away by the false policy of his councillors, which all the prophets since Isaiah had combated, he entered into negotiations with Egypt, where Uahprahet —the Hophra of the Bible, the Apries of the Greeks—then reigned. Having received the promise of help from him, Zedekiah thought himself strong enough to throw off the Babylonian yoke, which he had borne for eight years, and therefore refused his tribute. The Chaldæans again invaded the kingdom of Judah in 590 B.C., and occupied the whole country, with the exception of the strong cities of Lachish and Jerusalem, which, reckoning on the speedy arrival of the Egyptian troops, prepared for resistance. The siege of Jerusalem commenced in the first days of January, 589. Jeremiah, questioned by order of the king by Zephaniah the priest, delivered a threatening prophecy. Foreseeing that the city would be forced to surrender sooner or later, he again insisted that the king should repair his fault towards Nebuchadnezzar by a voluntary submission, giving him to hope that in that case he might die in peace, and rest in the sepulchre of his fathers; but he was not heeded. To increase the number of combatants, and to regain

the affections of the people, who were discontented at seeing the king subject to the exclusive influence of the aristocracy, Zedekiah bethought himself of the provisions of the Mosaic law, so little observed during the period of the monarchy, which did not permit a Hebrew to be detained in slavery for more than six years; he ordered these regulations to be at once put in force, and released all Israelitish slaves.

7. At this time the Egyptian troops entered Judæa to attack the Chaldæans, who raised the siege of Jerusalem in order to meet them. Then the king and his nobles, believing themselves freed from all danger, revoked their decision relative to the slaves, and wished to reduce again to slavery those who had already been released. The indignation of Jeremiah at this sight knew no bounds. "Thus saith the Lord," said he, "Ye have not hearkened unto me in proclaiming liberty, every one to his brother, and every one to his neighbour: behold, I will proclaim a liberty for you, saith the Lord, to the sword, to the pestilence, and to the famine; and I will make you to be removed into all the kingdoms of the earth. * * * And Zedekiah, king of Judah, and his princes, will I give into the hand of their enemies, and into the hand of the king of Babylon's army, which are gone up from you. Behold, I will command, saith the Lord, and will cause them to return to this city; and they shall fight against it, and take it, and burn it with fire: and I will make the cities of Judah a desolation without an inhabitant." (Jer. xxxiv. 17, *seq.*)

Very soon, in conformity with the predictions of Jeremiah, the Egyptians retreated almost without fighting, and the Chaldæans recommenced the siege of Jerusalem, and pressed it with greater vigour than before. Jeremiah reiterated his prophecies of evil, and said openly that none should save their lives who did not give themselves up to the Babylonians, which irritated the officers of Zedekiah to the highest degree, as it induced many to desert, and so thinned the ranks of the defenders. They obtained an order from the king to throw the prophet into prison, where the military party wished to have him put to death. Zedekiah went to visit him there, and Jeremiah repeated to him his counsels of submission, which the king well knew to be wise counsels, but dared not adopt, for fear of the vengeance of Nebuchadnezzar.

8. Whilst provisions remained in the city, the inhabitants heroically resisted the Chaldæan army. The tenth year of the reign of Zedekiah passed away before the besiegers could make a breach. Many houses were demolished to fortify the walls against the war machines of the enemy, the approaches of which became more formidable every day. But at last the defenders of Jerusalem, whose courage had not yet for an instant failed, succumbed to hunger and fatigue. In July, 588 B.C., provisions were entirely exhausted in the city, and resistance was no longer possible. One night, profiting by the fatigue of the defenders,

the Chaldæans, without much difficulty, penetrated into the city on the north side. Zedekiah fled away with the remains of his troops by a postern gate giving access to the royal gardens. The fugitives made towards the Jordan, but the Babylonians pursued and overtook them in the Plains of Jericho. Zedekiah's little troop disbanded, and the unfortunate king was made prisoner, and conducted to Nebuchadnezzar's head-quarters at Riblah, on the territory of Hamath. Fearful treatment awaited him; his young sons, as well as the nobles of Judah who had encouraged him to revolt, were killed before his eyes, and he himself, with his eyes put out, was loaded with chains and carried to Babylon, where he remained in a dungeon till his death.

The fate of Jerusalem and of its inhabitants was next decided; and on enquiry it was found that every personage of importance had entered into the plot against the authority of the Babylonian monarch. A month after the conquest, Nebuzaradan, captain of Nebuchadnezzar's guards, entered Jerusalem. By his orders the Temple, the king's palace, and all the principal buildings of the capital of Judah were set on fire. In a few days the magnificent city was changed into a heap of ruins. The high priest Seraiah, and Zephaniah, the "second priest," were arrested with many of the great nobles and sixty of the principal inhabitants, and conducted to Riblah, where they were put to death. The majority of the citizens and of the soldiers had taken refuge in the country and in the neighbouring lands. The chief of those who remained were led captive to Babylon, but their number amounted to only 832 persons.

9. This frightful catastrophe, however, was not the last act of the sad tragedy of the fall of the kingdom of Judah. Nebuchadnezzar had confined himself to punishing Jerusalem, and had left the greater part of the inhabitants of the country unmolested. He had installed, as chief or satrap (under the surveillance of his general, Nebuzaradan, charged with maintaining for a time the military occupation of the country), not a Chaldæan or a Syrian, but a Hebrew, named Gedaliah, a pious man, a good patriot, beloved and esteemed by the people. He had fixed his residence at Mizpeh, where Jeremiah, who had been taken prisoner and afterwards released, joined him, and composed his sublime Lamentations on the destruction of Jerusalem. The installation of Gedaliah as governor, by re-assuring people as to Nebuchadnezzar's intentions, had caused the fugitives to re-assemble, and amongst them the chief captains who had directed the defence of the holy city. Order was re-established, agricultural labours again commenced, and a provisional worship organised in the ruins of the Temple. But a traitor soon destroyed the hopes of the last remnant of Judah. At the instigation of Baalis, king of the Ammonites, whose traditional hatred could not bear to see a compact nucleus of Hebrew nationality still subsisting, a

personage named Ishmael, of the race of David, assassinated Gedaliah; and as, after this useless crime, he could hope neither to succeed to his victim, nor to maintain himself against the Chaldæans, he fled to the land of the Ammonites.

A general panic followed the murder of Gedaliah. All the principal people who still remained in the land, fearing the vengeance of the Babylonians, emigrated to Egypt, taking with them by force Jeremiah, who did not wish to leave the land of Judah. The emigrants established themselves at Tahpanhes, in the eastern part of the Delta; and some years after, adding a new crime to those which had been the ruin of the Hebrews, they there stoned to death the prophet Jeremiah, who attempted to stem the progress of Egyptian idolatry among them. Nebuzaradan, as a punishment for the murder of Gedaliah, transported to Babylon 745 more of the chief inhabitants, and installed numerous foreign colonies in the land of Judah. From this moment till the return of Zerubbabel, under Cyrus, Judæa ceased to have the least vestige of national life, and obeyed Chaldæan governors sent from Babylon.

END OF BOOK II.

BOOK III.

THE EGYPTIANS.

CHAPTER I.

EGYPT—THE NILE AND ITS INUNDATIONS—THE KINGS OF THE OLD EMPIRE.

Chief Authorities for the Four Chapters on the History of Egypt.—Classical Writers:—The fragments of the *Dynasties* of Manetho, inserted in Vol. I. of *Fragmenta Historicorum Græcorum.* Didot.—Herodotus, Book II.—Diodorus Siculus, Book I.—The *Canon* of Eratosthenes, preserved by George Syncellus, the Byzantine Chronologer.—Josephus, *Against Apion.* Book I.

Collections of original Egyptian Texts:—Young, *Hieroglyphics*, London, 1823.—Burton, *Excerpta Hieroglyphica*, Cairo, 1828.—Champollion, *Monuments de l'Egypte et de la Nubie*, Paris, 1833—45.—Sharpe, *Egyptian Inscriptions from the British Museum*, London, 1837.—Leemans, *Monuments Egyptiens du Musée d'Antiquités des Pays Bas à Leyde*, Leyden, 1839—67.—Lepsius, *Auswahl der wichstigsten Urkunden des Ægyptischen Alterthums*, Leipzig, 1842.—Ungarelli, *Interpretatio Obeliscorum Urbis*, Rome, 1842.—Champollion, *Notices descriptives*, Paris, 1844.—Prisse d'Avennes, *Monuments Egyptiens*, Paris, 1847.—*Select Papyri of the British Museum*, London, 1844.—Lepsius, *Denkmäler aus Ægypten und Æthiopien*, Berlin, 1850—1858.—Brugsch, *Recueil de Monuments Egyptiens*, Leipzig, 1862.—*Matériaux pour servir à la reconstruction du Calendrier Egyptien*, Leipzig, 1864.—Dümichen, *Geographische Inschriften Altægyptischer Denkmäler*, Leipzig, 1864.—*Kalenderinschriften*, Leipzig, 1866.—*Historische Inschriften*, Leipzig, 1867.—*Tempelinschriften*, Leipzig, 1867.—De Rougé, *Album photographique de la Mission d'Egypte*, Paris, 1865.—Mariette, *Le Sérapéum de Memphis* (In course of publication).

Modern Works on Egyptology:—Champollion, *L'Egypte sous les Pharaons*, Paris, 1814.—*Lettres à M. le duc de Blacas*, Paris, 1824.—*Aperçu des résultats historiques de la découverte de l'alphabet hiéroglyphique*, Paris, 1827.—*Lettres écrites d'Egypte*, Paris, 1833 (2 edit. 1868).—Champollion Figeac, *L'Egypte ancienne*, Paris, 1840.—Ch. Lenormant, *Eclaircissements sur le Cercueil du roi Mycérinus*, Paris, 1837.—*Musée des Antiquités Egyptiennes*, Paris, 1841.—Barucchi, *Discorsi critici sopra la cronologia Egizia*, Turin, 1844.—Bunsen, *Ægyptens Stelle in der Weltsgeschichte*, Göttingen, 1845—1857. The English translation of this work enriched with the large additions due to the learned researches of Dr. Birch, London, 1867, 1868.—Brunet de Presle, *Examen critique de la succession des dynasties*

Egyptiennes, Paris, 1850.—Lepsius, *Chronologie der Ægypter*, Berlin, 1849.—*Briefe aus Ægypten und Æthiopien*, Berlin, 1852.—*Ueber die 12te Ægyptische Königsdynastie*, Berlin, 1853.—*Königsbuch der Alten Ægypter*, Berlin, 1858. The numerous and admirable Articles by Dr. Birch in the *Archæologia*, and *Transactions of the Royal Society of Literature.*—De Rougé, *Examen critique de l'ouvrage de M. Bunsen*, Paris, 1847.—*Mémoire sur l'inscription du tombeau d'Ahmès*, Paris, 1851.—*Mémoire sur la Statuette Naophore du Vatican*, Paris, 1851.—*Le Poëme de Pentaour*, Paris, 1856.—*Etudes sur une stèle de la Bibliothèque impériale*, Paris, 1858.—*Notice de quelques textes publiés par M. Greene*, Paris, 1856.—*Etude sur divers Monuments du règne de Toutmès III.*, Paris, 1861.—*Mémoires sur les Monuments des six premières dynasties*, Paris, 1866.—*Notice des Monuments Egyptiens du Musée du Louvre.*—Biot, *Recherches de quelques dates absolues sur les Monuments Egyptiens*, Paris, 1853.—*Sur un calendrier astronomique*, Paris, 1852.—Brusch, *Geographische Inschriften Altægyptischer Denkmäler*, Leipzig, 1857—1860.—*Histoire d'Egypte*, Leipzig, 1859.—Dümichen, *Bau-Urkunde der Tempelanlagen von Dendera*, Leipzig, 1865.—Marriette, *Renseignments sur les soixante quatre Apis trouvés au Serapéum*, Paris, 1855.—*Notice du Musée de Boulac*, Cairo, 1862.—*Abrégé de l'histoire d'Egypte*, Paris, 1867.—*Description du parc égyptien à l'Exposition Universelle*, Paris, 1867.—Chabas, *Inscription historique du règne de Seti Ier*, Paris, 1856.—*Mélanges Egyptologiques*, Chalons-sur-Saône, 1863.—*Les Papyrus hiératiques de Berlin*, Chalons-sur-Saône, 1863.—*Les Inscriptions des Mines d'Or*, Chalons-sur-Saône, 1862.—*Voyage d'un Egyptien en Syrie, Phénicie, Palestine*, Chalons-sur-Saône, 1867.—Th. Devéria, *Le Papyrus Judiciaire de Turin*, Paris, 1866.—F. Lenormant, *L'Antiquité à l'Exposition Universelle. L'Egypte*, Paris, 1867.—A large number of Articles on Egyptian Antiquities published in the *Revue Archéologique* by M. de Rougé, Dr. Birch, M. Mariette, and M. Devéria. The *Journal de linguistique et d'Archéologie Egyptiennes*, edited at Berlin by Dr. Brugsch and M. Lepsius.

SECTION I.—PHYSICAL GEOGRAPHY OF EGYPT—THE NILE—ITS INUNDATIONS.

1. EGYPT is a long narrow tract of country, stretching from south to north, occupying the north-east angle of Africa, or, as the ancients called it, Lybia, where it is joined to Asia by the Isthmus of Suez. Egypt is bounded on the north by the Mediterranean, on the east by the Isthmus and by the Red Sea, on the south by Nubia, which country the Nile traverses before it enters Egypt at the Cataracts of Syene, and lastly, on the west, by deserts containing a few scattered oases, or habitable spots, fertilised by fountains. The desert extends almost to the sea on the north-east of Egypt, as well as along the shores of the Red Sea.

But, moreover, much of the interior of Egypt itself is desert. Every part not watered by the annual inundations of the Nile is uninhabitable, and produces neither corn, nor vegetables, nor trees, nor even grass: no water is found there; the very utmost being here and there a well, more or less likely to be found dry, under a constantly burning atmosphere. In Upper, or Southern, Egypt rain is a phenomenon extremely rare, and the whole soil is sand or rock, except in the valley of the Nile, a valley which, as far as the place where the river bifurcates—that is, for three-fourths of the whole length of Egypt—has not a larger mean width than four or five leagues, and in some places far less.

Herodotus was then quite right in saying, "All Egypt is the gift of the Nile" (HER. ii. 5). If the course of the Nile were diverted, nothing would break the arid uniformity of the desert. If the Upper Nile were intercepted, Egypt would be annihilated. This idea did occur to an emperor of Abyssinia who lived in the thirteenth century, and in later times also to the Portuguese Albuquerque. In fact, the Nile throughout the whole of its lower course has the remarkable peculiarity of receiving no affluent, and, unlike all other rivers, of diminishing instead of increasing as it advances, for the water is employed in feeding canals, and there is nothing to restore what it thus loses.

2. Nearly the whole of the Nile valley is confined between two mountain chains, called on the east, Arabian, on the west, Lybian. These mountains, especially towards the south, approach each other so as almost to form actual defiles. The province called Fayoum, however, to the west of the Nile in Central Egypt, a short distance from the site of Memphis, is fertilised by canals and by a lake. Here Egypt, which north of the cataracts is a mere valley, widens very considerably. A little below the city of Cairo, the present capital of Egypt, situated not far from the ruins of Memphis, the Nile divides into two branches—one, that of Rosetta, runs north-west, and the other, that of Damietta, north and north-east. These were in former times called the "Bolbitine" and "Phatnitic," or "Bucolic," mouths. But the ancients mention also five others that have since been filled up, or at any rate have become useless for navigation. They were—1st, the Canopic, west of the Bolbitine, of which it was a branch; Herodotus thought that it was the ancient bed of a canal, and that the Bolbitine mouth was artificial; 2nd, the Sebennytic, running west of the Phatnitic; 3rd, the Mendesian; 4th, the Tanitic, which detached itself eastward from the same branch; and finally, the Pelusiac, the most eastern of all, and which during part of its course is the same as the Tanitic. These five channels were named from cities situated near their mouths. A great number of small canals intersected the interior of Lower Egypt, but the ground there being anything but solid, and much disturbed by the inundations, the natural or artificial watercourses have much changed in the lapse of ages, and are still frequently changing.

3. Near the sea, the Nile forms many great lagoons, enclosed by tongues of earth or sand, and communicating with the Mediterranean

by breaches in the banks. The chief are Lake Menzaleh to the east, which does not seem very ancient, at the mouth of the Tanitic and Mendesian branches ; Lake Boorlos, containing the ancient Lake Bonto, in the centre of the coast, and opening to the sea by the remains of the Sebennytic branch ; and finally to the west, near the famous city of Alexandria, founded by Alexander the Great, in a place already inhabited and called Racotis, the Lake Mareotis of the ancients. The space contained between the most distant branches of the river is called the Delta, on account of its almost triangular shape resembling that of the Greek letter Delta.

4. Each year in the summer solstice, that is, towards the end of June, the Nile commences to rise; its waters soon arrive at the height of, and overflow, its banks, and then spread suddenly over the whole valley which is in most parts lower than the river banks. An artificial system of irrigation has also been contrived to extend the benefits of the inundation to the soil beyond its natural limits. By the end of September the waters attain their greatest height, at which they remain only a few days, and then commence falling, and by the month of December have returned to their original level. Sowing commences, and continues as the waters fall, that is from the the beginning of October in Upper Egypt, and fifteen days later in the Delta; the fall as well as the rise of the water is later the lower we go down the course of the river. Harvest time is in March ; all agricultural operations are easy in a land so fertile and well prepared. During the overflow of the river, the inhabitants, shut up in their towns and villages built on natural or artificial elevations, and converted into islands in the midst of a vast lake, await with anxiety the moment when they can estimate the height of the year's inundation, for on that depends the abundance of the harvest.

This wonderful river, that leaves its bed at fixed periods to fertilise the ground, much excited the astonishment of the ancients, who did not know that all rivers rising in or flowing through the torrid zone present similar phenomena. They had recourse to a thousand absurd speculations to account for this periodical rise, which may be found in Herodotus and Diodorus Siculus. The true cause of the inundation, as some ancient geographers, such as Eratosthenes and Agatharcides, suspected, is the periodical rainy season inundating Upper Abyssinia, where the Nile takes its rise.

Section II.—Principal Sources of the History of Egypt.

1. For a very long time, to write the history of Egypt was but to repeat the tales of Greek authors, as no one had penetrated the deep mystery of the writing of the ancient Egyptians. And the accounts these Greeks have given of the land of the Pharaohs, and of its annals,

in no way agree with each other. In the midst of their contradictions, it has seemed that we ought in preference to give credit to the facts stated by Herodotus and Diodorus Siculus. The position of the historian has now, however, been completely changed by the invaluable discovery of Champollion, who has enabled us to read with certainty hieroglyphics that had for centuries been an insoluble problem. We turn now to the writings of the Egyptians themselves—to their monumental inscriptions, to their papyri—and ask them to reveal to us the annals of this ancient land. Since history has possessed the original documents of the banks of the Nile, the authority of these two classical writers, once almost exclusively followed as guides, has been entirely destroyed. Herodotus was a traveller of great truthfulness, who recounts with charming simplicity and also rare intelligence all that he himself saw. With respect to the description of the manners and customs of the Egyptians which he saw with his own eyes, his book is exceedingly valuable, and every day monuments are brought to light to confirm his testimony. But in all that is historical, knowing nothing of the language of Egypt, he could not refer directly to authorities, and was obliged to content himself with the stories of his guides, and of the priests of the temples that he visited. So he does not really attempt, and this he is himself the first to admit, even a complete and full essay on the history of the Pharaonic dynasties, but simply a series of "guide-book" stories relating to a few of those kings. These anecdotes, too, do not follow each other in real chronological order; it is easy to see that the ingenious Halicarnessian traveller has disarranged his sheets of notes taken at Memphis on the subject, and has, as a result, inverted epochs in a way otherwise inexplicable. As for the work of Diodorus Siculus, most valuable on the subject of manners and customs which he saw for himself, it is, as history, merely a compilation of facts gathered on all sides, and arranged without regard to order. His stories on the annals of Egypt have really no value; and it is with difficulty that we find among his anecdotes a few only of really Egyptian origin, such as we find in greater number in Herodotus. Of all the Greek writers who have treated of the history of the Pharaohs, there is only one whose testimony has, since the deciphering of the hieroglyphics, preserved any great value—a value which increases the more it is compared with the original monuments; we speak of Manetho. Once he was treated with contempt; his veracity was disputed; the long series of dynasties he unfolds to our view was regarded as fabulous. Now, all that remains of his work is the first of all authorities for the reconstruction of the ancient history of Egypt.

2. Manetho, a priest of the town of Sebennytus, in the Delta, wrote n Greek, in the reign of Ptolemy Philadelphus, a history of Egypt, founded on the official archives preserved in the temples. Like many

other books of antiquity, this history has been lost; we possess now a few fragments only, with the list of all the kings placed by Manetho at the end of his work—a list happily preserved in the writings of some chronologers of the Christian epoch. This list divides into dynasties, or royal families, all the kings who reigned successively in Egypt down to the time of Alexander. For the greater number of dynasties Manetho records the names of the kings, the length of each reign, and the duration of the dynasty; for the others, and the fewer number, he contents himself with a brief notice of the origin of the royal family, the number of its kings, and the years during which the family reigned.

We cannot here give the complete lists, in which, moreover, the names of the kings have frequently been so altered by Greek copyists, entirely ignorant of the Egyptian language, that they can be restored only by the direct study of Egyptian monuments. But we give an abstract of its chief features in the following table:—

Dynasty.	Seat.	Modern Name.	Duration.	Date, B.C.
I.	This . . .	Harabat el Madfouneh	253 years	5004
II.	,,	,,	302 ,,	4751
III.	Memphis . .	Mit-Rahineh	214 ,,	4449
IV.	,,	,,	284 ,,	4235
V.	,,	,,	248 ,,	3951
VI.	Elephantine .	Gezyret Essouan. . .	203 ,,	3703
VII.	Memphis . .	Mit-Rahinneh . . .	70 days	3500
VIII.	,,	,,	142 years	3500
IX.	Heracleopolis	Ahnas el Medineh . .	109 ,,	3358
X.	,,	,,	185 ,,	3249
XI.	Thebes . .	Medinet Abu. . . }	213 ,,	3064
XII.	,,	,,		
XIII.	,,	,,	453 ,,	2851
XIV.	Xois . . .	Sakha	184 ,,	2398
XV.	(Shepherds) .	San . . . . . . }	511 ,,	2214
XVI.	,,	,,		
XVII.	,,	,,		
XVIII.	Thebes . .	Medinet Abu. . . .	241 ,,	1703
XIX.	,,	,,	174 ,,	1462
XX.	,,	,,	178 ,,	1288
XXI.	Tanis . . .	San	130 ,,	1110
XXII.	Bubastis . .	Tel Basta	170 ,,	980
XXIII.	Tanis . . .	San	89 ,,	810
XXIV.	Sais. . . .	Sa el Hagar	6 ,,	721
XXV.	(Ethiopian) .		50 ,,	715
XXVI.	Sais. . . .	Sa el Hagar	138 ,,	665
XXVII.	(Persians). .		121 ,,	527
XXVIII.	Sais. . . .	Sa el Hagar	7 ,,	406
XXIX.	Mendes . .	Ashmoun	21 ,,	399
XXX.	Sebennytus .	Se'menood.	38 ,,	378
XXXI.	(Persians). .		8 ,,	340

3. "Every one must be struck with the enormous total of years to which the duration of the dynasties of Manetho amounts. The lists of the Egyptian priest, in fact, carry us back to times which are mythical among all other people, but which are in Egypt certainly already historical.

"Embarrassed by this fact, and, moreover, unable in any way to cast a doubt on the authenticity and veracity of Manetho, some modern authors have supposed that Egypt had been at some periods of its history divided into more than one kingdom, and that Manetho had represented, as *successive*, dynasties which were really *contemporaneous*. According to them, the fifth dynasty, for example, was reigning at Elephantine at the same time that the sixth was enthroned at Memphis. The convenience of this system, for certain combinations fixed at leisure and in view of preconceived ideas, need not be pointed out. By reconciling some dates and correcting others, we may, by an ingenious and even scientific arrangement of dynasties, contract almost as we wish the length of the lists of Manetho. It is thus that, where we in the preceding table place the foundation of the Egyptian monarchy in the year 5004 before our era, other authors, such as Baron Bunsen, place the same event only as far back as the year 3623.

"On which side lies the truth? The larger the amount of study given to the subject, the greater is the difficulty of answering. The greatest of all the obstacles in the way of establishing a regular Egyptian chronology is the fact that the Egyptians themselves never had any chronology at all. The use of a fixed era was unknown, and it has not yet been proved that they had any other reckoning than the years of the reigning monarch. Now these years themselves had no fixed starting point, for sometimes they began from the commencement of the year in which the preceding king died, and sometimes from the day of the coronation of the king. However precise these calculations may appear to be, modern science must always fail in its attempts to restore what the Egyptians never possessed. In the midst of these doubts, the course which seems the most prudent and scientific, the least likely to be a departure from truth, is to accept as they stand the lists of Manetho. It would certainly be contrary to established facts to pretend that from the days of Menes to the Greek conquest Egypt always formed one united kingdom; and it is possible that unexpected discoveries may one day prove that throughout nearly the whole duration of this vast empire there were even more collateral dynasties than the partisans of that system now contend for. But everything shows us that the work of elimination has been already performed on the lists of Manetho, in the state in which they have reached us. If in fact these lists contained the collateral dynasties we should find in them, either before or after the twenty-first, the dynasty of high priests who reigned at Thebes whilst the twenty-first occupied Tanis: in the same way we should have to count, either before or after the twenty-third, the seven or eight independent kings who were contemporary with it, and who, if Manetho had not rejected them, would have added as many successive royal families to the lists of the Egyptian priest; the dodecarchy would have counted for one at least between the twenty-fifth and twenty-sixth dynasties, and finally the Theban kings, rivals of the shepherds, would have taken rank before or after the seventeenth.

"There were, therefore, incontestably contemporaneous dynasties in Egypt; but Manetho has thrown them out and admitted those only whom he regarded as legitimate, and his lists contain no others. If it were not so, it would not be thirty-one dynasties that we should have to reckon, in the list of royal families previous to Alexander, but probably nearer sixty.

"The scholars who have attempted to compress the dates given by Manetho have never yet been able to produce one single monument to prove that two dynasties named in his lists as successive were contemporary. On the contrary, there are superabundant monumental proofs, collected by very many Egyptologers, to convince us that all the royal races enumerated by the Sebennytic priest occupied the throne in succession."—MARIETTE.

4. There is in fact no country the history of which can be written on the testimony of so many original documents as that of Egypt. Egyptian monuments are found not only in Egypt itself, but in Nubia, in Soudan, and even in Syria. To this series, already very numerous, we may add the large number of antiquities that for the last fifty years have been placed in the Museums of all large capitals, and among which the Museum of Cairo holds one of the first places, thanks to the energetic researches of M. Mariette. The historical monuments of Egypt may be divided into two classes, those belonging to history generally, and those peculiar to one particular dynasty, the history of which they tell, and serve as proofs of its existence.

We shall now say a few words on the most important monuments that throw light on the general history of ancient Egypt.

5. "The first is a papyrus preserved in the Turin Museum, purchased from M. Drovetti, consul-general of France. If this papyrus were entire, the science of Egyptian antiquities could not possess a more valuable document. It contains a list of all the mythical or historical personages who were believed to have reigned in Egypt, from fabulous times down to a period we cannot ascertain, because the end of the papyrus is wanting. Compiled under Ramses II. (nineteenth dynasty), that is, in the most flourishing epoch of the history of Egypt, this list has all the characteristics of an official document, and gives us the more valuable assistance, as the name of each king is followed by the duration of his

reign, and each dynasty by the total number of years during which it governed Egypt. Unfortunately this inestimable treasure exists only in very small pieces (164 in number), which it is often impossible to join correctly.

6. "A most valuable monument has been brought from the Temple of Karnak and deposited in the Imperial Library at Paris. This is a small chamber on the walls of which Thothmes III. (eighteenth dynasty) is represented making offerings before the images of sixty-one of his predecessors; it is called the 'Hall of the Ancestors.'* Here we have no longer to deal with a regular and uninterrupted series; Thothmes III. has made a choice among his predecessors, and to those of his choice alone he makes his offerings. At first sight, then, the 'Hall of the Ancestors' cannot be treated as an extract from the royal lists of Egypt. The compiler, actuated by motives of which we are ignorant, has taken here and there the names of some kings, sometimes accepting an entire dynasty, sometimes passing over long periods. It must be observed also that the artist charged with the execution of the Hall conceived the plan from a decorative point of view, without concerning himself to give everywhere a strictly chronological order to the figures he introduced. Lastly, unfortunate mutilations (twelve royal names are missing) have taken from the record preserved at Paris a part of its importance. It follows, then, that the 'Hall of Ancestors' has not afforded to science all the help that might have been expected from it. It has, however, assisted to define more precisely than any other list the names borne by the kings of the thirteenth dynasty.

7. "There is another choice of the same kind, made also under the nspiration of motives beyond our knowledge, offered us by the 'Tablet of Abydos,' found in the ruins of that celebrated city, and preserved in the British Museum. In this case it is Ramses II. who pays homage to his ancestors. There were originally fifty names, but only thirty, more or less complete, now remain. This deplorably mutilated state deprived the 'Tablet of Abydos' of nearly all its real historical value, till M. Mariette discovered quite recently, in another temple of the same city, another copy much more perfect, and which supplies nearly all the vacancies in the first, dated in the reign of Seti I., father and predecessor of Ramses II. This 'Second Tablet of Abydos' furnishes a list of the kings of the first six dynasties almost as complete as Manetho's list, which it entirely corroborates. It also shows that the royal names found on the mutilated monument preserved in London, hitherto defying classification, must henceforth serve to bridge over part of the monumental gulf between the sixth and eleventh dynasties.

---

* Frequently called also the "Tablet of Tuthmosis."

8. "The testimony of the 'Second Tablet of Abydos,' as regards the primitive dynasties, is confirmed by the 'Tablet of Sakkarah,' (discovered also by M. Mariette, and now deposited in the Museum of Cairo.) This monument is not, like the others, of royal origin. It was found in the tomb of a simple priest who lived under Ramses II., and was called Tunar-i; according to the faith of the Egyptians, one of the good things reserved for the dead who had merited eternal life was to be admitted to the society of kings. Tunar-i is represented as entering the august assembly; fifty-eight kings are there present, those no doubt whose memories were most honoured at Memphis. The selection is similar to that of the Tablet of Abydos. There are, nevertheless, some interesting differences. Once or twice a king omitted in one list is registered in the other, even sometimes of two princes, whose reigns were incontestably simultaneous, one figures at Sakkarah and the other at Abydos. Thus, in the time of the nineteenth dynasty, among the competitors who are represented in the Egyptian annals, we cannot positively pronounce as to which were at the time considered legitimate sovereigns, and the list varies according to the locality, and no doubt to the limits within which they exercised authority."—MARIETTE.

9. As for documents relating only to the history of one dynasty or one reign, they are so immensely numerous that it is easy to see how impossible it is for us to attempt even their enumeration. Moreover, we shall naturally be led to mention the most important in the course of our narrative. They are of two sorts, manuscripts on papyrus, poems on the exploits of the kings, literary compositions, correspondence or registers of accounts of the public administration, and monumental inscriptions. These last must be again divided into two principal heads, public and private monuments. The official inscriptions engraved on detached steles or on the Temple walls, often accompanied by great coloured bas-reliefs, relate especially striking events and military exploits; there are some really long poems, relating quite in Biblical style the events of several campaigns even to their smallest details. The private inscriptions open to us the internal life of Egyptian society, and initiate us into all the machinery of its organisation: they furnish also the most solid and valuable basis for chronology, as it is not uncommon to find epitaphs relating that a person was born on a certain day of one month in some particular year of some other person's life, and that he lived so many years, months and days.

SECTION III.—FOUNDATION OF THE MONARCHY—FIRST DYNASTIES.

1. As we have already said in the First Book of our Manual, in speaking of the ethnographical table of the Book of Genesis, the Egyptians

were a branch of the race of Ham. They came from Asia through the desert of Syria to settle in the valley of the Nile. This is a fact clearly established by science, and entirely confirms the statements of the Book of Genesis. As for the opinion once generally admitted, that the Egyptians belonged to an African race whose first centre of civilisation was at Meroe, and who had gradually descended the banks of the Nile to the Sea, it cannot now be sustained. We know, in fact, from the monuments, that the most ancient centre of Egyptian civilisation was in the neighbourhood of Memphis, in Lower and Central Egypt, before even the foundation of Thebes; and we can follow the gradual march of culture, ascending the Nile towards Ethiopia, in a way exactly the reverse of what has hitherto been supposed.

All remembrance of the early days of the residence of the sons of Mizraim, in the land where they settled, is lost in the mist of mythical traditions. This epoch Manetho fills with the fabulous dynasties of "Gods, Heroes and Manes," and the hieroglyphic inscriptions frequently call it the times of Hor Shesu—that is, "Servants of Horus," the national deity and special guardian of the Egyptian people. Did they arrive in this land with a civilisation already developed during their stay in Asia, and closely resembling that of the early Cushites of Babylonia, of the empire of Nimrod? Or, having emigrated in a state of barbarism, was that civilisation developed by their own exertions, uninfluenced by other nations? These are questions science will probably never be able to answer, and which will always remain an open field for speculation.

What alone seems evident is, that the population of Egypt was at first composed of distinct tribes, who, although of the same origin, had each a separate existence. The tenth chapter of Genesis mentions four of them, each represented by a son of Mizraim. These are first the "Ludim," the true and dominant Egyptian race, called in their language Rut or Lut—that is, "men" *par excellence.* Next the Pathrusim, or people of the southern country—that is, of the Thebaid, in Egyptian P-to-res. The Naphtuhim, or people of Memphis, the sacerdotal name of which was Na Phtah, the "Part of Phtah," and lastly the Annamim, the Anu of the Egyptian monuments, who seem originally to have been dispersed throughout the whole Nile valley, and who have left traces of their name in the cities of Heliopolis (in Egyptian An), Tentyris or Denderah (also sometimes called An), and Hermonthis (An-res, southern An); a branch of this race maintained for a long time a separate existence in a part of the Sinaitic peninsula. But Egyptian history only really begins from the time when these different peoples were welded into one under a single sceptre, when a purely political hereditary power, strongly marked by military character, replaced the theocratic authority, by which till then the various tribes had been governed.

2. The author of this revolution belonged originally to the city of This (in Egyptian Teni), called in later times Abydos, in Central Egypt. Herodotus says (HER. ii. 99), "The Priests said that Menes was the first king of Egypt, and that it was he who raised the dyke which protects Memphis from the inundations of the Nile. Before his time the river flowed entirely along the sandy range of hills which skirts Egypt on the side of Lybia. He, however, by banking up the river at the bend which it forms. about a hundred furlongs south of Memphis, laid the ancient channel dry, while he dug a new course for the stream half-way between the two lines of hills. * * Having thus, by turning the river, made the tract where it used to run dry land, he proceeded in the first place to build the city now called Memphis, * * he also built the temple of Vulcan (Phtah) which stands within the city, a vast edifice, very worthy of mention." All classical authors who have written about Egypt mention the name of Menes, and the monuments confirm their testimony by also mentioning him as the founder of the empire. The dyke he constructed still exists under the name of Dyke of Kosheish, and regulates the course of the water in that region.* The city built by Menes was called Men-nefer, "the pleasant residence," which name the Greeks corrupted into "Memphis."

The direct descendants of Menes form the first dynasty, which, according to Manetho, reigned 253 years. No monument contemporary with these princes has come down to us. The immediate successor of Menes, Teta (the Athothis of Manetho), is mentioned as having built a palace at Memphis, and as having written books on surgery. The name of the fifth king of the dynasty Hespu, or Hesep-ti (Usaphaidos, M.)† is frequently mentioned in the "Funeral Ritual" as the author of sacred writings. Lastly, the fragments of Manetho record under the reign of the seventh king, Semempses, a terrible plague. A comparison of the lists of Manetho with the second Tablet of Abydos and the Tablet of Sakkarah proves that the empire founded by Menes was not extended to the whole of Egypt at once, and without a struggle, but that, on the contrary, a great part of the time of the first dynasty was passed in conflicts between princes who reigned—some at Memphis and others at Abydos.

3. The second dynasty, to which Manetho assigns nine kings, lasted 302 years. It was also originally from This, and probably related to the first, for no distinction is made between them in the Turin papyrus.

---

* The remains of the Dyke of Menes were discovered by M. Mariette, and its existence is mentioned by Dr. Brugsch in his "Histoire d'Egypt."

† The forms of the names in the lists of Manetho will be indicated in this way (M).

It seems very probable that the great Pyramid, built in steps at Sakkarah, was intended for the sepulchre of the second king of this dynasty, Kekeu (Cechous, M.), by whom also was established, it is said, the worship of some sacred animals, amongst others the bull Apis, who was considered to be a living manifestation of the god Phtah, and was worshipped at Memphis. This Pyramid, therefore, is the oldest monument in Egypt, and with the exception of the ruins of the Tower of Babel, the most ancient in the world. The low and narrow door, with a lintel of white limestone covered with hieroglyphics, the jambs decorated in a manner unknown elsewhere, with alternate small pieces of limestone and cubes of green enamelled earth, which formed the entrance to the sepulchral chamber of this Pyramid, was, in 1845, carried by M. Lepsius to the Museum at Berlin. It is highly characteristic of an art still in its infancy and attempting its first steps; but it shows that the ingenious system of Egyptian writing was even then fully established.

To the third king of this second dynasty, Ba-neter-en (Binothris, M.), is attributed a law declaring females capable of ascending the throne of Egypt; this law, in fact, was often re-enacted in the course of history. Legendary prodigies are related of the reign of the seventh king, Neferkera (Nepherkeres, M.).* Lastly, it is said that the eighth king, Sesocris, was a giant. We possess some remains of sculpture, which we may venture, perhaps, to refer to the last reigns of this dynasty: first, the tomb of a high functionary called Thoth-hotep, discovered by the excavations of M. Mariette in the Necropolis of Sakkarah, where the dead of the great city of Memphis were buried; also three standing statues of limestone, representing Sepa, another functionary, and two of his sons, with which the Museum of the Louvre is enriched. In studying them we remark a rudeness and indecision of style, showing that at the end of the second dynasty Egyptian art was still feeling its way, and was still imperfectly formed.

4. When this family had become extinct, a dynasty, originally from Memphis, seized the throne, forming the third, and to it a duration of 214 years is attributed. The second of its kings, Tses-hor-tsa (Tosorthrus, M.), is said to have occupied himself specially with medical science, writing, and the art of stone cutting. In this royal family we meet with the first of the many conquerors who went out from the land of the Pharaohs; Manetho says that the head of this family, Seker-nefer-ke (Necherophes, M.), subdued a part of the Lybians, who were terrified by an eclipse.† On the rocks of Sinai a

* The Nile flowed for eleven days with a mixture of honey and water.—TR.

† "The Lybians revolted from the Egyptians and submitted through fear, on a sudden increase of the moon." MANETHO (*Syncellus*).—TR.

bas-relief has been found, which represents Snefru (Sephouris, M.), last king but one of the dynasty, subduing the nomadic tribes of the Anu of Arabia Petræa.

The tomb of one of the great officers of this king, named Amten, has been discovered at Sakkarah, and transported to the Museum of Berlin. Art has advanced since the last reign, but is still far from perfection. The pictures on this tomb, which is of an antiquity so great as to surpass imagination, assist us in penetrating the interior life of the epoch when it was constructed. It shows us Egyptian civilisation as completely organised as it was at the time of the Persian or Macedonian conquest, with all the marks of individuality and of a long previous existence. The inhabitants of the Nile valley had already domesticated nearly all kinds of animals which are useful to man, and even some that we know only in a wild state. The ox, the dog, aquatic birds, had long since been brought into use, and the skill of breeders had been able to produce numerous varieties of each species. The only beast of burden is the ass; neither the horse nor the camel seem to have been as yet known in Egypt. The Egyptian language was completely formed, with its peculiar characteristics, distinct from other allied idioms. Hieroglyphic writing is found on the monuments of the first dynasties, distinguished by all the complexity that it preserved to the last day of its existence.

Section IV.—Fourth and Fifth Dynasties—Age of the Great Pyramids.

1. With the fourth dynasty, Memphite, like the third, and which reigned 284 years, history becomes clearer, and monuments more numerous. This was the age of the three Great Pyramids, built by the three kings, Khufu (the Cheops of Herodotus), Shafra (Chefren), and Menkara (Mycerinus). Khufu was a warlike king; the bas-reliefs of Sinai celebrate his victories over the Anu, who harassed the colonies of Egyptian workmen established on the peninsula for working the copper mines.* But it is to the Pyramid that he owes the immortality of his name, which will be remembered as long as man exists. Herodotus gives us (Her. ii. 124) some details of the construction of this gigantic monument, mixed up, however, with puerile anecdotes that seem to belong to an exact and authentic tradition. 100,000 men, who were

* Dr. Brugsch, in a little work, *Wanderung nach den Türkis-Minen und der Sinai Halbinsel*, contends that the mines chiefly worked in the Sinaitic Peninsula by the Egyptians were the Turquoise Mines, recently rediscovered and worked by our countryman, the late Major Macdonald. —Tr.

relieved every three months, were, he says, employed for thirty years in building this artificial mountain; the king, in his pride, intended it for his tomb, and it has remained, at any rate as regards bulk, the greatest of all the works of man. The whole of the people of the country were successively forced to the work; and the labour was the harder, in that the Egyptians had no machinery but ropes and rollers, and were compelled to drag the stones by main force on causeways, on an inclined plane, to the required height. The causeway which served to bring the stone from the quarries of Toora, on the other bank of the Nile, to the summit of the Pyramid plateau, still remains, and has been preserved as in itself alone worthy of the admiration of future generations. Little less must have been the work of building the Pyramids of Shafra and Menkera. The science in construction which these monuments exhibit is wonderful, and has never been surpassed. With all the progress of knowledge, it would be, even in our days, a problem difficult to solve, to construct, as the Egyptian architects of the fourth dynasty have done, in such a mass as that of the Pyramid, chambers and passages, which, in spite of the millions of tons pressing on them, have for sixty centuries preserved their original shape without crack or flaw.*

The Pyramids are not, however, the only great architectural works that these kings have left us. The great Sphinx at Gizeh, in the neighbourhood of the three great Pyramids, an immense rock, sculptured and built into this form, seems to have been finished in the reign of Schafra. Close by it M. Mariette has discovered, buried in the sand of the desert, a vast temple, which seems from sure indications to belong to the same reign. It is entirely constructed of enormous blocks of black or rose-coloured granite, and of oriental alabaster, without any sculpture or even ornament of any kind. Straight lines alone, in the severest purity, are used in its decoration.

2. The early reigns of the fourth dynasty mark the culminating point in the primitive history of Egypt. The splendour and riches of the country seem to have been very great under these princes, as is sufficiently proved by the immense buildings erected during the period. The boundaries of the monarchy then extended as far as the cataracts; the capital was Memphis, and the whole vitality of the empire was concentrated in that neighbourhood.

But the enormous works of the Pyramids could only have been accomplished at the cost of frightful oppression. Forced labour laid an insupportable burden on the people. Manetho, Herodotus, and Diodorus Siculus repeat traditions proving that these princes, who

---

* On the Pyramids, see the splendid work of Colonel Howard Vyse, *The Pyramids of Ghizeh.* London, 1800—1812.

had laid such heavy burdens on their people, were remembered with hatred even after the lapse of ages. According to these traditions, Khufu not only oppressed the people in taking them from the occupations of their daily life, but even shut up the temples and stopped the sacrifices; he afterwards, however, repented, and became the author of a much esteemed religious book. Shafra is said to have followed the example of the tyranny and impiety of his predecessor, and by the popular verdict, the bodies of both kings were excluded from the splendid tombs they had prepared. Menkera did the same at the commencement of his reign, but afterwards amended his ways, re-opened the temples, and conducted public worship with a great degree of splendour; this last fact agrees with the statement that one of the most important mystical chapters of the "Funereal Ritual" is said to have been discovered, in an ancient manuscript, during the reign of Menkera, and to have been published by that king. There is no doubt that these stories are only popular and fabulous legends; for example, the closing of the temples by Khufu and Shafra is expressly denied by inscriptions dated in their reigns. But the legend is not, however, entirely without historical foundation. Everything seems to show that the end of the fourth dynasty, immediately after the reigns of the Pyramid-building kings, was a time of revolution and trouble, caused by preceding oppressions. A comparison of the lists of Manetho with the monuments of the Necropolis of Sakkarah, shows that there were violent competitions for the throne during this period. The splendid statues of Shafra in diorite, rose-coloured granite, alabaster, and basalt, which decorated the temple near the Sphinx, have been found in pieces in a well, into which they had been thrown during a revolutionary movement evidently not long after his reign.

3. The fifth dynasty came originally from Elephantiné, at the southern extremity of Upper Egypt, and there possibly the kings generally resided, though at the same time Memphis was not deprived of its importance. This dynasty numbered nine kings, whose names are all found on the monuments, and who occupied the throne for 248 years. Their reigns seem to have been prosperous and peaceable, but we cannot refer to anyone in particular as distinguished by any remarkable event.

The private monuments of the time of this dynasty are, like those of the fourth, very numerous. Near Memphis, particularly at Gizeh and Sakkarah, excavations have brought to light the tombs of a great number of personages of high rank at the courts of one or other of the kings of these dynasties.

4. By the aid of the inscriptions on these tombs science is able to reconstruct the "Peerage" of Egypt under Khufu, Shafra or Menkera, as well as under the kings of the Elephantiné dynasty. In

those ancient times Egyptian society was formed on an entirely aristocratic basis. It seems that Menes, in establishing royalty, had been the chief of a revolution, similar to those in ancient India, which frequently subjected the Brahmins to the absolute supremacy of the Kchatryas or warriors. The monuments of the primitive Egyptian dynasties show us all power concentrated in the hands of a small military caste, of an aristocracy to a certain extent apparently composed of conquerors, and to whom the people quietly submitted. Were not these the Ludim of Genesis, who, by establishing their supremacy over the Pathrusim, the Naphtuhim, and the Anamim, first made Egypt one united country? The families of this aristocracy were but few in number, and all more or less related to the royal family, owing to the number of children brought up in the royal harems. The members of these families, like the great feudatories of Europe, succeeded to all the higher military and political offices, and transmitted from father to son the government of provinces. Like all ancient pagan aristocracies, they even possessed themselves of and monopolised all priestly functions.

We constantly find representations of scenes from domestic or agricultural life on the walls of Memphite tombs of the fourth and fifth dynasties. These pictures help us to investigate all the secrets of the patriarchal feudal life of the nobles of Egypt sixty centuries ago. We seem to visit the large and flourishing farms scattered over their estates; we may know the numbers of their flocks, and the heads of cattle counted by thousands; their parks where antelopes, storks, geese of every species were domesticated and kept. We may even see them in their elegant villas, surrounded by respectful and obedient vassals, or rather serfs. We can know the flowers cultivated in their gardens; see the troops of dancers and singers maintained in their mansions to supply amusement. The minutest details of their field sports are depicted on these tombs. We see that they were passionately fond both of hunting and fishing; and for both of these amusements they found as many opportunities as they could desire on the numerous canals by which the country was everywhere intersected. For the service also of these great personages of the aristocracy, the large square-sailed barks, frequently depicted on the tombs, floated on the Nile, to be employed in a commerce which everything proves to have been most extensive.

5. In these monuments of the fourth and fifth dynasty, art attains to the most remarkable degree of perfection. It is entirely realistic, it strives above all for truth to nature, with no attempt at the ideal. The figures of men are somewhat more thickset and rude than in the works of later schools, the relative proportions of different parts of the body are less exactly preserved, the muscles of the legs and arms are exaggerated. But in these sculptures of the primitive Memphite tombs there is nevertheless an elegance of composition, a simplicity and reality

of movement, a life in all the figures, which the immutable laws of the priestly "Canon of Proportions" destroyed in later times, however much in other respects art may have improved. In this first and free development of Egyptian art, imperfect though it was, there were the germs of more than Egypt ever possessed, even in its most brilliant period. Art then had a life, afterwards destroyed by sacerdotal restrictions. If the Pharaonic artists could have preserved this secret, when acquiring that incomparable harmony of proportion and majesty which they possessed in a greater degree than any other artists in the world, they would have equalled the Greeks, and two thousand years before them would have attained to absolute perfection in art. But this phase of genius was never allowed full scope; and thus their style remained imperfect, and the glory of reaching that point which can never be surpassed was reserved for others.

6. In the decoration of the subterranean tombs of which we speak, and of the sarcophagi sometimes found in them, there is a peculiar architectural style, different from that of more recent monuments—a style characteristic of the Pyramid period. In this system of architecture, all the decoration consists of an arrangement of narrow vertical and horizontal bands with a convex surface. This is in imitation of buildings constructed of light timber, such as sycamore and palm, the two most common trees of Egypt, whose trunks were not even squared before being used. Also very often in tombs the sepulchral chamber is roofed by beams of stone, rounded so as to represent the trunks of palm trees. The Egyptians therefore had not commenced, as was long believed, by leading the life of troglodytes, or cavern-dwellers. Their most ancient edifices were constructed of wood, built in the midst of the Nile valley; and in the first subterranean tombs in the flanks of the Arabian and Lybian mountains, they copied the style and arrangement of these slight buildings, and this type always remained in use for their dwellings.

7. But we have not only monumental inscriptions of ages, when we might be inclined to believe that the whole human race must have been still in a state of complete barbarism, for, favoured by the climate of Egypt, so miraculously preservative, even sheets of fragile papyrus have lasted fifty centuries, and come down to us almost entire. The Imperial Library of France possesses a book dated in the reign of Assa-Tatkera (Tatkeres, M.), last king but one of the fifth dynasty, written by an old man of the royal family, named Phtah-hotep. It is a sort of handbook of good manners for young people, a treatise on practical morality, teaching them how to pass through the world with propriety and success; it does not belong to a higher moral sphere than the books of the Chinese Confucius. We find in it the rules to be observed in a community, and rules for making one's way in the world, without restraining

any of the passions, or, as the jargon of a false philosophy now says, any of the instincts of nature. The basis of all morality and good order in the book of Phtah-hotep is filial obedience, obedience also to the established government, supposed to be invested with a truly paternal authority. "The son who obeys the word of his father," it says, "will therefore live to a good old age." "The obedience of a son to his father is a joyful thing. . . . . He is dear to his father, and his fame shall be known to all men on earth." "The disobedient sees knowledge in ignorance, virtue in vice; every day he without fear commits every kind of wickedness, and thus is dead while he lives. His daily life is what the wise man knows to be death, and curses follow him as he walks in his ways." The reward of him who observes these precepts follows,—long life and the king's favour. "The obedient son shall be happy in his obedience; he shall grow old and shall obtain favour." The author cites himself as an example, "Thus I have become an old man on earth; I have lived 110 years in favour with the king, and with the approval of the elders: I have done my duty to the king, and stood in the place of his favour."

A second treatise contained in the same manuscript, but of which only a few pages remain, was a collection of proverbs similar to those of king Solomon. Some of the maxims are as follows:—"Happiness finds every place alike good, but a little misfortune will abase a very great man." "A good word shines more than an emerald in the hand of a slave who finds it in the mire." "The wise man is satisfied with his knowledge: good is the place of his heart; sweet are his lips."

SECTION V.—FROM THE SIXTH TO THE ELEVENTH DYNASTY—TEMPORARY DECLINE OF EGYPTIAN CIVILISATION.

1. ON the death of the last king of the fifth dynasty, a new family, of Memphitic origin according to Manetho, came to the throne. The first king Ati (Othoēs, M), was, it is said, after a reign of thirty years assassinated by his guards. A great portion of his reign was no doubt occupied by internal dissensions, for the monuments name two competitors for the throne, Teta,* and Userkera, who were probably descendants of the former dynasty. But his son and successor, Pepi Merira (Phios, M.), was one of the most glorious and powerful kings. The whole country was subject to his sceptre, for his monuments have been found in all parts of Egypt, from Syene to Tanis. Like Khufu,

* In illustration of the remarks of M. Mariette, quoted in secs. 2, 3, it may be mentioned that Teta seems to have been accepted as the legitimate king by the compilers of the Tablet of Sakkarah and of the second Tablet of Abydos.—TR.

Pepi I. was a warlike king: at this epoch, the cataracts of the Nile, particularly the second, at Wady Halfa, did not, as they now do, present an insurmountable obstacle to navigation, and towards the south the frontier of Egypt was open to the incursions of the Wa-Wa, a migratory negro people. Pepi reduced these enemies to obedience. An unknown tribe of southern Bedouins (possibly the present Bischaris), were also subdued by the Egyptian arms. Finally, to the north, the hostile nomadic tribes received from Pepi the chastisement they had drawn on themselves by their aggressions on Egyptian workmen engaged in the copper mines, in the Sinaitic Peninsula. We may remark, in the inscriptions relative to the campaigns of Pepi Merira, a fact of great importance in the history of the migrations of races: the negroes are there represented as immediately adjoining the Egyptian frontier, and we find no trace of the Cushite Ethiopians, whom subsequent evidence shows us to have occupied just that part of the Nile valley, after having driven the negroes southward. When the sixth dynasty ruled Egypt, the Hamitic race of Cush had not established itself in Africa, to which country it came no doubt by the Straits of Bab-el-Mandeb, but still remained in Asia, where it had founded a powerful empire at Babylon. Pepi Merira was not, moreover, a mere warrior king, he occupied himself in public works. It is proved from one of his monuments that he opened the route across the desert from Gheneh in Upper Egypt, to the port of Kosseir on the Red Sea, established stations, and dug wells for the benefit of caravans. A second Pepi, surnamed Nefer-kera (Phiops, M.) is remarkable as having (a fact unique in history) reigned one whole century; of the events of this long reign we, however, know next to nothing.

But immediately after this long reign, and probably even in its later years, troubles and civil discord broke out, more serious and more violent than had ever before been seen in Egypt. Mentemsaf (Menthesuphis, M.), the successor of Pepi-Neferkera was assassinated after a reign of only one year. His sister Neit-aker (whose name signifies "victorious Neit," or Minerva), the Nitocris of the Greeks, then seized the reins of government. Manetho calls her "the red-cheeked beauty," and agrees with Herodotus in praising, according to the sacerdotal traditions, her wisdom as well as her beauty. She struggled energetically against the revolutionary spirit which tended to divide the country, and had even reached the capital. At the same time, during a reign of twelve troubled years, Neit-aker repaired, or rather completed, the third pyramid of Gizeh, intending, it is supposed, to make it her own sepulchre, without, however, disturbing the sepulchral chamber of Menkera. She seems to have been obliged, during part of her reign, to temporise with the murderers of her brother, but without resigning the intention of revenging his death. She one day invited them to a subterranean gallery, and while they were enjoying a feast, the waters of the Nile, let in through a secret culvert, drowned them all. She was herself obliged to commit suicide to escape the reprisals of their partisans. Neit-aker was the last of her dynasty.

2. History, though so very fragmentary during the following epoch, gives us reason at any rate to think that Egypt then entered on a long period of convulsion, dismemberment, and political weakness. The seventh dynasty numbered in one version of the story, five kings in less than three months, and in another and still more expressive tradition, seventy kings in seventy days. Primitive art attained its highest point under the sixth dynasty. In the tombs of this period are found those beautiful and graceful statues with rounded smiling face, thin nose, broad shoulders, and muscular legs, of which the museum of the Louvre possesses a remarkable specimen in the sitting figure of a scribe, now in the centre of one of the rooms on the ground floor. But from the time of the civil commotions in which Neit-aker perished, Egyptian civilisation underwent a sudden and unaccountable eclipse. From the end of the sixth dynasty to the commencement of the eleventh Manetho reckons 436 years, and for this whole period the monuments are absolutely silent. Egypt seems then to have disappeared from the rank of nations; and when this long slumber ended, civilisation commenced a new career, entirely independent of the past. Did the empire of the Pharaohs during this interval of absolute darkness suffer from some invasion unknown to history? and do the lists of Manetho contain only the indigenous and legitimate dynasties who remained shut up in their capital? Doubtless, in treating of Egypt, the idea of invasion naturally occurs to us. Its geographical position and the inexhaustible resources of its soil rendered this country peculiarly liable to the attacks of its neighbours. It is also to be observed, that by comparing the skeletons of mummies from the tombs anterior to the sixth with those subsequent to the eleventh dynasty, we may observe, in the shape of the skulls, differences sufficient to lead us to the conclusion that the type of the population had been much modified in the interval by the introduction of a new element.

But as monumental proofs are absolutely wanting, it would be rash to affirm that this sudden eclipse of Egyptian civilisation, unaccountable after the sixth dynasty, was not due to one of those almost inexplicable seasons of weakness occurring sometimes in the life of nations, as well as of men. That a period of absolute decadence did then occur is certain, and the primitive civilisation of Egypt died with the sixth dynasty, to be resuscitated in later days.

3. Thus ends that period of nineteen centuries, which modern scholars know as the "Old Empire." "The spectacle then presented by Egypt," says M. Mariette, in his excellent history of that country,

"is worthy of close attention. At a time when all the rest of the world was plunged in barbaric darkness, when nations who in later times were to play so considerable a part in the world's history were still in a savage state, the banks of the Nile were peopled by a wise and polished race, and a powerful monarchy, supported by a formidable organisation of functionaries and employés, already governed the destinies of the nation. From the very earliest times, we see that Egyptian civilisation was complete, and future ages, however numerous they might be, could do but little to improve it. In some respects, Egypt, on the contrary, retrogrades, for no other period has been able to produce monuments like the Pyramids."

The Egyptian priests then were right in saying to Solon, when he visited their sanctuaries, "You Greeks are but children."

CHAPTER II.

THE MIDDLE EMPIRE.

SECTION I.—ELEVENTH AND TWELFTH DYNASTIES—THE LABYRINTH AND LAKE MOERIS.

1. THEBES did not exist in the days of the glory of the Old Empire. The holy city of Amen seems to have been founded during the period of anarchy and obscurity, succeeding, as we have said, to the sixth dynasty. Here was the birthplace of that renewed civilisation, that new monarchy, we are accustomed to call the Middle Empire, the middle age in fact of ancient Egypt—a middle age anterior to the earliest ages of all other history. From Thebes came the six kings of the eleventh dynasty, called alternately Entef and Muntuhotep, who struggled energetically with the separatists of the Delta, represented by the ninth and tenth dynasties of Manetho, perhaps even against foreign conquerors, and in the end subjected all Egypt to their sceptre. One of these Princes is constantly designated by the epithet "great" (Aa), and was doubtless the one who achieved this result. Here we again quote the excellent remarks of M. Mariette: "When with the eleventh dynasty, we see Egypt awake from her long slumber, all old traditions appear to be forgotten, the proper names used in ancient families, the titles of functionaries, the style of writing, and even the religion all seem new. This, Elephantine, and Memphis, are no longer the favourite capitals. Thebes for the first time becomes the seat of sovereign power. Egypt, moreover, has lost a considerable portion of her territory, and the authority of her legitimate kings hardly extends

beyond the limited district of the Thebaid. The study of the monuments confirms these general views; they are rude, primitive, sometimes coarse; and when we look at them we may well believe that Egypt, under the eleventh dynasty, again passed through a period of infancy, as she had already done under the third dynasty."

2. A dynasty, probably related to, and originally from, the same place as these first Theban princes, succeeded them. Manetho designates this as the twelfth. All the monarchs are called Osortasen, or Amenemhe, except the last, a queen named Ra-sebek-nefru (Skemiophris, M.). This twelfth dynasty reigned for 213 years, and its epoch was one of prosperity, of peace at home and glorious achievements abroad. In the time of the second king, Osortasen I., not only had Egypt regained its natural frontiers, but had reconquered Arabia Petræa, lost to her during the time of the civil discords. Nubia also was subjected to the authority of the Pharaohs. Osortasen I. engraved on a stele at Wady Halfa, in the south of Nubia, and on the rocks of Sinai, a record of his exploits.

The Pharaohs of the twelfth dynasty commenced the attempt to carry out that great political scheme, persisted in for more than thirty centuries, that led them to claim as their right every country watered by the Nile. At this time a state was established between the first cataract and the south of Abyssinia, which was to ancient, what Soudan is to modern, Egypt. This was "the land of Cush," or Ethiopia. With no precisely defined boundaries, with no unity of organisation or territory, Ethiopia was inhabited by numerous peoples differing in origin and race, but the bulk of the nation was composed of Cushites of the race of Ham, who had established themselves there since the time of the sixth Egyptian dynasty. These Cushites seem to have been, under the twelfth dynasty, formidable enemies to Egypt; towards Ethiopia the forces of the empire at that time marched; to oppose the Cushites, were built the fortresses of Kumneh and Semmeh on either bank of the Nile, beyond the second cataract, marking the southern limit of the empire of the Pharaohs. Whatever at this period may have been the political state of other parts of the world, the Egyptian forces under the twelfth dynasty never left the banks of their sacred river.

Amenemhe II. continued the southern wars of Osortasen I., with whom he had been associated in power; but the real conqueror of Ethiopia, the great military prince of the dynasty, was Osortasen III., the founder of the fortress of Semneh. The Temple erected there many centuries later in his honour, a temple where two other gods served as his subordinates, testifies to the reality of his power, and to the profound impression the grandeur of his reign had left in the country. The very steles placed by him at Semneh to mark the frontier of Egypt have also been found. On them is an inscription forbidding negroes to enter the land except to trade in cattle. This prince was buried in the brick pyramid of Dashur; his religious name was Ra-sha-keu, and he may be identified with the ancient and wise legislator, Asychis, of whom Herodotus speaks as having regulated the law of mortgages.* Two inscriptions of the reign of his successor Amenemhe III. speak of a great victory he gained over the negroes, and state that the Asiatic copper mines always belonged to him.

3. During these wars, which have conferred a never-fading lustre on the names of the Osortasens and Amenemhes, Egypt was strengthened internally by the vigour then apparent in all branches of civilisation. Works as marvellous as those of the fourth dynasty, but, in part at any rate, more useful—the Labyrinth and Lake Moeris, were then executed. We shall speak of the Labyrinth (ch. v. sec. 9. 2,) when we enumerate the principal monuments of Egypt. As for Lake Moeris, it was, in the estimation of those of the ancients who saw it, one of the wonders of the Pharaonic ages, and nothing could better prove the high state attained by engineering skill under the twelfth dynasty, than this work, of which a Frenchman, M. Linant, was the first to find the remains.

We have already spoken of the importance of the Nile to Egypt. "If its periodical rise is insufficient, a portion of the land is not inundated, and consequently remains uncultivated; if, however, the river leaves its bed with too much violence, it carries away the dykes, submerges the villages, and injures the land it ought to fertilise. Egypt thus perpetually oscillates between two equally dreaded scourges. Impressed with a sense of these dangers, Amenemhe III. conceived and executed a gigantic project. On the west of Egypt there is an oasis of cultivable land, the Fayum, buried in the midst of the desert, and attached by a sort of isthmus to the country watered by the Nile. In the centre of this oasis is a large plateau about the same level as the valley of the Nile; to the west, however, a considerable depression of the land produces a valley occupied by a natural lake more than ten leagues in length, the 'Birket Kerun.' In the centre of this plateau Amenemhe undertook the formation of an artificial lake with an area of ten millions of square metres. If the rise of the Nile was insufficient, the water was led into the lake and stored up for use, not only in the Fayum, but over the whole of the left bank of the Nile as far as the sea. If too large an inundation threatened the dykes, the vast reservoir of the artificial lake remained open, and when the lake itself overflowed, the surplus waters were led by a canal into the Birket Kerun.

"The two names given in Egypt to this admirable work of

* HER., Book II., ch. 136.

Amenemhe III. deserve to be recorded. Of one, Meri, that is 'the Lake' *par excellence,* the Greeks have made Moeris, a name erroneously applied by them to a king; whilst the other, P-iom, 'the Sea,' has become, in the mouth of the Arabs, the name of the entire province, Fayum, gifted by the genius of one of the kings of the twelfth dynasty with this precious element of fertility."—MARIETTE.

4. The time of the twelfth dynasty is thus, as we see, one of the most splendid periods in Egyptian history; it marks, perhaps, the highest point attained by, and the most flourishing epoch of, Pharaonic civilisation. The invasion of the Shepherds occurred some time afterwards; and their ravages, principally directed to all that recalled the princes of this dynasty, have left none of their great edifices standing. Of the public buildings of the Osortasens and Amenemhes, nothing remains beyond two obelisks at Heliopolis and the Fayum, and some beautiful colossal statues, discovered in the excavations of M. Mariette at Tanis and Abydos. We have, however, magnificent specimens of the art of this period in the numerous private funereal steles now preserved in our museums, and also in the celebrated tombs of Beni Hassan, where the façades show the first and original type of the Doric order, subsequently adopted by the Greeks. We may judge from these tombs that the architecture of the twelfth dynasty had no relation to that of the primitive ages. It is an entirely new art, and we shall see that its rules were again followed, when, after a second eclipse, Egyptian art once more revived at the dawn of that historical period called the "New Empire."

What we know most of in the art of the twelfth dynasty is its sculpture, which, favoured by a period of peace, arrived at a degree of perfection hardly surpassed by the best works of the eighteenth and nineteenth dynasties. The predominant feature in sculpture of this age is delicacy, elegance, and harmony of proportion. The reality and life of the primitive school no longer exist. Art has no longer the same liberty; it is subject to the fetters of priestly rule. The hieratic "canon of proportion" has already been established in the form we shall meet with after the expulsion of the Shepherds; no vestige remains of the primitive art but the energy and boldness with which the muscles of the arms and legs are rendered. The hardest, the least promising materials, are worked with such delicacy and finish of execution as, even in colossal works, to resemble a cameo. But if the sculpture of the twelfth dynasty surpasses in delicacy the most perfect monuments of the eighteenth dynasty, it has not the monumental grandeur of the productions of the latter epoch.

5. The curious subterranean tombs of Beni-hassan, already mentioned, are those of great personages, high functionaries of state, and governors of provinces, who led a life similar to that of the great lords

of the old empire, and who probably also constituted an hereditary aristocracy. Perhaps the most interesting is that of Ameni, where the Egypt of the twelfth dynasty is, so to speak, photographed. On one side we see the beasts they are fattening; the land is being cultivated with ploughs constructed like those now in use by the Fellahs of modern Egypt; corn is being harvested and trodden out by cattle, who tread the sheaves under their feet. On another side we see the navigation of the Nile; large ships being built or loaded; elegant furniture being made of precious woods, and garments being prepared. In a long inscription Ameni himself speaks, and relates the story of his life. As a general he had made a campaign in Ethiopia, and had been charged with the protection of the caravans bringing to Coptos across the desert the gold from the mines. As governor of the province he thus sums up his administration:—"The whole land was sown from north to south. Thanks were given me by the king's household for the tribute of large cattle. Nothing was stolen from my stores. I myself laboured, and all the province was in full activity. No little child was ever ill-treated, nor widow oppressed by me. I have never troubled the fisherman, nor disturbed the shepherd. No scarcity took place in my time, and a bad harvest brought no famine. I gave equally to the widow and married woman, and in my judgments I did not favour the great at the expense of the poor."

Section II.—Thirteenth and Fourteenth Dynasties.

1. Although the history of the twelfth dynasty is clear and well known, illustrated by numerous monuments, there is, nevertheless, no period in the annals of Egypt more obscure than the one closing with the thirteenth dynasty. It is one long series of revolutions, troubles, and internal dissensions, closed by a terrible catastrophe, the greatest and most lasting recorded in Egyptian history, which a second time interrupted the march of civilisation on the banks of the Nile, and for a while struck Egypt from the list of nations. The dynasties of this epoch are represented in the extracts from Manetho merely by the total duration of the government of each; and, moreover, the different versions we possess of these extracts do not agree as to the number of kings and the length of their reigns, or even sometimes of their origin.

2. The thirteenth dynasty was of Theban origin, like the two preceding. Manetho assigns to it sixteen kings, and a duration of 453 years. The names of the kings have for the most part been found on the monuments, nearly all being either Sevek-hotep or Nofre-hotep. No building of this dynasty has been preserved; but we may judge by the steles and statues of this time, discovered in the excavations at Tanis

and Abydos, as well as by some fragments of admirable sculpture preserved in the museums of Europe, that Egypt, at any rate during the early ages of the dominion of this new royal family, had lost nothing of its ancient prosperity, that she still remained mistress of her whole territory, and was internally as prosperous as under the twelfth dynasty. The silence of the monuments does not permit us to form even a conjecture on the subject of the wars of these kings. We may conclude, however, from the presence of a colossus of the thirteenth dynasty in the island of Argo, near Dongolah, that Egypt had at this time extended her frontier towards the south. Moreover, a fragment of a colossus in rose-coloured granite, which was in later times appropriated by King Amun-hotep III., of the eighteenth, would seem, from its style, to belong to the time of the thirteenth dynasty. This fragment is now in the Museum of the Louvre, and bears on its base a long list of subjugated negro nations. An inscription of the same date, engraven on a rock at El Hammamat, a station on the route to the port of Kosseir on the Red Sea, speaks of the extensive commerce then carried on in precious stones with Southern Arabia, and shows that Egyptian influence was then undisputed in the latter country.

3. A curious peculiarity belonging to this epoch deserves notice, and throws new light on the physical history of the valley of the Nile. There are at Semneh lofty rocks near the river, bearing, at a height of seven metres above the present water level, hieroglyphic inscriptions. Now the translation of these inscriptions proves that the Nile, which under the eighteenth dynasty was at its present level in the time of the inundation, under the twelfth and thirteenth dynasties rose seven metres higher. This enormous change must be attributed to the gradual wearing away of the granite rock, the natural dam that formerly kept the upper part of the river at a much higher level, and at one of the cataracts of the Nile, probably at Semneh, produced falls like those of Niagara, or of the Rhine near Schaffhausen. At that time the Nile, forming a deep and wide sheet of water above Semneh, must have watered vast regions, now partly desert, such as Dongolah, Fazoql, Southern Nubia, and the Isle of Meroe. But the river, by the long continued action of its waters, wore away piece by piece the natural barrier of rocks opposed to it, the remains of which even now obstruct the current. In the same way the Amazon has cut through the living rock the celebrated defile of Manzeriche; the Danube has, one after the other, drained its five basins or primitive lakes; the Rhine has worn a passage between the Black Forest and the Vosges; and lastly, the Niagara, ceaselessly wearing away the rock over which it falls, recedes insensibly, at a rate that may be calculated within a few hundred years, towards Lake Erie, and when it has reached this point, the lake as well as the famous cataract will cease to exist. The study of the alluvium of the

Nile has revealed the existence of three successive levels. The learned Sir Gardner Wilkinson, from his geological observations, has fixed the date of the chief of these changes at from fifteen to seventeen centuries before our era. But as positive monumental statements prove that the change had already taken place before the expulsion of the Shepherds, we must ante-date the rupture of the natural barriers of the Upper Nile three or four centuries, and place it in the interval between the thirteenth and eighteenth dynasties.

4. All the monuments of the thirteenth dynasty that we have mentioned, proving that its dominion extended over the whole territory of Egypt, are those of its earlier kings. We have no contemporary monuments of the princes who continued this line; their names are only known from royal lists like that of the "Hall of Ancestors" at Karnak, or the fragments of papyrus of Turin. Nothing, therefore, expressly forbids our adopting the opinion proposed by many modern scholars, and in itself probable enough, that towards the close of the thirteenth (Theban) dynasty, the fourteenth (the Xoite of Manetho) established itself as a rival in the Delta. The division of Egypt into two rival and hostile kingdoms, as well as the weakness necessarily resulting from the contest, may have been among the chief causes that facilitated the success of the Shepherd invasion. We know nothing of the history of this Xoite dynasty. The extracts from Manetho mention seventy kings, a statement evidently exaggerated; the number of years assigned for its duration differs, the most probable is 184 years. The thirteenth Theban dynasty, admitting that it was thus partly contemporary, would have reigned only 269 years over all Egypt, and the rest of the time over the southern provinces alone, and in antagonism with the rebels of the Delta.

Section III.—Invasion and Dominion of the Shepherds.

1. Manetho, in a fragment preserved by the historian, Josephus, says (Against Ap., i. 15), "There was a king of ours whose name was Amintimaos" (an evident corruption of the Greek copyists). "Under him it came to pass, I know not how, that God was averse to us; and there came, after a surprising manner, men of ignoble birth out of the eastern parts, and had boldness enough to make an expedition into our country, and with ease subdued it by force, yet without our hazarding a battle with them. So when they had gotten those that governed us under their power, they afterwards burned down our cities and demolished the temples of the gods, and used all the inhabitants after a most barbarous manner; nay, some they slew, and led their children and wives into slavery." He adds also, "This whole nation was called Hyksos, that is, 'shepherd kings'; for in the sacred language Hyk signifies King,

and Sos, in the ordinary dialect, Shepherds." The two words here given have been found in the hieroglyphic inscriptions: the first under the form Hak, as the name of the chiefs of Semitic tribes; the second under the form Shasou, as the designation of Bedouins. Nevertheless, all Egyptian monuments known up to this time describe the invaders, called in the fragment of Manetho Hyksos, by the name of "Mena," Shepherds.

The study of the monuments proves the reality of the frightful devastations consequent on the invasion. With one single exception, all the temples built prior to that event have disappeared, and nothing can be found of them but scattered ruins, bearing traces of a violent destruction. Very soon, however, after the first subjugation of the whole land by the invaders, the native kingdom of the Thebaid was re-constituted, and afforded refuge to all the patriots who had at first fled to Ethiopia; Lower and Central Egypt alone remained under the direct tyranny of the strangers. During four centuries the princes of the Thebaid, who formed two successive dynasties, the fifteenth and sixteenth, had for neighbours, and probably for masters, these barbarous invaders. It would be impossible to estimate the extent of the ruin which fell on Egypt during these 400 years. The only certain fact we can mention is, that no one monument remains to teach us what became of the ancient splendour of Egypt under the Hyksos. We see, therefore, under the fifteenth and sixteenth dynasties Egyptian civilisation was again interrupted. Vigorous as it was, the impetus given by the Osortasens was suddenly arrested, the series of monuments broken, and this silence even tells the calamities Egypt underwent.

2. Who were the Shepherds? We may say that their history, long obscure from the absence of any contemporary document, is partly elucidated by the recent discoveries of M. Mariette. They were a collection of all the nomadic hordes of Arabia and Syria; but the chief part of them, as also the extracts from Manetho say, were Canaanites. Those who held the first rank—the tribe directing the movement—were the Khitas of the Pharaonic monuments, the Hittites of the Bible, whom Abraham had found already established in the land of Canaan. We shall see in the Book of this Manual treating of the Phœnicians, that the invasion of Egypt was the last episode in the great migration that, some generations earlier, had led the Canaanitish race from the shores of the Persian Gulf, their original seat, into Palestine. When Abraham arrived, the Canaanites had been but a short time in the land. And, in fact, a papyrus in the Berlin Museum contains the report of an Egyptian explorer sent into Palestine under the twelfth dynasty, who found there none but nomadic Semitic tribes, and his narrative does not once mention the Canaanites.

3. "At length," says Manetho, in the continuation of the fragment

already quoted, "they made one of themselves king, whose name was Saites (in some other versions, Salatis); he also lived at Memphis, and made both the upper and lower regions pay tribute, and left garrisons in the places most proper for them. He chiefly aimed at securing the eastern parts, fearing that the Assyrians, then stronger than himself" (and this, in fact, as we shall see, was precisely at the time of the first great Chaldæan Empire), "would be desirous of that kingdom and invade it. And as he found in the Tanitic province" (the manuscripts have, in error, "Saitic") "a city very proper for his purpose, called Avaris, after an old religious tradition, he rebuilt it, and made it very strong by the walls which he built about it, and by a garrison of 240,000 armed men. Thither he came in the summer, partly to gather his corn and pay his soldiers their wages, and partly to exercise his soldiers and thereby terrify foreigners." Some details are added as to the successors of Saites; the list is preserved in the extracts made by the chronologer, Julius Africanus, who says that they reigned 284 years, names them Anōn (otherwise Bnōn), Pachnan (or Apachnas), Staan, Archles, and Apophis. The same extracts mention the existence of a contemporary native dynasty, the seventeenth, in the Thebaid.

We see by the monuments that, after a long time of absolute barbarism and savage devastations, the Shepherds in Lower Egypt, like the Tartars in China, allowed themselves to be conquered by the superior civilisation of the people they had subdued, and formed themselves into a regular dynasty, adopting Egyptian manners and names. The first king of the dynasty—the Saites of Manetho, who was really called Set-aa-peh-i-Nubti—is mentioned in a stele of Ramses II. (nineteenth dynasty), discovered at Tanis, identical with Avaris, as having, 400 years before the time of the latter prince, rebuilt the city, and founded there the temple of the god Set, or Sutekh, the national god of the Hittites. The name of Anōn in Manetho's lists is found as Annoub in the fragments of the papyrus of Turin, followed by the commencement of another name, Ap . . ., which must be Apachnas. Lastly, the real form of the name of the last king of the dynasty, Apepi (in Greek, Apophis), has been found on many monuments. In the reign (which lasted sixty-one years) of this Apepi, according to the express testimony of the extracts from Manetho, Joseph came into Egypt, and was made "governor over all the land of Egypt." We see by the narrative of the Book of Genesis that the court of this king was entirely Egyptian.

As for the contemporary Theban kings, we know the names of only the last two, Tiaaken, and Kames. A most important coincidence in relation to Biblical history is connected with this last king. In a royal proclamation we read the title "Sustainer of the World" written precisely in the same form (Tsaf-en-to, transcribed into Hebrew Zaphnath) recorded in the Book of Genesis as the surname Joseph received at the same period, when he had saved the people of Lower Egypt from famine. May we not conclude that the economic reforms of Joseph, and his wise precautions against dearth, had been imitated by the national sovereign of Upper Egypt?

4. The moment when Egyptian civilisation, at first almost annihilated by the invasion, thus revived in the Thebaid under a completely national form, and in the Delta under the government of rulers of foreign origin, is fully represented on the monuments. "The renaissance which is seen at Thebes," says M. Mariette, on whose great experience we are always glad to rely, "offers a singular analogy to that attributable to the commencement of the nineteenth dynasty. The same vases, the same arms, the same furniture is found in the tombs." The type of the sarcophagus became again what it had been under the eleventh dynasty—a type entirely peculiar, and found only at these two epochs. In allusion to the myth of the goddess Isis protecting the body of her brother Osiris (with whom the dead person is identified) by stretching over him her winged arms, the coffin is covered with a system of wings, painted with varied and brilliant colours. Moreover, at the time of this new Theban renaissance, ending in the national deliverance, individuals had, as under the eleventh dynasty, the names Entef, Ameni, Ahmes, and Aahhotep, so that we can hardly now distinguish between monuments separated by many centuries and a long period of foreign rule.

The discovery of the monuments of the kings of the Shepherd dynasty, is one of the most valuable results of the excavations of M. Mariette. They were found at Tanis, in the city where the Shepherds had fixed the capital of their monarchy, and which they strove to embellish more than any other. The style of art is better, and the workmanship more finished than in the monuments of the contemporary Theban dynasty. And, in fact, at this time the states governed by the kings of the invading race were more wealthy and peaceful than the states of the South, who were struggling hard to throw off the foreign yoke. These monuments show us to what extent the Shepherds had become real Pharaohs, adopting as their own the titles of the old dynasties. They had embraced the religion of Egypt, compelling only the admission of their own god Set, or Sutekh, into the pantheon, who, in the end remained there definitely, losing, however, the first rank which they had given him. Their manners and those of their subjects were Egyptian, with a small number of distinguishing customs brought from Asia.

We have, finally, of the age of the Shepherds, only the remains of sculpture, but not one single architectural work; the principal fragments, all in the museum at Cairo, are, first, a group in granite of most perfect execution, representing two personages in Egyptian costume, but with a large beard, and long hair, absolutely unknown to the true Mizraite blood, holding in their outstretched hands a table of offerings of fish, lotus flowers, and aquatic birds, in a word, of the various natural productions of the lakes of the Delta. Also four large Sphinxes (human-headed lions) in diorite, bearing the name of Apepi, the king whom Joseph served. These, in place of the ordinary head-dress of the Egyptian Sphinxes, have the head covered with a thick lion's mane, giving them a very peculiar appearance. The sculptures of the Shepherd period represent, moreover, a race of radically different type to that of the Egyptians, a race evidently Semitic, with angular and sharply cut features. The excavations at Tanis have also resulted in proving the fact that the last Shepherd kings had restored in the temples reconstructed by them, the statues of former ages belonging to the religious edifices overturned in the first period of the invasion, engraving on them their own names alone, as a new consecration.

SECTION IV.—EXPULSION OF THE SHEPHERDS—AHMES.

1. THIS position of affairs could not, however, last long, a great crisis was impending. As the power of the native and legitimate kings of the Thebaid increased, they attempted to throw off the yoke imposed on them by the strangers, to attack them in their fortresses in the Delta, and to free the sacred soil of Egypt from the presence of the barbarians. An invaluable papyrus in the British Museum, apparently a fragment of a detailed chronicle of the national deliverance, relates the commencement of the struggle. It begins thus—"It happened that the land of Egypt fell into the hands of enemies, and there was no longer any king (of the whole country) at the time when this happened. And so the king Tiaaken was only Hak (vassal king) of Upper Egypt. These enemies were in Heliopolis, and their chief in Avaris . . . The king Apepi chose the god Sutekh as his Lord, and did not serve any other god in the whole land. He built him a well constructed temple to last for ever." The chronicle next relates that the Shepherd, Apepi, learned that the Theban prince, Tiaaken, refused to acknowledge and worship his god Sutekh, which was equivalent to a formal rejection of the supremacy previously admitted. Apepi was indignant, and summoned his rebellious vassal. Tiaaken replied to him with contempt. Armaments were made on both sides, and the war commenced.

2. It was long and sanguinary, and doubtless marked by vicissitudes unknown to us. It occupied the remainder of the reign of Tiaaken, the entire reign of Kames, which seems, however, to have been very short, and great part of that of his son, Ahmes, the Amosis of Manetho, and terminated under this last prince. The struggle had its alternations

of successes and reverses; but the Egyptians, step by step, gained on the territory occupied by the invaders. "At last," says Manetho, in a fragment which Josephus also (Against Apion, i. 14) has preserved, "the Shepherds, subdued, were driven out of the rest of Egypt, and shut up in a place that contained 10,000 aroura (a superficial measure), called Avaris. The Shepherds had built round all this place a high and strong wall, in order to keep in safety all their possessions and plunder. The son of the king attempted to take this place by force, and besieged it with 480,000 men; but, despairing of success, he made a treaty on these conditions: That the enemy should leave Egypt, and go in safety wherever they wished. They then went away, carrying with them all their property; their number amounted to 240,000, and they took the road for Syria through the desert. But fearing the power of the Assyrians, who were then masters of Asia, they built a city in that country, which is now called Judæa, and that large enough to contain this great number of men, and called it Jerusalem."

Here again the authority of Manetho is confirmed, not in all the details, it is true, but in the general facts, by the testimony of the monuments, and particularly by the funeral inscription of a superior Egyptian officer, Ahmes, chief of the seamen, who took part in the war of liberation. This inscription, of immense historical value, relates the whole life of this personage, and has been deeply studied by that eminent Egyptologist, M. de Rougé. "When I was born in the fortress of Ilithyia" (in Upper Egypt), says the deceased Ahmes, in his epitaph, "my father was the lieutenant of the late king, Tiaaken. . . . I was lieutenant in turn with him in the ship named 'The Calf,' in the time of the late king Ahmes. . . . I went to the fleet to the north to fight; I had the duty of accompanying the king when he mounted his chariot. And when the fortress of Tanis (Avaris), was besieged, I fought on foot before his majesty. This is what happened on board the ship called 'The Enthronisation of Memphis.' A naval battle took place on the water, called the Water of Tanis (Lake Menzaleh). . . . The praises of the king were bestowed on me, and I received a golden collar for bravery. . . . The battle was south of the fortress. . . . The fortress of Tanis was taken, and I carried off a man and two women, three in all, whom his majesty assigned to me as slaves." The capital of the Shepherds once taken, the body of the nation passed the isthmus, and took refuge in Asia, where it rejoined its fellow countrymen, the Canaanites of Palestine. Some of them, Ahmes permitted to retain and cultivate a portion of the land of which their ancestors had taken possession. They formed a foreign colony in the east of Lower Egypt, tolerated in the same way as the Israelites. Only they had no Exodus, and, by a singular coincidence, we find the same people, in those strangers with robust limbs, grave and elongated faces, who still inhabit the banks of Lake Menzaleh.

3. Ahmes, seeking for support during this contest against the Asiatic invaders, had turned to the south, and had married an Ethiopian princess, named Nofre-t-ari, whom the monuments always represent with regular features and straight nose, but black in colour. This marriage gave rise to the pretensions of his successors to the sovereignty of Ethiopia. Ahmes, moreover, ruled over Nubia, as did the Theban princes of the seventeenth dynasty. But the Nubians had profited by the vicissitudes and embarrassments of the Northern war to revolt. No sooner was Tanis taken, than Ahmes returned towards Nubia; and, as we know from the epitaph of Ahmes, chief of the sailors, who also took part in this expedition, in a few battles completely subdued the rebels.

The end of this reign was occupied in works of peace, in rebuilding the ruins and healing the wounds inflicted on the country by foreign dominion. An inscription at Mount Mokattam, near Cairo, tells us that Ahmes re-opened the quarries there in the twenty-second year of his reign, in order to restore the Temples of Memphis and Thebes. The deliverance of the country and the total destruction of the foreign power were the signal for an immediate and remarkable expansion of the long-fettered national life and civilisation. In a few years Egypt regained the five centuries lost through the Shepherd invasion. From the Mediterranean to the cataracts both banks of the Nile were covered with edifices. New roads were opened for commerce; and trade, agriculture and the arts received a fresh and vigorous impetus. The incomparable jewels discovered by M. Mariette on the mummy of the Queen Aah-Hotep, widow of Kames, and mother of Ahmes, jewels now the pride of the Museum of Cairo, and which were to be seen at the Great Exhibition at Paris, in 1867, prove the high degree of excellence art and workmanship had attained to in Egypt a few years only after the end of the Shepherd invasion. It is difficult to believe that this long gold chain, this breast-plate of open work, this diadem with two golden sphynxes, this dagger chased with ornaments in damascened gold, and the various articles composing this treasure, could have come from the workshop of a Theban jeweller at a time when the country had hardly emerged from the disasters of so many centuries.

4. The chronology as well as the history of this period becomes clearer at this time; the list preserved by Josephus, and containing the duration of the reigns from Thothmes I. to Ramses II., may, in spite of some errors, in general easily rectified in the present state of knowledge, conduct us nearly to the reign of Ramses III., fixed by an astronomical observation as contemporary with the end of the fourteenth century before our era. It results, therefore, that the eighteenth

dynasty must have commenced nearly with the seventeenth century, and this is the date we must assign to the expulsion of the Shepherds.

CHAPTER III.

THE GREAT CONQUERORS OF THE NEW EMPIRE. FOREIGN INFLUENCE OF EGYPT.

SECTION I.—THE EIGHTEENTH DYNASTY.—FIRST SUCCESSORS OF AHMES.—(*Seventeenth Century B.C.*)

1. THE entire deliverance of the land inaugurates the reign of the great and glorious dynasty, reckoned as the eighteenth. Ahmes, though descended from the former Theban kings, owes it to his own glorious exploits that he is counted the founder of a new dynasty. He also opens the third historical period,—known as the New Empire.

From this time for many centuries, the power of Egypt was extensively felt in the world. The monarchy of the Pharaohs henceforth devoted its chief efforts to the conquest of Asia. It was known, by the sad experience of five centuries, that danger to Egypt was always to be apprehended from Asia. So, to prevent a new Shepherd invasion, policy led her to seek on their own territory all possible enemies and invaders, to fight them to the uttermost and subdue them to her own sceptre. But she nevertheless did not abandon the traditional policy inaugurated by the kings of the twelfth dynasty, of claiming the whole valley of the Upper Nile as an inheritance belonging legitimately to Egypt. Warlike expeditions therefore were constantly made either to the south or to the north-east, and were continued during the whole period of the eighteenth dynasty.

2. Almost immediately after the capture of Tanis, or Avaris, from the Shepherds, we find Ahmes following them into the land of Canaan, where they had commenced to reorganise themselves, conquering them again, dispersing them, and taking from them some fortified towns, amongst others the town of Sharuhen, belonging in later times to the tribe of Simeon (Jos. xix. 6). His successors followed the same road, and advanced with rapid steps. Before long they had subdued all Western Asia. But before relating their wars and conquests according to the testimony of the monuments—very numerous for this period—we think it necessary to explain briefly the position in which the Egyptians of the eighteenth dynasty found these Asiatic countries and nations, and to give a short sketch of the geography of these historical inscriptions.

We shall then be able to judge what were the facilities and what the obstacles found by the Pharaohs in the way of their enterprises.

Immediately on the north-east frontier of Egypt, the desert between it and Syria was occupied by Bedouin tribes, whom the hieroglyphic inscriptions always call Shasu. The most important of these, and the nearest to Egypt, were the Amalekites of the Bible, the Amalika of the Arabian historians, though this name applied equally to the Edomites, or Idumæans, and Midianites who are sometimes mentioned among the Shasu, and even generally to all the nomadic tribes of the desert. Palestine was entirely in the hands of the Canaanites, who, after the defeat of the Shepherds, were unable to form a powerful monarchy, but were in the divided state in which Joshua found them when, a little later, he conducted the Hebrews into that country. They formed an almost infinite number of petty principalities; every city had its own king, often in rivalry with, or hostile to, his neighbours. This state of division and local isolation made the Canaanites of Palestine an easy prey to every conqueror, for it hardly permitted them to unite against a common enemy. But at the same time it rendered a complete and perfect conquest of the country difficult, for it was necessarily favourable to partial insurrections, incessantly liable to break out.

The Syrian populations, who, to the north of the Canaanites, occupied the provinces called in the Bible by the general name of Aram, as far as the River Euphrates, belonged to the confederation of the Rotennu, or Retennu, extending beyond the river and embracing all Mesopotamia (Naharaina). What we have already said of the Cushites may be applied to this confederation. The Rotennu had no well-defined territory, nor even a decided unity of race. They already possessed powerful cities, such as Nineveh and Babylon, but there were still many nomadic tribes within the ill-defined limits of the confederacy. Their name was taken from the city of Resen, apparently the most ancient, and originally the most important, city of Assyria. The germ of the Rotennu confederation was formed by the Semitic Assyro-Chaldæan people, who were not yet welded into a compact monarchy, but were an aggregation of petty states, each having its own sovereign, and united by ties of a nature unknown to us. The first great Chaldæan empire, founded many centuries earlier, and which had exercised authority over the whole Tigro-Euphrates basin, was in fact at this moment so crippled in power that the last descendants of its early kings, reduced to the possession of Babylon, and perhaps even to Erech, the first seat of their power, were nothing more than mere members of the Rotennu confederacy. With the Assyro-Chaldæans, who were at its head, were joined in this confederation, the Aramæans on both sides of the Euphrates, whom history shows to have been always friendly to, and in strict alliance with, Assyria. The mountains to the north of Mesopotamia were inhabited by the

Remenen or Armenians, of Japhetic race. Finally, west of the Rotennu, in the valley of the Orontes, and the vast space contained between the left bank of the Euphrates, the Taurus and the sea, that Canaanitish tribe, apparently always the strongest and most powerful, the Khitas or Hittites (a small branch of whom remained in Palestine, near Hebron), had founded a warlike and formidable empire, a strongly centralised monarchy. These latter were still living in Palestine in the time of Solomon, who contracted an alliance with them, and married their king's daughter. But the power of the Hittite kingdom does not seem under the eighteenth dynasty to have been sufficiently great to be dreaded by the Egyptians, and it is not until the time of the following dynasty that we see them playing a considerable part in the affairs of Western Asia.

3. The first successor of Ahmes was Amen-hotep (Peace of Amen), called Amenophis by the Greeks. Under his reign the Shasu of the desert were subdued, at any rate as far as that is possible with Bedouin, for nearly all the other kings, even the most powerful, were obliged from time to time to send out expeditions to repress their plundering propensities. The conquest of the land of Canaan made great progress during this reign, aud Egyptian troops were almost constantly engaged in reducing the little forts of the petty kings of Palestine. The Pharaohs did not, however, change the organisation of the country, nor did they even suppress these small principalities, but confined themselves to exacting an acknowledgment of supremacy, the payment of tribute and military service. The inscription on the tomb of Ahmes, chief of the sailors, already more than once quoted, relates another war of Amen-hotep I., directed this time to the south. "I conducted," says he, "the vessel of king Amen-hotep when he made an expedition towards Ethiopia to extend the frontiers of Egypt. His majesty took captive the chief of the mountaineers in the midst of his warriors."

4. Thothmes I. (called Tuthmosis by the Greek copyists of Manetho) then ascended the throne. He followed up the successes of his predecessor in Ethiopia; and we may judge how much he enlarged the boundaries of the Egyptian empire by an inscription of the second year of his reign, engraven on the rocks opposite the island of Tombos, nearly as high up the course of the Nile as that of Argo. But the greatest enterprise, and the one which rendered the name of Thothmes illustrious, was to the north. Having reduced the Canaanites of Palestine to submission, he pushed on, and in the neighbourhood of Damascus encountered the Rotennu, who had assembled a large force to repel an enemy whose rapid increase of power they must have seen with terror. The Rotennu were conquered; but king Thothmes, who had felt their strength, judged that Egyptian dominion in Syria could never be established on a solid basis unless he reduced them still further by seeking them out on their own territory, and compelling the provinces

of Mesopotamia to submit to his sceptre. Crossing the desert, he marched upon the Euphrates, and passed the river at Carchemish, the Circesium of classical geography. Assyria, like Ethiopia, then felt the weight of the Egyptian arms; and, as on the Upper Nile so on the Euphrates, Thothmes placed inscriptions to record his passage. His reign thus marks another step in advance; he inaugurated the era of great Asiatic expeditions, of distant conquests. It was also in this war of Thothmes I. in Mesopotamia that the Egyptians first became acquainted with horses, then first appearing in their sculptures, and till then probably unknown to them. The king established studs in the pastures of Lower Egypt; this animal, one of the most valuable results of the conquest, prospered there, and in a short time the valley of the Nile became celebrated for its breed of horses. As well as horses, the Egyptians borrowed from the Asiatics the use of war-chariots, so important an element in after days in the armies of the Pharaohs.

Thothmes I. reigned twenty-one years, and at his death left the throne to his son, Thothmes II. We now find that Ethiopia was definitely subdued, and remained so for many centuries. We begin to find on the rocks of Syene the names of the "Princes governors of the South," a title then given to functionaries, generally chosen from the royal family, who represented the authority of the Pharaohs beyond the cataracts. It does not seem that Thothmes II., whose reign was very short, was a warlike prince. His successor was his brother, Thothmes III.

SECTION II.—CONTINUATION OF THE EIGHTEENTH DYNASTY.—THOTHMES III.—GREATEST MILITARY POWER OF EGYPT.

(*About* 1600. *Reign of about half a century.*)

1. ON his accession to the throne, Thothmes III. was still a child. His elder sister, Hatasu, who had already played a part in public affairs under the former king, became the guardian of the young prince. But her regency was really a usurpation during the seventeen years that her government lasted. Hatasu assumed all the prerogatives of the royal power. Her reign was, however, brilliant. Egyptian history knows no monarch who, when aggrandised by conquest and political influence, has not left behind proofs of taste for the arts and magnificent monuments. Hatasu was of this number. Among the principal works due to this queen are the two gigantic obelisks, one of which still stands among the ruins at Karnak. The inscriptions inform us that the queen erected these two obelisks to the memory of her father, Thothmes I. The legends on their bases mention some peculiarities worthy of notice. We see, for example, that the summit of the obelisk was originally formed by a pyramid made of gold taken

from the enemy. In another passage the inscription relates that the erection of the entire monument, from the time it was cut in the quarries of Syene, only occupied seven months. We may judge by these details of the efforts necessary to transport and set up in so short a time a mass thirty metres high, and weighing 374,000 kilogrammes (368 tons). The temple of Deir el Bahri is also a monument of the magnificence of Hatasu. The warlike exploits of the queen are the subject of the representations on the walls of that edifice. Great bas-reliefs, engraved with an astonishing boldness and freedom, tell us all the incidents of the conquest of the land of Pun, that is, of Yemen, or Arabia Felix, a country fertile and rich in itself, and which, being the depôt of Indian commerce, was the object of the desires of the Egyptian monarchy, as the possession of it was necessarily an almost inexhaustible source of wealth. A copy of these interesting representations was to be seen at the Exhibition in Paris of 1867. In conclusion, Hatasu was a sister worthy of the Thothmes, and occupies not the lowest place in the series of illustrious sovereigns of the eighteenth dynasty, who have left such mighty traces on the soil of Egypt. For seventeen years, as we have seen, she assumed all the royal power; but even when her brother, Thothmes III., attained his majority, she did not retire. As under Thothmes II., she continued for many years to take part in the government. At length she died, leaving him whose power she had usurped sole master of Egypt.

2. Of all the Pharaohs of this age, and perhaps of all Egyptian history, Thothmes III. is unquestionably the greatest. Under him Egypt attained to the summit of her power. In internal affairs, a wise foresight in administration ensured everywhere order and progress. Abroad, Egypt became by her victories the arbitress of the whole civilised world; and according to a poetical expression of the time, "She placed her frontier where it pleased herself." Her empire extended over the countries now called Abyssinia, Soudan, Nubia, Syria, Mesopotamia, Arabia, Kurdistan, and Armenia.

Thothmes III. himself relates in the annals of his reign inscribed on the walls of the sanctuary of Karnak, that he made his first expedition for conquest in the twenty-second year of his reign, including his minority. It is undoubtedly difficult, and sometimes impossible, in spite of the learned labours of Dr. Birch, Dr. Brugsch, and M. de Rougé, who have specially applied themselves to this long text, to recognise in our geography the exact equivalent of all the names of towns and peoples successively enumerated in the history of the wars of Thothmes. But we know sufficient to be enabled to give a satisfactory general idea. We borrow from the works of the authorities whom we have just named an analysis of the facts stated on the monument, usually designated "The Annals of Thothmes III.," or the "Wall Catalogue of Karnak," because of the lists giving the number of prisoners taken and amount of booty carried off. These definite and unexaggerated accounts are an invaluable guarantee of the truth of the relation, which may be called official and statistical, and which bear no traces of the inflated style so common to oriental monarchs.

3. The Rotennu refused their tribute, supposing, no doubt, that the young king, deprived of the experienced councils of his sister Hatasu, would be unable to reduce them to obedience. Moreover, a formidable insurrection, fomented and supported by them, broke out among the Canaanites of Palestine, whose petty kings united in an effort to throw off the yoke of the Pharaohs, and so successfully, that only a few strongholds, such as Gaza, were left in the possession of the Egyptians. The whole of the twenty-second year of the reign of Thothmes was occupied in preparations for the war, and in the siege of a few places of strength in the south of Palestine, in later times belonging to the tribe of Simeon; and having captured them, the king re-opened his communications by land with Gaza. This last-named place was selected as the base of the operations of the following year.

In the spring of his twenty-third year, on the 3rd or 4th of the month "Pachons,"* the king arrived at Gaza, and took command of his troops in person. On the 5th a neighbouring fortress surrendered, and Thothmes then advanced. On the 16th he learned that the Syrian and Canaanite princes, who were confederated against him under the king of Kadesh, had commenced their march, and were concentrating their forces at Megiddo, in the plain of Esdraelon, the field where many a battle has decided the fate of Syria. Rejecting the advice of his officers to circle round the base of the mountains separating him from the enemy, and thus to avoid the risk of attacking them in front, Pharaoh marched straight at the confederates, and encamped, on the 19th, on the first rise of the mountains at the entrance of a difficult ravine, which the enemy had not taken the precaution to occupy with a sufficient force. He burst through, in spite of all difficulties, and on the 20th appeared with his troops on the bank of the brook Kanah, in later times the boundary between the tribes of Ephraim and Manasseh (Jos. xvi. 8; xvii. 9), and flowing across the plain of Esdraelon to the south of Megiddo. The Annals of Karnak contain here a short pro-

* The 1st Pachons, properly and theoretically, should correspond with the summer solstice, which really was the case in the years 1785 and 280 B.C. But as the Egyptian year consisted of 365 days without bissextile years, at the end of 400 years there would be an error of 97 days, and under Thothmes III. the 1st Pachons must have fallen about the middle of May. See note at the end of this Chapter.

clamation, addressed by Pharaoh to his troops on the eve of battle. On the 21st Pachons, at break of day, he arranged his army for the attack; his right wing rested on the Kanah, and his left was extended to the north-west of Megiddo. Thothmes himself commanded the centre. The enumeration of the contingents the enemy opposed to him comprises the names of all the important cities of Palestine and of the Aramæan provinces between the Anti-Lebanon and the Euphrates. At the very first shock of battle the Asiatics were overthrown, and fled towards Megiddo; but the garrison of the place was terrified, and shut the gates, and the chiefs were obliged to be drawn with cords up the ramparts, to escape the pursuit of the Egyptians.

The very moderate numbers, as given in the text, of enemies killed and taken prisoners in the battle, show a spirit of truth which much enhances our interest in the narrative. Eighty-three killed and 340 prisoners only are reckoned for the battle of Megiddo. The pursuit was nevertheless hot, for the text says, that at the time when the chiefs of the enemy gained the fortress "the king's warriors paid no attention to the booty, and let it fall." The small number of killed may be explained by the vicinity of the mountains, where the vanquished found refuge from the pursuit of the Egyptians; in ancient times, in consequence of the use of defensive armour, and of the manner in which they fought, a pursuit was productive of much more slaughter than a battle. But the capture of 2,132 horses and of 924 war-chariots, as well as long lists of booty, attest the entire dispersion of the Asiatic army. Some days afterwards the city of Megiddo, blockaded and reduced to famine, was obliged to surrender without a struggle; and as all the allied princes had found refuge there, its fall decided the campaign. Thothmes encountered no further serious resistance; the remainder of his march through Palestine as far as Lebanon, and through the Syrian provinces to the Euphrates, was merely a triumphal procession. The chiefs who had not been at Megiddo hastened to make their submission; and to protest their fidelity, most of the fortresses opened their gates, and the few that attempted resistance were quickly taken. Even before the end of the campaign, Thothmes had incorporated with his own army large bodies of soldiers, taken from the enemy, who eagerly asked permission to enlist. Having garrisoned the three chief cities of the Rotennu on this side of the Euphrates, he returned to Egypt with thousands of prisoners and hostages. But in the following spring he passed the Euphrates at Carchemish at the head of his troops, and built, to secure at all times the easy passage of the river, a powerful fortress, the ruins of which still exist. This time he had no need to fight; the Rotennu beyond the Euphrates, that is, the Assyro-Chaldæans, submitted without an attempt at resistance, and Thothmes received tribute from their princes, amongst whom are named the king of Nineveh and the king of Asshur, or Ellasar, now Kileh Sherghât.

4. Four years of perfect peace succeeded these victorious campaigns. But the Annals of the Temple of Karnak make the wars recommence in the twenty-ninth year of the reign of Thothmes. Until then, the Egyptian conquerors, desirous of reaching the Euphrates as quickly as possible, so as to strike at the heart of the power of the Rotennu, had passed without turning aside to the mountain mass of the two parallel chains of Lebanon and Anti-Lebanon, containing between them the fertile plain called by the Egyptians Tsahi, and by classical geographies Cœle-Syria, or Hollow Syria. Thothmes III. penetrated into and subdued that country as well as the Phœnician coast to his sceptre. Wine (doubtless the famous golden wine of Lebanon), wheat, cattle, honey, and iron, are mentioned among the tribute that he exacted. Tunep, a city in the Anti-Lebanon, not far from Damascus, and Aradus in the southern extremity of Phœnicia, are enumerated among the cities then taken.

The following year, a new expedition, the sixth of his reign, was directed against the land of the Rotennu, where some insurrections had taken place. Aradus had revolted, and was again compelled to submit. Kadesh, a strong city, noted in later times in the wars of the kings of the nineteenth dynasty, the ruins of which have been found on the Orontes, not far from Emessa, was taken by assault. At the news of this success, the Assyrian princes beyond the Euphrates hastened to renew their submission; the terms used in relating this event in the great Karnak inscription, show us the nature of the power exercised by the Pharaohs over the Asiatic countries they had conquered. "Here they are bringing the sons and brothers of the chiefs to put them in the power of the king, and to be led into Egypt. If any one of the chiefs should die, his majesty will set free his successor to occupy the place." As we see, this was exactly the organisation of the subject kingdoms of the Roman Empire. Each country preserved a national government and king, but recognised the supremacy of Pharaoh, paid him tribute, and furnished to his army a contingent of auxiliary forces. The young princes were retained as hostages at the court of Thebes, where they received, doubtless, an entirely Egyptian education, and amongst them Pharaoh chose, and invested with power, the successors of vassal kings who died.

In the thirty-first year of his reign, Thothmes went into Mesopotamia to receive personally the tribute and homage of the Assyro-Chaldæan kings. On his return to Egypt, he received also tribute from several African people—ivory, gold dust, ebony, lions' and panthers' skins. In the following years Thothmes returned again to Mesopotamia, took some prisoners, and set up an inscription to commemorate his having "enlarged the frontiers of Egypt." Nineveh, Singar, and Babylon then formed parts of his empire, and in Syria, the cities beyond Jordan, Heshbon, and Rabbath Ammon, were for the first time forced to pay tribute. Some partial revolts in Mesopotamia and in the north of Syria were victoriously repressed. Finally, a great expedition was made into the mountainous district, north of Mesopotamia, in which the king does not seem to have been present, against the Remenen or Armenians, who submitted and became tributaries during the last years of his reign.

5. Such are the facts related by the Annals, engraven on the walls of the sanctuary at Karnak. But they only comprise the events of the Asiatic wars. Whilst Thothmes with his legions pushed on to Babylon, and even to Armenia, he was also the first of the sovereigns of Egypt to create a considerable fleet on the Mediterranean, and had acquired absolute supremacy on its waters. This fleet was undoubtedly manned by Phœnicians, for the Egyptians have never at any time been skilful sailors ; and moreover we find from the monuments, that from the date of their submission to Thothmes III., the Phœnician cities to which no doubt the Egyptian monarch had granted very favourable conditions, preserved for many centuries towards that kingdom an unshaken fidelity, in complete contrast with the conduct of other Canaanitish people. The results of the naval campaign of Thothmes, and his conquests in the basin of the Mediterranean, are chiefly known from an inscribed monumental stele discovered at Karnak by M. Mariette. The inscription, which is in poetry, and very biblical in style, has been translated by M. de Rougé. We quote here a few verses as specimens of the grand lyrical Egyptian style. Amen, the Supreme god of Thebes, is speaking:—

"I am come—to thee have I given to strike down Syrian princes;
Under thy feet they lie throughout the breadth of their country.
Like to the Lord of Light, I made them see thy glory,
Blinding their eyes with light, the earthly image of Amen.

"I am come—to thee have I given to strike down Asian people;
Captive now thou hast led the proud Assyrian chieftains;
Decked in royal robes, I made them see thy glory;
All in glittering arms and fighting, high in thy war-car.

"I am come—to thee have I given to strike down western nations;
Cyprus both and the Ases have heard thy name with terror.
Like a strong-horned bull, I made them see thy glory;
Strong with piercing horns, so that none can stand before him.

"I am come—to thee have I given to strike down men of the sea-board.
All the land of the Maten is trembling now before thee!

Fierce as the huge crocodile, I made them see thy glory;
Terrible Lord of the waters, none dare even approach him.

"I am come—to thee have I given to strike down island races;
Those in the midst of the sea have heard the voice of thy roaring.
Like an avenger of blood, I made them see thy glory,
When by his victim he stands prepared to strike with his falchion.

"I am come—to thee have I given to strike down Lybian archers,
All the isles of the Greeks submit to the force of thy spirit.
Like a lion in prey, I made them see thy glory,
Couched by the corpse he has made down in the rocky valley.

"I am come—to thee have I given to strike down the ends of the ocean.
In the grasp of thy hand is the circling zone of waters;
Like the soaring eagle, I made them see thy glory,
Whose far-seeing eye there is none can hope to escape from."

We see by the inscription on this Theban stele that the fleets of the great Pharaoh had conquered, first Cyprus and Crete, and had subjected the southern islands of the Archipelago, a large part of the coasts of Greece and Asia Minor, and possibly even the south of Italy. It seems that we ought to infer from the same monument, that the ships of Thothmes III. were often in the Black Sea, where Herodotus tells us that the Egyptians had founded a colony at Colchis to work the mines.* It is probable that the ancestors of the German Ases, who then lived by the banks of the Mæotic Gulf—the descendants of the Askenaz of the tenth chapter of Genesis—may be recognised in the list of northern people who paid tribute to the fleet of Thothmes. In another direction the same fleets had established the sovereignty of Pharaoh over the whole Lybian coast. Monuments of the reign of Thothmes have been found at Cherchel, in Algeria, and it is far from impossible that they marked the limit of Egyptian rule on the northern coast of Africa.

6. Other facts show that the supremacy of Thothmes was peaceably admitted in the whole of Cush, or Ethiopia. A cave at Ibrim, in Lower Nubia, shows us the "Governor of the South" presenting to Pharaoh tributes of gold, silver, and the grain of the country. Thothmes III. built and dedicated to the Sun the Temple of Amada. At Semneh, he restored the Temple where Osortasen III. of the twelfth dynasty was worshipped. Kumneh, opposite Semneh, Mount Doshe and the Isle of Sai, a little below that of Tombos, and also, nearer Egypt itself, Korte, Pselchis, Talmis, have preserved his memory. Beyond the limits of Ethiopia Proper, in the country of the negroes, frequent and victorious expeditions were made under the same king. In a bas-relief at Karnak

* HER. II. 103, 104.

we see 150 African prisoners defiling before Pharaoh, each one bearing the name of a subject tribe. As far as we can judge—for the identification of the names of African nations is more difficult than that of names in Asia and Europe—the list on this monument embraces the greater part of what is now Abyssinia, and extends far to the west in Soudan.

7. A reign so glorious and prosperous must necessarily have left in Egypt many magnificent monuments. Those of Thothmes III. are in fact very common from the Delta to the Cataracts, all in admirable style, tasteful in design, and admirably finished. At Heliopolis, Memphis, Ombos, Elephantine, and, above all, at Thebes, we still find most important remains of the great buildings erected by this king.

SECTION III.—LAST KINGS OF THE EIGHTEENTH DYNASTY—RELIGIOUS TROUBLES.—(*Sixteenth Century B.C.*)

1. AMEN-HOTEP (or Amenōphis) II. was the successor of Thothmes III. He repressed an attempt of the Mesopotamians to shake off the Egyptian yoke, and received the submission of Nineveh. An inscription in the Temple of Amada, in Nubia, relates that he fought with his enemies in the land of Asshur; that seven kings fell before him, and were brought [their embalmed bodies it is to be supposed] to the banks of the Nile, where six were hung against the walls of Thebes, and the seventh at Napata, the capital of Ethiopia, "that the negroes might see the victories of the ever-living king over all lands and all people upon earth, since he had possessed the people of the south and chastised the people of the north." In a grotto at Ibrim there is a statue of the king, seated as an equal among the gods of the land, and also an inscription enumerating the tributes paid by "the Prince Governor of the land of the South." But everything shows that the reign of Amen-hotep was short. The extracts from Manetho do not name him, and he is known only from the inscriptions. The reign of Thothmes IV., who succeeded him, was not much longer. The lists of Manetho assign him nine years, and no inscription is known later than his seventh year; the latest mentions this prince as the conqueror of the black people. On another monument he is receiving tribute from Mesopotamia. The limits of the empire were maintained.

2. The epoch of great wars was renewed with Amen-hotep III. A date of his thirty-sixth year is known, and a long list might be made of the Asiatic and African countries which, by policy or force, were subjected to him; his empire, says one inscription, extended from north to south, from Mesopotamia to Karo in Abyssinia. But it must be confessed that the expeditions of his troops do not seem to have always been very chivalrous, and appear sometimes to have had for their object

merely a chase after slaves (especially in expeditions to Soudan), if we may judge from an inscription at Semneh, where mention is made of 740 negro prisoners, of whom half were women and children. Amen-hotep III. throughout his long reign was especially a builder. He covered the banks of the Nile with monuments remarkable for their grandeur, and for the perfection of the sculptures with which they are adorned. The Temple at Djebel Barkal, the ancient Napata, capital of Egyptian Ethiopia, is the work of this reign, as well as that of Soleb, near the third cataract. At Syene, Elephantine, Silsilis, Eileithya, in the Serapeum of Memphis, and in the Sinaitic Peninsula works of Amen-hotep III. are found. He made considerable additions to the Temple at Karnak, and built that part of the Temple of Luxor, now covered by the houses of the village of that name. The dedicatory inscription which he placed on it deserves to be inserted as a specimen of the customary style and title of Egyptian sovereigns. "He is Horus, the strong bull, who rules by the sword and destroys all barbarians; he is king of Upper and Lower Egypt, absolute master, Son of the Sun. He strikes down the chiefs of all lands, no country can stand before his face. He marches, and victory is gained, like Horus, son of Isis, like the Sun in heaven. He overturns even their fortresses. He brings to Egypt by his valour tribute from many countries—he, the lord of both worlds, Son of the Sun."

But it is not by his conquests, it is not even in his real name, that this Pharaoh has attained his greatest celebrity. It is by the colossal statue he erected at Thebes, and still to be seen there, the statue which, under the name of Memnon, took such hold of the imaginations of the Greeks and Romans in the two first centuries of the empire. They believed that they saw or rather heard Memnon, the Ethiopian, one of the defenders of Troy, each morning saluting his mother, Aurora. A learned pamphlet by Letronne, founded on the physical observations of M. de Rosiere, has completely explained this pretended prodigy, which the emperor Hadrian himself witnessed. The mysterious noise was produced when the first rays of the sun fell on the granite stone of the Colossus, covered before sunrise with dew which had penetrated into the many fissures of the stone. Similar phenomena are by no means uncommon in natural history. It had not been produced in this Colossus before the earthquake that, about the time of Tiberius, threw down the upper part of the statue, and thus uncovered the fissures most exposed to the action of the dew; it ceased when the statue was repaired by Septimus Severus and put into the state in which we now see it.

3. Amen-hotep III. was succeeded on the throne by his son, Amen-hotep IV. He, in his foreign policy, followed the example of his predecessors, and some of his monuments show him standing in his chariot, and followed by his seven daughters, who fought with him, trampling

under his horses' feet the vanquished Asiatics. But in internal administration, the reign of this prince presents peculiar facts, which render it one of the most extraordinary episodes in the Pharaonic annals. His face has nothing of the Egyptian type; and his features on all the monuments bear the marks of perfect imbecility, such as must have subjected him entirely to the influence of anyone who desired to control him. He was probably the first since the foundation of the Egyptian monarchy to touch the religion of the country, and to attempt to reform, or rather destroy, it entirely, and substitute another form of worship. In place of the religion, up to that time unaltered, he wished to establish the worship of one single god, represented by the Sun's disc, and named Aten, which word has been compared, not without some apparently good cause, with the Semitic *Adonai.* A regular persecution broke out throughout the whole empire. The temples of the ancient gods were closed, and their images, as well as names, everywhere effaced from the monuments, especially the image and name of Amen, the supreme god of Thebes. The king himself changed his name, which was compounded of the name of the proscribed deity, and in place of Amen-hotep called himself Chu-en-Aten—"Glory of the Solar disc." Wishing to make an end of all the traditions of his ancestors, this reforming king abandoned Thebes, and built another capital in Upper Egypt, in a place now called Tell-el-Amarna. The ruins of this city, abandoned after his death, have preserved for us many monuments of his reign, displaying very advanced art, and where we see him presiding over the ceremonies of his new worship. It seems now to be proved that the mother of Amen-hotep IV., Queen Taia, a woman more than usually strong-minded, and who was all-powerful with her son, was the leader in this religious movement. This queen was not an Egyptian; the monuments represented her with light hair, blue eyes and rosy cheeks, like the women of northern climates. An inscription, preserved at the Cairo Museum, mentions her father and mother by names which are not Egyptian, and not even belonging to any foreign royal family. She was then the child of one of those families of foreigners who then lived in the Delta, and was married for her beauty by Amen-hotep III. In dedicating altars to a god whom Egypt had not before known, Chu-en-Aten was merely following the traditions of the foreign race whose blood ran in his veins. He did for Aten or Adonai what the Shepherds had done for Sutekh. He gave supremacy to a foreign faction; and this may perhaps explain why, in the bas-reliefs of Tell-el-Amarna, we find this king surrounded by officers whose physiognomy is as foreign and as little like the Egyptians as his own.

Had not the Hebrews, whose number had enormously increased during the ten generations of their residence in Egypt, some connection with this strange attempt, and the imperfect monotheism of Amen-hotep IV.? We have perhaps a right to suppose that they had. There are curious resemblances between the external forms of Israelitish worship in the desert, and those revealed by the monuments of Tell-el-Amarna. Some of the sacred furniture, such as the "Table of Shew-bread," described in the book of Exodus as belonging to the Tabernacle, is seen in the representations of the worship of Aten, but not at any other period. But what is still more significant is, that the commencement of the persecution of the Hebrews coincides exactly with the termination of the religious troubles excited by the attempts of the son of Taia at reform, or rather absolute revolution in religious worship. We have already seen, in the second chapter of our Manual, that during their sojourn in Egypt, and previous to the mission of Moses, the monotheism of the descendants of Jacob had become much corrupted. In particular it was tainted with materialism. Surrounded by idolaters, the Hebrews with difficulty only retained the worship of Jehovah, even under a visible and material form. And corrupted in this way, their religion was not much better than that which Amen-hotep attempted to establish.

4. After the death of this king, Egypt remained disorganised and a prey to factions. The history of the empire of the Pharaohs for this period is full of obscurities, which further discoveries alone can clear up. We find that many personages, some of them great officers at the court of Amen-hotep Chu-en-Aten, and husbands of his daughters, successively seized on the supreme power, and followed each other at very short intervals. The most important, the one whose authority seems to have been best assured, is one Amen-tu-t-ankh, another son of Amen-hotep III., whose mutilated monuments are found in Ethiopia, at Thebes, and at Memphis, who was therefore in possession of all Egypt, except perhaps the Delta. He made campaigns in Asia, and received an ambassador from Assyria.

In the midst of these disorders, apparent even in the lists of Manetho, we find mention of the last son of Amen-hotep III., Har-em-Hebi, the Horus of Manetho, who in the end was recognised as the only legitimate king of this period. The commencement of his reign was brilliant. An inscription, dated in his second year, is at Silsilis attached to a representation of his triumphal return from a victorious campaign on the Upper Nile. One of the Egyptian chiefs is reproaching the captives with having refused to hear those who told them "the lion is approaching the land of Ethiopia." In another place, the inscription says to the king, "The gracious god returns, borne by the chiefs of all the land . . . the king, director of the worlds, favoured by the Sun, Son of the Sun . . . The king's name is known in the land of Cush; he has chastised it as he had promised his father, Amen." After this second year, history is quite silent, although Har-em-Hebi still nominally reigned, and, according to the statements of later lists, for thirty-six or thirty-seven years. We know only of a few monuments erected by this prince. We find, also, traces of violent reactions against the reforms of Amen-hotep IV., and all that belonged to him. The names of the pretenders, his successors, are everywhere defaced; and the buildings erected by them are thrown to the ground, and the new city, Tell-el-Amarna, purposely and systematically destroyed. Everything shows us a time of trouble, of continual revolution, and of civil discord. No doubt part of the disturbances, of which the monuments bear traces, must have been contemporary with Har-em-Hebi, and have lasted during the whole of his official reign. In that period, we repeat, there are obscurities still impenetrable in the present state of knowledge, and which new discoveries alone can dissipate. In the midst of these obscurities, in the midst of the troubles we have mentioned, the eighteenth dynasty terminates with the reign of Har-em-Hebi, having occupied the throne of Egypt for 241 years, and carried the glory and power of Egypt to its highest point.

Section IV.—Commencement of the Nineteenth Dynasty—Seti I.—(*Fifteenth Century B.C.*)

1. Under the nineteenth dynasty, which acquired the throne after the death of Har-em-Hebi, the fortune of Egypt maintained to some extent its ascendancy; but, though the reigns of some warlike kings throw a bright gleam on this epoch, the shade of approaching trouble already darkens the horizon. Egypt, under the eighteenth dynasty, had been a standing menace to all nations of the earth; she was henceforward doomed to be herself constantly endeavouring to ward off threatened danger.

The king who commenced this series was Ramses I.; he seems to have been grandson on the mother's side of Har-em-Hebi, and possibly son of one of the pretenders who disputed the throne at the close of the eighteenth dynasty, so that he is sometimes counted as the last king of that dynasty. We have but a small number of monuments of his reign. In the midst of the disorders which for nearly half a century followed the death of Amen-hotep III., the Asiatic dominions of the Egyptian monarchy were much disturbed. Revolts occurred in most of the provinces; the petty local princes almost entirely ceased to pay tribute: the conquests of Thothmes III. needed in great part to be recommenced. Syria especially was threatened; Egyptian supremacy in that country was much more precarious than in the more distant Mesopotamia. On the banks of the Orontes, in the whole of that vast district comprised between the left bank of the Euphrates, the Taurus, and the sea, a region hitherto untrodden by the Egyptian conquerors, the country of the Khitas, or Hittites, of Canaanitish race, who seem never to have given offence to the Thothmes or Amen-hoteps, had suddenly become very powerful, had taken the lead of other neighbouring nations, had drawn round them other Canaanitish tribes, and even extended their influence over the south of Asia Minor. Formed now into one single monarchy, possessing a numerous and formidable army, the Khitas, descendants of the Shepherds, openly aspired to rule all Syria, and to take their revenge for the exploits of Ahmes, by crushing the foreign dominion of Egypt. Their pretensions were the more dangerous because the Canaanites of Palestine were induced by community of race to prefer them to the Egyptians as rulers.

Ramses I. made one campaign against the Khitas on their own territory; and an inscription at Karnak states that he was the first of the Pharaohs who sought them out in the valley of the Orontes. The war was concluded by a treaty between Ramses and Seplul, king of the Hittites. Very few passages of arms marked the reign of this Pharaoh, which was very short. His successor was Seti I., the Sethos of Greek tradition.

2. Although an inscription in the palace of Medinet Abu at Thebes describes Seti as the son of Ramses I., he seems to have been only his adopted son, and son-in-law. In the Temple of Abydos, recently uncovered by M. Mariette, it is said of his son, Ramses II., that he was "King in the womb of his mother before he was born"; also that Seti governed merely in the stead of his son Ramses, even before his birth. From such strange and unusual expressions, it seems certain that Seti I. was a general of repute—a soldier of fortune—a stranger by birth to the royal family, who, by marriage with the heiress to the crown, seated himself on the throne; whilst, from the legitimist point of view, he was regarded as a regent only, by whom the throne was preserved for his son Ramses, in whose veins, through his mother, ran the blood of the ancient kings of the eighteenth dynasty.

Not only was Seti I. a stranger to the royal family, but he seems not even to have been of pure Egyptian race. His features, and those of his son Ramses, are too handsome, and of a regularity too classical, for the pure blood of Mizraim; they denote an origin drawn from another people. But what is more extraordinary still is, that some indications, to which it is difficult to refuse belief, show that the strange race from which descended Seti, and, consequently, all the kings of the nineteenth dynasty, was that of the Shepherds, who still remained as colonists in the Delta. Thus only can we explain the surprising conclusion which results from an inscription discovered by M. Mariette at Tanis. This inscription is relative to the re-establishment by Ramses II. of the worship of Sutekh, the national deity of the Hyksos, in their ancient capital. Now the son of Seti I. gives to King Set-aa-pehti, the founder of the regular dynasty of the Shepherds, the title of "Father," or "Ancestor," and dates an era from the reign of this prince.

3. Seti I., surnamed Merenphtah, was one of the greatest and most warlike of the sovereigns of Egypt. He was also distinguished as a builder. He built the whole of the great Temple of Osiris at Abydos, more than 560 feet long, one of the wonders of Egypt brought to light by recent excavations. At Thebes he founded a magnificent palace, that of Kurnah, so called from a modern village partly built in the very court of that edifice. The subterranean tomb of the same king, built on so bold a plan that we can hardly imagine how an architect could have conceived it, must be classed among the most remarkable works of Pharaonic art. But the most astonishing of the monumental remains of Seti is the famous "Hall of Columns" in the immense palace of Karnak at Thebes, where so many successive generations have laboured. Travellers of our days have exhausted the language of admiration in their descriptions of this marvellous building, of which we shall have occasion to speak in a future chapter.

The exploits of Seti himself are represented on the sculptured walls of this gigantic hall. All these sculptures have inscriptions. One represents Seti attacking the Arabs of the desert, the Shasu, whom we already know; others show the Remenen, or Armenians, whom the king conquered, with their neighbours, the Assyrians, cutting down the trees in their forests, as if to open a passage for him. The Assyrians were cut to pieces, and submitted to pay tribute. Great battles were fought with the Khitas of the north of Syria, and at last the king returned to Egypt with numerous captives. He was received with great ceremony at the frontier by the grandees of the empire, and afterwards he presented his Asiatic prisoners to the god Amen, at Thebes. The whole of this period of wars—the complete "Setiad"—is depicted in an immense series of sculptures on a most magnificent scale.

Thus the most perfect work of art of this reign is at the same time an historical monument of the highest importance, contributing largely to our knowledge of Egyptian history. By comparing the facts recorded on these sculptures, and in their inscriptions, with the records of inscriptions found elsewhere, we arrive at a result which, unfortunately, we can only present in a hasty sketch.

4. Before carrying his arms into Syria, Seti was previously compelled, in the first year of his reign, to ensure the tranquillity of the frontier of Egypt itself, on the side of the Isthmus of Suez, by chastising the Shasu, or Bedouins, whose depredations had for some time been exceedingly annoying, and who had the audacity even to attack Zal,

the chief town of the fourteenth nome, or province of Lower Egypt, the Heliopolis of the Greeks, near the Bitter Lakes. Pharaoh repulsed them with ease, and drove them back into the desert; and pursuing them there, compelled the tribes to submit. In the following year, Seti repaired in person to Syria at the head of a large army. He seems to have met with no resistance in Palestine, where all the petty Canaanitish princes hastened to pay their tribute and to furnish contingents of troops. Desirous of first confronting the most menacing danger, instead of passing on, like his predecessors, to the Euphrates, he marched against the Khitas, and attacked the southern frontier of their country. The war at this point was long and desperate; and it seems that the Egyptians were unable to penetrate far into the enemy's territory. However, Seti at length carried by assault the chief fortress of the country of the Khitas, Kadesh, the key to the whole valley of the Orontes; it was not occupied by the Hittites, but by another tribe of Canaanitish race, vassals of the Hittite king, the Amorites, related to the nation of the same name whom the Hebrews at a later date found in Palestine. After this success a treaty of peace was made between Seti and Mautnur, king of the Hittites, by which the latter nation preserved their possessions entire. Even Kadesh was restored to them; but they engaged never again to attack the Egyptian provinces or foment rebellion against the authority of Pharaoh, and to leave him at liberty to attack and reduce to subjection the revolted nations who had obeyed his predecessors, and whom he had always regarded as subjects.

Secure in this quarter, Seti turned back to attack the Rotennu, who no longer acknowledged Egyptian supremacy, and had discontinued paying their tribute. Those between Lebanon and the Euphrates, that is the Aramæans, were easily subdued. The Rotennu beyond the Euphrates gave more trouble to the Egyptian conqueror; but some great battles brought about the complete submission of Mesopotamia, Assyria, and Chaldæa. Seti admitted to an interview the chiefs of Nineveh, Babylon, and Singar. A last campaign in the mountains of Armenia, re-established the supremacy of Pharaoh in that country. The whole of the conquests of Thothmes III. were recovered, and the Asiatic empire of Egypt was completely reconstructed. On the other hand, Seti I. does not seem to have made any attempt to recover the maritime conquests of Thothmes. We have no reason to suppose that he had any considerable fleet on the Mediterranean, or that he endeavoured to regain supremacy over the islands that had become independent in the troublous times at the close of the eighteenth dynasty. It is true that a formidable power had grown up, soon to be able to measure itself with Egypt—the navy of the Pelasgi, which it seems did not exist in the days of Thothmes III.

5. In the south, religious and political troubles had never shaken the peaceable possession of Ethiopia by the Pharaohs. Seti had therefore no need to undertake any serious expedition in that quarter. He confined himself to sending out from time to time, like his predecessors, a few expeditions, more for slave hunting than war, against the semi-barbarous populations bordering on Ethiopia, particularly against the negroes. In the sculptures of a temple near the frontiers of Nubia, at a place now called Radesieh, this king is represented holding a group of negro prisoners by the hair—a representation intended to express that the tribes were entirely at his mercy.

On the north-west frontier of Egypt, Seti repulsed the incursions of the Lybians, and despatched some successful expeditions into their country. Finally, he reconstructed the Egyptian fleet on the Red Sea which cruised on the shores of the Pun, or Yemen, where he re-asserted the supremacy of the Pharaohs, first established by Hatasu.

6. There is nothing to show that Seti I. had occasion to renew his great expeditions into Asia. On the contrary, everything indicates that, up to the time of his death, the supremacy he had re-established in Syria and Mesopotamia remained undisputed. The terror inspired by his name and by the superiority of his arms no doubt sufficed during his life to keep the people in submission.

The Khitas faithfully observed the treaty, and, while silently preparing for new and more formidable attacks on the Egyptian power, scrupulously respected for the time the provinces subject to Egypt. We have no monument of the reign of Seti subsequent to his thirtieth year, although, according to the lists of Manetho, he appears to have reigned more than fifty years. It seems, therefore, that no great events occurred during the latter part of his reign, and that Egypt must have enjoyed that happy repose during which people have no history. Unless, however, and this perhaps is most probable, we ought to correct the lists of Manetho and write thirty years only, instead of fifty, for the reign of Seti I.

In any case, it is certain that campaigns into Asia and the building of sumptuous edifices were not the only occupations of the Egyptian monarchy under this reign. Knowing that the gold mines in the desert south of Egypt were difficult of access, and that it was almost impossible to sustain life there because of the extreme dryness of the country, Seti I. ordered, in the 9th year of his reign, an Artesian well to be constructed (a most important fact as bearing on the skill of the Egyptian engineers of the period), whence water in abundance was obtained. Encouraged by this success, the king resolved to build a fortress and a temple where he himself often went to adore his gods. Care had been taken to place him among the divinities of the place. Such is the account given in a long inscription.

"But however important may have been the creation of a habitable place in the midst of the desert, a still more important fact is revealed to us by a monument of another kind. The bas-relief in the Hall of Columns at Karnak, representing Seti returning from his conquests and re-entering Egypt, shows us the towns or castles east of the Delta, or Isthmus of Suez, that he passed on his route. Now one of these, Zal (Heroopolis), is represented on a canal containing crocodiles, and opening into a great mass of water, probably a lake. Dr. Brugsch, the highest authority on Pharaonic geography, in describing this curious representation declares that, in his opinion, this is no other than the famous canal from the Nile to the Red Sea, passing the lake still called the Crocodile Lake (Timsah). He reminds us, that in later times the Greek tradition often confused the two reigns of Seti and of his son; and we know that Sesostris has passed for the original author of that magnificent enterprise, taken up again and completed in later times by the Greek kings of Egypt, and, though destroyed by the barbarism of another age, once more successfully carried out by the genius and indomitable perseverance of a Frenchman."—ROBIOU.

SECTION V.—RAMSES II. (SESOSTRIS).

(*Close of the Fifteenth and first half of the Fourteenth Century* B.C.).

1. RAMSES II., surnamed Meriamen, beloved of Amen, had been, as we have said, associated on the throne with his father from his birth, and even, we may say, before his birth. "Such thou hast been," say the gods to him in an inscription, "from thy birth; no monument was erected without thee, and no order was executed without thy consent." Nevertheles he counted the years of his reign only from the death of Seti and from the time when he became sole master, at the age of about eighteen or twenty. His reign was one of the longest in the annals of Egypt; he governed alone for sixty-seven years.

Among the Pharaohs he is *the* builder *par excellence.* It is almost impossible to find in Egypt a ruin, or an ancient mound, without reading his name. The two magnificent subterranean Temples at Ipsamboul, in Nubia, the Ramesseum of Thebes, a large part of the temples of Karnak and Luxor, the small temple at Abydos, are all his works; he built also large edifices at Memphis, where a magnificent Colossus bears his likeness, in the Fayum, and at Tanis. Ramses II. was enabled to complete these works, owing to the great length of his reign; and to his wars, which gave him the large number of prisoners whom, according to Egyptian usage, he employed on these edifices. To these causes we may add the presence of numerous tribes of foreign races on the banks of the Nile, whom the fertility of the soil, and the policy of former kings, had attracted from the plains of Asia into the Delta. These foreigners repaid the hospitality Egypt had extended to them by the workmen whom they furnished for the works on the temples, the construction of cities and the cleansing of canals. In this way we find, in the Bible story under this same Ramses II., the Israelites employed in the east of the Delta in the construction of two cities, one called after the king Ramses (Ex. i. 2).

2. Ramses II. was celebrated in Europe long before our era, long before the monuments of Egypt were understood by us. Herodotus had called him Sesostris, and the name had become famous; but the Greek writer did not invent it. Ramses had received during his life, and for some reason we are ignorant of, the popular surname of Sestesu, or Sesu, and with the addition of the word Ra (the Sun), a common addition to the names of Egyptian kings, this must have produced a sound, rendered agreeable in later times to Grecian ears, as Sesostris.

Round these popular surnames a legend gradually formed in the course of ages, attributing to one person all the exploits of the conquerors and warlike princes of Egypt, both of Thothmes and Seti as well as of the various Ramses, and magnifying these exploits by extending them to every known country, as legends always do. It is these legendary traditions, these fabulous stories, current among the populace, that the Greeks, the intelligent and correct Herodotus as well as the mere compiler Diodorus Siculus, greedily received from their guides in Egypt, being incapable of referring directly to the true sources of history. These are the stories from which from age to age the history of Egypt was written; a history as real and true up to the time of Champollion's discovery, as would be one of Charlemagne drawn from the Ballads of the middle age.

Sesostris, according to the legends collected and repeated by these Greeks, was prepared in an extraordinary way by his education to play the part of a conqueror. From his infancy his father had gathered round him all the boys born on the same day, and made him as well as his companions serve an apprenticeship to war, by violent exercise, by long journeys, and by constant conflicts with the wild animals and barbarous inhabitants of the desert. After his father's death, Sesostris aspired to other exploits and greater conquests. Ethiopia was the first country he conquered. He imposed on it a tribute of gold, ebony, and elephants' tusks. He next equipped a fleet of 400 long ships on the Arabian Gulf, the first of their kind the Egyptians had seen. Whilst this fleet subjugated the banks of the Red Sea, Sesostris at the head of his army invaded Asia. He subdued Syria, Mesopotamia, Assyria, Media, Persia, Bactria, and India, and penetrated even to the Ganges. Returning then towards the north, he subjugated the Scythian tribes as far as Tanais, and established in the Isthmus, separating the Black Sea from the Caspian, a colony, the origin of the state of Colchis; passed into Asia Minor, where he left monuments of his victories;* lastly, crossing the Bosphorus, he advanced into Thrace, where scarcity of food, the rigor of the climate, and the difficulties of passage put an end to his triumphs. At the end of nine years Sesostris returned to his kingdom, followed by a host of captives, loaded with booty and covered with glory.

Such is the legend. The reader will have already perceived that it attributes to Sesostris the conquest of countries already long subject to Egypt, such as Ethiopia; and the credit of deeds by preceding sovereigns, such as the creation of a navy and the reduction of the shores of the Red Sea; but above all it makes this prince march triumphantly over countries where Egyptian armies were never at any time seen, such as India, Persia, and generally the Arian countries beyond the Tigris, as well as the provinces to the north of Armenia. This is an exact parallel to those middle age poems that always enhance the exploits of Charlemagne and magnify his victories, making him the conqueror of Jerusalem and the deliverer of the Holy Sepulchre.

If we now investigate the real facts, from the testimony of the official monuments of Ramses Sesostris, though they are very emphatic in their language and often suspected of exaggeration, we see the whole fabric of these prodigious conquests vanish away. Ramses II. was no doubt a warlike prince, who passed the greater part of his reign in fighting, but he was not a conqueror. He did not add one single province to Egypt; in the south, north, and west, he was always compelled to stand on the defensive, and exposed every instant to the revolts of the people whom the Thothmes and Amen-hoteps had subdued. The only glory of his reign was to have maintained, at the expense of enormous efforts, the integrity of the empire. Far from having penetrated to the banks of the Ganges, he never carried his arms in Asia further than Thothmes III. and Seti, and nearly all his campaigns were confined to Northern Syria. In a word, the great renown of Sesostris is entirely fabulous; it is one of the baseless tales of glory accepted so readily by

---

* HER. ii. 106. One of these monuments attributed by the legend to Sesostris, and which Herodotus says that he saw, still remains at Ninfi, near Smyrna, and the author of this Manual having seen it, can confidently pronounce that it has no appearance of a work of Egyptian art.

Consult a dissertation by M. Perrot in the *Revue Archéologique*, 1867.

[See also description and plate in Rawlinson and Wilkinson's *Herodotus*, vol. ii., p. 149. 2nd ed.]

the Greeks, and which disappear before criticism and the progress ot knowledge as to the positive facts of history.

3. Let us see now what the reign of Ramses II. really was, according to the monuments of the banks of the Nile. A change of reign is always a critical time for vast empires established only by conquest, and extending over an immense extent of territory. The change is generally followed by the revolt of the less completely subjugated and more distant provinces—of those that have suffered most from oppression, and think themselves best able to procure their freedom by force of arms. The accession of Ramses, on the death of his father Seti, passed off quietly in Asia. The new prince was recognised peaceably as far as Mesopotamia, and an inscription of the second year of his reign, says that his orders were then obeyed there with fidelity. But affairs were not in the same state on the banks of the Upper Nile. The south of Ethiopia revolted, and with this part of the Ethiopians all the negro tribes who had been subject to the sceptre of the Pharaohs. It required a long, bloody, and furious war to reduce things to their former order and subdue the rebels. The walls of the subterranean temples of Ipsamboul and Beit Walli, in Nubia, are covered with great sculptured and painted tablets, representing the victories gained by his Ethiopian viceroys over his revolted subjects on the Upper Nile. On some of them Ramses is personally represented, and, in fact, to encourage his army he must have been present with it in one campaign in the south of Ethiopia in the second or third year of his reign.

4. The embarrassment caused by this revolt of the people of the Upper Nile drew for some years the attention of the government and the military forces of Egypt to the south, and, therefore, appeared to the Khitas, or Hittites, who henceforth were to play the first part in the affairs of Western Asia, to afford a favourable occasion for recommencing war and provoking a general insurrection of those Asiatic provinces first reduced to obedience by Seti. Armenia, Assyria, Mesopotamia, Chaldæa, and Aramæan Syria all revolted at once, and drove out the Egyptian garrisons.

The Khitas put themselves at the head of the movement, and a numerous and formidable confederation gathered round them, composed not only of the revolted nations, but also of the greater part of the tribes of Asia Minor, who dreaded the growth of the Pharaonic power, and had already felt the weight of its arms by sea, under Thothmes III. A great army was assembled in Northern Syria, menacing both Palestine, where already partial revolts had broken out among the petty Canaanitish princes governing different cities, and also the frontier of Egypt itself. The monuments of the reign of Ramses have preserved the names of the twelve states whose united troops formed this army. They were first the Khitas, or Hittites; the kingdom of Kadesh, or of the northern Amorites; the Gergesenes of Peræa (inhabitants ot the present Djerash), all of the race of Canaan; the Phœnicians of Aradus, the only ones of their nation unfaithful to the Egyptian monarch, to whom those of Byblos and Sidon always remained attached; the Aramæan people were represented by the States of Helbon (Aleppo); of Carchemish, where Thothmes III. had built his fortress to guard the passage of the Euphrates; of Katti (also mentioned in the Bible, but whose precise position is unknown); of Aloun (Elon, Jos. xix. 43), a town afterwards belonging to the tribe of Dan; of Gadara, in Cœle Syria; of Anaugas, chief city of the Rotennu on this side the Euphrates; and of Gazauatan, a place the site of which is unknown. Mesopotamia, mentioned here as always by the name of Naharaina, had furnished very numerous contingents. Finally, the nations of Asia Minor, who had sent soldiers to the army commanded by Mautnur, king of the Hittites, were the Mysians, the Lycians, the Pisidians, the Dardanians of Troy, and last, a people called Mushanet in the Egyptian texts, who may, perhaps, be identified with the Mosynœci of classical geography.*

All this occurred towards the end of the fourth year of the reign ol Ramses. The young king could not resign himself to the loss of the greater part of his empire, and of its most valuable provinces. In the spring of the following year, having assembled his whole military force, and gathered round him the experienced captains who had taken part in his father's wars, he commenced a campaign to recover the Asiatic possessions of his predecessors, and, above all, to humble the pride of the Khitas, who were the life and soul of the Asiatic insurrection.

The army of Ramses traversed first the land of Canaan. There is no inscription recording the first part of the campaign; but it is probable that Pharaoh had to fight more than once, to repress several revolts in this country, for centuries subject to the sovereigns of Egypt, as he engraved triumphal steles on the rocks; these still remain at Adloun, near Tyre, and at the passage of the Nahr El Kelb (Dog River), near Beyrut. But he arrived in the neighbourhood of Kadesh and the valley of the Orontes without meeting the grand army of his enemies. It was there that the personal exploit of Ramses occurred which is constantly commemorated on the monuments, where he was praised to satiety up to the end of his reign, and by the sculptures on the walls of all the temples built by this prince—an exploit proving the personal courage of the king rather than his possession of real military talent. This episode in the history of the Sesostris of the Greeks was made the subject of an epic poem, about as long as one book of the Iliad, composed by a scribe named Pentaour. Its text, always unfortunately

* HER. iii. 94; vii. 78.

much mutilated, is found in three places—engraven at length on the wall of the Ramesseum at Thebes and on that of the temple of Ipsamboul, and also written in the cursive style, called Hieratic, in a papyrus in the British Museum. This valuable text was in 1856 translated by M. de Rougé. We think it well to give here an analysis, with some quotations, that our readers may have some idea of an Egyptian poem, an epic written by one of the best literary men of the period, and only two years after the event it records.

5. It was in the fifth year of the reign of Ramses, Pharaoh, seeking his enemies, who retired slowly before him to make head only on their own territory, had penetrated as far as Cœle Syria, not far from Kadesh, and was encamped under the fortress of Shebetun (a place still unknown), when two Bedouins (Shasu) presented themselves before him. They said they were sent by their chiefs to join the Egyptian army, and to bring certain intelligence as to the movements of the Khitas, who had compelled the tribe to march with them.

They stated that the enemy, alarmed, had retreated towards Aleppo, where they were concentrating. But this was treachery, false intelligence contrived by the chiefs of the Khitas to cause Pharaoh to fall into a trap. They, with their numerous allies, had placed themselves in ambuscade a little to the north-east of Kadesh.

Deceived by the reports of these pretended fugitives, Ramses marched on without suspicion, accompanied only by his body guard, whilst the main portion of his army proceeded by the road on Aleppo, hoping to find the enemy there, when two men, who had been seized by the king's servants, were led into his presence. Compelled by blows to speak, they confessed that, far from retreating, the Khitas, confident in the numbers of their soldiers and allies, among whom were the people of Mesopotamia and Asia Minor, were close at hand, hoping to surprise the king. The Egyptian generals, assembled by Ramses, were much disconcerted at having allowed themselves to be deceived by the first report, and thus having led the king into so dangerous a position. Messengers were sent in all haste to recall the army to the place where the enemy was posted. But before the arrival of the troops the whole of the Khita forces sallied forth from their ambuscade, and fell on the small body which accompanied Ramses, hoping to make a prisoner of Pharaoh.

With the rash courage of youth, Ramses, who was then only twenty-three years old, rejected with scorn the prudent councils of his officers, who wished him to retire to the rear, and without waiting for the main body of his army, commenced the fight. "The footmen and horsemen then," says the poet, "recoiled before the enemy, who were masters of Kadesh, on the left bank of the Orontes. . . . Then his majesty, in the pride of his strength, rising up like the god Month, put on his fighting dress, completely armed, he looked like Baal in the hour of his might. . . . Urging on his chariot, he pushed into the army of the vile Khitas; he was alone, no one was with him. . . . He was surrounded by 2,500 chariots, and the swiftest of the warriors of the vile Khitas, and of the numerous nations who accompanied them, threw themselves in his way. . . . Each chariot bore three men, and the king had with him neither princes nor generals nor his captains of archers or of chariots." In the presence of such a danger the king was for an instant troubled. He invoked Amen, the great god of Thebes, asking help, and recalling the pomp with which he had surrounded his worship and the magnificent temples he had built to him, just as Homer's heroes reminded Zeus of all the hecatombs they had slain in his honour. "My archers and horsemen have abandoned me! There is none of them to fight by my side! What, then, is the intention of my father, Amen? . . . Did I not march at thy word?* Has not thy mouth guided my expeditions, and have not thy councils directed me? Have not I celebrated magnificent feasts in thy honour, and have not I filled thy temple with my booty? . . . I have slain for thee 30,000 bulls. . . . I have built for thee temples of blocks of stone, and have erected for thee everlasting trees. . . . I set up the obelisks of Elephantine; by me were the eternal stones set up.† . . . Thee I invoke, O my Father! I am in the midst of a host of strangers, and no man is with me. My archers and horsemen have abandoned me; when I cried to them, none of them has heard when I called for help. But I prefer Amen to thousands of millions of archers, to millions of horsemen, to myriads of young heroes all assembled together. The designs of man are nothing, Amen overrules them."

Here the deity intervenes in the midst of the strife, just as in the Homeric combats; Amen has heard the prayer of Ramses, he raises his sinking courage, gives him strength, and encourages him with these words: "I am near thee, I am thy father, the Sun, my hand is with thee. I will be more to thee than millions of men assembled together. I am the Lord of hosts, who loves courage; I have found thy heart firm, and my heart has rejoiced. My will shall be accomplished. I will be to them like Baal in his might. The 2,500 chariots, when I am in the midst of them, shall be crushed before thy horses. Their hearts shall sink in their bosoms, and their limbs shall be weak. They shall be able to shoot no more arrows, and shall have no strength to hold the spear. I will make them leap into the water, as the crocodile springs in; they shall be thrown one on another, and kill each other before thee."

---

* Doubtless on the faith of an oracle.

† Amongst others the one now at Paris, in the Place de la Concorde.

Strengthened and encouraged by the divine word, the king rushed on the Khitas, who halted, astonished at his boldness. He made the bravest of their warriors bite the dust, and opened for himself a blood-stained passage over their corpses. But the enemy, though terrified for a moment, regained courage, seeing that the Egyptian army did not come up at the shouts of the king. Ramses was again surrounded by the war-chariots of the bravest chiefs of the Hittite army. "When my armour-bearer saw that I was surrounded by such a number of chariots, he was afraid, his heart failed him, and his terror extended itself to all his limbs. He said to his majesty, 'My good master, generous king, sole protector of Egypt in the day of battle, we are alone in the midst of the enemy, stay and let us save the breath of our lives.' "*

But the king did not listen to these timid counsels, the greatness of his danger raised his courage ; trusting in the protection of Amen, he urged on his car. Six times he crossed the ranks of the enemy. Six times he struck down all who opposed his passage. He then rejoined his guards, and in severe terms reproached the generals and soldiers who had abandoned him. He recalled to them all the favours which he had bestowed upon them ; all the good he had conferred upon Egypt from the height of his throne. "Every day," said he, "I sit in judgment on every complaint made to me." Addressing particularly the officers charged with the government of the province of Syria and with watching the frontiers, he bitterly reproached them with their negligence in not getting information as to the movements of the enemy. Lastly, he reproached them all with their cowardice, contrasting it with the courage he himself had shown. "I have displayed my valour, and neither footmen nor horsemen went with me. The whole world has made way before the strength of my arm; I was alone, no one with me, neither princes, nor generals, nor chiefs of archers, nor of cavalry. . . . The warriors have stopped; they have retreated on seeing my exploits, their myriads have taken flight, and their feet can no more be stopped. The shafts launched by my hand dispersed their warriors as soon as they came near me."

The Egyptian soldiers praised the valour of their king by unanimous acclamations, and contemplated with astonishment the victims slain by his hand. But Ramses only replied by reproaches to the praises of his generals, and contrasted with their inconsiderate and pusillanimous conduct the constancy of the two faithful animals who had borne him out of danger; he ordered them to be covered with honours, and like Alexander who, after the defeat of Porus, founded a city and called it

* The Egyptian poet, in accordance with the emphatic form very common in the texts of that language, changes the person, and now puts the words into the king's mouth.

Bucephalus, after the horse that had carried him through the whole battle, and had several times extricated him from serious danger, "These (my horses)," he said, "I found with me when I was alone in the midst of the enemy. . . . I will that they shall be fed with grain before the god Ra (the Sun), every day when I am in my palace, because they have been with me in the midst of the enemy's army."

During the night the main body of the army arrived. As soon as day appeared, Ramses re-commenced the battle. It raged with fury, for the Khitas wished to avenge their bravest officers, and the Egyptians to wipe away the reproach of cowardice thrown on them by their king. They burned to efface their shame of the previous day. Very soon the Hittite army was overcome, the best of their soldiers fell under the blows of the "Children of the Sun." Ramses again performed prodigies of valour. "The great lion who marched by his horses fought with him, rage swelling all his limbs, and whoever approached him was overthrown. The king mastered them and killed them, and none could escape him. Cut to pieces before his horses, their corpses formed one great bleeding heap."

The king of the Khitas, seeing the flower of his army destroyed, and the rest flying on all sides, resigned himself to submission to the king of Egypt, and asked, "Amaun." He sent a herald, who addressed Pharaoh, "Son of the Sun . . . the Egyptians and the Khitas are slaves beneath thy feet. Ra has given thee dominion over them. . . . Thou mayest massacre thy slaves, they are in thy power, none of them can resist. Yesterday didst thou arrive and kill an infinite number of them; again to-day thou hast come; do not continue the massacre. . . . We are prostrate on the earth, ready to execute thy orders; O valiant king! flower of warriors, give us the breath of our lives."

The king consulted his chief officers on the message from the king of the Khitas, and on the answer he should make. In accordance with their unanimous advice, satisfied with the glory conferred on his arms by the double victory he had gained, and not wishing to drive his warlike enemies to despair, Ramses made peace, and, taking the road southward, directed his march to Egypt with his companions in glory. He entered his capital in triumph, and the god Amen welcomed him to his sanctuary, saying to him, "Hail to thee my much-loved son Ramses. We give thee years innumerable. Rest for ever on the throne of thy father, Amen, and let the barbarians be crushed beneath thy feet."

This piece of court poetry, attributing to the single arm of Ramses exploits so fabulous, and impossible from their very greatness, must not of course be taken literally. But it seems to show, that near Kadesh, Ramses, having fallen into an ambuscade, was abandoned by a part of the troops who accompanied him, and that with a weak escort he received the first shock of the enemy, or prevented it by an impetuous charge, thus giving his army time to come up and rescue him from danger; it may undoubtedly be easy to exaggerate an event, especially for a poet and a courtier, but it would be a difficult task to invent the whole story.

6. But where the poet had decidedly overlooked facts in recording his king's victory, was in announcing the complete and final submission of the Khitas and their allies. The confederation was not yet broken. Ramses had contented himself with the nominal submission of the chiefs and with the request for "Amaun" after the battle of Kadesh, and had at once returned to Egypt without going personally into the provinces of Aramæa, or Mesopotamia, without rebuilding the fortresses and garrisoning them, or levying tribute at the head of his army. So the pretended peace concluded in his fifth year was in reality only a very short truce. Two years afterwards—that is, in the same year that Pentaour wrote his epic on the prowess of the son of Seti—Mautnur, king of the Khitas, died, and was succeeded by his brother, Khitasar, and war recommenced with more fury than ever. It lasted fourteen whole years with no truce or interruption. Unfortunately we have very few details of the successive events that distinguished it, but at least we know that the vicissitudes of successes and reverses were great.

Thus, in the eleventh year of the reign of Ramses, the Egyptians were driven back by the Asiatics almost to the valley of the Nile, the greater part of Palestine was lost, and they were reduced to consider the capture of Ascalon as a great success, worthy of being represented on public monuments. Three years earlier they had besieged Salem, the city of the Jebusites, of which Melchisedek had been king in the time of Abraham, identified by many commentators with Jerusalem, and afterwards the siege of Debir at the foot of Mount Tabor, a northern Amorite city. These exploits are represented on the Pylon of the Ramesseum of Kurnah, as well as the capture of Beth Anath, and Kamon, two other cities of Canaan. Afterwards, it is true, fortune smiled on the Egyptian arms, and they drove the allied armies out of Palestine, Phœnicia, and Cœle Syria; took Kadesh by assault, descended the valley of the Orontes to its extremity, and thus penetrated into the heart of the Khita country, pushing on even further in the direction of Cilicia and Pisidia. Ramses, during this long war, several times personally took command of his army in Asia.

One of the historical tablets of the Ramesseum at Thebes shows him, after a great battle against the Khitas and their allies, receiving from his generals an account of the number of enemies slain, whose amputated hands are piled at his feet. In another he is engaged in the fight, two of his sons are pursuing the routed enemy, who fly towards a city under whose ramparts are already two other sons of the king preparing to make an assault.

7. At last, in the twenty-first year of the king's reign and fourteenth of the war, a real and final treaty of peace was concluded between the two belligerents, with conditions as favourable to the Hittites as to Pharaoh. The text of this treaty, undoubtedly the oldest diplomatic document extant, has been preserved in an inscription at Thebes, and translated by M. de Rougé. We there read that the king of Egypt received, in the fortress he had built in Cœle Syria to prevent any new invasion of Palestine, and had called by his own name, a visit from the king of the Khitas, who came to propose conditions of peace. They stipulated for perpetual peace and alliance between the two nations, in such terms as showed that they treated on a footing of absolute equality. The clauses prohibiting either direct or indirect hostility are identical on both sides; the two kings reciprocally promise to give no asylum to servants or subjects of the other who may have left their country. Entire freedom of trade is established between the Egyptians and Hittites. Such was the treaty terminating the war. After fourteen years of uninterrupted fighting, confined within the bounds of Syria, the famous Sesostris, far from having subjugated his enemies, recognised their independence and the integrity of their territory; a result very different from the legends of Herodotus and Diodorus Siculus. As a pledge of the alliance, Ramses receives among his wives a daughter of king Khitasar, who received an Egyptian name, meaning "Gift of the great Sun of Justice." To show his good will to the Hittites, he re-established at Tanis the worship of Sutekh, the national deity of these people as well as of the Shepherds, and built in his honour one of the largest and most magnificent temples of Egypt; whilst Khitasar seems to have done nothing similar in his country in honour of the gods of Egypt.

In making this treaty with Ramses, the king of the Hittites had separated himself from his allies; he had made no stipulation with regard to them, and, contented with favourable conditions for himself, had left them to manage for themselves. The people of Asia Minor, Pisidians, Lycians, Mysians, Dardanians, retreated peaceably to their own countries, and were under no apprehension, for the Hittite country was between them and Egypt. The people of Mesopotamia and of the countries between Lebanon and the Euphrates, however, were in no position to continue the war, and hastened to submit to the king of Egypt, before he invaded their country. One of the tablets of the Ramesseum represents Ramses giving investiture to the chiefs of the Rotennu—that is, of the Aramæans, Assyrians, and Chaldæans—who recognised his suzerainty.

The Asiatic conquests of Thothmes and Seti were thus recovered without the king being obliged to cross the Euphrates; Mesopotamia again paid tribute, and Egyptian residents were sent to the courts of all the native princes to exercise supervision over them. Garrisons of Pharaoh's soldiers were reinstated in some of the most important places, amongst others at Carchemish, but the bonds of subjection in which these countries were held were much lighter than they had been under Thothmes III.; and the Egyptian king prudently contented himself with gratified self-love as a substitute for real power.

From this time to the end of the reign of Ramses—that is, for nearly half a century—peace was preserved in Western Asia, once the scene of such long and sanguinary wars. Hostilities did not again break out between the Egyptians and Khitas, and the good understanding between these rival empires seems to have been uninterrupted. We find no trace on the monuments of any further revolts in Mesopotamia or Syria; these countries remained in a state of partial subjection just as they were at the end of the Hittite war. A papyrus in the British Museum contains a letter from an Egyptian officer who at this time was sent on a mission into Phœnicia; he describes the towns he passed through that were subject to the sceptre of his master in that country, Gebal, or Byblos, "the city of mysteries," Berytus, Sidon, Sarepta, and Tyre, at that time merely a fishing village. Another papyrus in the same collection contains orders relative to preparations for the march of a body of troops in the south of Palestine. Segor, or Zoar, the only city that had survived the destruction of the five doomed cities of the plain of Sodom, is mentioned in this document.

8. Having thus reduced the famous conquests of Sesostris to their true proportions, we must now speak of his internal government. The legends contain stories equally fabulous respecting this also. The more intimately we come to know the history of Ramses II., the less he seems to deserve the title of Great, conferred on him by the first decipherers of Egyptian inscriptions on the faith of Greek tradition. We now know enough to pronounce him a man of very ordinary capacity, intoxicated with the possession of absolute power, a licentious despot, ambitious and ostentatious to the extreme, a man so vain as actually to efface, wherever he could do so, the names of his predecessors from their monuments in order to substitute his own.

This Sun-king of Egypt increased the royal harem to an unprecedented extent. During the sixty-seven years of his reign, he had 170 children, fifty-nine of them sons. Considering himself superior to all moral laws, he even went so far as to marry one of his own daughters, the princess Bent-Anat.

The Book of Exodus represents Ramses as a tyrant because of his persecution of the Hebrews. He it was who attempted to crush them finally and completely by the labours he imposed, and by the cruel edict dooming all their male children to death. The Hebrews, moreover, were not the only sufferers under his reign, and the calm judgment of history confirms the stigma fixed on him by the Bible.

We cannot, without horror, think of the numbers of captives who must have died under the taskmaster's stick, or fallen victims to excessive fatigue and privations of every kind, while employed as slaves on the gigantic works erected to minister to the insatiable pride of the Egyptian king. In all the monuments of Ramses, there is hardly a stone, so to speak, that has not cost a human life. When, however, the Asiatic wars were ended, captives were wanting for the works. Then man-hunting expeditions among the unfortunate negroes of Soudan were organised on a monstrous scale, unknown in former periods. There was no longer any intention, as under the Thothmes and Amen-hoteps, of extending the frontier of the Egyptian empire so as to include the ivory and gold producing countries. The chief and in fact only aim was to procure slaves. Nearly every year grand *razzias* were made into Ethiopia, returning with thousands of captives of every age, and of both sexes, loaded with chains.

The principal incidents of these negro-hunting expeditions were actually sculptured as glorious exploits on the walls of the temples! Ramses was also the first of the kings of Egypt to practise the system, adopted in later times by the kings of Assyria and Babylon, of transporting conquered people from their own land so as to obviate the danger of rebellion. He carried into Asia entire tribes of negroes, and sent to Nubia the Asiatics whose lands he had given to the negroes. This barbarous system was not without its dangers. Diodorus Siculus heard in Egypt a story, apparently authentic, although naturally it has found no place in the official inscriptions of Ramses, being by no means glorious to the name of Pharaoh. According to this story, a large body of Assyrian and Chaldæan prisoners, who were working in the quarries near Memphis, revolted, being unable to support the excessive labour imposed on them. They possessed themselves of a strong place in that neighbourhood, whence they made incursions into the adjacent country. After having in vain attempted to reduce them by force, the proud Sesostris was obliged to make an agreement with them. He accorded them a general amnesty, and left them in possession of the fortress they had seized, named by them in remembrance of their fatherland, "Babylon." It is now called Old Cairo.

All the foreign tribes of Semitic race, attracted by the policy of the predecessors of Ramses into the Delta to colonise the land reclaimed from the water, were subjected to the same oppression, to the same routine of forced labour as the Hebrews. Even the indigenous rural population, Egyptian by birth, did not escape. The reign of a warlike despot, who is also possessed with a mania for building, is always a deplorable calamity for this class. Egypt under Ramses II. was no exception to this general rule. A papyrus in the British Museum has preserved the correspondence between the chief librarian of Ramses, Ameneman, and his pupil and friend, Pentaour, the author of the epic poem we have already given extracts from. One of the letters describes as follows the state of the country, and the life of its agricultural people:—"Have you ever conceived what sort of life the peasant leads who cultivates the soil? Even before it is ripe, insects destroy part of his harvest. . . . Multitudes of rats are in the fields; next come invasions of locusts, cattle ravage his harvest, sparrows alight in flocks on his sheaves. If he delays to get in his harvest, robbers come to carry it off from him; his horse dies of fatigue in drawing the plough; the tax collector arrives in the district, and has with him men armed with sticks, negroes with palm branches. All say, 'Give us of your corn,' and he has no means of escaping their exactions. Next the unfortunate wretch is seized, bound, and carried off by force to work on the canals; his wife is bound, his children are stripped. And at the same time his neighbours have each of them his own trouble."

9. In every nation, and at all times, it has been found that art has been unable to resist the degrading influence of a certain amount of despotism. The monuments of Ramses II. exhibit a serious falling off in Egyptian sculpture, increasing with incredible rapidity as this long reign advances. It commenced with some works worthy of all admiration as the *ne plus ultra* of Egyptian art—such are the Colossi of Memphis and Ipsambul, but soon the universal oppression which weighed like a yoke of iron on the whole country dried up the source of the great art inspiration. All the inventive genius of the country seems to have been exhausted in gigantic constructions, conceived by boundless pride. No new generation of artists grew up to replace those who had been formed under earlier kings. At the end of this reign, the degradation was complete, and in the last days of Ramses, as under his son Merenphtah, we meet with really barbarous works, and sculptures of extraordinary coarseness.

10. The close of this long and pretentious reign of Ramses-Sesostris was, moreover, a period of decadence in every respect, a time of disasters but imperfectly known to us, resembling in some respects the end of the reign of Louis XIV., but without a battle of Denain to gild its last moments with glory.

The country, enervated by sixty years of unrestrained despotism, and governed by the feeble hand of an octogenarian king, was in no condition to resist its enemies. But on this occasion the danger did not come from Asia; the invasion was from Northern Africa, and from the Mediterranean Sea. New adversaries were about to enter the lists with the Egyptian power.

Since the time of Thothmes III., who had possessed the whole coast of Lybia and the Archipelago, a great change had occurred in the population of these countries. A fleet, manned by light-haired, blue-eyed barbarians belonging to the Japhetic or Indo-European race, had arrived on the African coast, and, driving the old inhabitants of the Hamite race of Phut into the interior of the country, had fixed their own residence there. These were the ancestors of the light-haired people whom the French soldiers found still remaining in the mountains of the Kabyles, the Lybians, properly so called, the Lebu of the hieroglyphic inscriptions, and the Mashuash, the Maxyans of Herodotus. The Egyptians designated them by the two generic names of Tamahu, "Northern men," and Tahennu, "men of the mist;" they were closely allied with, and undoubtedly related to, the Pelasgic nations, who had just created a naval power, and were dominant in the Mediterranean, and also to the inhabitants of some of the islands, such as Sardinia, Sicily, and Crete.

The fleets of these northern invaders constantly advancing, soon coasted along Lybia, and towards the end of the reign of Seti began to threaten Lower Egypt from the west. The fertile plains of the Delta were the object of their desires. During the first part of the reign of Ramses, the Egyptian troops succeeded, although with difficulty, in keeping them back. During his wars in Asia, the king had several bodies of soldiers recruited among the prisoners of these nations. But when Ramses had become old, he was no longer able to arrest the progress of these Japhetic Lybians. The frontiers of the land of Mizraim were violated, and continual incursions laid waste all Lower Egypt. The mass of the nation then seized on the fertile lands laid open to their depredations, and driving back the Egyptian population, occupied the whole western part of the Delta. Thus the proud Sesostris died, leaving a considerable part of the possessions of his fathers, the very heart of the kingdom, in the hands of barbarians.

SECTION VI.—END OF THE NINETEENTH DYNASTY.—FOREIGN INVASIONS—THE EXODUS. (*Fourteenth Century B.C.*)

1. RAMSES II. was succeeded by his thirteenth son, named Merenphtah (beloved by Phtah). His monuments and inscriptions are generally found at Memphis, a city famous for the worship of the god Phtah, where he seems to have moved his residence. His reign was one of the most unfortunate in the history of Egypt; it presents one long succession of disorders, invasions, and miseries of every kind, the necessary consequences of the tyranny of his father.

The first with whom Merenphtah had to deal were the Lybians and their allies, the Pelasgians. His war against them is related in a long inscription on the Temple of Karnak, translated by M. de Rougé. We will give extracts to convey the chief features of the story.

The northern people of Lybia and of the Archipelago, who had already for some time been masters of part of the Delta, saw in this change of government a favourable opportunity for invading and subjugating all Egypt. A formidable army was organised under the command of Maurmuiu, son of Batta,* king of the Lybians. The Lybians and Mashuash formed the bulk of the invaders, with the Pelasgian Tyrrhenians from Italy, ancestors of the Etruscans; but with them they had numerous bands of Sardinians, Sicilians, Achæans of the Peloponnesus, and Laconians. The Egyptian narrative gives us the valuable information that "the Tyrrhenians had commenced the war, and that each warrior had brought his wife and children," thus clearly showing their intention of making a new settlement. A speech placed by the composer of the inscription in the mouth of Pharaoh himself, describes the evils brought by these invaders upon Egypt: "These barbarians are plundering the frontiers; every day these evil men are violating them; they are robbing. They plunder the ports, they invade the fields of Egypt, coming by the river; they are establishing themselves; the days and months pass away and still they remain." The sufferings of the country are described as even greater than during the invasion of the Shepherds. "Nothing like this has been seen, even in the times of the kings of Lower Egypt, when the land of Egypt was in their power, and misfortune continued, and when the kings of Upper Egypt had not strength to drive out the strangers."

The barbarians advanced without meeting any serious resistance. Already Memphis and Heliopolis were reached, and the invading army had arrived at the city of Paari, in Central Egypt. It was necessary to stop them at once, if Egypt was to be saved. Merenphtah, who had taken refuge at Thebes, assembled an army in Upper Egypt. But he did not venture to expose his person to the consequences of a defeat, by putting himself at the head of his soldiers. He sent one army under the command of the surviving generals of his father, whilst he despatched a second body through the desert into Lybia, to create a diversion in the rear of the enemy. A great battle took place near Paari. It lasted six hours, and ended in the complete defeat of the Lybians and their allies.

The official narrative gives the particulars of the loss of the foreign invaders; the very moderation of the numbers proves their correctness, as is almost always the case with Egyptian computations. The Lybians had 6,359 killed; the Mashuash, 6,300; the Kehak, another Japhetic tribe from Northern Africa, 2,362; the Tyrrhenians, 790; the Sicilians,

* This is the name "Battus," borne in later times by some of the Greek kings of Cyrene.

250; the numbers of the losses of the Sardinians, Achæans, and Laconians have been unfortunately destroyed. 9,376 prisoners were made, and a large booty was found in the enemy's camp, amongst other things 1,307 head of fat cattle, as well as a large quantity of bronze arms, found on the field of battle, abandoned by the fugitives, who were pursued even beyond the frontier, where the fortresses were restored and the garrisons replaced. Maurmuiu, king of the Lybians, had disappeared in the battle, without any one being able to say what had become of him, and the nation elected a new chief, who hastened to treat with Pharaoh.

Thus was repulsed this formidable invasion, which had covered great part of Egypt with ruins. The victory, however, was not so complete but that Merenphtah was obliged to adopt the expedient of the later Roman emperors, who, unable to drive the barbarians entirely away, assigned them lands in the provinces of the empire, after having conquered them in battle. The foreign tribes, belonging chiefly to the Mashuash, who for some time had been settled in the Delta, and had formed colonies there, were not driven out; they were allowed to remain in the country on recognising the authority of the Egyptian king, and they were even permitted to furnish a special body of troops, who always formed part of the body guard of Pharaoh.

2. A short time after this invasion of the Lybians and Pelasgians we must place the Exodus of the Israelites. This again was a disastrous event for Egypt, depriving the country of three million souls, of a hard-working and useful people, besides the injury caused by the plagues brought down on the land by the obstinacy of Pharaoh in resisting the Divine orders communicated by Moses, and by the destruction of the flower of his army in the Red Sea. We shall not here repeat the story, as it has been given in the Second Book of this Manual. The official monuments are silent on this subject, as they are on all disasters that were not retrieved by subsequent successes. But the Bible narrative bears unmistakable marks of absolute historical truth, and agrees perfectly with the state of things in Egypt at this period. Thus the continual coming and going of Moses and Aaron to the presence of Pharaoh from the land of Goshen, necessarily supposes the residence of the king at Memphis. Now Merenphtah is precisely the only king of the nineteenth dynasty who made this second capital of Egypt his constant residence. We have already remarked that the Bible does not in any way say or imply, as has often been supposed, that Pharaoh perished with his army in the Red Sea. We have shown that the reverse clearly follows from its language, and, in fact, Merenphtah long survived the calamities of the Exodus. He reigned thirty years, and his tomb is to be seen among the royal sepulchres at Thebes.

3. Towards the end of the reign of Merenphtah, another event, very

unfortunate for Egypt, occurred—a new foreign invasion. We know of it only from Manetho. The narrative has been preserved by Josephus*; but, unfortunately, the Jewish historian, with the bad faith so common with controversialists, has evidently made considerable alterations, in order to bring in the name of Moses, and to transform this into a story of the Exodus of the Israelites, with which the event has no real connection. Nevertheless, in spite of the interpolations of Josephus, we may distinguish the original features of the story. The king, Amenophthis (Merenphtah), having brought together into one part of Egypt all the lepers and unclean persons, to employ them in forced labour at the quarries, they, to the number of 80,000, revolted, under the conduct of a priest of Heliopolis, named Osarsiph. Searching everywhere for allies, they called to their aid the descendants of the Shepherds who had retired to Asia, that is, evidently the Khitas, possessors of a "holy city," made by Josephus, as well as the Cadytis of Herodotus, to stand for Jerusalem, whilst in reality it ought, as well as the latter, to be the Kadesh (the holy) of the hieroglyphic inscriptions, the famous fortress on the banks of the Orontes. The descendants of the Shepherds answered their call with alacrity. To the number of 200,000 they came to the help of the unclean who had revolted, and threw themselves into the valley of the Nile. "They practised towards the inhabitants of Egypt the most cruel and sacrilegious tyranny. Not only did they burn towns and villages, pillage temples and carry oft the statues of the gods, but they even used the sacred animals for food, compelling their priests and prophets to kill them themselves, and then, after having stripped them, drove away the priests." The king did not consider it possible to resist this invasion, and resolved to allow the torrent to pass without opposition. He therefore retired into Upper Egypt with his army of 300,000 men, having sent his son and heir Sethos (Seti), five years old, into Ethiopia, where he found a safe asylum. Amenophthis (Merenphtah) died soon after, while the invaders were still in the country.

4. If the Egyptian monuments remaining to us do not mention this invasion, they bear numerous traces of the troubles it caused. Merenphtah having died, leaving the country full of foreigners, and his legitimate successor hidden in the provinces of the Upper Nile, a prince of the royal family, named Amenmeses, whose exact place in the royal genealogy is not known, assumed the crown in the city of Chev, the Aphroditopolis of the Greeks, near the Fayum. He seems to have succeeded at the end of a few years in recovering the greater part of Egypt. His son, proclaimed after his death in the city of Chev, as Merenphtah II. (Siphtah), succeeded him. To render his occupation

* JOSEPHUS, *Cont. Ap.*, i. 28.

of the throne legitimate, he married a daughter of Merenphtah I., the princess Tauser, whose rights the great chancellor Bai caused to be recognised by the whole country, though they were at first contested by a large party. On all monuments the king gives precedence to his wife, as if recognising the fact that she had more right than himself to the throne.

Prince Seti, the legitimate heir of Merenphtah, still in Ethiopia, recognised the royalty of Merenphtah Siphtah, and received from him the title of Viceroy of the Southern Provinces. But after some time, thirteen years according to Manetho, he altered his resolution, and insisted on his rights to the crown. Having assembled an army, he descended the Nile, entered Thebes and Memphis in triumph, and possessed himself of the throne. The two kings, who had been successively proclaimed at Chev, were then treated as usurpers, and their names erased from the monuments. But, on the other hand, Amenmeses and Tauser stand in the lists of Manetho as legitimate sovereigns, the final judgment of posterity having thus evidently recognised them as such. The reign of Seti II. must have been long, but we know no particulars of it, and possess hardly any monuments. This king died without children, and with him ended the nineteenth dynasty, which had lasted 174 years.

5. The entry of the Hebrews into Palestine and the conquest of the Promised Land by Joshua were events contemporary with the reign of Seti II. The Egyptians opposed no obstacle, and do not seem to have been at all disquieted. They considered themselves, nevertheless, as sovereigns of the land of Canaan; and the more distant provinces of Syria and Mesopotamia continued to pay them tribute. But we have already noticed the system of the Egyptian kings with regard to the government of their Asiatic provinces. They allowed the native princes to govern their own states under the inspection of an Egyptian resident. Like the Assyrians and Persians in later times, and the Turkish government in our own day, so long as the suzerainty of Pharaoh was recognised, the tribute punctually paid, and the required military contingents furnished, they gave themselves no trouble about the internal wars of the different tribes; and rather encouraged, as a guarantee for the maintenance of their own supremacy, the disputes of petty local chiefs and the wars that employed their forces.

The Israelites in establishing themselves in the Promised Land must have accepted the conditions of Egyptian suzerainty. The Book of Joshua certainly does not say so, but it contains nothing expressly to the contrary. The king of Egypt asked nothing more. Occupied with his own troubles, it would have been difficult and highly imprudent to attempt to oppose the Israelitish force, excited and rendered almost irresistible by religious enthusiasm. Moreover, on the eve of a new invasion of Canaanitish Khitas, the Egyptian king would with pleasure see the nations of Canaan (who from community of race were always disposed to take part with his enemies) cut to pieces. One thing alone would have, doubtless, brought about a direct intervention of the Egyptians in the affairs of the land of Canaan, and led them to oppose the Israelites, namely, any interference with the military road along the shore of the Mediterranean, the route between Egypt and the Syrian and Mesopotamian provinces. There the Egyptians exercised a more direct authority; there they had fortresses and garrisons; there they could not tolerate any conflicts. But Joshua did not feel sufficiently strong to attack the coast cities, and they therefore remained in their previous condition. And as their military road was untouched, unthreatened, the Egyptians remained quiet spectators of the conflicts between Israel and the Canaanites.

SECTION VII.—COMMENCEMENT OF THE TWENTIETH DYNASTY—RAMSES III.

(*Close of the Fourteenth Century B.C.*)

1. SETI II. having died without heirs, a new dynasty, designated by Manetho as Theban, mounted the throne. We do not know what was its relationship to the preceding dynasty, or by what title it succeeded to power. Its founder was called Nekht-Set, and had only a short reign, undistinguished by any important event.

2. But this insignificant reign was followed by that of a glorious king, who shed a last radiance on the arms of Egypt on the eve of its entire decline. Ramses III., son of Nekht-Set, seems, from one of the titles in his royal ring, to have exercised during the lifetime of his father a sort of vice-royalty over Lower Egypt, with Heliopolis as his capital. He was very young when he mounted the throne, and had before him a very difficult task. The troubles and reverses of the preceding epoch had seriously compromised the preponderance of Egypt in Asia, the frontiers of the empire were attacked, and it was necessary to fight again for a great part of the conquests of former dynasties. Ramses III. was an able and valiant warrior, but his campaigns were entirely defensive. Like Trajan, Marcus Aurelius, and Septimus Severus, his efforts were confined to making head against the constantly increasing stream of barbarians, who from all quarters rushed on the frontiers of the empire, and foreshadowed its approaching ruin. His struggles, however, were successful, and he succeeded in preserving entire the great empire constructed by Thothmes III. and Seti. The palace at Medinet Abu at Thebes is the Pantheon erected to the glory of this great Pharaoh. Every pylon, every gate, every chamber, gives us an account

of his exploits, and great sculptured compositions illustrate his principal battles.

3. The first war took place in the fifth year of the reign of Ramses III. The Lybians of the white race joined with the Takkaro, a people from the islands or northern shores of the Mediterranean, whose country is not yet ascertained (possibly Thracians), and who, like the Tyrrhenians, had a considerable fleet, attacked by land the western frontier of Egypt. They were repulsed with loss. Unfortunately, the details of the struggle are unknown. Three of the immense bas-reliefs at Medinet Abu give us the chief features, but the inscription accompanying them is so short that it tells us little or nothing.

4. A very long inscription, however, has been preserved, and, in spite of deplorable mutilations, contains all the essential points of a narrative of another war, the most important of the reign of Ramses, which took place in his ninth year, in Asia. In spite of the successive defeats they had sustained, the Pelasgic nations of the Mediterranean had not given up the project of making a settlement in some of the fertile countries belonging to Egypt. But two disasters, one after the other, had taught them that there was little hope of success if they disembarked in Lybia and attacked the western part of the Delta. They resolved therefore to try a new road, and throw themselves into Syria, where they might find some support among the determined enemies of Egypt in that country. An alliance was made between the Khitas on one side, the Pelasgians and the Lybians, their allies, on the other. It was agreed that the Khitas should attack the Aramæan provinces, and attempt to get possession of them, whilst the people from the Mediterranean, arriving by sea, would land on the coast. Among these last, the Philistines, then settled in Crete, and the Takkaro seem to have taken the initiative in the projected expedition, as the Tyrrhenians had done in the time of Merenphtah; for they furnished the great body of invaders, coming with their wives and children as though in search of new homes; the other nations furnished only auxiliary detachments.

Ramses, warned of the attack of the Khitas, and of the disembarkation of the first detachment of the invaders from the sea, saw clearly that his only safety was in rapidity of movement, and that he had no chance of success but in fighting the enemy successively, in detail, before they could unite their forces. He made the utmost possible haste. One of the great bas-reliefs of Medinet Abu represents his departure from Thebes. "The king," says the inscription, "is leaving for Cœle Syria, like the image of the god Month, to trample under foot the people who have violated the frontier. His soldiers are like hawks in the midst of little birds." A second tablet shows us the king marching with his army against the enemy across a mountainous country wooded and haunted by lions, no doubt one of the spurs of the Lebanon. He arrived thus in Cœle Syria, the land of Tsahi, where the Khita army had penetrated. These Hittites had for allies the people of Aradus, of Carchemish, and the Katti: the nations of Asia Minor took no part in this struggle, as under Ramses II.; and it does not appear that there was any insurrection in Mesopotamia, for its people are not mentioned among those then combined against Egypt. The battle with the Khitas and their confederates is represented on a bas-relief. It took place in the country of the Amorites in the valley of the Orontes, probably before Kadesh. Victory declared for the Egyptians. Ramses haughtily says in the long inscription containing the story of the whole campaign, "I have made these people and their country, as though they had never existed at all."

The Khitas beaten and driven back into their own country, Ramses hastened towards the coast, where the first detachment of the northern nations had disembarked some time before, and was slowly journeying southward. It was chiefly composed of Philistines, accompanied and supported by the Mashuash or Maxyans of Africa in great numbers. The sculptures of Medinet Abu relative to this part of the war show us that the Philistines were accompanied by their wives and children riding in rough cars drawn by oxen. It is thus that the Latin writers describe the march of the Cimbri and Teutones. Attacked by the disciplined and practised troops of Egypt, this disorganised mass was easily routed; 12,500 men were killed, the camp was surrounded and carried by assault, and the whole mass of Philistine invaders had no alternative but to surrender at discretion.

On the site of this victory, which was the place where the second detachment of northern invaders were to land, Ramses hastened to build a fortress, called "The Tower of Ramses." His fleet joined him at that place. It was numerous, and the inscription says that it "looked like a strong wall on the waters." Everything was ready to receive the ships bringing the new army of invaders. These soon arrived with the Takkaro, who formed the bulk of the second army of invaders, but with them were a greater number of Sardinians, Lybians, Sicilians, Tyrrhenians, and people from the Peloponnesus, whom the inscriptions at Medinet Abu no longer call Achæans, but Dardanians, the dynasty of Danaus having supplanted the Achæan dynasty of Inachus on the throne of Argos, in the interval between the reign of Merenphtah and of Ramses III. A gigantic bas-relief shows us the naval battle before the Tower of Ramses, and the defeat of the allied fleet. The Egyptian ships manœuvre both with sail and oar, and the prow of each ship is decorated with a lion's head. One Takkaro ship is already sunk, and their fleet is driven between the Egyptian ships and the shore, whence king Ramses and his infantry shoot a cloud of darts against the enemy's vessels.

The recital of the great inscription exactly agrees with this picture, unique among Egyptian monuments. "The vessels were manned from stem to stern with brave and well-armed warriors. On the shore, the infantry, the chosen men of the Egyptian army, stood like young lions roaring on the mountains. The horsemen eagerly ranged themselves by the side of their brave captains. The very horses seemed to collect all their strength to trample down the barbarians. 'As for me,' says the king, in whose mouth the narrative is placed, 'I was as brave as the god Month; I remained at their head, and they saw the exploits of my arm. I, king Ramses, bore myself like a hero conscious of his strength, who stretches out his arm to defend men in the day of slaughter. Those who approached my frontiers will reap no more in this world, the time of their souls is reckoned in eternity.'"

In consequence, however, of this victory over the Philistines, Ramses found an entire nation prisoners in his hands. This was a serious embarrassment; he could not kill them, old and young together, and was compelled to assign them lands in his dominions, thus realising the object of their emigration. Ramses settled the Philistines in the land of Canaan, near the cities of Gaza, Ashdod, and Ascalon, where he thought the Egyptian garrisons could keep them in order. There it was that, strengthened by new immigrations from Crete, they, in the decline of the Egyptian monarchy, founded a state so formidable for some time to the Israelites and Phœnicians.

5. Other bas-reliefs at Medinet Abu represent more battles of the Egyptians with the Asiatics, the assault of one of the Khita fortresses, and Ramses marching out to a new war with them. Several engagements in the eleventh and twelfth years of his reign are represented on the monuments as victories gained over both Asiatics and Lybians. One inscription states that the southern chiefs carried their tribute into Egypt. "I grant," says the god Harmachu to the king, in this text, "that people who know not Egypt shall come to thee laden with gold, silver, lapis lazuli, and every precious stone." In the east, Ramses III., having re-established his fleet on the Red Sea, sent it to the coasts of Yemen, or the land of Pun, and again subjected that country to tribute. Lastly, the revolts of the tribes of the Upper Nile, of Soudan and Abyssinia were vigorously repressed.

These military successes were, however, balanced by internal troubles. The Museum at Turin and the Imperial Library at Paris possess part of a judicial process relative to a serious conspiracy set on foot in the reign of Ramses III. The political aim of the plot is not clearly stated in the documents, but we see that the royal harem took a large part in it. A great number of the king's concubines, and the eunuchs who guarded them, were involved in this plot. Magical incantations, "an abomination to all the gods and all the goddesses," held a prominent place in the charges against the conspirators. They were judged by a special commission and treated in the most severe manner. Ramses, finding the sentence pronounced by the first judges too lenient, altered it by his supreme authority to death, and ordered the judges themselves to be decapitated, as an example how magistrates should perform their duty. We owe the translation of these valuable documents to M. T. Deveria.

The fact of a violent opposition breaking out in political plots in the reign of Ramses III., no doubt explains a curious papyrus in the British Museum. This is an album of caricatures in which the principal bas reliefs on the walls of the palace of Medinet Abu are parodied by figures of animals. The war pictures become fights between cats and rats.* Scenes in the harem are represented by a lion and gazelles. These pictures are licentious in the extreme.

We at present know of no monument of Ramses III. dated later than his twelfth year. His tomb, a vast excavation, made after the custom of the kings of Egypt, in his lifetime, is one of the most splendid in the valley of Biban-el-Moluk, at Thebes.

6. From the date of the reign of Ramses III., Egyptian chronology for the first time finds a sure and fixed starting point, the result of an astronomical date furnished by the monuments of Medinet Abu. On the walls of that palace Ramses caused to be engraved a great calendar of religious festivals. Now the day on which the feast of the Heliacal rising of the star Sothis† is marked indicates that it was engraven in

---

* The Egyptians are the rats and the Asiatics the cats.

† The whole chronology of Egypt was regulated by the "Sothic Cycle," or the periods when the star Sothis, or Sirius—the Dog-star—rose with the sun. Herodotus says (ii. 4), "The Egyptians were the first to discover the solar year, and to portion out its course into twelve parts. They obtained this knowledge from the stars. To my mind, they contrive their year much more cleverly than the Greeks, for these last intercalate a whole month every other year [διὰ τρίτου ἔτους, but compare HER. i. 32]; but the Egyptians, dividing the year into twelve months of thirty days each, add every year a space of five days, whereby the circuit of the seasons is made to return with uniformity."—RAWLINSON'S Translation.

It is evident that this year of 365 days would not in the lapse of time bring back the seasons with uniformity, as the year would be wrong by one day every four years, and the error would in time entirely reverse the seasons.

The Egyptians had found by experiment that the Heliacal rising of Sothis recurred at the end of 1461 years of 365 days, or "vague" years, and that these 1461 years were, in fact, equal to 1460 true, or Sothic years.

From this cycle the Sothic, or true year of 365¼ days, was obtained; and as the vague year is indicated in hieroglyphics by the symbol of the

commemoration of the twelfth year of Ramses III., being one of the years occurring only at intervals separated by long ages, and serving as the point of departure for the great astronomical period of the Egyptians; at these periods only their vague year of 365 days coincided with the solar year. The calculation's of the celebrated Biot have proved that this rare coincidence occurred in the year 1300 B.C. Consequently, we can with mathematical and absolute certainty fix the accession of Ramses in the year 1311 B.C.

CHAPTER IV.

DECLINE AND FALL OF THE EGYPTIAN EMPIRE.

SECTION I. — END OF TWENTIETH DYNASTY — TWENTY-FIRST ROYAL FAMILY.

(*From Thirteenth to the commencement of Tenth Century B.C.*)

1. AFTER the warlike king, to whom we owe the palace at Medinet Abu, fourteen, and possibly more, kings named Ramses continued the twentieth dynasty for more than a century and a half. But they did not all form a continuous series; the lists of Manetho only admit eight among the number of legitimate kings. In the midst of the obscurities surrounding this historical period, of which we have so few monumental records, we may discern troubles and competitions for the throne, and especially, on several occasions, amicable partitions of Egypt between several princes. This, for example, is what occurred among the younger sons of Ramses III. after the death of his first heir, Ramses IV., who appears to have governed the whole country, and to have died childless.

---

palm branch and sun's disc, so this Sothic or square year (*annus quadratus*) is marked by the palm branch and a square.

The Egyptians also used a lunar year, which agreed with the civil solar year at each "Apis period" of twenty-five years. They had also calculated a great Siderial year of 36,525 solar years, or the number of days in 100 Sothic years.

Herodotus says above, that the Egyptian month consisted of thirty days; but from the fact that the month is represented in hieroglyphics by the symbol of the moon, we may infer that in early times they used a lunar month.

It is remarkable that Moses, in his account of the Deluge, uses this Egyptian month of thirty days, as he makes five months to equal 150 days (Gen. vii. 11, 24; viii. 3, 4), although the Jews used the lunar month.—TR.

None of these numerous kings added any lustre to the name of Ramses. The timid successors of the hero of Medinet Abu knew not how to preserve entire the glorious heritage of his traditions. It was in vain that Ramses III. had by his victories arrested for a moment the decline of Egypt, for now the full time had come.

Although the monarchy of the Pharaohs still governed Syria, the subordination of that country became more and more merely nominal. From its prolonged contact with Asiatics, Egypt had, moreover, lost that unity essential to its power. Semitic words had been admitted into the language; foreign gods had invaded the sanctuaries previously inaccessible. During this period of general decline another cause of weakness appeared. The high priests of Amen at Thebes, with whom that dignity was hereditary, attempted to play the part taken in later times by the mayors of the palace under the Merovingian kings of France; they possessed themselves successively of all the supreme functions, civil and military, gradually undermined the royal authority, and aspired to dethrone the legitimate king. Egypt thus paid the penalty of the ambition of the conquerors of the eighteenth and nineteenth dynasties.

Depressed now in direct proportion to her former exaltation, she was to see her territory again trodden down by foreigners; and after having ruled over the Cushites, Lybians, and Asiatics, to be compelled to serve the kings of those nations. As M. Mariette so well says, "It was because she would not remain on the territory really her own, the Nile valley, as far south as it extends—it was because she endeavoured to impose her authority (in Asia) where a thousand questions of race and climate tended to compromise it, that her too vast empire was dismembered." Here ends the most brilliant period of the history of Egypt. Powerless to face so many dangers, the empire of Menes after Ramses III., entered on the miserable road to ruin. In the north as in the south, her conquests were one by one torn from her; and at the time when, under the last king of the twentieth dynasty, the high priests assumed the crown of the Pharaohs, we see Egypt reduced to the smallest possible frontier, and surrounded by enemies henceforth more powerful than herself.

2. The nominal submission of Western Asia and the payment of tribute by Mesopotamia were continued, however, till late in the time of the twentieth dynasty. Not only under Ramses IV. do we find the Assyrians paying homage to Pharaoh, but nearly a century and a half later, under Ramses XII., about 1150 B.C., we know positively that Mesopotamia still recognised the suzerainty of Egypt, and paid tribute. This is proved by a stele discovered at Thebes, and preserved in the Imperial Library at Paris; its long inscription has been studied both by Dr. Birch and M. de Rougé. The subject matter of the inscription is

so curious that it deserves mention. Ramses XII. had gone to make the tour of Mesopotamia, and receive tribute, when he met with the daughter of one of the chiefs, and married her. Some years later, when Ramses was at Thebes, he was informed that a messenger had come from his father-in-law, requesting the king to send a skilful physician to the queen's sister, who was sick of an unknown malady. An Egyptian physician was accordingly sent back with the messenger. The young princess was suffering from a nervous attack, and according to the usual belief of the period, it was supposed that she was possessed by an evil spirit. In vain the physician employed all the resources of his art; the spirit refused to obey, and the physician was obliged to return to Thebes without curing the queen's sister. This occurred in the fifteenth year of Ramses. Eleven years later, in the twenty-sixth year, another ambassador presented himself. This time it was not a physician that the queen's father required; in his opinion it was the direct intervention of one of the gods of Thebes that alone could cure the princess. As on the first occasion, Ramses consented to the request, and the sacred ark of one of the gods of Thebes, named Chons, was sent to perform the miracle requested. The journey was long; it lasted a year and six months. At last the Theban god arrived in Mesopotamia, the evil spirit was conquered, and compelled to leave the body of the young princess, who immediately recovered her health.

But the story engraven on the stele does not end with this cure. A god whose mere presence brought such miraculous cures was inexpressibly valuable; and at the risk of a rupture with his powerful ally, the father of the young princess resolved to keep the ark in his palace. For three years and nine months the ark of Chons was kept in Mesopotamia. But at the end of that time this treacherous chief had a dream. He seemed to see the captive deity fly away towards Egypt under the form of a golden sparrowhawk, and at the same time he was suddenly taken ill. The father-in-law of Ramses accepted this dream as a warning from heaven. He immediately gave orders for sending back the ark of the god, who in the thirty-third year of the reign of Ramses returned to his temple at Thebes.

What adds much to the interest of this curious story, related by a contemporary monument, is, that the event took place but a few years at most after the adventures of the Ark of the Covenant among the Philistines, recounted in the Book of Samuel (1 Sam. iv., v., vi.). The two narratives have striking points of contact that can hardly escape the reader. Ramses XII., as we see by the commencement of this stele, in the Imperial Library, still in the twelfth century B.C., considered himself as the legitimate master of Mesopotamia, performed acts of suzerainty there, and received tribute. But beyond this mark of vassalage, the authority of the kings of Egypt over the Asiatic provinces was from that time merely nominal.

Beyond the Euphrates, they were unable to prevent the formation of the empire of the Assyrians, whose power, commencing in the beginning of the fourteenth century, gradually progressed and increased. Even nearer to their frontier they had allowed the Philistines to possess themselves of Gaza, Ashdod, Ascalon, Gath, and Ekron, and thus render themselves masters of the military road, hitherto so carefully guarded, by which Egypt communicated with Syria and Mesopotamia. They had not intervened in the quarrels of the Philistines with the Israelites and Phœnicians, even when the former took and destroyed Sidon; nor had they interfered when a king of Aramæan Mesopotamia, Cushan-Rishathaim conquered, for the time, Northern Syria and all Palestine. A short time only after Ramses XII., the high priest of Amen, Her-Hor exercised the supreme power; and during that period we find the last trace of the power of the Pharaohs in Asia.

3. About the same time (in the second half of the twelfth century B.C.) the power of the Assyrian empire suddenly increased; the kings of Nineveh began their career as great conquerors, and before long no authority but theirs was recognised between the Tigris and the Euphrates. In the interior of Egypt Her-Hor (Horus, the supreme), having united to his sacerdotal titles those of superintendent of public works and of generalissimo of the troops, ended by usurping on the monuments the title and marks of royalty, all the while retaining the high priesthood. He was the first who renounced all pretension to the sovereignty of Asia, and abandoned the traditional policy of every Pharaoh since Thothmes I. Adopting an entirely different course, he allied himself closely with the kings of Nineveh, hoping thereby to obtain support in his usurpation. This intimate alliance is marked by the Assyrian names he gave to most of his children. After the death of Her-Hor, the line of the legitimate descendants of Ramses III., who were still in existence, seems for a short time to have regained the ascendancy, as the title of high priest only is given to the son of that personage, named Piankh. But soon after, with Pinetsem I., the royal titles reappear in that family, to continue for many generations. The race of Ramses is finally dethroned; and in order to legitimatise themselves, the usurping priestly family allied themselves by marriage with a descendant of one of the competitors of Seti II., the princess Isi-em-Chev. This family preserved, moreover, the politic alliance with the Asiatics, inaugurated by its founder. A cuneiform inscription in the British Museum tells us of an ambassador whom Pinetsem, or one of his successors, sent to Tiglath Pileser I., king of Assyria, who had become master of the Phœnician cities. Amongst the presents borne by this ambassador is mentioned a crocodile, an animal probably new to the inhabitants of the banks of the Euphrates or Tigris.

4. In the meanwhile a rival dynasty arose in Lower Egypt, at Tanis,

according to the lists of Manetho, where also are found the few monuments it has left. It seems now proved that it assumed the crown in that city whilst the last of the Ramses reigned nominally, and the High Priests of Amen in reality, at Thebes. It was during competitions between this dynasty and the family of the priest, Her-Hor, that David reigned over Israel, and succeeded in creating for a time a great territorial power, then rendered possible by the weakening of Egypt, and by the fact that the Assyrian empire, still but imperfectly developed, was not at that time strong enough to cross the Euphrates with its armies.

The Tanite kings succeeded, after a prolonged struggle, in triumphing over their adversaries and in establishing their dominion over all Egypt. It was these whom later historians, such as Manetho, considered as continuing the series of legitimate kings. One of them, Psiu-en-san, a contemporary of Solomon, gave him his daughter in marriage—an evident proof that this dynasty had renounced all hope of re-asserting its ancient power in Asia. It did not reign, however, much more than a century, and was succeeded by another family, also of Lower Egypt, from Bubastis.

When the Tanite dynasty finally triumphed in Egypt, the descendants of Her-Hor, who continued to unite the titles of the high priesthood with those of royalty, retired to Ethiopia, where they formed and carefully fortified an independent and rival state to Egypt, though with the same language and civilisation. The town of Napata (now Djebel Barkal) was chosen for their capital, and there they founded a sanctuary of Amen, with an oracle in rivalry with that of Thebes, and pretended to have transferred there the rights of the legitimate priesthood.

SECTION II.—TWENTY-SECOND, TWENTY-THIRD, AND TWENTY-FOURTH DYNASTIES.

(*Tenth, Ninth, and Eighth Centuries B.C.*)

1. A MOST important fact to be remarked with regard to the twenty-second dynasty, called by Manetho Bubastic, is, that in the series of its kings and in the paternal ancestors of its founder, who are known from some monuments, nearly all the names are incontestably Asiatic in form, and especially Assyrian—Nimrod, Tiglath, Uaserken, Nabonasi, Shapheth—and therefore a decisive indication of its origin. Moreover, from the time of the defeat of the priestly sovereigns of the family of Her-Hor, the preponderance of Thebes finally ceased. All subsequent dynasties sprang from Lower Egypt and resided there. Henceforth the kings are real Mamelukes, such as those who governed Moslem Egypt in the Middle Ages; all sprang from bodies of foreign soldiers, whom we

find from this time exclusively employed as body-guards to the sovereigns who reigned on the banks of the Nile.

The manner in which the foreign family of the twenty-second dynasty succeeded to the throne, we know from the monuments. A certain Uaserken, of Semitic origin, a superior officer in the army, whose family had previously been connected by marriage with the Theban usurpers descended from Her-Hor, married the daughter of a king who seems to have been the last of the Tanitic dynasty. The child born from this union, Sheshonk, adopted by his maternal grandfather, first governed as regent of the empire, and finally as king. He was the head of the new dynasty.

2. Sheshonk, called in the Bible Shishak, gave an asylum at his court to the fugitive Jeroboam towards the end of the reign of Solomon; and afterwards, when that personage had put himself at the head of the ten tribes, Sheshonk, following the same policy and in alliance with him, invaded the kingdom of Judah. Thus, as we have already seen, in the fifth year of Rehoboam (973) he entered the land of Judah with 1,200 chariots, 60,000 horsemen, and an immense body of infantry, Egyptians, Lybians, Ethiopians, and Troglodytes; he penetrated to Jerusalem and carried off the treasures of the temple, as well as those of the king. These conquests are recorded on a great bas-relief at Karnak, dated in the reign of Sheshonk himself, on which are inscribed the names of 133 cities of the kingdom of Judah taken by the Egyptian army. The greater part of the names are mentioned in Scripture, amongst others Rabbith (Jos. xix. 20), Taanach (xii. 21, xvii. 11), Shunem (xix. 18), Rehob (xix. 28), Haphraim (xix. 19), Adoraim (2 Chron. xi. 9), Mahanaim (Jos. xxi. 38), Gibeon (ix. 3), Bethhoron (x. 10), Kedemoth (xiii. 18), Ajalon (x. 12), and Megiddo (xii. 21). The capital is not mentioned on the monument by its ordinary name Jerusalem, but is recognised under the title Jehudah Malek—"Royalty of Judah."

3. The exact duration of the reign of Sheshonk I. is not known with certainty, but we know at any rate that it lasted twenty-one years. The history of Uaserken I., or Osorchon, as the Greeks wrote the name, is still full of obscurity. We have only reason to think that it was in his reign, or in that of his successor, that Azerch-Amen, king of Ethiopia, starting from Napata, invaded Egypt and traversed its whole length to the mouth of the Nile, subjected it for the time to his sceptre, and penetrated into Palestine at the head of an army of Ethiopians and Lybians. We have already related [Book II.] how he was conquered on the territory of the kingdom of Judah by Asa, grandson of Rehoboam.

The defeat of the king of Ethiopia was so complete that he does not seem even to have attempted to maintain his position in Egypt, but to have retired at once to his own states. However, the road opened by his invasion was soon to be followed by other Ethiopian conquerors.

4. We shall not stop to enquire into the genealogy and chronology of the Bubastic dynasty, although completely cleared up by the discoveries of M. Mariette at the Serapeum of Memphis; for none of the Sheshonks, Uaserkens, or Tiglaths, who continued it, have made any mark in history by any notable deed. We shall merely state that the twenty-second dynasty lasted for more than a century after Uaserken I., and that the kings were generally so associated in the government, that their reigns occupied in reality a much less time than the addition of their several durations would amount to.

5. The twenty-third dynasty, Tanitic, like the twenty-second, consists of only four kings in Manetho's lists. The names of three are found on known monuments, one of whom, called Uaserken, like one of the preceding family, brings us down to the eighth century B.C.; and there is reason to think that the same system of associating the heir-apparent on the throne during the life of his father, prevailed during this as well as during the twenty-second dynasty. But the lists of Manetho give only a very incorrect idea of the history of Egypt at this epoch. At this period, as in all times of trouble, the Sebennyte priest has only registered the dynasty considered by him and the authorities he followed to be legitimate; he makes no mention and takes no account of its rivals and competitors. But in reality the age of the twenty-third dynasty was a time of contention and revolution; the land was divided between rival families, and full of civil discord. The monuments furnish a certain number of royal names, necessarily belonging to this epoch, and give us some information as to the kings proclaimed in various parts of Egypt in antagonism with the sovereigns of Tanis. The existence of several families who disputed the throne, each possessed of a portion of territory, is, moreover, clearly alluded to in a passage in the Book of the prophet Isaiah, who then lived and predicted that this anarchy would soon bring Egypt under a foreign rule. "And I will set the Egyptians against the Egyptians: and they shall fight every one against his brother, and every one against his neighbour: city against city, and kingdom against kingdom. . . . . And the Egyptians will I give over into the hand of a cruel lord; and a fierce king shall rule over them. . . . . The princes of Zoan [Tanis] are become fools, the princes of Noph [Memphis] are deceived; they have also seduced Egypt" (Isaiah xix. 2, 4, 13).

The state of complete disorder and anarchy in which Egypt, torn by conflicting factions, then was, may easily be proved from the long inscription on a stele, discovered by M. Mariette in the ruins of Napata, erected to commemorate the submission of the whole of Egypt to a king, named Piankhi, who made the Thebaid a simple province dependant on Ethiopia, and imposed a tribute on Lower Egypt. The inscription, translated by M. de Rougé, relates all the details of that event, the battles with the chiefs of the Delta, and the final assumption of the throne at Thebes by the Ethiopian king, who was favourably received there by the people. It seems that the family of the high priests of Amen, even after its retirement into Ethiopia, had retained many partisans in the priestly city, and during the whole period of Egyptian history we are now considering, Thebes showed itself better disposed towards the Ethiopian kings and their pretensions, than towards the princes who reigned in the Delta. The situation of Lower Egypt at the moment when Piankhi peaceably entered Thebes, and took Memphis by force, is known from the stele at Napata. The two contemporary dynasties alluded to by Isaiah, that of Tanis, registered by Manetho as legitimate, and that of Memphis, three kings of which have become known in consequence of the excavations at the Serapeum, were not the only ones who strove for power. Lower and Middle Egypt, and especially the Delta, were divided into thirteen petty rival states, with princes at their head who, for the most part, had come from the ranks of the Lybian Mashuash guard—Janissaries in fact—who by slow degrees had ascended the steps of the throne under the obscure and inglorious kings of the close of the twenty-second dynasty. Five only among them bore the title of king. The most powerful at the time of the invasion of Piankhi were Uaserken of the Tanitic line, considered legitimate by Manetho, Tafnekht of Sais, the Tnephactus of Diodorus Siculus, and Pefaabast, who reigned at Heracleopolis in Middle Egypt. Such a state of anarchy must naturally have made Egypt an easy prey to the attack of every foreign invader. Thus it was that Piankhi was enabled without serious obstacles to subject for the time the whole country, and to hold the southern part; and that the national existence was for some time interrupted by a new invader from the banks of the Upper Nile.

6. The twenty-fourth Saite dynasty comprised but one king, Bokenranf, the Bocchoris of the Greeks, son of Tafnekht, contemporary with the invasion of Piankhi, who reigned only six years. Whether this king succeeded in expelling the Ethiopians from Upper Egypt, or whether he was only one of the petty kings of the north who united Lower Egypt under one sceptre, we cannot tell. We know as yet nothing positive about his reign—the monuments contain no record on this subject. A new Ethiopian invasion placed the crown of Egypt for a long time on the heads of the kings of Napata, and soon swept away the power of Bokenranf, together with the independence of Egypt.

SECTION III.—ETHIOPIAN DYNASTY (725 *to* 665 *B.C.*).

1. WE have now long passed the period of the great battles of the Osortasens and Thothmes, of those tributes imposed by the Pharaohs, conquerors of the "vile race of Cush," of those victories reducing the whole Nile valley as far as Abyssinia to the state of an Egyptian province. Cush now treats Egypt as a conquered country, and comes to reign in those palaces of Thebes, full of the glories of Thothmes, Amenhotep, and Ramses.

Bokenranf had occupied the throne but a few years when Shabaka, king of Ethiopia, the Sabacon of the Greeks, the So (Sua) of the Bible,* descended from the neighbourhood of the cataracts at the head of a formidable army of Ethiopians and negroes, and conquered all Egypt even to the shores of the Mediterranean. Having taken the unfortunate Bokenranf prisoner, he had him burned alive, in order probably, by this terrible example, to discourage all resistance. But even in this barbarous act the natives were not sufficiently terrified to prevent them from making efforts to disquiet the Ethiopian government. Then, as in the time of the Shepherds, a national royalty continued to exist and struggle against the conquest in some districts of the kingdom. The family who afterwards founded the twenty-sixth dynasty (called Saite), exercised authority, to all appearance, in the western part of the Delta, a district easily defended in a partisan war. Herodotus† here gives us a clue to the truth by telling us of a king who took refuge in the marshes during the Ethiopian government. We know also, not from Egyptian monuments, but from Assyrian inscriptions, that the petty local dynasties of the cities of the Delta recovered their authority towards the end of the Ethiopian dominion.

2. Nevertheless, this partial resistance did not prevent the Ethiopian dynasty from obtaining great consideration abroad. Shabaka was called on by Hoshea, king of Israel, for assistance against the Assyrians. The appeal was in vain as far as Hoshea was concerned, but it seems that Pharaoh made an expedition when it was too late to save Samaria, for an inscription at Karnak flatters him by naming Syria as a tributary. But soon after Sargon, king of Assyria, inflicted a crushing

---

* The syllable *ka*, terminating the names of all the kings of the Ethiopian dynasty, was the article in the Cushite language. It may therefore either be added or omitted. The Egyptian monuments and the lists of Manetho give, as the name of the conqueror and founder of the dynasty, Shabaka, or Sabacon, with the article; the Bible transliterates from Shaba, or Shava, without the article; in both cases the name is the same in its essential elements.

† HER. ii. 137.

defeat on him at Raphia. The third king of the dynasty, Tahraka, whilst yet only prince royal, but no doubt sent by his father, king Shabatoka (the Sabacon II. of some Greek writers, the Sethos of Herodotus),* marched against Sennacherib, when that king of Nineveh invaded the kingdom of Judah. We have related in the book on the history of the Hebrews, the miracle which then destroyed the army of Sennacherib, and delivered Egypt as well as Palestine from a formidable danger. The same Tahraka, when a little later he became king, during the twenty-six years that he occupied the throne, undertook considerable wars in Lybia. He is reported to have carried his arms even to the straits of Gibraltar, to the north-west extremity of the continent of Africa. A bas-relief at Medinet Ábu represents him holding a number of conquered chiefs together by the hair of their heads, whilst threatening them with his mace.

But the end of the reign of Tahraka, so fortunate in its commencement, was full of troubles and disasters. His own official inscriptions, as we might suppose, do not tell us so; we learn this from Nineveh. In 671 B.C., Esarhaddon, son of Sennacherib, adopting his father's policy, entered Egypt at the head of a numerous army, and in alliance with one of the petty kings of the Delta. He conquered before Memphis the troops of the king of Ethiopia, and possessed himself of all Egypt, as far as the first cataract.

Esarhaddon reorganised the country on the principle generally applied by Assyrian kings to conquered provinces. He divided it into twenty small kingdoms, tributary to the king of Nineveh; twelve were comprised in the Delta, among them we remark Tanis, Athribis, Heroopolis, Sebennytus, Mendes, and Busiris. Upper Egypt formed eight others, one of the names given in the Assyrian inscription has not as yet been identified; the seven others are Aphroditopolis, Heracleopolis, Hermopolis, Lycopolis, Chemmis, This and Thebes. The kings of the Delta were the vassal dynasties of Tahraka continued in power, those installed in Upper Egypt were in part natives, and in part Assyrians; the king of Thebes was called Month-Mei-Ankhi. Necho, prince of Sais, whose family had always energetically opposed the Ethiopians, and who had displayed great courage in his assertion of the national independence, was made superior to the others, and received possession of Memphis.

In conformity with the usual custom of the Ninevite kings in conquered lands, Esarhaddon gave Assyrian names to some of the chief cities of Egypt. Sais was named Dur-Bilmati (the Fortress of the Lord of the Land), Athribis, Limur-patis-Asshur (Dwelling of the Vicegerent

* Herodotus has followed the form Shabato or Shavato without the article, the final *ka*.

of Asshur), Memphis, Dur-Asshurakhiddin (Fortress of Esarhaddon), and Tanis, Dur-Banit. He then returned to Nineveh, and on his way caused to be engraved on the rocks at Nahr el Kelb near Beyrut, a stele, still remaining there to commemorate his conquest of Egypt.

3. The country remained two years in the hands of the Assyrians, and Esarhaddon entitled himself in official documents, "king of Egypt and Ethiopia." But in 669 B.C., when he was attacked by the illness that proved fatal to him, Tahraka profited by the circumstance to reconquer the whole Nile valley. Thebes welcomed him with enthusiasm as the defender of the cause of Amen, and the priests, very hostile to the Assyrians, opened to him the gates of Memphis. Pursuing his course of success, he attacked the kings of the Delta, beat them in several encounters, drove most of them from their cities, and compelled them with their partisans to take refuge in the country near Sais, intersected with canals, where they with difficulty maintained their position.

In the meantime, Asshur-bani-pal succeeded his father on the throne of Nineveh. He assembled a numerous army, and marched to Egypt to restore the position of affairs. The Assyrians took possession of the city of Tanis, or Dur-Banit, without striking a blow. Tahraka was then at Memphis; he dispatched his army northward, and a great battle was fought before Tanis. The Ethiopians were defeated with enormous loss. When Tahraka received intelligence of the defeat of his troops, he gave up all idea of holding Memphis, and fled in haste to Thebes, where he hoped to find a firmer support in the attachment of the people.

The kings who had retired towards Sais, came to meet Asshur-bani-pal, and pay their homage. He made with them a triumphal entry into Memphis, and then marched without loss of time into Upper Egypt. In forty days he arrived at Thebes, where, however, Tahraka did not venture to await him. The Ethiopian king retreated beyond the cataracts, and all Egypt was again in the possession of the Assyrians. Asshur-bani-pal, having re-established the organisation created by Esarhaddon, and left fresh garrisons in the fortresses, returned to Assyria.

But he had hardly left the country, when the princes of the Delta, who had not found any real advantage in exchanging an Ethiopian for an Assyrian sovereign, conspired to recall Tahraka under the condition that he should continue them in power. The chiefs were Necho, prince of Sais and Memphis, Saretikdairi, prince of Tanis, and Pakrur, prince of the Arabian nome. The plot was discovered, and they were arrested, loaded with chains, and conveyed to Nineveh. There they protested their repentance, and Asshur-bani-pal, no doubt from policy, forgave them.

During this time a great insurrection had broken out in the Delta. The Assyrian generals succeeded in quelling it, but only after having taken by assault Sais, Mendes, Tanis, and Heroopolis. Tahraka had re-entered Egypt, having again subdued all the upper region, and fixed his capital at Thebes. Marching towards Lower Egypt, he had blockaded Memphis, and pushed his troops into the Delta, the greater part of which they occupied, and the Assyrians were almost driven out of the country.

Asshur-bani-pal now sent Necho into Egypt with an Assyrian army. The Saite prince recovered the Delta from the Ethiopians, and installed as local king in Athribis, his son Psammetik, who had then adopted the Assyrian name Nabo-sezib-anni. Memphis was then relieved, and Tahraka reduced to the possession of Upper Egypt, where he soon after died.

4. Rot-Amen, son-in-law of Tahraka, succeeded him on the thrones of Thebes and Napata. With all the ardour of youth, he undertook the expulsion of the Assyrians. He succeeded at first in winning a great battle, in taking Memphis, making the Assyrian garrison prisoners, and even in rendering himself master of the Delta. Necho, taken prisoner in Memphis, was put to death by Rot-Amen.

But Asshur-bani-pal, having been informed of the misfortunes of his army in Egypt, undertook a new expedition to that country, as the Assyrians attached the highest value to its possession, for it appeared to them the only guarantee for their supremacy in Syria. The king of the Arabs, as vassal, furnished the Assyrian army with camels to carry a supply of water across the desert. The troops of Rot-Amen were beaten near Pelusium, and the Ethiopian prince then abandoned Memphis, and Asshur-bani-pal entered that city without striking a blow. The petty kings of the Delta hastened to make their submission to him.

Asshur-bani-pal then marched on Thebes, and Rot-Amen abandoned it, although he had hastily erected fortifications for its protection. The city of Amen was given up to be pillaged by the Assyrians, and the devastation was so great that it never recovered the blow. Asshur-bani-pal carried off as trophies, and sent to Nineveh, the two obelisks erected before one of the principal temples. But this success did not lead to any lasting result, for he was soon compelled to see the impossibility of maintaining himself in Egypt, and decided on evacuating the country.*

---

* On the subject of these events, see Mr. George Smith, in the *Journal d'Archéologie Egyptienne de Berlin*, September and October, 1868.

5. The records of this epoch, however, do not all relate exclusively to wars. Herodotus attributes to Sabacon the abolition of the punishment of death, and the substitution of hard labour. Diodorus Siculus speaks of the numerous canals, and Herodotus* of the embankments intended to raise the mounds on which towns were built to keep them above the level of the inundation, works all due to the Ethiopian dynasty. It has been objected that this legislation and these works do not correspond with the violent and fierce character of the murderer of Bokenranf, and that they must be assigned to one of his successors; but, leaving out the question whether Bokenranf had not drawn on himself this terrible punishment, possibly by ordering some cruelties to be inflicted on Ethiopian prisoners, or whether he was treated by Shabaka as a rebel vassal, it must be remarked that the works connected with the inundation of the Nile were works of necessity, and requiring prompt execution in order to remedy the damage consequent on the conquest. We see, at Luxor, Shabaka making offerings to the gods of Thebes, in the same way as a native sovereign, and he and his successors adopted Egyptian prenomens.

The Greek historians relate† that in the twenty-sixth year of his reign Tahraka suddenly evacuated Egypt and retired to Ethiopia. This voluntary retreat of the Ethiopians seems to be a fact, but not as relating to Tahraka, who died king of Upper Egypt. It must be ascribed to his son-in-law, Rot-Amen. Herodotus asserts that it was in consequence of a dream. No doubt some superstitious motive contributed to this unexpected resolution, but it is probable that the special reason was a powerful insurrection in Lower Egypt.

SECTION IV.—THE DODECARCHY—THE SAITE KINGS—(665—527 B.C).

1. AFTER having related the end of the Ethiopian dynasty, Diodorus Siculus says, "There was then in Egypt an anarchy lasting two years, during which the people gave themselves up to disorder and intestine wars. At last twelve of the principal chiefs laid a plot. They met at Memphis, and, having entered into reciprocal treaties, proclaimed themselves kings. But at the end of fifteen years the whole power fell into the hands of one of them."

The chief event of the two years of complete anarchy following on the retreat of the Ethiopians is related by an inscription on a stele, discovered by M. Mariette at Napata. The son-in-law of Tahraka having

---

* HER. ii. 137. † HER. ii. 139.

died without direct heirs after a a very short reign, a personage named Amen-meri-Nut, who must have been more or less distantly related to him, caused himself to be proclaimed in his place. A prophetic dream had announced this elevation to him, and also that he should re-unite the crown of Egypt to that of Ethiopia. Consequently, profiting by the fact that Egypt had no supreme king, he entered the country at the head of a numerous army in order to claim the sovereignty. Thebes received him joyfully; but at Memphis matters assumed a different aspect. The chiefs of the Delta, composing their differences, formed a coalition against the Ethiopian invader, disputed his entry into the sacred city of Ptah, and it required a bloody battle to open its gates to him. After having remained there some time, Amen-meri-Nut pursued his enemies as far as the marshes of the Delta; but he could not take their cities, and the inundation soon forced him to retire to Memphis. Whilst he was preparing a new expedition, the chiefs, who had successfully resisted him, hoping that he would retire when his avarice was satiated, sent him a considerable tribute. Contented with this result the Ethiopian king, who seems only to have wished in reality to make into Egypt one of those great razzias of which war in the east so often consists, took the road for his own states, leaving the greater part of the country, that is, the Delta and Lower Egypt, to itself.

2. The invasion of Amen-meri-Nut, by showing the danger of anarchy, had been one of the chief means of bringing about a state of comparative order, as well as the regular establishment of the Dodecarchy. The twelve chiefs or kings who then amicably divided Lower Egypt, and who were for the most part identical with those of the time of Tahraka, belonged probably to the Mashuash soldiery, Lybian by origin, who had been established in the Delta since the reign of Merenphtah (nineteenth dynasty), and had become the chief military strength of the country. The fact appears the more certain in the case of Psammetik, the one of the chiefs who ended by reigning alone; his name is not at all Egyptian, and its form is, on the contrary, entirely Lybian. But though of foreign origin, his family had identified itself with the interests and patriotic passions of the people. His father and grandfather, in the country of Sais, had continued to resist during the greater part of the Ethiopian invasion. His father, too, Necho, as we have seen, fell a victim to the national cause. As for himself, he had, under an Assyrian name, been made king of the city of Athribis, by Asshur-bani-pal.

Whilst the Dodecarchy thus governed Lower Egypt, the Thebaid continued to belong to the Ethiopian kings. It was in the hands of Piankhi II., successor of Amen-meri-Nut, who seems to have occupied the throne but for a very short time. This king, whom everything proves to have been merely a parvenu, shared the power with his wife,

Amen-iritis, sister of Shabaka, whom he had married to legitimate his pretensions in the absence of direct heirs of Tahraka. Amen-iritis, moreover, was a woman of rare intelligence and superior merit; she had on many occasions been charged with the regency of Egypt under the three sovereigns of the Ethiopian dynasty, and had made herself very popular in Thebes and its neighbourhood.

3. The good understanding between the twelve confederate kings lasted fifteen years. Herodotus says an oracle had predicted that all Egypt should belong to him who should first make libations to Ptah from a vessel of bronze. One day, when the twelve princes were offering a sacrifice, the high priest brought them the golden cups they were in the habit of using; but he had mistaken the number, and brought only eleven for the twelve kings.* Then Psammetik, who possibly had prepared the scene beforehand, in order to appear to be the man intended by the oracle, finding that he alone was without a cup, took his bronze helmet and used it for his libation. Exile in the marshes was the consequence of this action, noticed by the other kings.

Psammetik resolved to resent this outrage, and sent to consult the oracle for himself. The answer he received was that he should be avenged by brazen men issuing from the sea. A short time afterwards some Greeks, who had been shipwrecked on the coast, came on shore, clothed in armour. An Egyptian ran to bring the news to Psammetik, still in the marshes, and, having never seen men armed in that way, said that brazen men had issued from the sea and were plundering the country. The king, understanding from this that the oracle was accomplished, made an alliance with the Greeks, and engaged them by large promises to take his part. Afterwards, with these auxiliaries and the Egyptians who had remained faithful to him, Psammetik commenced the campaign, gained a decisive battle at Mo-Memphis, dethroned the eleven kings his colleagues, expelled the Ethiopians from the Thebaid, and restored to Egypt its ancient territory, from the Mediterranean to the first cataract.

To conciliate the numerous partisans whom the Ethiopians, as we have already said, had in Upper Egypt, he married the princess Shap-en-ap, daughter and heiress of Piankhi II. and Amen-iritis. The suzerainty of Assyria had been recognised by the kings of the Dodecarchy. By dethroning them, Psammetik put an end to this vassalage, and re-established the complete independence of Egypt. Gyges, king of Lydia, assisted him in this enterprise.

4. Psammetik I., the Psammetichus of the Greeks, when once in possession of supreme power, ignored all that occurred since the death of

* Her. ii. 151.

Tahraka, independently of himself, during the two years of anarchy and fifteen years of the Dodecarchy, and dated his monuments from the seventeenth year of his reign. Owing his elevation to the assistance of foreigners, he continued to invite numbers of them to come to Egypt. He brought mercenaries from Arabia, Caria, and Ionia, gave them handsome pay, and assigned them lands between the Pelusiac mouth of the Nile and the city of Bubastis, in one of the Nomes where the military class was already established. At last he entrusted to foreigners some of the highest dignities of the country. In an expedition into Syria he went so far as to give the auxiliary troops all the posts of honour, and placed them on the right of the army. The military caste, wounded in its honour and injured in its interests, emigrated in a body, and formed an establishment in Ethiopia. This desertion of 200,000 men, who represented nearly the whole military strength of the country, must naturally have seriously weakened Egypt. In vain Psammetik humbled his pride sufficiently to invite their return: they preferred to remain in Ethiopia. Psammetik then allied himself still more closely with foreigners, and to ensure the good-will, at any rate, of the sacerdotal class, he was prodigal in his gifts to the temples of the gods. He built at Memphis a pylon before the temple of Ptah, and built, or rather added to, the sacred edifice in which Apis was kept when he manifested himself. Owing to these works, Egyptian art had one final renaissance, lasting during the time of the Saite dynasty. It did not attain to the truth and grandeur of the ancient schools, but, nevertheless, produced a great number of beautiful works remarkable for their exquisite finish. It seems also that at this time a portion of the sacred books, particularly the famous Funereal Ritual, were revised.

This founder of the real power of the twenty-sixth dynasty also occupied himself actively in the administration of the State, augmented the revenue by encouraging foreign commerce, facilitated intercourse with Greece and Phœnicia, and thus brought Egypt out of the mysterious isolation which the policy of many centuries had maintained. "Psammetichus," says Diodorus Siculus, "received with hospitality strangers who came to visit Egypt. He was so fond of Greece that he had his children taught the language of that country. Lastly, he was the first Egyptian king to open to other nations the centres of commerce, and give security to traders; for his predecessors had made Egypt inaccessible to foreigners, killing some and condemning others to slavery."

Desirous of strengthening his dynasty by military glory, Psammetik wished to imitate the policy of the eighteenth and nineteenth dynasties in Asiatic countries, and to conquer Syria; for the rich Phœnician cities, where commerce had for ages accumulated the treasures of the world, excited his cupidity. But he was arrested at the first step, nearly on the frontier of Egypt, by the city of Ashdod, which cost a twenty-nine years' siege before he succeeded in taking it.

5. Necho, his son, continued the war, and at first made more rapid progress. Near Megiddo, on the ancient battle-field of Thothmes III., he conquered the Syrians and Jews commanded by Josiah, king of Judah, who wished to oppose his progress (609 B.C.), and for the moment possessed himself of all Syria. But at this time, between the Tigris and Euphrates, a redoubtable empire had arisen, and had attained under Nebuchadnezzar I. the highest degree of power. This was the Chaldæo-Babylonian monarchy. A contest between these two powers, both claiming supremacy in Asia, was inevitable. The kings of Egypt and Babylon met on the banks of the Euphrates, near Circesium, or Carchemish. Necho was overcome and put to flight; one single battle stripped him of all his conquests, and compelled him to retire to Egypt (604 B.C.).

Foreign wars were not the only occupation of this king. Like his father, he had devoted himself to the peaceful work of the extension of Egyptian commerce. Intercourse with foreigners, now become more common, and rendered more easy by the institution of a new body of interpreters, had enlarged the king's ideas and inspired him with the most noble projects, amongst others that of re-opening the canal of Seti I., from the Red Sea to the Nile, obstructed for ages by the sands of the desert, through the carelessness of the worthless kings of the twentieth dynasty. The work had thus become as difficult as if undertaken anew, and Herodotus states* that 120,000 men perished whilst engaged on it, from epidemics breaking out among the crowds of workmen; but it was never finished. Necho after a few years suddenly suspended the work, on account of an oracle that warned him that he was working for the barbarian.

Although the canal was abandoned, the expeditions by sea were continued. Wishing to extend the commercial relations of Egypt, Necho undertook the circumnavigation of Africa. He directed some Phœnicians to make the circuit of the African continent, over seas then unknown to the whole world, sailing down the Arabian Gulf and returning through the Straits of Hercules. The voyage lasted three years, and the history of it is accompanied by circumstances that the Phœnicians cannot have invented, thus proving that it really was accomplished.† But it produced no results, and the knowledge acquired by this adventurous voyage was soon forgotten.

---

* HER. ii. 158.

† "That in sailing round Lybia they had the sun on their right hand"; or, in other words, that the sun at noon was to the north instead of to the south. A fact recorded by Herodotus (iv. 42), though he admitted that he considered it incredible.—TR.

6. Psammetik II., the Psammis of the Greeks, who succeeded his father, Necho, reigned only six years, and died on his return from an expedition against the Ethiopians. He put forward pretensions to the crown of Ethiopia; and, in order to create a right to it by allying himself to their royal line, he married his own aunt, the princess Net-aker, daughter of the queen, Shap-en-ap, and grand-daughter of Amen-iritis.

His expedition against Ethiopia has left some curious monuments in the Greek and Carian inscriptions, engraved by the mercenaries of his army on the legs of one of the famous colossi, ornamenting the façade of the Temple of Ipsambul, in Nubia.

7. After him, his son, Uahprahet (the sun enlarges his heart), called by the Greeks Apries, mounted the throne, and reigned twenty-five years. He recurred to the old policy of Asiatic wars; and with a numerous fleet, after an unsuccessful attack on the island of Cyprus, assailed Phœnicia, took the city of Sidon by assault, and spread terror through all the Phœnician cities. This is the king named Hophra in the Bible, who came to the help of Zedekiah, king of Judah, when threatened by Nebuchadnezzar. But his interference was useless, and only drew down a Babylonian invasion on the eastern provinces of the Delta.

Some time after this Uahprahet, having sent an army against Cyrene, and the expedition ending unfortunately, the army revolted. He sent a certain Ahmes, the Amasis of the Greeks, to appease the tumult. He went to the insurgents; but while he was haranguing them, an Egyptian, who was behind him, placed a helmet on his head, exclaiming that he had crowned him king. Ahmes made no objection, and marched against Uahprahet, who put himself at the head of his mercenaries. The two armies met at Mo-Memphis and commenced battle. The mercenaries fought with courage, but, outnumbered, they were defeated. Uahprahet, made prisoner, was conducted to Sais, and confined in the magnificent palace he had inhabited as king. He was at first treated with generosity; but the Egyptians, whom the unfortunate prince had much wounded in their national pride by his preference for foreigners, required Ahmes to give him up to them. They no sooner had him in their power than they strangled him.

8. Ahmes, or Amasis, in imitation of the policy of his predecessors, married the heiress to the rights of the Saite dynasty, the princess Ankhs-en Ranofrehet, daughter of Psammetik II. At the commencement of his reign the Egyptians, as we learn from Herodotus,* had but little consideration for him, as he was of obscure parentage; but he raised himself in their opinion by his prudence and ability: he compared himself, speaking to a large assembly, to a golden vase,

* HER. ii. 172.

employed at first for common purposes, but afterwards worked up into the statue of a god, when it becomes an object of adoration to all.

This king was a clever man, and knew perfectly how to combine pleasure with a due regard to affairs of state. He said to his friends,* "Bowmen bend their bows when they wish to shoot, and unbrace them when shooting is over. Were they always kept strung they would break, and fail the archer in the time of need. So it is with men. If they give themselves constantly to serious work, and never indulge awhile in pastime or sport, they lose their senses and become mad or moody." According to the testimony of Herodotus,† "the reign of Amasis was the most prosperous time that Egypt ever saw; the river was more liberal to the land, and the land brought forth more abundantly for the service of man than had ever been known before, while the number of inhabited cities was not less than 20,000." This number, furnished by the priests, comprised, no doubt, even villages and hamlets; for under the Persian rule, they were desirous of exaggerating the splendour of Egypt before the conquest.

The extensive commerce then carried on by the land of the Pharaohs with foreigners, and above all with Greece, was one of the principal causes of the prosperity of the country in the last days of its independence. Amasis extended his special protection to the industrious and active Greek people, and not only permitted them to make a settlement at Naucratis, but authorised the free exercise of their religion, and gave them sites for the erection of temples and altars to their divinities. The largest and most celebrated of these temples was called the Hellenium. It was built by the Greek cities of Asia Minor; of the Ionians, Chios, Teos, Phocæa, Clazomenæ; of the Dorians, Rhodes, Cnidus, Halicarnessus, Phaselis; and of the Æolians, Mytelene.‡ The Æginetans had also built a temple to Jupiter, the Samians to Juno, and the Milesians to Apollo. Amasis even contributed a sum of a thousand talents of alum§ for the reconstruction of the temple at Delphi, which had been destroyed by fire. At the same time he allied himself to the Greeks of Cyrene by marrying Laodice, a daughter of one of their princes, and sent to the city of Cyrene a gilt statue of Minerva, together with his own portrait. He, moreover, gave to different Grecian temples many statues and some very valuable works of art, as Herodotus, who had seen them, testifies.|| The Greek historian also tells us that the island of Cyprus was conquered and re-united to Egypt by Amasis.

This magnificent prince was not likely to forget in his liberality the gods of his own country. The temple of Isis, in the city of Memphis,

* HER. ii. 173. † Ibid. ii. 177. ‡ Ibid. ii. 178.
§ Ibid. ii. 180. || Ibid. ii. 182.

mentioned by Herodotus* as most admirable; that of Neith at Sais, the porticoes of which surpassed, it is said, any work of the kind, both in elevation and in the size of the columns; and lastly, the monolithic chamber which he had made at Elephantine — all prove that in his reign art had not retrograded since the times of the Psammetiks.

Egypt, then, in the time of Amasis seems to have been as flourishing as at any period of her history, though this prosperity but thinly veiled the decline of public spirit and of national institutions. The Saite kings hoped to breathe new life into Egypt, to infuse new blood into the veins of the old monarchy of Menes, by allowing free current to the liberal ideas already propagated by the Greeks. Unconsciously they had in this way introduced new elements of decay into the empire of the banks of the Nile. The basis and safeguard of Egyptian civilisation was its immutability. Its very foundation consisted in preserving its traditions intact in spite of the lapse of ages, and thus only could it last. From the moment that it came in contact with the spirit of progress, personified in the Greek race and civilisation, it was doomed to destruction. It could neither enter on a new road contrary to the letter and spirit of its laws, nor yet continue immovable.

Thus when Greek influence began to make itself felt, Egyptian civilisation at once began to decline, and collapsed into a state of death-like decrepitude. The military caste having almost entirely emigrated, the nation was disarmed. Foreigners, disliked by the people, were charged with its defence, and had even been employed in foreign wars and conquests ending in disaster. The public indignation culminated in revolt. A bold adventurer had possessed himself of the throne, and had found the country so committed to these new ways, that he himself favoured the foreigners, thus contributing to the riches of Egypt, but also exciting the cupidity of conquerors. When these arrived, Egypt could oppose to them only a people who had lost all aptitude for arms. So the son of Amasis, Psammetik III., the Psammenitus of the Greeks, mounted the throne to see, almost immediately on his accession, the independence of Egypt succumb finally to the attack of the Persians under Cambyses.

---

* HER. ii. 175.

CHAPTER V.

CIVILISATION, MANNERS, AND MONUMENTS OF EGYPT.

Chief Authorities.

For Manners and Social Organisation: — Herodotus, Book II.—Diodorus Siculus, Book I.—Caillaud, *Recherches sur les Arts et Métiers de l'ancienne Egypte*, Paris, 1829.—Rosellini, *Monumenti dell' Egitto e della Nubia; Monumenti civili*, Florence, 1833.—Wilkinson, *Manners and Customs of the Ancient Egyptians*, London, 1847.—The great works of Champollion and Lepsius.

For Language and Writing:—Champollion, *Précis du Système Hiéroglyphique*, Paris, 1828.—*Grammaire Egyptienne*, Paris, 1836.—*Dictionnaire Egyptien*, Paris, 1841.—Lepsius, *Lettre à M. Rosellini sur le Système Hiéroglyphique*, Rome, 1837.—*Grammar, Dictionary, and Chrestomathy*, by Dr. Birch, in the 5th vol. (2nd ed.) Bunsen's "*Egypt's Place*," etc., London, 1868.—Brugsch, *Scriptura Ægyptiorum Demotica*, Berlin, 1848.—*Grammaire Démotique*, Berlin, 1856.—*Hieroglyphisch Demotisches Wörterbuch*, Leipzig, 1868.—De Rougé, *Lettre à M. de Saulcy sur l'Ecriture Démotique*, Paris, 1849.—*Grammaire Egyptienne*, 1*st* part, Paris, 1867.—*The Journal of Egyptian Philology and Archæology of Berlin.*

For Religion:—Champollion, *Panthéon Egyptien*, Paris, 4°.—Birch, *Gallery of Egyptian Antiquities from the British Museum*, London, 1844.—De Rougé, *Notice des Monuments Egyptiens du Musée du Louvre.—Mémoire sur la Statuette Naophore du Vatican*, Paris, 1851.—Mariette, *Mémoire sur la mère d'Apis*, Paris, 1856.—Chabas, *Hymne à Osiris*, Paris, 1857.—Lepsius, *Das Todtenbuch der Ægypter*, Leipzig, 1842.—De Rougé, *Etudes sur le Rituel Funeraire*, Paris, 1860.—F. Lenormant, *Les Livres chez les Egyptiens*, Paris, 1857.

For the Monuments:—The volumes on Antiquities, in the great French work, "*Description de l'Egypte.*" — Champollion, *Lettres écrites d'Egypte*, Paris, 1833; 2nd ed. 1868.—Nestor, L'Hote, *Lettres d'Egypte*, Paris. Lepsius, *Briefe aus Ægypten und Æthiopien*, Berlin, 1852.—The two first volumes of *Denkmäler aus Ægypten und Æthiopien*.—Ampère, *Voyage en Egypte*, Paris, 1868.—Ch. Lenormant, *Beaux Arts et Voyages*, vol. ii.

SECTION I.—SOCIAL CONSTITUTION.

1. The division of the people into classes was the foundation of the social constitution of Egypt, of which royalty formed the summit. The number of these classes varies in the accounts of Herodotus and Diodorus Siculus. The first* mentions seven,—priests, warriors, cow-

* HER. ii. 164.

herds, swine-herds, tradesmen, interpreters, and boatmen; the second* divides the people into only five classes,—priests, warriors, husbandmen, shepherds, artizans. This difference between two historians, who had both seen and travelled in Egypt, shows that the information they have transmitted to us on this point was incompletely and carelessly collected. Moreover, many of the occupations we find mentioned on the monuments cannot be easily included in any of the classes enumerated by the two Greek writers.

It has long been supposed, on the faith of testimony imperfectly understood, that the Egyptian people was divided distinctly into castes. A modern scholar, J. J. Ampère, has completely disproved this idea.† Caste, in fact, only exists when three conditions are imposed on its members—to abstain from certain forbidden occupations, to contract no alliance beyond the limits of the caste, and to continue to practise the profession of their fathers. Now to speak only of the sacerdotal and military classes, in which, according to Herodotus and Diodorus, occupations were handed down from father to son, we learn from the monuments, first, that the sacerdotal and military functions, far from being exclusive, were often joined one to the other, and either or both of them with civil positions, as the same person is known to have had a sacerdotal, a military, and a civil title; secondly, that a personage invested with a military title could marry the daughter of a sacerdotal dignitary; thirdly, that the members of one family, father and sons, might fill, some military, others civil positions, and the offices did not necessarily pass to their children.

There was then no sacerdotal caste, in the true meaning of the word, for priests might also be generals, governors of provinces, architects, or judges. It was the same with the military class; one man might be both commander of archers and governor of Southern Ethiopia, superintendent of the royal buildings and also commander of foreign mercenaries. Hereditary transmission was not the general law of Egyptian society. Doubtless, the son often did inherit the office of the father, and more often in the sacerdotal and military classes than in the others; but this occurs in very many other nations, and is far from proving absolute and exclusive inheritance. There was formerly in France a class, the nobles, exclusively devoted to war, and another to the magistracy, and in these classes offices were nearly always transmitted from father to son; but we should not conclude from this that the people of France was ever divided into castes. It would therefore be better, as Ampère has done, to translate by "corporation," the Greek word usually rendered caste.

---

* DIOD. SIC. i. 74.

† In an essay re-published at the end of his *Voyage en Egypte.*

2. Of all the classes of Egyptian society those of the warriors and priests were esteemed most honourable. The priests, especially under the later dynasties, formed a sort of privileged nobility in the state. They filled the highest offices, and possessed the largest and best part of the land. To render this property inalienable, they represented it as the gift of the goddess Isis, who, when she was on earth, assigned to them a third part of the kingdom. These estates were free from every tax (Gen. xlvii. 22); they were generally let for a rent, which was paid into the treasury of the temple to which the land belonged, and was employed in the expenses of the worship and on the support of the priests and their numerous subordinates. These, the classical writers say, spent nothing of their own property, each of them received a portion of the sacred food given them ready cooked; they even had every day a large quantity of beef and goose flesh; wine also was given them, but they were not permitted to eat fish.*

The priests were obliged to be scrupulously clean in their persons and clothes. "They shave the whole body every other day," says Herodotus, and his account quite agrees with the monuments. "Their dress is entirely of linen, and their shoes of the papyrus plant; and it is not lawful for them to wear either dress or shoes of any other material. They bathe twice every day in cold water, and twice each night, besides which they observe, so to speak, thousands of ceremonies."

3. After the sacerdotal class, in order of importance came the military. This also enjoyed great privileges. According to Herodotus, the warrior class was divided into two bodies, the Calasirians and Hermotybians. They were distributed in the different nomes of Egypt in the following manner† :—The nomes of the Hermotybians were Busiris, Sais, Chemmis, Papremis, the island called Prosopitis, and half of Natho: these nomes furnished 160,000 men. The Calasirians occupied the nomes of Thebes, Bubastis, Aphthis, Tanis, Mendes, Sebennytus, Pharbæthus, Thmuis, Onuphis, Anysis, Myecphoris, and Athribis: these nomes could, when fully peopled, furnish 250,000 men.

We see, by the designation of the different nomes occupied by the warrior class, that the facts collected by Herodotus relate to an epoch posterior to the twenty-first dynasty, when the whole military power of Egypt was concentrated in Lower Egypt. In the interior of the Delta four and a half nomes were then occupied by the Hermotybians, and twelve others by the Calasirians, and they had each of them only one in Upper and Central Egypt, that is Chemmis and Thebes. The corps of foreign origin, who had been settled for many generations in the Delta, such as the Mashuash, were probably enrolled in one or other of these lists.

---

* Her. ii. 37. † Ibid. ii. 165, 166.

The warrior class, like that of the priests, was richly endowed, and possessed nearly a third of the soil; each of them, as Herodotus states,* had twelve aruræ of land (about nine acres) exempt from all taxes. Every year 1,000 men from the Calasirians, and the same number from the Hermotybians, served as the king's guards, and to each of them was given daily five minæ of bread (about 6½ lbs.), and two minæ of beef (about 2½ lbs.), and four measures (about one quart) of wine.

Such was the organisation of the Egyptian army under the last dynasties of the monarchy of the Pharaohs. For many ages the Egyptians employed chiefly native troops, and among them military service was considered as a privilege and distinction. The foreign auxiliaries then held a very inferior position to the native troops, and it was only after hereditary service for many generations had made them at last (like the Matoi under the Middle Empire and the Mashuash under the New) really Egyptian citizens, that their position was assimilated to that of Egyptian troops. Psammetik disorganised the whole constitution of the army by giving his hired Greek mercenaries precedence over the native troops. The soldiers of Egyptian birth saw in this a flagrant violation of their privileges, and 200,000 warriors deserted the garrison, where the king had designedly placed them, to go off and form a colony beyond the cataracts.

From that time the sinews of the Egyptian military power were broken. The Greek and Carian mercenaries, who composed the majority of the Egyptian armies, became rather the instruments of the king than the defenders of the nation. A feeling of rivalry sprang up between them and the rest of the soldiery, and Egypt was given over to intestine strife and anarchy. When the Persian invasion took place, the country was defenceless, and one single battle sufficed to render Cambyses master of the whole Nile valley.

4. All the free population, belonging neither to the military nor sacerdotal class, formed in Egypt a sort of third order subdivided into many smaller classes not well defined by ancient writers.

In this respect lies the chief discrepancy between Herodotus and Diodorus Siculus. The former divides the people into five classes, the latter only into three—shepherds, husbandmen and artisans. On some points it is easy enough to make these conflicting statements agree. Thus the artisans, tradesmen and interpreters, of whom Herodotus makes three distinct bodies, belonged apparently all to one class, and were only subdivisions—the cow-herds, and swine-herds, mentioned by the same author, also belong to one class—the shepherds. But there always remains this important difference between Herodotus and

* Her. ii. 168.

Diodorus, that the latter admits one special class of husbandmen whom the former excludes. Heeren believes that they are included by Herodotus under the name κάπηλοι (tradesmen), and that we must class the husbandmen among the artisans. The nature of the tenure of landed property in Egypt authorises this explanation. In fact, as Diodorus tells us, and the monuments confirm the statement, the whole soil of Egypt was in the hands of the king, the priests, and the warriors, and the husbandmen were only serfs attached to the land, who cultivated, paying a rent, the estates of the privileged classes. They were sold with the ground, and could not leave the district where they lived without the permission of government. The forced labour for public works pressed on them with all its weight. Their position was very like that of the modern *fellahs* who have no property of their own, and cultivate the land of Egypt for their sovereign.

The class of shepherds naturally included all who made the care of cattle their principal occupation. Those who lived in villages and tended large herds of cattle in the interior of the country must not be confounded with the nomad shepherds who wandered near the frontiers. These were generally hated by the Egyptians, as Moses and Herodotus both state. This antipathy, as old as the earliest times of the monarchy, and always existing in the east between the inhabitants of cities and the Nomads or Bedouins, extended also to the foreign settlers in the marshes of the Delta, most of whom were descended from the Shepherds of Avaris. These tribes had completely adopted Egyptian manners and customs; but as they remained barbarians at heart, they were addicted to brigandage, and by their depredations kept alive the old hatred felt towards them by all other people of the country.

The swine-herds, whom Herodotus particularly distinguishes from cow-herds, were looked down upon and regarded as unclean. They were not only forbidden to have access to the temples, but even to mix with other classes. The pig was in Egyptian, as in Jewish eyes, an unclean animal. Nevertheless, according to ancient custom, an animal of that species was sacrificed on one of the feasts of Osiris.

The class of sailors, or pilots, must have been composed of men employed in the navigation of the Nile. The inundation, periodically transforming Egypt into a vast lake, rendered their services indispensable. Moreover, there were on the Nile, and on the numerous canals intersecting the country, a great number of vessels of all kinds, as all merchandise and building materials were transported by water. The river was the great, almost the only, road for internal commerce. The Egyptians regarded the sea as unclean, and had a great disinclination to venture on it, so that it is very doubtful whether they ever had real seamen among them, and whether, when the Pharaohs maintained considerable fleets on the Mediterranean and Red Seas, the ships were ever manned by any but Phœnicians.

The interpreters, of whom Herodotus speaks, were another separate class, indispensable to the necessities of commerce; but they seem to have been first organised into a body under the Saite kings, when intercourse with foreigners had assumed a development and an activity unknown to earlier ages.

Section II.—Political Organisation and Administration.

1. The political constitution of Egypt never varied during the whole of the enormous period of the duration of the empire of the Pharaohs. The country always remained one united monarchy, the most absolute probably that has ever existed in the world. Neither changes of dynasties, nor the struggles of rival competitors for the throne, ever effected any change. "The Egyptians," says Diodorus Siculus, "respect and adore their kings as the equals of the gods. The sovereign authority with which Providence has invested kings, together with the will and the power to confer benefits, seems to them a manifestation of the deity."

This passage of the Greek historian is in complete accordance with the facts resulting from the study of the monuments. From the time of the very oldest dynasties, we find that such an unbounded respect for royalty existed, that it was transformed into religious worship, and Pharaoh became the visible god of his subjects. The Egyptian monarchs were more than sovereign pontiffs, they were real deities. The sacerdotal class depended absolutely upon them. The epithet "Son of the Sun-God" is as a matter of course attached to the name of each Pharaoh. They also styled themselves "the great God, the good God"; they identified themselves with the great deity Horus; for, as one inscription says, "The king is the image of Ra (the Sun-God) among the living." A prince in mounting the throne was, so to speak, transfigured in the eyes of his subjects. During his lifetime he attained a complete apotheosis. And this is why he assumed a symbolical and mysterious name at the time of his coronation. This name is found, from the earliest epochs, inscribed among the royal titles on a banner surmounted by a crowned hawk. The king was also called "The Sun, Lord of Justice," because from him was believed to emanate all regulations for moral and material order; he controlled everything, as the star of the day was believed to preside over cosmic phenomena.

The divinity of the king, thus commencing on earth, was, in a manner, completed and perpetuated in another life. All the Pharaohs when dead became gods; so, after each reign, the Egyptian pantheon was enriched by a new god. The series of Pharaohs thus constituted a series of gods, to whom the reigning monarch addressed homage and invocations. This gave rise to the monuments where we see Pharaoh addressing prayers to his predecessors. The list was so long that, in the inscriptions commemorative of their piety, the kings are obliged to make a selection among the names of these deified princes. This worship of the Pharaohs was so lasting and so devoutly believed in by the people, that we find the adoration of the kings of the primitive age extends even into the time of the Ptolemies. These kings had their particular priests, sometimes attached to the altars of two or more monarchs at once. But this was not all. Pharaoh was equally man and god; he, in the opinion of the Egyptians, so completely united the two natures, that he himself addressed worship to himself. Several monuments represent the prince making, in his own name, offerings to his own image.

We may imagine what prestige such an exaltation of royalty gave in Egypt to the sovereign power. That power, so great even among the neighbouring Asiatic nations, became in this country a real idolatry. The Egyptians, in the eyes of the king, were but trembling slaves, compelled, even from religious motives, to execute his orders blindly; the highest and most powerful functionaries were only the humble servants of Pharaoh. His most trifling favours are mentioned in their epitaphs as their most brilliant titles of glory. One, for instance, was permitted to touch the knees of the king instead of the usual prostration to the earth before him. Another had obtained the privilege of wearing his sandals in the king's palace. To accommodate themselves to such a regime, to consent to sink so completely their individuality, and to be only the docile instruments of their master's glory, the Egyptians, like almost all oriental people, must have been entirely devoid of that feeling of independence and of personal dignity, constituting the strength and nobility of modern nations, that first appeared in the Greeks and Romans. But that this regime could have lasted so many ages, with no sensible modification, proves also that the Egyptians were thoroughly imbued with the idea that their government was an emanation from the Divine will. A lively religious faith, perverted in this degrading way, could alone have reconciled them to such a servile condition.

2. Around this divine king etiquette must indeed have been rigorous. Not only were all the public acts of the kings regulated by invariable rules, but also those of their private daily lives. On awaking in the morning, the king first received and read dispatches from all parts of the country, so as to know all that was going on in his empire. Next, after having bathed and assumed his insignia of royalty, he offered sacrifice to the gods. The victims were led to the altar, the high priest stood near the king as his assistant, and in the presence of the people he prayed with a loud voice to the gods for the health and well-being of

the king. At the same time he enumerated his virtues, spoke of his piety towards the gods and his goodness to men. He spoke of him as temperate, magnanimous, truthful, benevolent; in a word, every virtue and all good qualities were attributed to him, and nowhere more than in Egypt was it an established principle that "the king can do no wrong."

The popular assemblies to sit in judgment on the deceased king, spoken of by some Greek authors, are all pure fictions. The king when dead was as much a god as when living. If in the series of Egyptian annals we find some kings deprived of burial, and whose names have been effaced from the monuments, it has not been from any popular judgment, but by order of another king who wished to treat a rival as a usurper.

3. The administration of Egypt, from the most ancient times to that of the Persian conquest, was in the hands of a powerful and numerous official body wisely constituted, with a hierarchy unsurpassed in the most bureaucratic countries in the modern world, who constituted the very large class of scribes. This administration was full of routine, and its records were kept in the most precise and methodical way. Among the papyri we now possess are a large number of administrative reports, and of fragments of registers of public accounts.

The departments administered by the most numerous and well-organised staff were those of public works, war and of the superintendence of the revenue of the state. Coined money was unknown, and all taxes were levied in kind. The land was divided under three heads according to the nature of its contribution to the state. The canals (mau) paid tithe in fish; the arable land (uu) in grain; and the marshes (pehu) in cattle. Statistical records, carefully adapted to all the changes that took place, contained a list for each district of all the various sorts of property with the names of the proprietors.

4. The territory of Egypt Proper was divided, for administrative purposes, into a certain number of districts, called by the Greeks, *Nomes*. The chief place of each nome was the sanctuary of some divinity; and each principal temple formed, with the territory belonging to it, a particular nome, distinguished from the others by its worship and ceremonies. This is what Herodotus tells us, and the monuments confirm his statement. Under the rule of the Greek Ptolemies, the number of nomes or cantons was thirty-six in Upper Egypt, sixteen in Central and ten in Lower Egypt. In the time of the Pharaohs, only two regions were distinguished, Upper and Lower, and each comprised twenty-two nomes, in all forty-four. Lists have been found on the walls of some temples, from which we have constructed the following table of the nomes and of their tutelary deities :—

No.	Egyptian Name.	Greek Name.	Modern District.	Protecting Deity.
1	Kens	Nubian	Nubia	Chnum-Ra
2	Tes-Hor	Apolinopolite	Edfu	Har Hat
3	Ten	Latopolite	Esneh	Suvan (Goddess)
4	Tsam	Diospolite	Medinet Abu	Month
5	Horti	Coptite	Keft	Min
6	Emsuh	Tentyrite	Dendera	Isis (Goddess)
7	Seshesh	Phathyrite	Hon	Hathor (Goddess)
8	Abot	Thinite	Arabat el Med-funeh	Anhur
9	Sechem	Panopolite	Achmim	Min
10	Tsets	Aphroditopolite	Edfeh	Har siesis
11	Shes-hotep	Anteopolite	Kau el Kebir	Chnum
12	Tuf	Hypselite	Sotb	Anubis
13	Chesf-chent	Lycopolite Upper	Siout	Ap-heru
14	Chesf-pehu	Lycopolite Lower	Manfalut	Hathor (Goddess)
15	Un	Hermopolite Upper	Ashmunein	Thoth
16	Sah	Hermopolite Lower	Minieh	Horus
17	Anup	Cynopolite	El Kais	Anubis
18	Seb	Oxyrynchite	Behnesa	Anubis
19	Tsebets	Aphroditopolite		Nephthys (Goddess)
20	Neha-chent	Arsinoite Upper	Fayoum	Sevek
21	Neha-pehu	Arsinoite Lower	Fayoum	Hathor (Goddess)
22	Seft	Heracleopolite	Anasieh	

LOWER EGYPT.

No.	Egyptian Name.	Greek Name.	Modern District.	Protecting Deity.
1	Sebt-het	Memphite	Menf	Phtah Sokar Osiris
2	Aa	Latopolite	Ausim	Bast (Goddess) (Bubastis)
3	Ament	Lybian		Hathor (Goddess)
4	Sai-res	Saite Upper	Ssa	Neith (Goddess)
5	Sai-mehit	Saite Lower	Alexandria	Neith (Goddess)
6	Ka	Athribite	Etrib	Horus
7	* * ament			Sevek
8	* * abt			
9	Ati	Canopic (?)		Osiris
10	Ka-kem			Apis
11	Ka-hebs			Osiris
12	Ka-she			
13	Hak	Heliopolite	Matareeh	Atum
14	Chun-abt	Heroopolite	Wady Tumilat	Horus
15	Habu	Bubastite	Tell Basta	Hathor (Goddess)
16	Chev	Thmuite		Hatmehi ,,
17	Sam-hut			Samta
18	Chrud-chen			
19	Chrud-pehu	Bouto		Buto (Goddess)
20	Sept-hor	Arabian		Sept Achem
21	An			Horus
22	Men	Mendesian		Ba-n-ded (Mendes)

At the head of each nome was a governor, whom the Greeks called "Nomarch." The whole administration depended on this officer. Under the Nomarchs were other magistrates, subordinate to them, called by the Greeks "Toparchs," who governed smaller districts. A marked spirit of local jealousy prevailed in these nomes; they had frequent quarrels with one another, both political and religious, often giving rise to revolts and sanguinary struggles.

5. The judicial organisation was almost independent of the royal power; the kings themselves only judged cases as a last appeal, but very rarely, and, as a rule, only in such cases as had some political bearing. The common and regular administration of justice belonged to the ordinary tribunals, which were bound strictly to observe the laws. The sacerdotal class furnished the Egyptian magistracy. The great cities of Memphis, Heliopolis, and Thebes, where the most flourishing sacerdotal colleges were situated, supplied most of the judges; ten came from each. The thirty judges chose from amongst them a president, and the place he vacated was filled by another judge from the same city. These magistrates were maintained at the expense of the royal treasury, and the president enjoyed a large income. All business was transacted in writing, never *vivâ voce*, in order, it was said, that nothing might excite the feelings of the judge, and thus prejudice his impartiality. The plaintiff in civil processes, the prosecutor in criminal cases (for there was no public prosecutor), presented his complaint in writing, and stated the amount of damage he required, or the extent of punishment he desired to be inflicted on the accused. The defendant, or accused, was informed of the demand, or accusation of the opposite party, and was obliged to make a written defence to each of its heads. The plaintiff might make one rejoinder, and the defendant another reply, and the tribunal was then obliged to pronounce judgment in writing, sealed with the seal of the president. This officer had a gold chain round his neck, from which hung an image of the goddess Ma (Truth and Justice), distinguished by the attribute of the ostrich feather on her head. It was necessary for the president to put on this chain before the sitting could commence. When judgment was pronounced, the president placed this image of truth on one of the parties brought into his presence, and the case was concluded. We possess the proceedings in two Egyptian criminal cases; the first, tried by a commission specially appointed by the king, is that of the conspirators in the reign of Ramses III.; the second, tried by the ordinary tribunals, is that of a band of robbers, who, under Ramses IV., had been organised to plunder the tombs at Thebes. The report of the enquiry into this last case is preserved in a papyrus in the British Museum. Unfortunately, among the papyri as yet found and translated, there is no original and authentic document with regard to a

civil trial. A special tribunal took cognisance of all cases relating to religion, such as the practice of magic.

SECTION III.—LAWS.

1. THE Egyptian laws were too remarkable to be passed over in silence. "Egypt," says Bossuet, "was the source of all good government." In fact, however imperfect may be the information we possess on this head, it is easy to see from ancient writers that Egyptian legislation respected all the best feelings of the human mind, and answered the highest wants of social order. We are about to review some of these laws according to the account given by Diodorus Siculus, who was thoroughly well informed on this subject.

2. In the first place perjury was punished with death, because it comprises the two greatest crimes that can be committed, one against the gods and the other against men. He who saw in the road anyone struggling with an assassin, or subjected to any violence, and did not do all that he could to help him, was punished with death. If he had really been unable to help, he was obliged to denounce the criminals and accuse them before the tribunals. If he did not do this, he was condemned to receive a given number of blows from a stick, and to be kept without food for three days. Those who made false accusations were condemned, when discovered, to undergo the punishment of calumniators. It was directed that every Egyptian should deposit with the magistrate an account in writing of his means of subsistence; he who made a false declaration, or who gained his livelihood by unlawful means, was condemned to death.* The wilful murderer, whether a freeman or a slave, was punished with death; for the object of the law was to punish according to the crime and intention of the offender, not according to his station in life; at the same time, the arrangements with regards to slaves was such as to prevent their being guilty of an offence towards a freeman. A woman condemned to death while *enceinte*, was not executed until her child was born; as it was thought the height of injustice to make the innocent participate in the punishment of the guilty, and to visit the crime of one person upon two. The judges who put to death an innocent person, were held as guilty as if they had acquitted a murderer.

Among the laws regarding soldiers,—he who had deserted his ranks, or had not obeyed the orders of his officers, was punished, not with death, but with infamy. If afterwards he wiped away his shame by

---

* See HER. ii. 177.

any glorious action, he was reinstated in his rank. Thus the law made dishonour a punishment more dreadful than death, in order to accustom the soldiers to regard infamy as the greatest of all evils; and at the same time those who had been punished in this way were incited to attempt great actions to recover their former position, whilst if they had been put to death, they could have been of no more use to the state. A spy, who had betrayed secret plans to the enemy, was condemned to have his tongue cut out. Coiners, makers of false weights and measures, those who made false scales, those who forged documents or falsified public records, were condemned to have both hands cut off. The laws with regard to women were very severe. Whoever was convicted of offering violence to a free woman was condemned to mutilation—for this crime included three great evils, insult, corruption of manners, and confusion in families. Adultery without violence was punished, in a man by 1,000 blows with a stick, and in a woman by the loss of her nose. The law desired to deprive of her attractions one who only employed them in seduction.

3. Some of the civil laws were not less remarkable. Many regulations as to commercial transactions are attributed to King Bokenranf (Bocchoris). Thus a debt was null if the debtor affirmed on oath that he did not owe anything to a creditor who was unprovided with a bond. The interest also was not allowed to amount to more than the principal. The property of a debtor could be seized for a debt, but not his person; the law considered that the person of a citizen belonged to the state, which might at any moment claim his services, either in war or peace. Imprisonment for debt, therefore, was in no case allowed. Herodotus mentions also a very singular law, attributed to Osortasen III.* (Rashakeu-Asychis), permitting an Egyptian to borrow money on the security of the mummy of his father. The lender at the same time entered on possession of the tomb of the borrower. Whoever had not paid his debts was deprived of the honour of burial in the family tomb, and so also were those of his children who died during the continuance of the arrangement.

Numerous contracts for the sale or hire of lands and houses, written on papyrus, have been preserved in the cave-tombs among the family papers of the deceased. They show us with what guarantees, with what a number of protective formalities, the rights of property were surrounded in ancient Egypt.

---

* HER. ii. 136.

SECTION IV.—MANNERS AND CUSTOMS.

1. IT would require a lengthened description to explain all that the monuments have recorded of the customs and private life of the Egyptians. The people were at once commercial, agricultural, and warlike. The fertile soil of the Nile valley was at all times highly cultivated by its numerous population; and if machinery, properly so called, was at all times unknown in Egypt, if the manufacture of articles of daily and general consumption seems to have been conducted by processes as simple as those of their agriculture, objects of luxury—luxury both elegant and expensive—were largely produced in Egypt. The museums of Europe contain proofs of this fact, too numerous and decisive to leave any doubt on the subject. A great number of workmen were employed in weaving and dyeing rich stuffs. The arts of working in metals, of making porcelain and glass, and of preparing enamel and mastic for mosaics, had, on the banks of the Nile, attained to a high degree of perfection; lastly, the productions of Egyptian industry were exported by land and sea to the most distant countries. The nation, however, did not know the use of coined money; all commerce was carried on by exchange, or rather by employing ingots of metal, estimating value by weight.

Herodotus* remarks two peculiarities in the industrial and commercial customs of the Egyptians, exactly the reverse of those of the Greeks—the *men* worked at the loom and carried on their trades, while the *women* frequently transacted business.

2. In general, the character of the Egyptians was mild, their manners polished, and such as might be expected from a people naturally obedient, profoundly religious, and early civilised. "There is another custom," says Herodotus,† "in which the Egyptians resemble a particular Greek people, namely, the Lacedemonians; their young men, when they meet their elders in the street, give way to them and step aside; and if an elder come in where young men are present, these latter rise from their seats. In a third point, they differ entirely from all the nations of Greece. Instead of speaking to each other when they part in the streets, they make an obeisance, dropping the hand to the knee."

The same author also says, and the study of the monuments completely confirms his testimony, "The Egyptians are, I believe, next to the Lybians, the healthiest people in the world. . . . They are persuaded that every disease to which men are liable is caused by the substances whereon they feed. . . . They live on bread made of spelt. . . . Their drink is beer made from barley. . . . Many

---

* HER. ii. 135. † Ibid. ii. 80.

kinds of fish they eat raw, either salted or dried in the sun. Quails, also, ducks, and small birds they eat uncooked, merely first salting them. All other birds and fishes, excepting those which are set apart as sacred, are eaten either roasted or boiled."*

"They wear a linen tunic fringed about the legs, and called *calasiris;* over this they have a white woollen garment, thrown on afterwards. Nothing of woollen, however, is taken into their temples, or buried with them, as their religion forbids it."†

3. "In social meetings among the rich," Herodotus also states,‡ "when the banquet is ended, a servant carries round to the several guests a coffin, in which there is a wooden image of a corpse, carved and painted to resemble nature as nearly as possible, about a cubit or two cubits in length. As he shows it to each guest in turn, the servant says, 'Gaze here, and drink and be merry; for when you die, such you will be.'"

"Medicine is practised among them on a plan of separation; each physician treats a single disorder, and no more: thus the country swarms with medical practitioners, some undertaking to cure diseases of the eye, others of the head, others again of the teeth, others of the intestines, and some those which are not local."§

Care for the body, the desire to guard it after death from all chance of destruction, was again a subject of serious consideration among the Egyptians. Thence arose the custom of embalming, growing out of their religious ideas of the destiny of the soul after death. It was necessary that the body should be preserved from all injury, from all corruption, so that the soul might find it uninjured on the day of resurrection. Hence the infinite precautions for the preservation of the corpses—hence the enormous quantity of mummies now in our museums, and found in all parts of Egypt. The curious description of the processes employed in embalming, differing according to the rank and fortune of the deceased, may be read in Herodotus, Book II. 86, 87, 88.

SECTION V.—WRITING.

1. THE Greeks gave the name of Hieroglyphics, that is, "Sacred Sculpture," to the national writing of the Egyptians, composed entirely of pictures of natural objects. Although very inapplicable, this name has been adopted by modern writers, and has been so completely accepted and used, that it cannot now be replaced by a more appropriate appellation. Neither the Greeks nor the Romans, whilst masters of Egypt, attempted in any way to learn the method of reading this

* HER. ii. 77. † Ibid. ii. 81. ‡ Ibid. ii. 78. § Ibid. ii. 84.

writing. It appeared to them an unattainable secret, although the natives under their authority still continued to use it. For a long series of ages the decipherment of the hieroglyphics, for which the classical writers furnish no assistance, remained a hopeless mystery. The acute genius of a Frenchman at last succeeded, not fifty years since, in lifting the veil. By a prodigious effort of induction, and almost divination, Jean François Champollion, who was born at Figeac (Lot), on the 23rd of December, 1790, and died at Paris on the 4th of March, 1832, made the greatest discovery of the nineteenth century in the domain of historical science, and succeeded in fixing on a solid basis the principle of reading hieroglyphics. Numerous scholars have followed the path opened by him; the chief of them are, in France, C. Lenormant, Ampère, de Rougé, Mariette, and Chabas; in Germany, Dr. Lepsius and Dr. Brugsch; in England, Dr. Birch. By their profound and persevering studies the discovery of Champollion has been completed and perfected, and its results have been extended. It can now no longer be doubted by any one that the hieroglyphics of ancient Egypt may be translated with almost as much certainty as the works of any classic author.

2. In our present state of knowledge it cannot now be maintained that, as for a long time was believed, the hieroglyphics were a mysterious system of writing, reserved exclusively for the priests, who alone were in possession of the key. Hieroglyphic writing is found everywhere, on the public monuments and on articles of domestic use, in historical narratives and in the praises of the kings, intended for the greatest publicity and destined to last to remotest posterity, as well as in the explanations of the most subtle doctrines of the Egyptian religion. It would also be very far from the truth to regard hieroglyphics as always, or even generally, symbolical. No doubt there are symbolical characters among them, generally easy to understand; as also there are, and in very great number, figurative characters directly representing the object to be designated; but the majority of the signs found in every hieroglyphic text are characters purely phonetic, that is, representing either syllables (and these are so varied as to offer sometimes serious difficulties) or the letters of an only moderately complicated alphabet. These letters are also pictures of objects, but of objects or animals whose Egyptian name commenced with the letter in question, while also the syllabic characters (true rebusses) represented objects designated by that syllable. It is in this way that Champollion succeeded in reconstructing the whole system of the Egyptian writing and language, from the moment that the comparison of the royal names (pointed out by a frame, cartouch, or ring) in texts with a Greek translation, like the famous Rosetta inscription, permitted him to take the first step towards deciphering the alphabet, assisted afterwards by the Coptic, a language

derived from, and still very much resembling, the ancient Egyptian, and which has continued to our days to be the liturgical language of the Egyptian Christians.

3. The following table contains a selection of the most commonly used alphabetical characters from hieroglyphic texts:—

Phonetic Power or Sound.	Characters in common use.	Characters rarely used.	Phonetic Power or Sound.	Characters in common use.	Characters rarely used.
A			D		
Â			TS		
I			M		
U or OU			N		
F			R or L		
B			S		
P			SH		
K			KH		
Q			HH		
G			H		
T					

4. Words written phonetically, that is, with characters representing sound or pronunciation, whether by means of the letters of this alphabet or of the numerous syllabic signs used by the Egyptian scribes, compose the greater part of every hieroglyphic text. But from time to time words are found expressed by means of an ideographic character, that is, a figure depicting the idea contained in the word, independently of its sound and of its pronunciation in reading the text. A mixture of such absolutely differing elements in one system of writing is not so strange a fact, nor so entirely at variance with our own practice as at first sight it seems. We also have our ideographic signs; we often use them in the middle of a sentence, all the other words of which are

written alphabetically. Such are our Algebraic signs, + plus, — minus; such especially are our numerical figures, conveying the same idea to all European nations, quite independently of the pronunciation, for each nation calls the symbol by a different name.

Thus, as we have already said, these ideographic signs are of two sorts, figurative and symbolical. The first are pictures of the object itself desired to be expressed, and have no other meaning when so employed, as may be seen in the following examples:—

As for the symbols, they also are representations of concrete things, employed to embody abstract ideas; and sometimes also concrete ideas, when the direct pictorial representations would necessarily be too large and complicated. They are formed in the four following methods:—

I. By *synecdoche*, depicting a part for the whole; being simply abbreviations of characters, which would otherwise become too complicated. Thus the idea of building is expressed by a representation of the act of building up a wall. The two eyeballs sometimes represent the idea of *eyes*, and the ox is sometimes described by drawing the head instead of the entire animal.

II. By *metonymy*, taking the cause for the effect, the effect for the cause, or the instrument for the effect produced by it. Thus, *month* is expressed by the moon; *day*, by the sun; *fire*, by a column of smoke issuing from a chafing dish; *to see*, by two eyes or two eyeballs; *writing*, by a reed pen, with an ink-jar and palette.

III. By *metaphor*, by depicting an object that has some generally admitted and easily understood likeness to the idea to be expressed. The vulture expressed the idea of *maternity*, because that species of bird was believed to consist entirely of females, and to be reproduced without any male. The picture of the Nile goose represented *son*, because of the popular idea ascribing to that bird an amount of filial regard worthy of imitation by mankind. *Priority*, *pre-eminence*, or *superiority* were expressed by the fore-parts of a lion. The ideas of *vigilance* or *bravery*, by the head of the same animal, which was supposed to sleep with his eyes open. The bee stood for *king*, because those insects have a regular and apparently monarchical government.

IV. By *enigma*, by employing the picture of some physical object having only a very obscure, very distant, and often entirely conventional connection with the idea to be expressed. By this inevitably very vague method an ostrich feather signified *justice*, because the feathers of that bird were supposed to be all of equal length; a palm branch represented the *year*, because it was supposed that the palm every year put forth twelve branches, one in each month; a basket woven from reeds conveyed the ideas of *Lord* and *all*, and the uræus serpent was equally *royalty* and *divinity*.

There is a third and very important class of hieroglyphics, called "Determinatives," as they determine the nature of the idea conveyed by a word written in phonetic characters, and occasionally the pronunciation of the word,

In the ancient Egyptian language, as in most others, there were many words of the same sound, but with very different meanings; and to these words the determinative sign is added to distinguish the sense in which the word is used; for instance, the word *af* may mean *food*, *end*, or *viper;* and so, whenever the word is employed, the proper determinative is added to define the meaning. Names of objects of wood and metal are distinguished by determinatives; names of places in Egypt are marked by a sign, usually called a "cake," but which would appear to be a "cross-staff," or surveying instrument, peculiarly characteristic of Egypt, where re-surveys of property were needed after each inundation. It is remarkable that a determinative sign, evidently originally the same figure, was employed in cuneiform writing to distinguish names of towns and districts in Assyria, Babylonia, Chaldæa, and Susiania, exclusively. Names of foreign places also are distinguished by a representation of "hills," the peculiar feature of foreign lands, as compared with the dead level of the Nile valley.

These signs may be divided into two classes:—

a. Special determinatives, the figure of the object, or the symbol of one particular idea.

b. Generic determinatives, applying to a large number of words, or a large class of ideas.

The first class it would seem difficult to separate from ideographics; the principle of the classification of these signs is, that every determinative is applicable to more than one word or idea; the ideographic to one only.

In some cases, also, the pronunciation of a word or part of a word is fixed by adding to it the representation of an object in ordinary use, and with a well-known name; and in these cases the signs are always used in such a way as to prevent their being understood to refer to the meaning in place of the sound. The most apposite instance is perhaps in the name of the foreign god Set (introduced by the Shepherds into the Egyptian pantheon); the name is spelt with the phonetic signs for ST, and the figure of a block of stone (in Egyptian *Set*) is added to fix the pronunciation.

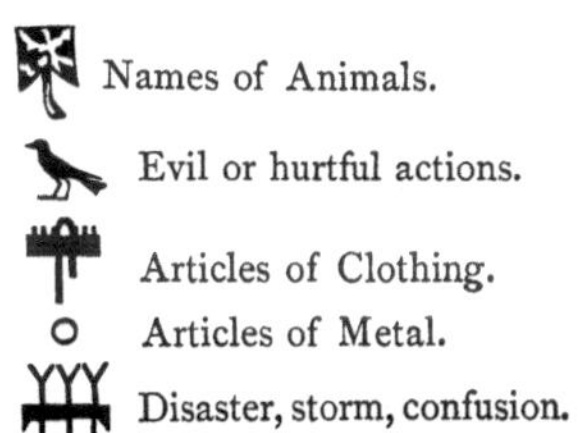

Names of Foreign Countries.

Names of Places in Egypt.

Encloses Royal Names.

Names of Enemies.

Objects in Wood.

Names of Animals.

Evil or hurtful actions.

Articles of Clothing.

Articles of Metal.

Disaster, storm, confusion.

5. Besides hieroglyphics, properly so called, the nature of which we have been endeavouring to explain, the Egyptians used a cursive character, called by the Greeks, though inappropriately, the Hieratic. The characters are abbreviated, and more or less altered hieroglyphics. In this character nearly all the books on papyrus that we now possess are written, as well as the records of accounts and contracts of the eighteenth and nineteenth dynasty. Lastly, in the seventh century B.C. (at any rate we do not know an earlier example), a still more abridged style came into use, named by the Greeks Demotic. Although no trace whatever of the primitive pictures can be recognised, this system of writing still contains the same mixture of phonetic and ideographic characters as the hieroglyphics.

SECTION VI.—LITERATURE AND SCIENCE.

1. THE productions of Egyptian literature were both numerous and celebrated; classical authors often speak of the books of Egypt. In the Ramesseum at Karnak, the hall of the library has been found, placed under the protection of Thoth, the god of science, and of the goddess

Saf, patroness of literature. Unfortunately we now possess but little of that rich literature, considered worthy of consultation by some of the greatest geniuses of the ancient Greeks; but from what we have as yet been able to discover and read of manuscripts on papyrus, we may form some idea of the variety of the subjects treated of in the Egyptian books.

2. The first rank belongs to religious books, and especially to the one of which we possess most copies—to that great sacred book, containing the complete explanation of the belief of the Egyptians as to the destiny of the soul after death, called by modern scholars the "Funereal Ritual," but in reality bearing the title of "The Book of the Manifestation to Light." A copy of this, more or less complete according to the fortune of the deceased, was deposited in the case of every mummy. The book was revised under the twenty-sixth dynasty, and then assumed its final definite form. But many parts of it are of the highest antiquity. Some chapters are spoken of as composed under King Hesepti, of the first dynasty, and others as dating from the reign of Menkera (fourth dynasty), and very many chapters of the Ritual are found on monuments long anterior to the invasion of the Shepherds.

The whole series of pilgrimages which the soul, separated from the body, was believed to accomplish in the various divisions of the lower regions, are related in this book; it also contains the hymns, prayers, and formula for all ceremonies relative to funerals and to the worship of the dead. The doctrine of the immortality of the soul forms the basis of it, although the idea of its personality, as distinct from the body, is not clearly defined.

The reader will no doubt be interested by a short analysis of a book holding so important a place in the literature of Egypt, and containing the principal philosophical opinions and religious doctrines of the Pharaonic civilisation.

3. The Funereal Ritual opens by a grand dialogue taking place at the very moment of death, when the soul separates from the body (Ch. i.). The deceased, addressing the deity of Hades, enumerates all his titles to his favour, and asks for admittance into his dominions. The chorus of glorified souls interposes, as in the Greek tragedy, and supports the prayer of the deceased. The priest on earth in his turn speaks, and implores also the divine clemency. Finally Osiris, the god of the lower regions, answers the deceased, "Fear nothing in making thy prayer to me for the immortality of thy soul, and that I may give permission for thee to pass the threshold." Reassured by the divine word, the soul of the deceased enters Kar-Neter, the land of the dead, and recommences his invocations.

After this grand commencement, which we have epitomised, come many short chapters (Ch. ii.—xiv.), much less important, relative also to the dead and to the preliminary ceremonies of his funeral. When at last the soul of the deceased has passed the gates of Kar-Neter (Ch. xv.), he penetrates into that subterranean region, and at his entry is dazzled by the glory of the sun, which he now for the first time sees in this lower hemisphere. He sings a hymn to the sun under the form of mixed litanies and invocations. After this hymn, a great vignette, representing the adoration and glorification of the sun in the heavens, on earth, and in hades, marks the end of the first part of the Ritual, serving as a sort of introduction. The second part traces the journeys and migrations of the soul in the lower region. "The Egyptians," says Horapollo, in his "Hieroglyphics," "call knowledge *sbo*, that is, 'food in plenty.'" This passage certainly contains an allusion to the religious ideas as to the destiny of the dead. Knowledge and food are, in fact, identified on every page of the Ritual. The knowledge of religious truths is the mysterious nourishment the soul must carry with it to sustain it in its journeys and trials. A soul not possessing this knowledge could never reach the end of its journey, and would be rejected at the tribunal of Osiris. It was therefore necessary, before commencing the journey, to be furnished with a stock of this divine provision. To this end is destined the long chapter at the commencement of the second part (Ch. xvii., "The Egyptian Faith"). It is accompanied by a large vignette, representing a series of the most sacred symbols of the Egyptian religion. The text contains a description of these symbols, with their mystical explanation. At the beginning of the chapter, the descriptions and explanations are sufficiently clear, but as it advances we get into a higher and more obscure region; at the end of the chapter we lose the clue almost entirely, and, as often happens in such cases, the explanation ends by being more obscure than the symbols and expressions explained.* Next come a series of prayers to be pronounced

* There is a remarkable peculiarity in this chapter, first pointed out by Baron Bunsen. The original text is, after every sentence, followed by a commentary, explanation, or gloss, prefaced in every case by a group of characters in red, meaning "The explanation is this," or "Let him explain it." From this necessarily arises, first, that the text had by a certain time become so unintelligible as to require an explanation; second, that the explanation itself had in its turn become unintelligible; and finally, that the text and gloss, equally obscure, had been jumbled together and written out as one continuous document. The enormous length of time indicated by these several steps can hardly be estimated, and we know that they had all occurred before the time of the eleventh dynasty, as the text of this seventeenth chapter is found on a coffin of that period exactly in the same state as in the Turin papyrus. See BUNSEN'S *Egypt*, 2nd ed., English translation, vol. v., pp. 89, 90; and Dr. BIRCH'S *Translation of the Ritual*, in the same book.—TR.

during the process of embalming, whilst the body was being rolled in its wrappers. These invocations are addressed to Thoth, the Egyptian Hermes, who, as among the Greeks, played the part of Psychopompe, or conductor of souls. They are of the highest interest, for in each allusion is made to the grand myth of Osiris and his contest with Typhon, of which Plutarch and Synesius have given us the most recent versions. The deceased, addressing the god, asks him to render to him again the service he once rendered on that solemn occasion to Osiris and his son Horus, "avenger of his father."

The body once wrapped in its coverings, and the soul well provided with a store of necessary knowledge, the deceased commences his journey. But he is still unable to move; he has not yet the use of his limbs; it is necessary to address the gods, who successively restore all the faculties he had during his life, so that he can stand upright, walk, speak, eat, and fight (Ch. xxi. to xxix.—" The reconstruction of the deceased"). Thus prepared, he starts; he holds his scarabæus over his heart as a passport, and thus passes the portal of Hades (Ch. xxx.).

From the first step, terrible obstacles present themselves in his way. Frightful monsters, servants of Typhon, crocodiles on land and in the water, serpents of all kinds, tortoises and other reptiles, assail the deceased and attempt to devour him. Then commences a series of combats (Ch. xxxi. to xli.). The deceased and the animals against which he contends, mutually address insulting speeches to each other, after the fashion of Homer's heroes. Finally, the "Osiris" (the name applied to all the deceased, as we shall explain in the succeeding paragraph) has conquered all his enemies; he has subdued the Typhonic monsters and forced a passage, and, elated by his victory, sings on the spot a song of triumph (Ch. xlii.), likening himself to all the gods, whose members are made those of his own body. "My hair is like that of Nu (the firmament); my face is like that of Ra (the sun); my eyes like those of Athor (the Egyptian Venus);" and so on for every part of his body. He has even the strength of Set, that is, of Typhon, for the strife between the good and evil principle is but in appearance; in reality they are one and the same, and equally receive the adorations of the initiated.

After such labours the deceased needs rest; he stays for a time to recruit his strength and to satisfy his hunger (Ch. xliii. to lvi.). He has escaped great dangers, and has not gone astray in the desert, where he would have died of hunger and thirst (Ch. li.—liii.). From the tree of life, the goddess Nu gives him refreshing waters, which invigorate him and enable him to recommence his journey in order to reach the first gate of heaven (Ch. lix.).

Then commences a dialogue between the deceased and the personification of the divine Light, who instructs him (Ch. lxiv.). This dialogue presents most remarkable resemblances to the dialogue, prefixed to the books given by the Alexandrian Greeks as translations of the ancient religious writings of Egypt, between Thoth and the Light, the latter explaining to Thoth the most sublime mysteries of Nature. This portion is certainly one of the best and grandest of the Ritual, and may almost be classed with the invocations to the sun at the close of the first part.

The deceased, having passed the gate, continues to advance, guided by this new Light, to whom he addresses his invocations (Ch. lxv. to lxxv.). He then enters on a series of transformations, more and more elevated, assuming the form of and identifying himself with the noblest divine symbols. He is changed successively into a hawk (Ch. lxxvii., lxxviii.), an angel or divine messenger (Ch. lxxix., lxxx.); into a lotus (Ch. lxxxi.); into the god Ptah (Ch. lxxxii.); into a heron (Ch. lxxxiii.); into a crane (Ch. lxxxiv.); into a human-headed bird (Ch. lxxxv.), the usual emblem of the soul; into a swallow (Ch. lxxxvi.); into a serpent (Ch. lxxxvii.); and into a crocodile (Ch. lxxxviii.).

Up to this time the soul of the deceased has been making its journeys alone; it has been merely a sort of εἴδωλον (*eidolon*), if we may be permitted to employ this untranslatable Greek phrase; that is, an image, a shade, with the appearance of that body now stretched on the bier. After these transformations the soul becomes re-united to its body, which is needed for the rest of the journey. It was on this account that careful embalming was so important; it was necessary that the soul should find the body perfect and well preserved. "Oh," cries the body, "that in the dwelling of the master of life I may be re-united to my glorified soul, do not order the guardians of heaven to destroy me, so as to send away my soul from my corpse, and hinder the eye of Horus, who is with thee, from preparing my way" (Ch. lxxxix.).

The deceased traverses the dwelling of Thoth, who gives him a book containing instructions for the rest of his way, and fresh lessons of the knowledge he is soon to require (Ch. xc.). He arrives on the banks of the subterranean river separating him from the Elysian Fields, but there a new danger awaits him. A false boatman, the envoy of the Typhonic powers, lays wait for him on his way, and endeavours by deceitful words to get him into his boat, so as to mislead him and take him to the east instead of to the west (Ch. xciii.), his true destination, and where he ought to land and rejoin the sun of the lower world. The deceased again escapes this new danger; he unmasks the perfidy of the false boatman, and drives him away, overwhelming him with reproaches. He at last meets the right boat to conduct him to his destination (Ch. xcvii., xcviii.). But before getting into it, it is necessary to ascertain if he is really capable of making the voyage, if he possesses a sufficient amount of the knowledge necessary to his safety. The divine boatman therefore makes him undergo an examination, a preliminary initiation, seemingly corresponding to the lesser Eleusinian mysteries. The deceased passes the examination, each part of the boat then seems successively to become animated, and to demand of him its name, and the mystical meaning of the name. *The stake for anchoring the boat.* Tell me my name! "The Lord of the earth in thy case" is thy name. *The rudder.* Tell me my name! "The enemy of Apis" is thy name. *The rope.* Tell me my name! "The hair with which Anubis binds up the folds of the wrappers" is thy name; and so on for twenty-three questions and answers (Ch. xcix.).

After having thus victoriously passed through this trial, the deceased embarks, traverses the subterranean river, and lands on the other bank, when he soon arrives at the Elysian Fields in the valley of Aoura or Balot (Aahlu or Bat), the position of which the ritual gives in these terms, "The valley of Balot (abundance), at the east of heaven, is 370 cubits long and 140 cubits broad. There is a crocodile lord of Balot in the east of that valley in his divine dwelling above the enclosure (Ch. cviii.). There is a serpent at the head of that valley thirty cubits long, his body six cubits round. In the south is the lake of sacred principles (Sharu); the north is formed by the lake of Primordial Matter (Rubu) (Ch. cix.). A large picture here shows us this valley (Ch. cx.), a real subterranean Egypt, intersected by canals, where we see the "Osiris" occupied in all the operations of agriculture; preparing the ground, sowing and reaping in the divine fields an ample provision of that bread of knowledge he is now to find more necessary than ever. He has, in fact, arrived at the end of his journey; he has before him only the last, but also the most terrible of all his trials.

Conducted by Anubis (Ch. cxiii. to cxxi.), he traverses the labyrinth, and by the aid of the clue, guiding them through its windings, at last penetrates to the judgment-hall where Osiris awaits him seated on his throne, and assisted by forty-two terrible assessors. There the decisive sentence is to be pronounced, either admitting the deceased to happiness, or excluding him for ever (Ch. cxxv.). Then commences a new interrogatory much more solemn than the former. The deceased is obliged to give proof of his knowledge; he must show that it is great enough to give him the right to be admitted to share the lot of glorified spirits. Each of the forty-two judges, bearing a mystical name, questions him in turn; he is obliged to tell each one his name, and what it means. Nor is this all; he is obliged to give an account of his whole life. This is certainly one of the most curious parts of the Funereal Ritual; Champollion called it the "Negative Confession;" it would perhaps be better described by the word "Apology." The deceased addresses successively each of his judges, and declares for his justification that he has not committed such and such a crime. We have therefore here all the laws of the Egyptian conscience.

"I have not blasphemed," says the deceased; "I have not stolen; I have not smitten men privily; I have not treated any person with cruelty; I have not stirred up trouble; I have not been idle; I have not been intoxicated; I have not made unjust commandments; I have shown no improper curiosity; I have not allowed my mouth to tell secrets; I have not wounded anyone; I have not put anyone in fear; I have not slandered anyone; I have not let envy gnaw my heart; I have spoken evil, neither of the king, nor my father; I have not falsely accused anyone; I have not withheld milk from the mouths of sucklings; I have not practised any shameful crime; I have not calumniated a slave to his master."

The deceased does not confine himself to denying any ill conduct; he speaks of the good he has done in his lifetime. "I have made to the gods the offerings that were their due. *I have given food to the hungry, drink to the thirsty, and clothes to the naked.*" We may well be astounded on reading these passages, at this high morality, superior to that of all other ancient people, that the Egyptians had been able to build up on such a foundation as that of their religion. Without doubt it was this clear insight into truth, this tenderness of conscience, which obtained for the Egyptians the reputation for wisdom, echoed even by Holy Scripture (1 Kings iv. 30; Acts vii. 27).

Besides these general precepts, the apology acquaints us with some police regulations for public order, raised by common interest in Egypt to the rank of conscientious duties. Thus the deceased denies ever having intercepted the irrigating canals, or having prevented the distribution of the waters of the river over the country; he declares that he has never damaged the stones for mooring vessels on the river. Crimes against religion also are mentioned; some seem very strange to us, especially when we find them classed with really moral faults. The deceased has never altered the prayers, nor interpolated them. He has never touched any of the sacred property, such as flocks and herds, or fished for the sacred fish in the lakes of the temples; he has not stolen offerings from the altar, nor defiled the sacred waters of the Nile.

The Osiris is now fully justified; his heart has been weighed in the balance with "truth," and not been found wanting; the forty-two assessors have pronounced that he possesses the necessary knowledge. The great Osiris pronounces his sentence, and Thoth, as recorder to the tribunal, having inscribed it in his book, the deceased at last enters into bliss.

Here commences the third part of the Ritual, more mystical and obscure than the others. We see the Osiris, henceforth identified with the sun, traversing with him, and as him, the various houses of heaven and the lake of fire, the source of all light. Afterwards the Ritual rises to a higher poetical flight, even contemplating the identification of the deceased with a symbolical figure comprising all the attributes of the deities of the Egyptian pantheon. This representation ends the work.*

4. Precisely the same doctrine, as in the Funereal Ritual, though in a much more abridged form, is found in the "Book of Transmigrations," a very short work sometimes deposited in sepulchres of not very remote antiquity.† We possess also some copies of a book consisting almost entirely of pictures with but little text, on the course of the sun in the lower world, and numerous fragments of collections of hymns, sometimes in the highest style of poetry.

All this knowledge of men and of the world, all these ideas of another life, had been communicated to the Egyptians, as the priests said, by

---

* In this translation the numbers of the chapters are given for convenience of reference from Dr. Birch's translation in Bunsen's "Egypt," Second Edition, vol. v.

It need hardly be pointed out that the origin of the belief in the doctrine of Metempsychosis is probably to be found in the chapters of the Ritual on the transformations of the soul (Ch. lxxvi. to lxxxviii.). This seems very clear (as M. Lenormant has pointed out) from the representation of the soul of the glutton changed into a pig, to be found in many vignettes.—See also "The Alabaster Sarcophagus of Oimenepthah (Seti), king of Egypt, drawn by Joseph Bonomi, and described by Samuel Sharpe." London, 1864.

Some passages in the "Ritual" also furnish a probable explanation of a passage in Herodotus, which has puzzled most commentators. In the rubric to Chapter i., it is said, "Let this book be known on earth; it is made in writing on the coffin. It is the Chapter by which he comes out every day as he wishes, and he goes to his house. He is not turned back. *Then are given to him food and drink, slices of flesh off the altar of the sun*," etc. (Dr. Birch's translation), and this is repeated with a slight variation in the rubric to Chap. lxxii. Herodotus (Book iii. 17, 18) says that Cambyses sent spies into Ethiopia charged especially to observe whether there was really in Ethiopia what was called the "table of the sun;" and this he describes (according to the accounts given to him) as "a meadow in the skirts of the city full of the boiled flesh of all manner of beasts, which the magistrates are careful to store with meat every night, and where, whoever likes, may come and eat during the day. The people of the land say that the earth itself brings forth the food." The same story is repeated by other classical writers, and many attempts have been made to explain it. Heeren ("African Nations," Chap. i., p. 333) supposes it to be a reference to the dumb trading very common on the African coast; but it seems very probable that the tale, as related by Herodotus, is derived from this altar of the sun, from which the "Osiris" was supplied with food in Hades.—Tr.

† Translated by Dr. Brugsch, *Sai an Sinsin, sive liber Metempsychosis*." Berlin, 1831.

Thoth, the first Hermes Trismegistus, or "thrice greatest," who wrote all these books by the order of the supreme God. The first Thoth was the celestial Hermes, or the personification of the divine intelligence. The second Hermes, who was only an imitation of the first, passed for the author of all the social institutions of Egypt. He it was who had organised the Egyptian nation, established religion, regulated the ceremonies of public worship, and taught men the sciences of astronomy, numbers, geometry, the use of weights and measures, language and writing, the fine arts, and, in short, all the arts of civilisation. This knowledge had been included in the sacred books to the number of forty-two, and the Egyptian priests, who had the custody of them, were obliged to know their contents wholly, or in part, according to the nature of their functions, and their rank in the hierarchy. It seems most probable that the Funereal Ritual was one of these Hermetic books. As Osiris was the prototype of kings, so Thoth, or Hermes, was the type of the priests, the minister of science and religion. He personified all discoveries made by the members of the sacerdotal class, of which he was at once the founder and the representative. Thoth, in fact, was the learned class itself; that is, according to Egyptian ideas, the personification of science.

5. We have already given an analysis of the epic poem of Pentaour, on the exploit of Ramses II. against the Khitas, and quoted a fragment of a chronicle of the expulsion of the Shepherds. We have also mentioned the existence at Turin of a papyrus, containing a complete list of the kings, with the duration of their reigns. History—sometimes in the form of a poem, sometimes in that of a chronicle, or chronological abstract—formed a great part of the literature of ancient Egypt. Unfortunately, we have but very few examples.

The Museum of Turin possesses a fragment of a geographical chart of the time of Seti I., containing the region of the Nubian gold mines. Other papyri, chiefly in the British Museum, contain collections of the letters of celebrated writers, preserved as models of style, and in more than one place interesting to the historian. We have also collections of literary exercises, analogous to the orations of the Greek or Latin rhetoricians. As a specimen of this style we quote a fragment on the fatigues of the profession of arms, written in the time of the great wars of the nineteenth dynasty, and arranged in parallel lines in Biblical style:—

"When you receive the verses I have written, may you find the work of the scribe agreeable.
I wish to depict to you the numberless troubles of an unfortunate officer of infantry.
While still quite a youth he is entirely shut up in a barrack,
A tight suit of armour encases his body, the peak of his helmet comes over his eyes;

The visor is over his eyebrows; so that his head is protected from wounds.
He is wrapped up like a papyrus roll, and can hardly move his limbs in fight.
Shall I tell you of his expeditions into Syria, his marches in far distant lands?
He is obliged to carry water on his shoulder, as an ass bears its burden;
His back is bent like that of a beast of burden, his back bone is bowed.
When he has quenched his thirst with a drink of bad water, he is obliged to mount guard for the night.
If he meets the enemy he is like a bird in a net, his limbs have no strength left.
When he returns to Egypt, he is like a piece of worm-eaten wood.
If he is too ill to stand, they put him on the back of an ass;
His baggage is plundered by robbers, and his servant deserts him."

What we should least expect to find among the literature of grave and solemn Egypt are works of pure imagination, romances. There are, however, some, and M. de Rougé has translated the more important of those as yet discovered by us. These romances are, however, all of an essentially religious character, for Pagan religions have invariably chosen to teach their doctrines in the form of stories or fables. We might quote many and very curious examples in the stories preserved by popular tradition down to our days, commencing with that of Cinderella, so admirably modernised by the pen of Perrault, and in its old form preserved by Lucian, one of the myths of Asiatic religions.

6. Scientific literature, if we may judge by what classical writers have said, was largely developed in Egypt. We have a few specimens.

Two treatises on medicine, one of which is preserved in the museum at Berlin,* give an idea of the very low state of this science in the Pharaonic civilisation. It consisted entirely in the employment of purely empirical prescriptions, often the strangest that can be imagined. There are, however, traces of a somewhat extensive acquaintance with symptoms, and a certain amount of knowledge of the anatomy of the human body; but the theories show most fantastic ideas on physiology.

A papyrus, recently acquired by the British Museum, contains a dozen theorems of a treatise on practical geometry, extending beyond the essential and elementary problems of plane trigonometry. The Egyptians had a really scientific knowledge of astronomy; from the remotest antiquity they used a year of 365 days, and in later times invented a very ingenious astronomical period, to make this vague year accord from time to time with the real fixed year of 365¼ days.† But

* See BRUGSCH, *Etudes sur un Papyrus Médical de Berlin*, Leipzig, 1853. CHABAS, *Mélanges Egyptologiques*, vol. i.

† See note to page 268.

they had not advanced beyond what a patient and attentive observation with the naked eye alone could achieve, insufficient even under the clearest sky to permit the precise moment of the occurrence of every phenomenon to be noted. Instruments they had none. Moreover, their method of designating the constellations was different from ours. It was only in the latter days of their history that they borrowed the zodiac from the Greeks; thus the interpretation of the astronomical monuments belonging to Pharaonic ages becomes exceedingly difficult, and only in a very few cases have the names of stars been identified with those known by us. Dr. Brugsch, however, has translated a catalogue of planetary observations, the precise date of which is unknown.

The Egyptians believed in astrology, and reckoned this fallacious superstition among the sciences. A papyrus in the British Museum has been found to contain fragments of an astrological calendar, compiled under the nineteenth dynasty, and containing for each day a list of things not to be done, because of the adverse influence of the stars.

SECTION VII.—RELIGION.

1. HERODOTUS,* when he visited Egypt, was struck with the extreme devotion of the people, and represents them as the most religious of mankind, and surpassing all other people in the reverence they pay the gods. Without speaking of those pompous sacred ceremonies, producing such an effect on strangers—of those magnificent fêtes where the naos, or ark of the deity, was carried in procession with their consecrated vessels, fêtes without number, a calendar of which was often inscribed on the porch of the temple—without recalling the vast sanctuaries, where bas-reliefs, paintings, and decorations covered the walls in profusion—everywhere on the banks of the Nile one was in the immediate presence of a religious sentiment. All Egypt bore the impress of religion; its writing was full of sacred symbols and of allusions to sacred myths, so that its use beyond the influence of Egyptian religion became, as it were, impossible. Literature and science were but branches of theology. The fine arts were only employed with a view to religion and the glorification of the gods or deified kings.

The prescriptions of religion were so multiplied, so constantly repeated, that it was not possible to exercise a profession to provide for one's subsistence, or to satisfy one's commonest wants without being constantly reminded of the laws laid down by the priests. Each province had its special gods, its peculiar rites, its sacred animals. It seems that the priestly element had presided even over the distribution

* HER. ii. 37.

of the country into nomes, and that these had originally been ecclesiastical districts.

2. The Christian religion has not feared to reveal itself to all, and in spite of the profundity of its doctrines, it is open to great and small, ignorant and learned; because, being eternal truth, it is addressed to the whole human race. But this was not the case with the false religions of antiquity. Whatever in them was most elevated and most philosophical, always remained hidden in the sanctuary, for the honour and profit of the priests and of a small number of initiated. In Egypt, as in all pagan countries, there were in reality two religions; one held by the people in general, consisting only of the outer form of the esoteric doctrine, and presenting an assemblage of the grossest superstitions; the other known only to those who had sounded the depths of religious science, containing some of the more elevated doctrines, and forming a sort of learned theology, having for its basis the great idea of the unity of God. Herodotus tells us that the Egyptians of Thebes recognised one only God, who had had no beginning, and would have no end. This statement of the father of history is confirmed by the reading of the sacred texts of ancient Egypt, where it is said of that God "that He is the sole generator in heaven and on earth, and that He has not been begotten . . . That He is the only living and true God, who was begotten by Himself . . . He who has existed from the beginning . . . who has made all things, and was not Himself made."

This sublime idea, the echo of a primitive revelation, has possibly been the secret of the construction of some of the most curious temples of Egypt. Thus at least might we be able to explain those great religious edifices of the primitive ages, without sculptured images, without idols, such as M. Mariette has discovered near the Pyramids. Unfortunately the idea was very early obscured and disfigured by the conceptions of the priests, as well as by the ignorance of the multitude. The personal idea of God was by degrees confounded with the various manifestations of His power; His attributes and qualities were personified in a host of secondary agents, distributed in a regular hierarchy, in agreement with the general organisation of the world, and the preservation of its inhabitants. Thus originated that polytheism which, in its varied and strange symbolism, finally embraced the entire creation.

3. The mind of the Egyptians was especially directed to speculations on the destiny of man in another life. Of this future state they fancied they saw symbols and images in a thousand natural phenomena, but it seemed to them especially represented by the daily course of the sun. The sun seemed to them, in the course he each day accomplished, to prefigure the transformations reserved for the human soul. For a

people ignorant of the true nature of the celestial bodies, such an idea was by no means strange. The sun, or as the Egyptians called it, Ra, passed alternately from his stay in darkness, or with the dead, to an existence in light, or with the living. His life-giving warmth produced and supported all existence. The sun, then, in the universe was the general progenitor and father; he was the cause of life, but had received his life from no one; self-existent, and therefore his own creator. This symbolism, once admitted, became by degrees more and more developed, and the imagination of the Egyptians sought in the succession of solar phenomena, an indication of the several phases of human existence. Each change in the course of the planet was regarded as corresponding with a different stage in that existence. Ra, moreover, was not considered solely as the celestial type of man, who was born, lived, and died to be born and live again: like other pagan nations the Egyptians considered him a deity, the supreme deity, because he was the greatest of all the heavenly bodies, and the source of all light and life. The theological ideas of the Egyptians did not stop at this; they subdivided him, so to speak, into several deities. Considered in his different positions, and under his different aspects, he became in each a different god with distinct name, attributes, and worship; in this feature the Egyptian agrees with almost every other mythology. Thus the sun during the night is Atum; when shining at midday, he is Ra; in his character of the producer and sustainer of life, he is Kheper. These were the three principal forms of the solar divinity, but they also imagined many others. As the night precedes the day, Atum was considered as born before Ra, and as having at first alone proceeded from the abyss, or chaos. These three manifestations of solar power were united into a divine triad, the prototype of a host of other triads composed of deities who personified the various relations of the sun with nature, and his different influences on cosmic phenomena.

4. Anthropomorphism, that is, the conception of gods under a human shape, obtained a place among these early Sabean ideas, and the Egyptians supposed that the generation of gods was produced in the same way as the generation of men. This is why they introduced into their theogony ideas on the respective parts of the sexes in this mysterious act of nature. Diodorus Siculus says that, in the opinion of the Egyptians, the father is the sole parent of the child, the mother merely supplies nourishment. This is the part assigned by their theogony to the female principle, personified at Thebes by the goddess Maut; at Sais by the goddess Neith, mother of the sun. This principle represented only purely inert matter—the lifeless mass in which generation took place.

Thus, to borrow the mystical language of the Egyptian priests, the mother of the gods was a creation of the god Num, or Chnuphis, a personification of the divine breath-animating matter, symbolised by the rain; for what happened to the sun was considered, in a more general and abstract sense, to have happened to the deity. Each of his acts was personified by a separate god, a new divine personage. Chnuphis is divinity, animating matter and giving it life; he is the first of the demiurgi, or secondary creators. We may see by this, that, in Egyptian doctrine, inert matter, the receptacle of life, identified with the female principle, was not co-eternal with the god, but created by his breath, as was Chaos in the narrative of Genesis, and the patriarchal tradition, of which we find here a distorted remembrance. The assimilation of the course of the sun with generation was thus complicated by a new symbolism. The lower hemisphere, where he descends on setting, was personified by the goddess Hathor. She was consequently considered as the mother of Ra, as having borne in her bosom the father of all beings, and her symbol was the cow. In later times the Greeks imagined that they had discovered in her their own Aphrodite. Worshipped as issuing from the divine cow, the sun took the name of Horus, and was represented as a child lifted above the waters on a lotus flower. At his entry into the world, he was received by the same cow, then deified under the name of Nub.

5. As in Egypt, navigation was the ordinary mode of locomotion—the Nile, as we have said, being the great artery of communication—it was in a boat that the sun was represented in his course, whether as the solar triad, or in the lower hemisphere, as the emblem of another life. This subterranean sun specially took the name of Osiris. There were given him as companions, and assessors, the twelve hours of the night, personified by so many gods, at the head of whom was placed Horus, that is, the rising sun himself; and the story went that this god had pierced with his dart the serpent Apophis, or Apap, the personification of the morning mists pierced and dispersed by the first rays of the sun. This contest of Osiris, or of Horus his son, with darkness, was very naturally connected with that of good with evil, a symbol found in all mythologies.

Thence arose a fable, very popular in Egypt, and alluded to by a great number of monuments; evil was personified by one particular god, Set, or Sutekh, called also sometimes Baal, who was the supreme god of neighbouring Asiatic nations, and in later times, that of the Shepherds. The Greek confounded him with their Typhon, and it was said that Osiris had fallen beneath his blows. Resuscitated by the prayers and invocations of Isis, his wife, who reunites the features of Maut, of Neith, and Hathor, this good god found an avenger in his son Horus. The death of Osiris, the grief of Isis, and the final defeat of Set, furnish an inexhaustible theme for legendary creations, resembling those of various Eastern religions, and specially the stories of Cybele and Atys, and Venus and Adonis.

6. When once the course of the sun was regarded as the type of existence in the lower world, the doctrine of another life needed only a reproduction of the same symbolism in order to establish it among the Egyptians. Man descends to the tomb only to rise again. After his resurrection he enters on a new life, in company with, or in the sun. The soul is immortal, like Ra, and accomplishes the same pilgrimages. Thus we see sometimes on a sarcophagus the soul figured by a human-headed hawk, holding in its claws the two ring-symbols of eternity, and beneath, as an emblem of the new life reserved for the deceased, the rising sun, assisted in his course by the goddesses Isis and Nephthys.

This explains why the solar period, symbolised by the bird *bennu* (the lapwing), called by the Greeks phœnix, represented the cycle of human life; the mysterious bird was supposed to accompany the soul during its course in the lower world. The deceased was to be resuscitated after this subterranean pilgrimage; the soul was to re-enter the body again, to give it movement and life, or, to use the language of the Egyptian mythology, the deceased was to arrive finally at the boat of the sun, to be received there by Ra—the Scarabæus god—and to shine with a brightness borrowed from him. The tombs and mummy cases abound with pictures showing the various scenes of this invisible life. One of the vignettes of the Funereal Ritual represents the mummy on its bier, the soul or human-headed hawk flying towards it, bearing the Crux Ansata, the emblem of life (Ch. lxxxix.).

This doctrine was perhaps imported from Asia into Egypt, and can be traced back to the most remote antiquity. It necessarily conduced to inspire great respect for the remains of the dead, as they were one day to be recalled to life, and was the origin of the custom of embalming. The Egyptians desired to preserve entire, and to protect from destruction, the body, since it was destined to enjoy a new and more perfect existence. They also imagined that the mummies, even when enclosed in wrappers, were not entirely deprived of life; and the Ritual (Ch. clxiii.) shows us that the deceased was supposed still to avail himself of his organs and members; but to ensure the preservation of vital heat, they had recourse to mystical formulæ pronounced at the time of the funeral, and to certain amulets which were placed on the mummy (Ch. clvi.—clxi.). In general, the greater part of the funereal ceremonies, the various wrappers of the mummies, the subjects painted on the interior or exterior of the coffins. have reference to the different phases of the resurrection, such as the cessation of the corpse-like rigidity, the reviving of the organs, the return of the soul.

7. Belief in the immortality of the soul is never separated from the

idea of a future recompense for deeds done in the body, and this is particularly to be observed in ancient Egypt. Although all bodies were to descend into the lower world, Kar-Neter, as it was called, they were not, however, all assured of resurrection. To obtain this it was necessary never to have committed any great sin, either in act or in thought, as is proved by the scene of the Psychostasy, or weighing of the soul, figured in the Funereal Ritual, and on many mummy coffins. The deceased was, as we have seen, to be judged by Osiris and his forty-two assessors; his heart was put into one of the scales of the balance held by Horus and Anubis, and weighed against the image of Justice; the god Thoth registered the result. On this judgment, delivered in the "Hall of Double Justice," depended the irrevocable lot of the soul. If the deceased was convicted of inexcusable faults, he became the prey of a terrible monster with a hippopotamus's head; he was decapitated by Horus, or by Smu, one of the forms of Set, on the *nemma*, or block, of Hades.

Annihilation was believed by the Egyptians to be the punishment reserved for the wicked. As for the righteous, purified from venial faults by means of a fire guarded by four genii with apes' faces, he entered "Pleroma," or perfect happiness, and as the companion of Osiris, the good being *par excellence* (Ounnofre), was fed by him with delicious food. In all cases the justified, because in his human nature he must necessarily have been a sinner, could not arrive at final beatitude without passing through many trials. The deceased, in descending into Kar-Neter, found himself compelled to pass fifteen gateways or porticos, guarded by genii, armed with swords (Ch. cxlvii.), whom he could pass only by proving his good deeds and his knowledge of divine things, that is his initiation. He was subjected to the severe trials we have recounted in our analysis of the Ritual; he had to sustain terrible combats with monsters and fantastic animals, and only triumphed by being furnished with sacramental formula and exorcisms, filling twelve chapters of the Ritual (Ch. xxxi.—xlii.). One of these creatures defeated by the soul at the gate was a real demon, the great serpent Refrof, or Apap, the enemy of the sun.

Amongst other singular means resorted to by the deceased to conjure these diabolical phantoms, was that of likening every one of his members to those of various gods, and thus, as it were, to invest his person with a sort of divinity (Ch. xlii.). The wicked, in his turn, before being annihilated, was compelled to undergo every sort of torture, and under the form of an evil spirit he returned to the world, to mislead men and lure them to ruin; he inhabited the bodies of unclean animals.

The sun, personified by Osiris, was, as we see, the foundation of the Egyptian Metempsychosis. From a god who gave and preserved life, he had become a retributive and saving god. They even came to consider Osiris as accompanying the deceased in his pilgrimage in Hades, as receiving the soul on its entrance into Kar-Neter, and guiding it to the eternal light. Himself the first raised from the dead, he assisted to raise those who were justified, after having aided them to overcome all their trials. The deceased, in the end, was even completely identified with Osiris, and so absorbed into his substance as to lose all individuality; his trials became those of the god himself, and thus from the moment of his death the deceased was called "The Osiris."

8. In this hasty sketch of the essential and fundamental doctrines of ancient Egypt we have noticed only the most prominent features, only the principal personages of the pantheon formed by the sub-division of the unity of the first principle—an idea always preserved in the sanctuaries, where combinations more or less ingenious were invented to reconcile this fact with polytheism. We cannot here enumerate the secondary personages of the Pharaonic pantheon, as from their number the list would be too long. In fact, these gods, who were originally only attributes and qualities of one sole absolute and eternal being, and who by degrees were invested with an individual and personal existence, might be indefinitely multiplied, and undoubtedly popular superstition did its best to do so. Often many of these personages proceeded from one single conception, and may be traced back to the same original. Frequently, when they are studied closely, their apparent differences disappear, and they may be identified one with another; and we may soon arrive at the conclusion that Egyptian mythology and all the tribe of its gods may be reduced to a very small number of elements, infinitely diversified in outward expression.

But in the popular and visible religion—in that presented by the outward ceremonies in the temples to the eyes of the people—all these divine beings were considered as absolutely distinct, and the people believed them to be so; the priests only and those whom they had instructed in the secrets of religion knew the true foundation of religious faith. Thus the Egyptian religion, although originally based on a distinct acknowledgment of the divine unity, a last relic of the primitive revelation, assumed the form of an unlimited polytheism, with strange, often monstrous, deities; and to the people, to the uninitiated, it was nothing else.

9. In the external and public worship the indefinitely multiplied deities were grouped into triads, or series of three, who represented to the people an image of the mystery of divine generation, a family comprising, like a human family, a father, mother, and son. These groups, these divine families, reproduced in a material and tangible form a mysterious and primitive doctrine, and were supposed to have given birth successively the one to the other, thus forming a continuous chain of emanations from the supreme deity, each link approaching

nearer the earth, and descending at last almost to the level of humanity.

Here policy had intervened, and very cleverly too, in the organisation of public worship. Each triad was worshipped in the sanctuary of one of the capital cities of the nomes, and no two cities worshipped the same triad. Now the rank held by the triad enshrined in the sanctuary in the scale of the divine emanations, was in direct relation with the political and administrative importance of the city. We can scarcely find even two or three exceptions to the rule, that when cities of great importance in very ancient times, and where a worship had been officially constituted, lost their old importance, the gods who were there worshipped lost also their rank in the divine hierarchy.

The supreme triad was that of Thebes, composed of Amen-Ra (Amen the Sun), who became officially the greatest god of Egypt, from the time that the twelfth dynasty established its native city as the capital of the country; Maut, the divine mother *par excellence;* and Chons, son of Amen, who was also a form of Amen himself, for in these groups of divinities the son is always identified with his father. Amen is, however, the most elevated, the most spiritual form of the deity presented by the Egyptian priests for the adoration of the crowds in the temples. He is the invisible and incomprehensible god, his name means "the hidden"; he is, in fact, the mysterious power who created, preserved, and governed the world. An invaluable passage in the Ritual distinctly represents him as the original and only first principle, the other divine personages being merely his attributes or emanations. "Amen-Ra," it is there said (Ch. xvii.), "is the creator of his members; they become the other gods who are associated with him."

The parent god in the triad of Memphis was Phtah, the second demiurgus, the personification of creative energy (but inferior in the scale of emanations to Chnuphis), lord of justice, and regulator of the worlds, believed in as the author of the visible universe; his attributes, however, show entire confusion between the creator and the created, between the author of order in the world and chaos. His wife was Pasht, the great goddess of Bubastis, sometimes with a lion's and sometimes a cat's head, considered to be the avenger of crimes, and also one of the forms of Maut. The sun was considered her son in the sanctuary of the old capital of the primitive dynasties.

Month, with the hawk's head, was the terrible and hostile form of the sun, when his rays strike like arrows and are sometimes fatal. He was specially worshipped at Hermonthis, with the goddess Ritho his wife, and their son Harphre (Horus, the sun), another example of the identity of the divine father and son.

But of all these triads, the one most closely related to humanity in external form and worship, although the conception, as we have seen, was one of the most exalted, was that of Osiris, Isis, and Horus, who were the object of universal worship in all parts of Egypt. They were said to be the issue of the god Set, the personification of the earth, and of the goddess Nut, the vault of heaven. Osiris, said the tradition, had manifested himself to men and had reigned in Egypt. The whole of the legend of his death from the violence of Set, of his resurrection, and of the vengeance taken by his son Horus on his enemies, was said to have taken place on earth; and every city on the banks of the Nile professed to have been the scene of one of the episodes of this great drama.

10. Symbolism was the very essence of the genius of the Egyptian nation, and of their religion. The abuse of that tendency produced the grossest and most monstrous perversion of the external and popular worship in the land of Mizraim. To symbolise the attributes, the qualities, and nature of the various deities of their Pantheon, the Egyptian priests had recourse to animals. The bull, the cow, the ram, the cat, the ape, crocodile, hippopotamus, hawk, ibis, scarabæus, and others, were each emblems of a divine personage. The god was represented under the figure of that animal, or more often by the strange conjunction peculiar to Egypt, of the head of the animal with a human body. But the inhabitants of the banks of the Nile, instinctively averse to the idolatry of other pagan nations, preferred to pay their worship to living representatives of their gods rather than to lifeless images of stone or metal, and they found these representatives in the animals chosen as emblems of the idea expressed by the conception of each god.

Hence arose that worship of sacred animals, which appeared so strange and ridiculous to the Greeks and Romans. Each of these animals was carefully tended during its life in the temple of the god to whom it was sacred, and after death its body was embalmed. Certain cities were peculiarly set apart for each species, for it must not be supposed that every animal of each sacred species was considered sacred. A few only were maintained at the expense of the state, and under the care of the greatest personages. Thus the sacred cats, after having been embalmed, were carried to Bubastis, the hawks to Buto, the ibis to Hermopolis. The same animals, moreover, were not held sacred in all provinces. The hippopotamus was only worshipped in the Papremis nome. The inhabitants of Thebes held crocodiles in great veneration; in other places they were hunted.

We repeat that in the original conception, and for those who understood the basis of their religion, these sacred animals were only the living representatives of the deities, but popular superstition made them into real gods; and the worship of these animals was, perhaps, that part of their religion to which the people were most invincibly attached.

"When," says Herodotus,* "a man has killed one of the sacred animals, if he did it with malice prepense, he is punished with death; if unwittingly, he has to pay such a fine as the priests choose to impose. When, however, an ibis or a hawk is killed, whether it was done by accident or on purpose, the man must needs die." A Roman soldier under the Ptolemies, who had accidentally killed a sacred cat, was put to death by the enraged mob, in spite of the king's interference and the terror of the name of Rome. It is said that Cambyses, when he invaded Egypt, caused a number of sacred animals to be ranged before his army, and that the Egyptians allowed themselves to be put to flight without resistance, for fear of injuring them.

11. There were, however, three of these sacred animals more venerated and more celebrated than any others, which, from the very commencement of their worship, were considered, by a most degrading conception, not merely as representatives but as incarnations of the deity. The worship of these had been established, it was said, by the King Kekeu, of the second dynasty—the bull Mnevis, worshipped at Heliopolis; the goat of Mendes, the incarnation of the god Khem, or Min, in whom was personified in the most brutish manner the reproductive power, and who then received the special name of Ba-n-ded, "the spirit of the region of stability," of which the Greeks have made Mendes; and lastly, the bull Apis, the incarnation of Phtah, whose worship held the first rank in the religion of Memphis. Apis was born of a cow, mysteriously impregnated by lightning descending from heaven. He was to be black, with a white triangle on his forehead, a mark like a half moon on the back, and a sort of lump or thickening of the skin, in the form of a scarabæus, under the tongue. When this god died, all Egypt was in mourning, and solemn lamentations were everywhere made. As soon as he was manifested anew, the Egyptians put on their richest clothes, and gave themselves up to the greatest rejoicings.† But the divine bull was not allowed to live more than a determined number of years, and at the end of that time, if he did not die a natural death, he was killed; still, however, they mourned for him.

The dead Apis was embalmed and deposited in the magnificent caves of the temple, called by the Greeks "the Serapeum," discovered by M. Mariette. He then became the object of a new worship. By the very fact of his death, he had become assimilated with Osiris, the god of the lower world, and received the name of Osir Hapi, converted by the Greeks into Serapis. Of only secondary importance under the Pharaohs, the worship of Apis, or Serapis, took a sudden development, and became of primary importance under the Ptolemies. Changing completely its nature and features, it became a mixed worship, made by

---

* HER. ii. 65. † Ibid. iii. 27, 28, 29.

the policy of the Lagides, the point of contact between the two nations, Greek and Egyptian.

12. Such, then, was in reality the religion of the Egyptian people, a strange and almost inextricably confused mixture of sublime truths (vestiges more or less obliterated of a primitive revelation) with metaphysical or cosmological ideas, often confused, always grandiose; a refined morality, an abject form of worship, and popular superstitions, coarse to the last degree. "If you enter a temple," says Clement of Alexandria, "a priest advances with a solemn air, singing a hymn in the Egyptian language; he raises the veil a little to let you see the god; and what then do you see? A cat, a crocodile, a snake, or some other noxious animal. The god of the Egyptians appears! . . . It is but a wild beast, wallowing on a purple carpet."

Section VIII.—Arts.

1. The Egyptians were, even before the time of the Greeks, that nation of antiquity who had carried the plastic arts to the highest degree of perfection and grandeur. The Greeks alone have been able to surpass them. The genius of the Egyptian people is completely depicted in the general character of their architecture. The sons of Mizraim, as we have just seen, firmly believed in the immortality of the soul, and attempted to ensure the immortality of matter, with the idea that the soul would one day re-enter the body. They regarded life in this world as only a prelude to a better life. Thus, while they took little pains with the houses of the living, they displayed extreme magnificence in the resting-places of the dead. A people thus convinced of a future life, a people who preserved corpses for 4,000 years, had therefore adopted in their architecture such dimensions as would ensure solidity, and almost endless duration. The immense size of the base was the distinguishing feature of their monuments. Walls, pillars, columns, everything, in fact, is short and thick in Egyptian buildings. And to add to the appearance of this indestructible solidity, the size of the base is augmented still more by a sloping method of construction, giving to all buildings a pyramidal tendency. The Pyramids themselves, those of Memphis, the largest of which is the loftiest building in the world, stand on an enormously large base; their height is much less striking than their breadth. Thus making their height, as well as that of all the Egyptian structures, even the most elevated, less striking in this respect than for the greatness of their breadth.

2. In relating in the preceding chapters the annals of Egypt, we have mentioned the chief epochs of its sculpture, and its essentially characteristic features; the first phase of development under the primitive dynas-

ties, entirely free, and attempting always an exact imitation of nature, the introduction of the hieratic and invariable canon of proportion about the time of the twelfth dynasty; the culminating point of the grand religious style, under the eighteenth and the beginning of the nineteenth; the absolute decadence commencing with the close of the reign of Ramses II.; and finally the last "renaissance" under the Saite kings.

Considered as a whole, and without reference to the differences between various epochs, Egyptian sculpture exhibits a peculiarly symbolical character, always recalling its original intention—to embody religious ideas and to be their visible representative. Its birth-place was the Temple. There it is at first found in the condition of merely outline drawing. Next, the drawing is cut into the wall, or stands out in relief. Afterwards it is almost, but not quite, detached from the wall, and when finally the statue is completely isolated,—though this is very seldom the case, for it almost always has a pilaster at its back,—it bears unmistakable traces of its original architectural origin, and the symbolical purpose for which it was made. If we look at an Egyptian statue its lines are invariably marked by conciseness or brevity, not without finish, but without detail. The lines are straight and broad; the attitude is stiff, imposing, and fixed; the legs are generally parallel and joined; the feet touch, or rather stand one before the other in the same direction, and are also exactly parallel; the arms hang down by the sides, or are crossed over the breast, unless they are detached sufficiently to hold some attribute, a sceptre, crux ansata, or a lotus flower: but in this solemn and cabalistic pantomime, the figure makes signs rather than gestures; it is in position rather than in action; for whatever movement the statue seems about to make will be its last, and followed by no other.

Egyptian art seems in some respects to have remained in perpetual infancy; it is an art essentially grand, majestic, governed by the severest rules. It is majestic and grand from the very absence of detail; an absence voluntary and predetermined. Whether in bas-relief or in the round, the Egyptian statues are modelled, not rudely, but concisely; they are not cut out merely as a rough draught, but, on the contrary, admirably designed with studied simplicity in their lines and design, an elegant delicacy in their form, or rather, mathematical formula.

Two things are evident and plainly intentional, the sacrifice of the small parts to the large, and the non-imitation of real life. The nude figure is seen as through a veil; the drapery of clothed figures sticks to them like a second skin, so that the naked figure can be seen when the statue is clothed, and seems clothed even when nude. The muscles, veins, folds and contractions of the skin are not rendered, not even the bony framework. The variety that distinguishes living beings, the essence of nature is replaced by a religious and sacerdotal symmetry, replete with skill and majesty.

All groups of more than one figure are arranged on a parallelism of double members, and seem to obey a certain mysterious rhythm regulated by the sanctuary. The surest mode of expression in Egyptian art was, in fact, repetition. However natural and graceful a movement may be, it becomes formal when repeated intentionally and in an identical manner, as we see so often in the sculptures of ancient Egypt. This persistent repetition, making every walk a procession, every movement a religious symbol, every gesture a sacred cadence, becomes sublime.

The Egyptian style is therefore monumental in conciseness of expression, the austerity of its lines, and their resemblance to the vertical and horizontal lines of architecture. It is imposing, because it is a pure creation of the mind; it is colossal even in the smallest examples, because it is supernatural and superhuman. It always presents the same recognisable character, because it represents an invariable faith. Lastly, Egyptian style is the result of a principle quite apart from imitation, it has voluntarily discarded all attempt at imitative truth; for the faculty of copying nature faithfully was as strong among the Egyptians as among the Greeks, as is proved by the faithfulness of some of their copies of animals compared with their conventional and artificial expressions of the human figure, as well as by contrasting the works of the primitive schools of art, with productions after the reign of the twelfth dynasty and the establishment of the priestly canon of the proportions of the human body.

In modelling the human head, the Egyptian sculptor was more faithful in his imitation than in the human body, and showed how strong would have been his power of imitation, if art had remained free. With what power is the physiognomy of the various races expressed whom the artists wished to represent! No other people have in their works of art so closely adhered to ethnographical truth.

Is there any further need to insist on the tendency to symbolism prevailing in all Egyptian sculpture to such an extent that we find figures with the monstrous combination of human bodies and the heads of animals? "In exhibiting to us," Raoul Rochette has well said, "a man's body with a lion's, a crocodile's or jackal's head, the Egyptians certainly never intended us to believe in the existence of such a being; it was the embodiment of an idea they wished to exhibit rather than a representation of any real thing. The mixture of the two natures was employed to make it plain that this human body supporting an animal's head was a written thought, a personified idea, but never intended to pass for any real being."

Thus, we may say, that Egyptian sculpture was one form of their writing, an essentially symbolical art, and this was one reason why it could not progress. Symbolism was for this great school of art, what the aromatic spices were to the embalmed dead; it made it a mummy, but in so doing rendered it everlasting.

3. Painting was hardly ever used by the Egyptians except for decoration, to accompany and set off architecture and sculpture; all buildings and statues were coloured. Nevertheless some small wooden steles have been found on which the subjects are merely painted, often with great delicacy and in admirable style; and even some tombs, where the nature of the rock did not admit of the execution of finished sculpture, have had the internal walls covered with plaster and painted. This painting, however, is entirely sculptural in its character, and executed quite in the style of a bas-relief. The papyrus manuscripts of the Funereal Ritual frequently present vignettes designed with the pen with wonderful freedom, firmness and boldness, and sometimes with a purity of outline recalling the decorations of Greek vases.

Section IX.—Principal Monuments.

1. The Pyramids. The most imposing monuments of Egypt, from their size, and the most curious from their antiquity, are undoubtedly the pyramids of Gizeh. We have already mentioned the enormous amount of labour required for their construction; but we may be able perhaps to form a more precise idea when we know that the largest—the pyramid of Khufu (Cheops)—is formed of more than 200 steps or layers of enormous blocks. When entire it was 480 feet high, nearly double the elevation of the towers of the cathedral of Notre Dame at Paris; its base measured 756 feet, and it was composed of the truly astonishing mass of more than ten millions of cubic yards of stone material, sufficient to build a wall six feet high, a foot thick, and nearly 3,000 miles long. To relieve the enormous weight that the chamber intended for the royal sarcophagus had to support, open spaces have been left in the mass of the monument above it, forming five small chambers. A second sepulchral chamber is situated almost exactly below the first, and a third at a great depth below, excavated in the rock and forming no part of the building. The orientation of this gigantic monument is perfect, its four sides exactly facing the four cardinal points.

The arrangement of the other two pyramids is similar, with the exception that their masonry is solid, and the chambers they cover are cut in the rock. The second is not so high as the first, and the difference is rendered more apparent from the height of the rocky platform on which the first stands; its construction is also far from equalling in beauty that of the first. It was built to receive the body of Shafra

(Chefren), and is the only one still retaining a part of its original outer casing. The third pyramid is not more than a third of the height of the first, but was more highly ornamented; in it was found the wooden coffin of the king Menkera (Mycerinus), by whom it was built. The chamber where it was found, was entirely faced with granite. Now, to find that stone, it is necessary to go up the Nile as far as the first cataract, and thence it must have been brought in boats. This pyramid had also an exterior casing of granite from Syene, but less ancient, it seems, than the pyramid itself, and added by the queen Net-aker (Nitocris) of the sixth dynasty.

The colossal Sphinx at the foot of the Great Pyramids, to which it is subsidiary, is a monument completed if not commenced under the reign of Shafra. It is nearly ninety feet in length and about seventy-four feet high. The face measures twenty-six feet from the chin to the top. It is carved out of the rock it rests on; the stratification of the rock has divided the face into horizontal bands. Advantage has been taken of one of these divisions to form the mouth. The great Sphinx was the image of the god Har-ma-chu, the setting sun, a deity of an essentially funereal character; between its two front paws was placed a small sanctuary, consecrated to that deity, reconstructed by Thothmes III. "This huge, mutilated figure," says Ampère, "has an astonishing effect; it seems like an eternal spectre. The stone phantom seems attentive; one would say that it hears and sees. Its great ear appears to collect the sounds of the past; its eyes, directed to the east, gaze as it were into the future; its aspect has a depth, a truth of expression, irresistibly fascinating to the spectator. In this figure, half statue, half mountain, we see a wonderful majesty, a grand serenity, and even a sort of sweetness of expression."

Besides Gizeh, many other localities, at various distances from Memphis, possess pyramids, though smaller. Altogether sixty-seven have been found, and, in fact, sepulchres of this kind were in use until the time of the twelfth dynasty. At Gizeh there are nine in all. We find important groups of them at Zauiet-el-Arrian, and at Abousir, S.S.E. of Gizeh; one in the latter place bears the names of three kings of the fifth dynasty, who were buried there. At Sakkarah there are also several pyramids, the largest, built in stages, is, as we have already said, the oldest monument in Egypt, for it appears to have been the tomb ot king Kekeu of the second dynasty; another had apparently a very large platform on the summit, and was the tomb of king Unas, of the fifth dynasty; its ruins are now called by the Arabs, Mastabat-el-Faraoun. Lastly, the village of Dashur has five of these monuments, the largest 326 feet high; one of these pyramids is of sun-dried brick, and was the tomb of Osortasen III. (thirteenth dynasty); it has in front of it a small temple, where the worship of the deceased king was conducted.

2. THE LABYRINTH. The Labyrinth, founded, as Manetho tells us, by a king of the twelfth dynasty, Amen-emhe III., but possibly completed or repaired after the departure of the Ethiopians, had, if we believe the testimony of Herodotus, attracted the attention and excited the surprise of Greek travellers almost as much as the Pyramids. Herodotus (ii. 148) even considers it superior, and describes it as formed of "twelve courts, all of them roofed, with gates exactly opposite one another, six looking to the north, and six to the south. A single wall surrounded the entire building. There are two different sorts of chambers throughout, half under ground, half above ground, the latter built up on the former; the whole number of these chambers is 3,000, 1,500 of each kind. He adds that he has seen only the first, as the priests were unwilling to take him into the subterranean chambers containing, as they said, the sepulchres of the kings who built the labyrinth, and those of the sacred crocodiles, "the passages through the houses and the varied windings of the paths across the courts," says he again, "excited in me infinite admiration, as I passed from the courts into chambers, and from the chambers into colonnades, and from the colonnades into fresh houses, and again from these into courts unseen before. The roof was throughout of stone, like the walls, and the walls were carved all over with figures. Every court was surrounded with a colonnade, which was built of white stones exquisitely fitted together. At the corner of the Labyrinth stands a pyramid forty fathoms high, with large hieroglyphics engraven on it, entered by a subterranean passage."

Twenty-three centuries after Herodotus, on the 25th June, 1843, M. Lepsius wrote from the ruins of the same monument*—"These lines are written from the distinctly recognised Labyrinth of Mœris and of the Dodecarchy, not from the doubtful spot whose identity is still contested, of which I myself was unable to form any conception rom the hitherto more than deficient descriptions even of those who have removed the labyrinth hither. An immense cluster of chambers still remains, and in the centre lies the great square, where the courts once stood, covered with the remains of large monolithic granite columns, and of others of hard white limestone, shining almost like marble. . . . At the first superficial survey of the ground a number of complicated spaces, of true labyrinthine forms, immediately presented themselves, both above and below ground. . . . We literally find at once hundreds of them, as well next to as above one another, small, often diminutive ones, besides greater ones; and large ones, supported by small columns, with thresholds and niches in the walls, with remains of columns and single casing stones, connected by corridors, without

---

* *Letters from Egypt* (Eng. Trans., Bohn), pp. 89, 90.

any regularity in the entrances and exits, so that the descriptions of Herodotus and Strabo in this respect are fully justified. . . . The whole is so arranged that three immense masses of buildings, 300 feet broad, enclose a rectangular place, which is 600 feet long and 500 feet wide. The fourth side, one of the narrow ones, is bounded by the pyramid, which lies behind it; it is 300 feet square. . . . But the chambers lying on the farther side, especially their southern point, where the walls rise nearly ten feet above the rubbish, and about twenty feet above the base of the ruins, are to be seen very well, even from this, the eastern side; and viewed from the summit of the pyramid, the regular plan of the whole design lies before one as on a map." The learned traveller found the name of the builder, Amen-emhe III., inscribed in several places on the monument.

3. Funereal Grottoes.—"The Egyptians," says Diodorus Siculus, "called the dwellings of the living, lodgings, because they were only occupied for a short time; the tombs, on the contrary, they called 'eternal houses,' because their occupants never left them. This is why they took so little pains to decorate their houses, whilst they neglected nothing that could enhance the splendour of their tombs." We cannot here enumerate and describe the innumerable private rock-tombs, all decorated with sculpture, to be met with throughout the entire length of the Nile valley. The most remarkable are those of the neighbourhood of Memphis (Gizeh and Sakkarah), those of Beni Hassan in Central Egypt, and those of Gurnah, the principal necropolis of Thebes. But we must at least give a short account of the celebrated royal tombs of Thebes, described by every antiquarian traveller who has visited Egypt. These subterranean constructions are almost as astonishing as the magnificent edifices near them. The most ancient of the Theban tombs belong to the eleventh dynasty; they are those of the Entefs, discovered near the village of Drah abu'l Neygah.

At the period these tombs were constructed, the sarcophagus alone was ornamented. The kings of the twelfth dynasty, although Theban by origin, appear to have been buried at Fayum, and in the neighbourhood of Memphis, under the Pyramids. The period of decline, and even disaster, following this has left no great monuments. We know no sepulchres, either of the Sevek-hoteps nor yet of any of the Theban princes, who contended with the Shepherds. At Drah abu'l Neygah has been discovered that of Queen Aah-hotep, mother of Ahmes. The sepulchres of the valley of Assassif belong to the eighteenth dynasty, where Amen-hotep III. and Ai, one of the usurpers towards the close of this period, were buried. It is not, however, to the time of the eighteenth dynasty, but to the age of the Ramses of the nineteenth and twentieth, that the most magnificent of the royal sepulchres of Thebes belong, those of Biban-el-Moluk, called by the

Greeks the Syringes, and reckoned by them among the wonders of Egypt.

The tomb of Ramses V. is most remarkable, for the long series of sculptures or paintings adorning a succession of halls or galleries, excavated in the side of the mountain, and forming the approach to the Sarcophagus Hall. They are mythological and astronomical scenes, representing the sun's course, and the rewards or punishments to be awarded to the soul in a future life. The Sarcophagus Hall, described in great detail in the letters of Champollion, shows us the course of the sun, and the walls are covered with thousands of hieroglyphics. Among the sixteen tombs of the valley of Biban-el-Moluk, a part only have their decorations completed throughout their whole extent, and these belong to princes who had a long reign, for the construction of the royal sepulchre was begun at the commencement of the reign, and, more or less, was accomplished according to the length of time that the king occupied the throne. When once the corpse was deposited in the sepulchre, the door was closed, to be re-opened no more.

Among the best furnished and most curious sepulchres we may reckon those of Seti I. and Ramses III. In the first are represented the various human races according to Egyptian ideas; the sculptures of the second represent (as do those of the primitive ages) incidents in private life; but there is also a symbolical picture of the Egyptian year, represented by six figures of the Nile and six of Egypt personified, each bearing productions peculiar to the division of the year they were intended to represent. We know that the waters of the Nile determined in Egypt the succession of the agricultural seasons.

4. Temples and Palaces.—The division of the French army commanded by General Desaix, hastening into Upper Egypt in pursuit of Mourad Bey and his Mamelukes—in want of everything, without food, fainting with the heat—no sooner got the first sight of the ruins of Thebes than they forgot at once their fatigue, their sufferings, and the proximity of the enemy, and seized with enthusiasm, unanimously began to clap their hands. Thebes, in spite of all the disasters which have successively for so many ages fallen on this sacred city of Amen—in spite of all the ravages of time and of the barbarians—still presents the grandest, the most prodigious assemblage of buildings ever erected by the hand of man.

At Karnak, first, in the north-east part of the ancient city, and on the right bank of the Nile, is found a series of buildings erected by the labours of nearly all the dynasties from Osortasen I. to Ptolemy, father of the famous Cleopatra. The description of this immense assemblage of buildings would alone require an entire volume. To give an idea of its extent, it is enough to say that the sacred enclosure at Karnak is 1,170 feet long, without measuring the avenues of sphinxes, extending in front of the outer portico, or the second temple, built in the same direction by Ramses II., but behind the back wall of the first, so that the total length is about 2000 feet. There is found that Hall of Columns of Seti I., of which no words can convey a just conception.

"Imagination," says Champollion, "that, in Europe, may well conceive something superior to our porticoes, sinks abashed before the 140 columns of the Hall of Karnak. . . . I shall be careful to describe nothing, for my expressions cannot convey the thousandth part of what ought to be said in speaking of such objects, or rather, were I to attempt a feeble sketch, far from highly colored, I should pass for an enthusiast, and perhaps for a fool." "Imagine," says also Ampère, "a forest of towers; represent to yourself 140 columns as large as that of the Place Vendôme, the highest seventy feet high (as tall as the obelisk of the Place de la Concorde), and eleven feet in diameter, covered with bas-reliefs and hieroglyphics, the capitals sixty-five feet in circumference; a hall 319 feet long and 150 wide—this hall entirely roofed over, and one of the windows it was lighted by still to be seen." "It is impossible," writes also M. Lepsius, "to describe the overwhelming impression experienced upon entering for the first time this forest of columns, and wandering from one range to the other, between the lofty figures of gods and kings on every side represented on them, projecting sometimes entirely, sometimes only, in part. Every surface is covered with various sculptures, now in relief, now sunk, which, however, were only completed by the successors of the builder (Seti), most of them, indeed, by his son, Ramses Miamun." *

A series of colonnades of colossal rams of granite, forming avenues, and of paved roads, connect the buildings of Karnak with those of Luxor. Here again we meet with an assemblage of monuments of various dates, to which each generation has contributed a stone. The most ancient part, the principal temple, is the work of Amen-hotep III.; to the north of this principal temple a gallery of columns leads to another built by Ramses II., and still covering an area of 4,000 yards. It is in front of the court before this temple that Ramses set up two obelisks; one of them now ornaments the Place de la Concorde at Paris.

On the left bank of the Nile, not far from the village of Gurnah, is found a building every part of which recalls Ramses II. and his family; and therefore called by Champollion "the Ramesseum." It is quite clear that it was the palace of that prince. It is composed of a suite of courts surrounded by, or filled with, columns, covered with hieroglyphic inscriptions, recounting the exploits of the king. A granite colossus,

* *Letters from Egypt* (English translation, Bohn), p. 249.

fifty-five feet high, represents Ramses seated on his throne. This is the largest ruin of a statue that has ever been known; the foot alone is more than thirteen feet long.

Of the Palace of Amenhotep III., very near this, nothing remains but shapeless masses of ruins, and the famous colossal statues, called by the Greeks "Memnon." At Gurnah itself are the ruins of another important edifice, commenced during the minority of Thothmes III., and continued by Seti and his son. Lastly, a little further south we meet with the immense and magnificent palace of Medinet Abu. We have already had occasion to speak of this building, when referring to the historical tablets found there, relating the chief events of the reign of Ramses III.

The ruins of Thebes are the most extensive and majestic in the whole of Egypt. We have therefore spoken of them at some length. But we must not imagine they are the only ones existing on the banks of the Nile. Numerous other localities—Philæ, Ombos, Edfu, Esneh, Hermonthis, Denderah—possess splendid temples; some remain in their original condition, but the greater number were reconstructed under the Ptolemies in conformity with the traditions of the Pharaonic age. At Abydos the excavations of M. Mariette have brought to light one of the largest and most beautiful temples of the best period of Egyptian art, a temple dating from the reign of Seti I.; it measures 486 feet in length. The ruins of the sanctuary of Sutekh, at Tanis, the work of Ramses II., of Merenphtah, and of Seti II., have been discovered by the same learned explorer; and eleven obelisks, numerous monolithic granite columns, and colossal steles taken from the ruins, prove that this building may be ranked almost with the erections of the same epoch at Thebes.

No monument of Memphis still exists standing: any remains there may be are hidden under ground. One only of the temples of this great city has been disinterred—the Serapeum, discovered by M. Mariette. It contains in its enclosure the sepulchres of the Bulls Apis, from the time of the nineteenth dynasty to that of the Roman supremacy.

Before closing this chapter, we must lastly notice in a few words the numerous buildings of the Pharaonic age to be found on the banks of the Nile in Nubia, between the first and second cataracts, and especially the prodigious subterranean temple of Ipsambul, with historical and religious sculptures covering its walls, and its façade ornamented by four colossal statues of Ramses II., seated, each sixty-five feet high, and carved out of the rock. "These more than gigantic masses," says Charles Lenormant, "are treated in a manner rather grand than finished, with the exception of the heads, and nothing can be seen for truth, life and modelling, more perfect than these. Winckelman has laid down no other rules for that calm beauty regarded by him as the highest aim of art. The Ludovisi Juno, one-fourth of their size, does not excel them in the expression of the whole, or in the harmony of combination of so many parts. Give but movement to these rocks, and Greek art would be surpassed."

Additional Note to Page 239.

With reference to the possible connection of the Hebrews with the religious revolution under Amenhotep IV. or Chu-en-Aten, it may be observed that there is mention in 1 Chron. iv. 18 of "Bithiah, the daughter of Pharaoh, which Mered took"; and this name, Bithiah, seems to be particularly contrasted with Jehudijah (the Jewess), Mered's other wife.

The passage seems to have excited the attention of some Rabbinical and early Christian writers, and various speculations have been made as to who both *Mered* and *Bithiah* were, the general opinion being that Bithiah (daughter of Jehovah) must have been a proselyte.

The genealogy in 1 Chron. iv. is so fragmentary and confused that it is difficult to determine the exact date of Mered; it seems, however, that he must have lived before the Exodus.

The question will naturally occur. Under what circumstances could a Hebrew, even a Prince of the House of Judah, before the Exodus, have married a daughter of Pharaoh?

Is it not possible that this circumstance may point to the connection of the Hebrews with the reforms of Chu-en-Aten. May not Mered (Rebel) have taken a leading part in the revolution and been the husband of one of that king's many daughters?

It may be observed that as "Aten," or "Aten-ra" (the sun's disc) was, at this period, used as the symbol of one supreme deity, the title Su-t-ra or Su-t-aten, a name not unlikely to have been given to one of the daughters of Chu-en-Aten, might very naturally have been transcribed into Hebrew as Bithiah.

It is possible that future researches may throw some light on this point, which is not without interest as belonging to a very obscure period of the history of the Hebrews.—TR.

END OF BOOK III.

BOOK IV.

THE ASSYRIANS AND BABYLONIANS.

CHAPTER I.

THE PRIMITIVE CHALDÆAN EMPIRE.

Chief Authorities.

Classical Writers:—The fragments of *Berosus*, in Vol. II. of *Fragmenta Historicorum Græcorum.* Didot.—Herodotus, Book I.—Diodorus Siculus, Book II.—Eusebius, *Chronicles*, Book I., Chap. xiv., xv.—The *Canon of the Kings of Babylon* of Ptolemy.

Collections of Assyrian Monuments:—Botta, *Monuments de Ninive*, Paris, five Vols.—Layard, *Monuments of Nineveh*, London, 1851; *Monuments of Nineveh*, 2nd Series, London, 1853; *Nineveh and its Remains*, London, 1851; *Discoveries in the Ruins of Nineveh and Babylon, with Travels in Armenia, Kurdistan, and the Desert*, London, 1853.—Loftus, *Travels in Chaldæa and Susiana*, London, 1856.—Victor Place, *Ninive et l'Assyrie*, Paris (in course of publication).

Collections of Cuneiform Texts:—Botta, *Inscriptions de Khorsabad*, Paris, 1848.—Layard, *Inscriptions in the Cuneiform Character from Assyrian Monuments*, London, 1851.—Rawlinson and Norris, *Cuneiform Inscriptions of Western Asia*, London, 1861 and 1866.

Works of Modern Scholars on the Decipherment of the Writing and the Language:—Botta, *Mémoire sur l'Ecriture Cunéiforme Assyrienne*, Paris, 1849.—De Saulcy, *Recherches sur l'Ecriture Cunéiforme Assyrienne*, Paris, 1849.—Hincks, *On the Khorsabad Inscriptions*, Dublin, 1850; *On the Assyro-Babylonian Phonetic Characters*, Dublin, 1852; *On the Personal Pronouns of the Assyrian and other Languages*, Dublin, 1854; "On the Assyrian Verb" in the *Journal of Sacred Literature*, July, 1855: as well as a large number of dissertations published in the *Memoirs of the Royal Irish Academy*, in the *Transactions of the Royal Society of Literature*, and in the *Journal of the Royal Asiatic Society.*—Rawlinson, *On the Inscriptions of Assyria and Babylonia*, London, 1851; *Babylonian Translation of the Great Persian Inscription at Behistun*, London, 1851.—Oppert, *Etudes Assyriennes, Inscription de Borsippa*, Paris, 1857; *Expédition en Mésopotamie*, vol. ii.; *Eléments de la Grammaire Assyrienne*, Paris, 1860; *Commentaire de la Grande Inscription du Palais de Khorsabad*, Paris, 1865.—Menant, *Les Ecritures Cunéiformes*, 2nd ed., Paris, 1864; *Exposé des Eléments de la Grammaire Assyrienne*, Paris, 1868.—Norris, *Assyrian Dictionary*, London (in course of publication).

Works of Modern Scholars on History:—De Saulcy, *Mémoire sur la Chronologie des Empires de Ninive, de Babylone, et d'Ecbatane*, Paris,

1849.—Guigniaut, Article "Chaldée" in the *Encyclopédie Moderne.*—Heeren, *Politique et Commerce des Peuples de l'Antiquité*, French trans., vol. ii.—George Rawlinson, *The Five great Monarchies of the Ancient Eastern World*, London, 1862—1868.—Sir H. Rawlinson, *Note on the Early History of Babylonia*, London, 1856; *On the Orthography of some of the late Royal Names of Assyrian and Babylonian History*, London, 1856; and numerous Articles in the *Athenæum* and in the *Journal of the Royal Asiatic Society.* "Inscription of Tiglath Pileser I., king of Assyria," as translated by Sir H. Rawlinson, Fox Talbot, Esq., Dr. Hincks, and Dr. Oppert, London, 1857.—Oppert, *Rapport au Ministre de l'Instruction Publique*, Paris, 1857; *Expédition en Mésopotamie*, vol. i.; *Les Inscriptions des Sargonides*, Paris, 1862; *Histoire des Empires de Chaldée et d'Assyrie, d'après les Monuments*, Paris, 1865; Articles "Babylone" and "Babyloniens" in the 2nd edit. of the *Encyclopédie du XIXe Siècle; La Chronologie Biblique fixée par les Eclipses des Inscriptions Cunéiformes*, Paris, 1868.—Oppert and Ménant, *Les Fastes de Sargon*, Paris, 1865.—Ménant, *Les Briques de Babylone*, Caen, 1859; *Inscriptions de Hammourabi Roi de Babylone*, Paris, 1863.—Brandis, *Ueber den Historischen Gewinn aus der Entzifferung der Assyrischen Inschriften*, Berlin, 1856.—F. Lenormant, *Essai sur un Monument Mathématique Chaldéen, et sur le Système Métrique de Babylone*, Paris, 1868.

SECTION I.—THE TIGRO-EUPHRATES BASIN.

1. THE immense deserts extending from west to east across the entire eastern hemisphere of the globe, from the Atlantic Ocean to the Yellow Sea, intersected first, on the frontier of Asia and Africa, by the valley of the Nile, are again broken near their centre by a second oasis, larger and not less fertile than that of Egypt, in the exact place where the desert changes its geological character, and from a low plain becomes an elevated plateau. To the west of this fortunate spot, the solitudes of Asia and Africa are mere seas of sand, scarcely above, even where not below, the level of the ocean. To the east, on the contrary, in Persia, Kirman, Seistan, Chinese Tartary, and Mongolia, the desert consists of a series of terraced plateaux, from 3,000 to 10,000 feet above the sea level. The two great rivers, Tigris and Euphrates, form and surround with their waters this great oasis, called by the ancient Semites Naharaim, and by the Greeks Mesopotamia; and in the most ancient narrative of the Bible Shinar. These two rivers, about equal in volume, take their rise near each other on the sides of the ancient Mount Niphates (the modern Keleshin); in Armenia they run at first in exactly opposite directions, and enter the plain at the two extremities of the chain of Mount Masius (now Karadjeh Dagh), the Tigris to the east, the Euphrates to the west. From this point they gradually approach each other until, in the thirty-fourth degree of latitude, they

run parallel for thirty leagues, and afterwards unite into one stream, now called Shat-el-Arab, and flow into the Persian Gulf.

2. By the geological formation of the soil, as well as by the aspect of the country and its fertility, Mesopotamia is divided into two very distinct parts, the north and the south, the boundary being where the rivers begin to run parallel at Hit, on the Euphrates, and Samarah, on the Tigris. The northern part is divided in two by the river Chaboras (the modern Khabur), taking its rise in Mount Masius, running from north to south, and flowing into the Euphrates at Carchemish, separating Assyria on the east from Aramæan Mesopotamia, the Osrhoene of the Greeks on the west. All the northern part, as we have said, is one great plain of secondary formation, fertile only where springs and water-courses are abundant, as in Osrhoene and the neighbourhood of Mount Sinjar; but in the rest of its extent resembling the neighbouring deserts, and like them, must always have been sterile and unfit for cultivation. The southern portion, on the contrary, comprising Babylonia and Chaldæa, is a still lower plain entirely formed of the modern alluvium (in the geological sense of the word) of the two rivers. The distance from one to the other is not more than a day's journey; and the country has the appearance of an immense prairie, only needing water to produce enormous harvests. The summer heat in this region is excessive, even for the east, but the winter is temperate and pleasant.

The waters of the Euphrates and Tigris rise every year and inundate the low land, though they do not, like the Nile, deposit fertilising mud; nevertheless, this natural irrigation, if directed and controlled as it was in ancient times, would again make Chaldæa the garden of Asia. Rice and barley at one time returned an increase of 200 for one; but now-a-days that the canals are neglected, the produce is but a tenth of what it once was. The country has no trees but the date-palm; this, however, forms entire forests, sometimes of enormous extent.

3. From this hasty sketch we may see the resemblance of the natural features of the Tigro-Euphrates Basin to the land of Egypt, especially as regards Chaldæa, its southern part.* This country also is the gift of the river, a land of incomparable fertility, yielding its fruits almost without labour, and is an oasis in the midst of the deserts. Nature herself has prepared these two countries for the theatre where the two earliest human societies might form themselves and enter on the road of civilisation. Thus it is that in the plains watered by the two great rivers of Western Asia all the races of the ancient world have successively encountered each other, and from the days of Nimrod to those of the successors of Mahomet, have disputed the Empire of Asia.

* See page 194.

Egypt and Mesopotamia have been the two great centres of civilisation, the one almost as ancient as the other, although priority belongs to Babylon rather than to Memphis; they have been the two rivals, in whose hands has alternately been placed the dominion of Western Asia. The Euphrates and the Nile have an easy communication with each other by roads fit for the passage of great armies. Whenever Egypt has been governed by an energetic ruler, she has endeavoured to subjugate Mesopotamia, as though an inevitable law forbade the existence of two rival empires, possessed of equal resources and placed in analogous circumstances. A Thothmes or a Seti at Thebes, like a Saladin at Cairo, or a Mehemet Ali at Alexandria, have never pursued any other object so steadily as to march their troops on the Euphrates, and attempt the conquest of Mesopotamia. In the same way, whenever a strong power has arisen on the banks of the Tigris or the Euphrates, whether at Bagdad, Babylon, or Nineveh, it has menaced Egypt and attempted its conquest. The history of Ancient no less than that of Modern Asia, is little more than one continuous record of political struggles between Egypt and Mesopotamia, ending only when the military power of Western Europe, with its great moral superiority, entered the lists, as in the days of Alexander the Great and in the times of the Crusades.

SECTION II.—PRIMITIVE POPULATION OF CHALDÆA.

1. THE Bible places the commencement of the history of mankind in the Tigro-Euphrates basin. "And it came to pass," says the Book of Genesis, "that as they journeyed from the east, they found a plain in the land of Shinar; and they dwelt there." There Scripture places the building of Babel, the first great city founded after the Deluge, and there occurred the confusion of tongues and the dispersion of races. We have already shown that this story was preserved in the Babylonian tradition, as well as in the Mosaic narrative.*

After the dispersion of the sons of Noah, who originally were all living together in the plains of Shinar, there remained in the country a considerable body of people of various and mixed races. This follows from the Bible narrative, and is also attested by the Babylonian traditions carefully collected in the time of the Seleucidæ by the historian Berosus, a Chaldæan priest, who translated the annals of his country into Greek. "There were at first," says he, "at Babylon, a great number of men of different nations who had colonised Chaldæa."

2. To the earliest date that the monuments carry us back, we can

---

* See page 23.

distinguish in this very mixed population of Babylonia and Chaldæa two principal elements, two great nations, the Shumir and the Accad, who lived to the north and to the south of the country. As soon as a monarchical government was introduced there, the first title of the sovereigns was "King of the Shumir and Accad," a title preserved in official documents by the Assyrian and Babylonian kings to the last days of their empire, though it had then no real meaning. The Accad occupied the southern districts, and had as their capital a city called after them, Accad, to be identified apparently with Nipur, the modern Niffer. The position of the Shumir was more northern; they had also a city of their name, Sumere, mentioned by Ammianus Marcellinus* as situated on the Tigris, and not far from Ctesiphon.

Of these two great nations who constituted the mass of the population of Chaldæa, one was of the race of Ham and of the Cushite branch. The presence of Cushites in Chaldæa and Babylonia is attested by the Bible, by Berosus, and by the universal testimony of antiquity. To them, as we have already said,† properly belonged that language ot the family called Semitic, to which scholars have given the name *Assyrian.* This language was common to both Babylon and Nineveh, and it is found in use in Chaldæa as far back as the monuments enable us to go. We have proved that the greater part of the Hamitic people, particularly those of the Cushite branch and the Canaanites, spoke languages analogous to each other. Lastly, it is in vain to seek in the primitive annals of Babylon or the neighbouring countries for an event of sufficient importance to have suddenly given the Semites a preponderance so great as to enable them to impose their language on the other races.

The other principal element in the original population of the lower course of the Tigris and Euphrates belonged to the Turanian race. It spoke a language of the Uralo-finnish family, made use of, as we find, in some of the most ancient inscriptions of the Chaldæan monarchs, and, as is proved by the monuments, spoken as late as the time of Nebuchadnezzar.

3. The fact of the existence of an ancient Turanian civilisation, and the presence of people of that race in Chaldæa, is one of the newest and least expected results of the decipherment of the cuneiform inscriptions, and of the study of the original monuments of the Assyro-Chaldæan world. It is, nevertheless, incontestable, and throws valuable light on the most ancient history of Asia. We have already seen ‡ that the Turanians were one of the first races to spread out into the world, before the time of the great Semitic and Arian

* xxv. 6. † See page 72. ‡ See page 58.

migrations, and that they covered a great extent of territory both in Asia and Europe. They then occupied all that district between the Tigris and Indus, afterwards conquered by the Iranians, and they also held the greater part of India. When the Semites on the one hand, and the Arians on the other, had finished their migrations, and were finally established, there always remained between them a separating belt of Turanian people, penetrating like a wedge as far as the Persian Gulf, and occupying the mountains between Persia and the Tigro-Euphrates basin.

Media was not, as is often represented, peopled entirely by the Indo-European race. On the contrary, the greater number of its people belonged, then as now, to the Turanian race. Even the name "Media" is a purely Turanian word, Mata signifying "land, country." This alone would prove, even if other positive indications had not been found to demonstrate it, that the basis of the population of that country has always been, down to our days, of the Tartaro-finnish race, although from an early period the dominant aristocratic class has been Arian. And it was long before this Turanian Media ceased to struggle with varying success against the dualism of the religion of Zoroaster.

More to the south, the Turanians formed a notable portion of the population of Susiana, on the left bank of the Tigris in its lower course, and for a long time their language was predominant there. This remarkable country, situated on the common boundary of all the various races of Western Asia, had these several people inextricably mixed up together on its soil. There were at the same time Elamites of Semitic race, Susianans proper, and Arphasæans of the Turanian family, Uxians, a branch of the Arians, and Cossæans, descendants of Ham of the Cushite branch, each preserving their distinct nationality, and living side by side with each other, as do now the various races of Hungary.

The Turanians of Chaldæa formed the last link of the chain, and were connected with those of Susiana.

The primitive centre, whence all the Turanian people had spread into the world, was towards the east of Lake Aral. There, from very remote antiquity, they had possessed a peculiar civilisation characterised by gross Sabeism, peculiarly materialistic tendencies, and complete want of moral elevation; but at the same time an extraordinary development in some branches of knowledge, great progress in material culture in some respects, whilst in others they remained in an entirely rudimentary state. This strange and incomplete civilisation exercised over great part of Asia an absolute preponderance, lasting, according to the historian Justin, 1500 years.* All the Turanians of Asia carried

* ii. 3.

this civilisation with them into the countries they colonised; those of Europe, at any rate the branch now represented by the Esthonians seem to have separated from the main stock before making any advances in civilisation. This peculiar culture was introduced by the Shumir on the banks of the Tigris, and by the Dravidians into India. This also it was that the hundred families carried into the midst of the Miao-Tseu, and other indigenous people of the Celestial Empire, and thus it became the starting point for the development of the civilisation of China, so different from that of all other nations of the world.

Moreover, the Turanian nations, who, as we have said, maintained themselves between the Arian and Semitic races in Media, Susiana, and Chaldæa, did not all belong to the same branch of the Turanian race. We have proof of this in the difference of their idioms. The Median language has left numerous remains; its essential characteristics have been established by the researches of Westergaard, de Saulcy, and Norris, and it is decidedly a Turkish language. That of the Turanian tribes of Chaldæa, the key to which has been furnished by the labours of M. Oppert, and elsewhere designated by us as "Chaldæan," presents, on the contrary, the closest analogies with the idioms of the Uralo-finnish group. Many of the words, and the greater part of its grammatical forms, particularly resemble the Finlandish. As for the Susianian, although very imperfectly known, the little we do know seems to bear a likeness to both the Uralo-finnish and the Dravidian group. We may be allowed to suppose that it will one day furnish the connecting link, so long sought by scholars, between these two groups of languages, the original parentage of which is certain. It is in perfect agreement with the geographical situation of the Susianans, for they must originally have been Dravidians, and appear to have extended over Ariana and Persia, and were in later times driven out by the Arians of these countries, as they were from the basins of the Indus and Ganges, ending by being pushed into the peninsula of Hindostan, far from any other Turanian people.

4. Among the Shumir and Accad it is easy to distinguish between the Turanians and Cushites. Their respective geographical position alone is enough to determine this. The Accad were the most southern; they bordered on the sea, and continued the chain of Cushite peoples, who extended from the Straits of Bab-el-Mandeb to Malabar, occupying the whole shore of the Persian Gulf and Indian Ocean. They were the first to attempt navigation on these waters in the dawn of the historical period. The Shumir, on the contrary, were from their northern position connected with the Turanians, and occupied a continuation of their territory. But though these two nations were the most important in Chaldæa and Babylonia, and formed the greatest part of the population there, they were not the only ones; other races mixed with them by

slow degrees almost everywhere, without having a distinct and well-defined locality.

In that country there were large numbers of Semites, both nomadic and settled. There were first the Assyrians, the great bulk of whom went out of the land of Shinar, as recorded by the author of the Book of Genesis, leaving some of their number, however, who mixed with the Shumir and Accad. There were also the Tarechites, or descendants of Heber and Terah, who lived in the neighbourhood of the city of Ur, and did not quit it to make an establishment in Haran (where the call of Abraham took place) until after the birth of that patriarch; and lastly, a large number of families of the race of Aram, who inhabited the north-west of Mesopotamia between the Chaboras and Euphrates, and had firmly established themselves at an early period at Babylon and the district dependent on that city; their language became the vulgar tongue there in common with the Assyrians, from the ninth or tenth century before the Christian Era. Some expressions in the most ancient royal titles seem to admit of the explanation that the population of Chaldæa contained four elements of different origin, like those whom we have shown to have existed in Susiana. We must therefore allow that, at any rate at one period, some Arian tribes were there, although we are unable to fix the exact limits of their habitation. We shall, moreover, see that at one time the Arians had a military predominance in the primitive history of Babylonia.

5. This mixture of the genius and peculiar institutions of these differing people, united on one territory, gave rise to the great Babylonian and Chaldæan civilisation, which played so considerable a part in Western Asia, and extended its influence over the whole of that country. The two elements, Cushite and Turanian, had the preponderance, but it is very difficult to decide, in this mixed race, already completely formed when we first became acquainted with it, what belongs to the Shumir, and what to the Accad. There are reasons, however, to believe that religion, astronomy, and industrial culture were brought by the Cushites. This is indicated by the Babylonian tradition, placing the origin of its religious faith on the banks of the Persian Gulf, whence the Fish-god, Oannes, issued to teach men the precepts of religion.

As to the Turanians, they brought to Babylon and Assyria that singular system of writing called cuneiform, each character being formed of a number of marks having the form of a wedge or nail. The valuable researches of M. Oppert have incontestably established this fact. It is only within the last few years that cuneiform writing has been deciphered, and we shall in a future chapter explain its principles in detail. The characters represent ideas either ideographically or syllabically, and very often, according to the position in which they are placed they are even capable of being employed in both ways. Originally they presented a rude picture or symbolical image—subsequently much modified—of the object or of the abstract idea expressed by or contained in the syllable constituting their phonetic value, not in the Assyrian language, but in the idiom of the Turanians of Chaldæa. Thus the word for "God" in the Assyrian language is *Ilu*, but the character representing it ideographically had originally the form of a star, and was pronounced *an* when employed as a syllabic sign, because, in the Chaldæan language the word for God was *Annap*. Again, the character employed for "ear" is found in other cases with the pronunciation *pi*, because the Turanians of Chaldæa expressed that idea by the word *Pil* (Magyar *Fül*). The same sign represents "fish," and also the syllable *ha*, because fish was called *hal* (Finlandish *Hal*). Another combined the meaning of "two" and the sound of *kas*, because in Turanian *kas* meant "two" (Magyar *Ket*). A third was employed both to mean "nose," and for the sound *ar*, because, always in the same idiom, "nose" was called *ar* (Magyar *Orr*). These examples will suffice, but they might be indefinitely multiplied.

Cuneiform writing is then originally Turanian, and was the principal contribution of the Shumir to the Babylonian civilisation. Thus this people are often designated ideographically by a group composed of two characters, meaning "language" and "arrow," evidently designating them as the people whose language was written in arrow-headed or cuneiform characters. Did the Shumir or Chaldæan Turanians invent this system of writing on the banks of the lower Tigris, or was it already formed before their final immigration? I would be rash perhaps to attempt in the present state of knowledge to give a decidedly affirmative answer to this question. But whoever studies the symbols forming the cuneiform writing, and attempts to trace them back to the objects they originally represented, will find that the nature of these objects apparently points, as the place where that system of writing was invented, to a region very different from Chaldæa, a more northern region, whose fauna and flora were markedly different, where, for example, neither the lion nor any other large feline carnivora were known, and where there were no palm trees.

6. Are we to suppose that a branch of the Shumir, or Turanians of the north of Chaldæa, was the dominant tribe there from the beginning, or that the Chaldæans proper were another Turanian nation, whose establishment is still surrounded by the greatest obscurity? What is certain is, that the Chaldæans imposed themselves equally on the two great constitutional elements of the population of the country, no doubt by conquest, and that they remained there as a superior and learned caste, having both sacerdotal and military supremacy. They belonged neither to the race of Shem, like the Assyrians, nor to the race of

Ham, like the Accad, or Cushites of the Lower Euphrates; but they were already established in the midst of the Accad in the time of Abraham, when the great city of Ur was already called "Ur of the Chaldees," and even earlier, when the Semitic tribe, whence the Hebrews sprung, was designated by the name Arphaxad, which, as we have already said,* signifies "border of the Chaldæans." Their original country seems to have been the mountains north-east of Mesopotamia, where the classical geographers place nations of the name of Chaldæi, Carduchi, Gordiæi, and where the Kurdish tribes still live.

The Chaldæans succeeded in establishing their political government and moral ascendancy in so decided a manner as to outlast all the revolutions the country was to undergo. They had the talent of assimilating themselves with the populations at the head of whom they had placed themselves, and maintained their position as a dominant aristocracy. They adopted its language and civilisation, amalgamating it with their own, and thus preserved their own superior position. But while adopting, for ordinary use and in their intercourse with the rest of the population, the Semitic idiom of Nineveh and Babylon, they did not, even down to the last days of Babylonian independence, give up the use amongst themselves of their own peculiar language of the Uralo-finnish family; that Chaldæan language we have already mentioned as apparently that of the original inventors of cuneiform writing, the language of the Shumir. The laws regulating Babylonian society were compiled in that language. There are in the British Museum some fragments relative to the organisation of families in a double text, Turanian-Chaldæan and Semitic-Assyrian. The comparative study of these two versions proves that the Turanian is the original and primitive text, and that the Assyrian is a later translation, in which it is easy to detect several solecisms.

SECTION III.—ORIGIN OF THE STATES OF ASSYRIA AND CHALDÆA—NIMROD—FIRST CUSHITE EMPIRE.

1. THE various populations residing together on the soil of Babylonia and Chaldæa must at first have lived in separation from each other. There was certainly a primitive epoch of tribal existence, of petty local kingdoms; and some records of this state of existence have been preserved in Babylonian traditions, as for instance that of Sharyukin, king of the city of Agani, who appears in some texts as a legendary hero and almost a demi-god. But true history in the Tigro-Euphrates Basin commences only, as also does that of Egypt, with the formation in Chaldæa and Babylonia of one united empire, including

* See page 60.

all its tribes under one sceptre—an empire dating from such high antiquity, that it seemed almost legendary to the author of the Book of Genesis. In this state, the first regularly organised government in the world, the preponderance and dominion among the various tribes belonged at first to the Hamites of Cushite race. "And Cush," says the Book of Genesis, "begat Nimrod; he began to be a mighty one in the earth. He was a mighty hunter before the Lord; wherefore it is said, Even as Nimrod, the mighty hunter before the Lord. And the beginning of his kingdom was Babel, and Erech, and Accad, and Calneh, in the land of Shinar. Out of that land went forth Asshur, and builded Nineveh and the streets of the city (*margin*), and Calah, and Resen, between Nineveh and Calah; the same is a great city."

This invaluable passage in the inspired book furnishes us with facts of the highest importance in the primitive history of Mesopotamia. We see there, first, that the Semites of the race of Asshur remained there a long time mixed with the Cushites of Chaldæa, and did not leave it until after the commencement of historical times, when they emigrated to the north, undoubtedly to escape the Cushite dominion, formed a new state distinct from the first, and founded the Assyrian cities. This lengthened sojourn together explains why the Assyrians and Babylonians had the same language and civilisation, in spite of the difference of their origin.

The Book of Genesis also reveals to us the existence of a Tetrapolis, or confederation of four cities, who ruled over the rest of the land that had been the empire of Nimrod. These four cities were, 1st, Babylon;—2nd, Erech, the Orchoe of the classical geographers, the Warka of our days, situated on the left bank of the Euphrates, forty leagues south of Babylon; its religious name was "the city of the moon";—3rd, Accad, the ancient centre of the Accad tribes, called also Nipur and "the city of the Lord of the world"; its site was exactly in the centre of Chaldæa proper, on the banks of the famous Royal Canal;—4th, Calneh, "the dwelling of Oannes," also called Ur,* a Chaldæan name, meaning "the city" *par excellence*, and also designated by the religious names of "the city of the God who watches over the moon," and "the city of the house of the world"; its ruins are now called Mugheir, and are near the first confluence of the Tigris and Euphrates, at some distance from the river and on its right bank. They all four seem to have simultaneously held the rank of capitals during the entire time of the existence of the first Chaldæan Empire, and the kings resided alternately in each. This Tetrapolis, moreover, had a sacred as well as a political character; the four cities were, according to Chaldæan ideas, a representation on earth of the four regions of heaven, or the four

---

* See note, page 80.

cardinal points, just as in Egypt its two divisions, Upper and Lower, represented the two hemispheres of the world. Thence arose the term, "king of the four regions," an essential part of the royal title of the ancient kings of Chaldæa, and only in later times abandoned by the Assyrian kings. Instead of four regions, four languages are sometimes understood; and this seems to indicate that there was also a connection between the number of cities of the Tetrapolis and the constituent elements of the population of the country.

2. The foundation of the Cushite state of the lower Euphrates was almost coincident with that of the other branch of the sons of Ham in Egypt, and with the appearance of the first signs of civilisation on the banks of the Nile. The fragments of Berosus mention this first dynasty, said to have consisted of eighty-six kings (and, therefore, to have existed about fifteen centuries), and the founder is called Evechous. In the last syllable of this name it seems that we may recognise that of Cush. Possibly this name, preserved by Berosus, may be a traditional surname of the chief of the Hamite dynasty, and may have meant something like son of Cush* just as the name given in the Book of Genesis to that personage, *Nimrod*, is a Semitic word, meaning "Rebel." Evechous, according to Berosus, had for his successor Chomasbelus; the original form of this name Shamash bel, "servant of Bel," seems to admit of easy restoration.

3. We know nothing from literary sources, either sacred or profane, of the history of the kings who succeeded Nimrod, or of the early times of Assyria. We may perhaps dimly perceive through the medium of the more or less fabulous traditions preserved by Berosus, that Chaldæa and Assyria had at first a separate existence. The Semitic Assyrians occupied the sterile plains extending south of the mountains of Armenia, between the Chaboras and the Tigris, as far as Media. In this district, on the left bank of the river, they founded Nineveh. Material civilisation with all its refinements seems to have been more slowly developed among them than in Chaldæa; inhabiting a country less fertile, and a climate less enervating, they remained always less polished, but at the same time more manly and warlike than their southern neighbours. All appearances seem to indicate that the Assyrians did not at first form one united empire, a great monarchy, but merely a confederation of tribes with essentially military chiefs. Their principal cities—Nineveh, Resen, Calah, Asshur or Ellasar,† and

* May not Evechous be the Assyrian *Avil Kush*, "man of Kush"?

† Sir H. Rawlinson has identified the ruins of Senkereh in Southern Chaldæa, called in the cuneiform inscriptions Larrak or Larsa, with the Biblical Ellasar (Gen xiv. 1). The author's reason for the identification in the text is, that the name of the city is written in the inscriptions with ideographic characters, meaning "City of Asshur," and the

Singar, for the most part on the east of the Tigris, certainly had each of them, in primitive times, a separate king.

The Hamites of Babylon, on the other hand, spread themselves over the fertile plains of Chaldæa as far as the Persian Gulf. Their supremacy was marked by progress in industrial arts and in science, united with those superstitions and mythological ideas and traditions to be met with wherever the Cushites have established themselves; their contribution to the history of the development of humanity: by agriculture, mining of both common and precious metals, and commerce by land and sea. The population increased rapidly on that fertile soil; cities were multiplied, arts and sciences began to be developed; astronomy took its rise under that clear sky; while at the same time on the ruins of the ancient primitive faith, revealed to the ancestors of the human race, arose a system of worship of the sun and other heavenly bodies, the foundation of the religion of those lands. The Assyrians had carried with them some part of this civilisation in their emigration to the north. They continued to live under the direct and almost exclusive influence of the Babylonians, who had preceded them in the march of civilisation, and were their instructors in everything that belonged to it.

Thus at a very early date, and undoubtedly long before the time when the Chaldæan monarchs conquered Assyria by force of arms, there was, in spite of the diversity of origin, but one nation of mixed character, the Chaldæo-Assyrians, in the whole extent of the plains watered by the Tigris and the Euphrates. From this time, however, this great and numerous nation appears to us as already sometimes divided into two empires. Nineveh and Babylon were not universally subject to one sceptre. But an irresistible tendency to union always appears from this time amongst them, and most frequently the two are united under the authority of one monarch. The chief changes in operation during the long series of Chaldæa-Assyrian kings may be referred to fluctuations in the seat of their power, which oscillated between Babylonia and Assyrian. Transferred sometimes from the south, where it had first arisen, to the north, and again from the

---

character meaning "city" certainly had the sound of *Al*, and the group must therefore have been pronounced *Al Asshur*.

The identification of Ellasar with the northern city may perhaps be supported by the text above quoted. The ruins at Senkereh were certainly within the land of Shinar, and therefore would probably be within the dominions of the king of Shinar. The northern Asshur was far beyond the limits of that kingdom, and the centre of a district, and head of a people, whose king was equal in rank and power to the kings of Shinar and Elam, and to the great chief of the Nomad tribes.—Tr.

north to the south, the Mesopotamian empire was called according to its position at the time, the Chaldæan, or the Assyrian empire. But the religion, the customs, the language, and the boundaries of these two alternately preponderating kingdoms remained always the same in all essential points.

SECTION IV.—DYNASTIES OF THE CHALDÆAN EMPIRE ACCORDING TO BEROSUS.

1. AFTER a duration that we have no means of estimating, the first Cushite, or Accad dynasty of Babylon was overturned by a foreign invasion rather more than 2,500 years before our era. The invaders were Arians of Japhetic race; and this event appears to have coincided with the great migration, when the Iranian people, sprung from Japhet, leaving their original country on the banks of the Oxus, directed their course to the west, to seek new habitations in Media or Persia, whilst another branch of the same great race made a descent on India.

Berosus names the people who came thus into Mesopotamia, Medes, that is, Iranians. After having destroyed the Cushite kings they reigned in Babylon for 224 years. With this conquest he connects a name, very celebrated in Eastern tradition, that of Zoroaster, chief of the Bactrians, who was both conqueror and legislator, and whose doctrine, propagated by war, left so deep an impress in the countries bordering on the Euphrates and Tigris, and particularly in Persia and Media. That Zoroaster was ever at Babylon seems very improbable, and doubtless the appearance of his name at that time in the Chaldæan historical traditions merely proves that the Arian invaders already possessed the dualistic form of religion that we shall speak of in another book. However, although the ancient Persian tradition informs us that Zoroaster himself taught his religion in Bactria, where was the centre of that faith previous to the migration of the Iranians towards Persia, it tells us nothing positive either as to the original country of Zoroaster himself, nor especially as to the precise period when he lived.

2. But the domination of the Arians at Babylon and in Mesopotamia was soon to be brought to a close; their supremacy could never be established otherwise than temporarily in Asia on this side Mount Zagros; it was brought to a final close in Chaldæa, and suspended for some centuries in Media, by the defeat of the Arians, over whom the Turanians, antagonistic from time immemorial, regained the upper hand.

After the Median or Arian, Berosus records a new dynasty as having supplanted it. Unfortunately such fragments as have come down to us mention neither the duration nor the origin of this royal family of eleven kings. Scholars, as for example Sir H. Rawlinson and M. Oppert, are agreed in admitting that it must have reigned rather more than two centuries, and have occupied the throne from about the year 2300 to the year 2100 before the Christian era. As to the native country of these kings, the proofs of their decisive valour show that they were Elamite or Susianian, and had gained the country by conquest. It is at this period that we find from the Bible that Chedorlaomer, king of Elam, was master of the whole Tigro-Euphrates basin. He had as vassals Amraphel, king of Shinar, or Chaldæa, Arioch, king of Ellasar, the chief of the Assyrian cities of that time, and Thargal, "king of nations," and with them made an expedition towards the west, temporarily subjected the whole of Syria, even as far as the frontier of Egypt, plundered the cities of Sodom and Gomorrah, led Lot away captive, and was at last defeated by Abraham.

The name of Chedorlaomer unquestionably belongs to the language of the Susianian Turanians, and is composed of elements found in names of a later period in the native inscriptions of the country. With regard to the name "king o. nations," the Hebrew text has it written Tidal, and the Greek version of the LXX., Thargal; this last form seems undoubtedly preferable, as it agrees with the form Turgal, meaning in one of the oldest Turanian idioms found in the cuneiform inscriptions (the Chaldæan) "great chief." The "nations" over whom this personage ruled were probably nomadic tribes of Scythians, or Turanians.

Such are the arguments which have hitherto sufficed to prove that the third dynasty of Berosus was Elamite or Susianian. But the fact is now clearly proved by the direct testimony of cuneiform texts, containing the name of the founder of this dynasty and the approximate date of his reign. Asshur-bani-pal, the last of the Assyrian conquerors, mentions, in two inscriptions, that he took Susa 1635 years after Kedornakhunta, king of Elam, had conquered Babylonia. He found in that city the statues of the gods taken from Erech by Kedornakhunta, and replaced them in their original position. It was in the year 660 B.C. that Asshur-bani-pal took Susa. The date, therefore, of the conquest of Babylon by Kedornakhunta, and the establishment of the Elamite dynasty in Chaldæa, must have been 2295 B.C.

3. A new dynasty follows this in the lists of Berosus. The dates of this historian, apparently reliable, and based upon a regular and correct chronology, place its accession in the year 2017 B.C. This dynasty is specified as Chaldæan, and Berosus says that it reigned 458 years, and consisted of forty-nine kings; it governed down to the time of the conquest of Mesopotamia by the Pharaohs of the eighteenth dynasty.

The fragments preserved by the Byzantine chronologers do not, however, contain one single name of the kings registered by the historian Berosus in this part of his canon.

SECTION V.—ROYAL NAMES SUPPLIED BY THE INSCRIPTIONS.

1. THE ruins of Chaldæa have as yet been but very imperfectly explored. It has not been practicable to carry out continuous excavations on a large scale; but the results of the labours of Mr. Loftus and Colonel Taylor lead us to the conclusion that, when a complete and careful investigation of the ruins of the ancient cities on the Lower Euphrates can be made, they will yield treasures as valuable as those of Egypt. The ruins undoubtedly contain an immense number of remains, some of enormous size, and some belonging perhaps to the age of the primitive Chaldæan Empire.

The inscriptions known in Europe, generally stamped on bricks, have at present supplied us with about fifty names of the kings of that empire. These do not form a continuous series, but seem to be dispersed over a very long series of ages. The Palæographical variations observed in the mode of writing in these inscriptions lead us to attribute them to several different periods, separated by very long intervals of time. In general, the names we know may be arranged in groups of two or three, leaving between them enormously long intervals, reserved for future discoverers to fill up.

In this position of things it is impossible to classify the royal names recovered from the ruins of Ur, Erech, Larsam (now Senkereh), the Larancha of Berosus, of Nipur (now Niffer), and of Sippara, the Heliopolis of the Greek geographers (now Sufeira), or to assign them their true place in the four dynasties mentioned by Berosus. We are, however, even now in a position to determine to some extent the relative antiquity of these kings, and to establish some landmarks in monumental history concordant with the facts collected by the Chaldæan priest for the information of the Greeks of the Seleucidan era.

2. The most ancient monarch of Chaldæa mentioned in the inscriptions we possess is Ur-Hammu, whose name signifies "light of the sun." He was known to classical antiquity, and considered so completely legendary, that Ovid related the mythological story of Clytie and Leucothea as having occurred in his family.* He was said to be the seventh king of the empire. His inscriptions present the most

* "Rexit Achæmenias urbes pater Orchamus isque,
Septimus a prisci numeratur origine Beli."
Metaph. iv. 212, 213.

ancient type of cuneiform writing at present known, the types most nearly approaching the original hieroglyphical figures. His monuments have all the characteristics of very remote antiquity, an antiquity unsurpassed by the monuments of the third or fourth Egyptian dynasty. He was the builder of the great pyramid at Ur, or Calneh,* where, as we have seen, as well as at Borsippa, was laid the scene of the events connected with the "Tower of Tongues."† Lastly, some of his buildings had already fallen into ruin by the time of the Elamite dynasty, and one of its kings, Burnaburyash I., restored those that he had built in honour of the sun at Larsam. These facts enable us with little doubt to place Ur-Hammu at the very commencement of the empire—in the Cushite, or Accad dynasty of Nimrod, and rather towards its commencement than its end.

Recent discoveries withdraw this king from the realms of fable, and place him in the full light of historical truth. He was the great builder among all the kings of the old Chaldæan empire; he built at Ur, in addition to the great pyramidical temple dedicated to Sin, the Moon-god, the fortified walls of the city; in Nipur, a temple to the Air-goddess, and another to Bilit-Taauth, mother of the gods; in Erech, a second temple to Bilit; and lastly, at Sippara and at Larsam, monumental sanctuaries in honour of the sun. His name, stamped on building-bricks, has been found in the ruins of all the cities of Lower Chaldæa; but there is no trace of his reign to the north of Babylon. Ilgi, son of Ur-Hammu, completed the temple of Sin at Ur.

At a short interval after these kings must be placed Shagaraktiyash, who was considered a very ancient monarch by the Elamite king Kurigalzu I. He it was who built at Sippara the largest temple of that sacred city, described at length by Berosus, on the site where it was said that the mythical King Xisuthrus had, at the time of the deluge, buried the tables containing the story of the early days of mankind, and the revelation of the mysteries of the cosmogony. An alabaster vase bearing the name of his son, Naram-Sin (he who exalts Sin, the Moon-god), presents a type of writing almost as archaic as that of the inscriptions of Ur-Hammu. A king who may dispute the palm of antiquity with Naram-Sin and his father is Sin-Said (Sin is his lord), who executed considerable works at Erech. The close analogy in the formation of their names seems to indicate that a large group of princes, evidently, however, many generations later, belonged to the same royal family. These all, as the chief element in their names, have the name of the god Sin, the great god of the city of Ur, whose worship seems to have been peculiar to the Cushite race, for they carried the observance with them wherever they went, whilst Sin played only a secondary

---

* See note, p. 80.

† See page 22.

part in the Pantheon of later times in Chaldæa. These were Irshu-Sin, Rim-Sin, Amar-Sin, Sin-Inun, Sin-baladan, who have all left monumental remains at Ur.

We may remark that all the names we have mentioned, with the exception of that of Shagaraktiyash, are derived from the Assyrian language, and in that tongue are easily translated. The royal names we meet with in the later days of the existence of the empire have an entirely different character. Now we have already attempted to show that this idiom, of the family improperly called Semitic, was the national language of the Cushites of the monarchy of Nimrod.

Under the primitive kings whom we have named, the birthplace of the political life of the empire, its focus and centre, appears to have been in the south of Chaldæa, near the Persian Gulf, in the very heart of the exclusively Cushite, or Accad country. The great city, the political capital where the sovereigns usually resided, and which each of them endeavoured to embellish with new buildings, was Ur. Babylon was therefore evidently under the supremacy of Ur in matters of government, but it was nevertheless the sacred city, the learned city, the religious metropolis. Just as the four cities of the Tetrapolis we have already mentioned, took the lead of all others in the country, so Ur was supreme over the other three cities of the Tetrapolis.

2. The invasion of the Arian Medes has left but few monuments; like the Canaanitish Shepherds in Egypt, they were mere barbarians compared with the civilised Chaldæans. The period of their rule will therefore probably always remain a gap in the monumental series. At any rate in the inscriptions as yet discovered, no one royal name is mentioned of an Arian character, such as those of the princes of the Median dynasty must have been. But this is not the case with the Elamite or Susianian dynasty that overthrew them.

We have no inscription of Chedorlaomer, nor of Kedornakhunta, but we have some of a king, proved by the analogy of his name derived from the Susianian language to have belonged to the same family, Kedormabug. He calls himself, in an inscription at Ur, "Conqueror of the West"; and in another text his son says of him, "My father enlarged the empire of the city of Ur." He was therefore a conqueror like Chedorlaomer, whose warlike example he followed. Kedormabug had a son who succeeded him on the throne, and who bore the purely Assyrian name of Zikar-Sin (servant of Sin); as the dynasty had become nationalised and had adopted the language of the country.

Two kings with Susianian names, Burnaburyash I. and his son, Kurigalzu I., both of them great builders, must undoubtedly be assigned to the same royal family. But they seem to have been more ancient still; anterior even to Chedorlaomer, and to the establishment of the sovereignty of the Elamite dynasty in Assyria. In fact, Kurigalzu, wishing to cover the northern frontier of Chaldæa on the side of the Assyrians, built there an important fortress which, fifteen centuries after, under Sargon (Sharyukin), was considered the key of the country; it was called Dur-Kurigalzu, "The Castle of Kurigalzu," and its large ruins still exist at Akkerkuf, west of Bagdad.

3. We now come to kings whose date we are able to fix. Ishmi-Dagan (Dagon hears him) and his sons Gungun and Shamshi-Bin, who succeeded him on the throne. Under these princes the Chaldæan empire included all Assyria, and the limits of the extended empire of the Elamite dynasty were maintained.

Their inscriptions have been found at Ur, where the royal residence was still fixed, but at the same time the temples of Oannes at Ellasar (now Kileh Sherghat), on the Upper Tigris in Assyria, had been built by Ishmi-Dagan, who thus proved himself sovereign of that country. Tiglath Pileser I. (Tuklat Pal-ashar) gives us this information in the official records of his reign, stating that he rebuilt this temple 701 years after its first foundation. Tiglath Pileser I., as we shall see, reigned in the year 1100 B.C.; the chronological fact furnished by this inscription therefore clearly indicated about the year 1800 B.C. for the reign of Ishmi-Dagan. This king may therefore with certainty be assigned to the dynasty called by Berosus Chaldæan. During his reign the ancient empire attained the height of its greatness, in consequence of the union of Assyria to Chaldæa; and this is the very time when Manetho records that Set-aạ-pehti-Noubti, the first king of the regular Shepherd dynasty, was under apprehensions of danger from the increase of the Chaldæan empire, and fortified Avaris to avert a possible attack from the nations on the banks of the Euphrates.

At this time both the power and the prosperity of the first Chaldæan empire, then including all Mesopotamia, reached their culminating point. At least five reigns after Ishmi-Dagan must be placed Hammurabi, who, of all the kings of this ancient empire, is the best known from the labour bestowed on his inscriptions by a French Assyriologist, M. Menant. Hammurabi was a powerful king who erected numerous buildings in various parts of the country, especially in Chaldæa and in Irak. He appears to have resided more often at Babylon than at Ur.

The chief work of his reign, at once the greatest and the most beneficial, was the famous Royal Canal of Babylon, the principal artery and centre of the system of irrigation of Upper Chaldæa, repaired by Nebuchadnezzar in later times, and considered by Herodotus as one of the wonders of Babylon. This canal was at first known by the name of its constructor. "I have caused," says this king in an inscription, "to be dug the Nahar-Hammurabi (canal of Hammurabi), a benediction for the men of Babylonia. . . . I have directed the waters of its branches over the desert plains; I have caused them to run in the dry channels and thus given unfailing waters to the people. . . . I have distributed the inhabitants of the land of the Shumir and Accad among distant cities. I have changed desert plains into well-watered lands. I have given them fertility and abundance, and made them the abode of happiness." The inscription from which we quote these passages is the most ancient text in our possession, and written phonetically in the Assyrian language, like all the later inscriptions of the kings of Assyria and Babylon.

The monumental inscriptions of more ancient kings, and even part of those of Hammurabi himself, are exclusively written in ideographic characters, and the few grammatical forms written phonetically that are found in them prove that they were intended to be read in the Turanian Chaldæan, as the others were in the Semitic Assyrian; this difference of style distinguishing them from texts of later date renders the ancient inscriptions very difficult to interpret.

Hammurabi had succeeded to a queen, the only female sovereign known among the various empires of the Euphrates Basin. This fact is ascertained from a fragment of the royal list in cuneiform writing inscribed on a tablet of baked clay, now in the British Museum. It records after Hammurabi thirteen names of kings, of whose history we know nothing; they were all Chaldæan in the most restricted sense of the word—that is, Turanians—thus confirming the statements of Berosus as to the origin of the dynasty; some of the names much resemble those of a later date found in the inscriptions of Susiana; a fact that need not excite surprise, as the Chaldæans, properly so called, and the dominant race in Susiana, were equally of Turanian origin. The tablet contains a translation of these names into the Assyrian language. Unfortunately it is very much mutilated. The series of kings, successors to Hammurabi, furnished by this "London list" must bring us down to nearly the close of the Chaldæan dynasty, ending according to Berosus about 1559 B.C.

SECTION VI.—MONUMENTS OF THE PRIMITIVE CHALDÆAN EMPIRE.

1. THE first Chaldæan empire has left very many monumental remains of very large size in the most southern part of the Tigro-Euphrates Basin. The ruins of Ur, Erech, Sippara, Nipur, and Larsam belong for the most part to this remote period. The kings of the later Babylonian empire, Nebuchadnezzar [Nabu-kudur-ussur] and his successors have merely repaired the temples and the walls of these cities, and were not the original builders.

Stone is entirely wanting in the alluvial plains of Chaldæa; it could only be obtained from a great distance, and at a great expense. Thus all the buildings of the kings of the first empire, like the Tower of Babel, and like those of Babylon in all ages, were constructed exclusively of bricks. On each of these bricks is stamped the name of the king who erected the building, and the greater part of the inscriptions of the early Chaldæan kings in our possession are of this kind. In general the interior of these edifices is of merely sun-dried bricks, with here and there layers of reed matting cemented with bitumen, to give greater cohesion; this mode of construction is described by Herodotus * in speaking of the walls of Babylon. Sometimes also courses of baked bricks are alternated, to give greater stability to the work. The body of masonry, composed of sun-dried bricks, is almost invariably cased with burnt brick, to protect it from the action of rain and to prevent disintegration.

2. The sacred edifices of this period are all of the same type; a pyramid built in stages, a series of square terraces one above the other, each terrace smaller than the one beneath it, so that while the base of a building occupied a large site, its upper story was very small.

This is how the Tower of Babel had been built; and also the most ancient of the Pyramids of Egypt, that of Sakkarah for instance. This mode of construction for sacred edifices was connected with the essentially astronomical character of the original form of the religion of the Chaldæans. They thus thought to approach nearer to the heavenly bodies, the objects of public worship; and the temples were really observatories for watching their motions. On the upper platform was built a small chapel or square chamber, richly ornamented, containing the image of the deity of the temple. The casing of each terrace was of bricks, differing in dimensions and colour from the rest. Sometimes, as in the great temple at Ur, the lower stage that supported the weight of all the others, and therefore required great solidity, was strengthened by buttresses built of burnt bricks and arranged in a very scientific manner.

Constructed of such materials, so liable to disintegration, the palaces and houses of the primitive epoch in Chaldæa have left nothing on their sites but shapeless masses of ruins, where we are unable to make out the original plan of the building. The results of the excavations of Colonel Taylor enable us, however, to state that the halls were long and narrow, little better than mere passages, for it was impossible to put any great weight on vaults built of earth or sun-dried bricks. The inside of the walls was plastered with a thick coat of mortar; and in this were fixed cones of coloured terra-cotta, with the base outwards, arranged so as to produce patterns of lozenges, chevrons, or squares. At short

---

* HER. i. 179.

distances were semicircular projections in the walls, like half-detached pillars, but without bases, and probably also without capitals.

Tombs of the same age have been found in great number at Ur, each consisting of a small chamber 7 feet long, 3½ feet wide and 5 feet high, built of burnt bricks. In these there has been observed an attempt at a pointed arch, formed by courses of bricks overlapping each other, a system of construction that has been met with in Egypt and in the Pelasgic buildings in Greece.

3. The pottery discovered in these tombs is in general rude, and for the most part hand-made, without the assistance of a wheel. This useful implement was, however, then already known, for some vases of better workmanship have been found bearing traces of its use.

The utensils found in the tombs prove that the Chaldæans from the time of their earliest kings knew the art of working metals, gold, bronze, lead, and even iron; and this knowledge they owed to the Cushite element of the population. But metals, though known and easily worked, were nevertheless too scarce to be in general use, and implements of chipped and polished flint, knives, arrow heads, axes, and hammers were still employed. The most common metal was bronze, and all metal implements and utensils were made of it. Iron was still so rare as to be regarded as one of the precious metals, and was used not for tools, but for making bracelets and other rude ornaments.

4. With regard to the plastic arts, properly so called, having for their object the imitation of living nature, and particularly of the human figure, we have no sculpture and no painting either Babylonian or Chaldæan of early date, excepting a small bronze figure of a goddess bearing the legend of Kedormabug, now in the Museum of the Louvre, and a fragment of a statuette of alabaster in the British Museum, representing the god Nebo. But a number of those small engraved cylinders of hard stone that were used as seals, cylinders of Babylonian manufacture, with archaic inscriptions in cuneiform characters, must belong to the time of the Chaldæan empire. This fact is certain, at any rate with regard to two: the first, one that was in the possession of Sir R. Ker Porter, and is engraved in his "Travels,"* (this was the seal of King Ur-Hammu); the second, the cylinder of his son Ilgi, now one of the most valued treasures of the British Museum. In these, art is the same as in the engraved Babylonian stones of much later days, down to the time of Nebuchadnezzar and the Persian dominion, and is at least as far advanced.

5. We have already said that Astronomy had risen to the rank of a real science among the people of Chaldæa from the most remote times,

---

* Vol. ii. pl. 79.

and that its first advance dated back to the almost legendary epoch of Nimrod. In the most ancient times that the monuments permit us to investigate, astronomy was more advanced in Babylon and Chaldæa than it ever was in Egypt. The utmost progress that it was possible to make in this science with the naked eye, unaided by optical instruments, was made by the Chaldæans. They had even discovered the annual displacement of the equinoctial point on the ecliptic, a discovery usually attributed to the Greek astronomer, Hipparcus. But for want of correct instruments there was an error in their calculation, as, moreover, there was in that of Hipparcus. They had assigned it an annual precession of thirty seconds, whilst in reality it is fifty. On this basis they calculated their great astronomical period of 43,200 solar years, representing, according to their calculation, the total period of the precession of the equinoxes (the true period being 26,000 years); and the divisions of this period, called Sar, 3,600, Ner, 600, and Soss, 60, were the foundation of all their chronological computations.

The science of Arithmetic, indispensable to all real astronomy, was also very far advanced among this people. We might have inferred this from the establishment of these periods, but we have further and positive proof in a clay tablet discovered in the ruins of Larsam, and now preserved in the British Museum, bearing a list of the squares of fractional numbers, calculated with perfect correctness from $\frac{1}{60}$ to $\frac{60}{60}$.

Section VII.—Period of Egyptian Preponderance and of the Arab Kings.

1. We have already shown that, from about the twenty-second to the eighteenth century before the Christian era, Ur was the capital of the Chaldæan empire, then embracing the whole of Mesopotamia, and comprising the Assyrians among its subjects. This widely-extended power did not last more than three or four centuries, and Assyria escaped from the dominion of Chaldæa to return to its former state of independence. For the 400 succeeding years the history of Mesopotamia is written on the monuments of Egypt.

When, in the second half of the seventeenth century, Thothmes I., the conqueror of Syria, crossed the Euphrates at Carchemish, and, first of all the Pharaohs, poured his legions into Mesopotamia, there no longer existed one great empire embracing the whole basin of the two great Asiatic rivers. Assyria, in the records of the Egyptian campaigns, is represented as having a political existence of its own apart from that of Babylon, and does not even form a kingdom, in the proper sense of the word, as the Rotennu (the Egyptian name for the Assyrians) were then merely a confederation of petty states, governed by princes on an equality with each other, none of whom exercised suzerainty over the others; and this confederation extended its influence over Osrhoene, or Aramæan Mesopotamia, as well as over the plains extending from the Euphrates to Anti-Lebanon. The Syrian princes of these last countries made part of the league, and held in it the same rank as the Assyrian chiefs. The successors, therefore, of powerful monarchs, such as Ishmi-Dagan and Hammurabi, were no more than simple "kings of Babel," and equals of the kings of Nineveh, Asshur (Ellasar), and Singar.

2. Thothmes I. had made only a flying expedition across the Euphrates, and had not attempted in earnest to establish his supremacy there. Towards the middle of the sixteenth century, during the course of the great wars, the history of which we have related as given in the hieroglyphic inscriptions, Thothmes III. subjected all Mesopotamia, from Nineveh to Babylon, and placed garrisons in all the places of strength to ensure the submission of the country. We have already explained in what manner he organised the internal administration of the Asiatic countries subbdued by his arms.* The Pharaohs did not reduce them to the position of provinces governed directly by Egyptian rulers; they everywhere protected the petty local sovereigns, but reduced them to the position of vassals, compelling them to pay tribute and to furnish contingents of troops; these local princes were obliged to receive their investiture from the king of Egypt and to send their sons to the court of Thebes, to receive there an Egyptian education, and to remain as hostages until the time arrived for their being installed on the throne. Of course, Pharaoh, as suzerain, reserved to himself the right of dethroning, and replacing by another, any vassal prince who revolted or gave cause for suspecting his fidelity. This was exactly the method employed in later times by the Romans in dealing with allied kingdoms.

3. It is evident that the campaigns of Thothmes III. were the means of overturning the dominion of the Chaldæan dynasty. The year 1559 B.C., the date assigned by Berosus for the end of this dynasty, agrees exactly with his reign. We may even regard the year 1559 as identical with the thirty-first year of Thothmes, the time, as we know from the inscription on the walls of Karnak, when that king took Babylon. Berosus says that the Chaldæan princes were succeeded by nine Arab kings, who reigned 245 years; that is, from 1559 to 1314. Many scholars have attempted to identify these Arab kings with the Khitas of the Egyptian monuments; but, however great may be the authority of those who propound this, we are unable to admit the identification. In 1559 B.C. there was no mention of the Khitas, or Hittites,

* See page 233.

who had no weight in the affairs of Western Asia until more than a century later. Moreover, the territory of the Khitas and the limits of their power are perfectly defined by the Egyptian historical texts; they sometimes advanced a long way southward on the western bank of the Euphrates, but they did not cross that river; the Khitas are never mentioned in Mesopotamia, the people there are always called Rotennu.

We consider the Arabian kings of Berosus merely as Semitic princes installed at Babylon by the kings of Egypt, to represent them there in the place of the Chaldæan dynasty. Their reign commenced, as we have seen, simultaneously with the first establishment of Egyptian supremacy at Babylon, and they remained in power as long as the substantial authority of Egypt extended east of the Euphrates during the latter part of the eighteenth and the whole of the nineteenth dynasty; and, finally, their power ended in 1314 B.C., that is, just when the annals of Egypt record a general revolt of the Asiatic provinces, coincident with the accession of the twentieth dynasty, a revolt that the last Egyptian conqueror, Ramses III., successfully repressed in Syria and northern Mesopotamia, but does not seem to have ventured to follow up his success as far as Babylon.

We must remark, however, that the most recent Assyriological discoveries do not permit us to suppose with Berosus that the Arabian kings occupied the throne during the whole period of Egyptian supremacy—the whole interval between 1559 and 1314. Towards the close of that period, and previous to 1314 B.C., as we shall show in the proper place, the Assyrian inscriptions mention some kings of Babylon, whose names belong to the Chaldæo-Turanian language. We must then admit that in the fifteenth century B.C., possibly in consequence of the troubles in Egypt about the close of the eighteenth dynasty, a Chaldæan royal family supplanted the Arabian dynasty on the throne of Babylon, still, however, recognising Egyptian supremacy.

4. We have some doubts as to the correctness of the designation "Arabian" for these kings, as that word had in classical antiquity a very vague and extended meaning, and was not unfrequently applied to all Semitic tribes. It seems more probable that the princes who were put at the head of the Babylonian government by the Pharaohs were of Canaanitish origin; and the book on "Nabathæan Agriculture," written in Arabic in the tenth century, and containing, amongst a great deal of utterly worthless matter, some valuable extracts from native traditions, or rather from works written under the successors of Alexander, and now lost, mentions at this very period of Babylonian history, a dynasty of Canaanitish kings who, "after long combats," had overturned and supplanted the Chaldæan sovereigns.

The Byzantine chronologer, George Syncellus, mentions, we do not know on what authority, the names of six kings attributed to this so-called Arabian dynasty, and the purely Babylonian forms of these names give rise to serious doubts as to the correctness of the statement. We may nevertheless remark that one of them Nabu (the Nabius of Syncellus) has been found stamped on bricks at Erech and Babylon, which seem to the learned M. Oppert to belong certainly to the time of the Arabian kings of Berosus. The British Museum possesses a mutilated statue, in black basalt, of king Nabu, and the Louvre has several inscriptions of the same prince. These monuments certainly belong to a very ancient period, but the titles of the king differ completely from those of the monarchs of the primitive epoch; their modesty seems to indicate a prince who was not an independent sovereign, but merely the vassal of a more powerful suzerain.

5. To this period also must be attributed a most valuable head in limestone, bearing traces of having been coloured, which was discovered at Babylon, and is now in the museum of the Louvre. This head, rudely worked, but vigorously treated, and very lifelike in type, clearly represents an Egyptian. There is an evident intention of imitating the style of Egyptian works, and, moreover, the Pharaonic art at this period of Egyptian supremacy has left monuments in many parts of the Euphrates Basin. The Theban conquerors, as their inscriptions tell us, had erected steles to commemorate their victories, and undoubtedly the progress of explorations may bring some of these to light.

The ruins of the fortress built by Thothmes III. at Carchemish, to secure the passage of the Euphrates, have been discovered, and a great number of small objects of Egyptian manufacture bearing hieroglyphic inscriptions have been found there. Some also have been found in other places, and even at Babylon itself.

It is certain that at this period, Egyptian art exercised a powerful and dominant influence on Assyro-Chaldæan art, then in a state of infancy, almost of barbarism. In later times Assyrian art emancipated itself entirely from this influence, and assumed a distinct originality under the influence of principles diametrically opposed to those that governed the Egyptian sculptor. But the example of the Egyptians who had so many centuries before the Assyrians and Babylonians begun to cultivate true art, was followed for some time after their domination over the country had ceased. This is proved by many monuments, and especially by those remarkable dishes of chased bronze, now in the British Museum, discovered by Mr. Layard at Calah, in the palace of king Asshur-nazir-pal; they are certainly older than that king, and may be attributed to the eleventh or twelfth century B.C. The workmanship of these dishes shows us a peculiar style decidedly not Egyptian; but the ornamentation is entirely so, both as to the figures and the symbols drawn on them; it is Egyptian art transformed and imitated by Assyrian hands.

CHAPTER II.

THE FIRST ASSYRIAN EMPIRE.

SECTION I.—FOUNDATION OF THE FIRST ASSYRIAN EMPIRE—FABULOUS STORIES ABOUT THAT EMPIRE—NINUS AND SEMIRAMIS.

1. WE have now arrived at the period where we must place the origin of the Assyrian Empire. The Greek writers at this epoch introduce into history the fabulous names of Ninus and Semiramis. Diodorus Siculus, following Ctesias, has left us a brilliant picture of the reign of these two personages. The progress of knowledge, the direct study of the Assyrian monuments and inscriptions, enable us now to assert positively that neither Semiramis nor her husband Ninus ever existed, that their history is entirely mythical—a fable with no real foundation—and must therefore henceforth be erased from the annals of Asia. But it has obtained credit for so many centuries; it is so often alluded to in classical literature, that we cannot pass over it in silence and with the contempt it deserves; we find it necessary to tell the story even while declaring it entirely apocryphal.

2. According to the legend first related to the Greeks by Ctesias, Babylonia had been dismembered by an invasion of the Arabians, when Ninus, chief of the Assyrians, undertook to free the country from the barbarians. Before attacking Babylonia, he organised a large body of picked young men and prepared them by all sorts of exercises for the fatigues and dangers of war. He next made an alliance with an Arab chieftain, like himself, jealous of the power of Babylon, and with a strong army then attacked the Babylonians. "Their country," the story taken from Ctesias goes on to say, "contained many well-peopled cities; but the inhabitants, inexperienced in the art of war, were easily subdued and compelled to pay tribute." Ninus took the king and his children prisoners, and put them to death. Thence he marched on Armenia, and terrified the natives by the sack of some towns. Barzanes, the king of that country, finding that he was unable to resist, sent presents to the enemy and offered his submission. Ninus treated him generously, allowed him to retain his kingdom, and only required him to furnish a contingent of auxiliary troops. The king of Media, next attacked, attempted to resist; but, abandoned by his troops, was made prisoner and crucified. In seventeen years Ninus thus made himself master of all the countries between the Mediterranean Sea and the Indus.

"On his return from these conquests, to give his dominions a capital worthy of himself, he built Nineveh, and called it after his own name. This city was in the form of a parallelogram, the longest sides were 150 stades, and the shortest ninety; so that the whole circuit of the walls was 480 stades (about fifty-five miles)! The towers built to defend this wall were 15,000 in number, and were each nearly eighty yards high! Besides the Assyrians, who formed the richest and most powerful part of the population, Ninus admitted into his capital a great number of strangers, and Nineveh soon became the largest and most flourishing city in the world.

"These works of peace did not destroy the taste of Ninus for warlike enterprises; he undertook the conquest of Bactria, which he had already once attempted in vain. In the course of this war we first encounter Semiramis, whose name was soon to attain to such great celebrity. She was the daughter of Derceto, or Atergatis, the goddess of reproductive nature, the chief seat of whose worship was at Ascalon. Derceto had exposed her child, the fruit of a clandestine amour with a young mortal, and a shepherd named Simas had found and brought up Semiramis. Oannes, governor of Syria, had married her for her beauty, and she had followed him to the royal army in the Bactrian war. An act of bravery raised her to the rank of queen. Ninus, after having vanquished the Bactrians in the field, besieged their capital without success, when Semiramis, disguised as a soldier, found means to scale the wall, and by a signal announced her success to the troops of Ninus, who then stormed the place. Ninus, astonished at her bravery, took her from Oannes and made her his wife; a short time afterwards he died, and left her sole mistress of the empire.

"Semiramis, once in possession of supreme power, indulged her naturally enterprising genius. Desirous of surpassing the glory of all her predecessors, she conceived the idea of building a city in Chaldæa. Struck with the advantages of the situation of Babylon, she wished to make it one of the capitals of the Assyrian empire.

"The city was protected," still quoting Ctesias as reported by Diodorus Siculus, "by a wall 360 stades long (more than forty miles), flanked by many towers; the Euphrates passed through the middle. Such was the magnificence of the work, that the width of the walls permitted six chariots to drive abreast." The height, according to Ctesias, was one hundred yards; but, according to other Greek writers, thirty yards only, and the width sufficient for only two chariots. The same authors estimate the circumference at 365 stades, because Semiramis wished it to correspond with the number of days in the year. These walls were built of sun-dried bricks cemented with asphalt. The towers, of proportionate height and size, were only 250 in number.

"When the first part of the work was finished, Semiramis fixed on the place where the Euphrates was narrowest, and threw across it a bridge five stades long. She contrived to build in the bed of the stream pillars twelve feet apart, the stones of which were joined with strong iron cramps fixed into the mortises with melted lead. The side of these pillars towards the run of the stream was built at an angle, so as to divide the water, cause it to run smoothly past and lessen the pressure against the massive pillars. On these pillars were laid beams of cedar and cypress, with large trunks of palm trees, so as to form a platform thirty feet wide. The queen then built at great cost on either bank of the river a quay with a wall as broad as that of the city, and 160 stades long (nearly twenty miles). In front of each end of the bridge she built a castle flanked by towers, and surrounded by triple walls. Before the bricks used in these buildings were baked she modelled on them figures of animals of every kind, coloured to represent living nature. Semiramis then constructed another prodigious work; she had a huge basin, or square reservoir, dug in some low ground. When it was finished, the river was diverted into it, and she at once commenced building in the dry bed of the river a covered way leading from one castle to the other. This work was completed in seven days, and the river then was allowed to return to its bed, and Semiramis could then pass dry shod under water from one of her castles to the other. She placed at the two ends of the tunnel gates of bronze, said by Ctesias to be still in existence in the time of the Persians. Lastly, she built in the midst of the city the temple of the god Bel.

"Semiramis, after having completed these works in Babylonia, made an expedition against the Medes, who had revolted. She subjected the country afresh, and left there an everlasting monument of her presence. At the foot of Mount Bagistan she built a palace. One of the faces of the mountain is formed of perpendicular rocks of enormous height; on this rock she caused to be sculptured her own likeness, surrounded by those of a hundred of her guards, with an inscription recounting her achievements." Diodorus attributes to her also the foundation of Ecbatana, where the kings of Assyria were, he says, in after times in the habit of passing every spring. As the city required water, and there was no sufficient spring in the neighbourhood, she conducted, at great cost and by enormous works, a plentiful supply of pure water into all parts of it. For this purpose she tunnelled through Mount Orontes, and dug a canal, ten feet wide and forty feet deep, communicating with a lake on the other side of the mountain.

From Media, Semiramis passed on to Persia, and visited all her possessions in Asia. In Armenia she built, near Lake Van, a city with an immense palace. Wherever she went, says Ctesias, she pierced mountains, levelled rocks, and coustructed large and good roads. In the plains she constructed artificial hills for the tombs of the generals who died during the expedition, or for the foundation of her new cities.

According to the same author, she also subdued Egypt and the greater part of Ethiopia. She also undertook an expedition against India, attracted by the riches of that country. Stratobatis, the king of the Indians, having heard of the extensive preparations of the Babylonian queen, assembled a considerable force, and then defied Semiramis by a letter, in which he reproached her with the immorality of her private life, and threatened, if he were victorious, to crucify her. Semiramis did not, however, abandon her intention of attacking the Indian king. But his war elephants secured the victory to Stratobatis, the army of Semiramis was put to flight, and two-thirds of it destroyed.

After this defeat she retired to her own kingdom, and did not again quit it. She devoted herself to the completion of her great works; and such were the enterprise and renown of this queen that, after her time, according to Strabo, every great work in Asia was popularly attributed to her. Alexander found her name, it is said, inscribed on the frontiers of Scythia, then considered the extreme verge of the habitable world. The pretended text of this inscription has been preserved by Polyænus. Semiramis herself speaks, and thus expresses herself—"Nature gave me a woman's body, but my deeds have equalled those of the most valiant men. I ruled the empire of Ninus, which reaches eastward to the river Hinaman (the Indus); southward, to the land of incense and myrrh (Arabia Felix); northward, to the Saces and Sogdians. Before me no Assyrians had seen a sea; I have seen four, that no one had approached, so far were they distant. I compelled the rivers to run where I wished, and directed them to the places where they were required. I made barren land fertile, by watering it with my rivers. I built impregnable fortresses. With iron tools I made roads across impassable rocks; I opened roads for my chariots, where the very wild beasts had been unable to pass. In the midst of these occupations I have found time for pleasure and love."

Having learned that her son Ninyas was plotting against her, she formed the resolution of abdicating. Far from punishing the conspirator, she left the government of the empire to him, directed all the governors to obey the new sovereign, and disappeared, changed into a dove. She was worshipped as a goddess.

3. Such is the legend that Ctesias first related to the Greeks. We repeat that there is not one word of truth in it; the Assyrian monuments contradict it on all points. Such personages as Ninus and Semiramis belong in no way to real history; they never existed in fact. Ninus, as the name clearly indicates, is only a personification of the whole history of the city of Nineveh, and of all its power; under this name, popular stories grouped together all the exploits and conquests

of all Assyrian kings, and even (for these legends always have a tendency to magnify) conquests that no Ninevite king ever made. Just as the whole of the military exploits of the Assyrians have been grouped round the name of Ninus, although also attributed to Semiramis, so all the useful or gigantic works, whatever their origin, executed at different periods by various Asiatic sovereigns, have contributed to the glory of the name of Semiramis. To her have been attributed all the buildings of Babylon, from the Tower of Babel, identical with the Temple of Bel, to those of the age of Nebuchadnezzar and his successors, even the works of king Deioces at Ecbatana, and the great sculptures at Mount Bagistan (Behistun), in Media.*

The name of Semiramis has been borrowed from a really historical queen, who lived five centuries after the period where the legend places the fabulous Semiramis, Sammuramat, wife of Bin-lik-his III., a queen who had some important works executed at Babylon, but who in no other respect resembles the portrait drawn by Ctesias. In point of fact, with all modern scholars, we must recognise in the famous Semiramis one of the mythological personages of the religion of the Euphrates valley. The story itself speaks of her as a goddess, for it makes her the daughter of Derceto, and mentions her final metamorphosis and the worship subsequently addressed to her. All the fundamental features of her character, and of the adventures attributed to her, agree in showing that she was only the personification of the heroic form of the great goddess of the Babylonian religion, uniting in herself the most apparently opposite attributes, a patroness both of pleasure and of war, and who had for one of her principal symbols a dove. With her husband, Ninus the warrior, and her son Ninyas, the effeminate prince shut up in his harem, Semiramis represented on earth exactly the supreme triad of Babylonian worship. This idea, too, was not originally Assyro-Chaldæan; it was borrowed, as was also the greater part of their religion, from the Cushites; the same group of mythical personages being placed by popular tradition at the head of all primitive dynasties, wherever the first steps in civilisation are due to the Cushites, in India as well as in Mesopotamia.

4. Moreover, the legend of Ninus and Semiramis is by no means of early origin. It is neither Assyrian nor Babylonian, but Persian. Berosus, who compiled from the official archives of Assyria and Chaldæa, was ignorant of it, as also was Herodotus, in general so well

* The sculptures at Behistun, here referred to, are probably those described by Sir R. Ker Porter (*Travels*, vol. ii. p. 151, *seq.*) as still existing, though very much timeworn and barely distinguishable, on the same rock surface as the famous sculpture and inscriptions of Darius, but in a lower position.—TR.

acquainted with traditions, and who had been at Babylon and heard from the Chaldæans the history of their country. It was at the Persian court that Ctesias, physician to the king Artaxerxes Mnemon, had heard this story, received by him with implicit faith, and hastened to make it known to his countrymen, as preferable to the statements of Herodotus. It must be admitted that he was unfortunate in receiving his information from the Persians, for these people have always been, and still are (like their neighbours the Indians), incapable of recording true history. The historical instinct is entirely wanting in the famous annals engraven on the rocks at Behistun, where Darius records the days and months of the chief events of his reign, but has forgotten to mention the *years*. The same defect is apparent among the modern Persians, the only people who have no historian but the poet, and who have no record of their past history but a "Book of Kings," of an historical value about equal to that of our middle-age ballads. This has frequently struck the author when in conversation with Persians who passed for men of letters in their own country, but who had the strangest possible ideas as to the history of modern Asia. What could be the value of statements as to their conquered enemies furnished by a people who, in their own history, had soon forgotten the great Cyrus, the founder of their empire, and who represented, as closely related, personages separated by a distance of seventeen centuries.

5. The legend believed at the court of Persia as to Ninus and Semiramis, and generally as to the history of the Assyrian empire, probably partly originated from motives easy to penetrate, and which will become apparent in the course of this history.

Ninyas, it is said, succeeded his mother. He had none of the warlike character of his predecessors; occupied solely with his pleasures, he led a peaceful and obscure life buried in his palace; he confined himself to ensuring the security of his empire, and maintaining his subjects in obedience, by keeping on foot a numerous army annually levied in the several provinces. He assembled the troops near Nineveh, gave to each nation a governor devoted to himself, and at the end of each year dismissed these soldiers and replaced them by an equal number of fresh men. This constant renewal of the army prevented the formation of too intimate relations between the soldiers and their commanders, and precluded any plot against the sovereign. Moreover, by rendering himself invisible, he hid from all eyes the voluptuous life he led; and, as though he had been a god, no one dared to speak evil of him. His successors, down to Sardanapalus, adopted the same line of conduct, and thus these kings were enveloped in the most complete obscurity. For thirteen centuries one peaceably succeeded the other, their power was never disputed, and the extent of their dominions was never diminished.

The policy of the Persian monarchs was directly interested in thus attributing to the highest antiquity the origin of a system of Asiatic government, where obedience was ensured by the respect due to the mere name of the king, even when he was occupied entirely with his pleasures, and secluded from sight in his palace; a government maintained also by the suspicious policy that did not allow its various foreign subjects to acquire perfect experience as soldiers, or to become accustomed to camp life, but sent to each province representatives of its own absolute power. As these Persians pretended to have inherited the rights of the Assyrian empire, by attributing such a character to that empire, they gave to their own authority, established by force of arms, the sanction of a tradition many centuries old, and a character really legitimate. This intention will become still more manifest if we remember the extent attributed by the legend of Ctesias to the dominions and to the duration of the Assyrian empire. The conquests of Ninus and Semiramis very far exceed those of any, even the most powerful, Assyrian monarch, but they coincide exactly with the extent of the Achæmenian empire after the time of Darius Hystaspes. As to the question of duration, the reader will be able to judge, from what has been said, how absurd, how contrary to history, is this tradition of an empire dating back to thirteen centuries before the revolution that overthrew Sardanapalus—of a dynasty whose twentieth generation was contemporary with the Trojan war, and had suffered from no dismemberment, nor even revolt of its subjects, and had never had occasion to appear in arms before them. But this number of centuries represents almost exactly the total period of the duration of the various dynasties that succeeded each other, from the time of the establishment of the Chaldæan dynasty, properly so called, to the destruction of Nineveh in the time of Sardanapalus by the Medes or Babylonians. Thus the whole history of Mesopotamia was represented by the Persian kings for the instruction of their subjects, as the history of one and the same empire, whose unity had been unbroken and authority uncontested, and whose heirs and successors they themselves were. In this way among many nations official history has been written for political purposes.

Section II.—First Assyrian Dynasty.

(*Fifteenth to Eleventh Centuries B.C.*)

1. We have been compelled to speak of the legendary stories of Ctesias, in order to prove their fabulous character. But we have said quite enough on the subject, and it is time to return to real history, as we learn it from the study of the original monuments of the Assyrian kings.

Modern scholars, who have devoted themselves to the study of Assyrian history, generally place (according to the statements of Berosus, confirmed by a passage in Herodotus) the foundation of the Ninevite empire in the year 1314 B.C.; but the facts stated by Berosus apply to Babylon, and not to Assyria itself. The date 1314 is, then, that of the time when the kings of Assyria became masters of Babylonia, not of the time when they established themselves at Nineveh. The positive evidence of the monuments proves beyond doubt the fact that the Assyrian monarchy commenced in the fifteenth century before our era, whilst Egypt was supreme over the whole Tigro-Euphrates Basin.

Its beginnings, like those of all other things in the world, were but small. At the commencement of the dynasty it must have been simply the little kingdom of Nineveh, such as we find it in the confederation of the Rotennu. Far from commencing by conquests, such as those attributed to Ninus, it grew great by slow degrees, absorbed gradually other small neighbouring states of the same race, and thus united the whole Assyrian nation under one sceptre; and then, still gaining ground, extended its frontier on the Chaldæan side, and strove to unite all Mesopotamia in one united monarchy. The Armenian historian, Moses of Chorene, has preserved a most valuable document on this subject, that must have come from an ancient and authentic source; this is a list of names that he has taken for those of the first kings of Assyria—Ninus, Chalaos, Arbelus, Anebos, and Babios. In spite of some alterations, we recognise at a glance these names as being, not those of men, but of important and well-known cities, enumerated in the order in which they were incorporated with the states of the Assyrian monarchs—Nineveh, Calah, Arbela, Nipur, and Babylon. Thus this invaluable fragment, preserved by a historian who did not understand its true meaning, assists us in ascertaining the progress of the Assyrian empire and the successive extensions of its limits.

2. The history of the early period of the Ninevite kingdom, and of its connection with Babylon, is related in an invaluable tablet in the British Museum, a fragment of a historical manual for the use of Assyrian students; part of this only has been published, and none of it as yet translated; the author has, however, carefully studied the original in London, and we now proceed to give an account of the principal facts.

The record unhappily does not commence with the monarchy, and we therefore do not know its founder; but the first prince of whom it speaks reigned about 1450 B.C., a date not far from that of the establishment of Assyrian royalty. He was called Asshur-bel-Nishishu, and made a treaty with Karatadash, king of Babylon. This treaty was confirmed between his successor, Bushur-Asshur, and Burnaburyash, king of

Babylon. Next on the throne of Nineveh came Asshurubalat, who appears to have reigned about 1400 B.C. He gave his daughter in marriage to Burnaburyash, and his grandson, Karahardash, ascended the throne at Babylon while still quite young. But he was soon assassinated by a certain Nazibugash, who usurped the throne. Then the Assyrians made an expedition into Babylonia under the guidance of Asshurubalat, put Nazibugash to death, and installed Kurigalzu II., son of Burnaburyash, on the throne. These two names seem to be entirely Elamite, and we have already met with them among the successors of Kedornakhunta, but the common Turanian origin of the Chaldæans of Babylonia, and of the Susianians, explains the occurrence of similar names among the people.

There is here a short space of one or two reigns at most, of which we know nothing, and then we find the names of four kings on various monuments, of the incidents of whose reigns we know nothing, Bellikhish [or Belnirari], Budiel, Binlikhish I. [or Binnirari], and Shalmaneser I. [Shalmanuashir]. The son of this last king was Tuklat-Samdan I., who, as many Assyrian texts tell us, was the conqueror of Babylonia and Chaldæa. Sennacherib [Sinakherib], in one of his inscriptions, says that this king reigned 600 years before him, thus bringing the date up to about 1300 B.C. and fully coinciding with the date 1314 given by Berosus for the establishment of the authority of the Assyrian princes at Babylon.

3. The metropolis of Chaldæa was then, from the time of Tuklat-Samdan, reduced to the position of a dependency of the Assyrians. But neither then, nor at any time under the kings of Assyria, was this city treated as a simple provincial town subject to a governor appointed by the king. Babylon retained its own native princes who succeeded each other by hereditary right, and were vassals only of the king of Nineveh. It was the constant policy of the Assyrian monarchs in the government of conquered countries to maintain the native princes on the throne, but to reduce them to the position of vassals, thus constituting them, as we may say, hereditary satraps. This system was carried even further, and one of its principles (adopted in later times by the Persians) was to foster the regular hereditary transmission of power and of legitimate right to the throne amongst the royal families of conquered countries. When a vassal king revolted, his Assyrian suzerain treated him personally with the most extreme severity—not unfrequently he was impaled, or flayed alive—but his son and legitimate heir was always installed in the vacant throne. Under such a system, when immediately after making such a terrible example of a revolted prince, the suzerain could place the government in the hands of his son, without taking into account the hatred and desire for revenge that might be excited in his mind, revolts must have been frequent, and the unity of the empire

must, more or less, have depended on the firmness of the hand that held the reins of supreme power; the reconquest of some province or other must constantly have been in hand, for they periodically attempted to free themselves, the least sign of weakness in the sovereign state giving the signal for rebellion. Thus, to confine ourselves to the affairs of Babylonia and Chaldæa—if that great city was so early subjected to the suzerainty of Nineveh, its submission was at all times imperfect and precarious. Again and again, in the annals of Assyria, we find the Babylonian princes in revolt, attempting to reconquer their independence, constantly defeated, and, after each failure, again making preparations for a new attempt.

There was, moreover, between these vassals and their suzerains a curious dispute about titles, as we see by the monuments. The Ninevite kings styled themselves "Vicegerents of the Gods" at Babylon, and they did not wish to permit the princes who reigned in that city to call themselves sovereigns. These, on their own monuments, always called themselves "Kings of Babylon"; but at Nineveh they were officially called only Kings of Kar-Dunyash, or Lower Chaldæa.

But if Tuklat-Samdan, after taking Babylon, permitted a native king still to occupy the throne, it is evident that he changed the royal family. For, from this date, their names, instead of being Chaldæo-Turanian like those we have previously mentioned, have a purely Semitic character, and are borrowed from the so-called Assyrian language.

4. Tuklat-Samdan was succeeded by his son, Belkudurussur. Babylon revolted under this king, and the Chaldæan king, Binbaliddin, after having driven the foreigners from his dominions, invaded Assyria. Belkudurussur was killed in the contest, and the Babylonians carried off numerous trophies, amongst others the royal signet of Tuklat-Samdan. Binbaliddin is known from many inscriptions to have constructed the fortifications of Nipur, and made it one of the outworks of Babylon.

A king then mounted the throne named Adarpalashir (Adar, the Assyrian Hercules, protects his son), of whom it is said in an inscription that "he organised the country of Asshur, and that he first established the armies of Assyria." Binbaliddin having attempted again to invade Assyria at the commencement of the reign of Adarpalashir, was defeated in a great battle under the walls of Ellasar. This king, like his predecessors, must still have been partially under the yoke of the Egyptians, as even after the termination of the great Pharaonic campaigns, they continued to claim a supremacy over Assyria, that, day by day, became less real.

We have seen already, by a distinct statement in an inscription, that under Ramses XII., about 1150, the king of Egypt still continued to receive, with more or less regularity, tribute from Mesopotamia; but we have also seen that almost immediately after this date, all supremacy and even all pretensions to it ceased in consequence of the usurpation of the high priest, Her-Hor.* The king of Assyria, in whose time this event occurred, must have been Asshurdayan, son and successor of Adar-palashir; it is in fact, to the termination of the last vestiges of foreign dominion, that we must naturally attribute the expressions applied to him in the inscription where all these kings are mentioned. "He bore the supreme sceptre, he ennobled the nation of Bel . . . he outshone all who had preceded him." We know, moreover, that this king invaded Babylonia in order to take revenge for the defeat of his grandfather, and caused his supreme authority to be recognised in the whole of that country, whence he brought back immense booty.

His son Mutakkil-Nabu (trusting in Nebo), succeeded him; next came Asshur-rishishi (Asshur lifts his head); "a powerful king," says the inscription, "who attacked revolted countries, and annexed the lands of the whole world." We know also that he repressed the revolt of a Babylonian prince, named Nebuchadnezzar [Nabukudur-ussur], who on two occasions attempted to invade Assyria : but the expressions we have quoted, prove that he aggrandised the empire by new conquests. His son, Tiglath-pileser I. [Tuklat-palashar], was also a conqueror, who rendered himself illustrious during his tenure of power. A long inscription on a cylinder of baked clay, of which four copies were found in the foundations of a temple at Ellasar (Kileh Sherghat), relates the campaigns of the first part of his reign. This inscription has become celebrated because it was selected by the Royal Asiatic Society as a test of the value of the method employed in the translation of Assyrian inscriptions by the most eminent Assyriologists. Copies of the inscription (then unpublished) were in 1857 supplied to General Sir H. C. Rawlinson, Mr. Fox Talbot, Dr. Hincks, and M. Oppert, and the translations made by each of them separately were found substantially to agree.

The story in this inscription is very far from agreeing, either with the mode of life attributed by Ctesias to the successors of the fabulous Ninyas, or with the political geography of the period, such as it appears in his tale.

We find from the inscription that Tiglath-pileser commenced, in the very year of his accession to the throne, by conquering the Moschi in the neighbourhood of the Black Sea, who had come, with their five kings at their head, to the assistance of the people of Commagene who had revolted against Assyrian rule, and that he subjugated the latter country afresh. He next turned his arms against the districts of Armenia, situated above the sources of the Tigris ; the same year

* See page 272.

leading his troops in another direction, he crossed the Lower Zab, penetrated into the mountains, and subdued some tribes of Chalonitis and Western Media.

His next military efforts were directed to the north-east; he relates his battles with a great number of absolutely unknown tribes, who appear to have occupied the neighbourhood of Lake Urumiyeh, and the frontier between Armenia and Media, and at the close of these battles to have penetrated as far as the "Upper," the Caspian, Sea.

Finally, in the fourth year of his reign, Tiglath-pileser undertook the conquest "of the land of Aram where they did not worship Asshur my Lord." The first of his race, he crossed the Euphrates, possessed himself of Çarchemish, imposed tribute on the Khatti, the Khita of the Egyptian inscriptions, the northern Hittites of the Bible, and advanced as far as the mountain chain of Amanus (Kumani). In the midst of these great wars he did not neglect the arts of peace; by his orders the temples of the city of Ellasar, where was his usual residence, were rebuilt in magnificent style, amongst others the great temple of Oannes, originally constructed by Ishmi-dagan, and which king Asshurdayan had taken down in order to rebuild; but the work had been stopped for seventy years.

The cylinder ends with the fourth year of his reign; but an inscription, still partly unpublished, on a fragment of an obelisk, also in the British Museum, shows us Tiglath-pileser some years later, advancing with his army to Lebanon, and becoming master of Aradus. He entered a vessel of that city to fish in the sea, as no Assyrian king before him had ever done, and he records as one of his most brilliant exploits that he killed a dolphin with his own hand. At the news of his successes, the princes of Tanis, who also had made an alliance with Solomon, sent an embassy to request his friendship. "The king of Egypt," says the inscription, "sent him as an extraordinary present a crocodile from his river and whales from the great sea."

To these distant wars succeeded serious troubles in Babylonia, also mentioned in the tablet on the relations between the two countries, now in the British Museum. Mardukidinakhe, king of Babylon, revolted, and proclaimed his independence; Tiglath-pileser attempted to reduce him to obedience by invading Chaldæa, but was repulsed, and Mardukidinakhe, after gaining the first battles, entered Assyria, and took by assault the city of Hekali. The great Sennacherib boasts, in an inscription, of having brought back to Nineveh, after defeating the Babylonians, the statues of the gods taken from Hekali by Mardukidinakhe 418 years before, that is, about 1100 B.C.

Tiglath-pileser, after his defeat, did not assume the offensive for several years, but did so at last with great success, as he took successively Dur-Kurigalzu, Sippara, and Babylon. His eldest son, Asshur-belkala, ended the war by a treaty of peace, by which Nabushapikzir, successor of Mardukidinakhe, recognised the political supremacy of Nineveh over Babylon. This Asshur-belkala was the author of a dedicatory inscription on a mutilated statue of a goddess found at Nineveh, and now in the British Museum.

5. He was succeeded by his younger brother, Shamshi-Bin II., of whom we know only that he repaired one of the principal temples of Nineveh. Next comes Asshura-bamar, an unfortunate king, who about 1080 or 1070 was conquered in a decisive battle by the king of the Hittites, and lost all the conquests of Tiglath-pileser I. beyond the Euphrates. It was this event that facilitated, a short time afterwards, the formation of the empire of David and Solomon. But the dynasty to which Asshura-bamar belonged never recovered from the effects of this disaster. At the end of a short time, the superintendent of the royal gardens, Belkatirassu (Bel has strengthened my hand,)* the Belitaras of the Greek authors, put himself at the head of a conspiracy, dethroned his master, and became the head of a new line of kings.

SECTION III.—FIRST KINGS OF THE DYNASTY OF BELITARAS—ASSHUR-NAZIRPAL. 1070—905 *B.C.*

1. BELKATIRASSU, or Beletaras, is called "the origin of royalty" in an inscription of one of his descendants, from which we learn the series of the early successors of this head of the dynasty. Shalmaneser II. [Shalmanuashir] reigned immediately after him, and was the original founder of the magnificent palace in the city of Calah (now Nimrud), rebuilt afterwards by Asshur-nazirpal.

His successor was called Irib-Bin; next came Asshur-idinakhe (Asshur has given brothers), and then a third Shalmaneser [Shalmanuashir], and a king named Asshur-edililani (Asshur is the arbiter of the gods). Of these kings we know no certain fact nor date. We may conjecture with confidence, that some of them were the princes who possessed themselves of Media, and reunited it to the Assyrian empire. It is certain that this country had not been conquered in the time of Tiglath-pileser I., and we find it, under all kings subsequent to this period, enumerated among the dependencies of the empire.

With Binlikhish II. [or Binnirari], chronology becomes certain; the Assyrians had a special magistrate who gave his name to the year, as did the archons at Athens, and the consuls at Rome; and we possess

* By rendering the ideographic character for "hand" by a less frequently used synonym, we may read this name Belidiarassu — a form even nearer to the Beletaras of the Greek writers.

a nearly complete list of these Eponyms, with the names of the kings with whose reigns they correspond, commencing with Binlikhish II., a list in cuneiform characters on tablets of baked clay forming part of the British Museum collection. Binlikhish reigned twenty years, from 956 to 936; his son, Tuklat-Samdan II., six years, from 935 to 930. The annals of this last king have not been found, but he is referred to by his successors as a great warrior; he made one campaign amongst others towards the sources of the Tigris, in the mountains, and there set up a stele commemorative of his passage.

2. Although we have no documents of the reign of this king, those of his son, Asshur-nazirpal (Asshur protects his son), have been found in abundance. The great palace of Calah (Nimrud), with its magnificent halls decorated with sculptures, the great pyramid, used for astronomical observations, and the consecrated sanctuary at the top, explored by Mr. Layard, was rebuilt by this king; and relics of him have everywhere been found in the monument that was, as he himself said, "the glory of his name." In all the museums of Europe his bas-reliefs are to be seen, generally disfigured by a belt of inscription, containing in all cases the same text running across the figures of the sculpture. Gigantic human-headed bulls, and not less colossal lions, bear his texts engraved across their limbs. A stele, now in London, contains the narrative of his campaigns; the same story, but at greater length, is found on an immense stone forming the threshold of the temple of Adar-Samdan, the Assyrian Hercules, at Calah: this is the longest known Assyrian inscription.

Asshur-nazirpal is the only one of the Assyrian monarchs who has left us his statue, now in the British Museum. It is standing; in one hand he holds a sickle, in the other a mace. The inscription is written across his chest.

"Asshur-nazirpal, the great king, the powerful king, the king of the legions, king of Assyria, son of Tuklat-Samdan, great king, king of the legions, king of Assyria, son of Binlikhish, great king, powerful king, king of Assyria.

"He possessed the countries from the banks of the Tigris even to Lebanon; he subjected to his power the great seas and all lands, from the rising even to the going down of the sun."

3. This son of Tuklat-Samdan II. ascended the throne on the 2nd July, 930, a day marked by a partial eclipse of the sun, visible at Nineveh, a fact more than once mentioned on his monuments, and regarded as a very favourable augury for the new reign. He remained on the throne for twenty-five years, from 930 to 905. His reign secured the success of the Assyrians of the new dynasty, and gratified their desire for dominion over Asia, and especially the western countries.

The official narrative of the wars of this king up to the twentieth year of his reign, engraved on the monolith at Calah, gives us a clear idea of his warlike and ferocious character. He invariably caused his rebellious vassals to be flayed alive; and in an inscription on a stele set up over the ruins of a city he had destroyed, he said, "Over these ruins my image broods, in wreaking my vengeance I have found satisfaction.

Not one single year of his reign passed unmarked by a military expedition. The greater number were into the mountains of Armenia, to Commagene and Pontus, where the Moschi were then supreme, and finally into Media, and probably also part of Western Persia. But the names of the tribes and districts apparently belonging to these latter countries cannot as yet be identified with the names as given by other authorities; and therefore it is impossible, in the present state of knowledge, to determine how far eastward he carried his arms. Other campaigns took place on the banks of the Euphrates, and he subdued all the right bank, the Irak Arabi of our days, then divided into several flourishing kingdoms. Asshur-nazirpal was also called on to repress, especially during the first years of his reign, numerous revolts in the north of Assyria and in Lower Chaldæa, and he punished the rebels with implacable severity.

In 925 he conquered Nabubaliddin, king of Babylon, his brother Zabdan, and his general, Belbaliddin, who had had the temerity to rebel, and to send help to the people of Sukhi, on the eastern bank of the Euphrates. The chastisement inflicted in consequence of this rash attempt was so great that the Babylonians remained quiet for the remainder of his reign.

Crossing the Euphrates, Asshur-nazirpal reduced to obedience all Northern Syria, the land of the Khatti, or Hittites, the chains of Amanus (Kumani), and the basin of the Orontes (Aranta). Although he calls himself "Master of Lebanon," and states that in the year corresponding to 916, having himself visited Phœnicia, he advanced to the coast of the Mediterranean, to receive tribute from the cities of Tyre, Sidon, Byblos, and Aradus, he does not seem to have actually subjugated the Phœnician cities, but merely to have made a passing descent on the country. In this direction he did not dare to venture too far; the kingdoms of Judah and Israel were still too powerful, and by forming a coalition they might have opposed a very formidable resistance, as Jehoshaphat and Ahab, his contemporaries, had both been able successfully to carry on war against the Aramæans of the kingdom of Damascus, whom also Asshur-nazirpal did not attack.

SECTION IV.—FROM SHALMANESER IV. TO BINLIKHISH AND SAMMURAMAT (SEMIRAMIS). 905—828 B.C.

1. THE exploits of Asshur-nazirpal were surpassed by those of his son, Shalmaneser (Shalmanuashir) IV., who reigned from 905 to 865. From the commencement of the reign of this king Assyria begins to be closely and constantly connected with Bible history, and to bear invaluable testimony to its minute accuracy. Shalmaneser was the builder of the great central palace at Calah (now Nimrud), excavated by Mr. Layard. There have been found the inscriptions relating his annals; the most important is on an obelisk of black basalt, now in the British Museum, containing a summary of all the campaigns undertaken by him, or by his orders. He fortified, to guard Assyria proper, on the frontier of Chaldæa, always restless and disposed to rebel, the city of Asshur, or Ellasar (now Kileh Sherghat), as is proved by the inscriptions with his name on the bricks of the walls, and by the legend on the pedestal of an unfortunately mutilated statue.

The greater part of the expeditions of Shalmaneser IV., succeeding each other year after year, were directed, like those of his father, sometimes to the north, into Armenia and Pontus; sometimes to the east, into Media, never completely subdued; sometimes to the south, into Chaldæa, where revolts were of constant occurrence; and finally westward, towards Syria and the region of Amanus. In this direction he advanced further than his predecessors, and came into contact with some personages mentioned in Bible history. The part of his annals relating to the campaigns that brought him into collision with the kings of Damascus and Israel possesses peculiar interest for us, much greater than that attaching to the narrative of any other wars. Therefore, though we have simply mentioned the latter, we will quote what Shalmaneser, in his official records, himself says about his campaigns in Southern Syria:—

"In my sixth campaign (900) I advanced towards the cities of the banks of the Balikh (the Belias of the classical geographers, rising in the neighbourhood of Edessa, and flowing into the Euphrates above Thapsacus). I slew Giammu, the chief of their city. I passed the Euphrates in a ferry-boat, and received tribute from the kings of Syria."

"At this time Benhidri of Damascus, Sakhulina of Hamath, the kings of Syria, and those of the sea coast, trusting to the rapidity of their movements, advanced to give me battle. With the help of Asshur, the great master, my lord, I fought against them; I conquered them. I took from them their chariots, their cavalry, their arms, and I destroyed 20,500 of their soldiers."

It is in this battle, fought at Karkar, that the stele discovered near the sources of the Tigris, enumerating the confederate forces, mentions the presence of "10,000 men of Ahab of Israel," an invaluable record of the temporary alliance of Ahab and Benhidri mentioned in the Bible narrative (1 Kings xx. 34, and xxii. 1). Among the princes leagued against the Assyrians we also find the names of Matan-baal, king of Arvad, Adoni-baal, king of Sidon, Baasa, son of Rehob, king of Ammon, and consequently vassal of Ahab, and lastly an Arab sheik, named Djendib.

"In my tenth campaign" (896), says another inscription, "I crossed the Euphrates for the eighth time. I destroyed the cities of Sangar and Carchemish; I demolished them and burnt them with fire . . . Benhidri of Damascus, Sakhulina of Hamath, and twelve kings of the sea coast, putting trust in their . . . they advanced towards me to give battle. I fought with them and conquered them; I captured their chariots, their arms. They took to flight to save their lives."

"In my eleventh campaign (895) I marched out of Nineveh; I crossed for the ninth time the Euphrates in a ferry-boat . . . I advanced towards Mount Amanus; I attacked the land of Irak; I descended towards Hamath; I occupied Astamaku and eighty-nine other towns; I made a great slaughter there, and led away the inhabitants captive. At that time Benhidri of Damascus, Sakhulina of Hamath, and the twelve kings of the coast had confidence in their . . . they advanced towards me to give battle. I put them to flight; 10,000 soldiers fell before my arms; I captured their chariots, their cavalry, and their munitions of war."

"In my fourteenth year" (892), says the king, in another place, "I made enumeration of my vast and numberless territories; I crossed the Euphrates by a ford with 120,000 men. Then Benhidri of Damascus, Sakhulina of Hamath, and the twelve kings of the Upper and Lower Coast, who had assembled their innumerable armies, advanced to meet me. I fought them and put them to flight; I captured their chariots, their cavalry; I took their arms. They fled to save their lives."

These Syrian wars had been interrupted in 898 and 897, by a disturbance in Babylon. The local sovereign of that great city and of all Chaldæa, Mardukinaddinshu, had been dethroned by his illegitimate brother, Mardukbelusati. Shalmaneser marched towards the Lower Euphrates to re-instate Mardukinaddinshu. The war lasted two years, and the decisive operation was the siege of a town called Gananat, not at present identified. It was not till the second year of the siege that Shalmaneser entered Babylon, and dethroned the usurper.

The sixteenth campaign of Shalmaneser IV. (890) commenced a new series of wars; the king crossed the Zab, or Zabat, to make war on the mountain people of Upper Media, and afterwards on the Scythian tribes around the Caspian Sea. He did not, however, abandon the western countries, where he soon found himself opposed by the new king whom the revolution, arising from the influence of Elisha the prophet, had placed on the throne of Damascus in the room of Benhidri.

"In my eighteenth campaign" (886), we read on the Nimrud obelisk, "I crossed the Euphrates for the sixteenth time. Hazael, king of Damascus, came towards me to give battle. I took from him 1121 chariots and 470 horsemen, with his camp."

"In my nineteenth campaign (885), I crossed the Euphrates for the eighteenth time. I marched towards Mount Amanus, and there cut beams of cedar."

"In my twenty-first campaign (883), I crossed the Euphrates for the twenty-second time. I marched to the cities of Hazael of Damascus. I received tribute from Tyre, Sidon, and Byblus."

It evidently was at the end of this campaign that Jehu, king of Israel, whose territory Hazael had ravaged, appealed to Shalmaneser for help against his powerful enemy. The inscription on the obelisk says that the Assyrian king received tribute from Jehu, whom it names "son of Omri," for the great renown of the founder of Samaria had made the Assyrians consider all the kings of Israel as his descendants. One of the bas-reliefs of the same monument represents Jehu prostrating himself before Shalmaneser, as if acknowledging himself a vassal.

The annals of Shalmaneser say no more after this, either of the king of Damascus or of Israel. They record, as his twenty-seventh campaign, a great war in Armenia that brought about the submission of all the districts of that country that still resisted the Assyrian monarch. In the thirty-first campaign (873), the last mentioned on the obelisk, the king sent the general-in-chief of his armies, Tartan, again into Armenia where he gave up to pillage fifty cities, among them Van; and during this time he himself went into Media, subjected part of the northern districts of that country which were in a state of rebellion, chastised the people in the neighbourhood of Mount Elwand, where in after times Ecbatana was built, and finally made war on the Scythians of the Caspian Sea.

2. The official chronology of the Assyrians dates the termination of the reign of Shalmaneser IV. in 870, the period of his death. But during the last two years his power was entirely lost, and he was reduced to the possession of two cities, Nineveh and Calah. His second son, Asshurdaninpal, in consequence of circumstances unknown to us, raised the standard of revolt against his father, assumed the royal title, and was supported by twenty-seven of the most important cities in the empire. One of the monuments has preserved a list of these cities, and amongst them we find Arrapkha, capital of the province of Arrapachitis, Amida (now Diarbekr), Arbela, Ellasar, and all the towns of

the banks of the Tigris. War broke out between the father and his rebellious son, the army embraced the cause of the latter; he was recognised by all the provinces, and kept Shalmaneser until his death shut up and closely blockaded in his capital.

3. Shalmaneser died in 870 B.C.; his son, Shamash-Bin, continued the legitimate line. He succeeded in repressing the revolt of his brother, Asshurdaninpal, and in depriving him of the authority he had usurped. The monument recording the exploits of his first years gives no details, however, of the civil war; it merely records, after enumerating the cities that had joined the revolt of Asshurdaninpal, "With the aid of the great gods, my masters, I subjected them to my sceptre."

The usurpation of the second son of Shalmaneser, and a civil war of five years, had introduced many disorders into the empire and shaken the fidelity of many provinces. The early years of Shamash-Bin were occupied in reducing the whole to order. In the narrative which has been preserved, extending only to his fourth year, we find that the king overran and chastised with terrible severity Osrhoene or Aramæan Mesopotamia, where the people had been in rebellion, and reduced to obedience the mountainous districts, where are the sources of the Tigris and Euphrates, and finally Armenia proper. In his fourth year he marched against Mardukbalatirib, king of Babylon, who had taken advantage of the disorders in Assyria to assert his independence, and who was supported by the Susianians or Elamites. He completely defeated him, and compelled him to fly to the desert, killed very many of his army in the battle, took 200 war-chariots, and made 7,000 prisoners, of whom 5,000 were put to death on the field of battle as an example. Unfortunately our information ceases at that period, and we know absolutely nothing of the greater part of the reign of Shamash-Bin, or of the expeditions to the west of Asia, Syria, and Palestine, that must have been made after the termination of the campaigns by which the royal authority was re-established in all the ancient provinces of the empire. This king remained on the throne until 857. In 859 and 858 he had to repress a great revolt in Babylon and Chaldæa.

4. Binlikhish [or Binnirari] III., the next king, reigned twenty-nine years, from 857 to 828. An inscription of his, engraved in the first years of his reign, describing the extent of the empire, says that he governed on one side "From the land of Siluna, toward the rising sun, the countries of Elam, Albania (at the foot of Caucasus), Kharkhar, Araziash, Misu, Media, Giratbunda (a portion of Atropatene, frequently mentioned in the cuneiform inscriptions), the lands of Munna, Parsua (Parthia), Allabria (Hyrcania), Abdadana (Hecatompyla), Namri (the Caspian Scythians), even to all the tribes of the Andiu (a Turanian or Scythian people), whose country is far off, the whole of the mountainous country as far as the sea of the rising sun (the Caspian

Sea); on the other side from the Euphrates, Syria, all Phœnicia, the land of Tyre, of Sidon, the land of Omri (Samaria), Edom, the Philistines, as far as the sea of the setting sun (the Mediterranean);" on all these countries he says that "he imposed tribute."

"I marched," he says again, "against the land of Syria, and I took Marih, king of Syria, in Damascus, the city of his kingdom. The great dread of Asshur, my master, persuaded him; he embraced my knees and made submission."

Binlikhish III. was a warlike prince; every year of his reign was marked by an expedition. We have a summary of these in a chronological tablet, in the British Museum, containing a fragment (from the end of the reign of Shamash-Bin to that of Tiglath-pileser II.) of a canon of eponyms mentioning the principal events year by year. They nearly all occurred in Southern Armenia, and in the land of Van, where obedience was only maintained by incessant military demonstrations, and subsequently in the countries to the north of Media, as far as the Caspian Sea. Other expeditions were also made as far as Parthia, towards Ariana, and the various countries that, to the Assyrians, were the extreme east. We do not, however, know what that region was called by them, as it is always designated by a group of ideographic characters of unknown pronunciation. By the defeat of Marih, king of Damascus, the submission of the western provinces was secured for the remainder of this reign, for there is no record of any other campaign there.

The year 849 was marked by a great plague in Assyria; 834 by a religious festival, of which unfortunately no particulars are known; and, lastly, 833 by the solemn inauguration of a new temple to the god Nebo, in the capital.

5. But the most interesting monument of the reign of Binlikhish III. is the statue of Nebo, one of the great gods of Babylon, discovered by Mr. Loftus, and now in the British Museum; the inscription on the base of the statue mentions the wife of the king, and calls her, "the queen Sammuramat;" this is the only historical Semiramis, the one mentioned by Herodotus. He places her correctly about a century and a half before Nitocris, the wife of Nabopolassar, king of Babylon. "Semiramis," says the father of history, "raised magnificent embankments to restrain the river (Euphrates), which till then used to overflow and flood the whole country round Babylon."* But why did Herodotus, and the Babylonian tradition he has so faithfully reported, attribute these useful works to the queen, and not to her husband, Binlikhish? It was once supposed, as a solution of this problem, that Sammuramat had governed alone for some time, as queen regnant,

* HER. i. 184.

after the death of her husband. But this conjecture is absolutely contradicted by the table of eponyms in the British Museum, where it can be seen that Sammuramat never reigned alone. In our opinion the only possible explanation will be found in regarding Binlikhish and Sammuramat as the Ferdinand and Isabella of Mesopotamia. The restless desire of Babylonia and Chaldæa to form a state separate from Assyria grew more decided as time went on; in the time of Binlikhish it had already gained great strength, and the day was not far distant when the separation was definitely to take place, and to occasion the utter ruin of Nineveh. In this position of affairs it was natural for a king of Assyria to seek to strengthen his authority in Chaldæa by a marriage with a daughter of the royal line of that country, who were his vassals, and thus, in the opinion of the people of Babylon, acquire a legitimate right to the possession of the country by means of his wife, as well as the advantages to be derived from the attachment of the people to their own legitimate sovereign. We shall therefore consider Sammuramat as a Babylonian princess married by Binlikhish, and as reigning nominally at Babylon, whilst her husband occupied the throne at Nineveh, and as being the only sovereign registered by the Babylonians in their national annals. In fact, her position must have been a peculiar one, she must have been considered the rightful queen in one part of the empire, to have been named as queen, and in the same rank as the king, in such an official document as the inscription on the statue of the god Nebo. She is the only princess mentioned in any of the Assyrian texts, as we might naturally suppose; for unless under such very exceptional circumstances as we imagine in the case of Sammuramat, there can have been no queens, but only favourite concubines, under the organisation of harem life, such as it was under the Assyrian kings, and as it still is in our days.

SECTION V.—ASSHURLIKHISH [ASSHURNIRARI] OR SARDANAPALUS.—FALL OF THE FIRST ASSYRIAN EMPIRE, 828—789.

1. THE exaggerated development of the Assyrian empire was quite unnatural; the kings of Nineveh had never succeeded in welding into one nation the numerous tribes whom they subdued by force of arms, or in checking in them the spirit of independence; they had not even attempted to do so. The empire was absolutely without cohesion; the administrative system was so imperfect, the bond attaching the various provinces to each other, and to the centre of the monarchy, so weak, that at the commencement of almost every reign a revolt broke out, sometimes at one point, sometimes at another. It was therefore easy to foresee that, so soon as the reins of government were no longer in a

really strong hand—so soon as the king of Assyria should cease to be an active and warlike king, always in the field, always at the head of his troops—the great edifice laboriously built up by his predecessors of the tenth and ninth centuries would collapse, and the immense fabric of empire would vanish like smoke with such rapidity as to astonish the world. And this is exactly what occurred after the death of Bin-likhish III.

2. The tablet in the British Museum we have just mentioned allows us to follow year by year the events and the progress of the dissolution of the empire. Under Shalmaneser V., who reigned from 828 to 818, some foreign expeditions were still made, as for instance to Damascus in 819; but the forces of the empire were specially engaged during many following years, in attempting to hold countries already subdued, such as Armenia, then in a chronic state of revolt; the wars in one and the same province were constant, and occupied some six successive campaigns (the Armenian war was from 827 to 822), proving that no decisive results were obtained.

Under Asshur-edil-ilani II., who reigned from 818 to 800, we do not see any new conquests; insurrections constantly broke out, and were no longer confined to the extremities of the empire, they encroached on the heart of the country, and gradually approached nearer to Nineveh. The revolutionary spirit increased in the provinces, a great insurrection became imminent, and was ready to break out on the slightest excuse. At this period, 804, it is that the British Museum tablet registers, as a memorable fact in the column of events, "peace in the land." Two great plagues are also mentioned under this reign, in 811 and 805, and on the 13th of June, 809 (30 Sivan in the eponomy of Bur-el-salkhi), an almost total eclipse of the sun visible at Nineveh.

The revolution was not long in coming. Asshurlikhish ascended the throne in 800, and fixed his residence at Nineveh, instead of Ellasar, where his predecessor had lived after quitting Nineveh; he is the Sardanapalus of the Greeks, the ever-famous prototype of the voluptuous and effeminate prince. The tablet in the British Museum only mentions two expeditions in his reign, both of small importance, in 795 and 794; to all the other years the only notice is "in the country" proving that nothing was done, and that all thought of war was abandoned. Sardanapalus had entirely given himself up to the orgies of his harem, and never left his palace walls, entirely renouncing all manly and warlike habits of life. He had reigned thus for seven years, and discontent continued to increase; the desire for independence was spreading in the subject provinces; the bond of their obedience each year relaxed still more, and was nearer breaking, when Arbaces, who commanded the Median contingent of the army and was himself a Mede, chanced to see in the palace at Nineveh the king, in a female dress, spindle in hand, hiding in the retirement of the harem his slothful cowardice and voluptuous life. He considered that it would be easy to deal with a prince so degraded, who would be unable to renew the valorous traditions of his ancestors. The time seemed to him to have come when the provinces, held only by force of arms, might finally throw off the weighty Assyrian yoke. Arbaces communicated his ideas and projects to the prince then entrusted with the government of Babylon, the Chaldæan Phul [Palia?], surnamed Balazu (the terrible), a name the Greeks have made into Belesis; he entered into the plot with the willingness to be expected from a Babylonian, one of a nation so frequently rising in revolt. Arbaces and Balazu consulted with other chiefs, who commanded contingents of foreign troops, and with the vassal kings of those countries that aspired to independence; and they all formed the resolution of overthrowing Sardanapalus. Arbaces engaged to raise the Medes and Persians, whilst Balazu set on foot the insurrection in Babylon and Chaldæa. At the end of a year the chiefs assembled their soldiers, to the number of 40,000, in Assyria, under the pretext of relieving, according to custom, the troops who had served the former year. When once there, the soldiers broke into open rebellion. The tablet in the British Museum tells us that the insurrection commenced at Calah in 792. Immediately after this the confusion became so great that from this year there was no nomination of an eponym.

3. Sardanapalus, rudely interrupted in his debaucheries by a danger he had not been able to foresee, showed himself suddenly inspired with activity and courage; he put himself at the head of the native Assyrian troops who remained faithful to him, met the rebels and gained three complete victories over them. The confederates already began to despair of success, when Phul, calling in the aid of superstition to a cause that seemed lost, declared to them that if they would hold together for five days more, the gods, whose will he had ascertained by consulting the stars, would undoubtedly give them the victory.

In fact, some days afterwards a large body of troops whom the king had summoned to his assistance from the provinces near the Caspian Sea, went over, on their arrival, to the side of the insurgents, and gained them a victory. Sardanapalus then shut himself up in Nineveh, and determined to defend himself to the last. The siege continued two years, for the walls of the city were too strong for the battering machines of the enemy, who were compelled to trust to reducing it by famine. Sardanapalus was under no apprehension, confiding in an oracle declaring that Nineveh should never be taken until the river became its enemy. But in the third year rain fell in such abundance that the waters of the Tigris inundated part of the city and overturned one of its walls for a distance of twenty stades. Then the king, convinced that the oracle was accomplished and despairing of any means of escape, to avoid falling alive into his enemy's hands, constructed in his palace an immense funeral pile, placed on it his gold, and silver, and his royal robes, and then, shutting himself up with his wives and eunuchs in a chamber formed in the midst of the pile, disappeared in the flames.

Nineveh opened its gates to the besiegers, but this tardy submission did not save the proud city. It was pillaged and burnt, and then rased to the ground so completely as to evidence the implacable hatred enkindled in the minds of subject nations, by the fierce and cruel Assyrian government. The Medes and Babylonians did not leave one stone upon another in the ramparts, palaces, temples, or houses of the city that for two centuries had been dominant over all Western Asia. So complete was the destruction, that the excavations of modern explorers on the site of Nineveh have not yet found one single wall slab earlier than the capture of the city by Arbaces and Balazu. All we possess of the first Nineveh is one broken statue. History has no other example of so complete a destruction. The Assyrian empire was, like the capital, overthrown, and the people who had taken part in the revolt formed independent states — the Medes under Arbaces, the Babylonians under Phul, or Balazu, and the Susianians under Shutruk-Nakhunta. Assyria, reduced to the enslaved state in which she had so long held other countries, remained for some time a dependency of Babylon.

This great event occurred in the year 789 B.C.*

CHAPTER III.

THE SECOND ASSYRIAN EMPIRE.

SECTION I.—REIGN OF PHUL [PALIA?]—RE-ESTABLISHMENT OF THE ASSYRIAN EMPIRE. 789—721.

1. AFTER the destruction of Nineveh, the Medes, content with having regained their independence, retired into their mountains without concerning themselves further with the fate of Mesopotamia; and the Chaldæan Phul Balazu, otherwise called Belesis, possessed

* It must be mentioned that the opinions of many high authorities are opposed to the views expressed in the Text, and that the first destruction of Nineveh is believed not to be historical by Sir H. Rawlinson and Professor Rawlinson. See Rawlinson's *Herodotus*, vol. i. Essay 7, and *Five Great Monarchies*, vol. ii. pp. 385—395. The author is, however, in agreement with M. Oppert and the late Dr. Hincks.

himself of Assyria, and made it for a time a dependency of Babylon; he also seized on the western provinces of the Assyrian monarchy, that is of the Aramæan countries on both sides of the Euphrates.

No inscription of this king has as yet been found, and the classical historians do not mention him after the capture of Nineveh. All therefore that we know of his reign is the record in the Bible of his invasion of the kingdom of Israel in 770. Menahem had ascended the throne after murdering his predecessor, but there was a factious and strong opposition still existing. Incapable, in the midst of these domestic discords, of repulsing a foreign invasion, he could only avert the dangers that threatened him by submitting to be tributary to Phul, to whom he paid 1,000 talents of silver (2 Kings xv. 19), and by this humiliation obtained the support of the Assyrian monarch in retaining his usurped throne.

2. But the supremacy of the Chaldæans over Assyria did not last longer than the reign of Phul, who died in 747. The Assyrians were by far the most warlike of the nations of Mesopotamia; they were an essentially manly and military people, and in the eighth century B.C. the spirit of the great wars of the two preceding centuries was not yet extinct, in spite of the disaster of Sardanapalus. Assyria had been crushed only by a coalition of Medes, Susianians, and Babylonians, attacking the capital with the ardour inspired by deep-seated and unbounded hatred. But when the Medes and Susianians had retired to their own countries, where they remained quiet, satisfied with having destroyed the proud city that had so long oppressed them, when the Assyrians were only opposed by the Babylonians, who, though they had momentarily gained the upper hand, were too enervated, too little endowed with strength of character and warlike energy, as compared with their northern neighbours, to be able to preserve their supremacy long, the spirit of independence quickly awakened in the populous Assyrian cities, even if it had ever been lost, and forty-five years after the destruction of Nineveh a general insurrection drove the Babylonians out of Assyria. The royal race of the descendants of Belkatirassu had not become extinct with Asshurlikhish, when he ascended his funeral pile. There still remained some princes of this race concealed in different parts of the country. One of these, Tiglath-pileser II. [Tuklat-pal-ashar], was placed by the Assyrian insurgents at their head. The revolt evidently must have commenced immediately after the death of Phul, in 747. But it was not at once successful, the Babylonians would not abandon their conquests without resistance. There was a struggle prolonged for several years, and it was not till the 13th of the month of Air (May), in the year 744, that Tiglath-pileser, having surmounted all opposition, could date his accession to the throne. In this year the exclusively Assyrian custom of eponyms was re-established;

for during the time of Phul dates were reckoned in the Babylonian fashion, by the years of his reign.

3. Osrhoene and the north of Syria had been so completely crushed by the Assyrian conquerors of the tenth and ninth centuries, that they no longer had any distinct nationality or desire for independence. Mere dependencies of Nineveh, they changed masters with each revolution in Assyria, and obeyed whoever reigned there. After the fall of Asshur-likhish, or Sardanapalus, they were transferred to the rule of Phul; when the kingdom of Assyria was re-established, they quietly transferred their allegiance to Tiglath-pileser. The London chronological table informs us, that in the very year of his accession this king travelled as far as the Euphrates to re-establish his authority in the western provinces.

Two years after his accession in 742, Tiglath-pileser, having reduced to obedience both Babylonia and the country of the Scythian Caspians, made an expedition into Syria, as his authority had not been recognised in the south of that country. Eniel, king of Hamath, Rezin, son of Ben-hidri, king of Damascus, and Pekah, king of Israel, formed a confederation against him with Ashariah, son of Tabeal,* whom these princes had put forward as a pretender to the throne of Judah, in opposition first to Jotham, and subsequently to Ahaz. The confederates were defeated, the kingdoms of Hamath and Damascus ravaged, Pekah was dethroned, and his place filled by Menahem II. Tiglath-pileser carried everything before him. The city of Arpad alone resisted, and sustained a siege of three years ; this the king of Assyria left to the direction of his generals. Before leaving Syria, in 742, he received tribute from Hystaspes [Gustaspi], king of Commagene, Rezin, king of Damascus, Menahem, king of Israel, Hiram, king of Tyre, Sibitbaal, king of Gebal, Urikki, king of Kui (a city in some part of Syria, but not yet identified), Pisiris, king of Carchemish, and Eniel, king of Hamath.

After his return to Assyria, Tiglath-pileser, to assist in the re-organisation of the administration of the empire, took a census of the population. In the same year he conquered the Armenians who had, at the same time as the Medes, thrown off the burden of Ninevite supremacy, and his victory is termed a massacre in the tablet in the British Museum.

In 734 Pekah, taking advantage of the war in Armenia, then occupying the king of Assyria, again possessed himself of the throne, declared himself independent, and allied himself with Rezin, king of Damascus, in order to resist the power of Assyria.

Ahaz, king of Judah, threatened by Pekah and Rezin, begged for help from Tiglath-pileser (2 Kings xvi. 7, 9), who gladly availed himself of this pretext to chastise the two kings whom he regarded as rebels.

---

* In the Bible this personage is called merely the son of Tabeal, we learn his name only from the Assyrian inscriptions. See p. 172.

He advanced at the head of a numerous army into Syria, determined to take advantage of these occurrences in order to bring the nations of Palestine definitely into subjection. He commenced by destroying the kingdom of Damascus and putting Rezin to death. Marching next against the Philistines, he took Gaza; its king at first took refuge in Egypt, but afterwards returned and made his submission. Mitenti, king of Ashdod, also at first took to flight, and was provisionally replaced by his son, Rukiptu; he, moreover, at last returned and made his submission to Tiglath-pileser. The Assyrian king made also a great expedition against the Arabs of Dumah, took their city, and imposed on them a considerable tribute.

Towards the end of the year 731 Tiglath-pileser, before returning to Nineveh, held a grand court at Damascus. Twenty-three vassal kings came there to do him homage, and pay their tribute. These were, in the order in which the conqueror himself enumerates them, Hystaspes of Commagene, Urikki of Kui, Sibitbaal of Gebal, Pisiris of Carchemish, Eniel of Hamath, Pennamu of Samala in Armenia, Tarhula of Gamgum in the same country, Sulumal of Melitene, Dadil of Colchis, Wassami of the Tibareni, Uskhilti of Tuna, Tuham of Istunda, Urim of Hubisna (the four last are names of cities in the neighbourhood of the Caucasus and their precise situation is not yet determined), Mathanbaal of Aradus, Sanib of Ammon, Solomon of Moab, Pekah of Israel, Shamsie, queen of the Arabs, Mitenti, king of Ascalon, Ahaz of Judah, Kadu-malka of Edom, Hanun of Gaza.

The king of Tyre does not appear in this list. We do not know whether Hiram was still on the throne, or whether his son, Muthon, was king. But in the following year we have distinct mention of Muthon as sovereign.

Tiglath-pileser took from Pekah half of his territory, and also reduced him to the most abject vassalage, imposing on him a very considerable tribute. In this war, lasting three years (from 733 to 731), we meet with the first instance of the barbarous system of transplanting the whole people of a conquered country to places far distant from their native land—a system seemingly unknown to the kings of the first, but constantly practised by those of the second, Assyrian empire, and after them by the Babylonians, no doubt as being likely to prevent revolts. The principal inhabitants of the kingdom of Damascus were transported to Armenia, to the banks of the river Cyrus; the Israelitish tribes of Reuben, Gad and Manasseh were carried captive to Assyria. Military colonies of Assyrians and Chaldæans replaced them in their own countries (2 Chron. xxviii. 20). Ahaz, king of Judah, paid dearly for the services the king of Assyria had rendered him in delivering him from his enemies, he was obliged to acknowledge himself a vassal of the king, to go to Damascus to pay him homage, and to engage to pay a tribute, continued till his death, and the accession of Hezekiah.

In the interval between the two campaigns in Syria, in 736, Tiglath-pileser, not venturing to attack Media proper, took Atropatene, of which he had become master in his preceding wars, for his base of operations, and made a great expedition into those countries considered by the Assyrians as the extreme east, that is what classical geographers call Ariana. He advanced farther than any of his predecessors, and reached the frontiers of India. In an inscription towards the end of his reign he names among the countries that paid tribute to him, after the small Scythian states on the borders of the Caspian Sea, Parsuash (Parthia), Zikruti (Carumanian Sagartia), Nissha (the Nisâi of the Zend Avesta, the Nisæa of the classical geographers), Ariarva (Aria), and Arakuttu (Arachosia). It is impossible to mistake the identification of these countries.

Towards the end of 730, Muthon, king of Tyre, made an alliance with Pekah, king of Israel, and they both refused their tribute to the Assyrians. Tiglath-pileser did not consider this revolt of sufficient importance to require his own presence. He contented himself with sending an army into Palestine. On the approach of this force a conspiracy was formed in Samaria, headed by Hoshea, who, after killing Pekah, possessed himself of the crown. The Assyrian king confirmed him in this position, and Muthon, finding himself without an ally, attempted no resistance, and quietly submitted to pay his tribute.*

4. Shalmaneser [Shalmanuashir] VI. succeeded Tiglath-pileser in 727. We have no monuments of his reign except some bronze weights now in the British Museum; and we know its precise length only from the table of eponyms in the same collection. The only events that we know of this period are those related in the Bible. Hoshea, who had seized the throne after murdering Pekah in 730, had in the commencement of his reign paid the same tribute as his predecessor. But at the end of some years, having made an offensive and defensive alliance with the Ethiopian king, Shabaka, who in 725 became master of Egypt, he thought himself strong enough to revolt. Shalmaneser, desirous of putting an end to this rebellion before the Ethiopian conqueror could have time to fulfil his promises to Hoshea, hastily assembled an army, and marched on the kingdom of Israel. He captured and imprisoned Hoshea, and without difficulty, made himself master of the small territory left by his predecessors to the Israelites, and in December 724 laid siege to Samaria, the capital. This city, the last bulwark of Israelitish nationality, was defended with desperate energy. Shalmaneser, unable to take it by storm, resolved to reduce it by blockade, but he did not live to witness the fall of Samaria. In little more than a year after

* The details of these campaigns of Tiglath-pileser have been elucidated by Mr. George Smith and M. Oppert. The former is well known to Assyrian scholars as the discoverer of many important facts, and for his accomplishments as a decipherer of Assyrian inscriptions.

the commencement of the siege, in 722, he died; we do not know whether he had first returned to Assyria, leaving his generals before the place, or whether his death took place in the land of Israel.

SECTION II.—SARGON [SHARYUKIN].

1. SHALMANESER [Shalmanuashir] left only one son, who was under age. The Tartan, or general-in-chief of his troops, named Sargon [Sharyukin], and who was descended also from the royal family by another branch, then seized on the throne. But his accession was not unattended with difficulties; there were other competitors, and six months passed after the death of Shalmaneser before his reign commenced. A celestial prodigy, the famous eclipse of the moon on the 19th March, 721 (the same that plays so important a part in the construction of the astronomical tables of the Greek Ptolemy), exercised on the election of Sargon an influence the exact nature of which we cannot understand. In his inscriptions there is frequent mention of the princes who before Haran interpreted the eclipse in his favour, and gave in their adhesion in the midst of sacrifices offered to Oannes, and Dagon. For the first three years he ruled only as the guardian and co-regent of the young Samdan-malik (Samdan—the Assyrian Hercules—is king), son of Shalmaneser. The table of eponyms in the British Museum informs us, that it was only from 718 that Sargon reigned alone, but the years of his reign were reckoned from 721.

This usurper was a great king, a redoubtable conqueror, who restored to Assyria all its ancient glory, all the extent of territory it had possessed before the disaster of Asshurlikhish, and even added new domains, never previously subject to Nineveh. The long inscriptions found by M. Botta in the palace of Khorsabad, make us even better acquainted with the details of his reign, than with those of more than one of the Roman emperors.

2. "This is what I have done," says Sargon, in the longest of the inscriptions, in which he relates his annals, "from the commencement of my reign to my fifteenth campaign.

"I defeated in the plains of Kalu, Humbanigash, king of Elam.

"I besieged, took, and occupied the city of Samaria, and carried into captivity 27,280 of its inhabitants. I changed the former government of the country, and placed over it lieutenants of my own."

The fall of Samaria and the destruction of the kingdom of Israel took place, as we have already said, in July 721. The inhabitants of the capital, as well as the chief families of the Ephraimites, were removed to Calah (which, after the ruin of Nineveh, had become the usual residence of the kings), to the banks of the Chaboras, and to some of the recently reconquered Median cities. In their place Sargon established in the land of Israel colonies of captives from provinces of the lower Tigris, who had fallen into his power during the war against the king of Elam. The Bible, in complete agreement with the inscription, tells us that the land of Israel was not reconstituted as a tributary kingdom, but as a simple province, occupied by a military force, and governed by an Assyrian officer.

"Hanun, king of Gaza, and Sebeh (Shabak), "Sultan"* of Egypt came to Raphia to fight against me, they met me, and I routed them. Sebeh fled . . . . I took prisoner Hanun, king of Gaza.

"I imposed tribute on Pharaoh of Egypt, on Shamsie, queen of Arabia, and on Yathaamir the Sabæan, of gold, spices, horses and camels."

We omit the account given in the inscription of the conquest of countries that seem to belong to the interior of Asia Minor, but as yet have not been identified with the names known in classical geography, such as Sinukhta and Khulli. Sargon had given Cilicia to the king of this latter country, but as he subsequently revolted, he was kept prisoner in Assyria with all the grandees of his court.

"Yaubid [or Ilubid] of Hamath was not the legitimate king . . . . He persuaded the cities of Arpad, Simyra, Damascus, and Samaria to revolt against me, and prepared for battle. I led out all the forces of the god Asshur. I besieged him and his warriors in the city of Karkar, that had taken his part. I took Karkar and burnt it to ashes. I took him prisoner, and caused him to be flayed alive. I killed the chiefs of the rebels in each city, and destroyed the cities.

"Whilst Iranzu of Van lived, he was submissive and devoted to my empire, but he died. His subjects placed his son, Aza, on the throne. Urzaha the Armenian set on foot intrigues with the people of Mount Mildish (the Niphates of the Greeks), of Zikarta (Median Sagartia), of Misiandi (the Matieni of classical geography), and with the great men of Van, and persuaded them to revolt. They abandoned the body of their master, Aza, on the tops of the mountains. Ullushun of Van, his brother, whom they put on the throne, made an alliance with Urzaha, and gave him twenty-two strong places with their garrisons. In the wrath of my heart I counted all the armies of the god Asshur, and advanced to attack that country. Ullushun of Van, finding that I was approaching, came with his troops and occupied a strong position in the

---

* This unusual title "Silthan," or Sultan, of Egypt, is evidently contrasted in the inscription with the usual title of the Egyptian monarch Pharoah, or Pir'u, in the succeeding paragraph. Sir H. Rawlinson reads the word as Tardanu, "the high in rank," and considers the title as implying a position subordinate to the reigning monarch. The author, in accordance with M. Oppert, regards it as the title indicating the suzerainty of the Ethiopian, to whom the legitimate Pharaoh was a vassal.—Tr.

ravines of the high mountains. I occupied Izirti, his royal city, the cities of Isibia and Armit, his strong fortresses. I reduced them to ashes. I killed all that belonged to Urzaha the Armenian. I took captive 250 members of his family; I occupied fifty-five walled cities . . . . and reduced them to ashes. The twenty-two strong cities of Ullushun, of which Urzaha had become master, I annexed to Assyria."

Sargon next relates how he ravaged in Armenia the states of Mitatti, king of Zikarta, or Sagartia, and sacked twenty-three of his cities; how he took prisoner Sagadatti, king of Mount Mildish, and had him flayed alive: there is a representation of this on the bas-reliefs of the palace at Khorsabad. These are followed by a narration of other campaigns in Armenia, where king Urzaha for many years remained his irreconcilable enemy, constantly exciting fresh insurrections among the vassal kings, until at last he was compelled to commit suicide to avoid falling into the hands of Sargon; in Media also, where many districts were again brought under the Assyrian yoke; then in Parthia, where the great city of Surgadia was taken by assault; in Albania; in the Caucasus; in the mountains of Cilicia and Pisidia, where the inhabitants of one city, Papha, were transported to Damascus. This system of transportation of the inhabitants of conquered countries was continued throughout all the wars of Sargon.

"Azuri, king of Ashdod, obstinately refused to pay his tribute; he sent to the neighbouring kings messages hostile to the king of Assyria. As a punishment I replaced him by another. I placed on the throne his brother, Akhimit. But the people, bent on revolt, rejected the authority of Akhimit, and placed Yaman, who was not legitimate, master on the throne. In my wrath . . . I marched against Ashdod with my warriors, who followed close on my footsteps.

"Yaman learned from far the news of my approach, and fled into Egypt to Milukhi,* and no trace of him was ever found. I besieged and took Ashdod . . . I carried off captive his gods, his wife, his sons, his daughters, and his treasures, all the contents of his palace, and the inhabitants of his land. I rebuilt again his cities, and placed there the people whom I had conquered in the lands of the rising sun. I gave them an officer of mine as governor, and treated them like Assyrians." The date of this war against Ashdod is fixed by another inscription as the year 710. It is also mentioned in the Bible (Isaiah xx. 1).

"The king of Milukhi dwells in a desert land." He must not be

* The author had originally identified, as had M. Oppert, Milukhi with Meröe. He has, however, found proof in the Cylinder of Asshurbanipal that Milukhi was north of Memphis, and that it was the name given to the western portion of the Delta (Merekh in the Hieroglyphic texts), where at this time a small independent kingdom existed. The discovery was unfortunately made too late to appear in the French edition of this work.

confounded with the Ethiopian Shabak, whose capital was at Napata. This prince, as we learn from other documents of Sargon, had given an asylum to Yaman, thus explaining the sudden appearance of his name in the inscription. It seems that the king of Assyria made preparations for war against the king of Milukhi, who wished to avert the danger. "From the most distant ages his fathers had never sent ambassadors to the kings, my ancestors, to ask for peace and friendship, and to acknowledge the power of Merodach. But the great terror inspired by my majesty decided him, and fear caused him to act differently. He recognised the greatness of the god Adar, directed his steps to Assyria, and prostrated himself before me."

We next find the story of a revolt in Commagene, repressed with great severity, and of a civil war in Albania, about the succession to the crown; in this Sargon intervened, and placed one of the competitors on the throne.

"Merodach Baladan (Mardukbaliddin), son of Yakin (undoubtedly the Kinzirus of the canon of the kings of Babylon, preserved by the Greek astronomer, Ptolemy), king of Chaldæa, no longer respected the memory of the gods . . . he evaded their precepts and neglected their worship. He had allied himself for assistance with Humbanigash, king of Elam. He had excited to revolt the nomad tribes (of Irak Arabi). He prepared for a battle and was advancing." Sargon continues the narrative by telling how he assembled all his forces to fight with Merodach Baladan. He, becoming alarmed, evacuated Babylon, and retreated into Lower Chaldæa to the neighbourhood of a fortress built by his father, and called Dur-Yakin. There a sanguinary battle took place, and the inscription gives all its details; ending in the defeat of the Chaldæan king and his allies, who hastened to make their submission the very same evening.

"Merodach Baladan," continues Sargon, "abandoned in his camp his royal insignia, his golden tiara, his golden throne, his golden parasol, his golden sceptre, his silver chair . . . he escaped in disguise. I besieged and took his city of Dur-Yakin. I took as prisoners himself, his wife, his sons, his daughters. I took gold, silver, all his possessions. I punished for their faults all the families, and all the men who had revolted from my government. I reduced the cities to ashes. I undermined and destroyed the walls."

This war took place in winter, and Sargon re-entered Babylon in triumph in February. This battle at Dur-Yakin avenged the destruction of Nineveh, and again brought Babylon under the Assyrian yoke, from which Phul had freed her. It occurred in 709, according to the chronological canon of Ptolemy. Sargon after having dethroned Merodach Baladan did not again place a vassal king on the throne of Babylon, as other monarchs of Assyria had done, but merely a satrap of his own appointment, named Nabupakidilani. The prisoners previously made in Commagene were settled in Lower Chaldæa and Susiana or Elam; and, on the other hand, those taken in Chaldæa were sent to join the colonies established some years earlier in the kingdom of Israel.

"The seven kings of the land of Iatnan (Island of Cyprus), who had established themselves at a distance of seven days' sail in the sea of the setting sun, and whose name none among the kings my fathers in Assyria and Chaldæa had ever heard, having learned the great deeds I had done in Syria and in Chaldæa, and my glory that had spread far off even into the midst of the sea, humbled their pride and bowed themselves before me; they presented themselves before me at Babylon, bearing metals, gold, silver, vases, ebony, and the manufactures of their country; they bowed themselves before me." This submission of the Isle of Cyprus to the Assyrian king is referred by another inscription to the year 708. Some years ago there was discovered in this island, at Larnica, the ancient Citium, a large stele of granite with a cuneiform inscription and a representation of king Sargon.

3. The long inscription whence we have borrowed these quotations, known by the name of "The Acts of Sargon," mentions only the victories of the king, and is entirely silent on the serious check he received in the midst of his prosperity before Tyre. Another inscription converts this repulse into a victory, but only devotes one line to it, as not wishing to bring up a recollection so painful to the king's pride. After the story of the battle of Raphia, it proceeds, "Master of battles, I crossed the Sea of Jamnia in ships, like a fish. I annexed Kui and Tyre." Now the annals of Tyre, as quoted by the Jewish historian Josephus—and here we must in preference believe them—contain the following account:—

"Elulæus reigned thirty-six years; this king, upon the revolt of the people of Citium, sailed to them, and reduced them to obedience. Soon after the king of Assyria, at the head of his army, overran all Phœnicia, but retired when they made their submission. Sidon, Acco, Palætyrus, and many other cities revolted from Tyre, and gave themselves up to the king of Assyria. When the Tyrians would not submit to him, the king returned and made war upon them again, having received from the other Phœnicians sixty large ships with 800 rowers. The Tyrians, with only twelve ships, dispersed the enemy's fleet, and took from them 500 prisoners—a very high honour for the Tyrians. Then the king returned and blockaded their city by land, and intercepted the aqueducts that brought water into it, hoping thus to secure their submission. But the Tyrians, having dug wells inside their city, resisted five years" (Joseph. Ant., IX. xiv. 2). At the end of this long and fruitless siege, the Assyrians were compelled to retreat.

4. In 711, in the midst of his military successes, Sargon, "to replace Nineveh," not yet risen from its ruins, undertook the building of a new and large city, at a distance of fifteen miles from the site of the ancient capital, called Dur Sharyukin (the castle of Sargon). This place is now called Khorsabad; and here the first discoveries of works of Assyrian art were made, and the magnificent palace, entirely the work of Sargon, uncovered by the labours successively of M. Botta and M. Victor Place. The best of the sculptures from this place now ornament the Museum of the Louvre. We shall have occasion to mention, in another part of this work, the ruins of this city and palace, completed in 706. At present we shall simply quote what Sargon says in his "Acts." He there gives some details of the construction of some parts of an Assyrian palace that are of great value.

"At the foot of the Musri, to replace Nineveh, I have built, according to the will of the gods and the desire of my heart, a city, called Dur Sharyukin. Nisroch, Sin, Shamash, Nebo, Ao, Adar, and their divine wives, who reign eternally in Mesopotamia, have blessed the marvellous splendours, the superb streets, of the city of Dur Sharyukin. . . . . I built in the city a palace covered with seal skin, with woodwork of sandal, ebony, fir, cedar, cyprus, and pistachio—a palace of incomparable magnificence for the seat of my royalty. . . . There I wrote up the glory of the gods. The upper part I built of cedar wood. I cased the beams with bronze. . . . I made a spiral staircase, like that of the great temple in Syria, called Bethilanni. I sculptured with works of art stones from the mountain. To decorate the gates, I made ornaments on the lintels and jambs, and placed above them cross pieces of gypsum. . . . My palace contains gold, silver, vases of these two metals, colours, iron, the produce of various mines, stuffs dyed with saffron, blue and purple, ambergris, seal skins, pearls, sandal and ebony wood, horses from Egypt, apes, mules, camels, booty of all kinds."

5. In 706 the works at Dur Sharyukin were finished, and on the 22nd of the month Tasrit (in October), the solemn ceremony was held of the consecration of the new city, of its palace and temples. Two years afterwards, in 704, on the 12th of the month Ab (in August), Sargon was assassinated; it is not known by whom, but possibly by Chaldæan conspirators; for soon after his murder an insurrection took place in Babylon under a certain Agises. He was in turn put to death by a second Merodach-baladan, probably a son of the one who lost the battle of Dur Yakin, who took command of the Babylonians. During this time, in Assyria, Sennacherib [Sinakherib], son of Sargon, succeeded his father.

SECTION III.—SENNACHERIB [SINAKHERIB]. 704—681.

1. SENNACHERIB, or more exactly Sinakherib (Sin—the moon-god—has multiplied brothers), is the most celebrated of the Assyrian conquerors, owing to the concurrent mention of him in Herodotus and the Bible. We possess the official narrative of his wars up to 684 in an inscription of 480 lines of very close writing on the six faces of a cylinder of baked earth, now in the British Museum, without reckoning an immense number of other texts of great historical importance. We shall, as with the "Acts of Sargon," quote the most important passages; they will show us what was the reign of this king who made the proud boast, "I have brought under my power every one who carried his head high."

"In my first campaign I conquered Merodach-baladan, king of Chaldæa, and the armies of Elam, in the neighbourhood of Kish. In the midst of the battle he stole away quietly. . . . The chariots, the horses that were engaged, turned against him; he escaped alone, and fled to his palace at Babylon. But I opened his treasure-house, I seized gold, silver, his furniture, his robes, his wife, his men, his courtiers, his male and female slaves, his domestics of the palace, his soldiers; I brought them out and sold them for slaves. With the aid of Asshur, my lord, I besieged seventy-nine large strongholds in Chaldæa, and 820 small towns in the neighbourhood. . . . The tribes of Urbi, Aram, and Khaldu, who were in the cities of Erech, Nipur, Kish, of Calneh and Cutha, I brought out and sold for slaves."

The chronological canon of Ptolemy informs us that after this victory Sennacherib no longer allowed Babylon to be ruled, as his father had done, by a simple satrap, but placed there a vassal king, named Belibus, a young Ninevite, who had been brought up in the royal palace.

In his second campaign Sennacherib turned his arms against the warlike tribes of the north and east, in Armenia, Media, and Albania, among the Parthians, and in Commagene, and gained signal victories over them.

2. "In my third campaign I marched towards Syria; Eluli was king of the Sidonians. The great renown of my majesty affrighted him, and he fled to the isles in the midst of the sea and abandoned his country. The cities of Great Sidon and Lesser Sidon, Betzitti, Sarepta, Ecdippa, Acco, the great cities, the citadels, the places of pilgrimage and devotion, the temples, all had been affrighted by the glory of Asshur, my master, and gave themselves up to me. I established Ethbaal on the throne. I imposed on him tribute and the tenth part of his royal rents.

"Ethbaal of Sidon, Abdilit of Aradus, Mitenti of Ashdod, Peduil of Ammon, Kamoshnadab of Moab, Molochram of Edom, and the kings of the whole of Phœnicia, brought with them into my presence numerous tributes, and bowed themselves before me.

"But Sidka of Ascalon did not submit to me. I carried off his gods from the house of his fathers; I led captive himself, his wife, his sons, his daughters, his brothers, the scions of his race, and carried them into Assyria. . . . The rulers, dignitaries, and inhabitants of Migron* had betrayed the king, Padi, who was inspired by friendship and zeal for Assyria, and had given him up bound in chains of iron to Hezekiah of Judah. . . .

"But they were afraid of the kings of Egypt; for the archers, chariots, and horses of the king of Ethiopia, innumerable in multitude, assembled and marched against me. Their chiefs formed them in order of battle, in view of the city of Eltheca [Eltekon, Jos. xv. 59], and inspected their men. Adoring Asshur, my master, I fought against them, and put them to flight. The drivers of the chariots of the king of Meröe were taken alive by my hand in the midst of the battle. I besieged and took the cities of Eltheca and Thamna, and carried off their inhabitants captive.

"Then I returned towards Migron; I deposed the rulers and the dignitaries who had revolted, and killed them; I hung their bodies on crosses on the walls of the city. I sold for slaves all the men of the city who had committed violence and crimes. As for those who had not committed crimes or faults, and had not despised their masters, I pardoned them. I brought Padi, their king, out of Jerusalem, and restored him to the throne of his royalty. I imposed on him the tribute paid as acknowledgment of my suzerainty.

"But Hezekiah, king of Judah, did not submit. There were forty-four walled towns, and an infinite number of villages that I fought against, humbling their pride, and braving their anger. By means of fire, massacre, battles, and siege operations, I took them; I occupied them; I brought out 200,150 persons, great and small, men and women, horses, apes, mules, camels, oxen and sheep without number, and carried them off as booty. As for himself, I shut him up in Jerusalem, the city of his power, like a bird in its cage. I invested and blockaded the fortresses round it; those who came out of the great gate of the city

---

* The name given in the text as "Migron" is read by Sir H. Rawlinson as "Ekron." The word in the Assyrian text is read by the author as *Amgarrun*, and he regards it impossible to admit the identification of the name with Ekron. On the one hand may be urged the apparently very small importance of Migron, a town barely mentioned in Scripture, and the certainty that there was a king of Ekron; on the other hand, Migron is specially mentioned in the magnificent description of the advance of the Assyrian army in the 10th chapter of Isaiah.

were seized, and made prisoners. I separated the cities I had plundered from his country, and gave them to Mitenti, king of Ashdod, to Padi, king of Migron, to Ishmabaal, king of Gaza.

"Then the fear of my majesty terrified this Hezekiah of Judah; he sent away the watchmen and guards whom he had assembled for the defence of Jerusalem. He sent messengers to me at Nineveh, the seat of my sovereignty, with thirty talents of gold and 400 talents of silver, metals, rubies, pearls, great carbuncles, seats covered with skins, thrones ornamented with leather, amber, seal skins, sandal wood, and ebony, the contents of his treasury, as well as his daughters, the women of his palace, his male and female slaves. He sent an ambassador to present this tribute, and to make his submission."

These inscriptions of Sennacherib himself agree, as we see, in a most striking manner with the Bible narrative as to the ransom Hezekiah was compelled to pay in order to save Jerusalem, where the Assyrian conqueror had once appeared. But Sennacherib has not told us all; his annals are silent as to the disaster that befell his army on his second attempt on the capital of Judah. He has so completely passed over this episode, that he does not even mention the siege of Lachish, where he was when he sent to summon Hezekiah to surrender the city; the submission of Lachish is nevertheless represented on a great bas-relief in the palace at Nineveh, now in the British Museum.

3. Desirous of retrieving the reputation of his arms, temporarily compromised by the check received before Jerusalem, Sennacherib in the following year (699) marched against Babylon, where important events had occurred during his absence. Belibus had been driven away by an insurrection under Merodach Baladan, who had escaped from prison. This indomitable champion of Babylonian independence at once put himself into a state of defence against the Assyrian king, from whom he anticipated war to the knife. The Bible informs us that he solicited the alliance of Hezekiah, after the disaster of Sennacherib before Jerusalem. Unfortunately the portion of the inscription referring to the campaign against Merodach Baladan is much mutilated. We only learn from it that Sennacherib pursued the Chaldæan prince into the marshes of Lower Chaldæa, where he defeated him in a great battle; Merodach Baladan then fled into Elymais, where he soon died. "On my return," says Sennacherib, "I placed on the throne of royalty (at Babylon) Asshur-nadin, my eldest son, the child of my blessings." This is confirmed by Berosus, and by the canon of Ptolemy.

At the end of this war Sennacherib entered upon another, rendered very troublesome by the nature of the country, in the eastern mountains towards the frontiers of Media and Susiana. He there captured a great number of cities, "perched up on high like birds' nests"; but it is impossible as yet to identify these places with the modern localities.

Pressing his advantage still farther into countries that had not yet felt the weight of the Assyrian arms, Sennacherib attacked the land of Dayi, in which we recognise with Sir H. Rawlinson the territory of the Dahi, mentioned by Herodotus* as one of the Persian tribes. Their king is called Maniya, a name clearly of Iranian character. "I carried off," says the king, "the men, the beasts of burden, the cattle, the sheep; I destroyed the cities, I demolished them, I reduced them to ashes."

4. Some years of peace succeeded these devastating wars, and Sennacherib profited by them to put into execution the project he had conceived of rebuilding Nineveh, and re-establishing it as the capital, after the example of the great kings of the tenth and ninth centuries. This famous city had already begun to rise from its ruins, the inhabitants had returned to settle on its site, but it had not yet recovered its former prosperity, the ancient capital had become a simple country town. Sennacherib made it again the Queen of Asiatic cities; magnificent enough to rival the splendors of Babylon. "I rebuilt," he says, in an inscription, "all the edifices of Nineveh, my royal city; I rebuilt the ancient, I widened the narrower streets; I made the entire city splendid as the sun." Dur Sharyukin, built by his father, lost its importance, and a large part of its population came to settle at Nineveh. Nevertheless it continued to exist for three centuries later; Xenophon mentions it under the name of Mespila. In the midst of his renovated capital, Sennacherib rebuilt the royal palace "with alabaster and cedar" with extreme magnificence. The remains of this palace are called by the present inhabitants of the country Koyundjik. It has been excavated by Mr. Layard, and the greater part of the sculptures brought to the British Museum. In building it Sennacherib anticipated a long duration for his dynasty, and he addressed to his successors, in an inscription, words to which the second destruction of Nineveh, not long after, supplied a bitterly ironical commentary:—"This palace will in course of time grow old and fall to ruins; I will that my successors rebuild the ruins, renew the inscriptions containing my name, restore the paintings, and cleanse and replace the bas-reliefs. Then may Asshur and Ishtar hear their prayers. But should anyone erase my writing and my name, may Asshur, the great god, the father of the gods, treat him as a rebel, take from him sceptre and throne, and break his sword."

5. But before long it was again necessary to attack Babylon, always conquered, but always so rebellious that the repression of insurrections there formed great part of the business of every Assyrian king. Asshurnadin, eldest son of Sennacherib, whom he had installed as prince in that city, died in 693. He was succeeded by a certain Irigibel, who

* HER. i. 125. These people are referred to as Dinaites in Ezra iv. 9.

also died at the end of a year, and was replaced by a personage called Mesisimordach, the form of whose name reveals a Babylonian origin.

In the beginning of the year 688 an insurrection broke out in the country of Kar-Dunyash, the Characene of the classical geographers—that is, the part of Chaldæa nearest the sea; the great city of Bet-Yakin was the focus of the revolt. Sennacherib marched rapidly with his army to stifle the rebellion in its commencement. Not venturing to await his arrival behind their walls, the inhabitants of Bet-Yakin emigrated in a body to Susiana, where the king, Kedornakhunta, had promised them assistance. The Assyrian king pursued them; fearing to risk his troops in the almost impassable marshes to the east of the canal of Gambul, the Shat-el-Arab of our days, he coasted by sea along the shores of Susiana adjoining Chaldæa, and carried devastation with him.

But during this time Babylon revolted in concert with the king of Elam, in the rear of Sennacherib. A certain Suzub, son of Gatul, was proclaimed king there. When the Assyrian king, returning victorious from his expedition, was on his way to Nineveh, he found his passage disputed by Suzub; a battle then took place. "I conquered Suzub," says Sennacherib, "and took him alive. I spared him as a hostage and proof of the assistance of the god Ninip. I brought him to Assyria." The Babylonian rebel was shut up, well guarded, in the city of Lakhir. In the following spring Sennacherib marched again to Susiana, as the king of that country had been in concert with the rebels. He devastated all the southern part of the country, the plain through which the Choaspes, the Eulæus, and the Pasitigris flow before falling into the Tigris. Thirty-four cities in this district were taken and burnt. "I made," says the conqueror, "the smoke of these burning cities rise up to heaven like one vast sacrifice. Then Kedornakhunta, king of Elam, learned the capture of his cities and was affrighted. He caused the rest of his men to enter the lofty citadels to make resistance. He himself abandoned his capital, Madaktu (the Badaca of classical geographers, on the Eulæus), and retired towards Khailda, in the mountains. I ordered an expedition against Madaktu." But at the moment when this decisive enterprise was to be attempted, Sennacherib retreated, as the auguries were unfavourable. Three months afterwards Kedornakhunta died, and was succeeded by his brother, Ummanmimanu.

6. In 685, Suzub contrived to escape from his prison. He remained at first for some months in Susiana, and being promised help by the new king of that country, returned to Babylon.

"The Babylonians," says Sennacherib, "conferred on him the sovereignty of the Shumir and Accad. He opened the treasure of the pyramid, the gold and silver of the temples of Bel and Zarpanit; he plundered them to give to Ummanmimanu, king of Elam. He said to him, 'Prepare your army and organise your forces, march towards Babylon, and come to our help.' The Susian, whom in a former expedition I had attacked, and whose towns I had destroyed, gladly accepted the invitation. He taxed his cities, levied an army, and increased his power with chariots and horses. . . . They came to commit crimes, like a cloud of locusts when it alights on the fields to destroy them. . . . With a heart full of wrath, I hastily mounted my highest war chariot, that sweeps my enemies before it. I took in my hands the strong bow given me by the god Asshur. . . . I rushed like the devouring flame on all these rebel armies, like the god Bin, the overwhelming. By the grace of Asshur, my master, I marched towards them, to destroy them as my prey; like a devastating tempest, I terrified my adversaries. Through the protection of Asshur, and by the storm of battle, I shook the force of their resistance, and I made their confidence tremble. The army of the rebels, thrown into confusion by my terrible attacks, retreated, and their chiefs deliberated, reduced to despair."

Sennacherib then relates how he bribed the chief of the staff of the army of the king of Elam, named Humba-undasha, who, betraying the the plans of his master, enabled the Assyrian king to gain an easy victory over the combined army of Susians and Chaldæan rebels, numbering 150,000 men. "On the wet earth, armour and arms, taken in my attacks, floated in the blood of enemies as in a river; for the war chariots that struck down men and beasts, had, in their course, crushed the bleeding bodies and their limbs. I piled up the corpses of these soldiers like trophies, and I cut off their hands and feet. I mutilated those who were taken alive like straws, and as a punishment cut off their hands." Among the prisoners was found Nabubalarishkun, son of Merodach Baladan, who had joined the army. Ummanmimanu and Suzub both escaped with great difficulty from the conqueror, and took refuge in Susiana.

7. In 684, Sennacherib solemnly dedicated his new palace at Nineveh, the largest in all Assyria. He then thought himself freed from all anxiety with respect to Babylon; but in the following year Suzub returned once more to that city, where he was received with enthusiasm. As in the two preceding revolts, the king of Elam had supplied him with troops to assist him. Another great battle took place, which finally ruined the cause of Suzub, and gave Babylon into the power of the Ninevite king. Exasperated by these persistent and continued revolts, Sennacherib chastised Babylon with the most terrible severity. In spite of its sacred character, respected by the Assyrians almost as much as by the Chaldæans, the city was given up to be plundered, and in great part destroyed by fire. The most venerable religious monuments suffered from the fury of the Assyrian soldiers. Sennacherib

returned in triumph to Nineveh, carrying with him as the most precious trophies of his expedition the statues of the gods taken by Marduk-idinakhe from the city of Hekali 418 years before, when he conquered Tiglath-pileser I., as well as the royal signet of Shalmaneser I., a trophy of the wars of Binbaliddin. But when his first burst of anger was over, he dared not carry to extremity his vengeance on the city that was, in an especial sense, "the city of the gods," and take from it its ancient privilege of having a nominal king of its own, although dependent on the king of Nineveh. He therefore installed, in the half-ruined Babylon in 682, as king, his own fourth son, Esarhaddon [Asshurakhiddin] (Asshur has given brothers).

About this time, at the close of his reign, the troops of Sennacherib, according to the story of Berosus, came into serious collision in Cilicia, with the Greeks, who were then attempting to form colonies; the Assyrians were victorious, and set up a stele to commemorate the event. Berosus adds that the city of Tarsus, on the coast of Cilicia, was then founded by Sennacherib, though other authors attribute its building to Sardanapalus.

After a reign of twenty-three years, Sennacherib was, in 681, assassinated in the temple of his god Nisroch by his two sons, Adarmalik and Asshursarossor.

SECTION IV.—ESARHADDON [ASSHURAKHIDDIN] AND ASSHURBANIPAL. 681—647.

1. THE two assassins of Sennacherib derived no advantage from their crime. Esarhaddon [Asshurakhiddin] hastened from Babylon to Nineveh, compelled them to fly into Armenia, to escape the public indignation, and himself ascended the throne.

Esarhaddon (681 to 667), like his father, was a warlike king, who carried the victorious Assyrian arms into distant lands. We know in detail all the military exploits of the earlier years of his reign up to 672 (eponomy of Atarel, governor of Lakhir), the date of a cylinder of baked clay in the British Museum, on which these events are enumerated in their chronological order, but unfortunately without specifying the year of each occurrence.

The first campaign was towards Phœnicia, where the obedienee of the people, as in Babylonia, was always doubtful. "I attacked the city of Sidon, standing in the midst of the sea," says the king, in the cylinder just mentioned. "I put to death all its great men; I destroyed its walls and houses; I cast them into the sea. I destroyed the place of its altars. Abdimilkut, king of the city, had fled from my power even into the midst of the sea. Like a fish I traversed the waves, and humbled his pride. I carried away all that I could of his treasures:

gold, silver, precious stones, amber, seal skins, sandal wood and ebony, stuffs dyed purple and blue, all that his house contained. I transported into Assyria an immense number of men and women, oxen, sheep, and beasts of burden. I settled the inhabitants of Syria, and of the sea-shore in strange lands. I built in Syria a fortress called Dur-asshur-akhiddin, and there established men whom my bow had subdued in the mountains, and towards the sea of the rising sun (the Caspian)."

It was at the close of this Phœnician campaign that Esarhaddon attacked the kingdom of Judah. King Manasseh attempted to resist, but was conquered, made prisoner, and confined some time in Babylon. But the Assyrian monarch soon restored him, and replaced him on the throne as a vassal king; his inscriptions register Manasseh as one of his tributaries. Esarhaddon about the same time completed his colonisation of the Israelitish territory, establishing there large numbers of people from Lower Chaldæa and from Elam, reduced to captivity by his wars.

2. In fact, after two campaigns, briefly related, one in the land of Van and the other in the neighbourhood of the Black Sea, which brought about the submission of the Tibareni (Tabal), Mosynæci (Mashnaki), and of the Cimmerians (Gimirrai), who had already crossed the Caucasus, and commenced their invasions in Asia Minor, Esarhaddon was obliged to turn his arms against the part of Chaldæa bordering on the Persian Gulf—in later times called Characene—where Nabuzirshimtat, second son of Merodach Baladan, had succeeded in forming a small independent kingdom. The Assyrian king conquered and dethroned him, and placed his younger brother, Nahid-marduk, in his place, with the title of vassal king.

But during this time a new revolt occurred in Babylon, under a certain Shamash-ibni. Not feeling himself strong enough to attempt to hold that great city, as its fortifications had remained without repairs since its last capture by Sennacherib, he shut himself up in the neighbouring city of Bet-Dakkurri, carrying with him the astrological tablets from the temples of Babylon and Borsippa. Esarhaddon says, "Out of respect to my sublime master, and to Nebo, I restored these tablets, and entrusted them to the men of Babylon and Borsippa. I placed on the throne Nabushallim, son of Balazu, who respected the laws."

"The city of Ad-Dumu, the city of the power of the Arabians, that had been taken by Sennacherib, king of Assyria, the father who begot me, I again attacked, and led away the inhabitants captive into Assyria. . . . The ambassador of the queen of the Arabs came to Nineveh with many presents, and bowed himself before me. He implored me to restore their gods; I listened to his prayer. I restored the images of those gods that had been injured. I caused the praises of Asshur and the glory of my name to be engraved on those images. I brought them and gave them back to him. I nominated to the sovereignty of the Arabs, Tabuya, a woman from my harem. As the price of the gods I had restored to that land, I increased the tribute my father had laid on them by sixty-five camels which I imposed on them over and above." In the Book on the History of the Arabs we shall refer to the system of government of this country by queens invested also with the priesthood. Here we shall simply say that the capital, Ad-Dumu, is the Dumah of the Bible, the Daumat-el-djandal of the Arabian geographers of the Middle Ages.

At the end of this campaign, Esarhaddon also arranged the affairs of the Arabian kingdom of Hedjâz. The capital of this country, as we know by the inscriptions of Asshurbanipal, was Yathrib, now Medina. The king, named Haçan, having died, his son, Yala, was placed on the throne, and had to pay a considerable tribute.

Next comes the history of another much more distant expedition, into the Arabian peninsula. This marks the extreme point to which, in this direction, the Assyrian armies penetrated, and where, moreover, they appeared but once. The object of this expedition was a district called Bazu, situated in the south, beyond 140 schœnes (about 1,000 miles) of desert, and a mountain chain requiring forty hours for its passage. It must, from these facts as to the distance, necessarily be a district in the interior of Hadramaut, or of the Mahrah country.

On his return from this distant campaign, Esarhaddon was called on to put down a rebellion of the petty king of the district of Gambul, whose subjects "lived like fishes in the midst of waters and marshes" on the eastern bank of the Shat-el-Arab. He afterwards subdued, after a long and arduous war, part of Southern Media, and penetrated even into Western Persia, where he made prisoners the governors of two cities, who were named Sitraphernes and Hyphernes.

3. Although he had built at Nineveh a new palace, "a house of booty," where, in the foundations, was discovered the British Museum cylinder, Esarhaddon usually lived at Babylon. He exhibited a marked preference for that city, where he had lived as viceroy before the death of his father. Thus also he ensured the continued submission of Babylon, whilst he was always secure of the fidelity of Nineveh and Assyria. He it was who undertook to make Babylon the greatest and most beautiful city in the world. He commenced there the gigantic walls, and decided on the plan of those great works, resumed in after times by Nabopolassar and Nebuchadnezzar, which contributed so much to the glory of Babylon.

In the cylinder in the British Museum we find a list of the kings in the western countries who were paying tribute in the year 672. These were—Manasseh, king of Judah, the Phœnician princes (to whom we shall have occasion to refer again in our Book on the History of Phœnicia), the ten kings of the Island of Cyprus, the greater part of them with names easily recognised as Greek, a fact proving that the Hellenic element was then dominant in Cyprus, and that it submitted with a good grace to Ninevite suzerainty. The names are—Ægistus, king of Idalium; Pythagoras, king of Citium; Cius (?) king of Salamis; Ithodagon, king of Paphos; Ariel, king of Soli; Damas, king of Curium; Romis, king of Tamassus; Damus, king of Amathus; Onaerges, king of Limenium; and Baali, king of Upri.

Esarhaddon increased his empire on this side in 672 by a new and important conquest. He again adopted the policy of his father with regard to Egypt, taking advantage of the ill-feeling of the princes who then governed each of the cities of the Delta towards their suzerain, the Ethiopian king, Tahraka. The forces of the latter were defeated in a decisive battle, and Esarhaddon possessed himself of the whole of Egypt as far as the cataracts of Syene. From that time he styled himself, on the monuments, "King of Egypt and Ethiopia," as well as "King of Assyria," and "Vicegerent of the Gods at Babylon." Assyrian garrisons were stationed in the chief cities of Egypt, and new Assyrian names given to some of them. The country was divided into twenty petty principalities, under the supremacy of the Saite prince, Necho, to whom was assigned the town of Memphis.

This position of affairs continued until 668. Esarhaddon, being then seriously ill of the sickness of which he ultimately died, and finding himself unable to administer the affairs of so great an empire, decided on abdicating in favour of his eldest son, Asshurbanipal. In a proclamation, a copy of which has been discovered, bearing date the 12th Air, in the eponomy of Marlarmi (May 668), he announced his resolution to his subjects, and gave up to Asshurbanipal the government of Nineveh and of his whole empire, reserving to himself only his beloved Babylon, where he continued to reign. In the British Museum there is a fragment of a letter, written at this time by Asshurbanipal to his father, where he gives to Esarhaddon the title of king of Babylon, and entitles himself king of Assyria.

But the following year Esarhaddon died. His second son, Shamulshamugin (the Saosduchin of the canon of Ptolemy), succeeded him as king of Babylon and Chaldæa, separated from, but subordinate to, Nineveh. In 668, Tahraka, taking advantage of the illness and abdication of Esarhaddon, as well as of the feeling of insecurity produced by a change in the government, reconquered Egypt from the Assyrians.

4. Asshurbanipal (667—647) was a worthy son of his warlike father, and under him the Assyrian armies fully maintained their reputation. He commenced by directing his efforts towards Egypt, and even before the death of his father inaugurated his reign by three successive cam-

paigns on the banks of the Nile, advancing victoriously in each of them as far as Thebes. In the second he installed Necho on the throne of the city of Amen; in the third he came to avenge that prince, who had been put to death by Rot-Amen, son-in-law and successor of Tahraka. He then arranged the administration of Egypt on an entirely Assyrian basis; but after his departure his officers were unable to maintain themselves there, and his third campaign was thus nothing more than a razzia on an enormous scale. Nevertheless Assyrian supremacy was paramount for some time in Lower Egypt, and the kings of the Dodecarchy, in the Delta paid tribute to Nineveh, whilst the Ethiopians of Piankhi ruled Upper Egypt.

We have already spoken of the details of this war in our Book on the History of Egypt. It is the only one of the campaigns of Asshurbanipal that has as yet been studied by Assyrian scholars; a large number of historical texts of this king, now in the British Museum, have not been even published; and we are therefore compelled to mention very briefly the results of a hasty view of the original monuments in London, and of the more profound study of some portions made by M. Oppert.

Phœnicia had revolted at the same time that Rot-Amen invaded Egypt. After his third campaign on the banks of the Nile, in 666, Asshurbanipal, on his return to Assyria, chastised his rebellious vassals who governed the Canaanitish cities.

He first took Accho, next Tyre, admitting to mercy its king, named Baal. Aradus made a more stubborn resistance, the siege was difficult and cost many lives; but finally the city was taken, and its king, named Yakindu, killed himself to avoid falling alive into the conqueror's hands. Asshurbanipal made prisoners of the eight sons of Yakindu, a list of whom he gives; but he allowed Azbaal only, the eldest, to live, whom he installed as king of Aradus. The other seven were put to death. Phœnicia thus forcibly brought to obedience, Asshurbanipal marched on Cilicia, where also a revolt had broken out. A short campaign sufficed to quell the revolt, and the king of the country, as a mark of submission, gave up his daughter for the harem of the Ninevite monarch. It is during this war that a widely-spread tradition places the foundation of the city of Tarsus.

The following year (665), Asshurbanipal was at Nineveh, where he received an ambassador from Gyges, king of the Lydians, whose kingdom was invaded by the Cimmerians, and who, not being able to repulse them unaided, declared himself a vassal of the king of Assyria to obtain assistance against these formidable enemies. An auxiliary Assyrian force was sent to him, and by the aid of these troops Gyges gained a victory, and sent the two principal chiefs of the Cimmerians prisoners to Nineveh. The supremacy of the Assyrian empire was thus established over the whole of Asia Minor, as far as the Ægean Sea.

5. But during this time the most formidable storm that had threatened the Assyrian empire since the disaster of Asshurlikhish was impending. The younger brother of Asshurbanipal, Shamulshamugin, governed, as we have already said, Babylon and Chaldæa. He conspired to overthrow his elder brother and to seat himself on the throne of Nineveh. To accomplish this he conspired with the king of Susiana and the majority of the tributary princes of the southern states of the monarchy. In 663 he lifted the standard of revolt. To bring his ambitious projects into accordance with the feelings of nationality among the Chaldæans, he summoned to his side Nabubelshum, grandson of the great Merodach Baladan, the indomitable champion of Babylonian independence, and as king of Assyria invested him with the royalty of Babylon. Teumman, king of Elam, declared in his favour and marched into Babylonia to his assistance with a numerous army. Mathan, king of the Nabatheans, and Ywaite, king of the Arabs of Hedjâz, also joined in the revolt; and the latter sent troops to assist Shamulshamugin, under the command of a Sheikh, named Aym, son of Their. Psammetik, the Saite king, took advantage of this occasion to overthrow his colleagues of the Dodecarchy, and to re-establish the complete independence of Egypt. Gyges, forgetting the duties of the vassalage he had voluntarily assumed two years before, assisted Psammetik, and a force of Lydians contributed their assistance to drive out the Assyrian garrisons still remaining in the Delta.

This was a terrible position of affairs: the revolt broke out simultaneously almost at all points, in a way that proved a concerted plan; and unless its progress could be at once arrested before it extended to the northern provinces, the empire was lost. Asshurbanipal confronted the danger with energy and coolness, accepting the past as irrevocable; he gave up all fresh attempts on Egypt, and regarded the accession of Psammetik as an accomplished fact. In Lydia, not being able to go himself to punish the treason of Gyges, and also requiring to concentrate all the forces of Assyria in another quarter so as to crush the rebellion in its centre, he summoned the Cimmerians to invade that country again. They willingly responded to his call, devastated the whole of Lydia, and captured the city, but not the citadel, of Sardis. Gyges was killed in this invasion; his son, Ardys, who succeeded him, hastened to make his submission to Asshurbanipal, who then persuaded the Cimmerians to retreat.

Thus freed from all danger of a diversion on the side of Lydia, Asshurbanipal marched against his brother, with a view of crushing the revolt at its fountain head. The campaign seems to have been short and decisive. Asshurbanipal, in several encounters, decisively defeated the army of the Chaldæans and their allies, Teumman, king of Elam, and Aym, son of Their, forcing the one to retire on Susiana, and the other on Arabia. He then made his triumphal entry into Babylon. Shamulshamugin, terrified, felt unable to continue the struggle; he made his submission, and implored the clemency of his brother. Generally the kings of Assyria showed themselves pitiless in such cases; it was an established state rule to put conquered rebels to death. But Asshurbanipal remembered that he who had thrown himself at his feet was his brother; he pardoned him, and replaced him on the throne of the great Babylonian city, where Shamulshamugin remained for the rest of his life faithful to his Ninevite suzerain. No doubt the fraternal clemency of Asshurbanipal must be attributed to the entreaties and advice of his sister, Seruya-Edirat, who seems to have exercised great influence over him, and who is mentioned on several monuments with her two brothers.

6. But though the king of Babylon, the first author of this revolt, made his submission thus early, it was quite otherwise with his allies, who appeared resolved to carry on the war, and whom it was necessary that the king of Assyria should conquer, if he desired to ensure the tranquillity of his empire. Wishing to encounter the most serious danger first, Asshurbanipal advanced towards Susiana. Teumman, with four of his relations, Ummanibi, Tamaritu, Indabibi, and Ummanaldash, who commanded the four great divisions of the country, hastily assembled fresh troops, and prepared to invade Chaldæa. He had afforded refuge in his kingdom to Nabubelshum and his followers, who had promised him, as soon as his army had passed the frontier, to raise all the provinces of the Lower Euphrates in insurrection. Asshurbanipal anticipated his movements, and entered Susiana. After several engagements of minor importance, a great battle was fought on the banks of the Ulai (Eulæus); it ended in the defeat of the Susianians. Teumman and his son, a mere lad, were made prisoners. Asshurbanipal appeared before Susa, which opened its gates to him, and there installed on the throne, as an Assyrian vassal, Ummanaldash, who had been taken prisoner in one of the earlier battles of the campaign, and had entered the service of the Assyrian king.

Immense sculptured pictures, similar to those that decorate the pylons of the temples of Egypt, and, like them, containing hundreds of figures, give us all the details of this successful war; they were brought from the palace of Koyundjik, and are now in the British Museum. They contain a complete drama, with the story worked out in the most complete manner. We first see the battle that decided the fate of the country, a short distance in front of Susa. The Elamite warriors, in spite of their brave resistance, are cut to pieces and driven into the Eulæus, where numbers are swallowed up by the waves. In the next representation, Asshurbanipal, profiting by his victory, is marching on Susa. We next see the city (marked with its name), with its crenelated ramparts and its flat-roofed houses, in the midst of a forest of palm-trees. The Assyrian king has stopped his chariot at a short distance from the gate, and two of his officers present Ummanaldash to the people, as the king whom his sovereign will gives them, in place of the king who has dared to fight against him. Then, whilst the bodies of the last defenders of the national independence are still floating past the walls down the Eulæus, the people of the capital, terrified out of all reason, and hoping to appease the angry conqueror by the depth of their abasement, issue in a body, men, women and children, with harps, flutes and tambourines, and welcome with song and dance the new king installed by the foreign invader. During this time, and a short distance only from the scene of the rejoicings, the leaders of the vanquished army are expiating in tortures the crime of having dared to defend their king and country; one is flayed alive, the others have their ears cut off, their eyes put out, their beards and nails torn off. These scenes, comprising an immense number of figures, and executed with wonderful finish, have no more perspective than the Egyptian historical sculptures; nevertheless, we cannot but admire the life and movement exhibited by all the groups, the truth to nature, and the admirable simplicity of the attitudes.

Teumman was decapitated; an inscription, now in the British Museum, records the event. The war was not, however, concluded, but raged with great fury in the mountains of Susiana till the year 661. Ummanibi, Tamaritu, and Indabibi successively assumed the crown, and maintained the struggle in the most inaccessible parts of the country; whilst, under the Assyrian protection, Ummanaldash reigned at Susa. But all these three chiefs fell in succession on the field of battle; there was no longer anyone to head the national resistance, and the authority of Ummanaldash was recognised throughout the land. Asshurbanipal retired with his forces into Assyria, considering the war as concluded.

7. Nevertheless, the Assyrian army had hardly re-entered its own country when Ummanaldash, who had hitherto played the part of an obedient vassal of Assyria, suddenly changed his line of conduct. Throwing off the mask he had worn for two years, incited doubtless by the national spirit of the Elamites, who detested the rule of foreigners and had given up the struggle only for want of a chief to head them, he threw off his allegiance to the Ninevite monarch, and made great military preparations. Nabubelshum and the Chaldæan patriots who were concealed in the mountains were summoned to court, and entered into active correspondence with their partisans in the south of Babylonia. In the spring of 660, Asshurbanipal found himself obliged to undertake a new war in Susiana. Instead of entering the country by the way of Chaldæa, as in the preceding campaigns, he marched from the north-west directly from Assyria.

He first took the city of Rashi, capital of the district of Rash, situated in the northern part of Susiana, between the mountains of Mesobatene and the Tigris; next the city of Hamanu, in the same district, but further south. Ummanaldash was with his troops at Madaktu, the Badaca of the classical geographers; on learning the victorious advance of the Assyrians, he became alarmed and took refuge in Susa. The Assyrian army passed the river Itite, the Choaspes of the Greeks, without striking a blow, occupied Madaktu, and also Undashi, another city on the same river. Thence Asshurbanipal marched on Susa. Ummanaldash did not venture to await him there, and retired towards the mountains with the bulk of his army, leaving only a garrison in the capital. Asshurbanipal took Susa by storm, and then pushed on in pursuit of Ummanaldash, who retreated before him. He took the towns of Din, Pidilma, and Bubilu, the exact situation of which cannot be determined in the present imperfect state of our knowledge of the ancient geography of Susiana. The Elamite king then retreated to the mountains of Banun. The Assyrians overtook him there, and carried the town of Banun by assault; but he managed to escape them, together with Nabubelshum, who had not left him.

Then Asshurbanipal, tired of this fruitless pursuit, adopted other measures to compel the submission of the country and its king. He returned to Susa, and gave up the city to be pillaged by his troops. The royal treasures and archives were carried off to Nineveh. The temples were opened and systematically profaned; the statues of the gods, "that no eye had ever seen," as the cylinder in the British Museum says, were brought out to be sent to Assyria; and this seems to show that in the Susianian temples the images of the gods were placed in a sort of "holy of holies," inaccessible to the mass of worshippers. Asshurbanipal here gives a list of the gods whose statues he carried off, a list we think it well to repeat, as this is the only ancient document extant relative to the national Elamite gods. They were—Shumud, Bagamar, Parlikira, Amman-kashibar, Ansapata, Ragiba, Shimgam, Karsha, Kirshamash, Shudami, Aipaksina, Dilala, Panindimri, Shilagara, Napshu, and Kindakurbu. These strangely-named gods seem to have presented a great analogy with the gods of Chaldæa and Assyria, but under totally different names.

When he had thus pillaged and devastated Susa, and destroyed the temple, where was the oracle consulted by all the Elamite people with the greatest reverence, Asshurbanipal began to scour the country, carrying fire and sword on all sides, burning towns and villages and all the houses, destroying the crops, cutting down the plantations, slaughtering the flocks and herds, and reducing the populace to slavery. These frightful devastations went on uninterruptedly for a month and twenty-five days, and were spread over a great extent of territory. The terrified people from all quarters begged for peace. The soldiers who were with Ummanaldash deserted, in order to make their submission. He himself entered into negotiations with the Assyrian monarch. Nabubelshum of Chaldæa, in despair, fearing that he should be given up, made his armour-bearer kill him. Ummanaldash cut off the head of the dead man and sent it to the king of Assyria, imploring pardon for himself. Asshurbanipal received him with kindness, and having taken guarantees for his future fidelity, confirmed him in the kingdom with the title of vassal king.

A small bas-relief from Koyundjik, now in the British Museum, represents Asshurbanipal banqueting with his queen in the gardens of the harem at Nineveh. The head of Nabubelshum, salted and dried, is suspended from one of the trees of the garden facing the king, so that, during the feast, he might enhance his satisfaction by the view of this trophy.

8. The Elamite wars were now ended. The arms of Asshurbanipal had triumphed in this quarter, and he had come victorious out of a struggle that had all but overwhelmed the Assyrian empire. But the revolt still continued in Arabia and Nabathea. The king of Assyria resolved to reduce these countries to obedience, and to punish the conduct of the kings. Ywaite, son of Nuray, king of the Arabs, had taken advantage of the events of the last few years of the rebellion in Chaldæa and of the war in Susiana to increase enormously the extent of his states without opposition from the Assyrians; his two generals, Aym and Abyate, both sons of Their, had accomplished this by their conduct of the war, for we have no indication that the king himself was present in any one battle; he had acquired a vast empire, comprising not only Hedjâz, his hereditary kingdom, but also the greater part of the Arabian peninsula, the various parts of the Nedjed, Djebel Shammar, Djof, the desert of Syria, and even the whole western bank of the lower part of the Euphrates, that which is now called Irak Arabi.

The war commenced in 659, and lasted three years. The first campaign was occupied in the reconquest of Irak Arabi, and in the recapture of its towns one after the other. The most important was Hirata, on the site where was afterwards Hira, so celebrated in the Arabian histories of the first centuries of the Christian era. In the second campaign, 658, the Assyrian army commenced by crossing the Syrian desert, and advancing to the central plateau of Arabia; the whole of this plateau was overrun, and we shall follow the itinerary of the army in our Book on the History of the Arabians. A great number of fortified places were taken in these districts, and at last the Assyrians penetrated into Nedjed, to a city called Corassid, where the army awaited the opening of the third campaign. In this year, 657, Nedjed being completely subdued, Asshurbanipal attacked Hedjâz, thus striking at the heart of the power of Ywaite. From Corassid he advanced to the shore of the Red Sea, where he successively besieged and took Djisda (Djeddah) and Yanbo; and lastly crowned his successes by the capture of the great city of Yathrib (now Medina). Ywaite, in despair, implored *Aman*, which was granted him; his two generals, Aym and Abyate, were given up to Asshurbanipal, and flayed alive by the order of that king. Some bas-reliefs from Koyundjik, now in the British Museum, represent episodes of this Arabian war, the defeat of a tribe mounted on camels, and the surprise of an encampment where the warriors are being killed in their tents.

Asshurbanipal returned from Hedjâz into Syria, and on his way chastised the Nabatheans; their country was devastated, and their capital taken by the army that had conquered the Arabs. The king, Mathan, threw himself at the feet of the Ninevite king, and obtained pardon.

This final act in the great drama, opened by the revolt of Shamulshamugin, was short, and occupied only the latter months of the year 657.

In 655, Asshurbanipal was obliged once more to march his army into the land of Elam, to repress a revolt against Ummanaldash, who, since his submission, had remained a faithful vassal to Assyria. We have at present no information as to the last eight years of his reign.

9. His connection with Lydia, and his supremacy over the island of Cyprus, made Asshurbanipal known to the Greeks We have every reason to believe that he was the warlike and conquering Sardanapalus, of whom many classical writers speak, carefully distinguishing him from the voluptuous and effeminate king of the same name, under whom the first Ninevite empire came to an end.

With regard to this prince, the Greek historians of the Alexandrian period have fallen into two errors, sufficiently curious to be made the subject of remark, and plainly caused by a mistaken reading of Assyrian inscriptions; thus proving that there were among the Greeks some scholars who studied cuneiform writing and the monuments, though none of them attempted to read the Egyptian hieroglyphics.

Clitarchus* relates that in an inscription existing at Tarsus, where we may admit that this king might have been in the course of his expeditions, and have left a monument of his passage, that Sardanapalus calls himself "Son of Anakyndaraxes." But this supposed patronymic is nothing more than the common title almost always added to the name of Assyrian kings, "I, the great king of Assyria"—*Anakunadasharru-asshur*, from which an incompetent reader has made Anakyndaraxes, and taken it for the name of a man. Other writers say that Sardanapalus was surnamed *Conosconcoleros;* here again we find a common

---

* CLITARCHUS ap. ARRIAN, *Anab.* ii. 5; conf. STRAB. xiv. p. 672; ATHEN. viii., p. 335; xii. p. 529.

royal title mistaken for a proper name. The kings of Assyria were in the habit of styling themselves "I, the king, vicegerent of the god Asshur," and this title is almost always written ideographically by signs which, if mistaken for phonetics, and read phonetically, would give the pronunciation *Kunusskunkilasshur;* whence arose the supposed *Conoscoucoleros.* Very many of the errors of the Greek historians, especially those of the Alexandrian age, as to the history of the Assyrian kings, may be traced to erroneous readings of this kind.

Asshurbanipal completed the magnificent palace at Nineveh, commenced by Sennacherib, the sculptures of the part he built are the finest and best executed specimens of Assyrian art at present known. He had established there a well furnished library; its remains, discovered by Mr. Layard, are now in the British Museum, and have rendered invaluable assistance to the decipherment of the cuneiform inscriptions.

SECTION V.—END OF THE SECOND ASSYRIAN EMPIRE—FINAL FALL OF NINEVEH, 647—606 B.C.

1. Asshuredililani III. (647—625), son and successor of Asshurbanipal, reunited the crown of Babylon to that of Nineveh, probably dethroning Shamulshamugin, for he is found to have been master of the great Chaldæan city a few months after his accession, and it is very unlikely that both the sons of Esarhaddon died in the same year. In the reign of this king, the Cinneladanus of the Greek authors, Assyria gained her last military success. A single united kingdom had succeeded in Media, to the loose confederation of chiefs, that had afforded to Sargon and his son such facilities for their conquests. Phraortes ascended the throne in 657, and expelled the Assyrians from the positions they still held in the country, conquered Persia and all the Iranian lands on this side the Hindoo Koosh and the deserts of Carmania. Having thus erected the Median monarchy into a vast military empire, he thought himself able to undertake again the work of Arbaces, and to destroy the power of Nineveh. He therefore descended into Assyria, but Asshuredililani met him with a large army. A great battle took place at the foot of the mountains; Phraortes was killed, and the Median army dispersed.

Nevertheless the Assyrian empire approached its end, its military power fell into decay, its treasures were exhausted, whilst the neighbouring nations increased in power. In 625 Cyaxares, king of the Medes, and successor of Phraortes, who had subdued Asia Minor as far as the river Halys, taking advantage of the death of Asshuredililani and of the consequent disturbances in Assyria, laid siege to Nineveh, whilst the Chaldæan Nabopolassar raised an insurrection in Babylon where he proclaimed himself king, and restored independence to that country. Nineveh was in danger of falling, when it was saved for a time by the invasion of the Scythians, who, like a devastating torrent, overran the land of the Medes, and held the people in subjection for nineteen years.

2. Saruc or Assaracus, possibly another Esarhaddon [Asshurakhiddin], of whom we have no monuments, then ascended the throne, 625 to 606, and as the Scythian invasion had given a respite to Nineveh, governed during this time in tranquillity, but he ruled an empire weakened, debased and dismembered, without strength or vitality, and from this degraded state he did not even attempt to raise it. When Cyaxares had succeeded in clearing his kingdom of the hordes of Turanian invaders, he again appeared under the walls of Nineveh, more than ever resolved to complete the work of Arbaces, and to annihilate the city whose yoke had fallen so heavily on all Asia. Nabopolassar and his Babylonians advanced to his assistance, with all the good-will that Phul had brought to the help of Arbaces. After a long and close siege, Nineveh fell; and Assaracus, like his predecessor, Asshurlikhish, killed himself. The conquerors destroyed the city, burned its temples and palaces, and of the splendid Nineveh of Sennacherib, the glory of Asia, there remained only a heap of ruins (606). This great disaster that changed the face of Asia, is not recorded on any known monument, and is nowhere mentioned by any of the ancient classical writers (except Berosus), who have confused this capture and destruction of Nineveh with the ruin of the first Assyrian empire in 788. The Hebrew people alone, by the voice of their prophets, have handed down to us the memory of this great destruction; in it, lively faith and the remembrance of their own misfortunes made them see the terrible effects of Divine vengeance. The prophet Nahum says "(The burden of Nineveh). The Lord is a jealous God, and a revenger (*marg.*). The Lord revengeth and is furious. . . . He that dasheth in pieces is come up before thy face; keep the munition, watch the way, make thy loins strong, fortify thy power mightily. For the Lord hath turned away the excellency of Jacob, as the excellency of Israel: for the emptiers have emptied them out, and marred their vine branches. The shield of his mighty men is made red, the valiant men are in scarlet: the chariots shall be with flaming torches in the day of his preparation, and the fir-trees shall be terribly shaken. The chariots shall rage in the streets, they shall justle one against another in the broad ways: they shall seem like torches, they shall run like the lightnings. He shall recount his worthies: they shall stumble in their walk; they shall make haste to the wall thereof, and the defence shall be prepared. The gates of the rivers shall be opened, and the palace shall be dissolved. . . . But Nineveh is of old like a pool of water: yet they shall flee away. Stand,

stand, shall they cry; but none shall look back. Take ye the spoil of silver, take the spoil of gold: for there is none end of the store and glory out of all the pleasant furniture. She is empty, and void, and waste: and the heart melteth, and the knees smite together, and much pain is in all loins, and the faces of them all gather blackness. . . . The lion did tear in pieces enough for his whelps, and strangled for his lionesses, and filled his holes with prey, and his dens with ravin. Behold, I am against thee, saith the Lord of hosts, and I will burn her chariots in the smoke, and the sword shall devour thy young lions: and I will cut off thy prey from the earth, and the voice of thy messengers shall no more be heard. . . . And it shall come to pass, that all they that look upon thee shall flee from thee, and say, Nineveh is laid waste: who will bemoan her? whence shall I seek comforters for thee? . . . Thy shepherds slumber, O king of Assyria: thy nobles shall dwell *in the dust:* thy people is scattered upon the mountains, and no man gathereth them. There is no healing of thy bruise; thy wound is grievous; all that hear the bruit of thee shall clap the hands over thee: for upon whom hath not thy wickedness passed continually?" (Nahum i. 2; ii. 1—13; iii. 7, 18, 19).

This prophecy was literally accomplished: only two centuries after the terrible catastrophe, Xenophon, who with the Ten Thousand passed its site, does not even mention the name of Nineveh, nor do the historians of the age of Alexander. A colony was established on the ruins by the Romans, under the name of Ninus, and destroyed by the Sassanians. From that time every remembrance of Nineveh was entirely lost, even in the place where the city had stood. A town was built in the Middle Ages on the right bank of the Tigris, opposite the site of the royal city of Sennacherib, called by the Arabs Mosul. It is only in our own times that the ruins of the capital of Assyria have been discovered, buried under the soil that has covered them for 2,500 years.

CHAPTER IV.

CIVILISATION, MANNERS, AND MONUMENTS OF ASSYRIA.

SECTION I.—POLITICAL AND SOCIAL ORGANISATION.

1. THE Assyrian monarchy presented, undoubtedly, like the first Hamite empire of Babylon, whence it borrowed so much of its civilisation, a type of all later Asiatic monarchies, those of the Moslem caliphs,

as well as those of the Achæmenian and Sassanian Persians—a type we may still see in the Ottoman empire at Constantinople, and also in Russia, as opposing, even in our own days and in Europe, insurmountable obstacles to the progress of all liberty and civilisation; an unbounded, unrestrained despotism, interrupted from time to time only by revolutions plotted in the palace.

In Assyria, however, the king was not, as in Egypt, worshipped as a god; the monuments of Nineveh and of the neighbouring cities bear no trace of such religious worship as the Egyptian monuments prove to have been offered to the Pharaohs; we do not even find anything to lead us to suppose that the king was honoured by an Apotheosis.

The king was always considered as a mere man, and when in the inscriptions he addressed the gods, his language, in complete contrast with the common custom of pagan lands, is remarkable for exhibiting a strong feeling of the weakness of humanity in the presence of deity—that the king was as much a sinner as other men. An example of this is found in a beautiful prayer of king Asshurbanipal, on an unpublished tablet in the British Museum.*

"May the look of pity that shines in thine eternal face dispel my griefs.

"May I never feel the anger and wrath of the God.

"May my omissions and my sins be wiped out.

"May I find reconciliation with him, for I am the servant of his power, the adorer of the great gods.

"May thy powerful face come to my help: may it shine like heaven, and bless me with happiness and abundance of riches.

"May it bring forth in abundance, like the earth, happiness and every sort of good."

But this man, who was so humble in the presence of the gods, held in his hands, with regard to other men, the double power, spiritual and temporal; he was both a sovereign pontiff and an autocrat; he was called "the Vicegerent of the Gods on earth"; and his authority, thus emanating from a divine source, was as absolute over the soul as the body.

The monuments give us an insight into the daily life of the court of Nineveh; pictures of this nature alternate with scenes in the wars that raged unceasingly during the whole duration of the monarchy. In his palace, which was also a citadel, the king was surrounded by a numerous court, where the chief positions were filled by eunuchs. Their chief (Rab-saris), exercised a general supervision over the whole court, and, like the Kizlar Aga, or chief of the black eunuchs at Constantinople in our own days, was, next to the sovereign, the first dignitary of the empire. He followed the king to war, as also did the chief priest and

* Marked K, 163.—The name of the god to whom this prayer was addressed is unfortunately wanting.

the whole court, including the king's wives, who were carried in carefully-closed *arabas* in rear of the army. Among the great officers of the royal household are found also the controller of the palace (Mil-hekal), the grand cupbearer (Rab-sake), the captain of the guards, who also discharged the duties of provost-marshal, and of chief of the executioners. These officers of the palace, employed about the person of the king and in duties specially connected with him, were also at the same time the principal officers of state, the heads of the government. With the minister of state (Milik), the commander-in-chief of the army (Tartan), and the "governor of the land," a minister of the interior, or home secretary, they formed a sort of cabinet, to direct the affairs of the empire under the supreme authority of the king, who was frequently immersed in the pleasures of his harem, and indifferent to business. But they did not succeed to their offices by any hereditary title, as in a feudal monarchy; they were nominated and removed at the pleasure of the sovereign, whose caprice frequently led him to seek in the lowest ranks of the people for persons to fill the highest positions, and then to humble to the dust in a moment those whom he had exalted to honour.

2. The numerous provinces of the vast Assyrian empire were divided into two classes, those under governors directly appointed by the king, and those that were merely in a state of vassalage. We have already spoken of the organisation of these last, comprising the greater part of the conquered countries. The vassal states preserved, as the Assyrian inscriptions expressly say, their traditional organisation and their own peculiar laws, only occasionally modified by the suzerain; their own royal families remained on the throne, obliged only to recognise as master the king of kings, to pay him annually a considerable tribute, and to furnish a large contingent to his armies. We have already spoken of the extraordinary respect that the kings of Assyria, especially those of the old empire, showed for the legitimate hereditary succession to the crown in conquered countries, a feeling that constantly led them to reinstate on the throne the son and legitimate heir of a vassal king whose rebellion had been punished with death in its most terrible form. It was only after a long-continued series of rebellions, after repeated acts of high treason, that the king of Assyria deprived a tributary province of its privileges, and, according to the regular official formula, "treated it like the Assyrians"—that is, made it a province under the rule of a governor sent from Nineveh, as Sargon did to the kingdom of Israel and attempted to do in Babylon.

The provinces thus governed comprised Assyria itself and some conquered countries which it was necessary to hold in very close subjection. They were governed by satraps, or governors, appointed and recalled by the king, and selected from among the officers of his court;

their rank varied according to the importance of the province or city where each governed : the four highest in station seem to have been the governors of Nineveh, Calah, Ellasar, and Arbil. After them were reckoned in the first class, if we may use such an expression, the governors of Nisibis, Arabkha, Resen, Lakhir, Kirrur, Gozan, Rezeph, Mazamua, and Carchemish.

One of the principal duties of the satraps, or governors, was to receive the tribute either in money or in kind, and from it they made a deduction for themselves. Like the satraps of the Persian empire in later times, and the Turkish pachas of our own days, they had the command of the military garrisons of their provinces, and levied and organised the annual contingent for the army. They were assisted by a supreme judge and by a superintendent of the revenue; after whom came a large number of judges and subordinate functionaries, distributed over all the divisions and subdivisions of the provinces. The lowest class of officer in each town was a local magistrate, who was unable to act without the consent of a sort of municipal council, over which he presided.

3. For the business of the central administration, the government of the provinces and the quasi-diplomatic relations between the sovereign and his principal vassals, Assyria had a body of scribes, as numerous as that of Egypt, and an office system as complicated and carefully organised. Ruling over so many diverse races, the Assyrian monarchs could neither use one single official language, nor translate their official orders into all the languages of conquered provinces; it was necessary therefore to make a selection. Three languages were chosen for official use, and three separate "chanceries" for the business of the three great ethnographic divisions of the empire. This is a system necessarily adopted in all empires embracing a number of different races, instead of ruling over one single and distinct people, the system adopted now-a-days in Austria.

In the Assyrian empire the three chanceries, as is proved by numerous texts and monuments, were—the Chaldæo-Assyrian, the Turanian, and the Aramæan. The first managed the business of the central provinces, those of the Tigro-Euphrates Basin, Assyria and Babylonia. The second administered the affairs of the country to the north and north-east, where especially the Turanian, mixed it is true with some other and very diverse elements, was very numerous, and where, as the Assyrian kings found it most docile, submissive, less desirous of independence than either the Arian or Japhetic element, they always desired to give it the preponderance. The Aramæan chancery took charge of all the western provinces, Phœnicia, the kingdom of Israel, and the Arab tribes, who spoke dialects differing from the Syriac, but received the decrees of the king of kings in that language. The Syrian or Aramæan races, in fact, after having at first energetically resisted the Ninevite conquest in

Osrhoene and the north of Syria, had in the end identified themselves completely with the great Mesopotamian empire; and in later days gave to the Babylonians, and also to the Persians, the same support as they had done to the Assyrians. The Aramæans thus became the constant and devoted supporters of the great empire in the whole western part of the Semitic world; and in these countries an extension of the effective and military power of Assyria was always accompanied by an extension of the influence of the Aramæan language. When the kingdoms of Israel and Judah had fallen before the power, the one of Sargon, the other of Nebuchadnezzar, it required only a few generations under the yoke of the great empire to make these people forget the use of the Hebrew, and adopt a Syriac dialect.

4. In the hall of the archives in the palace of Koyundjik a number of petitions have been found, addressed to the king, and inscribed on tablets of baked clay. In spite of the servility of the form of address, these documents prove that the Assyrians, properly so called—the privileged population of the empire—assumed a certain amount of liberty in addressing their kings, and telling them the truth plainly. We give as an example a translation of a still unpublished tablet * in the British Museum, in which is denounced some peculation on the part of the controller of the palace and of the minister of state, dated apparently in the reign of Asshurbanipal:—

"Salutation to the king, my lord, from his humble petitioner, Zikar Nebo.

"To the king, my lord. May Asshur, Shamash, Bel, Zarpanit, Nebo, Tashmit, Ishtar of Nineveh, Ishtar of Arbela, the great gods, protectors of royalty, give a hundred years of life to the king, my lord, and slaves and wives in great number to the king, my lord.

"The gold that in the month Tashrit the minister of state and the controller of the palace should have given me—three talents of pure gold and four talents of alloyed gold, to make an image of the king and of the mother of the king—has yet not been given (to the workmen).

"May my lord, the king, give orders to the minister of state and to the controller of the palace, to give the gold, to give it from this time to the month of * * * to the army, and do it exactly."

We have also some petitions, addressed to superior officers of the court, hardly less humble in style than those to the king himself. An unpublished tablet in the British Museum contains one from a woman whose name seems to be Israelitish. It begins thus:—

"To my lord the controller of the palace, his humble slave, Sarah. May Bilit of Telit and Bilit of Babylon, Nebo, Tashmit, Ishtar of Nineveh, and Ishtar of Arbela, look favourably on him for many days, may happiness and worldly prosperity be the portion of my lord."

---

* Marked K, 538.

5. An institution peculiar to the Assyrian empire, and unknown in Chaldæa, was that of *eponyms*—an office precisely analogous to that of the consuls under the Roman emperors. Each year the king nominated a magistrate, who had no other duty than to give his name to the year in the chronological records. The eponym was always selected from the number of the superior officers of state. The highest officers of the crown had a right to this honour in regular rotation during the early years of a reign. The king reserved to himself the first eponymy, at the first commencement of a new year after his accession. The following year the commander-in-chief of the army was eponym; next the chief eunuch; after him the minister of state, and lastly the "governor of the country": this order of rotation evidently gives us the order of precedence among the superior officers of the Assyrian court. When once this series of eponyms by right was exhausted, the king made his choice among the governors of the first class. Such at any rate was the state of things in the first Assyrian empire. Under the second there was not perhaps so much regularity; the king chose the first year one from among the officers entitled to hold the eponomy, without even invariably reserving his own year.

The institution of eponyms, adopted by some countries, like the kingdom of Saba, in Yemen, in imitation of the Ninevite monarchy, must have been, like the consulship under the Roman emperors, a last traditional vestige of a time when the tribes of Assyria had a republican government, with magistrates elected annually.

6. We have no sufficient data for reconstructing the complete organisation and hierarchy of the sacerdotal and judicial professions. In the army the king was the supreme commander, and frequently directed military operations in person; but there was also a generalissimo, called in Assyrian Tartan, who seems to have been a sort of minister of war. The army was composed of two elements—the native Assyrian troops, who formed a nucleus of faithful and reliable soldiery, and the contingents of the vassal principalities. The Assyrians were an essentially military race, and also the dominant people of the empire, and appear to have been all, without exception, liable to military service for a certain number of years; but, unless they entered some permanent corps, such as the royal guard, they do not seem to have been retained under arms for any length of time. Each year a new call was made on a number of men, greater or less, according to circumstances and the wants of the empire, and distributed over the different provinces in such a way as not to put a stop to agricultural operations. The numbers only of the contingents furnished by the vassal kingdoms were fixed by the central government; and the king of each country was required to march them in by a certain date, getting the men where he would or could. Each of these contingents was commanded by officers

of its own nation. In war time the king usually gave the command of each corps of his army to one of the great officers of his court; and military exploits were, among a warlike people, and under princes almost always occupied in conquests, the readiest means of rising in political rank, and attaining to positions about the person of the king.

Military art had, moreover, made great progress among the Assyrians, especially in the engineering branch. What we know of their fortifications, both from the ruins still remaining of them and from the sculptures in the palaces, shows a large amount of science, great skill in placing the flanking towers and in arranging works to command various positions. They had also carried out the art of attack on fortifications and the construction of war machines with great success. In the bas-reliefs representing sieges of fortresses by Assyrian kings, we see them using the battering-ram, protected by a "tortoise" on rollers, and covered with hides kept constantly wet, as a protection against incendiary arrows; large moving wooden towers are also employed, filled with archers and slingers, and elevated above the crest of the enemy's rampart; the tortoises and towers are moved up an inclined plane, so as to get to the foot of the walls of the town; miners, in galleries, are sapping the ramparts, while others pull down the masonry of the counterscarp of the ditch, so as to fill it up with rubbish; skilful archers, each protected by a soldier holding a sort of mantelet, or large shield of wicker-work covered with leather, and as tall as a man, advance to the edge of the ditch, and aim at the loopholes to drive away the defenders, or shoot fire-tipped arrows over the walls to set fire to the houses; finally, the infantry fit together jointed ladders, raise them up against the walls, and prepare to make the assault under cover of the archers and moving towers.

7. In Assyria there were no castes, nor even rigorously defined classes, no hereditary or established aristocracy. There was complete social equality, such equality as despotism desires and establishes as most favourable to its own existence—an equality with a common level created by the yoke that bears equally on all, where there is no superiority but that of offices established by the will, often by the caprice, of an absolute master. In this empire there was not even an invariable and well-defined distinction between the Assyrians and the conquered nations. Men of these nations were often appointed by the royal will to the most eminent offices; and those high positions at court, that gave a potential voice in the affairs of the empire, were not always filled by Assyrians. In this way we find, in later times, the prophet Daniel, at Babylon, one of the ministers of Nebuchadnezzar, after having received the Babylonish name of Belteshazzar; and the three young Israelites, Hananaiah, Misael, and Azariah, after a similar change of name, were made superintendents of the buildings of the royal city.

The organisation of the triple chancery naturally conduced to this result, by attracting to the central seat of government, by the promise of posts of some importance in the administration, natives of subject countries, who thus found an opportunity of displaying their talents on a conspicuous stage.

8. The classical writers do not give us such detailed particulars on the subject of the Assyrian laws as they have done with regard to those of Egypt. In criminal cases we know only that the procedure was summary, the law draconian, and the punishments excessively severe; torture was applied to wring a confession from the accused, and the punishment of death was almost always inflicted with refinements in cruelty unknown, for example, in Egypt. Simple decapitation was a penalty unusually mild; in some cases the victims were crucified, in others impaled, in others flayed alive. Corpses of criminals were denied burial, and exposed to be devoured by wild beasts. For crimes less heinous than those deserving death, mutilation of one or more members, or loss of the eyes, was a common punishment.

We know rather more of their civil laws, as many contracts have been found for the sale or hire of landed property and slaves; these contracts are stamped on tablets of clay, and baked to preserve them. The oldest of these date from the earliest times of the primitive Chaldæan empire, in the reign of Sin Said; the most recent are of the Greek period, and the names of kings, Seleucus Philopator, Antiochus Epiphanes, and Demetrius Nicator, may be read on them. Some have been found relating to all periods during the whole of the long duration of the Chaldæo-Assyrian civilisation. We learn from them with how many civil and religious guarantees the possession of landed property was surrounded in Assyria. It could not be transferred except by solemn and sacred formula, as well as by a deed registered by a public officer, and bearing the signature of a certain number of witnesses. When it was necessary to deposit a sum of money as security for the performance of the contract, the deposit was made in the treasury of a temple, and the priests were present at the execution of the deed. A carefully-prepared register, in which every change was entered, served as a state record of the titles to estates, and also as a basis for the imposition of taxes. Irrigating canals, very numerous throughout the country, and the principal source of its agricultural prosperity, entailed a great number of reciprocal duties and obligations among the land-holders; and infringements of these arrangements gave rise to the majority of civil actions brought before the tribunals of Assyria.

As amongst all ancient nations, not only the goods but the person of the debtor were answerable for the debt to the creditor. He who was declared insolvent became the slave of his creditor, who could either sell him, or use his services; and this slavery was perpetual, for among the Assyrians there was no law, as among the Hebrews, limiting to any given number of years the slavery of one who fell into the power of a pitiless creditor. A portion, therefore, of the slaves in Assyria was composed of native Assyrians, reduced to that condition by the inability to pay their debts. The remainder were foreign prisoners captured in war, and sold by auction, or else brought from a distance by the slave merchants who flocked to Nineveh and the large cities. The people of the Caucasus, at that remote epoch, as now, were in the habit of selling their sons and daughters, who were specially educated for the purpose. The sale of slaves in Assyria was surrounded with the same formalities as the sale of landed property; a formal deed was required and the presence of witnesses. One of these deeds has been translated and published by M. Oppert.

9. Polygamy was allowed in all ranks of society, but the wealthy alone could afford to indulge in the practice. The royal harem ranked as an institution of the state, and was enormously large. The inscriptions found in the interior of the harem of Sargon, in the palace of Khorsabad, relating to the dedication of that building, contain the most extraordinary details, details so strange that it would be impossible to introduce them here. Marriages were placed under the special protection of the god Nisroch. The wife brought to her husband some real estate, given her as dowry by her father.

The celebrated Babylonian stone in the Imperial Library at Paris, known by the name of Cailloux Michaux, contains a deed of gift of one of these dowry estates, and the proprietorship is placed under the protection of the most terrible imprecations against all who should attempt to interfere with it.

A tablet in the British Museum contains a fragment of the civil law, in a double text, Turanian-Chaldæan and Semitic-Assyrian, on the subject of the rights and reciprocal duties of husbands and wives, fathers and children. From this we find that the Assyrian family was constituted on the basis of the most absolute and uncontrolled power of the husband and the father. No protection whatever is given to the weaker sex. The husband who wished to repudiate his wife, was obliged only to give her two minæ of silver; the wife who deceived her husband, or who wished to separate from him, was to be thrown into the river. The master was not compelled to do anything for a wounded or sick slave; but the steward through whose fault a slave died, or became temporarily unfit for work, had to pay compensation for the damage he had done to his master's property.

SECTION II.—MANNERS AND CUSTOMS.

1. THE Assyrians, who have been very happily termed "the Romans of Ancient Asia," were a people essentially fierce and warlike. Their own monuments exhibit them to us as short in stature, but thickset and strong, with every appearance of great muscular power; the nose prominent and curved, the eyes large, and the face of the most marked Semitic type.

In character, they may be regarded, both in their virtues and vices, as the complete type of the conquering races of Asia. Brave in battle, but cruel to the last degree; fond of slaughter and plunder; profoundly attached and implicitly obedient to their kings; haughty, and believing themselves immeasurably superior to all other people; patient under privations, inclined to falsehood and treachery, eminently endowed with the instincts of command, active and persevering; they formed one of the nations that Providence seems to raise up for the purpose of holding for a time other nations in subjection, and of serving as the instruments for inflicting divine chastisement. The strength and energy of their nature were such that they were for ages enabled to resist the enervating influence of the luxury, that, after so many conquests, pervaded their cities, where all the wealth of the world was accumulated; and such that, after the disaster of Sardanapalus, a half century sufficed them to recover from its effects, and again, more terrible than ever, to enter on the road to conquest. No other Asiatic people has ever been able so long to preserve military supremacy, and for so many centuries to escape the enervating influences of its own success, meeting with such persistent resistance from the nations it conquered, and surrounded by such powerful neighbours.

The Assyrians were naturally a highly religious people, and the worship of their gods held an important place in their daily life. Without being such absolute devotees as the Egyptians, everything proves that a feeling of piety existed among them, which, if it had been conjoined with any other religion than their degrading polytheism, would have proved the source of exalted virtues. They were, moreover, an intelligent as well as a warlike race, and exhibited an aptitude for varied occupations, and a superiority in widely different pursuits.

2. The soil of Assyria was and still is extremely fertile wherever it can be well watered. The Assyrians learned agriculture from their neighbours, the Babylonians, who were originally their masters; and

this art had been carried to the highest degree of perfection from the earliest times in the whole of Mesopotamia, as well in Assyria as in Chaldæa. They had all the best methods of cultivation in full use, founded both on the customs of remote ages, and on an ingenious and well-considered theory. No other ancient people made such advances in the art of agriculture; and on many points modern nations have, as it were, reinvented, but not improved on, the practice of the Babylonians and Ninevites. A system of irrigation extended over the whole country, absolutely necessary, since it seldom or never rains there; this was the foundation of their system of agriculture, and was carried to the highest point of perfection. It was first applied to the low and easily-watered plains of Chaldæa, but was afterwards extended to the whole of Assyria, where great difficulties had to be encountered in carrying it out, requiring much science, and a large amount of labour. All the rivers of the country contributed to it; and it may be said that the Assyrians did not allow one drop of that precious element to be lost—the main secret in all oriental countries of the fertility of the soil.

3. The industrial arts were not less well developed in Assyria, than was agriculture. Here again, at any rate in some manufactures, the Assyrians had been preceded by the Babylonians and had learned from them. The Assyrian woven stuffs, dyed in brilliant colours, were celebrated through the whole of the ancient world, especially for the beautiful embroideries of human or symbolical figures, processions of animals, divine symbols or flowers which covered them.

In the Assyrian sculptures all the important personages, the king, and the gods above all, have their garments decorated with these famous embroideries; and we may from this form an opinion of their beauty. These embroideries, distributed by commerce, served as models for decoration of the most ancient Grecian painted vases.

Metal work was carried to great perfection in Assyria. Furniture covered or cased with bronze was a conspicuous object in every palace. There is in the British Museum a very beautiful throne of bronze, found in the palace at Calah, in a hall where the bas-reliefs represent king Asshur-nazir-pal on a similar seat. In the decoration of halls, long friezes of sheets of bronze were used, worked in relief, and representing figures of animals or fantastic monsters; the projecting beams of the ceilings were also cased with sheets of bronze of the same kind. Vases of bronze were made in great numbers, as well as of gold and of silver, carefully chased and covered with figures; these specimens of Assyrian goldsmith's work were carried to great distances by commerce. A passage in the letters of Themistocles shows us that they were in great request at Athens, at the period of the Median wars, and they have even been found in Etruscan tombs.

The Assyrians had tools of iron and steel, but they do not seem to have manufactured them for themselves. They undoubtedly obtained them from the neighbouring provinces of the Caucasus, where the manufacture of steel, by the Chalybes, had been known from the most primitive ages. And these were not the only manufactures in common use among them that were obtained by foreign commerce. Textile fabrics, dyed purple or blue, came to them from Phœnicia, as well as some of their glass; transparent muslin from Egypt. All the carved ivory that has been found at present in the ruins of Assyrian palaces, where it was largely employed in the decoration of furniture, seems to be of Phœnician work. Assyria, however, exported to the countries with which she had commercial relations, manufactured produce to the full value of her imports. If articles evidently of Egyptian manufacture have been found at Nineveh, the sepulchres on the banks of the Nile have equally furnished their explorers with works of Assyrian manufacture, especially small articles of precious wood, and of enamelled pottery.

The Assyrian enamelled pottery, produced by a totally different process from that of Egypt—by means of a silico-alkaline glaze applied to ordinary clay, instead of to a sandy paste—and susceptible of being applied to a variety of uses, was in fact one of the most flourishing and best developed manufactures of Mesopotamia, and in the time of the eighteenth dynasty, part of the tribute to Pharaoh was paid in articles of this kind. The manufacture had been invented by the Babylonians, but in the end became as prevalent in Assyria, as in Chaldæa. The walls were encased with enamelled bricks, arranged so as to produce pictures; scenes of war or the chase, figures of deities, processions of animals, were among the chief means of decoration employed in Chaldæo-Assyrian architecture.

Ctesias describes these decorations in the palace at Babylon, and their remains have been found in the ruins of such Assyrian buildings as have been excavated, particularly at Khorsabad. The practice has been handed down traditionally from antiquity in this part of Asia, for enamelled tiles are at the present time the principal ornament of the palaces and mosques of Persia, and during the middle ages the productions of Ispahan in this art were marvellously beautiful.

The Assyrians also manufactured painted earthenware vessels and glass ware; there is in the British Museum a beautiful vase of the latter material, bearing the name of Sargon in cuneiform characters.

4. The costume of the Assyrians consisted of a robe open at the side, often with a border of fringe and decorated with rich embroidery, hanging down to the feet, and confined in the middle by a broad girdle,

precisely resembling the djubeh of the eastern people in the present day. The common people and soldiers used a shorter tunic, reaching only to the knees, so as to allow them to walk freely. The king, in his robes of ceremony, wore over all a sort of long mantle or chasuble, worn obliquely over one shoulder and splendidly ornamented; and this is also seen on the monuments on the figures of the gods; a high conical tiara surmounted his head, and in his hand he held a long sceptre or staff, nearly the height of a man. The insignia of his rank, when he appeared in public, were the same as those of Asiatic monarchs in the present day, the parasol and large feathered fly flaps carried behind him by slaves.

The Assyrians wore their hair long and curled at the end, the beard square, and with rows of curls. They were fond of wearing great quantities of jewelry, large earrings, rings, and bracelets. Some of the soldiers wore a cuirass of small pieces of metal protecting the body, and allowing the tunic to appear beneath it; these were probably light infantry. Others wore long coats of mail reaching to the feet, with a conical helmet to which was attached a sort of veil of chain mail, falling down on the neck and brought round to protect the chin, such as are now worn by the Circassians.

We can say nothing as to the costume of the Assyrian women, as we are almost entirely ignorant on the subject; the classical writers give us no information, and women are not represented in the sculptures of the palace, except among vanquished and captive people. This absence of the representations of women in the works of Assyrian art was a natural and almost inevitable consequence of the custom of shutting up women in the interior of the harem. We know of only one exception. A small bas-relief from the interior apartments of Asshurbanipal at Koyundjik, representing the king feasting in the harem garden; and in this case the queen wears a long-sleeved gown reaching to the feet; over it a fringed tunic or frock reaching below the knees; and over her shoulders a light cape or cloak, all richly decorated; on her head is a remarkable turreted diadem, very like that represented by the Greeks in the figures of their goddess Cybele, with earrings and bracelets of elaborate workmanship.

5. Among the customs still existing in Asiatic courts, and of which the earliest examples are found in Assyria, must not be forgotten the great hunting expeditions, where the Ninevite monarchs delighted to drive numbers of wild beasts together and pierce them with their arrows. In the immense plains of Assyria, however highly cultivated the land in general was, there were vast waste places, almost boundless steppes, where, as irrigation was impossible, there was no cultivation, and consequently no inhabitants. There lions, wild asses, wild bulls, and

ostriches increased and multiplied. Xenophon, who passed through the country with the Ten Thousand, tells us this, and the monuments add their testimony to his. These animals the king went out to hunt in very magnificent style, surrounded with all the pomp of a military expedition, as the Shahs of Persia still do, and as the descendants of the great Mogul did in the last century in India. Travellers who have been present at these gigantic chases, as were Taverner and Chardin, for instance, report them as regular butcheries, where animals are killed by hundreds, but where the king is not exposed to any danger. A large body of troops, spread as beaters over the plain, drive, by their shouts and all the noise they can possibly make, animals, both savage and inoffensive, into an enclosure prepared beforehand, and where they are crowded in enormous numbers. There the prince, safe in ambush and protected by strong palisades from the efforts of the lions and tigers, selected at leisure the animals he wished to kill, without being in any danger from them. It is probable that matters were arranged in this way in Assyria. But the flattery of the artists who drew the hunting scenes with which the monarchs were so fond of decorating the walls of their palaces, has represented the kings in a much more heroic position. They are traversing forests and plains in the chariots, with lions roaming all around them, and they fight face to face with the most formidable animals, exposing themselves to innumerable risks from monstrous beasts, and giving proofs of their courage as well as of their dexterity. All this is noble, grand, and poetical; but there is great reason to doubt that these scenes represent facts.

It is true that the secret of the comedy is revealed by several bas-reliefs of Asshurbanipal. This king was one of those who showed himself most addicted to hunting exploits. In all parts of his palace there are representations of his combats with lions, accompanied by inscriptions explanatory of the circumstances. On a bas-relief in the Louvre he says, "In one of my hunts a lion approached me; I seized him by the mane above his ears. Invoking Asshur, and Ishtar the lord of fights, I pierced his body with my lance, the word of my hand." On a bas-relief in the British Museum he says, "In one of my royal excursions I seized a lion by the tail, and, with the aid of Nergal and Adar, beat out his brains with my mace." There is scarcely any reason to doubt that the incident represented by the side of these inscriptions did really occur. But there is one part of some of these bas-reliefs that diminishes the value of these royal exploits. Slaves are shown, allowing the lion with which the king is about to fight to escape from a cage. He did not therefore attack these formidable animals when they were at liberty, but had them brought to his hunting ground, and they were most likely prepared beforehand so as to diminish the king's danger—lions whose claws had been cut and their teeth filed, or that had been stupefied by some beverage, so as to render them comparatively harmless.

In all cases when the kings of Assyria caused their official annals to be compiled in order to be sculptured on the walls of temples or palaces, they were as careful to mention the number of lions, wild bulls, and even wild boars, that they had killed with their own hands, as to enumerate their campaigns and the cities they had taken. This was one way of likening themselves to the gods who had been the destroyers of monsters.

The most curious inscription of this kind is that of the obelisk of Tiglath-pileser I. in the British Museum. We quote some passages from it:—"Adar and Nergal have increased his strength and have given him the glory of bravery. Embarked in the ships of Aradus, he killed a dolphin in the great sea. He killed wild boars, wild buffaloes, in the city of Arazik, opposite Syria, at the foot of Lebanon. He took the young of the wild boar alive; he dispersed a herd of them; he killed wild boars with his bow; he took wild boars alive and transported them to the city of Ellasar. He shut up 120 lions in the hunting enclosure; with his great courage he mounted his chariot and stretched them dead at his feet with his lance. He caught lions in traps. . . . He fished in the western sea, and in the sea of the rising sun, with harpoons of iron. In the countries of Ebech, Urashi, Azamari, Ankarna, Pizitu, Kashiyara, the mountains of Assyria and Khana, on the flanks of the land of Lulumi, and in the mountains where are the sources of the two rivers (Euphrates and Tigris), he caught wild goats, chamois, and wild asses."

The king who performed such famous hunting feats was a worthy successor of Nimrod, of him whose glory it was to be "a mighty hunter before the Lord."

SECTION III.—WRITING.

1. WE have already said a few words on the cuneiform writing of the Assyrian and Babylonian inscriptions, and have attributed its origin to the Shumir, the Turanian portion of the primitive population of Chaldæa. The system is perhaps the most complicated ever employed by man for depicting his thoughts. There were enormous difficulties in deciphering it, but this has now been accomplished; the interpretation rests henceforward on a secure and certain basis, and the result must be considered among the most magnificent and important discoveries of this age in the domain of historical science.

This achievement, however, is not like that of the interpretation of Egyptian hieroglyphics, due to the intellect of one man. The glory of the first decipherment of cuneiform writing must be shared among many scholars; and instead of being the result of a sudden inspiration of genius, followed from a long series of repeated and patient efforts. Even before the commencement of the excavations that revealed to the light of day the palaces buried under the soil of Assyria—even when but a very small number of specimens of this strange writing were known, Grotefend, one of the most ingenious of the men of science of modern Germany, had already established some points that have remained undisturbed by subsequent progress; by an effort almost of divination he succeeded in reading on some of the Babylonian bricks the name of Nebuchadnezzar. Soon afterwards, the successful researches of M. Botta and Mr. Layard brought to light the palaces of Khorsabad, Nimrud, and Koyundjik, and supplied an immense mass of documents for study. M. de Longperier and M. de Saulcy, the first to follow them up, contributed very important results; and if they did not finally complete the discovery of the method of interpretation, wonderfully smoothed the way for their successors. M. de Saulcy made the greatest advance; he determined the simple values of a large number of signs, first detected the syllabic character of the writings, and established the Semitic character of the language. Doubtless, had he not abandoned these studies so soon, he would have maintained the advantage he at first obtained over his fellow students.

Champollion found the key to the reading of the Egyptian hieroglyphics in the famous Rosetta stone, containing a part of a decree by the priests of Egypt under the Ptolemies, written in hieroglyphics, in the Demotic, and in Greek. Assistance of this kind was absolutely necessary, in order to arrive at any definite result in the reading of the cuneiform inscriptions. This was furnished by the inscription at Behistun, that lengthy text, in which Darius Hystaspes has related the events of his whole life, engraved on a rock in Media, in the language and writing of the Persians, of the Medes, and of the Assyrians. From the commencement of the present century the cuneiform inscription in the Persian language was read with tolerable certainty, and the portion of the Behistun monument engraved in that language gave the same assistance towards the analysis and decipherment of the Median and Assyrian inscription, as the Greek version in the Rosetta inscription. So from the date of the publication of the Behistun inscription by Sir H. Rawlinson, who had surmounted immense difficulties to make the copy, the study of cuneiform writing entered on a new phase of development, and advanced with great rapidity.

Three scholars of the highest attainments, General Sir H. Rawlinson in England, the late Dr. Hincks in Ireland, and M. Jules Oppert in France, pursued the study simultaneously, with noble emulation and equal success. In very many of the most essential points, it happened more than once that they simultaneously and independently arrived at and published the same results, so that priority of discovery could be awarded to neither; and as a result, in a few years the science of Assyriology has been established, and the decipherment of the ancient system of writing belonging to Nineveh and Babylon is an accomplished fact. To M. Oppert must be assigned the honour, after these discursive and perhaps confused attempts, of having reduced the discoveries to a system, of having separated the essential facts, and the laws to be deduced from them, and finally of having, before any one else, established the grammar of the writing and language of the Assyrians. These great and meritorious labours were acknowledged by the Imperial Institute of France in 1863, by awarding to him the prize that every tenth year is given for the most important discovery in the branches of science pursued in each of its academies.

2. Scholars have given the name of Anarian to the Ninevite and Babylonian system of cuneiform writing, as opposed to the Arian, or cuneiform writing of the Persians. It was necessary to choose a name equally general and vague, as the writing it designates is not only that of the idiom of the Chaldæo-Assyrians, but of at least five languages belonging to very different families: namely—

1st. The Assyrian, of the Semitic family, spoken both at Babylon and Nineveh.

2nd. The Armenian, an Arian or Indo-European language, used by the Armenian people from the ninth to the tenth century before our era; in this are written the numerous cuneiform inscriptions in the neighbourhood of Van.

3rd. The Susianian, or language of all the inscriptions of Susiana and Elam, belonging to the Turanian family.

4th. The Median, a Turanian idiom of the Turkish group, spoken in Media; all the official inscriptions of the Achæmenian Persians are composed in Persian, in Median, and in Assyrian.

5th. The Chaldæan, another Turanian idiom, of the Uralo-finnish group, the primitive national language of the Chaldæans before their establishment as the dominant caste in Babylon, where they continued to use it among themselves down to the last days of their supremacy, as we have already said.

There may have been, and probably were, other languages for which the Anarian system of cuneiform writing was used; but at present no others have been found on the monuments.

3. The Anarian cuneiform writing, as science has now proved, was

originally hieroglyphic, that is, composed of pictures of material objects, and these forms can in some cases be reconstructed. An inscription entirely written in these hieroglyphics exists at Susa, as is positively known; but it has not yet been copied, and is therefore unfortunately not available for study. In the course of time, by a very natural process, the pictured representation underwent a transformation in common use, in exact accordance with the process by which the Egyptian hieratic writing was formed from the hieroglyphic, and the present Chinese characters from the pictures originally used. The desire for simplicity contributed to replace the picture by some few lines which, without exactly copying its form, might serve to recall at any rate its most peculiar characteristics. The most ancient monumental remains of Babylonia and Chaldæa are inscribed with this form of writing, previous to its having assumed the cuneiform character, and this is called by scholars Hieratic.

From this was formed the true cuneiform writing, distinguished by the peculiarity of having its letters, whatever may have been their original shape, composed of a combination of marks like a nail, or wedge, 𒁹 or 𒀸 . The form of this constant element in all the signs of cuneiform writing was used among the Assyrians as one of the sacred symbols of divine intelligence, but took its origin from their method of writing. The Assyrians and Babylonians did not write with pen and ink or pencil on papyrus, prepared skins, or rolls of linen, nor with a hard point on boards, palm leaves or bark. For want of other available means they wrote on tablets of soft clay, afterwards baked when they wanted to preserve them.

Now the special distinguishing element, producing the very singular appearance of cuneiform writing, the nail, is nothing more than the mark made in the clay by the triangular stylus used for the purpose; many specimens have been found in the ruins of Nineveh. The nail would also be formed by two blows of the chisel, and was a more easy and expeditious method of engraving an inscription on stone, than by sculpturing the entire figure. The original Hieroglyphic writing thus transformed became simplified by degrees; the picture, the prototype of each character, was forgotten; the number of cuneiform marks composing each character was lessened, so that in the end they became purely conventional combinations.

Thus from the Hieroglyphic picture arose, first the Hieratic writing, and from this the first form of the cuneiform writing, termed the Archaic. This, however, itself was very complicated, but became simplified into a fourth type, the most commonly used of all, in which the greater part of the Assyrian inscriptions are written, called by scholars the Modern. Finally even this last, in its daily use, was still more abridged into a form capable of being written with greater rapidity, called the Cursive form.

The monumental remains of the primitive Chaldæan empire have no writing except in the Archaic form, apparently the only one then in use. In the time of the Assyrian kings, however, the period of the greater number of the monuments that have been preserved, that is, from the tenth to the seventh century B.C., the Cursive type was used for the writings on clay, the manuscripts of Chaldæa and Assyria; and in the monumental inscriptions, either the Archaic or Modern character was employed, at the choice of the sculptor; just as, among ourselves, inscriptions are cut sometimes in Gothic, sometimes in Roman, letters.

The Archaic type is the same in all countries where the Anarian cuneiform writing was in use; the Modern type, on the other hand, presents very apparent differences in Nineveh, Babylon, and Media.

4. In common with all hieroglyphic writing, the Anarian cuneiform commenced by a large employment of ideographics, of which very many vestiges remained to the end of its existence. The signs for ideas in this writing, like those of the Egyptian system, were doubtless originally while still hieroglyphics, some figurative, others symbolical. But there are only a very small number of these signs in the cuneiform writing which it has been possible to trace back to the ancient figurative representation, such for example as—

Sun. Shovel.

Fish. Ear.

The great majority, in the state in which we find them on the monuments, are merely conventional groups, and their meaning can be found only in an empirical manner.

5. With these ideographics are joined and mixed up, as in the Egyptian hieroglyphics, phonetic elements representing sounds and composing the majority of the texts of the Assyrian age, and a minority of those of the age of the primitive Chaldæan empire. But these phonetics are not alphabetic, as among the Egyptians; they are syllabic, for none of the nations who used the Anarian cuneiform writing had attained philosophical analysis of language sufficient to enable them to decompose the syllable, and to distinguish the mute consonant from the vowel

that gave it sound. The following table gives the usual syllabarium of the Anarian cuneiform writing—that is, the signs in most common use representing simple syllables, syllables formed of a single consonant and a single vowel; these form the chief part of every Assyrian inscription. The compound syllables with a vowel between two consonants are sometimes expressed by special signs, but more often by the juxtaposition of two simple syllables, one with a final and one with an initial vowel, thus, *Mat* was written *Ma-at*, *Bir—Bi-ir*, etc. The table is divided into three columns, giving the form of the same character in the three most commonly used varieties of the Modern form of writing, the type most common on the monuments: as under—

Number of the character in Norris's Dictionary.		Babylon.	Nineveh.	Media.
1	*a*			
40	*i*			
23	*u*			
21	*â*			
72	*e*			
24	*û*			
2	*ba*			
3	*bi*			
4	*bu*			
9	*ga*			

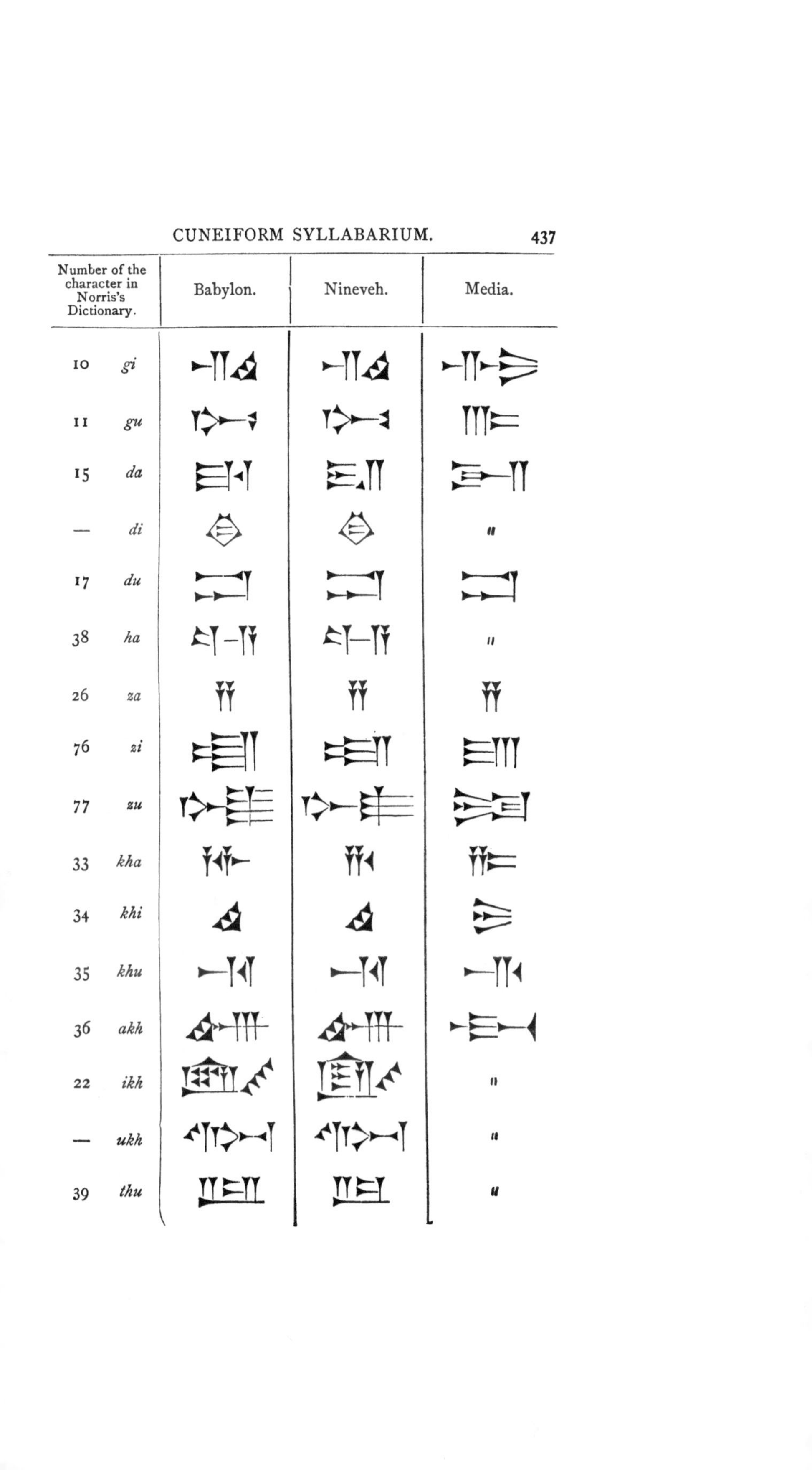

Number of the character in Norris's Dictionary.		Babylon.	Nineveh.	Media.
10	*gi*			
11	*gu*			
15	*da*			
—	*di*			"
17	*du*			
38	*ha*			"
26	*za*			
76	*zi*			
77	*zu*			
33	*kha*			
34	*khi*			
35	*khu*			
36	*akh*			
22	*ikh*			"
—	*ukh*			"
39	*thu*			"

Number of the character in Norris's Dictionary.		Babylon.	Nineveh.	Media.
42	*ka*			″
43	*ki*			
44	*ku*			
12	*ak*			
13	*ik*			
14	*uk*			
45	*la*			
46	*li*			
48	*lu*			
50	*al*			″
51	*il*			″
53	*ul*			
54	*ma*			
56	*mi*			
55	*me*			″
57	*mû*			

Number of the character in Norris's Dictionary.		Babylon.	Nineveh.	Media.
58	*am*			"
59	*im*			
60	*um*			
61	*na*			
62	*ni*			
6	*ne*			"
63	*nu*			
65	*an*			
66	*in*			
68	*un*			
69	*sa*			
70	*si*			"
91	*se*			"
71	*su*			
30	*as*			
31	*is*			

Number of the character in Norris's Dictionary.		Babylon.	Nineveh.	Media.
32	*us*			"
73	*pa*			
74	*pi*			
75	*pu*			"
5	*ap*			
7	*ip*			
8	*up*		"	
78	*qa*			
79	*qi*			"
80	*qu*			"
81	*ra*			
82	*ri*			
83	*ru*			
85	*ar*			"
86	*ir*			
87	*er*			"

Number of the character in Norris's Dictionary.		Babylon.	Nineveh.	Media.
88	*ur*			"
89	*ûr*			
90	*sha*			
93	*shi*			
95	*shu*			
92	*she*			
96	*shû*			"
97	*ash*			
99	*ish*			
100	*ush*			"
101	*ta*			
103	*ti*			
104	*tu*			
18	*at*			
19	*it*			"
20	*ut*			

NOTE.—English readers will naturally wish to compare this Syllabarium with that given in the excellent dictionary by Mr. Norris (Assyrian Dictionary, by Edwin Norris, Ph. D., Honorary Secretary of the Royal Asiatic Society, London, 1868); and as some differences will be found, the author desires to offer a few remarks on the subject.

The greater number of these differences are merely variations in the form of the character, such as are found on very many of the monuments themselves. Only two founts of movable Assyrian type have as yet been cast in Europe, one used by the Royal Asiatic Society, the other in the Imprimerie Impériale at Paris. In the first, the form of the characters is copied from the Behistun inscription; in the second from the inscriptions at Khorsabad. The author has preferred to use the second, even in this English edition of his work, as he considers the model on which the characters have been formed as better and, if such a term may be used in speaking of Assyria, more classical. Moreover, particularly desiring to show the fundamental identity of the Median system of writing with the Assyrian, he has selected among the varieties of the latter those forms which most clearly show that identity, as, for instance, in the characters *ak* and *il*, numbered 12 and 51, in Mr. Norris's list.

As no attempt has been made to introduce an Assyrian Grammar, and it was not considered desirable to make the syllabarium too extensive, the author has omitted some simple syllabic characters which are rarely used, or seem to be interchangeable with others. Thus the characters numbered in Mr. Norris's list 27, 28, *zi*; 29, *zu*; 47, *le*; 52, *el*; 67, *en*; 84, *ru*; 91, *sha*; 98, *ash*; 102, *te*; 105, *ta*.

49 seems to the author a simple variant of 48, and 94 also of 93, and found only on doubtful copies.

The author has not introduced any diphthongs, and has therefore omitted No. 25, regarding it not as a simple *u* but as *au*. The character 41, *ya*, seems also to him a combination of *i*, (40) and *a*, (1).

These variations, as will be seen, involve no differences in reading, and require no explanation to an experienced Assyriologist. The only real points of disagreement between the author and Mr. Norris, very few in number, are as follows:—

In No. 36, but the value, *akh*, still seems doubtful.

In No. 64, read by the author as *num*, or *nuv*, not *nu*.

No. 106 seems identical with 8, and to have the two sounds, *up* and *ar*, but not *ti*.

These points are of course merely mentioned and cannot be discussed here.

It may also be remarked, that syllables in which the consonant is represented in our list by *z*, include both of the Semitic articulations ז and צ. That in syllables in which the *m* occurs, that letter may be replaced by *v*. That in the characters representing syllables with an initial consonant and final vowel, one single character is used for all the articulations of the same class; thus, *ap* and *ab* are expressed by the same sign, as well as *ak*, *ag*, *aq* and *at*, *ad* and *ath*, etc.

6. With but very few exceptions, the ideographic and phonetic values of the written signs are the same, whether the language employed is Assyrian, Armenian, Susianian, or Median. But most frequently the

characters are capable, according to their position, of being used either as ideographics or phonetics; and in all the languages employing this system of writing, except the Turanian Chaldæan, the sound of the sign when used phonetically had no resemblance to the pronunciation of the word it represented ideographically. For example, in an Assyrian text, the character 𒀭 conveys, as an ideograph, the idea of "God," and was then pronounced "Ilu"; as a phonetic it represents the syllable "an." The character 𒀜 also, ideographically means father, and is read "abu," but it also stands for the syllable "at."

The explanation of this peculiarity is the foreign origin of this system of writing. We have already said that science has proved that the Anarian system of cuneiform writing was invented and introduced into Mesopotamia by a people of Turanian or Ugro-finnish race, the Shumir, who were the first inhabitants of a part of Chaldæa. Among these people the phonetic and ideographic values of the signs were identical; the one sprung from the other; the pronunciation of each character as a phonetic was the initial syllable of the word represented by the sign as an ideograph; 𒀭 represented *an*, because the word for God was AN*nap;* 𒀜 the syllable *at*, because the word for father was AT*ta*. When the system of writing passed from its Turanian inventors to other nations, Chaldæo-Assyrians, Armenians, Susianians, and others, they borrowed both the sound and the meaning; and as in the languages of the latter people the ideas were expressed by entirely different words, the concord between sound and meaning was at an end.

7. But the complications of the Anarian cuneiform writing did not end here. To these difficulties, already sufficiently embarrassing, of finding the same character with two directly opposed meanings, at one time phonetic and at another ideographic, and with no apparent connection between the double employment, must be added the peculiarity of *polyphony*—a fruitful source of difficulty. It consists in the existence of two or three different phonetic values for the same character. Thus, 𒉺 meaning as an ideographic *to anoint*, corresponding with the Assyrian word *nasak*, represents as a phonetic sometimes the simple syllable *pa*, and at others the compound syllable *khat*. This fact is so strange, that its first announcement was received with incredulity in the scientific world, but it has been established by such positive proofs, that it is now admitted as incontrovertible; an analogous fact has also been noticed in some Egyptian hieroglyphics. This has arisen from the fact that the ideographic characters, like the words of the spoken language,

sometimes received new though cognate meanings, one meaning, for instance concrete, another abstract—one meaning as a substantive, another as a verb; now these varied meanings frequently corresponded in the spoken language to words of totally different sound, and thence arose the various phonetic values.

We must not dwell longer on this subject, but we have said enough to show how complicated, how full of obscurities, how liable to error in the reading, was this system of Anarian cuneiform writing used in Assyria and Babylonia from a period more than thirty centuries before our era down to the time of the Seleucidæ. Of course, the Assyrians were better able than we are to disentangle this almost inextricable confusion; but even for them the difficulties were great. We find a proof of this in the number of fragments of lists of syllables and of grammatical vocabularies stamped on clay tablets, intended to teach the pupils of the Hiero-grammatists of Asshurbanipal the mysteries of the national system of writing that have been found in such abundance in the ruins of Nineveh. A large proportion of the remains of Anarian cuneiform writing are composed of school books, which assist us to decipher the remainder, and afford us the same assistance that they did 2,500 years ago to the students of the ancient land of Asshur. But though the remains of these lists of syllables, drawn up by the Assyrians themselves for their own assistance in reading their own writing, afford valuable help to modern students in deciphering the cuneiform system, they prove that it has always been complicated and obscure, and that to understand and employ it, even at the time when it was in common and extensive use, the very people, whose exclusive and national writing it was, were compelled to have recourse to help of the same kind.

SECTION IV.—LITERATURE AND SCIENCE.

1. BEROSUS tells us that the Babylonians and Assyrians had eight sacred books, and that they attributed the authorship of them to the god Oannes, the mythical founder of the first civilisation of Lower Chaldæa. From these books he drew the information he has given us on the cosmogony believed in Babylon; from the same source also, but indirectly, are derived the very correct ideas on the Chaldæo-Assyrian religion preserved by the Greek philosopher, Damascius.

No original fragment of the books of Oannes has been preserved, nor any portion of the chronicles relating the whole history of Nineveh and Babylon. But from their extraordinary length, some of the inscriptions of the Assyrian kings may almost be termed books, as they relate in detail the annals of their reigns, giving us an idea of the historical and literary style of the Assyrians. Even when translated, as the reader may have observed from the fragments we have quoted, these documents have a forcible and stately character. The style is magniloquent, the diction strong and vigorous, the metaphors bold and striking, the turn of thought poetic, a sort of epic air distinguishes the story told to gratify the pride of the monarchs of the Great Empire.

2. All the remains known to us of books, properly so called, of ancient Assyria, were found during Mr. Layard's excavations, and come from the library established by King Asshurbanipal in one of the halls of his palace at Nineveh. A curious library, consisting entirely of flat square tablets of baked clay, having on each side a page of very small and closely written cuneiform cursive letters, impressed on the clay while still moist; each was numbered, and formed a page of a book composed of a number of such tablets, probably piled one on another in the library.

The great majority of the tablets still preserved of the library of Asshurbanipal, and now in the British Museum, contain the remains of an immense grammatical encyclopædia, treating of the difficulties of the writing as well as of the language. We find from them that grammar had become among the Assyrians a very advanced science, and received much attention from them, the natural and almost inevitable consequence of the complication of their system of writing, requiring long and profound study. We find also from a notice appended to one of the treatises of the Grammatical Encyclopædia, that the library of the Ninevite palace was intended by its founder to be a public library—"Palace of Asshurbanipal, king of the world, king of Assyria, to whom the god Nebo and the goddess Tashmit (the goddess of wisdom) have given ears to hear, and eyes to see what is the foundation of government They have revealed to the kings, my predecessors, this cuneiform writing, the manifestation of the god Nebo, the god of supreme intelligence. I have written it upon tablets, I have signed it, I have placed it in my palace for the instruction of my subjects."

The Grammatical Encyclopædia, compiled by the orders of Asshurbanipal, was divided into several treatises; we have fragments of seven:—

1st. A lexicon of the Chaldæo-Turanian language, with the meaning of the words in Assyrian. This was used to interpret some treatises on religion and science, compiled by Chaldæan priests in their own language, to render them unintelligible to the common people. We have already mentioned that the original text of the fundamental civil laws of the empire was in the Chaldæan tongue.

2nd. A dictionary of synonyms in the Assyrian language.

3rd. A grammar of the same tongue, with paradigms of the conjugations of verbs.

4th. A dictionary of the signs of the Anarian cuneiform writing, with their ideographic meanings and phonetic values.

5th. Another dictionary of the same signs, arranged according to the primitive hieroglyphics whence they are derived.

6th. A lexicon of particular expressions, generally ideographic, employed in the inscriptions of the primitive Chaldæan empire. This exhibits a turn for archæology, and shows us that the Ninevite and Babylonian kings of later times must have made a careful search in the temples they repaired for the inscriptions of their original builders. Thus we have on a cylinder of Nabonahid, now in the British Museum, the translation of an inscription of Shagaraktiash, discovered in the foundations of the great temple at Sipparah.

7th. Tables of expressions illustrative of grammatical construction, and of the various methods of expression in ideographs and phonetics.

All these treatises, the fragments of which are of inestimable value to us, are not remarkable for the excellence of their method.

3. Nor do the riches of the library of the Ninevite palace end here. The fragments of the grammatical treatises, published many years ago by the authorities of the British Museum, have acquired the greatest celebrity, and have been chiefly used by scholars, as they furnish most invaluable assistance in deciphering cuneiform inscriptions. But the clay tablets discovered by Mr. Layard also contain parts of very many other books.

Fragments have been found, as we have said, relative to the laws. This subject is also represented by a number of contracts between private individuals that would hardly be found there unless intended to serve as "formulæ juris privati," and portions, still more numerous, of records of judicial proceedings, for the library was used also as a depositary for the archives of the palace. The remains of the table of the eponyms, embracing almost without interval a space of nearly three centuries, prove that there were also books on chronology. These are of four separate kinds, the two first containing only the list of the personages who gave their names to the years, divided by reigns; the two others, infinitely more valuable, and from which we have made many quotations, where this list was accompanied by a summary of the principal events of each year. One broken tablet is all that remains of a manual of the history of Nineveh and Babylon, arranged in parallel columns; it was especially an abstract of the political and diplomatic relations at different epochs. From this fragment we have quoted our statements as to the most ancient Ninevite kings, and their relations with the Babylonian kings.

Fragments have also been found on mythology, not yet translated, though some of them have been published in the "British Museum Inscriptions." They contain lists of the various epithets applied to the same god, and of his functions and attributes; tables of the localities in which were his principal temples; and, finally, highly important documents as to foreign gods. With them were found also the remains of collections of hymns, in a style sometimes recalling the Psalms of David. We find next the remains of a sort of encyclopædia, or geographical dictionary, enumerating the countries, towns, mountains, and rivers known to the Assyrians; also of a list of proper names in use in the country; and, lastly, statistical documents of the greatest interest on the hierarchy of the functionaries of the government, and on the different provinces of the monarchy, their productions and revenues. Several tablets contain remains of the lists of the tributary cities of Osrhoene, Taurus, Syria, Palestine, Arabia, and Egypt, with statements of the sums they paid, or the supplies they furnished in kind, particularly in grain. We have also a catalogue of the important buildings of Babylonia and Chaldæa, classified according to their kind, temples, pyramids, and fortified citadels.

4. Natural history also is represented in the remains of the library of the Ninevite palace. Lists of known plants and minerals have been found; of the timber trees employed in building or furnishing; of metals; of stones fit for architecture or sculpture. But perhaps the most interesting of all is a list of every species of animal known to the Assyrians, classified in families and genera. No doubt the great divisions of this classification are those of a very rudimentary science, but we may well be astonished to find that the Assyrians had already invented a scientific nomenclature similar in principle to that of Linnæus. Opposite the common name of the animal is placed a scientific and ideographic name, composed of one invariable sign, and of a characteristic epithet, varying with each species.

On the other hand, no trace has been found of a scientific and methodical system of medicine. This art had in reality no existence in the Chaldæo-Assyrian civilisation. Herodotus mentions* as one of the most remarkable peculiarities of the customs of the Babylonians, the absence of any physician. People meeting in the street accosted each other, to ask mutually for advice as to the complaints they suffered from. Sick people were carried into the public ways, and there consultations were held as to the treatment suitable for their maladies. The medical art, moreover, was confounded with that of magic, so much in vogue among the Chaldæo-Assyrians; and it appears that very often no other remedies were employed than conjurations and incantations, for

* HER. i. 197.

sickness was considered to be the result of the action of evil spirits, who injured the body.* One tablet contains a series of incantations of this kind, to avert the maladies likely to attack a woman before child-birth, or when nursing, and they are written in two languages, Turanian Chaldæan and Semitic Assyrian. Other formula against various evils, or against the power of magic charms, are to be found on tablets or on amulets. We are astonished to find amongst them exclamations that were used by magicians of the middle ages, and were then quite incomprehensible, such as the famous *Hilka, hilka, besha, besha;* these are simple Assyrian words, meaning *Go away, go away, evil one, evil one.* They came to the west with the Chaldæan magicians at the time of the decline of the Roman power, and adepts in the occult sciences transmitted them from generation to generation as mysterious words of sovereign efficacy against the spirits of darkness.

5. But the sciences, next to grammar, most frequently met with on these fragments, a small part only as yet having been published, are mathematics and astronomy. The library of Asshurbanipal contained many treatises on arithmetic, and the remains give us reason to think that Pythagoras borrowed the plan of his famous multiplication table from the Mesopotamian civilisation. It also contained catalogues of observations, both of fixed stars and planets, the remains of which have been found; amongst others, tables of the risings of Venus, Jupiter, and Mars; also of the phases of the moon from day to day during the month. We have, in the preceding chapter, spoken of the early progress of astronomical science at Babylon. The Assyrians were in this the pupils of the Babylonians, and their science was the same. The astronomers of ancient Mesopotamia had even determined the mean daily movement of the moon, as they had adopted the course of that planet as their measurement for time, and had succeeded, by their knowledge of the period of 223 lunations, in predicting eclipses. The most ancient calculation of this kind, that for the eclipse of 10th March, 721 B.C., was made by them, and differs from ours by a few minutes only. Eclipses of the sun, much more difficult to calculate, they did not, says Diodorus Siculus, venture to predict; they contented themselves with making and registering solar observations. Thus, as we have already seen, two solar eclipses, those of 2nd July, 930, and of 13th June, 809 B.C., are mentioned on the monuments.

We derive much that is still in use among astronomers from the civilisation and science of the Chaldæo-Assyrians, to which all writers of antiquity bear testimony. Thus the division of the ecliptic into twelve equal parts, forming the Zodiac, and even the figures of the constella-

* See page 271.

tions, seem to have originated with them. The division of the circle into 360 degrees, and the division of a chord of the circle, equal to the radius, into sixty equal parts, called degrees;* the division of those degrees into sixty minutes, of the minute into sixty seconds, and of the second into sixty thirds, as well as the invention of the mode of notation marking these divisions of the degree, are due to the Chaldæo-Assyrians. To them also is to be attributed the institution of the week of seven days, dedicated to the seven planetary bodies worshipped by them as divine beings, and the order assigned by them to the days has not changed from time immemorial. Having invented the gnomon, they were the first to divide the day into twenty-four hours, the hour into sixty minutes, and the minute into sixty seconds. Their great periods of time were calculated on this scale. The great cycle of 43,200 years, regarded by them as the period of the precession of the equinoxes, was considered as one day in the life of the universe. It was divided into twelve "sars," or cosmic hours, each of 3,600 years, and each subdivided into six ners, of 600 years; the ner again into ten sosses, or cosmic minutes, of sixty years; and thus the ordinary year was a second of the great chronological period.

This was all founded on the peculiar method employed by the Chaldæo-Assyrians in indicating fractions. They invariably divided unity into sixty equal parts, each such part again divided into sixty,

---

* See DELAMBRE, *Astronomie Ancienne*, tom. II., livre iii., chap. 2, "Construction de la Table des Cordes," where is explained the manner in which the Greeks expressed the subdivision of the arcs and chords of circles.

The curvilinear length of the circumference of a circle was divided into 360 equal parts, called degrees, and, consequently, the arc, which is the sixth part of that circumference, contained sixty degrees. Now the chord of that arc, as is well known, is equal to the radius of the circle; and the rectilinear length of the radius was, in like manner, divided into sixty equal rectilinear parts, which were also called *degrees*, but must be carefully distinguished from the *degrees* of the circumference.

For the subdivision of degrees of each of these kinds the *sexagesimal* system of notation was employed, each *degree* being divided into sixty *minutes*, each *minute* into sixty *seconds*, each second into sixty *thirds*, and so on.

And tables having been constructed, by which multiplication, division, and other numerical operations could be facilitated (Delambre, tom. ii., p. 32), and a system of trigonometry, both plane and spherical, having been invented and adapted to this notation (Delambre, tom. ii., chap. iii. iv.), complicated questions of arithmetic and trigonometry became capable of solution. Delambre gives several examples completely worked out.—Communicated by the Rev. Temple Chevallier.

and this sexagesimal division was continued to infinity. This it is very evident was the result of a wise combination of a very practical character, intended to combine the advantages of the two systems of dividing unity that have been in dispute at all times and among all nations—the decimal and the duodecimal. The number sixty, in fact, is divisible by all the divisors of ten and of twelve, and is among all the numbers that could be chosen as an invariable denominator for fractions, the one possessing the greatest number of divisors. Sexagesimal numeration regulated the scale of the divisions and of the multiples in the metrical system of Babylon and Nineveh, the wisest and best organised in the ancient world.

This is the only system, previous to the introduction of the French metrical system, where all proportions were scientifically concordant and founded on the fundamental plan of all unities of superficies, capacity and weight being derived from one primitive and typical linear measurement, an idea adopted also by the French republican commission on weights and measures. The cubit of 525 millimetres (=20·67 ins.) was the basis of the whole system. This was divided into 60 parts, corresponding to the 60 minutes of the degree. Multiplied by 360, the number of the degrees of the circle, it produced the stade of 189 metres (nearly 207 yds.), the unit of measures of distance. The foot of 315 millimetres (12·4 ins.) was to the cubit as 3 to 5, and was therefore 36 lines. The square of this foot (= 153·8 sq. ins.) became the lowest and fundamental unit, on which were founded all land and superficial measures. The cube of this foot was the metreta, or medimnus of 30½ litres (= 1,922·3 ins.), the standard of all measures of capacity; and the weight of the cube foot filled with water gave the talent of 30 kil. 650 grs. (=67·57 ozs.), the fundamental unit of weight; and the sexagesimal division of this produced the mina of 510·83 grs. (= 1·13 ozs.), and the drachma of 8·513 grs. (= ·019 ozs.). The greater part of these measures passed from the Tigro-Euphrates basin to the various neighbouring countries of Asia, and even to the Greeks, preserving often their names, for both μνᾶ and ὀβολὸς are Hellenised Assyrian words, losing, however, more or less in the transit their original character and scientific proportion.

6. The Chaldæo-Assyrians were acquainted with the solar year of 365¼ days, and made use of it in their astronomical calculations. But their ordinary civil and religious year was a lunar year, composed of twelve months, alternately of twenty-nine and thirty days. This year was borrowed by the Hebrews previous to the time of Moses, probably from the time of Abraham. The Jewish names for the months are the same as the Assyrian, as we may see by the following table, where the two calendars are arranged in parallel columns:—

Assyrian Months.		Jewish Months.	No. of Days.
Religious Name.	Common Name.		
1. Month of the Beginning .	Nisan	Nisan	30
2. ,, ,, Bull . . .	Air	Iyar	29
3. ,, ,, Brick . . .	Sivan	Sivan	30
4. ,, ,, Hand . .	Duz	Tammuz	29
5. ,, of Fire . . .	Ab	Ab	30
6. ,, of the Citadel . .	Ulul	Elul	29
7. ,, ,, Rampart .	Tashrit	Tisri	30
8. ,, ,, Foundation .	Arach Shamna	Marchesvan	29
9. ,, ,, Cloud . .	Kisiliv	Kislev	30
10. ,, ,, Rain . . .	Tebit	Tebet	29
11. ,, of Surveying .	Sabat	Sebat	30
12. ,, ,, End . . .	Addar	Adar	30

The greater part of the religious names refer to the season of the year in which the month occurs, such as those of Ab, corresponding to the summer heats; of Kisiliv and Tebit, when the winter rains fell. Others refer to the occupations of the people at the time, as, for religious reasons, they were to make bricks for buildings in the month of Sivan, to lay foundations in the month of Arach Shamna, and to conduct surveys of land in the month Sabat. The symbolical name of Air seems to indicate the sign of the Zodiac in which the sun was at that period of the year.

The Hebrews also borrowed from the Chaldæo-Assyrian civilisation their two-fold manner of commencing the year—the religious year began with 1st Nisan, about the spring equinox; the civil year with 1st Tashrit, about the autumnal equinox; the eponyms (limmu) followed the civil year, and commenced with the 1st Tashrit. This system originated with the Babylonian belief that the world had been created at the autumnal equinox.

The lunar year was made to agree with the solar of 365¼ days, by means of an intercalary cycle of eight years. Every fourth year a month called Magru-sha-Addari was intercalated after Addar, corresponding to the Ve-Adar of the Jews; every eighth year besides this they intercalated another called Magru-sa-Ululi after Ulul. This octennial cycle was introduced among the Greeks by Cleostratus of Tenedos, and remained in use until the great works of Meton and Calippus. We do not know how the Chaldæo-Assyrians applied to these inexact reckonings the corrections indispensable to their astronomical calculations.

SECTION V.—RELIGION.

1. THE skilful explorations of the last twenty-five years in the countries bordering on the Tigris and Euphrates have given us much more correct ideas on the subject of the Assyro-Babylonian mythology than had been handed down by the Greeks. Nevertheless many points still remain in great obscurity as to the religion common with a few exceptions to the two great Semitic cities of Mesopotamia.

The religion of Assyria and Babylonia was, in its essential principles and in the general spirit of its conceptions, of the same character as the religion of Egypt, and in general as all pagan religions. When we penetrate beneath the surface of gross polytheism it had acquired from popular superstition, and revert to the original and higher conceptions, we shall find the whole based on the idea of the unity of the Deity, the last relic of the primitive revelation, disfigured by and lost in the monstrous ideas of Pantheism, confounding the creature with the Creator, and transforming the Deity into a god-world, whose manifestations are to be found in all the phenomena of nature. Beneath this supreme and sole God, this great All, in whom all things are lost and absorbed, are ranked in an order of emanation, corresponding to their importance, a whole race of secondary deities, emanations from his very substance, who are merely personifications of His attributes and manifestations. The differences between the various pagan religions—the same in principle—is chiefly marked by the differences between these secondary divine personages and their reciprocal nature.

Thus, as we have already seen, the imagination of the Egyptians had been especially struck by the various stages of the daily and yearly course of the sun; in this they saw the most imposing manifestation of the Deity—that which best revealed the laws of the government of the world—and in this they sought their divine personifications. The Chaldæo-Assyrians, especially devoted to astronomy, saw in the Astral, and especially in the planetary system, a manifestation of the divine being. They considered the stars as his true external manifestation, and in their religious system made them the visible evidence of the subordinate divine emanations from the substance of the infinite being, whom they identified with the world, his work.

2. The supreme god, the first and sole principle from whom all other deities were derived, was Ilu, whose name signifies God *par excellence.* Their idea of him was too comprehensive, too vast, to have any determined external form, or consequently to receive in general the adoration of the people; and from this point of view there is a certain analogy between Ilu and the Chronos of the Greeks, with whom he was compared by the latter. In Chaldæa it does not seem that any temple was ever specially dedicated to him; but at Nineveh and generally throughout Assyria

he received the peculiarly national name of Asshur (whence was derived the name of the country, *Mat Asshur*), and this itself seems derived from the Arian name of the deity, *Asura*. With this title he was the great god of the land, the especial protector of the Assyrians, he who gave victory to their arms. The inscriptions designate him as "Master or Chief of the Gods." He it is who is to be recognised in the figure, occasionally found on the Assyrian monuments, but adopted in later times by the Persians to represent their Ormuzd, of a human bust wearing the royal tiara in the middle of a circle borne by two large eagle wings, and with an eagle's tail.*

3. Below Ilu, the universal and mysterious source of all, was placed a triad, composed of his three first external and visible manifestations, and occupying the summit of the hierarchy of gods in popular worship—Anu, the Oannes of the Greek writers, the primordial chaos, the first material emanation of the divine being; Bel, the demiurgus, the organiser of the world; Ao, called also Bin—that is, the divine "Son"

---

* There are many examples of this winged figure of Asshur in the British Museum, both on the sculptured monuments and on the signet cylinders. Eleven may be counted on the sculptures in the "Assyrian Gallery." It may be observed that in all examples the eagle's wings and tail are attached, not to the human bust, but to the circle; in some the figure is placed in the ring, in others merely imposed on it; in one, at the entrance of the Gallery, the figure is placed in what seems evidently intended for the sun's disc; in all others the ring is as distinctly formed as the tire of a wheel. There are also several examples, some very roughly executed, in which the human bust does not appear, but merely the winged ring.

In the war-scenes the figure of Asshur hovers over the king's chariot, and exhibits the same action as the king. If the king is shooting his arrow, the god does the same, using a three-pointed arrow (see the vignette to this volume); if the king holds out his right hand to promise pardon, so also does the god.

The translator had an opportunity (through the kindness of Dr. Birch) of inspecting the signet cylinders in the Museum, in search of this emblem. There are thirty-one examples, more or less complete and perfect, from the inexpressibly beautiful and perfect cylinder, labelled as that of Muses-Ninip, 800 B.C. [Mushishi-Adar], where the whole details of the wings and figure are rendered as perfectly as on any of the monuments, down to some on which the emblem is barely legible; of these there are eighteen without the human bust. Among the cylinders is the one usually termed the "Assyrian Trinity," as, besides the figure in the ring, there is a human head on each of the wings; there is also, on another cylinder, what appears to be a very rude attempt to produce the same figure.

The common occurrence of this emblem on some of the monuments and its entire absence on others may perhaps be explained by supposing that it was used only by kings or by private persons whose names were compounded of the name of the god.—TR.

par excellence—the divine light, the intelligence penetrating, directing, and vivifying the universe. These three divine personifications, equal in power and con-substantial, were not placed in the same degree of emanation, but were regarded as having, on the contrary, issued the one from the other, Ao from Oannes and Bel from Ao. Oannes, the "Lord of the Lower World, the Lord of Darkness," was represented on the monuments under the strange figure of a man with an eagle's tail, and for his head-dress an enormous fish, whose open mouth rises over his head, while the body covers his shoulders. It is under this form that Berosus tells us, according to Babylonian traditions, he floated on the surface of the waters of Chaos. Bel, the "Father of the Gods," was usually represented under an entirely human form, attired as a king, wearing a tiara with bull's horns, the symbol of power. But this god took many other secondary forms, the most important being Bel Dagon, a human bust springing from the body of a fish. We do not know exactly the typical figure of Ao or Bin, "the intelligent guide, the Lord of the visible world, the Lord of knowledge, glory, and life;" the serpent seems to have been his principal symbol.

Each god of this triad had a corresponding female deity—his reproduction in the passive form—to use the expression of many of the inscriptions, "his reflection." Anat, the Anaitis of the Greek writers, the passive reproductive matter, accompanied Oannes; Bilit, whose name was rendered by the Greeks as Mylitta, the mother of the gods, belonged to Bel; and lastly, Taauth, "the great lady," often confounded with Mylitta, was the female reproduction of Ao.

4. The first triad represented, as we have seen, the production of the material world, an emanation from the substance of the divine being; first the primordial chaos, uncreated matter, sprung from the fundamental and sole first cause of all things; secondly, intelligence—we may almost say "the Word"—animating and fertilising all; and lastly, the demiurgus, who ordains and brings into regulated order the universe, with which he himself is inextricably mixed up. The series of emanations is then continued, and a second triad is produced with personages no longer vague and indeterminate in character, like those of the first, but with a clearly defined sidereal aspect, each representing a known celestial body—those in which the Chaldæo-Assyrians saw the most striking external manifestations of the deity: these were Shamash, the Sun; Sin, the Moon god; and a new form of Ao or Bin, inferior to the first, and representing him as god of the atmosphere or firmament.

5. Below this second triad in the divine hierarchy, and in the order of emanations, are found the gods of the five planets—Adar (Saturn), Merodach (Jupiter), Nergal (Mars), Ishtar (Venus), and Nebo (Mercury). The worship of Merodach, though not much cultivated at Nineveh, was of primary importance at Babylon, where he was regarded as one of the

principal gods. He was a secondary form, another manifestation of Bel, in an inferior rank in the hierarchy; he was called "the ancient one of the gods, the supreme judge, the master of the horoscope"; he was represented as a man erect and walking, and with a naked sword in his hand. Adar,* "the fire," called also Samdan, "the powerful," although his planet had been called Saturn by the Greeks, was in reality the Assyrian Hercules; his appellations are—"the terrible, the lord of warriors, the strong one, the destroyer of his enemies, he who reduces the disobedient, the exterminator of rebels," and in other cases, "the son of the Zodiac." On some monuments he is represented in company with Merodach, and in the same manner. He is represented in the magnificent colossal figures in the Museum of the Louvre, and of the British Museum where he is seen as a god of terrible aspect, strangling in his arms a lion that appears quite small in comparison with him. With the surname of *Malik*, "king," *Adar Malik*, the Bible mentions him with "Oannes, the king," *Anu Malik* (2 Kings xvii. 31), as the principal god of Sippara, where the inhabitants "burnt their children in the fire" in their honor. In general these planetary gods are only forms, secondary manifestations, of the higher order. Such is the connection between Nebo and Ao; Nebo also is distinguished as the "supreme intelligence"; he is the god of prophetic inspiration, and of eloquence, and also the special guardian of royal prerogative, the protector of kings, and the prototype whom they reproduce on earth. Like Bel, he has on the monuments an entirely human form, with the tiara and the dress of a king; three pairs of horns, ranged one above the other, decorate his tiara, and four large wings are often attached to his shoulders; the sceptre also is one of his common attributes. Ishtar reproduces among the planetary gods Anat and Bilit, the great goddess of nature, the mother of all the gods and of all beings; she is their active and martial form, for she is called "the Goddess of Battles, the Queen of Victories, she who leads armies to the fight and is the judge of warlike exploits"; but she has a double form, uniting two characters—one fierce and sanguinary, the other voluptuous—for under the names of Zarpanit and Nana she presides over the reproduction of beings, and over sensual pleasures; she is in this last character always represented naked, always full face, and with the two hands on the chest. Moreover two Ishtars were always distinguished, that of Arbela (called also Arbail) and that of Nineveh, who presided over the two fortnights of the month.† The

* This is the divinity whose name has hitherto been read as Ninip. We shall give elsewhere the reasons and proofs of this new reading, Adar.

† Hence the common ideographic designation, "The goddess fifteen," just as Sin, who presides over the month, is called the "God thirty."

plural name of this double Ishtar, Ishtaroth, was the origin of the Phœnician Ashtaroth. Nergal, whose image is very uncommon, stands on the legs of a cock, and carries a sword in his hand. The application of the name of Mars to his star was quite natural, for the titles he receives in the inscriptions are "the great hero, the king of fight, the master of battles, champion of the gods," and also "god of the chase."

7. Such were the great gods of Nineveh and Babylon. Below them popular superstition believed in an immense number of personifications of inferior order, of lesser gods, or rather *geni*, whom it would be waste of time to enumerate. We must, however, mention some personages who are found on the monuments occupying an important position in the Chaldæo-Assyrian pantheon, and who were evidently other forms of the gods already named, but whose position has not as yet been precisely determined. Such is Nisroch, called also Shalman, the "king of fluids," he who "presides over the course of human destiny," and who is also the protector of marriages; this is the god with an eagle's head and large wings, whose image is so common on the sculptures of the Assyrian palaces. As we have already seen, it was in the temple of this god at Nineveh that Sennacherib was assassinated by his sons. Possibly we ought to consider this god as another form of Oannes.

The great gods are often all invoked one after the other at the beginning of the solemn inscriptions of the kings of Assyria. Sargon has given the names of eight of them on the gates of the city he founded. "Shamash has conferred on me all I possess," says he, in an inscription, "Bin gave me good fortune; I have named the great eastern gates after Shamash and Bin. Bel Dagon laid the foundation of my city, Bilit Taauth grinds like paint the elements of the world; I have named the great southern gates after Bel Dagon and Bilit Taauth. Oannes prospers the work of my hand, Ishtar leads armies to battle; I have called the great western gates after Oannes and Ishtar. Nisroch Shalman presides over marriages, the mistress of the gods presides over births; I have dedicated the great northern gates to Nisroch and Bilit."

SECTION VI.—ARTS.

1. UNTIL very lately it was necessary to rely entirely on the statements of authors such as Ctesias as to the great development of art among the Assyrians, and the splendour of the edifices of Nineveh and Babylon. It was only in 1844 that M. Botta, French consul at Mosul, made the first discovery of an Assyrian palace, on the site of a little village named Khorsabad, near that city. This discovery soon led to

others; and now a school of art, the very existence and greatness of which, a short time ago, rested only on the testimony of ancient authors, is known to every one. It is possible now, with the aid of the specimens that are to be found in all the large museums of Europe, and especially in the Louvre and British Museum—of the splendid works on the subject of Assyrian explorations, published in France and in England by M. Botta, M. Place, and Mr. Layard, and especially of the admirable essays of a French architect, M. Thomas, in M. Place's work—to sketch the essential characteristics of Assyrian architecture, sculpture, and painting.

2. The Assyrians were generally in the habit of piling up large mounds, or artificial hills, as platforms on which to erect temples, palaces, or cities. Nineveh was almost entirely built on artificial elevations, extending over an immense surface. Its walls were 360 stades in circumference, according to the testimony of one of Sennacherib's inscriptions; the outer casing was built of bricks, the interior was composed of earth; and this explains how, when the casing was removed, the mass of earth crumbled down and mixed with the soil. The enormous enceinte of the capital of Assyria was quadrilateral in shape, and may still be recognised, marked by a series of mounds in a regular line scattered over the plain.

These artificial hills, serving as the base of great edifices, and where the ruins are still buried, are met with in various parts of Assyria, to the number of several hundred. Three only have as yet been excavated, and these contained the palaces of Khorsabad (Dur Sharyukin), Nimrud (Calah), and Koyundjik (Nineveh).

These palaces, standing on artificial hills, were, from their mode of construction, in reality each a second artificial hill, erected above the first, with rooms excavated in their sides—an arrangement that seems to have originated from the nature of their building materials, and also from the necessity for placing dwellings in an airy situation in such a hot climate. The soil of Assyria supplied an abundance of stone fit for building, and also a coarse grey alabaster, very easily sculptured, but too soft to be used for the walls of gigantic edifices. The Babylonians, the original colonisers of Assyria, had been compelled by the nature of their soil, entirely composed of alluvial clay, to build all their edifices of bricks, some burned, others merely sun-dried.

The Assyrians never rose above the traditions of their original instructors, notwithstanding the difference in the nature of their soil; but they preferred to the dried or burnt brick a peculiar description of "pise" which they seem to have invented, composed of bricks used while still soft, so as to adhere closely to one another without cement, so that each wall or vault, when dry, formed one single compact mass. This is the only material used in any Assyrian edifice that has as yet been excavated; stone is found only as a casing, arranged in large thin sculptured slabs along the panels of halls, luxuriously decorated, and in paving arranged on the external facings of terraces. The nature of the materials employed must necessarily exercise great influence, and impose unalterable laws on the arrangements of any system of architecture. Building entirely with this "pise," the Assyrians were compelled to give an enormous thickness to the walls, to construct the halls very narrow and very low as compared with their length, for a vault constructed of "pise" could never be very strong; never to build edifices more than one story high; and lastly, to load the roof with a very thick mass of earth, so that the rain should not penetrate, and the heat of the sun should not cause it to crack throughout all its thickness. From these circumstances arose the essential characteristics and general aspect of Assyrian architecture, in which the base of a building bore a greater proportion to its height than even in Egypt.

3. Some of the Assyrian palaces occupy an enormous extent of ground. That of Sennacherib at Koyundjik covers a space almost equalling that of the great Temple of Karnak, in Egypt. The plan, however, is always the same; they are composed of a succession of immense square courts, more or less numerous, according to the extent of the building; around them are arranged halls or chambers, opening one into the other, with no other means of entry. Other courts, or esplanades, are placed between the building itself and the terraced wall bordering the artificial hill it stands on. The halls are never more than forty feet broad, but their length is frequently very great, so as to give them the appearance of mere galleries. The largest of those in the palace at Khorsabad is 116 feet long; in the palace of Asshurnazirpal, at Nimrud, one has been found 140 feet long; and finally, the length of the principal hall in the palace at Koyundjik is 180 feet. These long galleries were used for halls of ceremony, and were among the most characteristic peculiarities of Assyrian architecture. The internal walls of these great halls were, as we have already said, decorated up to a certain height by a panelling of sculptured slabs of stone, and above that by enamelled bricks. Other halls were ornamented entirely in the latter way. The chambers, or halls for common use, had the walls plastered with coloured stucco, sometimes painted in fresco. We also learn from the inscriptions that there were many rooms entirely panelled with wood, and that the most precious odorous kinds were employed for the purpose; the species enumerated as being used for panelling are the sea-pine, the fir, the cypress, the cedar, the wild pistachio, ebony, and sandal-wood. No remains of the panelling have as yet been found, for all the palaces that have been excavated were destroyed by fire during the disasters that occurred at the end of the Assyrian empire.

For assemblies too numerous for the great interior halls, the courts, ornamented all round by gigantic sculptures, were used; and on such occasions they were converted into halls by a *velum* stretched over them. Slender columns, sometimes of stone, more often of wood covered with metal, supported porticoes of wood painted in brilliant colours, extending across these courts. These were sometimes made to imitate palm or other trees, but more often crowned by voluted capitals, the origin of the Ionic order; sometimes, again, they were surmounted by metal figures of real or imaginary animals.

All the great gates opening into these courts, and the esplanades giving access to the principal parts of the building, were ornamented by colossal statues of winged, human-headed bulls; the faces of these symbolical figures always look outwards, and the bodies are attached to the side wall of the gateway. The size of these bulls, always colossal, varies according to the size and importance of the gateway where they stand. Some scholars have wished to identify these fantastic figures with the representation of the god Ninip, or Bel Merodach, placed as a protector at the entrance of the palace. We, however, believe these Ninevite bulls to be the prototypes of the cherubim of the Ark of the Covenant, representing no one particular divinity, but being the visible embodiment of an idea analogous to that expressed by the Egyptian sphinx; symbolising generally a divine protecting and guardian power, combining both physical force and intelligence, just as the symbolical figure combines the body of the strongest animal with a human head. These bulls are called Alapi and Kirubi, and the last name, Kirub, is applied, in an extended sense, to the gateway itself.

Sometimes lions are found in place of bulls, also with wings and human heads, the prototypes of the Grecian sphinx, a variety of the same symbol; these latter are called Nirgalli, in the inscriptions describing the works of the palace. Lastly, at the gate of one of the edifices of Nimrud, these emblematical figures are replaced by simple colossal lions, erect, and in the attitude of fierce and vigilant guardians. Above these bulls, or the figures which, as we have seen, sometimes replace them, the great gateways were built with an arched vault, with architrave outside decorated with enamelled bricks. One of these arched gateways was discovered entire, with all its decorations, in the excavations of M. Place at Khorsabad. It would have been brought to Paris, but by a most lamentable accident it was lost on the Tigris, with all the antiquities collected by the French expedition into Mesopotamia.

The roofs of Assyrian edifices were flat and terraced, surrounded by a crenelated battlement cut into gradines, and this plan was preserved in Arab architecture of the middle ages for the top of the external walls of buildings, as may be seen by the beautiful mosques at Cairo. This characteristic peculiarity is clearly indicated in all the pictures on the bas-reliefs; and thus M. Thomas was decidedly right in introducing it into his restorations. Nor is this the only thing that Arabian and Persian architecture borrowed from Assyrian art, for on looking at the plates where the accomplished artist who accompanied M. Place has restored the exterior of the palace at Khorsabad, we may almost fancy that they are drawn from modern Arab buildings. The common use of enamelled pottery for panelling walls in the Persian buildings of the middle ages originated in Assyria. The employment of cupolas in Arab and Persian architecture is due to the same source. Positive proofs were found in the excavations of M. Place that some of the square halls of moderate size were roofed by hemispherical cupolas, formed of "pise," and made in one piece, rising above the level of the terraces. Several bas-reliefs, moreover, represent these Assyrian cupolas.

The other halls had either a vaulted, or more probably a flat, roof, and the inscriptions inform us that the ceiling was formed of solid beams, sustaining the weight of the earthen roof. The timber was generally of resinous wood, as it was considered more durable than any other, such as sea-pine, fir, cypress, or cedar. This last wood was brought at great expense from the forests of Lebanon and Amanus, and military expeditions were sometimes made merely for the purpose of cutting cedars. The projecting beams, as we learn also from the monuments, were covered with sheets of bronze, no doubt stamped with figures and ornaments.

The halls must have been lighted by openings in the ceiling, as they still are in the houses in Armenia, for no trace has yet been found of a window; moreover, there are halls in the palaces that are surrounded on all sides by other halls, and therefore could be lighted only from the roof. But the power of the sun in summer, and the violence of the rain in winter, precluded the possibility of leaving these skylights entirely open to the air. I believe that I have discovered in the inscriptions the method by which they were covered, and that is by seal skins made into parchment, and thus made semitransparent and as translucent as unpolished glass. At the present day, the Danes of Greenland employ in a similar manner the skin of the nor-whale as a substitute for glass in their windows.

We must add one last fact of great importance in the history of the art of building; namely, that the Assyrians, from the time of Asshurnazirpal, were acquainted with the true arch, built with a key-stone, of a circular and also of an ogival form. A drain, built in this manner of burnt brick, has been found leading under the most ancient part of the palaces of Nimrud.

The courts and halls of Assyrian buildings were paved with larg furnace-baked bricks, the door-sills with stone, sculptured so as to represent a richly designed mat. The walls rested on a bed of sand, mixed, according to a superstitious custom mentioned in many inscriptions, with various amulets, chiefly necklaces of large cornelian beads. Under the door-sill were hidden clay idols, placed there to prevent any evil influence from entering.

4. One only of the Assyrian palaces has as yet been completely and in all parts uncovered, that at Khorsabad (Dur Sharyukin), and this is of great interest from its complete unity of plan, having been built in a few years, in one reign, and with no departure from the original conception. It therefore may be taken as an excellent type of the usual Assyrian plan and arrangement of a palace. It is composed of three great buildings entirely distinct, of different dimensions, connected with each other and forming one single royal dwelling, placed on the summit of an enormous artificial mound. These buildings correspond exactly to the three divisions still found in the houses of the wealthy and luxurious at Bagdad and Bassorah. The seraglio, or palace properly so called, inhabited by the men, and where the halls for ceremonial reception, the *selamlik*, were; the harem; and the khan, or servants' apartments, what may be called the common hall. The resemblance is so exact that, as we do not know the Assyrian names of each, it is impossible not to apply to the divisions of these Assyrian palaces the names now in use in the country to designate the great divisions of the dwellings.

The different buildings of the palace of Khorsabad were built on two platforms of different heights, arranged in the form of the letter T. One, the highest, was square, with its corners adjusted exactly to the four cardinal points; the other, very much less elevated, is in the form of an elongated rectangle, standing at the S.E. face of the square terrace, and lower than it at its two extremities. On the loftier terrace stood the palace, properly so called, with its entrance to the N.E., facing the open country, and opening on to the ramparts of the city wall. This entrance, however, was not in the middle of the façade, for no people were ever less particular than the Assyrians as to regularity and parallelism in their architecture; thus all the courts of their palaces have four great gates in their four sides, but none of them is placed exactly opposite the one to which it ought to correspond. The general mass of the buildings of the seraglio, or palace, forms a square, with some few irregularities, very trifling for an Assyrian building. The principal gateway to the north-east gives access to an immense court, rectangular in shape, and surrounded on all sides by buildings. Those on three of the faces seem to have been slight, and to have been lodgings for slaves and for the body-guard of the king; those on the fourth side were the main buildings of the palace. What is very unusual, there was a perfectly regular façade, with a gateway, the most highly ornamented in all the building, placed exactly in the centre.

In the interior arrangements of this building, the largest of all the edifices of Khorsabad, there was neither regularity nor symmetry. Two-thirds to the north-west part of the building was occupied by the grand reception hall, or selamlik, and its large and sumptuous galleries, with walls cased with bas-reliefs; one-third to the south-east by the inhabited apartments, with smaller and less decorated rooms. Passages opened into two of the sides of the large court; one on the north-west led to a square esplanade, or court, occupying the northern angle of the artificial mound of the palace, in front of a building touching the north-west face of the seraglio, with which it had no internal communication. This building was most lavishly ornamented; it comprised six immense halls decorated with sculpture, and some other smaller rooms. It was, we may almost say, a second palace grafted on to the first—a second selamlik, rivalling in splendour that of the seraglio. What could have been its purpose? It would be rash to make any assertion on the subject, but we may conjecture that it might have been the palace of the heir apparent; for Sennacherib was a great personage, even during the lifetime of his father Sargon, and must have had his own palace among the buildings of the royal dwelling. The passage opening into the south-east side of the reception-hall of the seraglio led to the lower platform, and to the great court of the offices.

The lower platform of the artificial hill built up for the foundation of the palace of Sargon, was occupied by the khan and by the harem. This portion of the edifice looked towards the city, and communicated directly with it. In the midst was the khan properly so called, that is, an immense square court, surrounded on all its sides by buildings, stables, lodgings for grooms, and for the greater number of slaves. It was approached from the city by two enormous flights of steps, in the middle of the south-east face of the terrace. An elaborately decorated passage led, as we have said, from this court of the khan into the reception-hall of the seraglio; two small doors also gave direct communication with the inhabited rooms of the palace. To the right of the immense court we have just mentioned, the khan, was a building of some extent, with many courts and numerous chambers, forming part of the offices, or common rooms of the palace.

To continue the use of the names still applied in modern oriental palaces, so similar to those of Assyria, we must distinguish this from the khan, and call it the khazneh, or treasury; for there, as the excavations of M. Place have proved, were the stores of provisions and utensils for the use of the royal household, as well as places of custody for all the valuables that Sargon, in his dedicatory inscription, tells us he had acquired by force of arms and stored in his palace.

The harem was adjoining the khazneh. It was a building of moderate extent, containing three courts—the walls of one of them was covered with the richest decoration in enamelled bricks; many long galleries, intended no doubt for feasts or festivals; and lastly, a large number of rooms for habitation. This harem was shut in as closely as possible; all communication with the outer world was intercepted, and the women must have found themselves in a real prison. One single vestibule, guarded by eunuchs, gave access to it; this had two issues, one communicating with the great court of the offices, and was the entry by which people came in from outside; the other opening on a long narrow court leading to the inhabited apartments of the seraglio; through this the king had access to his harem without being seen by the public.

Behind the harem was an enormous tower, or pyramid in seven stages, nearly fifty yards high. Remains of similar constructions have been found at Nimrud (Calah), and Kileh Sherghat (Elassar); and there seems no doubt that they were attached to every Assyrian palace, for the inscriptions frequently mention the one belonging to the palace at Nineveh. The seven stages, equal in height, and each one smaller in area than the one beneath it, were covered with stucco of different colours, and thus presented to view the colours consecrated to the seven heavenly bodies, the least important being at the base: white (Venus), black (Saturn), purple (Jupiter), blue (Mercury), vermilion (Mars), silver (the moon), and gold (the sun). This was the ancient staged pyramid of the first Semitic Chaldæan empire, adopted and but slightly modified by the Assyrians, by giving a rather smaller base and less difference between the relative sizes of the stages, so as to make it resemble rather a tower than a pyramid. But buildings of this kind, called Zikurat, and so frequently mentioned by the kings in their annals as having been erected by them, were not used in Assyria for temples, as they had been in Chaldæa under the first empire, and as they continued to be used in Babylon down to the destruction of the city. The sanctuary crowning the summit of the Chaldæan pyramids had disappeared. The Assyrian Zikurat was simply an observatory, and on its summit the priestly astrologers, pupils of the Chaldæans, attempted to read the future in the stars. Astronomy had, in fact, quickly degenerated into astrology in Chaldæa; the belief in the direct influence of the stars on terrestrial affairs was one of the most deeply rooted articles of faith in Babylon, and had passed into Assyria. The Ninevite kings, like those of Babylon, undertook no enterprise without first consulting the presages of the stars, and for this purpose they always had within reach, in their palaces, astrologers and an observatory. We have already seen that Sennacherib himself says that he gave up an expedition, undertaken with every chance of success, and declined a decisive battle when everything seemed to promise him a victory, because the stars did not seem favourable. We have also stated the influence that, according to the monuments, two eclipses exercised, the one on the accession of Asshurbanipal, the other on that of Sargon.

The royal astrologers kept a constant watch from the height of the Zikurat on the state of the heavens and the movements of the stars, so as to interpret them by the aid of the astrological tables so often mentioned in the inscriptions. They furnished the king with an account of their observations; and some tablets bearing reports of this kind were found in the archives of the palace of Koyundjik. As an example, one of them records the observation of the exact day of the spring equinox:—"On the 6th of the month Sivan the day and the night were equal, six double hours for the day, and six double hours for the night. May Nebo and Merodach protect my lord the king."

Another on a tablet in the British Museum still unpublished (marked K., 86)—"To the founder of buildings, my lord the king, his humble servant, Naboiddin, chief astrologer of Nineveh. May Nebo and Merodach be propitious to the founder of buildings, my lord the king. On the 15th of the month we have observed the entry of the moon into the lunar node and the result. The moon was eclipsed."

Another, in the same collection (marked K., 78), runs thus:—"To the king, my lord, his humble servant Ishtar . . . . chief astrologer of Arbela: peace to my lord the king. May Nebo, Merodach, and Ishtar of Arbela be propitious to my lord the king. On the 29th of the month Sivan we observed the lunar node, but we have not seen the moon. The 2nd of the month Duz, in the year of Belsun, governor of the city of Hirmirdan." It follows from this last inscription that the Assyro-Chaldæan astrologers, not yet able to calculate eclipses of the sun, watched attentively at each new moon to see whether one would occur.

5. The Zikurat in Assyria was not therefore a sanctuary for religious worship, like those in Chaldæa, as some scholars have supposed. But the Assyrians had their temples built in a style much resembling their palaces. None of the large sacred edifices of Assyria have as yet been excavated, and their splendour may no doubt in some respects have rivalled those of Egypt. But explorers have found at Nimrud, at Khorsabad, and at Koyundjik, some temples, small indeed, but most beautifully decorated, forming part of the palaces; and these, doubtless, were copies of the larger structures. That at Khorsabad was at the western angle of the upper platform, behind the seraglio; those at Nimrud (for there were two in that palace) were adjoining the Zikurat. The principal part of these temples, the sanctuary proper, is always a large hall of great length; at one of its extremities is a square recess of

considerable dimensions, to contain the statue of the god. Sometimes a smaller hall—a vestibule, or *pronaos*—stands in front of the sanctuary, and then the entrance is at the end, opposite the recess for the statue; in some cases there is no vestibule, and then the entry is at the side of the sanctuary, or *cella*, so that the statue of the god could not be seen from outside. Some small chambers, for use in the temple service, or for custody of the sacred utensils, were arranged around the sanctuary, or cella. Bas-reliefs, representing only religious subjects, decorated the walls of the latter; on each side of the gateway were lions or bulls, just as in the palaces. The external walls of the temples were cased with enamelled bricks.

6. Sculpture had made more progress than any other art in Assyria, and had developed a distinctive originality of its own. We do not know what was its state at the commencement of the monarchy, but four centuries afterwards, under Asshurnazirpal, it still bore unquestionable marks of complete archaism — a rude and barbaric grandeur. Under Sargon and Sennacherib it had acquired more finish in detail and facility in execution, but still preserved its grand rough outline; its greatest excellence was in the execution of colossal figures. Finally, under Asshurbanipal, at the close of the monarchy, it attained its highest degree of elegance, finish, life, and perfection in the imitation of nature, losing, however, the grandeur of the more ancient works.

Assyrian sculpture is one of the greatest of ancient arts; its teachings, received and transmitted by the peoples of Asia Minor, presided over the first steps of Grecian sculpture. Between the works of Ninevite artists and the early works of the Greeks, even to the Æginetans, we may observe an astonishing connection; the celebrated primitive bas-relief of Athens, known by the common name of the "Warrior of Marathon," seems as if detached from the walls of Khorsabad or Koyundjik. Like all primitive art, Assyrian as well as Egyptian sculpture presents a very imperfect imitation of nature, an awkward, almost architectural, stiffness in the design of the figures, and many parts represented conventionally, much in the style that children of all countries first attempt to draw. In the bas-reliefs, for example, all figures are in profile, even when the composition of the group is injured, because it is easier to design in relief a profile than a full face.

But Assyrian art springs from a totally different principle to that of Egypt; it has not the solemn and monumental gravity of the latter. In place of dealing with great masses, and deducing, so to speak, algebraical formula from the forms of nature, simplifying the design and the lines through reducing the model by a systematic and intelligent selection of its characteristic and essential elements, as the Egyptians attempted to do, Assyrian art sought to give with the utmost care every minute detail; nothing was omitted; no embroidery of a garment, no curl of the hair or beard, no muscle of arm or leg; and thus in Assyria, though by a directly opposite road, art travelled as far from reality as in Egypt. Secondary things were exaggerated into matters of primary importance, to the destruction of the effect of the whole work; the muscles of the members were so developed as to become monstrous, the proportions of the different parts of the body were not correct, and from this point of view Assyrian sculpture always remained in a lower rank than the Egyptian. It never attained that ideality, that height of inspiration, that calm, religious grandeur; but, on the other hand, it possessed an energy, a life, a movement, that Egyptian art never knew. The substance on which the Assyrian sculptures are executed adds still more to this appearance of energy; the Assyrians did not use the chisel with facility, and succeeded only when using the gypseous alabaster, soft enough for slabs for panelling the palaces. When they attempted to work hard stone, such as basalt, which the Egyptian artists worked with the finish of a cameo, their work was exceedingly coarse, as may be seen in the Nimrud obelisk. But this awkwardness was redeemed by a surprising energy, by a strength full of grandeur and fire; sometimes they dashed at the stone, and struck out bold lines; lifelike forms flashed out into light, cut in as with a lion's paw.

Assyrian sculpture excelled more in the representation of animals than in the human figure. Here, too, its principle was the opposite of that of the Pharaonic art. The Egyptians, unable to compete with nature, who possessed the secret of life, raised themselves above by epitomising her. The distinctive features of the animal were put together and thus exaggerated; the minor details were omitted; and in this way was produced a sort of very expressive symbol. The whole family of lions was represented by one single lion, always the same; the model was always powerful, the image very grand. In place of this formidable, laconic, and solemn art, that dealing with great masses on a grand scale, modelling concisely the distinctive features, the Assyrians, in the representation of animals, attempted to produce more of a lifelike picture, sharply cut and shaded, reproducing every possible detail of nature. Far from giving one single conventional type for each species, they attempted to give individuality to each figure, depicting truthfully every action, and, if one may say so, the feeling of the moment. In this they attained to the highest perfection about the time of Asshurbanipal; and in the sculptures of the palace of Koyundjik we may see in hunting scenes figures of animals such as no other art, not even that of the Greeks, can surpass for expression. We may especially mention one work, incomparably lifelike—we might almost say touching—true both to the individual and to the type, in a great bas-relief representing a lion hunt, now in the British Museum, and especially one figure of a lioness, who has been wounded in the spine by arrows, and having already lost the use of her hind legs, raises herself painfully on her forepaws to roar at the hunters, and threaten them with her open jaws.

7. Assyrian sculpture is seen to least advantage in statuary; its highest achievements are in bas-reliefs. The few Assyrian statues we possess display a remarkable want of skill; absolutely flat, they can only be seen from the front. The Ninevite artists, therefore, avoided making them as much as possible, whilst they almost infinitely multiplied bas-reliefs, the best means they had for the display of art.

The three chief epochs we have already mentioned in the development of Assyrian art, so far as it is at present known, correspond to the three most marked systems of composition in bas-reliefs. Under Asshurnazirpal the figures are few, simply grouped, and very confused, if an attempt is made to introduce any considerable number of them, as in some representations of sieges; there is a complete absence of all perception of the laws of perspective; the movement of the figures is generally slow and slight, but full of truth and propriety. Under Sargon and Sennacherib artists were more ambitious; they attempted to represent large scenes and numerous personages, who are more clearly distinguished, but with no better perspective than in the older sculptures. In all hunting scenes the field of the landscape was very rudely represented, and they were compelled to indicate the nature of the country by its characteristic trees and animals, but with the strangest mistakes in their relative proportions. We see, for instance, in the water fishes as large as the ships; and in the woods birds half as tall as the soldiers. The action of the figures is more vigorous and marked than in the earlier period, and not less true to nature. Lastly, in the time of Asshurbanipal the bas-relief becomes more conformed to reality and to the sound principles of art, and the artists renounce all pretensions to represent scenes on a different level in the landscape; the nature of the place where the scenes of war or hunting occur is simply indicated by a few trees, drawn with striking truth to nature, or by some buildings, faithfully sketched, so that there is but little occasion for mistakes in perspective. There is also an improvement to be remarked on the preceding period in the life and movement of the figures, as well as in the grouping and balancing of the different elements in the composition.

8. All the Assyrian sculptures were brilliantly painted, and the remains of the colours may still be observed on the bas-reliefs in the Museums. Besides this, painting, properly so-called, formed an important part of the decoration of Assyrian edifices, whether in the form of casings of enamelled bricks or of frescoes. No large composition of this kind has been preserved; but there are nevertheless fragments

enough to prove that the Assyrian paintings resembled the bas-reliefs. The figures standing out on a ground of uniform colour were not shaded, but formed by flat colours, surrounded by a broad black or white band, defining the outline, and serving exactly the purpose of the lead surrounding figures in the painted glass of the thirteenth century.

9. An art much cultivated among the Assyrians, and carried to a high degree of perfection, was engraving on hard stone. It was principally applied to the manufacture of cylinders for signets, the impression being taken by rolling them over a soft surface. The subjects engraved on them were in general of a religious character, assemblages of sacred symbols, or of images of deities, with one or more persons in the act of adoration. Some of them represent hunting scenes. The great majority of these cylinders are evidently ordinary trade goods of very careless workmanship. But there are also some carefully executed and finely engraved that, in spite of their small dimensions, may be advantageously compared, for beauty of art, to the best specimens of bas-reliefs from Khorsabad and Koyundjik.

CHAPTER V.

THE NEW CHALDÆAN EMPIRE.

Section I.—Survey of the History of Babylon under the supremacy of the Assyrians. 1314—625 B.C.

1. Chaldæa was the seat of the most ancient empire of Mesopotamia. Its focus and centre was to the south of Babylon; and although that great city, the most ancient in the Tigro-Euphrates Basin, was always of considerable importance—although even it was the religious, yet it never became the political, capital of this empire. We have already seen that the Egyptians under Thothmes III. had overturned the Chaldæan dynasty, and installed at Babylon princes designated as Arabs by Berosus, who reigned there for two and a half centuries.

When the Assyrian empire, profiting by the declining power of Egypt, established itself towards the end of the fourteenth century before the Christian era, Babylon, as we have shown, was governed by a dynasty of princes whose names prove them to have been of Chaldæo-Turanian, or rather of Elamite, origin. We have already related the sanguinary struggles between Karatadash, Burnaburyash, Karahardash, and Nazibugash, kings of Babylon, and the first Ninevite monarchs, Asshur-bel-Nishishu, Bushur-Asshur, and Asshurubalat—struggles occupying the greater part of the fifteenth and fourteenth centuries B.C.

In 1314, Tuklat-Samdan I. conquered the countries of the Lower Euphrates, and made Babylon a dependency of Nineveh, settling there a new line of princes of Chaldæo-Assyrian origin, and with purely Semitic names. Thus, even after this conquest, the city of Nimrod had kings of its own, although but vassals of the king of Assyria. Even at this period, when its glory was almost entirely eclipsed, it could vie with Nineveh both as to importance and population, and was in consequence a possession that gave its conquerors much trouble to keep. Essentially a rebellious city, Babylon longed for independence, and at each opportunity rose in revolt; during the six centuries of the Assyrian empire we constantly find its princes warring against their suzerains. Even under Belkudurussur, the successor of Tuklat-Samdan, we have seen that Binbaliddin, prince of Babylon, not only revolted, but even invaded Assyria. It was this Binbaliddin who enclosed the city of Nipur with a wall called "Nivit Marduk"—"the dwelling of Merodach." Towards the close of the twelfth century he was defeated, and again reduced to obedience by Adarpalashir, king of Nineveh. His successor, Nebuchadnezzar [Nabuchudurussur], also revolted against the Assyrian monarch, Asshurrishishi. Still more important was the revolt of Mardukidinakhe (about the eleventh century B.C.) against Tiglath-pileser I. [Tuklat-pal-ashar]. Having first defeated his suzerain, the Babylonian prince entered Assyria and sacked the town of Hekali. Some years after, he in his turn sustained a defeat, and Tiglath-pileser carried Babylon by storm.

The monuments here fail us, and we therefore know nothing of what passed in Babylon after the disasters of the Assyrian king, Asshurrabamar. It is probable that for a time the city threw off the Ninevite yoke, and that the first princes of the dynasty of Belkatirassu [or Bilpasqu], perhaps even its founder, made it their first occupation to reconquer Babylonia. We have no documents on the subject of the wars that brought about this result: all we know is, that the success of the Assyrians was complete, and the great Chaldæan city was so severely punished that, for more than a century, it did not again attempt to revolt. Its princes during this period were in reality only hereditary satraps of the Ninevite monarch. We know but one of these satraps, Irib Marduk, whose name is found on some weights now in the British Museum. But, in following the history of Assyria, we have seen that Nabubaliddin, king of Babylon, attempted a revolt, repressed almost before it broke out, against Asshurnazirpal, and that disturbances in Babylon and Chaldæa broke out afresh with such violence under Shalmaneser IV. (Shalmanuashir), that he found himself compelled to fortify strongly the frontier town of Ellasar, and to station a formidable garrison there, in order to keep the country in check. During the revolt of Asshurdaninpal and the civil war that ensued, Chaldæa escaped from its northern masters and proclaimed its independence, placing a certain Mardukbalatirib on the throne; and Shamash-Bin, on his accession, found himself obliged to reconquer his rebellious vassal. Binlikhish III., his successor, in order to assure himself the possession of Babylon, and at the same time to gratify the desire of its inhabitants for independence, married a princess of the native royal family, Sammuramat, who was the nominal sovereign of Babylon whilst her husband reigned at Nineveh. At this period great works were undertaken in the Chaldæan city, especially the construction of the embankments of the Euphrates.

2. Thirty-four years later Phul-Balazu, the Belesis of the Greeks, a prince of Babylon, joined, as we have before said, the insurrection of the Mede Arbaces and of the Susian Shutruknakhunta against Asshur-likhish, the Sardanapalus of the Greeks, and took part in the total destruction of Nineveh (B.C. 788). He had been, of all the confederates, the most determined, the one most obstinately bent on the ruin of the Assyrian power. On the fall of Nineveh, the Medes and Susians were content with having merely reconquered their independence. Phul, on the contrary, took possession of Assyria and of the western provinces of the empire, and made them for a time subject to Babylon. It was at this time that he made an expedition into the kingdom of Israel. About 747, doubtless immediately on the death of Phul-Balazu, Assyria threw off the yoke of her temporary conquerors; Tiglath-pileser II., a descendant of the old royal family, was proclaimed king, drove out the Chaldæans, and re-established the authority of Nineveh over the western provinces, Osrhoene and Syria. But the complete independence of the kingdom of Babylon, the work of Phul, lasted some time longer before the Assyrians ventured to attack it.

Nabonassar, who succeeded Phul, in order to efface every trace of foreign dominion, burnt all the historical documents of those kings of Nineveh who had reigned over Babylon, and wished to commence a new era, to be called by his own name. The era of Nabonassar commences from his accession in 747 B.C., and from this date the Greek astronomer, Ptolemy, has preserved a canon of the kings of Babylon, and his statements are fully confirmed by the monuments.

Nevertheless, after Nabonassar, the kingdom of Babylon fell rapidly into decay; it was a prey to disorders of which we have but an imperfect knowledge. The canon of Ptolemy registers at this time four kings in twelve years, a sufficient indication of a time of troubles and revolutions. The kings of Assyria, who had become more powerful than ever, profited by all this to claim again their ancient rights of suzerainty. In 709 B.C. Sargon [Sharyukin], after the bloody battle of Dur-Yakin, reconquered Babylon and Chaldæa.

From this date the history of the Babylonian state is known only from its relations, almost always unfortunate, with the Assyrian empire, and by its incessant and fruitless revolts. The true national hero of this epoch, the indomitable champion of the independence of Babylon, was Merodach Baladan [Mardukbaliddin], dethroned once by Sargon, then again on many occasions, in contest with him and with his son, Sennacherib [Sinakherib], unfailing in his hatred to the Assyrian yoke, always conquered and always retrieving his disasters, imprisoned by the kings of Assyria, and always escaping to put himself at the head of the Babylonians, laying down his arms at last only with his life. Suzub, son of Gatul, was equally intrepid and persevering. Esarhaddon [Asshurakhiddin], the fourth son of Sennacherib, was viceroy of Babylon under his father when he succeeded to the throne of Nineveh; he habitually resided at Babylon, as we have already said, and it was to that city he carried prisoner Manasseh, king of Judah. Esarhaddon occupied himself in repairing the more important monuments of Babylon, much defaced and destroyed during the later wars, especially during the sack of the city, by order of Sennacherib in 683. He also designed the plan, and commenced the construction, of the two immense enclosures, the completion of which was the glory of the reign of Nebuchadnezzar. After his abdication of the throne of Nineveh in favour of his son, Asshurbanipal, Esarhaddon still remained for a short time king of Babylon. At his death, his second son, Shamulshamugin, succeeded him in that city, but as vassal to Asshurbanipal. We have already given the details of his revolt, in which he was joined by Nabubelshum, the grandson of the great Merodach Baladan. But the two states were afterwards again united, and there was no king of Babylon, when, about 626, the Chaldæan Nabopolassar was made by Asshuredililani III., the last king but one of Assyria, governor of Chaldæa and Babylon, in order to preserve the country from the barbarians who threatened it.

Section II.—Nabopolassar [Nabupalussur]. 625—604 B.C.

1. The true founder of the Chaldæo-Babylonian power was Nabopolassar. Babylon under his obscure predecessors had been subject to Nineveh. Now emerging at last from that state of dependence, she arrived at the highest point of power and grandeur. "For, lo," had said, some years before, the prophets in the name of Jehovah, menacing with divine judgments both Nineveh and the kingdom of Judah, "I raise up the Chaldæans, that bitter and hasty nation, which shall march through the breadth of the land, to possess the dwelling-places that are not theirs. They are terrible and dreadful: their judgment and their dignity shall proceed of themselves. Their horses also are swifter than leopards, and are more fierce than the evening wolves: and their horse-

men shall spread themselves, and their horsemen shall come from far; they shall fly as an eagle that hasteth to eat" (Hab. i. 6—8).

Sent to Babylon as satrap or prefect — for Asshuredililani had for twenty-two years deprived that proud city of the right of having a prince of its own, and had made it directly dependent on the throne of Nineveh—Nabopolassar, who without doubt had played his part as courtier to the Assyrian monarch to obtain this favour, conceived at once the project of substituting himself for his master, and of freeing for ever his native country. He sent an embassy to the king of the Medes, who was beginning to establish a considerable empire and a military power of the first rank, by the conquest of all those countries that had for many centuries formed the northern provinces of the Assyrian kingdom, penetrating even to Asia Minor. This king was Cyaxares, as we are told by Herodotus. Eusebius and Syncellus call him Astyages; but this appellation seems to have been, among the Medes, a title or surname rather than a proper name. Nabopolassar concocted with him a plot for the overthrow of the Ninevite power; and to seal the alliance, married his own son, Nebuchadnezzar, or more correctly Nabukudurussur, as Berosus wrote it (Nebo protects my crown), to the daughter of the Median king. Before long the death of the king of Assyria furnished them the opportunity they were waited for, to declare themselves independent. Cyaxares advanced to lay siege to Nineveh, and Nabopolassar, proclaiming himself king, sent large bodies of troops to assist him in the enterprise.

2. We have already related how the Scythian invasion, pouring suddenly on Media, achieved for the moment its subjection, and saved for a time the capital of Assyria from destruction. Babylon and Chaldæa remained safe from the ravages of the Scythians. Nabopolassar was more fortunate than his ally, for though obliged to postpone his scheme for the destruction of Nineveh, and to allow to what was now the mere shadow of the Assyrian kingdom a prolonged existence for nineteen years, still he remained in peaceable possession of his dominions, and profited by the delay to consolidate the independence he had achieved, establishing on a solid basis the power of the Babylonian kingdom. Profiting by the weakness and inaction of Assaracus, the last Ninevite king, he conquered the western or Aramæan portion of Mesopotamia—that is to say, Osrhoene—and reduced the descendant of Sargon and Sennacherib to the possession only of Assyria, properly so called. But he did not carry his arms beyond the Euphrates, avoiding, until the final fall of Nineveh, a contest with Necho, king of Egypt, who at that time, having vanquished Josiah, king of Judah, at Megiddo, had overrun the whole of Syria and seized his share of the spoils of the Assyrian empire.

3. Whilst he thus extended his territory, and gradually substituted the dominion of Babylon for that of Nineveh, Nabopolassar employed

himself actively in restoring the ancient splendour of his capital, which had suffered much in the late wars, and in reconstructing many of the public edifices that had fallen to ruin, notwithstanding the repairs of Esarhaddon. Nabopolassar had married a princess, whom Herodotus calls Nitocris, and whose name, purely Egyptian (Neith-aker—"Neith, the Victorious"), seems to point her out as born on the banks of the Nile, and belonging to the royal family, originally of Sais, then reigning over the land of the Pharaohs. Nitocris appears to have filled, in conjunction with her husband, Nabopolassar, a position in the state not less important than Sammuramat (the Semiramis of Herodotus) did with regard to Binlikhish III. It seems that she assumed the direction of the great works then being executed at Babylon, for Herodotus, correctly and well informed on all the history of the Chaldæan kingdom at that period, attributes to her the credit of them, whilst Nebuchadnezzar in his official inscriptions ascribes it to his father. "Nitocris," says Herodotus,* "not only left behind her, as memorials of her occupancy of the throne, the works which I shall presently describe, but also, observing the great power and restless enterprise of the Medes, who had taken so large a number of cities, and among them Nineveh, and expecting to be attacked in her turn, made all possible exertions to increase the defences of her empire. And first, whereas the river Euphrates, which traverses the city, ran formerly with a straight course to Babylon, she, by certain excavations which she made at some distance up the stream, rendered it so winding that it comes three several times in sight of the same village, a village in Assyria, which is called Ardericca; and to this day they who would go from our sea to Babylon, on descending to the river, touch three times, and on three different days, at this very place. She also made an embankment along each side of the Euphrates, wonderful both for breadth and height, and dug a basin for a lake a great way above Babylon, close alongside the stream, which was sunk everywhere to the point where they came to the water, and was of such breadth that the whole circuit measured 420 furlongs. The soil dug out of this basin was made use of in the embankments along the waterside. When the excavation was finished she had stones brought, and bordered the entire margin of the reservoir with them. These two things were done—the river made to wind and the lake excavated—that the stream might be slacker by reason of the number of curves, and the voyage be rendered circuitous, and that, at the end of the voyage, it might be necessary to skirt the lake and so to make a long round. All these works were on that side of Babylon where the passes lay, and where the roads into Media were the straightest; and the aim of the queen in making them was to prevent the Medes

* HER. i. 185, 186.

from holding intercourse with the Babylonians, and so to keep them in ignorance of her affairs.

"While the soil from the excavation was being thus used for the defence of the city, Nitocris engaged also in another undertaking, a mere by-work compared with those we have already mentioned. The city, as I said, was divided by the river into two distinct portions. Under the former kings, if a man wanted to pass from one of these divisions to the other, he had to cross in a boat, which must, it seems to me, have been very troublesome. Accordingly, while she was digging the lake, Nitocris bethought herself of turning it to a use which should at once remove this inconvenience, and enable her to leave another monument of her reign over Babylon. She gave orders for the hewing of immense blocks of stone, and when they were ready, and the basin was excavated, she turned the entire stream of the Euphrates into the cutting, and thus for a time, while the basin was filling, the natural channel of the river was left dry. Forthwith she set to work, and in the first place lined the banks of the stream within the city with quays of burnt brick, and also bricked the landing-places opposite the river gates, adopting throughout the same fashion of brick-work which had been used in the town wall; after which, with the materials which had been prepared, she built, as near the middle of the town as possible, a stone bridge, the blocks whereof were bound together with iron and lead. In the daytime square wooden platforms were laid along from pier to pier, on which the inhabitants crossed the stream; but at night they were withdrawn, to prevent people passing from side to side in the dark to commit robberies. When the river had filled the cutting, and the bridge was finished, the Euphrates was turned back again into its ancient bed; and thus the basin, transformed suddenly into a lake, was seen to answer the purpose for which it was made, and the inhabitants, by help of the basin, obtained the advantage of a bridge."

4. In 607, Nabopolassar, feeling himself already old and enfeebled, and seeing also that a serious contest with the Egyptian monarchy had become imminent on account of the progress of Necho, who, master of all Syria, already threatened the Euphrates, thought fit to associate with himself on the throne a younger and more active prince. Nebuchadnezzar reigned conjointly with his father during the three succeeding years, thus giving rise to a double method of computing the dates of the new reign; some reckoning from this association, others from the death of Nabopolassar.

The year 606 was the great epoch in the history of the Chaldæan monarchy founded by Nabopolassar. From that year it became unquestionably the sovereign power of Asia, and acquired that supremacy in war and politics which had belonged first to Egypt, then to Assyria.

This result was due to two great wars waged simultaneously by the kingdom of Babylon in this year, both terminating in brilliant success.

The Medes having at last succeeded in freeing themselves from their Scythian invaders, and in regaining their full independence and liberty of action, Nabopolassar renewed his alliance with Cyaxares, and they both again undertook the enterprise against Nineveh, which for nineteen years they had been compelled to postpone. This had become still more easy, for the Assyrian monarchy had been growing gradually weaker from that time in the incapable and feeble hands of Assaracus, and had successively lost every one of its provinces. Nevertheless, at the last moment, when the united armies of the Babylonians and Medes presented themselves under the ramparts of Nineveh, the ancient valour of the Assyrians appeared to revive again. The city resisted with vigour and obstinacy, a very long siege was required to reduce it, but at last it was taken and completely destroyed with systematic ferocity. The conquerors divided the territory of Assyria. The Medes acquired the mountainous districts to the north and east, that is to say, the lesser part of the country. The king of Babylon joined to his states all the immense plains of the southern region bordering his own dominions, embracing at once the largest and most fertile parts of Assyria.

Whilst he was himself occupied in the enterprise against Nineveh, Nabopolassar confided to his son the more difficult task—the one requiring the most courage and activity—the task of arresting the progress of Necho, who had already commenced the siege of Carchemish, with a view of seizing the passage of the Euphrates, and re-commencing in Mesopotamia the conquering expeditions of Thothmes, Seti, and Ramses. Nebuchadnezzar, at the head of the picked troops of the Chaldæan army, marched against the Egyptians, and inflicted on them a crushing defeat under the walls of Carchemish. "And the king of Egypt," says the Bible, "came not again any more out of his land, for the king of Babylon had taken from the river of Egypt unto the river Euphrates all that pertained to the king of Egypt" (2 Kings xxiv. 7).

Nebuchadnezzar pursued his adversary closely, as far as the frontier of Egypt; but having learned, whilst before Pelusium, that his father was dead (604), he retraced his steps, to take possession of a throne that, so recently established, might be shaken by a change of kings. Under these circumstances, says Berosus, the Babylonian historian, he put the affairs of Egypt, Syria, and the adjacent countries in order; and leaving in charge of his trusted generals the numerous prisoners he had taken, as well as the command of the garrisons left in the conquered provinces, he departed with a small escort, crossed the desert by forced marches, and thus arrived speedily at Babylon, where the chief of the caste of the Chaldæans resigned into his hands the government he had administered since the death of Nabopolassar.

SECTION III.—NEBUCHADNEZZAR [NABUKUDURUSSUR]. 601—561 B.C.

1. THE defeat of the king of Egypt had prepared the way for the ruin of the kingdom of Judah, the only part of Palestine that had not yet submitted to the power of the Chaldæan monarchy, and had escaped the consequences of the battle of Carchemish. Two years after the death of his father had left him in full possession of power (602), Nebuchadnezzar, once more in Syria, attacked Jehoiakim, king of Judah, imposed on him a tribute, and carried to Babylon numerous hostages, with a part of the sacred vessels of the Temple of Jerusalem. Three years, however, had not passed before the Hebrew prince again revolted, counting on the support of the king of Egypt (who in reality did nothing to assist him), and almost immediately died, leaving all the consequences of his rebellion to fall on the head of his son, Jehoiachin. Jehoiachin reigned but three months. Nebuchadnezzar sent an army against him, and soon himself arrived in Judæa; and the young king of Judah was compelled to put himself and all his house into the hands of his enemy (599). Nebuchadnezzar did not content himself with these royal captives; he entered Jerusalem, despoiled the Temple and palace of all their treasures, and made prisoners of the bravest men of the army to the number of 10,000, with a portion of the artisans, amongst others the smiths and armourers (a precaution dictated by prudence, in order that the country should not be able again to put itself into an effective state of defence); he left, in short, in the city only the poorest of the people. He carried also Jehoiachin, with his mother, his wives and his eunuchs, to Babylon, and there shut up the unfortunate king of Judah closely in prison. Then, affecting to leave the nation a shadow of independence, he placed on the throne of Jerusalem, Zedekiah, uncle to the young prince.

The new king, no less infatuated than his predecessors, remained deaf to the warnings of Jeremiah, who recommended to him a policy of prudence and submission to the king of Babylon. Having contrived to arrange a coalition with the king of Egypt and the Phœnician cities, he believed himself in a position to throw off the yoke, and broke into open rebellion, by refusing his tribute as a vassal (590). Nebuchadnezzar, enraged, marched again on Jerusalem; but he was obliged almost immediately to raise the siege, in order to offer battle to Pharaoh Uahprahet, who advanced to the relief of Zedekiah.

The king of Egypt having retired without striking a blow, the

Chaldæans returned into Judæa, took the cities of Lachish and Azekah, and again appeared before Jerusalem. During eighteen months the Hebrews in their capital repulsed all attacks, but famine triumphed over their endurance. The Chaldæans penetrated through a breach into the city, whence the king attempted to escape with some of his servants towards the Jordan; but he was taken in the plain of Jericho and carried to the king of Babylon, who put his sons to death in his presence, put out his eyes, and led him, loaded with chains, to Babylon (588). A month afterwards Nebuzaradan, captain of the guards of the Babylonian king, entered the city, and at once the work of destruction commenced. The Temple of the Lord and the royal palace were burned, the high priest was killed, with sixty of the principal inhabitants, and all the families of the upper class who had not fled to the desert were led into captivity.

Nebuchadnezzar had appointed a Hebrew, Gedaliah, governor of the territory of Judah; but he, after the lapse of a few months, was assassinated by one of the royal family, named Ishmael. The chief men of the Jews who still remained in the country, fearing the vengeance of Nebuchadnezzar, retired to Egypt, where they hoped to find some security; but Uahprahet, by giving them an asylum, drew down on his own country the wrath of the Babylonian king. The eastern part of the Delta was invaded, and given over to the ravages of the Chaldæan army.

2. The haughty king of Babylon was not yet satisfied; he aspired to the conquest of Phœnicia, coveting its immense riches. For a long time, too, the grand utterances of the prophets had announced to the people of Tyre, now in the sixth century of their supremacy over the other cities, the misfortunes impending over them. "Behold," said Ezekiel, "I will bring on Tyrus Nebuchadnezzar, king of Babylon, a king of kings, from the north, with horses, and with chariots, with horsemen, and companies, and much people. He shall slay with the sword thy daughters in the field: and he shall make a fort against thee, and cast a mount against thee, and lift up the buckler against thee. And he shall set engines of war against thy walls, and with his axes he shall break down thy towers" (Ezekiel xxvi. 7—9).

The Tyrians resisted for a long time, with the constancy and obstinacy they had already shown against Sargon, and the siege of their city lasted thirteen years. But at last Tyre was carried by assault, by the king of Babylon in person (574), who treated the Tyrians as he had the Jews, and carried into Chaldæa the most distinguished families of the country. The colonies Tyre then possessed on the northern coast of Africa and in Spain, such as Carthage, not yet independent, and Gades (now Cadiz), recognised the suzerainty of the conqueror of their mother country. From this originated the fabulous stories that obtained credence at a later time, that Nebuchadnezzar marched at the head of his legions as far as the columns of Hercules, and that attributed to him the glory of subjecting to his arms the Iberians of Spain.* Tyre once taken, Nabuchadnezzar, before returning to Babylon, attacked the people of Idumea, Moab, and Ammon, who had associated themselves with the last Jewish attempt at revolt, and compelled them to submission. He made also a campaign in Arabia, passed victoriously through Hedjaz and Nedjid, and penetrated as far as the Sabean kingdom of Yemen. These wars, predicted by the prophets, terminated the series of Chaldæan conquests in Western Asia.

3. Once more in his own states, Nebuchadnezzar rendered himself no less famous by his internal administration than by his foreign conquests. The fortune of war had placed at his disposal immense riches and innumerable captives; he employed both in the great works of embellishment and of public utility, which made Babylon the most celebrated city in the world. "The city stands on a broad plain," says Herodotus,† who visited it in the fifth century before the Christian era, "and is an exact square, a hundred and twenty furlongs in length each way, so that the entire circuit is four hundred and eighty furlongs. While such is its size, in magnificence there is no other city that approaches to it. It is surrounded, in the first place, by a broad and deep moat, full of water, behind which rises a wall fifty royal cubits in width, and two hundred in height. (The royal cubit is longer by three fingers' breadth than the common cubit.)

"And here I may not omit to tell the use to which the mould dug out of the great moat was turned, nor the manner wherein the wall was wrought. As fast as they dug the moat the soil which they got from the cutting was made into bricks, and when a sufficient number were completed they baked the bricks in kilns. Then they set to building, and began with bricking the borders of the moat; after which they proceeded to construct the wall itself, using throughout for their cement hot bitumen, and interposing a layer of wattled reeds at every thirtieth course of the bricks. On the top, along the edges of the wall, they constructed buildings of a single chamber, facing one another, leaving between them room for a four-horse chariot to turn. In the circuit of the wall are a hundred gates, all of brass, with brazen lintels and side-posts. The bitumen used in the work was brought to Babylon from the Is, a small stream which flows into the Euphrates at the point where the city of the same name stands, eight days' journey from Babylon. Lumps of bitumen are found in great abundance in this river.

---

* STRABO, xv. p. 687; JOSEPH., *Ant.* x. 11, 1; EUSEB., *Præpar. Evang.* ix. p. 456. The authority for all these passages is the historian Megasthenes.

† HER. i. 178, 179, 180, 181.

"The city is divided into two portions by the river, which runs through the midst of it. This river is the Euphrates, a broad, deep, swift stream which rises in Armenia and empties itself into the Erythræan sea. The city wall is brought down on both sides to the edge of the stream: thence from the corners of the wall there is carried along each bank of the river a fence of burnt bricks. The houses are mostly three and four stories high; the streets all run in straight lines, not only those parallel to the river, but also the cross streets which lead down to the water-side. At the river end of these cross streets are low gates in the fence that skirts the stream, which are, like the great gates in the outer wall, of brass, and open on the water.

"The outer wall is the main defence of the city. There is, however, a second inner wall, of less thickness than the first, but very little inferior to it in strength. The centre of each division of the town was occupied by a fortress. In the one stood the palace of the kings, surrounded by a wall of great strength and size: in the other was the sacred precinct of Jupiter Belus, a square enclosure, two furlongs each way, with gates of solid brass, which was also remaining in my time."

The great wall of Babylon, following the measures of M. Oppert who has completely elucidated the questions relative to the topography of the great Chaldæan city, enclosed a space of 513 square kilometres—that is a territory as large as the department of the Seine, fifteen times the extent of Paris in 1859, seven times of Paris at present. The inner and smaller wall enclosed a space of 290 square kilometres—much larger than the city of London.

But these walls were less the ramparts of a city, properly so called, than an immense entrenched camp. The territory enclosed by the inner, and much more the outer, wall was far from being entirely inhabited. Quintus Curtius mentions ninety stades as the extent of ground covered with houses: the remainder was under cultivation and was sufficient to supply the defenders for a long time with the means of avoiding famine, while at the same time the immense extent of the outer wall precluded the possibility of an investment. Aristotle, wishing to give an idea of a city such as he imagined it, says, "It is not by walls alone that a city is made; if so one would only have to enclose the Peloponnesus with a wall. That would be the same as Babylon, or any other place whose circuit encloses rather a nation than a city."

4. We have previously noticed the large works carried out at Babylon under Binlikhish III. and Sammuramat, and later under Nabopolassar and Nitocris. Nebuchadnezzar surpassed all the works of his predecessors; under his reign Babylon became the first city in the world. He almost entirely rebuilt the "royal city," situated on the eastern bank of the Euphrates, where had been the first germ of Babylon in the time of

the Cushite kings. A new palace was constructed there by his orders, conceived in the most gigantic proportions, and far more magnificent than the old one; we recognise its position in the tumulus called "Kasr," one of the most considerable ruins on the site of Babylon. He says of it, in the great inscription preserved in London, "Nabopolassar, king of Babylon, my father, had commenced the building of the palace with bricks, and had erected an altar in the centre. He had sunk its foundations deep in the waters. I laid the sub-structure with brick. I laid on it the foundation stone. I built as high as the level of the waters, and there I firmly fixed the foundation of the palace. I constructed it of bitumen and bricks. For its timber work I employed great beams, cedar wood, cased with iron. I employed in it enamelled bricks, forming inscriptions and pictures, and enamelled brick also framed the doors. I collected there gold, silver, metals, precious stones of every kind and value, a collection of valuable objects and immense treasures. I established there a valiant cohort, a royal garrison." In the vast enclosure of this palace, and on the very border of the river, Nebuchadnezzar caused to be raised and planted the famous "Hanging gardens," a sort of artificial mountain, to recall to the mind of his queen, Amytis—a Median by birth—the picturesque aspect of her own country. A succession of terraces rose in stages one above the other, like those of Isola Bella on Lake Maggiore. An enormous sub-structure supported the whole, and vast subterranean chambers were made under each cultivated terrace. The site of this construction, universally admired by the ancients, has been recognised by M. Oppert in the tumulus, called "Amram." In the royal city there was the building designated by the inscriptions themselves as the most ancient of the city, properly called Babylon, the pyramid in stages, called "the temple of the foundations of the earth," or rather "Val Saggatu," in Chaldæo-Turanian "Temple of the lofty head." The Chaldæan priests pretended to show the tomb of the god Bel Merodach, who had there his famous oracle. This pyramid, the work of the Cushite dynasty, had fallen into ruin from old age; Nebuchadnezzar repaired and partly reconstructed it. "Val Saggatu," says he, in an inscription, "is the great temple of heaven and earth, the dwelling of Merodach, the master of the gods. I have restored its sanctuary, the place of repose of the deity, plating it with pure gold." The pyramid of Babylon contained at its base a sanctuary of Nebo; half way up was the sepulchral chamber of Bel Merodach, where they consulted his oracle; lastly, at the top was another sanctuary, called "the mystic sanctuary of Merodach." The distinction of these three parts is indispensable to the right understanding of the circumstantial details which Nebuchadnezzar gives in his "standard inscription," of the restoration of the pyramid:—"I undertook in Val Saggatu the restoration of the chamber of Merodach. I gave to the cupola the form of a lily, and I covered it with chased gold, so that it shone as the day. On the high hill, where fates were foretold outside the town, was erected the Altar of Destinies. It was erected in Val Saggatu during the feasts of the new year. This altar—altar of the sovereignty of Merodach, the sublime master of the gods—had been made in silver by a former king; I covered it with pure gold of immense weight. I employed for the woodwork of the chamber of oracles the largest of the trees I had caused to be transported from the summit of Lebanon. I covered with pure gold the enormous beams of cypress, employed for the woodwork of the chamber of oracles; the lower portion of the woodwork I incrusted with gold, silver, other metals and gems. I had the vault of the mystic sanctuary of Merodach incrusted with glass and gems, so as to represent the firmament with the stars. The wonder of Babylon, I rebuilt and restored it: it is this temple of the base of heaven and earth whose summit I raised of bricks, and covered it externally with a cornice of copper."

5. Whilst these works were being executed in the royal city, the part of Babylon, called Hillat, or "the profane city," whose site is occupied by the present town of Hillah, was more than doubled in size by the numerous colonies of captives, whom the conquering monarch had brought from all the countries subdued by his arms. It is there that the Hebrews from Jerusalem and the neighbouring district were established. They had the privilege, in common no doubt with other communities of exiles, of having their own national judges; thus proving that in the system of government of the kingdom of Babylon, as in that of Merovingian Gaul, and of Turkey at present, the law was personal not territorial. They enjoyed there also complete liberty of religious worship, for Ezekiel was able to discharge among them, without hindrance, his prophetic mission, though he publicly announced the short duration of the Chaldæan power. It was at Babylon that certain of the Psalms were written for use in religious worship, such as that beautiful one, "By the rivers of Babylon" (Ps. cxxxvii.), in which Divine vengeance was invoked for the chastisement of the oppressors of Israel. Some of the Jews were advanced to very elevated posts in the administration, and that without ceasing to profess their own faith, as in the case of Daniel, who was one of the king's ministers. It was necessary only, on entering on public functions, to take a Babylonian name as the mark of a sort of naturalisation.

The walls of the enceinte of Babylon, commenced by Esarhaddon, were completed by Nebuchadnezzar, and commemorative inscriptions have been recently found, engraven in order to transmit to posterity the remembrance of that gigantic work. The exact agreement of the statements they furnish with the descriptions of Herodotus, which we have already quoted, is remarkable.

"Imgur-bel and Nivit-bel, the great walls of Babylon, I built them square . . . I repaired, with bitumen and bricks, the sides of the ditches that had been dug. I caused to be put in order the double doors of bronze, and the railings, and gratings in the great gateways. I enlarged the streets of Babylon so as to make them wonderful. I applied myself to the protection of Babylon and Val Saggatu (the pyramid), and on the most elevated lands, close to the great gate of Ishtar, I constructed strong fortresses of bitumen and bricks, from the bank of the Euphrates down to the great gate, the whole extent of the streets. I established their foundations below the level of the waters. I fortified these walls with art. I caused Imgur-bel, the great wall of Babylon, the impregnable, such as no king before me had made, to be measured, 4,000 mahargagar; that is the extent of Babylon." This measurement corresponds exactly with the 480 stades given by Herodotus as the circuit.

6. The construction of these walls had the effect of reuniting to the city of Babylon, properly so called, in one enclosure, the original Babel, anterior even to Nimrod, the city that had seen the confusion of tongues, and to which the tradition of that event was still attached—Borsippa—situated at some distance on the eastern bank of the Euphrates, and up to that time a separate city. It was there that he restored the Tower of Babel—existing from time immemorial as a mass of rubbish—and established the great temple of Bel, called by the Babylonians "Val-zida," a Chaldæo-Turanian word, with a meaning as yet unknown to us, and "the Tower of the seven celestial spheres."

We have given in our First Book the most striking passages of the inscription found in the ruins of the edifice, in which Nebuchadnezzar describes this restoration and quotes, for the origin of the monument, a tradition exactly agreeing with that of the Bible. Herodotus, who saw the Temple of Bel in the state in which it was left by the great Chaldæan conqueror, describes it in these words:—"It was a square enclosure, two stades each way. In the middle of the precinct there was a tower of solid masonry, a stade in length and breadth, upon which was raised a second tower, and on that a third, and so on up to eight." The basement was 75 feet high, and each of the stages 25, so that the whole structure was 250 feet in height. Excavations made by Sir H. Rawlinson enable us to state that the seven stages crowned by the sanctuary of the god had, like those of the Zikurat of the Assyrian palace at Khorsabad, facings of the colours of the seven planets, but differently arranged, that is to say, beginning from the bottom, black (Saturn), white (Venus), purple (Jupiter), blue (Mercury), vermilion (Mars), silver (the Moon), and gold (the Sun). Reckoning from the top, this is the order of the days of the week. "On the topmost tower there is a spacious temple, and inside the temple stands a couch of unusual size, richly adorned, with a golden table by its side. There is no statue of any kind set up in the place, nor is the chamber occupied at night by anyone but a single native woman, who, as the Chaldæans, the priests of this god, affirm, is chosen for himself by the deity out of all the women of the land . . . Below, in the same precinct, there is a second temple, in which is a sitting figure of Jupiter, all of gold. Before the figure stands a large golden table, and the throne whereon it sits, and the base on which the throne is placed, are likewise of gold. The Chaldæans told me that all the gold together was eight hundred talents' weight. Outside the temple are two altars, one of solid gold, on which it is only lawful to offer sucklings; the other a common altar, but of great size, on which the full-grown animals are sacrificed. It is also on the great altar that the Chaldæans burn the frankincense, which is offered to the amount of a thousand talents' weight every year at the festival of the god."*

All these particulars are confirmed by the Apocryphal Book of Daniel ("Bel and the Dragon," vv. 3 and 23, *seq.*), containing more interesting details of the worship of Bel in that sanctuary, of which the ancient Tower of Babel, the most venerable monument in the world, had furnished the nucleus. According to the sacred writer, seventy priests were attached to the service of the temple, and each day they offered to the god twelve large measures of the purest wheat-flour, forty sheep and six large vessels of wine; there was also in this temple, probably in the lower sanctuary, a great serpent, adored by the Babylonians as the living image of Bel, and said to have been killed by Daniel before the eyes of the king.

"Borsippa," says the London inscription, "is the town of those who exalt the god. I ornamented it. In the centre I caused to be constructed Val-zida, the eternal house; I completed its magnificence with gold, silver, other metals, stones, enamelled bricks, timber work of sea-pine and cedar. I covered with gold the woodwork of the place of repose of the god Nebo. The cross pieces of the door of oracles have been plated with silver. The uprights, the sill and the lintel, of the place of repose I encrusted with ivory. I encrusted with silver the uprights in cedar of the door of the women's chamber. I built the entrance to the place of repose and the square portico of the temple magnificently with bricks of various colours. I constructed the temple solidly. To astonish mankind, I reconstructed and renewed the wonder of Borsippa, the temple of the seven spheres of the world. I raised the top of bricks, and covered it with copper. I inlaid the sanctuary of the god with alternate bands of marble and other stones. . . . At Borsippa, in the body of masonry forming the base of Val-zida, I made a temple in the form of a cavern, in honour of Sin, who sustains my authority, the sanctuary of Oannes."

In the inscription found amongst the ruins of the tower there are

* HER. i. 181, 182.

some details of the construction agreeing with those quoted, and also some fresh ones.

"I did not change the site or alter the foundations. In a fortunate month, on an auspicious day, I pierced through with vaults the crude brick of the body of masonry, and the baked brick of the casing. I adjusted the circular inclines. I inscribed my name on the frieze of the terraces. I set my hand to reconstruct Val-zida, and to raise its head as it was in ancient times. I reconstructed and rebuilt it as it was in former times. I raised its summit."

Lastly, another inscription repeats the same information, but adds this detail, not found elsewhere, that the goddess Nana was supposed to be residing with the god in the upper sanctuary of the tower.

The cuneiform inscriptions of Nebuchadnezzar also give us valuable details of the interior administration of this sovereign, of the spoils torn from conquered peoples, and employed in the construction of all those edifices, the pride of the Chaldæan city. They enumerate the ancient temples he restored and the new ones he built, not only at Babylon and Borsippa, but at Cutha and numerous other towns of Chaldæa; for they had all suffered enormously under the later Assyrian kings, who had severely repressed their attempts at independence, and they all rose from their ruins at the same time as the capital under Nebuchadnezzar.

We will first relate the details given on this subject by the London inscription.

"I built at Babylon, in honour of the sublime sovereign (Bilit Zarpanit), the mother who bore me, *the temple of the goddess of the summit of the mountains*, which is the heart of Babylon."

Considerable ruins of this temple are found at a place called El Kolaïah, near Hillah. Amongst them has been found a dedicatory inscription bearing the name of Nebuchadnezzar.

"I caused to be built in Babylon, of bitumen and bricks, according to the rules of art, a temple in honour of the god Nebo, the supreme regent who bestows the sceptre of justice to govern the legions of men. *The temple of him who confers the sceptre.*"

"I built in Babylon, to the god Sin, who inspires me with judgment, *the temple of the great light*, his house."

"I built in Babylon, of bitumen and bricks, a temple in honour of the god Shamash, who inspires my body with the sentiment of justice, *the temple of the judge of the world.*" This edifice occupied the site, in the town of Hillah, now filled by a mosque, still called "Mosque of the Sun."

"I built, in the form of a square, a temple at Babylon, of bitumen and bricks, in honour of the god Bin, who showers down abundance on my country, *the temple of the dispenser of storms.*"

"I built at Babylon temples of bitumen and bricks, a vast body of masonry, in honour of the great goddess (Nana), who rejoices and sustains my soul. *The temple of the depths* and *the temple of the high mountains*."

"I built at the entrance of the wall of Babylon a temple in the form of a square, in honour of the sovereign of the house of heaven, the queen who has pity on me, *the temple of Kikupan*."

"I built at Borsippa a temple to the god Adar Samdan, who breaks the arms of my enemies."

"I built at Borsippa, in honour of the great goddess (Nana), who accepts my song, *the great temple*, *the temple of life*, and *the temple of the living soul*, its three wonders." These three temples, alluding to the lunar attributes of the goddess Nana, and to the phases of the planet—new, full, and waning moon—were all one body of masonry. The ruins form what is now called the Tel Ibrahim el Khalil, near Nimrud.

"I constructed at Borsippa, in masonry, the temple of the god Bin, who causes the prophetic thunder to sound in my country."

The details in this inscription refer also to other sacred edifices.

"The 8th of the month Ulul I consecrated the portico of the god Nergal and of the god Nibkhaz, the gods of the temple Valpitlam at Cutha. I accomplished the oracle of the great god; I added a new portico to that of the façade." Cutha to the north of Babylon had, like Borsippa, been included in the immense circuit of the exterior wall. The special god of this town was Nergal, and we learn from some mythological details given in the tablets of the library of Asshurbanipal, that he was worshipped there under the form of a lion.

"I founded and constructed the *temple of the day* at Sippara, in honour of Shamash and Sin, my lords."

"I founded and constructed at Sarsam *the temple of the day*, in honour of Shamash and Sin, my lords."

"I founded and built the temple . . . at Ur, in honour of the god Sin, the master who exalts my royalty."

"I founded and built the temple *Ikul Anu* at Nipur, in honour of the god Oannes, my master."

"I founded and constructed in the town of Ras *the temple of eternal adoration*, in honour of the god Bel Zarbi, my lord."

At Babylon itself this prince, as we learn from his inscriptions, completed the quays of the Euphrates, commenced by his father, Nabopolassar, and his mother, Nitocris. Not content with ornamenting and embellishing "the city of his royalty," as he calls it in his monuments, and the other cities subject to his sceptre, he was solicitous also for the fertility of Babylonia and the extension of its commerce. He repaired and put into working order the famous royal canal, or Naharmalcha, constructed 1,300 years before by the king, Hammurabi, but from lapse of time so much obstructed that these repairs were considered by the historians as, in truth, a new construction. He caused an immense lake to be dug below Sippara, to serve as a reservoir for watering the plain, and finally he secured the navigation of the Persian gulf by establishing a large port at the mouth of the river at Teredon, called by the Babylonians in their own language Kar Dunyash.

8. Nebuchadnezzar was then, in truth, a great king; but pride was his ruin, and led him to madness, as it has done other men of great genius, equally infatuated with their own success. Already, in the inscription commemorative of the restoration of the tower of Babel, he had said "Merodach, the great lord, has begotten me himself." A little later, when all his great works were accomplished, he thought himself a god, and willed that everyone should fall prostrate before a statue of himself, which he caused to be made of gold. Three Hebrews resisted him, and witnessing the miracle by which God preserved them from the flames, the king of Babylon, says the Bible, rendered homage to the God of Israel. But his pride was not abated, and one day while he walked in his palace, the king spake and said, "Is not this great Babylon, that I have built for the house of the kingdom by the might of my power, and for the honour of my majesty? Then a voice from heaven said to him, O Nebuchadnezzar, to thee it is spoken; The kingdom is departed from thee. And they shall drive thee from men, and thy dwelling shall be with the beasts of the field: and they shall make thee to eat grass as oxen, and seven times shall pass over thee, until thou know that the Most High ruleth in the kingdom of men, and giveth it to whomsoever he will" (Dan. iv. 30, *seq.*). This decree was at once accomplished; Nebuchadnezzar, struck with the most abject madness, fled from the society of men, and, imitating the beasts, tried, like them, to eat grass; his person, deprived of all care, and exposed to the inclemencies of weather, exhibited all the effects of this neglect. A personage, named Bellabarisruk, of whose origin we know nothing, and whose son was son-in-law to the king—in all probability the Archi-Magus, or chief of the Chaldæan caste—possessed himself of power, possibly as regent of the empire during the incapacity of the sovereign. An inscription shows, however, that he took the title of king, and thus consummated a real and complete usurpation. It was not until after the lapse of seven months that Nebuchadnezzar became himself again, and was able to reassume the exercise of power. A short time after this he died, having reigned forty-three years, predicting, says Berosus, the ruin of the Babylonian empire.

NOTE.—The Jewish historian, Josephus, has misinterpreted the words of the Bible, and enormously exaggerated the time of Nebuchadnezzar's madness, prolonging it to seven years. *Ant.* X. 6.

SECTION IV.—THE SUCCESSORS OF NEBUCHADNEZZAR—FALL OF THE BABYLONIAN EMPIRE. 561—533 B.C.

1. IT did not require a supernatural gift of prophecy to foresee that the Babylonian empire, arrived at such a high degree of splendour, was very near its fall, and that its power would take no longer time to crumble away than had been required to build it up: for this no more was requisite than a clear and prescient mind. This empire had, in truth, in itself no one real element of duration. The colossus, as in the vision explained by Daniel, had feet of clay. The Babylonian nation was not sufficiently energetic, or sufficiently military in character, to be able to maintain, as the Assyrians had done during many centuries, its dominion over a hundred different races. Its whole warlike force consisted of hordes of cavalry from the tribes of Irak Arabi and the people of Lower Chaldæa—hordes admirably fitted to overrun, with the impetuosity of a torrent that has burst its banks, a large extent of country in a very short time, but not to preserve their conquests and found a lasting dominion.

It may generally be observed in history that those people whose military strength consists entirely of cavalry are capable indeed of great and rapid conquests, but are never able to preserve them for any length of time.

From the very moment of the death of Nebuchadnezzar, disquieting rumours began to prevail at Babylon. It was said that a new dominant power had appeared in the world. Already the kingdom of the Medes had fallen before this people, but lately its subjects; the Persians, for so were these new conquerors called, had sallied from their rugged mountains under the guidance of a young chief, whom the events of the war had already raised to the rank of a great captain. The prophets of Israel, too, announced with startling voice that proud Babylon must ere long herself feel the miseries she had inflicted on Jerusalem. "Come down, and sit in the dust, O virgin daughter of Babylon, sit on the ground: there is no throne, O daughter of the Chaldæans: for thou shalt be no more called tender and delicate. Take the millstones, and grind meal: uncover thy locks, make bare the leg, uncover the thigh, pass over the rivers. Thy nakedness shall be uncovered, yea, thy shame shall be seen" (Isa. xlvii. 1—3).

2. Nebuchadnezzar was succeeded by his son, Evil-Merodach; this prince is distinguished in sacred history by an act of humanity (2 Kings xxv. 27). At the commencement of his reign he "lifted up the head" of Jehoiakin, king of Judah, and brought him forth out of prison, where for thirty-seven years he had been left in fetters; gave him a rank above the other captive kings who were at the capital; admitted him to his table, and assigned him a pension. But the rest of his reign did

not fulfil the promise of so honourable an action. Berosus represents him as having trampled under foot every law and all propriety. A plot was laid against him, and he was assassinated by his brother-in law, the son-in-law of Nebuchadnezzar, and the son of the Bellabarisruk who had usurped power during the madness of the great Chaldæan conqueror (559), who was named *Nergalsarussur* (Nergal protects the king), a name altered in the fragments of Berosus to Neriglissar. Evil-Merodach had reigned but two years. This domestic tragedy gave to Neriglissar a sceptre that he held without dignity, and did not long retain.

The son-in-law of the conqueror of Jerusalem built himself a new palace outside the royal city, on the western bank of the Euphrates, and placed statues of massive silver in the various sanctuaries of the pyramid of the tomb of Bel. He reigned only four years, and lost his life in a great battle against the Persians under Cyrus, the conquerors of Media, of which country, formerly subject to the kings of Assyria, he desired to dispute their possession (555).

3. The son and successor of this prince is called Laborosoarchod in the fragments of Berosus; it is probable that he was in reality called Bellabarisruk, after his grandfather. He was a child, and occupied the throne only a few months. The chiefs of the Chaldæan caste dethroned him, indignant at the vicious and cruel instincts he displayed, young as he was. They then proclaimed one of their number, named Nabonahid (Nebo is majestic), the Labynetus of Herodotus, son of a certain Nabobalatirrib (555). He reigned during the last seventeen years of the Babylonian empire. At Babylon itself he repaired the quays of the royal city. A curious inscription of the last year of his reign, discovered at Ur by the English traveller, Loftus, shows him to us, saying his "mea culpa" for having neglected the worship of the gods, and undertaking to repair the temple of Sin, in order to obtain the protection of that god. The terms employed are sufficiently curious to warrant our repeating them here:—

"Although I myself, Nabonahid, king of Babylon, have long sinned against the great divinity, yet save me, grant me a long existence, reaching even to the most advanced age that man can attain to. And since I have Belsharussur, the scion of my heart, my eldest son, propagate on his account the worship of thy great divinity. May his life be preserved from harm, so long as the destinies permit."

Everything points out this inscription as the work of a prince threatened with a great and pressing danger. And so it was; for in the year of the date of the Ur monument (538), Cyrus, who had already made himself master of all the rest of Asia, advanced against him at the head of the Medes and Persians, with the declared resolution of adding Chaldæa to his dominions.

Nabonahid advanced to meet Cyrus, but sustained a complete defeat;

and, followed by a small number of soldiers, threw himself into Borsippa, whilst Cyrus laid siege to Babylon. We gather from this fact, reported by Berosus, that the last Chaldæan monarch did not feel himself able to defend effectively the immense extent of the first great wall erected by Nebuchadnezzar, including both Babylon proper and Borsippa, and that he allowed it to be forced by the Persian army without opposition. Babylon, protected by the second wall, and by the impregnable citadel forming the royal city, was not to be reduced easily; provided with food for many years' consumption, its inhabitants disdained a besieger not so well supplied as themselves. But the time fixed by Providence for the chastisement of the Chaldæan city had arrived. Cyrus, who very recently had, by digging canals, exhausted the Gyndes, an affluent of the Tigris, resolved to adopt the same measures, and to enter Babylon by the bed of the Euphrates; he opened the sluices serving to divert the waters of the river into the artificial lake, dug by Nitocris, and his troops, going down into the Euphrates, with water to their knees only, entered the city, or rather between its two parts. The inhabitants might then have taken them as in a net, by shutting on them the bronze gates of the quays, and have crushed them from the height of their walls. But they were then engaged in celebrating a feast, and, drowned in revelry and carelessness, they permitted the enemy to obtain full occupation of the centre of the city before the more distant quarters were even informed of the attack. Thus were fulfilled the prophecies announcing the drying up of the river of Babylon; the orgies of the warriors and priests ending in the sleep of death; its gates set open before the ministers of divine justice; and Cyrus (named by Isaiah, Hezekiah's contemporary) taking possession of that proud city, whose capture Jeremiah had *described* at the period of its highest power.

Nabonahid, when he retired to Borsippa, had left in Babylon his son Belsharussur (Bel protects the king), the Belshazzar of the Book of Daniel,* who had been associated with himself in the government.

---

* In the Books of Baruch and of Daniel, Belshazzar is called "son of Nebuchadnezzar" (Baruch i. 11; Daniel v. 18), and this, until his name was found in the inscriptions, gave much trouble to all commentators. Here, however, the word "son" is used in its general and poetical sense of successor, just as we have seen on the Nimrud obelisk Jehu called the "son of Omri." It must, however, be borne in mind, in considering the historical facts contained in the Book of Daniel, that admitting the book to be perfectly authentic, and unquestionably written at Babylon, we no longer possess the whole of the original text, but merely the results of the re-arrangement and partial re-writing in Syro-Chaldee about the third century B.C.; and this by transcribers ignorant of history, who have fallen into several manifest errors as to the names of Babylonian kings.

It is on that festal night, when the Persians surprised Babylon, that we must place the scene of Belshazzar's feast, related in such thrilling terms in the Book of Daniel. The son of Nabonahid has profaned in his orgie the sacred vessels of the Temple of Jerusalem; a terrible sign—fingers writing on the wall the three famous words, Mene, Tekel, Peres—announces to him the destined chastisement of Providence; and so that very night he was killed by Darius the Mede, one of the generals of Cyrus, who having been charged by that prince with the nocturnal expedition, was rewarded for his success by the government of Babylon.*

Nabonahid escaped the unfortunate end of his son; he did not await in Borsippa a siege, that in all probability would not have lasted long, and surrendered to Cyrus, who sent him into Carmania, where he ended his days. From that time the kingdom of Babylon ceased to exist, though the ruin of the city was slowly and gradually accomplished.

Babylon continued, under the Persian kings, to be one of the capitals of their empire. Many times the proud city attempted again to raise its head, for it did not resign itself easily to the loss of independence; but their revolts served only to draw down on the inhabitants the vengeance of the conquerors. During the troubles following the death of Cambyses (522), a certain Nidintabel proclaimed himself king there, giving himself out as Nebuchadnezzar, son of Nabonahid. A Greek cameo in the Museum at Berlin, of archaic workmanship, carried to Babylon in the course of commerce, was dedicated by this Nebuchadnezzar to one of his gods, as is proved by the cuneiform inscription engraved round it. Four years later (518), Darius, son of Hystaspes, could only take Babylon after a siege of twenty months, and by help of the treason of Zopyrus. The following year saw a new insurrection, soon put down, by a man called Arakhu, who also passed himself off as son of Nabonahid. The Babylonians did not take the trouble to examine into the pretensions of these impostors; it was enough that they proclaimed independence, and called the people to arms against the Persians. In 508, a new insurrection was more successful than the

---

* The name of Darius the Mede has been, like that of Belshazzar, a veritable *crux interpretum*. There is no possible theory that has not been started on this subject, because we read in the Bible that he became king on the death of Belshazzar. "And Darius the Mede 'took the kingdom,'" a phrase that may be equally well applied to the investiture of a satrap as to the accession of a king. At any rate, if we must absolutely maintain the sense this phrase has hitherto received, Darius the Mede can have been no other than Darius, son of Hystaspes, whose name the author of the re-arrangement has substituted for that of Cyrus, as the former was much better known in the third century B.C.

preceding; it freed Babylon and all Chaldæa for twenty years from the Persian yoke. No Persian monuments are found there in that long interval. But Darius subdued it at last in 488; and to render any future revolt of Babylon impossible, he overturned its towers, its walls, and its immense fortifications. Xerxes, some years after, continued the work of his father, and regularly pillaged the city, carrying off the golden statue of Nebo and the treasures of the tomb of Bel Merodach.

Alexander, the conqueror of the Persians, adopted another policy. Struck with the beauty and the advantages of the situation of Babylon, he wished to make it rise from its ruins; but that great man died before he was able to carry out his plans.

The Seleucidæ wished to have a capital built by themselves, and bearing their name; they founded Seleucia on the banks of the Tigris, and the privileges given to those who came to settle there led to a general desertion of Babylon. The new capital numbered 600,000 inhabitants. This state of prosperity did not outlast the time of these new masters of the East. When the Parthians had seized the empire of Asia, they did to Seleucia what Seleucus Nicator had done to Babylon, they founded a new city, Ctesiphon; this in its turn was superseded by the Arab city of Bagdad, the capital of the Caliphs, still existing. Bagdad, the youngest, would equal her elder sisters in grandeur, in spite of Hulagu and Tamerlane, if the commerce of the world had not found out other channels.

In the time of Pliny Babylon was already a desert. At the present day there remains of the immense city nothing but huge masses of rubbish and an inexhaustible magazine of materials, whence the inhabitants of the neighbourhood constantly take what they require; above all, excellent and perfectly moulded burnt bricks, slabs of marble, and glazed tiles. The hills of rubbish, marking the sites of the principal edifices, palaces, hanging gardens, the Pyramid of Bel, the Tower of Tongues, furnish dens for the wild beasts of the desert. Thus is accomplished to the letter the prophecy of Isaiah:—"Behold, I will stir up the Medes against them, which shall not regard silver; and as for gold, they shall not delight in it. Their bows also shall dash the young men to pieces; and they shall have no pity on the fruit of the womb; their eye shall not spare children. And Babylon, the glory of kingdoms, the beauty of the Chaldees' excellency, shall be as when God overthrew Sodom and Gomorrah. It shall never be inhabited, neither shall it be dwelt in from generation to generation: neither shall the Arabian pitch tent there; neither shall the shepherds make their fold there. But the wild beasts of the deserts shall lie there; and their houses shall be full of doleful creatures; and owls shall dwell there, and satyrs shall dance there. And the wild beasts of the islands shall cry in their desolate houses, and dragons in their pleasant palaces" (Isa. xiii. 17—22).

CHAPTER VI.

MANNERS AND RELIGION OF BABYLON.

SECTION I.—MANNERS.

1. THE civilisation of Nineveh and of Babylon were one and the same. Between Assyria and Chaldæa there was complete conformity in all things fundamental and essential. What we have already said in the preceding chapter, on the manners, customs, and religion of the Assyrians, will be equally applicable here; and we may confine ourselves to some short remarks on a few points where the genius and civilisation of the two great Mesopotamian people separated, and took each its own peculiar aspect.

The clothing of the Babylonians, according to the testimony of Herodotus,* and the representations on the cylinders, was a linen tunic reaching to the feet; over this they wore another tunic of wool, and over that again a short white cloak. They wore the hair carefully curled, and on the head high-pointed tiaras. The soldiers wore conical helmets, like those of the Assyrians, breastplates of quilted linen, and used wooden bucklers. Their offensive arms were wooden maces studded with iron, lances, and short swords.

Each Babylonian had, as his personal emblem, a walking-stick with some figure carved on the top, serving as his symbol, or, as we might say, armorial bearing. Every one had also a seal, usually in shape of a cylinder. An immense number of these cylinders have been discovered; they bear some mythological symbols, and usually the name of the owner, of his father, and of the deity under whose protection he had placed himself. These cylinders were kept ready made in shops, only requiring the name to be filled in, and some have been found where the name-space is vacant.

2. Herodotus says† that the Babylonians buried their dead in honey, a statement rather difficult to understand. Some facts seem to indicate that they also used oil for this purpose.

Marriages were made once a year at a public festival,‡ where the maidens of age to marry were put up to public auction. The beautiful girls sold for large sums, and this money was employed as a dowry for the ugly ones. No one could marry his daughter except in this way. This marriage festival was celebrated in the month Sabat, and the principal day was the last of the month. They gave to each damsel

* HER. i. 195. † Ibid. i. 198. ‡ Ibid. i. 196.

they sold for marriage a model of an olive in baked clay, pierced with a hole so as to be worn round the neck; on this was inscribed her name, the name of her husband, and the date of the ceremony. Some of these olives have been found, and as specimens we give the inscriptions on three now in the Museum of the Louvre. 1. "Manutamat, whom Bakit-Alsi has taken the day of the feast of Sabat, the ninth year of Merodach Baladan, king of Babylon." 2. "Binit Nisukin, whom Ha...kan has taken, in the month Sabat, the tenth year of Merodach Baladan, king of Babylon." 3. "Halalat, whom Marnarih has taken, in the month Sabat, the eleventh year of Merodach Baladan, king of Babylon."

The Greek writers* mention, among the peculiarities of the manners and customs of the Babylonians, one festival in summer, called Sacees, resembling the Saturnalia at Rome. The slaves for five days took command of their masters, and one of them, clothed in a royal robe, received the honours of a sovereign. This, no doubt, is the great festival mentioned twice by Sargon [Sharyukin], and Esarhaddon [Asshur-akhiddin], in their inscriptions as peculiar to Babylon, and called Çak-muku, a name at present unintelligible, and probably borrowed from the Chaldæo-Turanian language. It is mentioned as falling in the month Nisan.

Section II.—The Caste of the Chaldæans.

1. The population in Babylonia and Chaldæa was not, as in Assyria, one single unmixed race. On the contrary, it was essentially mixed, and contained, as we have already said, Cushite, Turanian, and Semitic elements, imposed as it were one over the other. Thence arose, as in all such cases, the distinctions of castes, unequal in rank, and devoted to certain defined occupations. The merchants, artisans, and husbandmen formed each a caste. The fishermen of the marshes bordering on the Persian Gulf also formed a separate caste, and were at the bottom of the social scale. Herodotus† tells us that they lived entirely on dried fish, pounded and made into a species of cake. Assyrian bas-reliefs depict these people in the campaigning scenes of Sennacherib and Asshurbanipal as living in islands in the midst of the reeds, or rather, with their families, inhabiting rafts covered with earth, forming floating islands, such as may still be seen in some parts of China and on the lakes of Mexico.

The superior and dominant caste, entirely exclusive, was composed of the Chaldæans, properly so called, who, as we have already attempted to show, were strangers, and conquerors of the Turanian race.

---

* Athen. xix. p. 369. † Her. i. 200.

They had obtained exclusive possession of all priestly functions, and used them so as to govern the state. Classical writers give us some details on their organisation, functions, and power.

2. "The Chaldæans," says Diodorus Siculus, following Ctesias, who had seen them at Babylon, "are the most ancient of the Babylonians; they formed in the state a body resembling the priests in Egypt. Set apart for following up the worship of the gods, they passed their whole life in meditation on philosophical subjects, and had acquired a great reputation in astrology; they especially devoted themselves to the science of divination and to predictions of the future; they attempted to avert evil and procure good fortune, either by purifications, or by sacrifices, or by enchantments. They are accomplished in the art of predicting the future by observing the flight of birds; they explained dreams and prodigies. Skilled in the art of inspecting the entrails of victims, they were accounted capable of giving the true interpretation. But these branches of knowledge were not taught as among the Greeks. The learning of the Chaldæans was a family tradition; the son who inherited this from his father was exempt from all taxes. Having their relations for instructors, they had the double advantage of being taught everything without reserve, and that by masters in whose statements they could put implicit faith. Accustomed to work from infancy, they made great progress in the study of astrology, partly because learning is easy at an early age, and partly because they received a long course of instruction. . . . The Chaldæans always remained at the same point in science, maintaining their traditions without alteration; the Greeks, on the contrary, thinking of nothing but profit, were constantly forming new schools, disputing among themselves as to the truth of the most important doctrines, confusing the minds of their disciples, who, tossed about in continual doubt, ended in believing nothing at all."

We see by the Book of Daniel (Dan. i. 4; ii. 2; v. 7) what were the functions of the Chaldæans; they composed many distinct classes, of more or less elevated rank, in the hierarchy. Some of them were the sacred scribes, decipherers of writings; others the constructors of horoscopes, or interpreters of the stars, magicians who pronounced magical formulæ, conjurors who had power to avert malign influences. Their power of divination assured them great influence, as it made them, so to speak, masters of every one's destiny. They usually foretold in almanacks, a custom that seems to have lasted to our own times, all that our common almanacks now predict,—fluctuations in the temperature, physical phenomena, and historical events. The Chaldæans were not confined to Babylon, but were spread over all Babylonia. They had schools in various places, more or less flourishing: according to Strabo, that at Borsippa was the most celebrated. That at Orchoe, or Erech, was also well known, and maintained its reputation down to the times of the Romans. In the period of the Seleucidæ, the doctrine of the unity of God was distinctly taught there: as we know from tablets with cuneiform inscriptions, dated in the reign of several Greek kings, found at Warkah, and now in the British Museum. The only name of a Deity found in them, and this is many times repeated, is "God One."

3. But the Chaldæans did not confine themselves to the duties and positions of priests and astrologers, and to the unbounded influence derived from this position both over the state and over individuals. They became the absolute governing class in politics. Members of this caste commanded armies, and held all the chief offices of the state. From them came all the royal families who ruled Babylon, whether vassals of Assyria, or, after the time of Phul, completely independent. At the head of the hierarchy and caste was an Archi-Magus, whose national and proper title we do not yet know; he was, next to the king, the chief personage of the empire; he accompanied the sovereign everywhere, even in war, to direct all his actions according to priestly rule and presage. When the king died and the legitimate successor could not immediately assume the reins of power, this personage administered the government in the interim, as in the instance which occurred between the death of Nabopolassar and the arrival of Nebuchadnezzar.

Section III.—Commerce of Babylon.

1. Babylon, from its geographical situation, naturally enjoyed great commercial prosperity. Placed at the junction of Upper and Lower Asia, within reach of the two great rivers communicating with the Persian Gulf and the Indian Sea, the city necessarily became the depôt for the caravans, both of the east and west, and at the same time the port for ships arriving from Africa, Arabia, and India. Everything proves that this great city was, from remotest antiquity, one of the chief commercial centres of the east.

Babylon received the productions of the various Asiatic countries, and in return distributed to them the products of her own peculiar industry. Among the articles manufactured in great quantity by the Babylonians, woollen and linen fabrics were the most important. Robes and tapestry were nowhere made so fine or so brightly coloured, as in Babylon. These celebrated manufactures were produced not only in the capital, but also in the other cities and towns of Babylonia. According to Diodorus Siculus, there were, on the banks of the Euphrates and Tigris, a great number of depôts for storing both the manufactures of the country and imported goods. In the time of Strabo, the chief manufacture of linen was at Borsippa, at that time distinct from Babylon.

Besides robes and tapestry, the Babylonians made with great taste and skill articles of luxury, such as chased weapons, furniture, jewelry, amulets, and engraved cylinders of stone for seals. In exchange for these, Babylon received from the various countries of Asia everything required for the wants and luxuries of such a great capital. Armenia sent its wines down the Euphrates, and Herodotus * gives us a most interesting account of the voyage. India supplied precious stones and large dogs, and so great was the passion for the latter, that Tritantæchmes, satrap of Babylon under the Achæmenians, had set apart four cities or large villages, exempted from all other taxes, on condition of maintaining his dogs.† From the same country, as well as from Persia, were imported valuable woollen fabrics. From Arabia and Ethiopia came perfumes, spices, gold, ivory, and ebony.

2. Babylon was in communication with the different countries that furnished their merchandise by many roads, all meeting at the great city. One of these routes, starting from Babylon, went northward, passed Ecbatana, the capital of Media, then turning eastward, passed Rhagæ, traversed the famous defile of the Caspian gates, whence it descended into Hyrcania and passed by Hecatompylos, as far as the city called, in later times, Alexandria of Aria. There it divided into two branches—one of them tended northward to Bactria, the other turned southward towards India by way of Drangiana and Arachosia, passing the cities of Prophthasia, Arachosia, and Ortospana. At the latter place the road again divided in three, called by the ancient geographers the trivium of Bactria. The first, running directly east, entered India by way of the cities of Peucela (Pushkalavati), and Taxila (Takshaçila). From Taxila the road turned south, crossed the Hydaspes (Vitasta), the Hyphasis (Vipaça), and thence went on to the confluence of the Ganges and Iomanes (Yamuna) at Palibothra (Pataliputra). The second road leaving Ortospana arrived at the same termination, passing through Arachosia; the third, turning to the north, entered Bactria and went on through Marachanda, as far as the Iaxartes.

Another road connected Babylon with the border countries of the Mediterranean, passing due north through Mesopotamia to the Euphrates at Anthemusia, and thence turning westward to the sea. Again another road led first to Susa, turned north, and passed through Assyria towards Armenia, crossed the northern part of that country, passed the Euphrates, traversed Cilicia and through the "Cilician gates" entered Cappadocia. Thence it traversed Phrygia and ended at Sardis, in Lydia. "Royal houses," says Herodotus,‡ who had travelled over great part of this road, "exist along its whole length and excellent stations." These were the caravanserais of the present

* HER. i. 194. † Ibid. i. 192. ‡ Ibid. v. 52.

day. One hundred and eleven such stations were reckoned, Herodotus adds, between Sardis and Susa. This road is still employed by the caravans between Smyrna and Ispahan.

3. The Euphrates was the natural road for commerce between Babylon and Armenia and the countries of the Caucasus. Merchandise was transported, as Herodotus relates,* on round rafts supported by inflated skins, like the *keleks* still used in navigating the Tigris. These rafts were abandoned to the current; when they arrived at Babylon and the merchandise had been sold, the skins were emptied of air, and carried back by land, as well as the wood of the raft.

Great works had been undertaken to facilitate the navigation of the river; the banks had been raised to keep in the water and prevent it from overflowing the land; canals traversed the country, spreading fertility in every direction, as well as affording means of communication with all parts of Mesopotamia. Some of these canals, as for instance the Royal Canal, or *Nahar Malcha*, were so large and deep as to afford passage for large merchant ships. These numerous drains on the river had rendered the current slower and less impetuous. This canal system had also another object; it assisted in the defence of the country against hostile neighbours.

The capital of the empire had also in the days of its prosperity a powerful navy; its ships crossed the Persian Gulf in search of the precious commodities of the south, the productions of Arabia and India. If we may credit Strabo, the Babylonians had factories and colonies in those countries; and Gerrha, one of the richest markets in the world, was once, according to this celebrated geographer, a Chaldæan colony. The valuable and abundant pearls of the Persian Gulf, and the magnificent plantations of the Isle of Tylos, must have attracted their merchants. From this island they procured the light and strong canes so much esteemed all over Assyria. Thus the merchandise and productions of all Asia and Africa, flowed into Babylon, whence they were distributed to all parts of the empire.

SECTION IV.—RELIGION.

1. THE religion of Babylon was in all essential points the same as that of Assyria; it had followed the course of the Tigris, and its primitive seat had evidently been Chaldæa in the early days of the first empire of Nimrod. But although all the fundamental doctrines of the religious system, and all its divine personages, were the same among the Assyrians as among the Babylonians, there were differences of race and genius between the two peoples that gave rise to some differences in their religion.

---

* HEROD. i., 194.

Thus the Chaldæans had been led in the earliest times from Astronomy to Astrology; and this pretended science had received a greater development among them than ever at any time among other people. "According to them," says Diodorus Siculus, "the stars exercised an absolute and decisive influence on the birth of men, and determined their good or evil destiny. Changes in the heavens were thus so many signs of good or evil fortune for countries and nations, as well as for kings or individuals. The stars thus became the interpreters of the divine will, or rather of the decrees of destiny." With such preconceived ideas, their religious opinions necessarily took an astronomical and astrological form, even more markedly than at Nineveh. The Chaldæans supposed the divine hierarchy to be almost exclusively in relation to the sidereal world. Below the two superior triads—one of them essentially creative, the other cosmical—and below the deities of the five planets, they placed twelve councillors of the gods, each of whom presided over one of the months of the year, and over one of the signs of the zodiac. To these chief deities were also attached other powers, distributed in both a scientific and religious order, and forming essential elements in the Chaldæan worship. This sidereal pantheism was not only widely spread in Chaldæa, but had gained ground step by step among the neighbouring nations, and had become intimately mixed in their national faith. Thus, according to the testimony of the Book of Kings (2 Kings xxiii. 5, 11), the Israelites, who were frequently brought into contact with the Babylonians, offered incense to the Sun, the Moon, the twelve zodiacal signs, and all the host of heaven. We know also that several of the kings of Judah had dedicated horses to the sun, in imitation of the Babylonians.

2. Such a system was too learned, too complicated, to satisfy the gross desires and sensual passions of the multitude. But the forms that these refined and scientific ideas assumed in the popular worship, indicate to what an extent the primitive Hamitic depravity still tainted the people of Babylon; whilst on the contrary in Assyria, the Semitic genius of the people had invested the same ideas with the most spiritual and elevated character that they were capable of assuming. Everything proves that the most unbounded and shameless naturalism played a great part in the worship of the Babylonians. The stories of profane historians, the writings of the Hebrew prophets, the national monuments, such as cylinders and engraved stones of various kinds, testify to the number and variety of the idols they adored.

One of the chief features of the external and public organisation of the national worship in Chaldæa was the localisation of the worship of each divine personage in some particular city, where he was regarded as the first and greatest of the gods, whatever might be the place he filled elsewhere in the hierarchy of the Babylonian Pantheon. This privilege, by which each divine personage, even if holding only secondary rank, might become, in the place where he was specially adored, the first of the gods, is however common to all pantheistic religions.* In the spirit of these religions, the one sole deity, the first being, is incomprehensible, invisible, and manifested only in his varied attributes, each personified, each deified, and reflected in a variety of symbols. These symbols, found in nature, man observes and imitates. Immense bodies, such as the sun, the moon, the earth—impressive phenomena, such as thunder, volcanic eruptions, deluges, are more extended expressions for the deity; but these expressions are never complete, man is unable, either in his mind or by his eye, to appreciate the idea of the divine unity; the infinite inseparable from that unity, permitted him to see at one time as it were only one side of the divine character. Thus every symbol, every figure, name, manifestation, or emanation, bears a double character;—isolated they express only one of the qualities of the divine being, combined they express both the unity and the variety.

The deity who was the principal object of worship at Babylon and at Borsippa was Bel Merodach, with his wife, Bilit or Mylitta, the great nature-goddess, who assumed the two opposite forms of Taauth and Zarpanit—the one austere, the other voluptuous, like the two forms of the Venus of classical mythology. Bilit had a magnificent temple in the centre of Babylon, where an infamous custom compelled every woman once in her lifetime to give herself up to a stranger. At Ur, the god of the city, from the remote times of Ur-Hammu, was Sin, the Moon-god. At Sippara and Larsam, Shamash, the Sun. At Erech and Nipur, Bilit-Taauth, "Goddess of the firmament." At Cutha, Nana or Zarpanit was worshipped under the name of Succoth Benoth, a name referring to the prostitutions in honour of that goddess (see 2 Kings xvii. 29—31).

3. The materialistic and profoundly immoral worship at Babylon, naturally excited extreme horror in the worshippers of Jehovah, and provoked their vehement invectives against the idols of Chaldæa. We quote the eloquent words that portray so vividly an always materialistic, often obscene, worship that was in fact no more than a constant employment of popular superstition for the profit of the priests.

"Now ye shall see in Babylon gods of silver, and of gold, and of wood, borne upon shoulders, which cause the nations to fear. . . . And taking gold, as it were, for a virgin that loveth to go gay, they make crowns for the heads of their gods. Sometimes also the priests convey from their gods gold and silver, and bestow it upon themselves. Yea, they will give thereof to the common harlots, and deck them as men with garments, being gods of silver, and gods of gold and wood. . . .

---

* See page 324.

And he that cannot put to death one that offendeth him holdeth a sceptre (Nebo), as though he were a judge of the country. He (Bel Merodach) hath also in his right hand a dagger and an axe, but cannot deliver himself from war and thieves. . . . They light them candles, yea, more than for themselves, whereof they cannot see one. They are as one of the beams of the temple, yet they say their hearts are gnawed upon by things creeping out of the earth; and when they eat them and their clothes, they feel it not. . . . As for the things that are sacrificed unto them, their priests sell and abuse; in like manner their wives lay up part thereof in salt; but unto the poor and impotent they give nothing of it. . . . The priests also take off their garments and clothe their wives and children. . . . The women also with cords about them sitting in the ways burn bran for perfume."*

Section V.—Cosmogony.

1. The Chaldæans, like all other people, had deeply considered the problem of the origin of the world, and they had constructed a learned cosmogony, explained in the books of Oannes. The chief points have been preserved in the extracts from Berosus given by the Byzantine chronologers.

We have already seen, in the preceding chapter, that three successive divine emanations constituted the most exalted triad in the Chaldæo-Assyrian religion—Oannes, Ao, and Bel—representing the origin of the material world as an emanation from the substance of the divine being; first the primordial chaos, uncreated matter, sprung from the sole fundamental principle and cause of all things; next intelligence, or the word, that animates and renders it fertile; and lastly the demiurgus, who arranges and completes the organised universe, mixing himself up with this universe. We shall see now how the last act of this trilogy, the birth of the organised universe, its passage from the state of *indeterminate existence*, or of *non-existence with the power of existing* (to use the phrases of that philosophy of Hegel that, in our days, has had recourse to the conceptions of ancient pagan pantheists †), to the state of *determinate existence;* its creation, in a word, was symbolically related in the sacred books, and represented in paintings in the temple of Bel at Borsippa. The actors in this mythic cosmogony are Bel and his wife, the personages in the third divine emanation. We shall quote the text of some fragments of Berosus.

---

* Baruch VI. Epistle of Jeremiah.

† Compare the *Vedic Hymn* on this subject, translated in Max Müller's *Sanscrit Literature*, pp. 560—564.

"There was a time in which there existed nothing but darkness, and an abyss of waters, wherein resided most hideous beings, which were produced of a twofold principle. There appeared men, some of whom were furnished with two wings, others with four and with two faces. They had one body but two heads—the one that of a man, the other of a woman—and likewise in their several organs both male and female. Other human figures were to be seen with the legs and horns of goats: some had horses' feet: while others united the hind quarters of a horse with the body of a man resembling in shape the hippocentaurs. Bulls likewise were bred there with the heads of men; and dogs with fourfold bodies, terminated in their extremities with the tails of fishes. In short there were creatures in which were combined the limbs of every species of animals. In addition to these, fishes, reptiles, serpents, with other monstrous animals, which assumed each others' shapes and countenances, of all of which were preserved delineations in the temple of Belus at Babylon. The person who presided over them was a woman named Omorca, which, in the Chaldæan language, is Taauth;* in Greek Thalassa, the sea, but which might equally be interpreted the Moon. All things being in this situation, Belus came and cut the woman asunder; and of one-half of her he formed the earth, and of the other half the heavens; and at the same time destroyed the animals within her. All this (he says) was an allegorical description of nature. For the whole universe consisting of moisture, and animals being continually generated therein, the deity above mentioned took off his own head; upon which the other gods mixed the blood, as it gushed out, with the earth; and from thence were formed men. On this account it is that they are rational, and partake of the divine knowledge. This Belus, by whom they signify Jupiter, divided the darkness, and separated the heavens from the earth, and reduced the universe to order. But the animals, not being able to bear the prevalence of light, died. Belus upon this, seeing a vast space unoccupied, though by nature fruitful, commanded one of the gods to take off his head and to mix the blood with the earth; and thence to form other men and animals, which should be capable of bearing the air. Belus formed also the stars and the sun and the moon and the five planets."†

---

* The Greek text has Thalatth, a name not found in the cuneiform inscriptions. But now that we begin to know what were the original names of the Chaldæo-Assyrian deities, it is evident that the fragment of Berosus must be corrected by reading Θαυάτθ in place of Θαλάτθ, for reference is intended here to the goddess—mentioned also by the philosopher, Damascius, undoubtedly following Berosus—Bilit or Mylitta, Taauth, the wife of Bel, mother of the gods and of all beings, the great nature-goddess of Babylon, the passive and reproductive matter, organised by the demiurgus, and the source whence he drew the universe.

† CORY, *Ancient Fragments*, p. 22.

2. The narrative of Berosus, borrowed from the books of Oannes, goes on to relate the primitive history of the human race down to the dispersion of races. In the Babylonian tradition we find, among a host of purely mythical tales, some that present a very striking resemblance to the patriarchal revelation preserved in the Book of Genesis. The number of antediluvian patriarchs, the tradition of the deluge, that of the building of the Tower of Babel, and of the confusion of tongues, are almost identical in each.

"At Babylon there was, (in these times), a great resort of people of various nations, who inhabited Chaldæa, and lived in a lawless manner like the beasts of the field.

"In the first year there appeared, from that part of the Erythræan Sea which borders upon Babylonia, an animal endowed with reason by name Oannes, whose whole body (according to the account of Apollodorus) was that of a fish; that under the fish's head he had another head, with feet also below, similar to those of a man, subjoined to the fish's tail. His voice too and language was articulate and human, and a representation of him is preserved even to this day. This being was accustomed to pass the day among men, but took no food at that season, and he gave them an insight into letters and arts of every kind. He taught them to construct cities, to found temples, to compile laws, and explained to them the principles of geometrical knowledge. He made them distinguish the seeds of the earth, and showed them how to collect the fruits; in short, he instructed them in everything which could tend to soften manners and humanize their laws. From that time nothing material has been added by way of improvement to his instructions. And when the sun had set this being, Oannes, retired again into the sea, and passed the night in the deep; for he was amphibious. After this there appeared other animals like Oannes, of which Berosus proposes to give an account when he comes to the history of the kings. Moreover, Oannes wrote concerning the generation of mankind and of their civil polity." *

The Chaldæan historian next gives the history of the ten first antediluvian kings of Babylon—Alor (Ram of Light), Alapar (Bull of Light), Almelon of Sippara (the name of this town meaning "the city of books," seems to be here rendered by its Greek equivalent, Pantibibla, as it appears in the fragments of Berosus), Ammenon, Amelagar of Sippara, Daon of Sippara, Aedorach of Sippara, Amempsin of Larsam, Otiarte of Larsam, and lastly Xisuthrus. The legend of the cosmogomy assigns them collectively 432,000 years of life, and places in their days four new manifestations of Oannes, and one of Bel Dagon, each of whom had left to mankind a book explaining and completing that of the first Oannes.

* CORY, *Ancient Fragments*, p. 22.

"In the time of Xisuthrus happened a great deluge, the history of which is thus described. The deity Chronus (the Greeks thus translated the Chaldæo-Assyrian name Ilu), appeared to him in a vision, and warned him that upon the 15th day of the month Dæsius (Sivan) there would be a flood, by which mankind would be destroyed. He therefore enjoined him to write a history of the beginning, procedure, and conclusion of all things, and to bury it in the city of the sun at Sippara; and to build a vessel, and take with him into it his friends and relations, and to convey on board everything necessary to sustain life, together with all the different animals, both birds and quadrupeds, and to trust himself fearlessly to the deep. Having asked the deity whither he was to sail, he was answered, 'To the gods,' upon which he offered up a prayer for the good of mankind. He then obeyed the divine admonition, and built a vessel five stadia in length and two in breadth. Into this he put everything which he had prepared, and last of all conveyed into it his wife, his children, and his friends. After the flood had been upon the earth, and was in time abated, Xisuthrus sent out birds from the vessel, which, not finding any food, nor any place whereupon they might rest their feet, returned to him again. After an interval of some days he sent them forth a second time, and they now returned with their feet tinged with mud. He made a trial a third time with these birds, but they returned no more, from whence he judged that the surface of the earth had appeared above the waters. He therefore made an opening in the vessel, and upon looking out found that it was stranded upon the side of some mountain, upon which he immediately quitted it, with his wife, his daughter, and the pilot. Xisuthrus then paid his adorations to the earth; and having constructed an altar, offered sacrifices to the gods, and with those who had come out of the vessel with him disappeared.

"They who remained within, finding that their companions did not return, quitted the vessel with many lamentations, and called continually on the name of Xisuthrus. Him they saw no more, but they could distinguish his voice in the air, and could hear him admonish them to pay due regard to religion, and likewise informed them that it was upon account of this that he was translated to live with the gods; that his wife and daughter and the pilot had obtained the same honour. To this he added that they should return to Babylonia, and, as it was ordained, search for the writings at Sippara, which they were to make known to all mankind; moreover, that the place wherein they then were was the land of Armenia. The rest having heard these words offered sacrifices to the gods, and taking a circuit journeyed towards Babylonia. The vessel being thus stranded, some part of it yet remains in the Gordyæan mountain of Armenia; and the people scrape off the bitumen with which it had been coated, and make use of it by way of an alexipharmic and amulet. And when they returned to Babylon, and had found the writings at Sippara, they built cities and erected temples; and Babylon was thus inhabited again." *

4. We owe the preservation of the continuation of the narrative of Berosus, not to the Greek chronologers, but to the Armenian historian, Moses of Chorene.

"Before the Tower, and the multiplication of languages among mankind, after that Xisuthrus sailed to Armenia, Zervan, Titan and Japhetos were the lords of the earth. Scarcely had they divided the world among them, when Zervan made himself lord over his two fellows. Titan and Japhetos opposed themselves to him, and made war on him, for Zervan wished to make his children reign over them all. In the conflict Titan acquired possession of a part of the heritage of Zervan; but their sister Astlik interposed, and made peace between them.† Japhetos necessarily recalls the Japhet of the Bible; another fragment, also preserved by Moses of Chorene, identifies Zervan with Shem. The name of Titan seems a Greek translation of "Nimrod," "the rebel," the name given by the Semites to the originator of the primitive preponderance of the Hamite race at Babylon, clearly indicated in the narrative of Berosus by the conquest of a part of the inheritance of Zervan by Titan.

5. The story of primitive and fabulous times, the preface to early history, terminates in the work of the Chaldæan priest, who had translated into Greek the annals of his country, with the story of the Tower of Babel and of the confusion of tongues. We have already quoted,‡ in the first book of our Manual, the mention, apparently made in an inscription of Nebuchadnezzar, of the restoration of a building to which this tradition was attached. Berosus records this event as follows, in complete agreement with the Bible, and with the words of Nebuchadnezzar:—

"They say that the first inhabitants of the earth, glorying in their own strength and size, and despising the gods, undertook to raise a tower whose top should reach the sky, in the place in which Babylon now stands; but when it approached the heaven, the winds assisted the gods and overthrew the work upon its contrivers, and its ruins are said to be still at Babylon; and the gods introduced a diversity of tongues among men, who till that time had all spoken the same language; and a war arose between Chronus and Titan. The place in which they built the tower is now called Babylon, on account of the confusion of tongues, for confusion is by the Hebrews called Babel." §

---

* Cory, *Ancient Fragments*, p. 26.

† Moïse de Khoréne. *Histoire d'Arménie.* Texte Arménien, et Traduction Française. Venise, 1841.

‡ Page 23.

§ Cory, *Ancient Fragments*, p. 34.

A story exactly similar is told by Moses of Chorene, not from Berosus, but from another Greek work of Chaldæan origin, which he quoted from a Syriac version.

SECTION VI.—ARTS.

1. ALL writers of antiquity concur in stating that Babylon was always very superior to Nineveh in all that pertains to literary culture and the sciences. All the notions of the Assyrians on science, all the standard works of their literature, the best of their religious books, came to them from Chaldæa. But in all the plastic arts the Babylonians had not at any period the genius of their Ninevite neighbours, and were always far behind them. Assyria was the birthplace of the great school of ancient art, an art exercising deep and decisive influence on the opening period of the Grecian school. Babylon and Chaldæa had nothing to compare with this.

Undoubtedly Babylon, from the earliest days of its existence, from the time of the Tower of Babel, its first example, had her own peculiar architecture, imposing and grand in style from the very size of its conceptions, but with no variety; for temples, palaces, and hanging gardens, were all constructed as pyramids, in steps or terraces, one above the other, and the upper smaller than the lower. This had been, as we have already shown, the general type of the buildings of the first Chaldæan empire, some of them still existing in our times. This, with no modification at all, a thousand years later, when the Babylonian kingdom regained its ancient glory and became preponderant in Western Asia, was the invariable type of the buildings of Nebuchadnezzar. This architecture, employing no materials but crude or burnt brick, exercised, as we have shown, an absolute influence on that of Assyria, where it was copied even to the materials employed, though better materials were within easy reach. It seems, however, that the Assyrians introduced a little more variety in the exterior forms of their buildings than the Babylonians.

2. But if the Assyrians imitated the Babylonian architecture, their sculpture, in which they excelled, was peculiar to themselves. They represented human figures, and generally all living nature, with wonderful correctness. The Babylonians could not do this; and from the remote period when the cylinder of king Urchammu was engraved, down to the days of Nebuchadnezzar, the plastic arts seem to have made no real progress. An eminent scholar, Etienne Quatremère, many years ago remarked on the proportions of the colossal golden statue of Nebuchadnezzar, that, as given in the Book of Daniel, they "prove complete ignorance, entire forgetfulness of the proportions between the various parts of the human body," as the height was ten times the

breadth. And these are exactly the proportions to be found in the small number of remains of Babylonian art still preserved. No doubt the relative proportions of the various parts of the human body are not so accurately calculated or exactly observed in the works of Assyrian sculptors as in those of the Egyptians, but the errors found in them are nothing as compared to the really monstrous misproportions that seem to have been the rule at Babylon. Babylonian and Assyrian art are, moreover, so perfectly independent of each other that they each seem to have taken the type of their own race as their model for the human figure. In the Assyrian sculptures the figures are usually short, in Babylonian works they are generally tall and thin.

All that we at present possess of monuments of Babylonian art consists of cylinders and other engraved stones, and a few enamelled bricks with symbolical and religious subjects. Not only are the figures much too tall, but their gestures are awkward and untrue to nature, the composition is rudimentary, everything is stiff, and lifeless, showing art not yet advanced beyond a state of infancy. The execution of the Babylonian cylinders is much less finished than that of the Assyrian.

3. Painting, either in the form of frescoes or of casings of enamelled bricks, was the chief element in the decoration of Babylonian buildings. Ctesias gives a long description of the ornamentation of the great royal palace, attributed by him to Semiramis, but in reality dating from the reign of Nebuchadnezzar. These represented the same hunting and war scenes as the sculptures of the Assyrian palaces, and no doubt the capture of Jerusalem was depicted there. Berosus, in a fragment we have quoted,* gives some information as to the religious and cosmographical paintings in the temple of Bel, no doubt in the sanctuary. Many pictures on enamelled bricks covered the exterior walls of buildings, with long inscriptions in painted cuneiform characters, a practice that never seems to have prevailed in Assyria.

Coloured sculpture was also employed in the decoration of some Babylonian edifices, such as the royal palace, and many such remains have been found there. But this sculpture was not, as in Assyrian palaces, executed in stone, but in enamelled bricks. A slab of clay was taken sufficiently large to contain the whole subject intended to be represented. On this slab a bas-relief was modelled, and it was then cut into rectangles about 3 ins. × 5 ins., each forming one brick. The pieces, respectively marked with their position in the picture, were coloured separately with suitable pigments, and baked in a furnace. They were then put together with mortar according to the marks previously made. These were the first rude essays in those Mosaics which, in after times, the Greeks and Romans executed with such skill.

Stone of various sorts, usually of volcanic origin, such as basalt, was

* Page 501.

used in Babylonian monuments, but only for statues. A colossal group has been found in the ruins of the palace at Babylon, in the Kasr, representing a lion devouring a man. This, the only piece of Babylonian sculpture that has been preserved, and apparently occupying a place of honour in the palace of Nebuchadnezzar, is executed in a wonderfully rude manner.

List of Assyrian Royal Names as given by—

M. Lenormant, Manual of Oriental History.	Professor Rawlinson,* Five Great Monarchies.	Mr. George Smith,* Zeitschrift für Aegyptische Sprache, Nov. 1868.
		Bil-pasqu.†
Asshur-bel-nishishu.	Asshur-bel-nisis.	Assur-bilu-nisi-su.
Bushur-asshur.	Buzur-asshur.	Buzur-assur.
Asshur-ubalat.	Asshur-vatila.	Assur-upalit.
	Bel-sumili-kapi.	
Bel-tanagbal.‡	Bellush.	Bil-nirari.
Budiel.	Pudiel.	Budil.
Bin-tanagbal I.‡	Iva-lush I.	Vul-nirari I.
Shalmanu-ashir I.	Shalmaneser I.	Shallim-manu-uzur.
Tuklat-samdan I.	Tiglathi-nin I.	Tukulti-ninip I.
Bel-kudur-ussur.	Iva-lush II.	Bil-kudur-uzur.
Adar-pal-ashir.	Nin-pala-zira.	Ninip-pal-zara.
Asshur-dayan.	Asshur-dah-il.	Assur-dayan I.
Mutakkil-nabu.	Mutaggil-nebo.	Mutaggil-nabu.
Asshur-rish-ishi.	Asshur-ris-ilim.	Assur-ris-ilim.
Tuklat-pal-ashar I.	Tiglath-pileser I.	Tukulti-pal-zara I.
Asshur-bel-kala.	Asshur-bil-kala.	Assur-bil-kala.
Shamshi-bin.		Samsi-vul I.
Asshur-rab-amar.	Asshur-mazur.	Assur-rabu-amar.
Bel-kati-rassu.†		
Shalmanu-ashir II.		
Irib-bin.		Irba-vul.

* The editor has to acknowledge the kindness of the Rev. Professor Rawlinson and of Mr. Geo. Smith in revising these lists, and thus enabling him to present the latest views of these accomplished scholars.

† These two names belong to the same person. He is called (in an inscription of Bintanagbal III. in the British Museum) *qadma sarruti*, "the origin of Royalty," on which account Mr. Smith has placed him at the head of the Assyrian Royal List. But the author believes that the same text gives the number of generations between him and Bintanagbal III., fixing the place of the former where he appears in the author's list.

It therefore follows that the expression *qadma sarruti* does not apply to the origin of the Assyrian empire, but to the foundation of the dynasty to which Bintanagbal III., the husband of Sammuramit, himself belonged.

‡ In this table a new reading has been introduced for the

M. Lenormant, Manual of Oriental History.	Professor Rawlinson, Five Great Monarchies.	Mr. George Smith, Zeitschrift für Aegyptische Sprache, Nov. 1868.
Asshur-idin-akhe.	Asshur-iddin-akhi.	Assur-iddin-aχi.
Shalmanu-ashir III.		
Asshur-edil-ilani I.	Asshur-danin-il I.	Assur-dayan II.
Bin-tanagbal II.‡	Iva-lush III.	Vul-nirari II.
Tuklat-samdan II.	Tiglathi-nin II.	Tukulti-ninip II.
Asshur-nazir-pal.	Asshur-idani-pal.	Assur-nazir-pal.
Shalmanu-ashir IV.	Shalmaneser II.	Sallim-manu-uzur II.
Shamash-bin.	Shamas-iva.	Samsi-vul II.
Bin-tanagbal III.‡	Iva-lush IV.	Vul-nirari III.
Shalmanu-ashir V.	Shalmaneser III.	Sallim-manu-uzur III.
Asshur-edil-ilani II.	Asshur-danin-il II.	Assur-dayan III.
Asshur-tanagbal.‡	Asshur-lush.	Assur-nirari.
Tuklat-pal-ashir II.	Tiglath-pileser II.	Tukulti-pal-zara II.
Shalmanu-ashir VI.	Shalmaneser IV.	Sallim-manu-uzur IV.
Shar-yukin.	Sargon.	Sargina.
Sin-akhe-rib.	Sennacherib.	Sin-aχi-irba.
Asshur-akh-iddin.	Esarhaddon.	Esar-haddon.
Asshur-bani-pal.	Asshur-banipal.	Assur-bani-pal.
Asshur-edil-ilani III.	Asshur-emid-ilin.	Assur-ebil-ili-kain.
Asshur-akh-iddin II. (?)		

names given in the text of this work as Bellikhish, Binlikhish and Asshurlikhish.

The second element in these names, composed of two characters, unquestionably means "protect." There has been a doubt whether, with M. Oppert, we should read it as a phonetic *likhish;* or, with Mr. George Smith, as an ideographic, *nirari.* But in a syllabarium in the British Museum (Cuneiform Inscriptions of Western Asia, vol. 2, pl. 44. 4 l. 28) these two characters are found explained by *gablu;* they, therefore, form a complex ideographic representing a root connected with the Hebrew קָבַל *ante.*

If this word be used in Itanaphal, a conjugation peculiar to the Assyrian, but proved to exist by the grammatical tablets in the British Museum, though not yet introduced into Grammars, we have, in place of the present "Asshurlikhish" or "Asshur-nirari," the reading Asshur-tanagbal, whence, by a softening of the consonants, the Greek form Σαρδανάπαλος might easily have arisen, whilst with any other reading of the name the Greek form seems inexplicable.

Henceforth, therefore, we shall use the forms *Bel-tanagbal*, *Bin-tanagbal*, and *Asshur-tanagbal.*

END OF VOL. I.

INDEX TO VOL. I.

A.

B.

C.

D.

I.

L.

M.

N.

O.

P.

Q.

R.

S.

T.

Z.

END OF INDEX.

LIST OF SCRIPTURE TEXTS QUOTED.

REFERENCES TO HERODOTUS.

The Quotations from and References to HERODOTUS are so numerous and important, that it has been considered advisable to add a List of Passages, quoted and the pages where these will be found.

[All quotations are from the translation of the Rev. Professor Rawlinson. 2nd Ed.].

WERTHEIMER, LEA AND CO., PRINTERS, FINSBURY CIRCUS.

www.ingramcontent.com/pod-product-compliance
Lightning Source LLC
LaVergne TN
LVHW021240110826
845150LV00002B/363

* 9 7 8 1 4 2 5 5 6 1 8 0 2 *